Flask: Building Python Web Services

Unleash the full potential of the Flask web framework by creating small to large and powerful web applications

A course in three modules

BIRMINGHAM - MUMBAI

Flask: Building Python Web Services

Published on: Febuary 2017

Production reference: 1090317

Published by Packt Publishing Ltd.
Livery Place
35 Livery Street
Birmingham B3 2PB, UK.

ISBN 978-1-78728-822-5

www.packtpub.com

Credits

Authors

Gareth Dwyer

Shalabh Aggarwal

Jack Stouffer

Reviewers

Kyle Roux

Burhan Khalid

Rahul Shelke

Christoph Heer

Matthew Copperwaite

Ben Chaimberg

Munir Hossain

Priit Laes

Pedro Baumann

Ayun Park

Nidal Al Hariri

Ellison Leão

Rotem Yaari

Content Development Editor

Johann Barretto

Graphics

Jason Monteiro

Production Coordinator

Nilesh Mohite

Preface

Are you a fan of Python? Do you want to create powerful applications with it? Then Flask is the right choice for you and this course will take you through a journey where you will learn the intricacies of Flask Micro framework, use its components and elements, integrate it with useful third party libraries. Then as you move up the skill level, you will be treated to exciting recipes on creating powerful state of the art web applications. You will dive deep to exlpore the complete power that Flask has to offer and then you will create multiple Python apps from scratch on your own. This Learning Path combines some of the best that Packt has to offer in one complete, curated package.

What this learning path covers

Module 1, Flask By Example, This module will take you on a journey from learning about web development using Flask to building fully functional web applications. In the first major project, we develop a dynamic Headlines application that displays the latest news headlines along with up-to-date currency and weather information. In project two, we build a Crime Map application that is backed by a MySQL database, allowing users to submit information on and the location of crimes in order to plot danger zones and other crime trends within an area. In the final project, we combine Flask with more modern technologies, such as Twitter's Bootstrap and the NoSQL database MongoDB, to create a Waiter Caller application that allows restaurant patrons to easily call a waiter to their table. This pragmatic tutorial will keep you engaged as you learn the crux of Flask by working on challenging real-world applications.

Module 2, Flask Framework Cookbook, Flask Framework Cookbook takes you through a number of recipes that will help you understand the power of Flask and its extensions. You will start by seeing the different ways of configurations that a Flask application can make use of. You will learn how to work with templates and learn about the ORM and view layers. You will see how to write an admin interface followed by the debugging and logging of errors. Finally, you will learn about different deployment and post-deployment techniques on platforms such as Apache, Tornado, and Heroku.

By the end of this module, you will have gained all the knowledge required to write Flask applications in the best possible way, and scale them with best practices.

Module 3, Mastering Flask, Starting from a simple Flask app, this module will walk through advanced topics while providing practical examples of the lessons learned. After building a simple Flask app, a proper app structure is demonstrated by transforming the app to use a Model-View-Controller (MVC) architecture. With a scalable structure in hand, the next chapters use Flask extensions to provide extra functionality to the app, including user login and registration, NoSQL querying, a REST API, an admin interface, and more. Next, you'll discover how to use unit testing to take the guesswork away from making sure the code is performing as it should. The module closes with a discussion of the different platforms that are available to deploy a Flask app on, the pros and cons of each one, and how to deploy on each one

What you need for this learning path

Module 1:

You will need at least one Linux system, which could be a virtual machine as well.

Depending on specifi c features discussed, you might also benefi t from the following:

• Access to an SMTP (e-mail) server

• More Linux systems

• A device with SNMP support

• A Windows system

• A device with IPMI support

• A Java virtual machine

• A VMware instance

Some of these can be replicated on the same Linux box—for example, running snmpd or a Java VM will allow you to try out all the monitoring solutions without a separate system.

Module 2:

In most cases, you will just need a computer system with an average configuration to run the code present in this module. Usually, any OS will do, but Linux and Mac OS are preferred over Windows.

Module 3:

To get started with this module, all you will need is a text editor of your choice, a web browser, and Python installed on your machine.

Windows, Mac OS X, and Linux users should all be able to easily follow along with the content of this module.

Who this learning path is for

This learning path is ideal developers who know the basics of Python and want to learn how to use the Flask framework to build powerful web solutions in Python.

Reader feedback

Feedback from our readers is always welcome. Let us know what you think about this course—what you liked or disliked. Reader feedback is important for us as it helps us develop titles that you will really get the most out of.

To send us general feedback, simply e-mail `feedback@packtpub.com`, and mention the course's title in the subject of your message.

If there is a topic that you have expertise in and you are interested in either writing or contributing to a book, see our author guide at `www.packtpub.com/authors`.

Customer support

Now that you are the proud owner of a Packt course, we have a number of things to help you to get the most from your purchase.

Downloading the example code

You can download the example code files for this course from your account at
`http://www.packtpub.com`. If you purchased this course elsewhere, you can
visit `http://www.packtpub.com/support` and register to have the files e-mailed
directly to you.

You can download the code files by following these steps:

1. Log in or register to our website using your e-mail address and password.
2. Hover the mouse pointer on the **SUPPORT** tab at the top.
3. Click on **Code Downloads & Errata**.
4. Enter the name of the course in the **Search** box.
5. Select the course for which you're looking to download the code files.
6. Choose from the drop-down menu where you purchased this course from.
7. Click on **Code Download**.

You can also download the code files by clicking on the **Code Files** button on the
course's webpage at the Packt Publishing website. This page can be accessed by
entering the course's name in the **Search** box. Please note that you need to be logged
in to your Packt account.

Once the file is downloaded, please make sure that you unzip or extract the folder
using the latest version of:

* WinRAR / 7-Zip for Windows
* Zipeg / iZip / UnRarX for Mac
* 7-Zip / PeaZip for Linux

The code bundle for the course is also hosted on GitHub at `https://github.
com/PacktPublishing/Flask-Building-Python-Web-Services`. We also have
other code bundles from our rich catalog of books, videos, and courses available at
`https://github.com/PacktPublishing/`. Check them out!

Errata

Although we have taken every care to ensure the accuracy of our content, mistakes do happen. If you find a mistake in one of our courses—maybe a mistake in the text or the code—we would be grateful if you could report this to us. By doing so, you can save other readers from frustration and help us improve subsequent versions of this course. If you find any errata, please report them by visiting `http://www.packtpub.com/submit-errata`, selecting your course, clicking on the **Errata Submission Form** link, and entering the details of your errata. Once your errata are verified, your submission will be accepted and the errata will be uploaded to our website or added to any list of existing errata under the Errata section of that title.

To view the previously submitted errata, go to `https://www.packtpub.com/books/content/support` and enter the name of the course in the search field. The required information will appear under the **Errata** section.

Piracy

Piracy of copyrighted material on the Internet is an ongoing problem across all media. At Packt, we take the protection of our copyright and licenses very seriously. If you come across any illegal copies of our works in any form on the Internet, please provide us with the location address or website name immediately so that we can pursue a remedy.

Please contact us at `copyright@packtpub.com` with a link to the suspected pirated material.

We appreciate your help in protecting our authors and our ability to bring you valuable content.

Questions

If you have a problem with any aspect of this course, you can contact us at `questions@packtpub.com`, and we will do our best to address the problem.

Module 2: Flask Framework Cookbook

Module 3: Mastering Flask

Module 1

Flask By Example

Unleash the full potential of the Flask web framework by creating simple yet powerful web applications

1
Hello, World!

And hello, reader! Let's get started with building some Flask applications. Flask is minimalist enough to allow you choice and flexibility; unlike in larger frameworks, you choose what you want to do and then manipulate Flask to do your bidding, and it is complete enough to work right out of the box.

We'll walk together through the development of three web applications; the first one is straightforward and will allow you to cut your teeth on Flask and get used to the new technologies and terminology while building a nontrivial web application; the second will get you started with building a web application that makes use of a traditional SQL database; and the final, which has the most features, will make use of a **NoSQL** database and a frontend framework to create a useful and good-looking web application.

In this chapter, we'll take a brief look at what Flask is and, perhaps more importantly, what it isn't. We'll move on to setting up our basic development environment as well as a web server, and we'll install a Python package manager as well as Flask itself. By the end of the chapter, we'll have the outlines of our first app, and, as dictated by age-old tradition, we'll use our new skills to display the text "Hello, World!".

In brief, we will cover the following topics:

- Introducing Flask
- Creating our development environment
- Writing "Hello, World!"
- Deploying our application to production

Introducing Flask

Flask is a micro framework for Python web development. A framework, in the simplest terms, is a library or collection of libraries that aims to solve a part of a generic problem instead of a complete specific one. When building web applications, there are some problems that will always need to be solved, such as routing from URLs to resources, inserting dynamic data into HTML, and interacting with an end user.

Flask is a micro framework because it implements only core functionality (including routing) but leaves more advanced functionality (including authentication and database ORMs) to extensions. The result of this is less initial setup for the first-time user and more choice and flexibility for the experienced user. This is in contrast with "fuller" frameworks, such as **Django**, which dictate their own ORM and authentication technologies.

As we'll discuss, our Hello World application in Flask can be written in only seven lines of code, with the entire application consisting of a single file. Does that sound good? Let's get going!

Creating our development environment

A development environment consists of all the software that a developer uses while building software. For starters, we'll install a Python package manager (**pip**) and the Flask package. In this book, we'll show detailed steps for developing using **Python 2.7** on a clean installation of **Ubuntu 14.04**, but everything should be easy to translate to Windows or OS X.

Installing pip

For our Hello World application, we only need the Python Flask package, but we'll install several Python packages throughout the development process of our three applications. To manage these packages, we'll use the Python package manager pip. If you've developed in Python without a package manager until now, you'll love how easy it is to download, install, remove, and update packages using pip. If you already use it, then skip to the next step where we'll use it to install Flask.

The pip manager is included in Python's 3.4+ and 2.7.9+ versions. For older versions of Python, pip needs to be installed. To install pip on Ubuntu, open a terminal and run the following command:

```
sudo apt-get update
sudo apt-get install python-pip
```

To install pip on Windows or OS X, you can download and run the `get-pip.py` file from the pip homepage at `https://pip.pypa.io/en/latest/installing/#install-or-upgrade-pip`.

That's it! You can now easily install any Python package you need through pip.

Installing Flask

Installing Flask through pip could not be more straightforward. Simply run the following:

```
pip install --user flask
```

You might see some warnings in your terminal, but at the end, you should also see **Successfully installed Flask**. Now, you can import Flask into a Python program just as with any other library.

If you're used to using VirtualEnv for Python development, you can install Flask inside a VirtualEnv environment. We will discuss this further in *Appendix, A Sneak Peek into the Future*.

Writing "Hello, World!"

Now, we'll create a basic web page and serve it using Flask's built-in server to `localhost`. This means that we'll run a web server on our local machine that we can easily make requests to from our local machine. This is very useful for development but not suited for production applications. Later on, we'll take a look at how to serve Flask web applications using the popular Apache web server.

Writing the code

Our application will be a single Python file. Create a directory in your home directory called `firstapp` and a file inside this called `hello.py`. In the `hello.py` file, we'll write code to serve a web page comprising the static string "Hello, World!". The code looks as follows:

```
from flask import Flask

app = Flask(__name__)
```

```
@app.route("/")
def index():
    return "Hello, World!"

if __name__ == '__main__':
    app.run(port=5000, debug=True)
```

Let's break down what this does. The first line should be familiar; it simply imports Flask from the package `flask`. The second line creates an instance of the Flask object using our module's name as a parameter. Flask uses this to resolve resources, and in complex cases, one can use something other than __name__ here. For our purposes, we'll always use __name__, which links our module to the Flask object.

Line 3 is a Python decorator. Flask uses decorators for URL routing, so this line of code means that the function directly below it should be called whenever a user visits the main *root* page of our web application (which is defined by the single forward slash). If you are not familiar with decorators, these are beautiful Python shortcuts that seem a bit like black magic at first. In essence, they call a function that takes the function defined under the decorator (in our case, `index()`) and returns a modified function.

The next two lines should also seem familiar. They define a very simple function that returns our message. As this function is called by Flask when a user visits our application, the return value of this will be what is sent in response to a user who requests our landing page.

Line 6 is a Python idiom with which you are probably familiar. This is a simple conditional statement that evaluates to `True` if our application is run directly. It is used to prevent Python scripts from being unintentionally run when they are imported into other Python files.

The final line kicks off Flask's development server on our local machine. We set it to run on `port 5000` (we'll use `port 80` for production) and set debug to `True`, which will help us see detailed errors directly in our web browser.

Running the code

To run our development web server, simply fire up a terminal and run the `hello.py` file. If you used the same structure outlined in the previous section, the commands will be as follows:

```
cd firstapp/hello
```

```
python hello.py
```

You should get an output similar to that in the following screenshot:

Also, you should see the process continue to run. This is our web server listening for requests. So, let's make a request!

Fire up a web browser — I use Firefox, which comes packaged with Ubuntu — and navigate to `localhost:5000`.

The `localhost` part of the URL is a shortcut to the loopback address, usually `127.0.0.1`, which asks your computer to make the web request to itself. The number after the colon (`5000`) is the port it should make the request to. By default, all HTTP (web) traffic is carried over `port 80`. For now, we'll use `5000` as it is unlikely to conflict with any existing services, but we'll change over to `port 80` in production, which is conventional, so that you won't have to worry about the colon.

You should see the "Hello, World!" string displayed in your browser as in the following screenshot. Congratulations, you've built your first web application using Flask!

Deploying our application to production

It's great to have an application that runs, but inherent to the idea of a web application is the idea that we want others to be able to use it. As our application is Python-based, we are a bit limited in how we can run our application on a web server (many traditional web hosts are only configured to run PHP and/or .NET applications). Let's consider how to serve Flask applications using a **Virtual Private Server** (**VPS**) running Ubuntu Server, Apache, and WSGI.

From this point on, we'll maintain *two* environments. The first is our **development** environment, which we just set up and where we'll write code and view its results using the Flask server running on `localhost` (as we just did). The second will be a **production** environment. This will be a server to which we can deploy our web applications and make them accessible to the world. When we install new Python libraries or other software on our development environment, we'll normally want to mirror our actions in the production environment.

Setting up a Virtual Private Server

Although you could, in theory, host your web application on your local machine and allow others to use it, this has some severe limitations. First of all, every time you turned off your computer, your app would not be available. Also, your computer probably connects to the Internet via an Internet Service Provider (ISP) and possibly a wireless router. This means that your IP address is dynamic and changes regularly, which makes it difficult for your applications' users to keep up! Finally, chances are that you have an asymmetrical connection to the Internet, which means that your upload speed is slower than your download speed.

Hosting your application on a server solves all of these problems. Before "the cloud" became popular, the traditional way to host a web application was to buy a physical server and find a data center to host it. These days, things are far simpler. In a few minutes, you can fire up a virtual server, which to you seems just like a physical server—you can log in to it, configure it, and enjoy full control over it—but it is actually just a virtual "piece" of a machine owned and controlled by a cloud provider.

At the time of writing, major players in the cloud provider field include Amazon Web Services, Microsoft Azure, Google Cloud Compute, and Digital Ocean. All of these companies allow you to hire a virtual server or servers upon paying by the hour. If you are learning Flask as a hobby and are unwilling to pay anyone to host your web applications, you'll probably find a free trial at one of the providers quite easily. The smallest offering by any provider is fine to host all the applications that we'll run.

Select one of the preceding providers or another of your choosing. If you've never done anything similar before, Digital Ocean is often cited to have the simplest process of signing up and creating a new machine. Once you select a provider, you should be able to follow their respective instructions to fire up a VPS that runs Ubuntu Server 14.04 and SSH into it. You'll have full control over the machine with one slight difference: you won't have a display or a mouse.

You'll enter commands on your local terminal, which will in fact be run on the remote machine. Detailed instructions on how to connect to your VPS will be given by the provider, but if you use Ubuntu, it should be as simple as running the following:

```
ssh user@123.456.789.000
```

Alternatively, if you set it up with a public-private key authentication, where `yourkey.pem` is the full path to your private key file, here's the command to run:

```
ssh user@123.456.78.000 -i yourkey.pem
```

Here, `user` is the default user on the VPS, and `yourkey` is the name of your private key file.

SSH from other operating systems:

SSH from OS X should be the same as Ubuntu, but if you're using Windows, you'll have to download PuTTY. Refer to `http://www.putty.org/` to download and for full usage instructions. Note that if you use key files for authentication, you'll have to convert them to a format compatible with PuTTY. A conversion tool can also be found on the PuTTY website.

Once we connect to the VPS, installing Flask is the same process as it was previously:

```
sudo apt-get update
sudo apt-get install python-pip
pip install --user Flask
```

To install our web server, Apache, and WSGI, we will run the following:

```
sudo apt-get install apache2
sudo apt-get install libapache2-mod-wsgi
```

Apache is our web server. It will listen for web requests (which are generated by our users visiting our web application using their browsers) and hand these requests over to our Flask application. As our application is in Python, we also need **WSGI (Web Server Gateway Interface)**.

This is a common interface between web servers and Python applications, which allows Apache to talk to Flask and vice versa. An overview of the architecture can be seen in the following diagram:

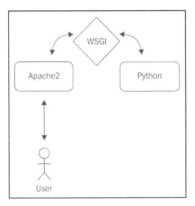

Configuring our server

Now that we've installed Apache, we can see our first results. You're probably used to visiting websites using a URL, such as `http://example.com`. We'll access our web applications using the IP address of our VPS directly. Your VPS should have a static public address. Static means that it doesn't change periodically, and public means that it is globally unique. When you connected to the VPS via SSH, you probably used the public IP to do this. If you can't find it, run the following on your VPS and you should see an `inet addr` section in the output, which contains your public IP:

```
ifconfig
```

The IP address should look similar to 123.456.78.9. Enter your IP address into your browser's address bar, and you should see a page saying "**Apache2 Ubuntu Default Page: It Works!**" or something similar, as in the following screenshot:

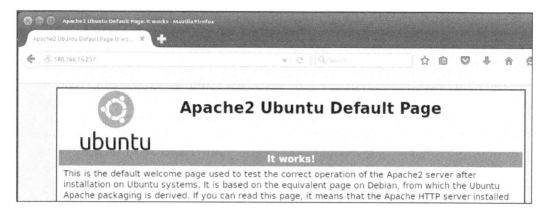

This means that we can now serve web content to anyone with an Internet connection! However, we still have to:

- Copy our code to the VPS
- Link up Apache and Flask
- Configure Apache to serve our Flask application

For the first step, we'll set up a Git repository on our local machine and clone the repository to the VPS. For the second step, we'll use the WSGI module that we installed with Apache. Finally, we'll take a look at how to write a virtual host to have Apache serve our Flask application by default.

Installing and using Git

Git is a version control system. A version control system, among other things, saves multiple versions of our code base automatically. This is great to undo accidental changes or even deletions; we can simply revert to a previous version of our code. It also includes lots of functionality for distributed development—that is, many developers working on a single project. We'll use it mainly for its backup and deployment features, however.

To install Git on your local machine and VPS, run the following commands on each:

```
sudo apt-get update
sudo apt-get install git
```

Make sure you're comfortable with the difference between running commands on your own machine using the terminal and on your server through the SSH connection. In many cases, we'll need to run the same commands twice—once for each environment.

Now that you have the software, you need a place to host your Git repositories or "repos". Two popular and free Git hosting services are GitHub (http://github. com) and Bitbucket (http://bitbucket.org). Head over to one of them, create an account, and create a new repository by following the instructions that they provide. When given the option to give your repository a name, call it firstapp to match the name of the directory that we will use for our code base. Once you create a new repository, you should be given a unique URL to your repository. Take note of this as we'll use it to push our **Hello, World!** application using git and then deploy it to our VPS.

On your local machine, open a terminal and change the directory to the Flask application. Initialize a new repository and link it to your remote Git repository via the following commands:

```
cd firstapp
git init
git remote add origin <your-git-url>
```

Tell git who you are, to allow it to automatically add metadata to your code changes, as follows:

```
git config --global user.email "you@example.com"
git config --global user.name "Your Name"
```

Git allows you full control over which files are part of your repository and which aren't. Even though we initialized the Git repo in our firstapp directory, our repo currently contains no files. Add our application to the repo, commit, and then push it, as follows:

```
git add hello.py
git commit -m "Initial commit"
git push -u origin master
```

These are the main Git commands that we'll use throughout this book, so let's take a brief look at what each does. The add command adds new or modified files to our repository. This tells Git which files are actually part of our project. Think of the commit command as taking a snapshot of our project in its current state. This snapshot is saved on our local machine. It is good to make a new commit with any major change to the code base as we can easily revert to previous commits if a later commit breaks our application. Finally, the push command pushes our local changes to the remote Git server. This is good for backup, and it will also allow us to fetch the changes on our VPS, thus keeping the code base on our local machine and that on our VPS in sync.

Now, SSH into your VPS again and get a copy of our code, as follows:

```
cd /var/www
git clone <your-git-url>
```

 Where the <your-git-url> part of the above command is actually a placeholder for the URL to your Git repository.

If you get a permission denied error on trying to clone the Git repository, you might need to take ownership of the /var/www directory for the Linux user that you're using. If you logged into the server with tom@123.456.789.123, you can run the following command, which will give your user ownership of /var/www and allow you to clone the Git repository into it. Again tom is the placeholder used in the following case:

```
sudo chown -R tom /var/www
```

If you used firstapp as a name for your remote repository, this should create a new directory called firstapp. Let's verify that our code is there using the following:

```
cd firstapp
ls
```

You should see your hello.py file. Now, we need to configure Apache to use WSGI.

Serving our Flask app with WSGI

First, we'll create a very straightforward .wsgi file in our application directory. Then, we'll create an Apache configuration file in the directory where Apache looks for available sites.

The only slightly tricky part about these two steps is that we'll create the files directly on our VPS, and as our VPS does not have a display, this means that we have to use command-line interface text editors. Of course, we could create the files locally and then transfer them to our VPS as we did for our code base, but for small changes to configuration files, this is often more effort than it's worth. Using a text editor without a mouse takes a bit of getting used to, but it's a good skill to learn. The default text editor on Ubuntu is Nano, and the other popular choices are vi or Vim. Some people use Emacs. If you already have a favorite, go with it. If not, we'll use Nano for the examples in this book (it is already installed and arguably the simplest to use). However, if you want to go the extra mile, I recommend learning to use Vim.

Assuming you're still connected to your VPS and have navigated to the /var/www/firstapp directory as in the most recent steps, run the following command:

```
nano hello.wsgi
```

This creates the hello.wsgi file, which you can now edit through Nano. Type the following:

```
import sys
sys.path.insert(0, "/var/www/firstapp")
from hello import app as application
```

This is simply Python syntax, which patches our application into the PATH system so that Apache can find it through WSGI. We will then import app (we named this in our hello.py app with the app = Flask(__name__) line) into the namespace.

Hit *Ctrl* + *X* to exit Nano and enter *Y* when prompted to save the changes.

Now, we'll create an Apache configuration file that points to the .wsgi file we just created, as follows:

```
cd /etc/apache2/sites-available
nano hello.conf
```

> If you run into permission issues while editing or saving files, you may need to take ownership of the apache2 directory too. Run the following command, substituting the username for your Linux user:
>
> ```
> sudo chown -R tom /etc/apache2
> ```

In this file, we'll create a configuration for an Apache virtual host. This will allow us to serve multiple sites from a single server, which will be useful later when we want to serve other applications using our single VPS. In Nano, enter the following configuration:

```
<VirtualHost *>
    ServerName example.com

    WSGIScriptAlias / /var/www/firstapp/hello.wsgi
    WSGIDaemonProcess hello
    <Directory /var/www/firstapp>
        WSGIProcessGroup hello
        WSGIApplicationGroup %{GLOBAL}
         Order deny,allow
         Allow from all
    </Directory>
</VirtualHost>
```

This might look quite complicated, but it's actually very straightforward. We will create a `virtualhost` and specify our domain name, where our `.wsgi` script is, the name of our application, and who is allowed to access it. We'll discuss domain names in the final chapter, but for now, you can just leave it as `example.com` because we'll access our application by its IP address.

 If you get stuck on this step, the Flask website has a great resource on configuring and troubleshooting Apache configuration. You can find it at `http://flask.pocoo.org/docs/0.10/deploying/mod_wsgi/`.

Hit *Ctrl* + *X* and enter *Y* when prompted again to save and exit the file. Now, we need to enable the configuration and set it as our default site.

Configuring Apache to serve our Flask application

Apache sites work as follows: there is a `sites-available` directory (where we created the new virtual host configuration file) and a `sites-enabled` directory, which contains shortcuts to all the configuration files that we want to be active. By default, you'll see a file in the `sites-available` directory named `000-default.conf`. This is the reason that we saw a default **It works** Apache page when we first installed Apache. We don't want this anymore; instead, we want to use our application as the default site. Therefore, we'll disable the default Apache site, enable our own, and then restart Apache for the changes to take effect. Run these commands to do this:

```
sudo a2dissite 000-default.conf
sudo a2ensite hello.conf
sudo service apache2 reload
```

The required Apache configuration and commands can vary quite a bit based on the platform you're using. If you use Ubuntu Server as recommended, the preceding should all work smoothly. If not, you may need to read up a bit on how to configure Apache for your specific platform.

You should note `reloading web server apache2` in the output. If errors are displayed, then you probably misconfigured something in the preceding command. If this is the case, read the error message carefully and go back over the previous steps to take a look at why things didn't work as expected.

To test that everything is working, open a web browser on your local machine and type your IP address into the address bar again. You should see **Hello, World!** displayed in your browser instead of the default Apache page that we saw before.

If you get **Error 500** instead, it means that our application fell over for some reason. Fear not; it's better that you get used to dealing with this error now, when the fix will probably be simple, than later on, when we've added more components that could break or be misconfigured. To find out what went wrong, run the following command on your VPS:

```
sudo tail -f /var/log/apache2/error.log
```

The `tail` command simply outputs the last several lines of the file passed as an argument. The `-f` is for follow, which means that the output will be updated if the file changes. If you can't immediately work out which lines are indicative of the error we're looking for, visit the site in your web browser on your local machine again, and you'll see the output from the `tail` command be updated accordingly. The following screenshot shows the output from the `tail` command when there are no errors; however, if anything goes wrong, you'll see the error output printed among all the info messages.

```
root@blank: ~
root@blank:~# tail -f /var/log/apache2/error.log
[Wed Mar 02 13:23:49.586889 2016] [mpm_event:notice] [pid 97
9:tid 140715828262784] AH00489: Apache/2.4.7 (Ubuntu) mod_ws
gi/3.4 Python/2.7.6 configured -- resuming normal operations
[Wed Mar 02 13:23:49.586923 2016] [core:notice] [pid 979:tid
 140715828262784] AH00094: Command line: '/usr/sbin/apache2'
[Wed Mar 02 13:23:52.141654 2016] [mpm_event:notice] [pid 97
9:tid 140715828262784] AH00493: SIGUSR1 received.  Doing gra
ceful restart
AH00558: apache2: Could not reliably determine the server's
fully qualified domain name, using 127.0.1.1. Set the 'Serve
rName' directive globally to suppress this message
[Wed Mar 02 13:23:52.194574 2016] [mpm_event:notice] [pid 97
9:tid 140715828262784] AH00489: Apache/2.4.7 (Ubuntu) mod_ws
gi/3.4 Python/2.7.6 configured -- resuming normal operations
[Wed Mar 02 13:23:52.194607 2016] [core:notice] [pid 979:tid
 140715828262784] AH00094: Command line: '/usr/sbin/apache2'
[Wed Mar 02 14:20:56.644223 2016] [mpm_event:notice] [pid 97
9:tid 140715828262784] AH00493: SIGUSR1 received.  Doing gra
ceful restart
AH00558: apache2: Could not reliably determine the server's
fully qualified domain name, using 127.0.1.1. Set the 'Serve
rName' directive globally to suppress this message
[Wed Mar 02 14:20:57.059385 2016] [mpm_event:notice] [pid 97
9:tid 140715828262784] AH00489: Apache/2.4.7 (Ubuntu) mod_ws
gi/3.4 Python/2.7.6 configured -- resuming normal operations
[Wed Mar 02 14:20:57.059449 2016] [core:notice] [pid 979:tid
 140715828262784] AH00094: Command line: '/usr/sbin/apache2'
```

Some possible tripping points are incorrectly configured WSGI and Apache files (make sure that your WSGIDaemonProcess and daemon name match, for example) or incorrectly configured Python (you may forget to install Flask on your VPS). If you can't figure out what the error message means, an Internet search for the message (removing the error-specific parts of your app, such as names and paths) will usually point you in the right direction. Failing this, there are strong and very friendly Flask and WSGI communities on Stack Overflow and Google Groups, and there's normally someone willing to help beginners. Remember that if you're having a problem and can't find an existing solution online, don't feel bad for asking; you'll help countless people facing issues similar to yours.

Summary

We got through quite a lot of material in this first chapter! We did some initial setup and house-keeping and then wrote our first web application using Flask. We saw this run locally and then discussed how to use Git to copy our code to a server. We configured our server to serve our application to the public; however, our application is merely a static page that prints the "Hello, World!" string to whoever visits our page. This is not useful to many people and could be achieved more simply using a static HTML page. However, with the extra effort we put in, we now have all the power of Python behind our application; we're just not using it yet!

In the next chapter, we'll discover how to take advantage of Python to make our web applications more useful!

2
Getting Started with Our Headlines Project

Now that our Hello World application is up and running, we have all the groundwork in place to create a more useful application. Over the next few chapters, we'll create a Headlines application that displays up-to-date news headlines, weather information, and currency exchange rates to our users.

In this chapter, we'll introduce RSS feeds and show how to use them to automatically retrieve recent news articles from specific publications. In the next chapter, we'll discuss how to use templates to display headlines and summaries of the retrieved articles to our users. *Chapter 4, User Input for Our Headlines Page Project,* will show you how to get input from users so that they can customize their experience and will also look at how to add weather and currency data to our application. We'll finish off the project in *Chapter 5, Improving the User Experience of Our Headlines Project,* by adding some CSS styles and looking at how to remember our users' preferences from one visit to the next.

By the end of this chapter, you'll have learned how to create a more complex Flask application. We'll pull raw data from real-world news stories and build up HTML formatting to display this to our user. You'll also learn more about routing—that is, having different URLs trigger different parts of our application's code.

In this chapter, we will cover the following topics:

- Setting up our project and a Git repository
- Creating a new Flask application
- Introduction to RSS and RSS feeds

Setting up our project and a Git repository

We could simply edit our Hello World application to add the desired functionality, but it's cleaner to start a new project. We'll create a new Git repository, a new Python file, a new .wsgi file, and a new Apache configuration file. We'll do this for each of the projects in the book, which means that all three of the projects as well as the original Hello World application will be accessible from our web server.

Setting up is very similar to what we did for our Hello World application in *Chapter 1, Hello, World!* but we'll briefly go through the steps again as we don't have to repeat a lot of the configuration and installation, as follows:

1. Log in to your GitHub or BitBucket account and create a new repository called headlines. Take note of the URL you're given for this blank repository.

2. On your local machine, create a new directory called headlines in your home directory or wherever you put the firstapp directory.

3. Create a new file in this directory called headlines.py.

4. In your terminal, change the directory to the headlines directory and initialize the Git repository by executing the following commands:

```
cd headlines
git init
git remote add origin <your headlines git URL>
git add headlines.py
git commit -m "initial commit"
git push -u origin master
```

Now, we're almost ready to push code to our new repository; we just need to write it first.

Creating a new Flask application

To begin with, we'll create the skeleton of our new Flask application, which is pretty much the same as our Hello World application. Open headlines.py in your editor and write the following code:

```
from flask import Flask

app = Flask(__name__)
```

```
@app.route("/")
def get_news():
    return "no news is good news"

if __name__ == '__main__':
    app.run(port=5000, debug=True)
```

This works exactly as before. You can run it in your terminal with `python headlines.py`. Open a browser and navigate to `localhost:5000` to see the **no news is good news** string displayed. However, although the old adage may be true, it's bad news that our app does not do anything more useful than this. Let's make it display actual news to our users.

Introduction to RSS and RSS feeds

RSS is an old but still widely used technology to manage content feeds. It's been around for such a long time that there's some debate as to what the letters RSS actually stand for, with some saying Really Simple Syndication and others Rich Site Summary. It's a bit of a moot point as everyone just calls it RSS.

RSS presents content in an ordered and structured format using XML. It has several uses, with one of the more common uses being for people to consume news articles. On news websites, news is usually laid out similarly to a print newspaper with more important articles being given more space and also staying on the page for longer. This means that frequent visitors to the page will see some content repeatedly and have to look out for new content. On the other hand, some web pages are updated only very infrequently, such as some authors' blogs. Users have to keep on checking these pages to see whether they are updated, even when they haven't changed most of the time. RSS feeds solve both of these problems. If a website is configured to use RSS feeds, all new content is published to a feed. A user can subscribe to the feeds of his or her choice and consume these using an RSS reader. New stories from all feeds he or she has subscribed to will appear in the reader and disappear once they are marked as read.

As RSS feeds have a formal structure, they allow us to easily parse the headline, article text, and date programmatically in Python. We'll use some RSS feeds from major news publications to display news to our application's users.

Although RSS follows a strict format and we could, with not too much trouble, write the logic to parse the feeds ourselves, we'll use a Python library to do this. The library abstracts away things such as different versions of RSS and allows us to access the data we need in a completely consistent fashion.

There are several Python libraries that we could use to achieve this. We'll select `feedparser`. To install it, open your terminal and type the following:

```
pip install --user feedparser
```

Now, let's go find an RSS feed to parse! Most major publications offer RSS feeds, and smaller sites built on popular platforms, such as WordPress and Blogger, will often have RSS included by default as well. Sometimes, a bit of effort is required to find the RSS feed; however, as there is no standard as to where it should be located, you'll often see the RSS icon somewhere on the homepage (look at the headers and footers), which looks similar to this:

Also, look for links saying **RSS** or **Feed**. If this fails, try going to `site.com/rss` or `site.com/feed`, where `site.com` is the root URL of the site for which you're looking for RSS feeds.

We'll use the RSS feed for the main BBC news page. At the time of writing, it is located at `http://feeds.bbci.co.uk/news/rss.xml`. If you're curious, you can open the URL in your browser, right-click somewhere on the page, and click on **View Source** or an equivalent. You should see some structured XML with a format similar to the following:

```xml
<?xml version="1.0" encoding="UTF-8"?>
  <channel>
    <title>FooBar publishing</title>
    <link>http://dwyer.co.za</link>
    <description>A mock RSS feed</description>
    <language>en-gb</language>
    <item>
      <title>Flask by Example sells out</title>
      <description>Gareth Dwyer's new book,
      Flask by Example sells out in minutes</description>
      <link>http://dwyer.co.za/book/news/flask-by-example</link>
      <guid isPermalink="false">http://dwyer.co.za/book/news/
      flask-by-example</guid>
      <pubDate>Sat, 07 Mar 2015 09:09:19 GMT</pubDate>
    </item>
  </channel>
</rss>
```

At the very top of the feed, you'll see a line or two that describes the feed itself, such as which version of RSS it uses and possibly some information about the styles. After this, you'll see information relating to the publisher of the feed followed by a list of `<item>` tags. Each of these represents a *story*—in our case, a news article. These items contain information such as the headline, a summary, the date of publication, and a link to the full story. Let's get parsing!

Using RSS from Python

In our `headlines.py` file, we'll make modifications to import the `feedparser` library we installed, parse the feed, and grab the first article. We'll build up HTML formatting around the first article and show this in our application. If you're not familiar with HTML, it stands for **Hyper Text Markup Language** and is used to define the look and layout of text in web pages. It's pretty straightforward, but if it's completely new to you, you should take a moment now to go through a beginner tutorial to get familiar with its most basic usage. There are many free tutorials online, and a quick search should bring up dozens. A popular and very beginner-friendly one can be found at `http://www.w3schools.com/html/`.

Our new code adds the import for the new library, defines a new global variable for the RSS feed URL, and further adds a few lines of logic to parse the feed, grab the data we're interested in, and insert this into some very basic HTML. It looks similar to this:

```
import feedparser

from flask import Flask

app = Flask(__name__)

BBC_FEED = "http://feeds.bbci.co.uk/news/rss.xml"


@app.route("/")
def get_news():
  feed = feedparser.parse(BBC_FEED)
  first_article = feed['entries'][0]
  return """<html>
    <body>
        <h1> BBC Headlines </h1>
        <b>{0}</b> <br/>
        <i>{1}</i> <br/>
```

```
        <p>{2}</p> <br/>
    </body>
</html>""".format(first_article.get("title"), first_article.
get("published"), first_article.get("summary"))

if __name__ == "__main__":
    app.run(port=5000, debug=True)
```

The first line of this function passes the BBC feed URL to our `feedparser` library, which downloads the feed, parses it, and returns a Python dictionary. In the second line, we grabbed just the first article from the feed and assigned it to a variable. The `entries` entry in the dictionary returned by `feedparser` contains a list of all the items that include the news stories we spoke about earlier, so we took the first one of these and got the headline or `title`, the date or the `published` field, and the summary of the article (that is, `summary`) from this. In the `return` statement, we built a basic HTML page all within a single triple-quoted Python string, which includes the `<html>` and `<body>` tags that all HTML pages have as well as an `<h1>` heading that describes what our page is; `<b>`, which is a *bold* tag that shows the news headline; `<i>`, which stands for the *italics* tag that shows the date of the article; and `<p>`, which is a paragraph tag to show the summary of the article. As nearly all items in an RSS feed are optional, we used the `python.get()` operator instead of using index notation (square brackets), meaning that if any information is missing, it'll simply be omitted from our final HTML rather than causing a runtime error.

For the sake of clarity, we didn't do any exception handling in this example; however, note that `feedparser` may well throw an exception on attempting to parse the BBC URL. If your local Internet connection is unavailable, the BBC server is down, or the provided feed is malformed, then `feedparser` will not be able to turn the feed into a Python dictionary. In a real application, we would add some exception handling and retry the logic here. In a real application, we'd also never build HTML within a Python string. We'll look at how to handle HTML properly in the next chapter. Fire up your web browser and take a look at the result. You should see a very basic page that looks similar to the following (although your news story will be different):

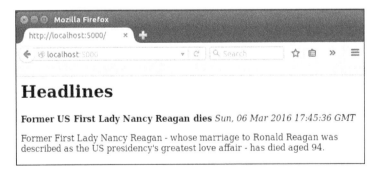

This is a great start, and we're now serving dynamic content (that is, content that changes automatically in response to user or external events) to our application's hypothetical users. However, ultimately, it's not much more useful than the static string. Who wants to see a single news story from a single publication that they have no control over?

To finish off this chapter, we'll look at how to show an article from different publications based on URL routing. That is, our user will be able to navigate to different URLs on our site and view an article from any of several publications. Before we do this, let's take a slightly more detailed look at how Flask handles URL routing.

URL routing in Flask

Do you remember that we briefly mentioned Python decorators in the previous chapter? They're represented by the funny `@app.route("/")` line we had above our main function, and they indicate to Flask which parts of our application should be triggered by which URLs. Our base URL, which is usually something similar to `site.com` but in our case is the IP address of our VPS, is omitted, and we will specify the rest of the URL (that is, the path) in the decorator. Earlier, we used a single slash, indicating that the function should be triggered whenever our base URL was visited with no path specified. Now, we will set up our application so that users can visit URLs such as `site.com/bbc` or `site.com/cnn` to choose which publication they want to see an article from.

The first thing we need to do is collect a few RSS URLs. At the time of writing, all of the following are valid:

* **CNN**: http://rss.cnn.com/rss/edition.rss
* **Fox News**: http://feeds.foxnews.com/foxnews/latest
* **IOL**: http://www.iol.co.za/cmlink/1.640

First, we will consider how we might achieve our goals using static routing. It's by no means the best solution, so we'll implement static routing for only two of our publications. Once we get this working, we'll consider how to use dynamic routing instead, which is a simpler and more generic solution to many problems.

Instead of declaring a global variable for each of our RSS feeds, we'll build a Python dictionary that encapsulates them all. We'll make our `get_news()` method generic and have our decorated methods call this with the relevant publication. Our modified code looks as follows:

```
import feedparser
from flask import Flask
```

```
app = Flask(__name__)

RSS_FEEDS = {'bbc': 'http://feeds.bbci.co.uk/news/rss.xml',
             'cnn': 'http://rss.cnn.com/rss/edition.rss',
             'fox': 'http://feeds.foxnews.com/foxnews/latest',
             'iol': 'http://www.iol.co.za/cmlink/1.640'}

@app.route("/")
@app.route("/bbc")
def bbc():
    return get_news('bbc')

@app.route("/cnn")
def cnn():
    return get_news('cnn')

def get_news(publication):
  feed = feedparser.parse(RSS_FEEDS[publication])
  first_article = feed['entries'][0]
  return """<html>
    <body>
        <h1>Headlines </h1>
        <b>{0}</b> </ br>
        <i>{1}</i> </ br>
        <p>{2}</p> </ br>
    </body>
</html>""".format(first_article.get("title"), first_article.
get("published"), first_article.get("summary"))


if __name__ == "__main__":
  app.run(port=5000, debug=True)
```

Common mistakes:

If you're copying or pasting functions and editing the @app.route
decorator, it's easy to forget to edit the function name. Although
the name of our functions is largely irrelevant as we don't call them
directly, we can't have different functions share the same name as the
latest definition will always override any previous ones.

We still return the BBC news feed by default, but if our user visits the CNN or BBC routes, we will explicitly take the top article from respective publication. Note that we can have more than one decorator per function so that our bbc() function gets triggered by a visit to our base URL or to the /bbc path. Also, note that the function name does not need to be the same as the path, but it is a common convention that we followed in the preceding example.

Following this, we can see the output for our application when the user visits the /cnn page. The headline displayed is now from the CNN feed.

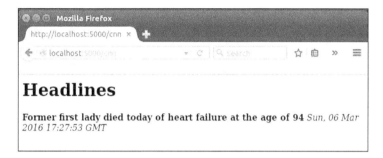

Now that we know how routing works in Flask, wouldn't it be nice if it could be even simpler? We don't want to define a new function for each of our feeds. What we need is for the function to dynamically grab the right URL based on the path. This is exactly what dynamic routing does.

In Flask, if we specify a part of our URL path in angle brackets < >, then it is taken as a variable and is passed to our application code. Therefore, we can go back to having a single get_news() function and pass in a <publication> variable, which can be used to make the selection from our dictionary. Any variables specified by the decorator must be accounted for in our function's definition. The first few lines of the updated get_news() function are shown as follows:

```
@app.route("/")
@app.route("/<publication>")
def get_news(publication="bbc"):
    # rest of code unchanged
```

In the code shown earlier, we added <publication> to the route definition. This creates an argument called publication, which we need to add as a parameter of the function directly below the route. Thus, we can keep our default value for the publication parameter as bbc, but if the user visits CNN, Flask will pass the cnn value as the publication argument instead.

The rest of the code remains unchanged, but it's important to delete the now unused `bbc()` and `cnn()` function definitions as we need the default route to activate our `get_news()` function instead.

It's easy to forget to *catch* the URL variables in the function definition. Any dynamic part of the route must contain a parameter of the same name in the function in order to use the value, so look out for this. Note that we gave our publication variable a default value of `bbc` so that we don't need to worry about it being undefined when the user visits our base URL. However, again, our code will throw an exception if the user visits any URL that we don't have as a key in our dictionary of feeds. In a real web application, we'd catch cases such as this and show an error to the user, but we'll leave error handling for later chapters.

Publishing our Headlines application

This is as far as we'll take our application in this chapter. Let's push the results to our server and configure Apache to display our headlines application instead of our Hello World application by default.

First, add your changes to the Git repository, commit them, and push them to the remote. You can do this by running the following commands (after opening a terminal and changing directory to the headlines directory):

```
git add headlines.py
git commit -m "dynamic routing"
git push origin master
```

Then, connect to the VPS with SSH and clone the new project there using the following commands:

```
ssh -i yourkey.pem root@123.456.789.123
cd /var/www
git clone https://<yourgitrepo>
```

Don't forget to install the new library that we now depend on. Forgetting to install dependencies on your server is a common error that can lead to a frustrating debugging. Keep this in mind. The following is the command for this:

```
pip install --user feedparser
```

Now, create the `.wsgi` file. I assume that you named your Git project `headlines` when creating the remote repository and that a directory named `headlines` was created in your `/var/www` directory when you did the preceding Git clone command. If you called your project something else and now have a directory with a different name, rename it to headlines (otherwise, you'll have to adapt a lot of the configuration we're about to do accordingly). To rename a directory in Linux, use the following command:

```
mv myflaskproject headlines
```

The command used earlier will rename the directory called `myflaskproject` to `headlines`, which will ensure that all the configuration to follow will work. Now, run the following:

```
cd headlines
nano headlines.wsgi
```

Then, insert the following:

```
import sys
sys.path.insert(0, "/var/www/headlines")
from headlines import app as application
```

Exit Nano by hitting the *Ctrl* + *X* key combo and enter *Y* when prompted to save changes.

Now, navigate to the `sites-available` directory in Apache and create the new `.conf` file using the following commands:

```
cd /etc/apache2/sites-available
nano headlines.conf
```

Next, enter the following:

```
<VirtualHost *>
    ServerName example.com

    WSGIScriptAlias / /var/www/headlines/headlines.wsgi
    WSGIDaemonProcess headlines
    <Directory /var/www/headlines>
       WSGIProcessGroup headlines
       WSGIApplicationGroup %{GLOBAL}
        Order deny,allow
        Allow from all
    </Directory>
</VirtualHost>
```

Save the file and quit nano. Now, disable our old site, enable the new one, and restart Apache by running the following commands:

```
sudo a2dissite hello.conf
sudo a2enssite headlines.conf
sudo service apache2 reload
```

Try and visit the IP address of your VPS from your local machine, and if all went as expected, you should see the news headline as before! If not, don't worry. It's easy to make a mistake in some piece of configuration. It's most likely that your `headlines.wsgi` or `headlines.conf` file has a small error. The easiest way to find this is by looking at the most recent errors in your Apache error log, which would have been triggered when you attempted to visit the site. View this again with the following command:

```
sudo tail -fn 20 /var/log/apache2/error.log
```

Summary

That's it for this chapter. The major takeaways of this chapter were taking a look at how routing, both static and dynamic, are handled in Flask. You also learned a fairly messy way of formatting data using HTML and returning this to the user.

In the next chapter, we'll take a look at cleaner ways to separate our HMTL code from our Python code using Jinja templates. We'll also have our app display more than a single news story.

3
Using Templates in Our Headlines Project

In the last chapter, we saw one way of combining static HTML with dynamic content for creating a web page. But it's messy, and we don't want to hack away at Python strings for building our web pages. Mixing HTML and Python is not ideal for a few reasons: for one, it means if we ever want to change static text, such as that which appears in our headings, we have to edit our Python files, which also involves reloading these files into Apache. If we hire frontend developers to work on HTML, we run the risk of them breaking the unfamiliar Python code by mistake, and it's far more difficult to structure any other frontend code such as JavaScript and CSS correctly. Ideally, we should aim for complete segregation between the frontend and backend components. We can achieve this to a large extent using Jinja, but as with most aspects of life, some compromise will be necessary.

By the end of this chapter, we'll have extended our application to display more than a single headline for the chosen publication. We'll display several articles for each publication, each one having a link to the original article, and our logic and view components will largely be separated. In this chapter, we'll cover the following topics:

- Introducing Jinja
- Basic use of Jinja templates
- Advanced use of Jinja templates

Introducing Jinja

Jinja is a Python template engine. It allows us to easily define dynamic blocks of HTML which are populated by Python. HTML templates are useful even for static websites which have multiple pages. Usually, there are some common elements, such as headers and footers, on every page. Although it is possible to maintain each page individually for static websites, this requires that a single change be made in multiple places if the change is made to a shared section. Flask was built on top of Jinja, so although it is possible to use Jinja without Flask, Jinja is still an inherent part of Flask, and Flask provides several methods to work directly with Jinja. Generally, Flask assumes nothing about the structure of your application except what you tell it, and prefers providing functionality through optional plugins. Jinja is somewhat of an exception to this. Flask gives you Jinja by default, and assumes that you store all your Jinja templates in a subdirectory of your application named `templates`.

Once we've created templates, we'll make calls from our Flask app to render these templates. Rendering involves parsing the Jinja code, inserting any dynamic data, and creating pure HTML to be returned to a user's browser. All of this is done behind the scenes though, so it can get a bit confusing as to what is being done where. We'll take things one step at a time.

Basic use of Jinja templates

The first step to using Jinja templates is creating a directory in our application to contain our template files, so navigate to your `headlines` directory, and create a directory called `templates`. Unlike the previous steps, this name is expected by other parts of the application and is case sensitive, so take care while creating it. At the most basic level, a Jinja template can just be an HTML file, and we'll use the `.html` extension for all our Jinja templates. Create a new file in the `templates` directory called `home.html`. This will be the page that our users see when visiting our application, and will contain all the HTML that we previously had in a Python string.

 We'll only be using Jinja to build HTML files in this book, but Jinja is flexible enough for use in generating any text-based format. Although we use the `.html` extension for our Jinja templates, the files themselves will not always be pure HTML.

For now, put the following static HTML code into this file. We'll look at how to pass dynamic data between Python and our templates in the next step.

```
<html>
    <head>
        <title>Headlines</title>
```

```
        </head>
        <body>
            <h1>Headlines</h1>
            <b>title</b><br />
            <i>published</i><br />
            <p>summary</p>
        </body>
    </html>
```

Now in our Python code, instead of building up the string and returning that in our routing function, we'll render this template and return it. In `headlines.py`, add an import at the top:

```
from flask import render_template
```

The `render_template` function is the magic which takes a Jinja template as input and produces pure HTML, capable of being read by any browser, as the output. For now, some of the magic is lost, as we'll give it pure HTML as input and view the same as output in our browser.

Rendering a basic template

In your `get_news()` function, remove the `return` statement, which contains our triple-quoted HTML string as well. Leave the previous lines which grab the data from `feedparser`, as we'll be using that again soon.

Update the `return` statement, so that the `get_news()` function now looks as follows:

```
@app.route("/")
@app.route("/<publication>"
def get_news(publication="bbc"):
  feed = feedparser.parse(RSS_FEEDS[publication])
  first_article = feed['entries'][0]
  return render_template("home.html")
```

Although our current HTML file is pure HTML and not yet using any of the Jinja syntax that we'll see later, we're actually already doing quite a bit of magic. This call looks in our `templates` directory for a file named `home.html`, reads this, parses any Jinja logic, and creates an HTML string to return to the user. Once you've made both the preceding changes, run your application again with `python headlines.py`, and navigate to `localhost:5000` in your browser.

Again, we've gone a step backwards in order to advance. If you run the app and view the result in your browser now, you should see something similar to our original page, except that instead of the real news data, you'll just see the strings **title**, **published**, and **summary** as seen in the following image:

Let's take a look at how to populate these fields inside our `render_template` call so that we can see real news content again.

Passing dynamic data to our template

First, in our Python file, we'll pass each of these as named variables. Update the `get_news()` function again, and pass all the data that you need to display to the user as arguments to `render_template()`, as follows:

```
@app.route("/")
@app.route("/<publication>"
def get_news(publication="bbc"):
    feed = feedparser.parse(RSS_FEEDS[publication])
    first_article = feed['entries'][0]
    render_template("home.html",
                    title=first_article.get("title"),
                    published=first_article.get("published"),
                    summary=first_article.get("summary"))
```

The `render_template` function takes the filename of the template as its first argument, and can then take an arbitrary number of named variables as subsequent arguments. The data in each of these variables will be available to the template, using the variable name.

Displaying dynamic data in our template

In our `home.html` file, we simply need to put two braces on either side of our placeholders. Change it to look like the following:

```
<html>
    <head>
        <title>Headlines</title>
    </head>
    <body>
        <h1>Headlines</h1>
        <b>{{title}}</b><br />
        <i>{{published}}</i><br />
        <p>{{summary}}</p>
    </body>
</html>
```

Double braces, {{ }}, indicate to Jinja that anything inside them should not be taken as literal HTML code. Because our *placeholders*, *title*, *published*, and *summary*, are the same as our Python variable names passed into the `render_template` call, just adding the surrounding braces means that the `render_template` call will substitute these for the real data, returning a pure HTML page. Try it out to make sure that we can see real news data again, as seen in the following image:

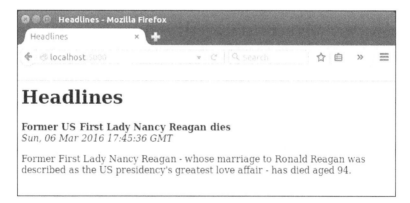

Advanced use of Jinja templates

Now we have perfect separation of our backend and frontend components, but our application doesn't do anything more than it did before. Let's take a look at how to display multiple news articles from a selected publication. We don't want to add three new arguments to our `render_template` call for each article (or dozens of additional arguments if we ever decide that we want to display more than just the title, date, and summary of an article).

Fortunately, Jinja can take over some of the logic from Python. This is where we have to be careful: we spent all that effort to separate our logic and view components, and when we discover how powerful the Jinja language actually is, it's tempting to move a lot of the logic into our template files. This would leave us back where we started with code that is difficult to maintain. However, in some cases it's necessary for our frontend code to handle some logic, such as now where we don't want to pollute our backend code with too many repeated arguments.

Using Jinja objects

The first thing to learn is how Jinja handles objects. All of the basic Python data structures, such as variables, objects, lists, and dictionaries, can be understood by Jinja and can be processed in a very similar way to what we are used to in Python. For example, instead of passing each of the three components of our article separately to our template, we could have passed in the `first_article` object and dealt with the separation in Jinja. Let's see how to do that. Change the Python code to pass in a single-named argument to `render_template`, that is `first_article`, and the frontend code to grab the bits we need from this.

The `render_template` call should now look like this:

```
render_template("home.html", article=first_article)
```

The template now has a reference called `article`, which we can use to get the same result as before. Change the relevant part of the home.html to read as follows:

```
<b>{{article.title}}</b><br />
<i>{{article.published</i><br />
<p>{{article.summary}}</p>
```

Note that accessing items from a dictionary is slightly different in Jinja as compared to Python. We use a full stop to access properties, so to access the title of the article, we use {{article.title}} as in the preceding example, instead of the Python equivalent `article["title"]` or `article.get("title")`. Our code is again neater, but yet again has no additional functionality.

Adding looping logic to our template

Without much extra effort, we can make the whole list of articles available to Jinja. In the Python code, change the `render_template` call to read as follows:

```
render_template("home.html", articles=feed['entries'])
```

You can remove the line directly above the preceding one in the code which defines the `first_article` variable, as we won't need it any more. Our template now has access to the full list of articles that we fetch through `feedparser`.

In our Jinja template, we could now add `{{articles}}` or `{{articles[0]}}` to see a full dump of all the information we're now passing, or just a dump of the first article respectively. You can try this as an intermediate step if you're curious, but in our next step we'll be looping through all the articles and displaying the information we want.

By giving our template more data to work with, we're passing along some of the logic responsibility that should ideally be handled by our Python code, but we can also deal with this very cleanly in Jinja. Similar to the way we use double braces, `{{ }}`, to indicate variables, we use the brace and percentage combination, `{% %}`, to indicate control logic. This will be clearer by looking at an example. Change the `<body>` part of the template code to read as follows:

```
<body>
    <h1>Headlines</h1>
    {% for article in articles %}
        <b>{{article.title}}</b><br />
        <i>{{article.published}}</i><br />
        <p>{{article.summary}}</p>
        <hr />
    {% endfor %}
</body>
```

We can see that the Jinja for loop is similar to Python. It loops through the *articles* list that we've passed in from the Python code, and creates a new variable, `article`, for each iteration of the loop, each time referring to the next item in the list. The `article` variable can then be used like any other Jinja variable (using the double braces). Because whitespace in Jinja is irrelevant, unlike Python, we must define where our loop ends with the `{% endfor %}` line. Finally, the `<hr />` in HTML creates a horizontal line which acts as a separator between each article.

Run the application locally with the new template file, and view the results in your browser. You should see something similar to the following image:

Adding hyperlinks to our template

Now we want to link each headline to the original article. Our user will probably find this useful—if a headline seems interesting, he or she can easily get to the full text of the article to read it. The owner of the RSS feed will also often require or request that anyone who uses the feed links back to the original articles. (Again, check for terms and conditions as published along with most big feeds.) Because we're passing the whole `article` object to our template already, we won't need to make any further changes to our Python code to achieve this; we simply need to make use of the extra data already available to us.

In the template file, search for the following:

```
<b>{{article.title}}</b><br />
```

Change this line to the following:

```
<b><a href="{{article.link}}">{{article.title}}</a></b><br />
```

If you're new to HTML, then there's quite a bit going on here. Let's pull it apart: the <a> tag in HTML indicates a hyperlink (usually displayed by default as blue and underlined in most browsers), the href attribute specifies the destination or URL of the link, and the link ends with the </a> tag. That is, any text between <a> and </a> will be clickable, and will be displayed differently by our user's browser. Note that we can use the double braces to indicate a variable even within the double quotation marks used to define the destination attribute.

If you refresh the page in your browser, you should now see the headlines as bold links, as in the following image, and clicking on one of the links should take you to the original article.

Pushing our code to the server

Now is a good time to push the code to our VPS. This is the last time we'll break down the steps of how to do this, but hopefully, you'd be familiar enough with Git and Apache by now that there won't be anything unexpected. On your local machine, from the headlines directory, run:

```
git add headlines.py
git add templates
git commit -m "with Jinja templates"
git push origin master
```

And on your VPS (SSH into it as usual), change to the appropriate directory, pull the updates from the Git repository, and restart Apache to reload the code:

```
cd /var/www/headlines
git pull
sudo service apache2 reload
```

Make sure everything has worked by visiting the IP address of your VPS from the web browser on your local machine and checking that you see the same output that we saw locally, as seen in the following image:

Summary

We now have a basic news summary site! You can display recent news from a number of different websites, see the headline, date, and summary for each recent article, and can click on any headline to visit the original article. You've only seen a tiny sample of the power of the Jinja language though—as we expand this project and other projects in future chapters, you'll see how it can be used for inheritance, conditional statements, and more.

In the next chapter, we'll add weather and currency information to our application, and look at ways to interact with our users.

4

User Input for Our Headlines Project

Remember how we allowed the user to specify the publication to be viewed by using `<variable>` parts in our URL? Although we were effectively getting input from our user, it's a way of retrieving input that has some pretty heavy limitations. Let's look at some more powerful ways to interact with our users, and add some more useful information to our application. We'll be making quite a few incremental changes to our code files from here on, so remember that you can always refer to the accompanying code bundle if you need an overview at any point.

In this chapter, we'll look at some more flexible and powerful ways to get input. We'll also bump into some more advanced Git features along the way, and take a moment to explain how to use them.

We'll cover the following topics in this chapter:

- Getting user input using HTTP GET
- Getting user input using HTTP POST
- Adding weather and currency data

Getting user input using HTTP GET

HTTP GET requests are the simplest way of retrieving input from the user. You might have noticed question marks in URLs while browsing the Web. When submitting a term in the search box on the website, your search term will usually appear in the URL, and look something like this:

```
example.com/search?query=weather
```

The bit after the question mark represents a named GET argument. The name is `query` and the value, `weather`. Although arguments like these are usually automatically created through HTML input boxes, the user can also manually insert them into the URL, or they can be part of a clickable link that is sent to the user. HTTP GET is designed to get limited, non-sensitive information from the user in order for the server to return a page as requested by the GET arguments. By convention, GET requests should never modify the server state in a way that produces side effects, that is, the user should be able to make exactly the same request multiple times and always be given exactly the same results.

GET requests are, therefore, ideal for allowing our user to specify which publication to view. Let's extend our Headlines project to incorporate selecting a headline based on a GET request. First, let's modify the Python code to do the following:

- Import the request context from Flask
- Remove the dynamic URL variable
- Check to see if the user has entered a valid publication as a GET argument
- Pass the user query and the publication to the template

Update the `headlines.py` file as follows:

```
import feedparser
from flask import Flask
from flask import render_template
from flask import request

app = Flask(__name__)

RSS_FEEDS = {'bbc': 'http://feeds.bbci.co.uk/news/rss.xml',
             'cnn': 'http://rss.cnn.com/rss/edition.rss',
             'fox': 'http://feeds.foxnews.com/foxnews/latest',
             'iol': 'http://www.iol.co.za/cmlink/1.640'}

@app.route("/")
def get_news():
        query = request.args.get("publication")
        if not query or query.lower() not in RSS_FEEDS:
                publication = "bbc"
        else:
                publication = query.lower()
        feed = feedparser.parse(RSS_FEEDS[publication])
        return render_template("home.html",
        articles=feed['entries']
```

```
if __name__ == "__main__":
    app.run(port=5000, debug=True)
```

The first new change is a new import for Flask's request context. This is another piece of Flask magic that makes our life easier. It provides a global context which our code can use to access information about the latest request made to our application. This is useful for us, because the GET arguments that our user passes along as part of a request are automatically available in `request.args`, from which we can access key-value pairs as we would with a Python dictionary (although it is immutable). The request context simplifies some other parts of request handling as well, which means that we don't have to worry about threads or the ordering of requests. You can read more about how the request context works, and what it does, at the following website:

`http://flask-cn.readthedocs.org/en/latest/reqcontext/`

We check to see if this has the publication key set by using the `get()` method, which returns `None`. if the key doesn't exist. If the argument is there, we make sure that the value is valid (that is, it is accounted for by our `RSS_FEEDS` mapping), and if it is, we return the matching publication.

We can test out the code by visiting our URL followed by the `get` argument, for example: `localhost:5000/?publication=bbc`. Unfortunately, from our user's experience, we've made the application less user-friendly, instead of more. Why did we do this? It turns out that our user doesn't have to modify the URL by hand—with a very small change, we can have the URL arguments populated automatically so that the user doesn't have to touch the URL at all. Modify the `home.html` template, and add the following HTML below the heading:

```
<form>
  <input type="text" name="publication" placeholder="search" />
  <input type="submit" value="Submit" />
</form>
```

This is quite straightforward, but let's pick it apart to see how it all works. First we create an HTML form element. By default, this will create an HTTP GET request when submitted, by passing any inputs as GET arguments into the URL. We have a single text input which has the name `publication`. This name is important as the GET argument will use this. The `placeholder` is optional, but it will give our user a better experience as the browser will use it to indicate what the text field is intended for. Finally, we have another input of type `submit`. This automatically creates a nice **Submit** button for our form which, when pressed, will grab any text in the input and submit it to our Python backend.

Save the template, and reload the page to see how it works now. You should see the input form at the top of the page, as seen in the following screenshot. We've gained a lot of functionality for four lines of HTML, and now we can see that, although GET arguments initially looked like they were creating more mission and admin, they actually make our web application much simpler and more user-friendly.

Getting user input using HTTP POST

The alternative to HTTP GET is HTTP POST, and it may not always be immediately obvious which one to use. HTTP POST is used to post larger chunks of data or more sensitive data to the server. Data sent through POST requests is not visible in the URL, and although this does not make it inherently more secure (it does not by default provide encryption or validation), it does offer some security advantages. URLs are often cached by the browser and suggested through autocomplete features next time the user types in a similar URL.

Data sent through GET requests may, therefore, be retained. Using POST also prevents someone from seeing the data by looking over the user's shoulder (shoulder surfing). Passwords especially are often obscured on input by using HTML password fields, making them appear as asterisks (********) or dots (••••••••) in the browser. The data would still be clearly visible in the URL if sent using GET however, and so POST should always be used instead.

Although our search query is hardly confidential or excessively long, we're going to take a moment now to see how we'd implement the same functionality using POST instead of GET. If you just want to get ahead with finishing off our Headlines application, feel free to skip this section, but keep in mind that we'll be using POST requests in later projects without extended explanation. Once we're done with the POST example, we'll revert our application to the state it is currently in (using the GET request), as this is much more suitable for our use case.

Creating a branch in Git

To make a change to our code base that we're not sure if we want, we'll use Git's branch functionality. Think of a branch as being like a fork in a road, except we can at any time change our mind and go back to the decision point. First, we need to make sure our current branch (master) is up to date—that all our local changes are committed. Open a terminal, and run the following commands from the headlines directory:

```
git add headlines.py
git add templates/home.html
git commit -m "Using GET"
git push origin master
```

We don't strictly need to push it to the server—Git keeps a full revision history locally, and our changes would still be theoretically safe without the push. However, our code is in a working state, so there's no harm making the backup to remote. Now we're going to create the new branch and switch to using it to make our next set of changes:

```
git branch post-requests
git checkout post-requests
```

We're now working in a new branch of our codebase. Usually, we'd eventually merge this branch back into our master branch, but in our case, we'll just abandon it once we're done with what we need. It's quite hard to visualize what's happening as Git does most things behind the scenes, so it's worth reading up about Git if you're interested, and are likely to use it for future projects. Otherwise, just think of this as a checkpoint so that we can freely experiment without the worry of messing up our code.

Adding POST routes in Flask

To use a POST request, we need to make some small changes to our Python and HTML code. In the `headlines.py` file, make the following changes:

- Change `request.args.get` to `request.form.get`
- Change `@app.route("/")` to `@app.route("/", methods=['GET', 'POST'])`

The reason for the first change is that we are now grabbing the user data from a form, so Flask automatically makes this available to us in `request.form`. This works the same way as `request.get` except that it gathers data from POST requests instead of from GETs. The second change is not quite as obvious. What we haven't mentioned before is that all route decorators can specify how the function can be accessed: either through GET requests, POST requests, or both. By default, only GET is permitted, but we now want our default page to be accessible by either GET (when we just visit the home main page and are given BBC as a default), or POST (for when we've requested the page through our form with the additional query data). The `methods` parameter accepts a list of HTTP methods which should be permitted to access that particular route of our application.

Making our HTML form use POST

Our template needs similar changes. Change the opening `<form>` tag in the `home.html` file to read:

```
<form action="/" method="POST">
```

Just as with Flask, HTML forms use GET by default, so we have to explicitly define that we want to use POST instead. The `action` attribute isn't strictly necessary, but usually, when we use POST, we redirect users to a confirmation page or similar, and the URL for the following page would appear here. In this case, we're explicitly saying that we want to be redirected to the same page after our form has been submitted.

Save the changes to the Python and HTML files, and refresh the page in your browser to see the changes take effect. The functionality should be exactly the same except that we don't see any data in the URL. This can be cleaner for many applications, but in our case, it is not what we want. For one, we'd like the search term to be cached by our users' browsers. If a user habitually makes a query for FOX, we want the browser to be able to autocomplete this after he begins typing in the URL for our application. Furthermore, we'd like our users to be able to easily share links that include the query.

If a user (let's call him Bob) sees a bunch of interesting headlines after typing **cnn** into our application, and wants to share all of these headlines with another user (Jane), we don't want Bob to have to message Jane, telling her to visit our site, and type a specific query into the search form. Instead, Bob should be able to share a URL that allows Jane to directly visit the page exactly as he saw it (for example, `example.com/?publication=cnn`). Jane can simply click on the link sent by Bob and view the same headlines (assuming she visits our page before the RSS feed is updated).

Reverting our Git repository

We need to revert the code to how we had it before. Because all the changes in the previous section were made in our experimental post-request branch, we don't need to manually re-edit the lines we changed. Instead, we'll commit our changes to this branch, and then switch back to our master branch, where we'll find everything as we left it. In your terminal, run the following:

```
git add headlines.py
git add templates/home.html
git commit -m "POST requests"
git checkout master
```

Open the `headlines.py` and `templates/home.html` files to be sure, but they should be exactly as we left them before experimenting with POST!

Adding weather and currency data

Now let's add some more functionality. We're showing media headlines from three different sources, but our user is probably interested in more than current affairs. We're going to see how easy it is to display the current weather and some exchange rates at the top of the page. For the weather data, we'll be using the OpenWeatherMap API, and for currency data, we'll be using Open Exchange Rates. At the time of writing, these APIs are freely available, although they both require registration.

Introducing the OpenWeatherMap API

In your web browser, visit the URL `http://api.openweathermap.org/data/2.5/` `weather?q=London,uk&units=metric&appid=cb932829eacb6a0e9ee4f38bfbf112` `ed`. You should see something that looks similar to the following screenshot:

This is the JSON weather data for London which is designed to be read automatically instead of by humans. Before looking at how to go about reading this data into our Headlines application, note that the URL we visited has an `appid` parameter. Even though the weather data is provided for free, every developer who accesses the data needs to sign up for a free account with OpenWeatherMap, and get a unique API key to pass as the value for the `appid` parameter. This is to prevent people from abusing the API by making too many requests, and hogging the available bandwidth. At the time of writing, OpenWeatherMap allows 60 calls to the API per minute and 50,000 per day as part of their free access plan, so it's unlikely that we'll be hitting these limits for our project.

Signing up with OpenWeatherMap

You should sign up for your own API key instead of using the one published in this book. Generally, your API key should remain a secret, and you should avoid sharing it (especially avoid publishing it in a book). To get your own API key, head over to `www.openweathermap.org` , and complete their sign-up progress by clicking the sign-up link at the top of the page. Fill out an e-mail address, username, and password. The registration page should look similar to the following screenshot:

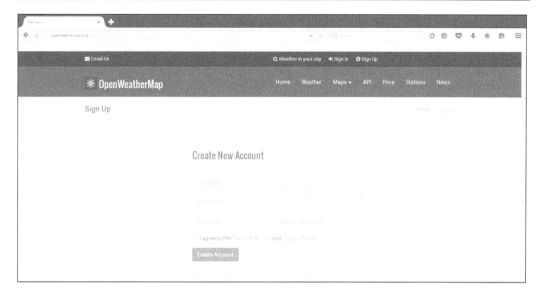

Retrieving your OpenWeatherMap API key

Once you've signed up, you'll be able to log into OpenWeatherMap. You can the find your personal API key by navigating to home.openweathermap.org and scrolling down to the **API key** text box. You should see your API key as indicated by the red rectangle in the following image:

Copy the key to your clipboard, as we'll be using it in our Python code soon.

Parsing JSON with Python

Now we can access structured weather data over HTTP by using a URL. But doing so in our browser isn't much good, as we want to read this data automatically from our Python code. Luckily, Python has a bunch of useful standard libraries for exactly this use case!

Introducing JSON

JSON is a structured data format very similar to a Python dictionary, as should be apparent from the preceding sample. In fact, in this case it's identical, and we could very simply convert it to a Python dictionary to use in our Flask application by loading it as a string and running the built-in Python `eval` function on it. However, JSON is not always identical to a Python dictionary. For example, it uses `true` and `false` instead of `True` and `False` (note the case difference) — and passing anything that we don't have full control over to `eval()` is generally a bad idea. Therefore, we'll use the `Python json` library to safely parse it. We'll also use the Python `urllib2` library to download the data from the web, and the Python `urllib` library to correctly encode URL parameters.

Retrieving and parsing JSON in Python

For retrieving and parsing JSON in Python, the first step is to add the three new imports that we need to our `headlines.py` file:

```
import json
import urllib2
import urllib
```

Style tip:

For good Python style, keep the imports ordered alphabetically. You can read more about the conventions for ordering imports at the following site: `https://www.python.org/dev/peps/pep-0008/#imports`

Now add a new function, `get_weather()`, which will make a call to the weather API with a specific query. It's pretty straightforward, and looks like the following code. Replace the `<your-api-key-here>` placeholder with the API key that you copied from the OpenWeatherMap page.

```
def get_weather(query):
api_url = "http://api.openweathermap.org/data/2.5/
weather?q={}&units=metric&appid="
```

```
query = urllib.quote(query)
url = api_url.format(query)
data = urllib2.urlopen(url).read()
parsed = json.loads(data)
weather = None
if parsed.get("weather"):
    weather = {"description":
                  parsed["weather"][0]["description"],
               "temperature":parsed["main"]["temp"],
               "city":parsed["name"]
               }
return weather
```

We use the same URL we looked at earlier in our browser, but we make the query part-configurable so that the city for which we retrieve the weather data is dynamic. We use `urllib.quote()` on the query variable, as URLs cannot have spaces in them, but the names of the cities that we want to retrieve weather for may contain spaces. The `quote()` function handles this for us by, for example, translating a space to "`%20`", which is how spaces are represented in URLs. Then we load the data over HTTP into a Python string by using the `urllib2` library. As in our feedparsing example, downloading data over the Internet is always potentially unstable, and for a real-world application, we would need to add some exception handling, and retry logic here.

We then use the json library's `loads()` function (load string) to convert the JSON string that we downloaded into a Python dictionary. Finally, we manually build up a simpler Python dictionary based on the JSON one returned by the API, as OpenWeatherMap supplies a whole bunch of attributes that we don't need for our application.

Using our weather code

Now make two small changes to the `get_news()` function in order to use our `get_weather()` function. We need to call the `get_weather()` function (for now we'll just pass in London as a constant), and then pass the weather data to our template. The `get_news()` function should now look as follows:

```
@app.route("/")
def get_news():
    query = request.args.get("publication")
    if not query or query.lower() not in RSS_FEEDS:
        publication = "bbc"
    else:
        publication = query.lower()
    feed = feedparser.parse(RSS_FEEDS[publication])
    weather = get_weather("London,UK")
```

```
      return render_template("home.html",
      articles=feed["entries"],
      weather=weather)
```

This now loads the simplified data for London into the `weather` variable, and passes it along to our template file so that we can display the data to our users.

Displaying the weather data

Now we just need to adapt our template to account for the extra data. We'll display the weather data just above the news headlines, and add some level 2 headings to keep the different sections of our application organized.

Add the following three lines to the `home.html` template, right after the opening `<h1>` tag:

```
<body>
  <h1>Headlines</h1>
  <h2>Current weather</h2>
  <p>City: <b>{{weather.city}}</b></p>
  <p>{{weather.description}} |{{weather.temperature}}&#8451;</p>
  <h2>Headlines</h2>
```

There's nothing here that we haven't seen before. We simply grab the sections we want out of our weather variable using braces. The funny `&#8451;` part is to display the symbol for degrees Celsius. If you're one of those people who is able to make sense of the notion of Fahrenheit, then remove the `&units=metric` from the API URL (which will tell OpenWeatherData to give us the temperatures in Fahrenheit), and display the *F* symbol for our users by using `&#8457;` in your template instead.

Allowing the user to customize the city

As mentioned earlier, we would not always want to display the weather for London. Let's add a second search box for city! Searching is usually hard, because data input by users is never consistent, and computers love consistency. Luckily, the API that we're using does a really good job of being flexible, so we'll just pass on the user's input directly, and leave the difficult bit for others to deal with.

Adding another search box to our template

We'll add the search box to our template exactly as before. This form goes directly under the *Current weather* heading in the `home.html` file.

```
<form>
  <input type="text" name="city" placeholder="weather search">
```

```
    <input type="submit" value="Submit">
</form>
```

The form defined in the preceding code snippet simply uses a named text input and a submit button, just like the one we added for the publication input.

Using the user's city search in our Python code

In our Python code, we need to look for the `city` argument in the GET request. Our `get_news()` function is no longer well-named, as it does more than simply getting the news. Let's do a bit of refactoring. Afterwards, we'll have a `home()` function that makes calls to get the news and the weather data (and later on the currency data), and our `get_news()` function will again only be responsible for getting news. We're also going to have quite a few defaults for different things, so instead of hard-coding them all, we'll add a `DEFAULTS` dictionary as a global, and whenever our code can't find information in the GET arguments, it'll fall back to getting what it needs from there. The changed parts of our code (excluding the imports, global URLs, and the main section at the end) now look like this:

```python
# ...

DEFAULTS = {'publication':'bbc',
            'city': 'London,UK'}

@app.route("/")
def home():
    # get customized headlines, based on user input or default
    publication = request.args.get('publication')
    if not publication:
        publication = DEFAULTS['publication']
    articles = get_news(publication)
    # get customized weather based on user input or default
    city = request.args.get('city')
    if not city:
        city = DEFAULTS['city']
    weather = get_weather(city)
return render_template("home.html", articles=articles,
weather=weather)

def get_news(query):
    if not query or query.lower() not in RSS_FEEDS:
        publication = DEFAULTS["publication"]
    else:
        publication = query.lower()
    feed = feedparser.parse(RSS_FEEDS[publication])
```

```
        return feed['entries']
def get_weather(query):
    query = urllib.quote(query)
    url = WEATHER_URL.format(query)
    data = urllib2.urlopen(url).read()
    parsed = json.loads(data)
    weather = None
    if parsed.get('weather'):
        weather =
        {'description':parsed['weather'][0]['description'],
         'temperature':parsed['main']['temp'],
         'city':parsed['name']
        }
    return weather
```

Now we have a good separation of concerns—our `get_weather()` function gets weather data, our `get_news()` function gets news, and our `home()` function combines the two and handles the user's input to display customized data to our visitors.

Checking our new functionality

If all went well, we should now have a site that displays customizable news and weather data. The weather search, as mentioned, is pretty flexible. Give it a go with some different inputs—you should see a page similar to the following image:

Handling duplicate city names

The OpenWeatherMap API handles duplicate city names well, although the defaults are sometimes a bit counter-intuitive. For example, if we search for Birmingham, we'll get the one in the USA. If we want to look for the Birmingham in the UK, we can search for Birmingham, UK. In order to not confuse our viewers, we'll make a small modification for displaying the country next to the city. Then they'll immediately be able to see if they get results for a city different from what they were expecting. If you examine the full API response from our weather call, you'll find the country code listed under `sys` — we'll grab that, add it to our custom dictionary, and then display it in our template.

In the `get_weather` function, modify the line where we build the dictionary:

```
weather = {'description': parsed['weather'][0]['description'],
           'temperature': parsed['main']['temp'],
           'city': parsed['name'],
           'country': parsed['sys']['country']
          }
```

And in our template, modify the line where we display the city to read as follows:

```
<p>City: <b>{{weather.city}}, {{weather.country}}</b></p>
```

Check that its working – if you restart the application and reload the page, you should see that typing `Birmingham` into to the **Current weather** search box now displays the country code next to the city name.

Currency

Currency data is considered more valuable than weather data. Many commercial services offer APIs that are frequently updated and very reliable. However, the free ones are a bit rare. One service that offers a limited API for free is Open Exchange Rates—and again, we need to register a free account to get an API key.

Getting an API key for the Open Exchange Rates API

Head over to openexchangerates.com, and complete their registration process. After clicking on the **Sign up** link, it may look like they only have paid plans, as these are more prominently displayed. However, underneath the large paid plan options, there is a single line of text describing their free offering with a link to select it. Click on this, and enter your details.

If you are not automatically redirected, head over to your dashboard on their site, and you'll see your **API key** (App ID) displayed. Copy this, as we'll need to add it to our Python code. You can see an example of where to find your API key in the following screenshot:

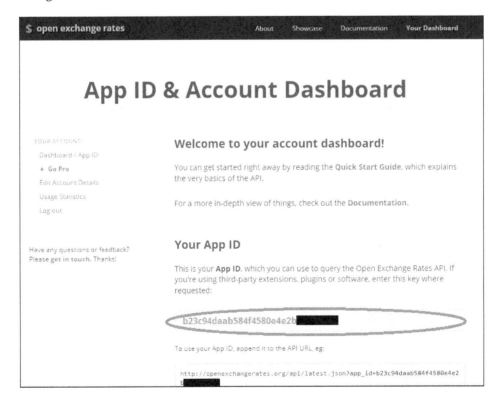

Using the Open Exchange Rates API

The `currency` API returns JSON just like the `weather` API, so we can integrate it into our Headlines application very easily. We need to add the URL as a global, and then add a new function to calculate rates. Unfortunately, the free version of the API is restricted to returning all the major currencies against the United States Dollar, so we will have to calculate our own approximate rates for conversions not involving the dollar, and rely on a perfect market to keep our information as accurate as possible (see `http://en.wikipedia.org/wiki/Triangular_arbitrage`).

Add the variable `CURRENCY_URL` to your globals below the existing `WEATHER_URL`, as seen in the following code snippet. You'll need to substitute your own App ID.

```
WEATHER_URL =
"http://api.openweathermap.org/data/2.5/weather?q={}
&units=metric&APPID=<your-api-key-here>"
CURRENCY_URL =
"https://openexchangerates.org//api/latest.json?
app_id=<your-api-key-here>"
```

Add the `get_rates()` function as follows:

```
def get_rate(frm, to):
        all_currency = urllib2.urlopen(CURRENCY_URL).read()

        parsed = json.loads(all_currency).get('rates')
        frm_rate = parsed.get(frm.upper())
        to_rate = parsed.get(to.upper())
        return to_rate/frm_rate
```

Note the calculation that we do at the end. If the request was from USD to any of the other currencies, we could simply grab the correct number from the returned JSON. But in this case, the calculation is simple enough, and it's therefore not worth adding the extra step of logic to work out if we need to do the calculation or not.

Using our currency function

Now we need to call the `get_rates()` function from our `home()` function, and pass the data through to our template. We also need to add default currencies to our `DEFAULTS` dictionary. Make the changes as indicated by the highlighted code that follows:

```
DEFAULTS = {'publication':'bbc',
            'city': 'London,UK',
            'currency_from':'GBP',
            'currency_to':'USD'
```

```
    }

@app.route("/")
def home():
    # get customized headlines, based on user input or default
    publication = request.args.get('publication')
    if not publication:
        publication = DEFAULTS['publication']
    articles = get_news(publication)
    # get customized weather based on user input or default
    city = request.args.get('city')
    if not city:
        city = DEFAULTS['city']
    weather = get_weather(city)
    # get customized currency based on user input or default
    currency_from = request.args.get("currency_from")
    if not currency_from:
        currency_from = DEFAULTS['currency_from']
    currency_to = request.args.get("currency_to")
    if not currency_to:
        currency_to = DEFAULTS['currency_to']
    rate = get_rate(currency_from, currency_to)
    return render_template("home.html", articles=articles,
    weather=weather,
                        currency_from=currency_from, currency_
to=currency_to, rate=rate)
```

Displaying the currency data in our template

Finally, we need to modify our template to display the new data. Underneath the
weather section in home.html, add:

```
<h2>Currency</h2>
1 {{currency_from}} = {{currency_to}} {{rate}}
```

As always, check that everything is working in your browser. You should see
the default currency data of the British Pound to US Dollar conversion as in the
following image:

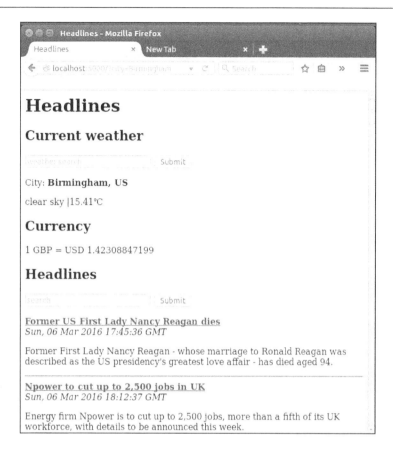

Adding inputs for the user to select currency

Now we need to add yet another user input to customize which currencies to display. We could easily add another text search like we did for the previous two, but this gets messy. We need two bits of input from the user: the *from* currency and the *to* currency. We could add two inputs, or we could ask the user to enter both into the same input, but the former makes our page pretty cluttered, and the latter means we need to worry about properly splitting the user input data (which is almost certainly not consistent). Instead, let's look at a different input element, the HTML select. You've almost certainly seen these on other web pages—they're drop-down menus with a list of values that the user can choose from. Let's see how to build them in HTML, and how to grab the data from them in Flask.

Creating an HTML select drop-down element

First, let's hard-code four currencies in each drop-down menu. The code should be inserted right below the **Currency** heading in the home.html template, and it looks like this:

```
<form>
    from: <select name="currency_from">
            <option value="USD">USD</option>
            <option value="GBP">GBP</option>
            <option value="EUR">EUR</option>
            <option value="ZAR">ZAR</option>
          </select>

    to: <select name="currency_to">
            <option value="USD">USD</option>
            <option value="GBP">GBP</option>
            <option value="EUR">EUR</option>
            <option value="ZAR">ZAR</option>
          </select>
          <input type="submit" value="Submit">
</form>
```

The name used for the GET request argument is an attribute of the select tag itself (similar to the name attribute used in our <input type="text"> tags). In our case, these are currency_from and currency_to, which we specified in our Python code earlier. The value is slightly more tricky — we have the value that's passed in our GET request (for example, currency_from=EUR), and then the value that is displayed to the user. In this case, we'll use the same for both — the currency code — but this is not compulsory. For example, we could use the full name of the currency, such as United States Dollar, in the display value, and the code in the value that's passed in the request. The argument value is specified as an attribute of the option tags, each a child of <select>. The display value is inserted between the opening and closing <option> and </option> tags.

Test this out to make sure it's working, by saving the template and reloading the page. You should see drop-down inputs appear, as in the following image:

Adding all the currencies to the select input

Of course, we could do what we did in the preceding section for the full list. But we're programmers, not data capturers, so we'll make the list dynamic, insert the options using a `for` loop, and keep our template up-to-date and clean. To get the list of currencies, we can simply take the keys of our JSON `all_currency` object, in order to make our `get_rate()` function return a tuple—the calculated rate and the list of currencies. We can then pass the (sorted) list to our template, which can loop through them and use them to build the drop-down lists. The changes for this are shown as follows:

Make the following changes in the `home()` function:

```
    if not currency_to:
        currency_to=DEFAULTS['currency_to']
rate, currencies = get_rate(currency_from, currency_to)
return render_template("home.html", articles=articles,
weather=weather,
currency_from=currency_from, currency_to=currency_to,
rate=rate,
currencies=sorted(currencies))
```

In the `get_rate()` function:

```
frm_rate = parsed.get(frm.upper())
to_rate = parsed.get(to.upper())
return (to_rate / frm_rate, parsed.keys())
```

And in the `home.html` template:

```
<h2>Currency</h2>
<form>
        from: <select name="currency_from">
            {% for currency in currencies %}
                <optionvalue="{{currency}}">
                {{currency}}</option>
            {% endfor %}
            </select>

        to: <select name="currency_to">
            {% for currency in currencies %}
                <option value="{{currency}}">
                {{currency}}</option>
            {% endfor %}

        </select>
        <input type="submit" value="Submit">
</form>
1 {{currency_from}} = {{currency_to}} {{rate}}
```

Displaying the selected currency in the drop-down input

After this, we should easily be able to see the exchange rate for any currency we want. One minor irritation is that the dropdowns always display the top item by default. It would be more intuitive for our users if they displayed the currently selected value instead. We can do this by setting the `selected="selected"` attribute in our select tag and a simple, one-line Jinja `if` statement to work out which line to modify. Change the `for` loops for the currency inputs in our `home.html` template to read as follows:

For the `currency_from` loop:

```
{% for currency in currencies %}
    <option value="{{currency}}"
    {{'selected="selected"' if currency_from==currency}}>
    {{currency}}</option>
{% endfor %}
```

For the `currency_to` loop:

```
{% for currency in currencies %}
    <option value="{{currency}}"
    {{'selected="selected"' if currency_to==currency}}>
    {{currency}}</option>
{% endfor %}
```

Reload the application and the page, and you should now be able to select any of the available currencies from both select inputs, and after the page has loaded with the desired currency data, the select inputs should automatically display the current currencies as well, as seen in the following image. After clicking on the select input, you should also be able to type on your keyboard and select the option based on the first letters of what you've typed.

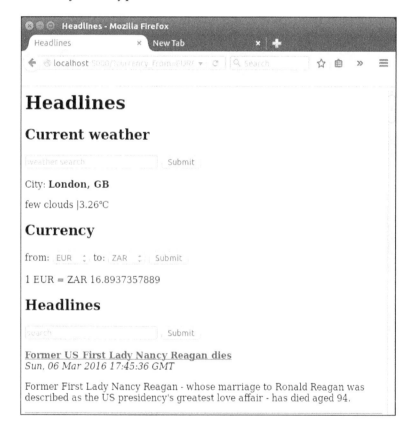

We can now see news, weather, and currency data at the same time! You can refer to the complete code from the code bundle of the chapter.

Summary

In this chapter, we've looked at the difference between the HTTP GET and POST requests, and discussed where it's good to use which. Although we have no good use for HTTP POST at the moment, we will use it in future projects where we will be getting login data from our users. Luckily, the explanatory work we did with HTTP POST is not lost—we also took a look at some more advanced ways that Git can help us with version control, and our unused code is safely stored in a different branch of our code repository in case we need to refer back to it later. Last but not least, we added weather and currency data to our application, and looked at a few different options for allowing our user to input data into our application. We're nearly done with our first project!

In the next chapter, we'll do some cosmetic touch-ups, and look at remembering our users so that they don't have to carry out exactly the same actions every time they visit our site.

5
Improving the User Experience of Our Headlines Project

Wealthy business people who have to constantly make a good impression to keep up profitable relations sometimes employ personal assistants to study their acquaintances. The PA then stands behind the wealthy person at social events and whispers a few choice words to him or her about someone who is approaching to converse. The words have to be succinct but informative, such as "Paul Smith. One child, Jill. Recently travelled, Mauritius". Now, our business person can pretend that whoever has approached is a dear friend and talk all about his children and travels at some length without having the faintest clue of who the person actually is. This makes other people feel important and liked, and this can help our hypothetical millionaire become even richer.

Why is this relevant to web applications? Well, we want to do exactly the same thing. Users of our site who feel important and remembered are more likely to come back, so we need a digital PA to make the user feel as though we've taken the time and effort to remember who they are and what they like. We could build a database of our users to store what currency conversions they usually calculate and which cities' weather they are interested in and then display these to them by default. The issue with this strategy is that we'd need them to identify themselves with every visit, and most users would find the extra step of entering a username, and possibly a password, tedious and off-putting.

Enter HTTP cookies. These sly little things will lurk on our users' computers and act as digital PAs for us when our users make a second visit to our site, giving us information that we've acquired before but haven't bothered to remember. This sounds pretty underhand. At one point, the European Union thought this way and attempted to regulate the use of cookies, but they are everywhere and are simple and useful, and the regulation attempts were a bit underwhelming (take a look at `http://silktide.com/the-stupid-cookie-law-is-dead-at-last/`).

In their simplest form, cookies are simply key-value pairs that we store on our users' machines and ask their browser to automatically send back to us whenever they visit our site. The pros of this are that we don't have to keep and maintain a database and we don't have to explicitly ask users to tell us who they are. However, the cons are that we don't have control of the information and if a user changes computers, web browsers, or even just deletes our cookies, we'll no longer be able to identify him or her. Cookies are, therefore, perfect for an application such as the one we've built; it's not the end of the world if a user has to click a few times to get back to the media, currency, and weather information he or she searched for the last time, but it's nice if we can remember previous choices and display these automatically.

While we're on the topic of user experience (or UX as it's often referred to), our site looks as though it was made in the 1980s. We'll have a stronger focus on aesthetics in later chapters, but for now we'll also take a look at how to add some basic layout and colors to our site. As we're focusing on functionality and simplicity, it'll still be far from "modern-looking", but we'll add some building blocks to our toolkit that we'll use more carefully later on. We'll use **Cascading Style Sheets** (normally just called **CSS**) to achieve this. CSS is a great tool to enable a further separation of concerns; we have already mainly separated our logic (that is, our Python script) from our content (that is, our HTML templates). Now, we'll take a look at how CSS can help us separate our formatting (that is, the color, font, layout, and so on) from the rest of our content, such as the static text in our template files.

Now that we've had an overview of cookies and CSS, we'll get to looking at implementing them in Flask. This is the final chapter of our first project, and by the end of it, we'll have a Headlines application that includes cookies and CSS.

In this chapter, we'll look at the following topics:

- Adding cookies to our Headlines application
- Adding CSS to our Headlines application

Adding cookies to our Headlines application

Our application, at this point, has a couple of issues. Let's imagine a user, Bob, who lives in Seattle. Bob visits our site and sees the defaults for BBC, London, and conversion of GBP to USD. Bob wants to see the weather for Seattle, so he types Seattle into the **Weather search** bar and hits Enter. He glances at the returned weather and feels pretty depressed that it's cold and raining as usual, so he looks away from the weather further down the page and sees the BBC headlines. He would prefer CNN headlines, so he selects this publication from the drop-down menu and hits **Submit**. He reads through a couple of headlines before realizing that current affairs are even duller and more depressing than the weather. So, his eyes move back to the top of the page again to cheer himself up. He's confused; since changing his publication preference, the weather has defaulted back to London, where the weather is even worse! He closes our application and doesn't come back. If he were to come back, everything would display the defaults again.

The two immediate problems are:

- Not remembering our users' choices even while they stay on our site
- Not remembering our users' choices after they close our site and revisit at a later stage

Let's fix both of these issues.

Using cookies with Flask

Cookies, as introduced earlier, can be thought of as key-value pairs that we may or may not receive by default from return visitors. We need to change our app so that when a user makes choices, we create or update their cookie to reflect these changes, and when a user requests our site, we check to see whether a cookie exists and read as much of the unspecified information from this as possible. First, we'll look at how to set cookies and have our user's browser automatically remember information, and then we'll look at retrieving the information that we previously used cookies to store.

Setting cookies in Flask

Flask makes dealing with cookies as easy as ever. First, we need a couple more imports; we'll use the `datetime` library from Python to set the lifespan of our soon-to-exist cookies, and we'll use Flask's `make_response()` function to create a response object that we can set cookies on. Add the following two lines to your imports section in the `headlines.py` file:

```
import datetime
from flask import make_response
```

Earlier, we were simply rendering our template with the custom arguments and then returning it to our users' web browsers. In order to set cookies, we need an extra step. First, we'll create a response object with our new `make_response()` function and then set our cookie using this object. Finally, we'll return the entire response, which includes the rendered template and the cookies.

Substitute the last line of our `home()` function in `headlines.py` with the following lines:

```
response = make_response(render_template("home.html",
  articles=articles,
  weather=weather,
  currency_from=currency_from,
  currency_to=currency_to,
  rate=rate,
  currencies=sorted(currencies)))
expires = datetime.datetime.now() + datetime.timedelta(days=365)
response.set_cookie("publication", publication, expires=expires)
response.set_cookie("city", city, expires=expires)
response.set_cookie("currency_from",
  currency_from, expires=expires)
response.set_cookie("currency_to", currency_to, expires=expires)
return response
```

This is quite a big change from the simple return statement we had, so let's break it down a bit. First, we will wrap a `make_response()` call around our `render_template()` call instead of returning the rendered template directly. This means that our Jinja templates will be rendered, and all the placeholders will be replaced with the correct values, but instead of returning this response directly to our users, we will load it into a variable so that we can make some more additions to it. Once we have this response object, we will create a `datetime` object with a value of 365 days from today's date. Then, we will do a series of `set_cookie()` calls on our `response` object, saving all the user's selections (or refreshing the previous defaults) and setting the expiry time to a year from the time the cookie was set using our `datetime` object.

Finally, we will return our `response` object, which contains the HTML for the rendered template, and our four cookie values. On loading the page, our user's browser will save the four cookies, and we'll be able to retrieve the values if the same user visits our application again.

Retrieving cookies in Flask

Remembering the information is not much good if we don't do anything with it. We now set cookies as the final step before we send a response to our users. However, we need to check for the saved cookies when a user sends us a request. If you remember how we got named arguments from Flask's request object, you could probably guess how to get saved cookies. The following line will get the cookie named `publication` if it exists:

```
request.cookies.get("publication")
```

This is simple, right? The only tricky part is getting our fallback logic correct. We still want explicit requests to take the highest priority; that is, if a user enters text or selects a value from a drop-down menu, this will be what he or she wants irrespective of what we expect from previous visits. If there is no explicit request, we will look in the cookies to check whether we can grab a default from there. Finally, if we still have nothing, we will use our hardcoded defaults.

Writing the fallback logic to check for cookies

Let's just implement this logic for `publication` first. Add a new `if` block to our publication logic in the `home()` function of `headlines.py` to make it match the following:

```
# get customised headlines, based on user input or default
publication = request.args.get("publication")
if not publication:
    publication = request.cookies.get("publication")
    if not publication:
        publication = DEFAULTS["publication"]
```

Now, we will look in the GET arguments, fall back if necessary on the saved cookies, and finally fall back on our default value. Let's take a look at this working. Open your web browser and navigate to `localhost:5000`. Search for `Fox` in the **Publication** search bar and wait for the page to reload with Fox News headlines. Now, close your browser, reopen it, and load `localhost:5000` again. This time, you should see the Fox headlines without having to search for them, as in the following screenshot.

Note that there is no `publication` argument in the URL, and yet the headlines themselves are now from Fox News.

Retrieving the cookies for other data

We have basic cookies working for our publication, but we still want to read the cookies we potentially saved for weather and currency options. We could simply add the same if statement to each section of our code, substituting `city`, `currency_from`, and `currency_to` for `publication` as relevant, but making the same changes in many parts of our code is a strong sign that we need to do some refactoring.

Let's create a `get_value_with_fallback()` function instead that implements our fallback logic on a more abstract level. Add the new function to the `headlines.py` file and call it from the `home()` function, as shown here:

```
def get_value_with_fallback(key):
    if request.args.get(key):
        return request.args.get(key)
    if request.cookies.get(key):
        return request.cookies.get(key)
```

```
        return DEFAULTS[key]

@app.route("/")
def home():
    # get customised headlines, based on user input or default
    publication = get_value_with_fallback("publication")
    articles = get_news(publication)

    # get customised weather based on user input or default
    city = get_value_with_fallback("city")
    weather = get_weather (city)

    # get customised currency based on user input or default
    currency_from = get_value_with_fallback("currency_from")
    currency_to = get_value_with_fallback("currency_to")
    rate, currencies = get_rate(currency_from, currency_to)

    # save cookies and return template
    response = make_response(render_template("home.html",
      articles=articles,
      weather=weather, currency_from=currency_from,
      currency_to=currency_to, rate=rate,
      currencies=sorted(currencies)))
    expires = datetime.datetime.now() +
      datetime.timedelta(days=365)
    response.set_cookie("publication", publication,
      expires=expires)
    response.set_cookie("city", city, expires=expires)
    response.set_cookie("currency_from",
      currency_from, expires=expires)
    response.set_cookie("currency_to",
      currency_to, expires=expires)
    return response
```

Now, we should be able to submit the forms in any order and have all our options remembered as we would expect. Also, whenever we visit our site, it will automatically be configured with our most recently used options. Give it a go! You should be able to search for currency, weather, and headlines; then, close your browser; and revisit the site. The inputs you used most recently should appear by default.

In the following screenshot, we can see that no arguments are passed in the URL, and yet we are displaying weather data for Port Elizabeth in South Africa; currency data from the **Chinese Yuan** (**CNY**) to **Saint Helena Pound** (**SHP**); and headlines from Fox News.

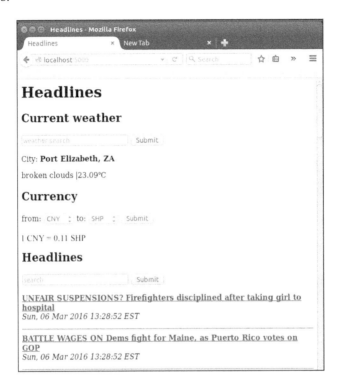

Adding CSS to our Headlines application

Our site remains pretty bare. There's a lot of white and some black. Most users prefer color, animations, borders, margins, and so on. As mentioned before, we're not really going to focus on aesthetics now, but we'll add some basic colors and styles.

External, internal, and inline CSS

There are a few ways that CSS can be added to a web page. The best way is to keep it completely separate from the HTML and save it in an external file, which is included in the HTML in a `<link>` element. This is sometimes referred to as the *external CSS*. The worst way is called *inline CSS*. Using the inline method, CSS is defined on a per element basis; this is considered bad practice as any changes to style require trawling through HTML to find the relevant sections.

Furthermore, many elements on a page often have the same or at least related styles to maintain color schemes and styles throughout the site. Using inline styles, therefore, often leads to a lot of code repetition, which we know to avoid.

For this project, we'll take a middle ground. We'll keep our CSS defined in our `.html` template files, but we'll define it all in a single place. This is because we haven't yet looked at how Flask handles files by convention, so keeping all our code in one place is simpler for now.

Adding our first CSS

CSS is quite straightforward; we will describe elements of our page by type, ID, class, and so on and define a number of properties for these, such as color, layout, padding, fonts, and so on. CSS is designed to *cascade*, that is, if we don't specify for a more specific element, it'll automatically inherit properties defined for a more general element. We'll go through the CSS itself fairly quickly, so if you've never heard of it before and would like to know more about it, now is the opportune moment to take a break and go through some CSS-specific resources. There are a lot of them online that a quick search will reveal; if you enjoyed the W3Schools HTML tutorial we mentioned earlier, you can find a similar CSS one here at `http://www.w3schools.com/css/`. Alternatively, dive in the deep end with the examples and brief explanations that follow!

First, let's add a better header to our site. We'll add a tagline beneath our top level heading, and surround it with a new `<div>` tag so that we can modify the entire header in the upcoming CSS. Modify the start of the `home.html` template to look as follows:

```
<div id="header">
    <h1>Headlines</h1>
    <p>Headlines. Currency. Weather.</p>
    <hr />
</div>
```

The `<div>` tag doesn't do anything by itself, and you can think of it as a container. We can use it to group logically related elements into the same element, which is very useful for CSS as we can then style all of the elements in a `<div>` tag at once.

CSS should be added into the `<head>` section of our template inside a `<style>` tag. Underneath the `<title>` tag in our `home.html` template, add the following code:

```
<style>
html {
    font-family: "Helvetica";
    background: white;
```

```
    }

body {
    background: lightgrey;
    max-width: 900px;
    margin: 0 auto;
}

#header {
    background: lightsteelblue;
}
</style>
```

We defined the styles explicitly for three elements: the outer `<html>` element, the `<body>` element, and any element with an `id="header"` attribute. As all of our elements are within our `<html>` element, the font cascades automatically down everywhere (although it could still be overwritten explicitly by subelements). We set everything in our body element (which contains all the visible items of the page) to have a maximum width of 900 pixels. The `margin: 0 auto;` line means that there will be no margin at the top and bottom of the body, and an automatic margin on the left- and right-hand sides. This has the effect of centering everything on the page. The `background: white;` and `background: lightgrey;` lines mean that we'll have a centered main element with a light grey background inside the larger window, which is white. Finally, our defined header `div` will have a lightsteelblue background. Save the page with the added styles and refresh to see the effect. It should look similar to the following image:

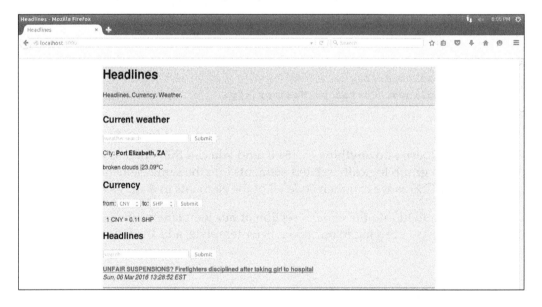

Let's take a look at how we can improve the aesthetics in the next section.

Browsers and caching

 Browsers often cache content that doesn't change often locally in order to display pages more quickly the next time you visit them. This is not ideal for development as you want to see the changes as you make them. If your styles don't seem to be doing what you'd expect, clear your browser's cache and try again. This can be done on most browsers by pressing *Ctrl + Shift + ESC* and selecting the relevant options from the menu that pops up.

Adding padding to our CSS

This is slightly more interesting than black on white, but it's still pretty ugly. One problem is that the text is right up against the margin of the color without any breathing room. We can fix this using *CSS padding*, which moves everything over from the top, right, bottom, left, or any combination by specified amounts.

We could add padding directly to our `<body>` tag as we want a nice left-hand side buffer for all the text. If you try this, you'll see the immediate issue; the padding will affect everything, including our `<div>` header and the `<hr>` tag that separates it from the rest of our content, which means that there will be a weird stripe of grey that isn't what we want. We'll fix the issue in a way that you'll soon use for nearly everything CSS-related—just add more divs! We need a *main* `<div>` header around all our subheadings and an inner header div so that we can pad the text in our header without padding the background color or the separator.

Adding more styles to our CSS

Add the following sections to your CSS to define left-hand side padding for our main and inner header divs and update the `#header` section to include some top padding:

```
#header {
  padding-top: 5;
  background: lightsteelblue;
}
#inner-header {
  padding-left: 10;
}
#main{
  padding-left: 10;
}
```

Adding the div tags to the template file

Now, let's add the divs themselves; the template code in `home.html` should be updated to look as follows:

```
<body>
    <div id="header">
        <div id="inner-header">
            <h1>Headlines</h1>
            <p>Headlines. Currency. Weather.</p>
        </div>
        <hr />
    </div>
    <div id="main">
        <h2>Current weather</h2>

... [ rest of the content code here ] ...

        {% endfor %}
    </div>
</body>
```

Styling our inputs

This makes the layout a bit more pleasant to look at because the text doesn't look like it's trying to sneak off the edge. The next major pain point is our input elements, which are very boring. Let's add some style to them as well. At the bottom of the CSS we have so far, add the following text:

```
input[type="text"], select {
    color: grey;
    border: 1px solid lightsteelblue;
    height: 30px;
    line-height:15px;
    margin: 2px 6px 16px 0px;
}
input[type="submit"] {
    padding: 5px 10px 5px 10px;
    color: black;
    background: lightsteelblue;
    border: none;
    box-shadow: 1px 1px 1px #4C6E91;
}
input[type="submit"]:hover{
    background: steelblue;
}
```

The first section styles our text input and select (that is, drop-down) elements. The text color is grey, it has a border that is of the same color as our heading, and we will make them a little bit bigger than the default ones we had before using height and line height. We also need to adjust the margins to make the text fit in the new size more naturally (if you're curious, leave out the margin line at the bottom of the first section and look at the result.) The second and third sections are to style our **Submit** buttons; one to define how they usually look and the other to define how they look when the mouse moves over them. Again, save these changes and refresh the page to see how they look. You should see something similar to the following screenshot:

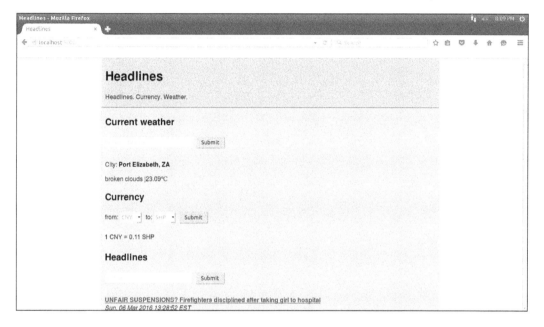

The final result will still not win any design awards, but at least you've learned the basics of CSS. One of the most frustrating parts of designing web pages is that each browser interprets CSS slightly differently (or in some cases, very differently). Cross-browser testing and validation is every web developer's arch nemesis, and in later chapters, we'll look at some tools and frameworks that can be used to mitigate the issues that arise from this potential lack of consistency.

Summary

We've made our site a bit more user-friendly in this chapter, both in terms of functionality (by remembering our users' choices through cookies) and aesthetics (using CSS). We'll come back to both of these topics in later projects, in which we'll use cookies to allow users to log in and some more advanced CSS. This is the end of our Headlines project; we have a functioning Headlines application that displays news, weather, and currency information.

In the next chapter, we'll start building a new project: an interactive crime map.

6
Building an Interactive Crime Map

Our first project notably lacked any sort of long term memory. Although we worked around the issues using cookies to simulate long-term storage, we also saw the limitations of these. In this project, we'll build an interactive crime map that allows users to tag locations with details of witnessed or experienced criminal activities. As we want to keep the data for the long term and make it available to many users, we cannot rely on our users' local and temporary storage.

Therefore, the first step to our project will be setting up a MySQL database on our VPS and linking this to a new Flask web application. We'll use the Google Maps API to allow users to view our map and add new markers to it (in which each marker represents a crime).

We'll also have some more advanced user input than in our previous project, allowing users to filter their view of the map and add fairly complex data to the map. Therefore, we'll have a stronger focus on input validation and sanitization.

Our goal for the project is a web page containing an interactive map. The user should be able to submit new crimes by choosing a location for the map and entering a date, category, and description of the crime. The user should also be able to view all the previously recorded crimes as icons on the map and more details about any specific crime by selecting the relevant icon from the map. The point of the map is to be able to easily view areas with high crime rates as well as to assist investigators in detecting patterns and trends in crime.

A substantial chunk of this chapter is devoted to setting up a MySQL database on our VPS and creating a database for the crime data. This will be followed by us setting up a basic page containing a map and text box. We'll see how to link Flask to MySQL by storing data entered into the text box in our database.

As in the previous project, we'll avoid the frameworks and automation tools that we'd almost certainly use in a "real-world" project. As we will focus on learning, a lower level of abstraction is useful. Therefore, we won't be using **Object-relational Mapping** (**ORM**) for our database queries or a JavaScript framework for user input and interaction. This means that there will be some laborious writing of SQL and vanilla JavaScript, but it's important to fully understand why the tools and frameworks exist and what problems they solve, before diving in and using them blindly.

In this chapter, we'll cover:

- Setting up a new Git repository
- Understanding relational databases
- Installing and configuring MySQL on our VPS
- Creating our Crime Map database in MySQL
- Creating a basic database web application

Setting up a new Git repository

We'll create a new Git repository for our new code base as, although some of the setup will be similar, our new project should be completely unrelated to our first one. If you need more help with this step, head back to *Chapter 1*, *Hello, World!*, and follow the detailed instructions in the *Installing and using Git* section. If you feel confident, check whether you can do this just with the following summary:

- Head over to the website for Bitbucket, GitHub, or whichever hosting platform you used for the first project. Log in and create a new repository
- Name your repository `crimemap` and take note of the URL you're given
- On your local machine, fire up a terminal and run the following commands:

```
mkdir crimemap
cd crimemap
git init
git remote add origin <git repository URL>
```

We'll leave this repository empty for now as we need to set up a database on our VPS. Once we have the database installed, we'll come back here to set up our Flask project.

Understanding relational databases

In its simplest form, a relational database management system, such as MySQL, is a glorified spreadsheet program, such as Microsoft Excel. We use it to store data in rows and columns. Every row is a "*thing*" and every column is a specific piece of information about the "*thing*" in the relevant row. I put "*thing*" in inverted commas because we're not limited to storing objects. In fact, the most common example of a thing, both in the real world and in explaining databases, is data about people. A basic database storing information about customers of an e-commerce website could look something similar to the following:

ID	First name	Surname	E-mail address	Telephone
1	Frodo	Baggins	fbaggins@example.com	+1 111 111 1111
2	Bilbo	Baggins	bbaggins@example.com	+1 111 111 1010
3	Samwise	Gamgee	sgamgee@example.com	+1 111 111 1001

If we look from the left to the right in a single row, we will get all the information about one person. If we look in a single column from the top to the bottom, we will get one piece of information (for example, an e-mail address) for everyone. Both can be useful; if we want to add a new person or contact a specific person, we will probably be interested in a specific row. If we want to send a newsletter to all our customers, we will just be interested in the e-mail column.

So, why can't we just use spreadsheets instead of databases then? Well, if we take the example of an e-commerce store further, we will quickly see the limitations. If we want to store a list of all the items we have on offer, we can create another table similar to the preceding with columns such as Item name, Description, Price, and Quantity in stock. Our model continues to be useful; however, now, if we want to store a list of all the items Frodo has ever purchased, there's no good place to put the data. We could add 1,000 columns to our customer table (as seen earlier), such as Purchase 1, Purchase 2, and so on until Purchase 1000, and hope that Frodo never buys more than 1,000 items. This is neither scalable nor easy to work with. How do we get the description for the item Frodo purchased last Tuesday? Do we just store the name item in our new column? What happens with items that don't have unique names?

Soon, we will realize that we need to think about it backwards. Instead of storing the items purchased by a person in the Customers table, we need to create a new table called Orders, and store a reference to the customer in every order. Thus, an order "knows" which customer it belongs to, but a customer has no inherent knowledge of which orders belong to him/her.

While our model still fits into a spreadsheet at a push, as we grow our data model and size, our spreadsheet becomes more cumbersome. We need to do complicated queries, such as "I want to see all items that are in stock, have been ordered at least once in the last six months, and cost more than $10".

Enter **Relational Database Management Systems** (**RDBMS**). They've been around for decades and are a tried-and-tested way of solving a common problem (such as storing data with complicated relations in an organized and accessible manner). We won't touch on their full capabilities in our Crime Map (in fact, we could probably store our data in a text file if we needed to), but if you're interested in building web applications, you will need a database at some point. So, let's start small and add the powerful MySQL tool to our growing toolbox.

I highly recommend that you learn more about databases! If the you experience in building our current project takes your fancy, go read and learn about databases. The history of RDBMS is interesting, and the complexities and subtleties of normalization and database varieties (including NoSQL databases, which we'll see some of in our next project) deserve more study time than we can devote to them in a book that focuses on Python web development.

Installing and configuring MySQL on our VPS

Installing and configuring MySQL is an extremely common task. You can, therefore, find it in prebuilt images or in scripts that build entire *stacks* for you. A common stack is called the **LAMP stack**, which stands for **Linux**, **Apache**, **MySQL**, and **PHP**, and many VPS providers provide a one-click LAMP stack image.

As we will use Linux and have already installed Apache manually, after installing MySQL, we'll be very close to the traditional LAMP stack; we will just use the P for Python instead of PHP. In keeping with our goal of "education first", we'll install MySQL manually, and configure it through the command line instead of installing a GUI control panel. If you've used MySQL before, feel free to set it up as you see fit.

MySQL and Git

 Keep in mind that neither our setup of MySQL nor the data we store in it is part of our Git repository. Be careful as any mistakes made at a database level, including misconfiguration or deleting data, will be harder to undo.

Installing MySQL on our VPS

Installing MySQL on our server is quite straightforward. SSH into your VPS and run the following commands:

```
sudo apt-get update
sudo apt-get install mysql-server
```

You should see an interface prompting you for a root password for MySQL. Enter a password and repeat it where prompted. Once the installation is complete, you can get a live SQL shell by typing the following:

```
mysql -p
```

Then, enter the password you chose earlier when prompted. We could create a database and schema using this shell, but we'd rather do this through Python; so, type quit and hit the *Enter* key to terminate the MySQL shell if you opened it.

Installing Python drivers for MySQL

As we want to use Python to talk to our database, we need to install another package. There are two main MySQL connectors for Python: *PyMySQL* and *MySQLdb*. The first is preferable from a simplicity and ease-of-use point of view. It is a pure Python library, which means that it has no dependencies. MySQLdb is a C extension and therefore has some dependencies, but it is a bit faster in theory. They work very similarly once installed. We'll use PyMySQL in our examples throughout this chapter.

To install it, run (while still on your VPS) the following command:

```
pip install --user pymysql
```

Creating our Crime Map database in MySQL

Some knowledge of SQL's syntax will be useful for the rest of this chapter, but you should be able to follow either way. The first thing we need to do is create a database for our web application. If you're comfortable using a command-line editor, you can create the following scripts directly on the VPS as this can make them easier to debug and we won't run them locally. However, developing over an SSH session is far from ideal; so, I recommend that you write them locally and use Git to transfer them to the server before running.

This may make debugging a bit frustrating, so be extra careful in writing these scripts. If you want, you can get them directly from the code bundle that comes with this book. In this case, you simply need to populate the user and password fields in the dbconfig.py file. correctly, and everything should work.

Creating a database setup script

In the crimemap directory in which we initialized our Git repository at the beginning of the chapter, create a python file called db_setup.py containing the following code:

```python
import pymysql
import dbconfig
connection = pymysql.connect(host='localhost',
                             user=dbconfig.db_user,
                             passwd=dbconfig.db_password)

try:
        with connection.cursor() as cursor:
                sql = "CREATE DATABASE IF NOT EXISTS crimemap"
                cursor.execute(sql)
                sql = """CREATE TABLE IF NOT EXISTS crimemap.crimes (
id int NOT NULL AUTO_INCREMENT,
latitude FLOAT(10,6),
longitude FLOAT(10,6),
date DATETIME,
category VARCHAR(50),
description VARCHAR(1000),
updated_at TIMESTAMP,
PRIMARY KEY (id)
) """
                cursor.execute(sql);
        connection.commit()
finally:
        connection.close()
```

Let's take a look at what this code does. First, we imported the PyMySQL library we just installed. We also imported dbconfig, which we'll create locally in a bit and populate with the database credentials (we don't want to store these in our repository). Then, we will create a connection to our database using localhost (because our database is installed on the same machine as our code) and the credentials that don't exist yet.

Now that we have connection to our database, we can get a cursor. You can think of a cursor a bit like the blinking object in your word processor that indicates where text will appear when you start typing. A database cursor is an object that points to a place in the database where we want to create, read, update, or delete data. Once we start dealing with database operations, there are various exceptions that could occur. We'll always want to close our connection to the database, so we will create a cursor (and do all the subsequent operations) inside a `try` block with `connection.close()` in a `finally` block (the `finally` block will get executed whether or not the `try` block succeeds).

The cursor is also a resource, so we'll grab one and use it in a `with:` block so that it'll automatically be closed when we're done with it. With the setup done, we can start executing the SQL code.

When we call the `cursor.execute()` function, the SQL code we will pass in will be run using the database engine, and the cursor will be populated with results if they are appropriate. We'll discuss later how we can read and write data using the cursor and the `execute()` function.

Creating the database

SQL reads similarly to English, so it's normally quite straightforward to work out what the existing SQL code does, even if it's a bit trickier to write new code. Our first SQL statement creates a `crimemap` database if it doesn't already exist (this means that if we come back to this script, we can leave this line in without deleting the entire database every time). We will create our first SQL statement as a string and use the `sql` variable to store it. Then, we will execute the statement using the cursor we created.

Looking at our table columns

Now that we know we have a database, we can create a table. The table will store the data for all the crimes that we record, with each crime in a row of the table. Therefore, we need several columns. Each column can be seen in our `create table` statement along with the type of data that will be stored in this column. To break these down, we have:

- **id**: This is a unique number that's automatically recorded for every crime we have. We don't need to worry too much about this field as MySQL will automatically insert it for us every time we add new crime data—starting at 1 and incrementing as required.

- **Latitude and longitude**: These fields will be used to store the location of each crime. We will specify `(10, 6)` after the floats which means that each float can be up to 10 digits and up to 6 digits can be after the decimal point.

- **Date**: This is the date and time of the crime.

- **Category**: We will define several categories to classify different types of crime. This will help in filtering the crimes later. VARCHAR(50) means that this will be data of variable length and up to 50 characters long.

- **Description**: This is similar to Category but with a maximum of 1000 characters.

- **Updated_at**: This is another field that we don't need to worry about. MySQL will set this to the current time when we insert the data or edit it. This could be useful if we want to, for example, remove a bunch of data that was inserted by mistake at a specific time.

Indexing and committing

The last line of our create table query specifies our id column as a *primary key*. This means that it'll be indexed (and therefore, we'll be able to find data very efficiently if we use it when we query our database), and will have various other useful properties, such as enforced existence and uniqueness.

Once we define this more complicated piece of SQL, we will execute it as well in the following line. Then, we will commit our changes to the database. Think of this as saving our changes; if we close the connection without the commit, our changes will be discarded.

SQL Commit:

> Forgetting to commit changes is a common error of SQL beginners. If you get to a point where your database doesn't behave as expected and you can't figure out why, check whether you forgot a commit somewhere in your code.

Using the database setup script

Save our script locally and push it to the repository. Refer to the following commands in this sequence:

```
git add db_setup.py
git commit -m "database setup script"
git push origin master
```

SSH to your VPS and clone the new repository to your /var/www directory using the following commands:

```
ssh user@123.456.789.123
cd /var/www
git clone <your-git-url>
cd crimemap
```

Adding credentials to our setup script

Now, we still don't have the credentials that our script relies on. We'll do two things before using our setup script:

- Create the dbconfig.py file with a database and password
- Add this file to .gitignore to prevent it from being added to our repository

Create and edit the dbconfig.py file directly on your VPS using nano, as follows:

```
nano dbconfig.py
```

Then, type the following using the password you chose when you installed MySQL:

```
db_user = "root"
db_password = "<your-mysql-password>"
```

Save it by hitting *Ctrl* + *X* and entering *Y* when prompted.

Now, use similar nano commands to create, edit, and save .gitignore, which should contain the following:

```
dbconfig.py
*.pyc
```

The first line prevents our dbconfig file from being added to our Git repository, which helps prevent an unauthorized use of our database password. The second line prevents compiled Python files from being added to the repository as these are simply runtime optimizations and are relevant to our project.

Running our database setup script

With this done, you can run:

```
python db_setup.py
```

Assuming everything goes smoothly, you should now have a database with a table to store crimes. Python will output any SQL errors, allowing you to debug if necessary. If you make changes to the script from the server, run the same git add, git commit, and git push commands that you did from your local machine.

git status:

 You can run `git status` from the terminal (make sure you are in your repository directory) to see a summary of the files that are committed. You could use this now (before `git push`) to make sure that you didn't commit the `dbconfig` file.

This concludes our preliminary database setup! Now, we can create a basic Flask project that uses our database.

Creating a basic database web application

We will start by building a skeleton of our Crime Map application. It'll be a basic Flask application with a single page that:

- Displays all the data in the `crimes` table of our database
- Allows users to input data and stores this data in the database
- Has a **Clear** button that deletes all the previously input data

Although what we will store and display can't really be described as *crime data* yet, we'll store it in the `crimes` table that we created earlier. We'll just use the `description` field for now, ignoring all the other ones.

The process of setting up the Flask application is very similar to what we did before. We will separate out the database logic into a separate file, leaving our main `crimemap.py` file for the Flask setup and routing.

Setting up our directory structure

On your local machine, change to the `crimemap` directory. If you created the database setup script on the server or made any changes to it there, make sure to sync the changes locally. Then, create the `templates` directory and touch the files we will use by running the following commands (or using the GUI file explorer if you prefer):

```
cd crimemap
git pull origin master
mkdir templates
touch templates/home.html
touch crimemap.py
touch dbhelper.py
```

Looking at our application code

Add the following code to the crimemap.py file. This contains nothing unexpected and should all be familiar from our Headlines project. The only thing to point out is the DBHelper() class, which we'll consider the code for next. We will simply create a global DBHelper instance right after initializing our application and then use it in the relevant methods to grab data from the database, insert data into the database, or delete all data from the database:

```python
from dbhelper import DBHelper
from flask import Flask
from flask import render_template
from flask import request


app = Flask(__name__)
DB = DBHelper()


@app.route("/")
def home():
    try:
        data = DB.get_all_inputs()
    except Exception as e:
        print e
        data = None
    return render_template("home.html", data=data)


@app.route("/add", methods=["POST"])
def add():
  try:
    data = request.form.get("userinput")
    DB.add_input(data)
  except Exception as e:
    print e
  return home()

@app.route("/clear")
def clear():
  try:
    DB.clear_all()
  except Exception as e:
    print e
  return home()

if __name__ == '__main__':
  app.run(port=5000, debug=True)
```

Looking at our SQL code

There's a little bit more SQL to learn from our database helper code. Add the following code to the dbhelper.py file:

```python
import pymysql
import dbconfig


class DBHelper:

  def connect(self, database="crimemap"):
    return pymysql.connect(host='localhost',
            user=dbconfig.db_user,
            passwd=dbconfig.db_password,
            db=database)

  def get_all_inputs(self):
connection = self.connect()
    try:
      query = "SELECT description FROM crimes;"
      with connection.cursor() as cursor:
        cursor.execute(query)
      return cursor.fetchall()
    finally:
      connection.close()

  def add_input(self, data):
    connection = self.connect()
    try:
      # The following introduces a deliberate security flaw.
      See section on SQL injection below
      query = "INSERT INTO crimes (description) VALUES
      ('{}');".format(data)
      with connection.cursor() as cursor:
        cursor.execute(query)
        connection.commit()
    finally:
      connection.close()


  def clear_all(self):
    connection = self.connect()
    try:
      query = "DELETE FROM crimes;"
      with connection.cursor() as cursor:
        cursor.execute(query)
        connection.commit()
    finally:
      connection.close()
```

As in our setup script, we need to make a connection with our database and then get a cursor from our connection in order to do anything meaningful. Again, we will do all our operations in `try: finally:` blocks in order to ensure that the connection is closed.

In our helper, we will consider three of the four main database operations. **CRUD (Create, Read, Update,** and **Delete)** describes the basic database operations. We will either create and insert new data, read the existing data, modify the existing data, or delete the existing data. We have no need to update data in our basic app, but creating, reading, and deleting are certainly useful.

Reading data

Let's start with reading, assuming that there is some data already in our database. In SQL, this is done using the `SELECT` statement; we will choose which data we want to retrieve based on a set of conditions. In our case, the query in the `get_all_inputs` function is `SELECT description FROM crimes;`. We'll take a look a bit later at how to refine a `SELECT` query, but this one just grabs the `description` field for every row in our `crimes` table. This is similar to the example we talked about at the beginning of this chapter, in which we wanted to send out a newsletter and needed the e-mail address of each of our customers. Here, we want the description of each of our crimes.

Once the cursor executes the query, it will point to the beginning of a data structure containing the results. We will perform `fetchall()` on our cursor, which transforms our results set to a list so that we can pass them back to our application code. (If you've used generators in Python, it may help to think of a database cursor as a generator. It knows how to iterate over the data but doesn't itself contain all the data).

Inserting data

Next up is our `add_input()` function. This takes the data input by the user and *inserts* it into the database. Creating data in SQL is done using the `INSERT` keyword. Our query (assuming `foobar` is our passed in data) is `INSERT into crimes (description) VALUES ('foobar')`.

This may look overcomplicated for what it actually does, but remember that we're still dealing with a single field (description). We'll discuss later how `INSERT` is designed to accept multiple but arbitrary columns, which can all be named in the first set of brackets, and then matching values for each of these, which are given in the second set of brackets, after `VALUES`.

As we made changes to the database, we will need to *commit* our connection to make these permanent.

Deleting data

Finally, we will take a look at how concise a DELETE statement in SQL can be. DELETE FROM crimes wipes all the data from our crimes database. We'll consider later how to make this keyword behave less like a nuke by specifying conditions to delete only some data.

Again, this makes changes to our database, so we need to commit these.

If all the new SQL commands seem to be a lot to take in, go play around with them for a bit in an online sandbox or even in our own live SQL shell that we discussed how to access earlier. You'll find that SQL comes quite naturally after a while as most of its keywords are taken from a natural language, and it uses very few symbols.

Finally, let's take a look at our HTML template.

Creating our view code

Python and SQL are fun to write, and they are indeed the main part of our application. However, at the moment, we have a house without doors or windows; the difficult and impressive bit is done, but it's unusable. Let's add a few lines of HTML to allow the world to interact without the code we wrote.

In templates/home.html, add the following:

```
<html>
<body>
  <head>
    <title>Crime Map</title>
  </head>

  <h1>Crime Map</h1>
  <form action="/add" method="POST">
    <input type="text" name="userinput">
    <input type="submit" value="Submit">
    </form>
  <a href="/clear">clear</a>
  {% for userinput in data %}
    <p>{{userinput}}</p>
    {% endfor %}
</body>
</html>
```

There's nothing we haven't seen before. Here, we had a form with a single text input to add data to our database by calling the /add function of our app, and directly below it, we looped through all the existing data and displayed each piece within <p> tags.

Running the code on our VPS

Finally, we need to make our code accessible to the world. This means pushing it to our git repo, pulling it onto the VPS, and configuring Apache to serve it. Run the following commands locally:

```
git add .
git commit -m "Skeleton CrimeMap"
git push origin master
ssh <username>@<vps-ip-address>
```

Now, on your VPS, run the following:

```
cd /var/www/crimemap
git pull origin master
```

Now, we need a .wsgi file to link Python to Apache, which can be created by running the following command:

```
nano crimemap.wsgi
```

The .wsgi file should contain the following:

```
import sys
sys.path.insert(0, "/var/www/crimemap")
from crimemap import app as application
```

Now, hit *Ctrl + X* and then enter *Y* when prompted to save.

We also need to create a new Apache .conf file, and to set this as the default (instead of headlines, the .conf file that is our current default). Run the following commands to create the file:

```
cd /etc/apache2/sites-available
nano crimemap.conf
```

Next, add the following code:

```
<VirtualHost *>
    ServerName example.com

    WSGIScriptAlias / /var/www/crimemap/crimemap.wsgi
```

```
    WSGIDaemonProcess crimemap
    <Directory /var/www/crimemap>
       WSGIProcessGroup crimemap
      WSGIApplicationGroup %{GLOBAL}
       Order deny,allow
       Allow from all
    </Directory>
  </VirtualHost>
```

This is so similar to the `headlines.conf` file we created for our previous project that you might find it easier to just copy the previous one and substitute as necessary.

Finally, we need to deactivate the old site and activate the new one, as follows:

```
sudo a2dissite headlines.conf
sudo a2ensite crimemap.conf
sudo service apache2 reload
```

Now, everything should be working. If you copied the code out manually, it's almost certain that there's a bug or two to deal with. Don't be discouraged by this; remember that debugging is expected to be a large part of development! If necessary, run `tail -f /var/log/apache2/error.log` while you load the site to note any errors. If this fails, add some print statements to `crimemap.py` and `dbhelper.py` to narrow down where things are breaking.

Once everything works, you should be able to see a web page with a single text input. When you submit text through the input, you should see the text displayed on the page, as in the example that follows:

Note how the data we get from the database is a tuple, so it is surrounded by brackets and has a trailing comma. This is because we selected only a single field, `'description'`, from our `crimes` table, while we could, in theory, be dealing with many columns for each crime (and soon we will do so).

Mitigating against SQL injection

Our application contains a fatal flaw. We take input from our users and insert it into our SQL statements using Python string formatting. This works well when the user enters a normal alphanumeric string as expected, but if the user is malicious, they can actually inject their own SQL code and take control of our database. Although SQL injection is an old attack and most modern technology automatically mitigates against it, there are still dozens of attacks against major corporations every year in which passwords or financial data are leaked due to a SQL injection vulnerability. We'll take a moment to discuss what an SQL injection is and how to prevent it.

Injecting SQL into our database application

Navigate to our web application and hit the **clear** link to remove any saved inputs. Now, in the input, type `Bobby` and click on the **Submit** button. The page should now look similar to the following image:

In this input, now type:

```
'); DELETE FROM crimes; --
```

All characters are important here.

The input needs to start with a single quote followed by a close bracket, followed by a semicolon, and then followed by the delete statement, another semicolon, a space, and finally two hyphens. You might expect to see a second line when the page refreshes, listing this strange-looking string beneath the **Bobby** output, but instead, you'll see a blank page that looks similar to the screenshot that follows:

This is weird, right? Let's take a look at what happened. In our `DBHelper` class, our insert statements have the following line:

```
query = "INSERT INTO crimes (description) VALUES
('{}');".format(data)
```

This means that the user's input gets added into the SQL code just before we run the code on the database. When we put the strange-looking input that we used previously into the placeholder of the SQL statement, we will get the following string:

```
"INSERT INTO crimes (description) VALUES (''); DELETE FROM crimes; --
');"
```

These are two SQL statements instead of one. We closed off the `INSERT` statement with an empty value and then deleted everything in the `crimes` table with the `DELETE` statement. The two hyphens at the end form an SQL comment so that the extra close quotation mark and bracket don't cause any syntax errors. When we input our data, we inserted a blank row into our database and then deleted all the data from the `crimes` table!

Of course, a creative attacker could run any SQL statement in place of the DELETE statement that we chose. They could drop an entire table (refer to https://xkcd.com/327/ for a humorous example), or they could run a select statement to bypass a database login function. Alternatively, if you store credit card information, a similar attack could be used to fetch the data and display it to the attacker. In general, we don't want the users of our web application to be able to run arbitrary code on our database!

Mitigating against SQL injection

Mitigating against SQL injection involves sanitizing user inputs and making sure that if the user inputs special characters that might be interpreted as SQL syntax, these characters are ignored. There are different ways to do this, and we'll use a simple one provided automatically by our Python SQL library. For more comprehensive information on this topic, take a look at https://www.owasp.org/index.php/SQL_Injection_Prevention_Cheat_Sheet.

In the dbhelper.py file, change the add_input() method to read as follows:

```
def add_input(self, data):
    connection = self.connect()
  try:
      query = "INSERT INTO crimes (description) VALUES (%s);"
      with connection.cursor() as cursor:
          cursor.execute(query, data)
          connection.commit()
      finally:
          connection.close()
```

The %s token that we used here is a string placeholder similar to %d, which is used in normal Python strings as a placeholder and an older alternative to braces. However, instead of using Python's str.format() function, we will pass the string and values that we want to insert into the placeholders to the PyMySQL cursor.execute() function. This will now automatically escape all characters that are meaningful to SQL so that we don't have to worry about them being executed.

Now, if you try the inputs again, you'll see them displayed as expected-special characters and all-as in the screenshot that follows:

In the final chapter of this book, we'll briefly talk about ORM techniques that can provide even stronger mitigation against SQL injection attacks. While it might seem to be a simple problem that we've solved by escaping some special characters, it can actually become quite subtle. Tools such as **sqlmap** (`http://sqlmap.org/`) can try hundreds of different variants on the same idea (that is, the idea of inputting special characters against a database) until one gets unexpected results and a vulnerability is found. Remember that for your application to be secure, it has to be protected against every possible vulnerability; for it to be insecure, it only has to be vulnerable to one.

Summary

That's it for the introduction to our Crime Map project. We discussed how to install a MySQL database on our VPS and how to hook it up to Flask. We looked at creating, reading, updating, and deleting data, and we created a basic database web application that can accept user input and display it back again. We finished off by looking at the SQL injection vulnerability and how to protect ourselves against it.

Next up, we'll add a Google Maps widget and some better aesthetics.

7
Adding Google Maps to Our Crime Map Project

In the previous chapter, we set up a database and discussed how to add and remove data from it through Flask. With a web application that can do input and output with long-term storage, we now have the building blocks needed for nearly all web applications and are limited only by the power of our imagination.

In this chapter, we will add more features than the text-only interface from the previous chapter; we'll add embedded Google Maps that will allow a user to view and select geographic coordinates in an intuitive way.

Google Maps is written in JavaScript, and we'll need to write some JavaScript code to adapt Google Maps to our needs. As always, we'll do a whirlwind tutorial for readers who haven't ever used JavaScript before, but if you're interested in solidifying your all-inclusive web application knowledge, now is a good time to quickly go through a couple of JavaScript-specific tutorials. If you've never seen any JavaScript code before, an easy introduction that is similar to the HTML and CSS tutorials we provided links to before can be found at `http://www.w3schools.com/js/default.asp`.

Arguably, the most important part of a crime map is the map itself. We'll use the Google Maps API, which is simple and powerful for developers and intuitive for users. As a first step, we'll just add a basic map that loads to an area and zoom level that we choose. Once we've seen to this, we'll add functionality to allow for markers. Markers will serve two purposes for our map: first, we'll display a marker on the map in the location of every crime we have saved in our database; second, when the user clicks on the map, it'll add a new marker and allow the user to submit a new crime report (eventually by adding a description and date in form fields).

However, first we need to be able to run our application locally again for development and debugging. Having linked it to the database, this is a bit tricky; so, we'll look at how to solve this common problem.

In this chapter, we'll cover the following topics:

- Running a database application locally
- Adding an embedded Google Map widget to our application
- Adding an input form for new crimes
- Displaying existing crimes on our map

Running a database application locally

In order to develop and debug locally, we need to be able to run the application. However, at the moment, this is not possible as MySQL is only installed on our VPS. There are three main options to develop our database application locally:

- Connecting to the database on our VPS even when running Flask on our local machine
- Installing MySQL on our local machine
- Creating a "mock" of our database in memory using Python

While any could work, we'll go with the third option. Connecting to our production database would cause us to be affected by latency if we develop in a location far from our VPS, and this would also mean that we'd run test code against our production database, which is never a good idea. The second option would limit the portability of our development environment, increase setup time if we switch to a new development environment, and in the worst case scenario, use up a significant amount of local resources.

Creating a mock of our database

If you try to run the `crimemap.py` file locally, the first error you will see is `ImportError` because of the `dbconfig.py` file that we don't have. In the previous chapter, we created this file directly on our VPS and didn't check it into git as it contained sensitive database credentials. We'll create a local copy of `dbconfig.py`, which indicates that our application should use a mock database. We'll update the `dbconfig.py` file on our VPS to indicate that the real database should be used when the app is run from there. We'll do this with a simple Boolean flag.

Adding a test flag

In your local `crimemap` directory, create a new `dbconfig.py` file and add a single line of code:

```
test = True
```

Now, SSH into your VPS and add the flag to the production configuration as well; although, here, the value should be set to `False`, as follows:

ssh user@123.456.789.123

cd /var/www/crimemap

nano dbconfig.py

Add the following to the top of the file:

```
test = False
```

Then, type *Ctrl* + *X* followed by *Y* to save and quit the file

Now, exit the SSH session. This will solve `ImportError` (the `dbconfig.py` file now exists on our VPS and locally), and our application is now aware of whether it is running in test or production.

Writing the mock code

Our flag doesn't actually do anything yet though, and we don't want to trigger all the exceptions when we test our app. Instead, we'll write a "mock" of our database code (the code in the `dbhelper.py` file) that'll return basic static data or `None`. When our application runs, it will be able to call database functions normally, but there will be no actual database. Instead, we'll have a few lines of Python to emulate a very basic database. Create the `mockdbhelper.py` file in your `crimemap` directory and add the following code:

```
class MockDBHelper:

    def connect(self, database="crimemap"):
        pass

    def get_all_inputs(self):
        return []

    def add_input(self, data):
        pass

    def clear_all(self):
        pass
```

As you can note, the methods we used for our basic database application all exist but don't do anything. The `get_all_inputs()` method returns an empty list, which we can still pass to our template. Now, we just need to tell our app to use this instead of the real `DBHelper` class if we are in a testing environment. Add the following code to the end of the imports section in `crimemap.py`, making sure to remove the existing `import` for `DBHelper`:

```
import dbconfig
if dbconfig.test:
    from mockdbhelper import MockDBHelper as DBHelper
else:
    from dbhelper import DBHelper
```

We use our test flag in `dbconfig` to specify whether or not to import the real `DBHelper` (which relies on having a connection to MySQL) or to import the mock `DBHelper` (which does not need database connection). If we import the mock helper, we can change the name so that the rest of the code can continue to run without conditional checks for the test flag.

Validating our expectations

Now, you should be able to run the code locally, just as before we added a database dependency. In your terminal, run:

python crimemap.py

Then, visit `localhost:5000` in your browser to take a look at your app loading. Check the output of the terminal to make sure that no exceptions are triggered (as would be the case if you attempted to run the real `DBHelper` code instead of the mock ones we just made). Although our application no longer "works", we can at least run it to test our code that doesn't involve the database. Then, when we deploy to production, everything should work exactly as in our tests, but with a real database plugged in.

Adding an embedded Google Maps widget to our application

Now, we want to add a map view to our app instead of the basic input box. Google Maps allows you to create a map without registration, but you will only be able to make a limited number of API calls. If you create this project, publish a link on the Web, and it goes viral, you stand a chance of hitting the limit (which is currently 2,500 map loads per day). If you think this will be a limiting factor, you can register for the maps API and have the option of paying Google for more capacity. However, the free version will be more than adequate for development and even production if your app isn't too popular.

Adding the map to our template

We want to display a map on the main page of our app, so this means editing the code in the `home.html` file in our `templates` directory. Remove all the existing code and replace it with the following:

```html
<!DOCTYPE html>
<html lang="en">
  <head>
    <script type="text/javascript"
      src="https://maps.googleapis.com/maps/api/js">
    </script>

    <script type="text/javascript">
      function initialize() {
        var mapOptions = {
          center: new google.maps.LatLng(-
          33.30578381949298, 26.523442268371582),
          zoom: 15
        };
        var map = new
        google.maps.Map(document.getElementById("map-
          canvas"),mapOptions);
      }
    </script>

  </head>
    <body onload="initialize()">
    <div id="map-canvas" style="width:80%;
      height:500px;"></div>
    </body>
</html>
```

Introducing JavaScript

Let's take a look at what happened here. The first line told our user's browser that we're using HTML5. Lines 4 to 6 include the map resources we need in our page. Note that this is between `<script>` tags, indicating that it's JavaScript. In this particular case, we did not actually write the JavaScript code – we simply linked to where it's hosted on Google's servers. Think of this a bit as a Python `import` statement, except we don't even have to install the package locally; it's simply "imported" at runtime by your user's browser.

Directly following this is our setup script to display a basic map. Again, this is between `<script>` tags to indicate that it's JavaScript instead of HTML. This time, we actually wrote the JavaScript code ourselves though. The syntax is similar to Java in terms of brackets, braces, and `for` loops. Apart from this and its name, there is little relation between it and Java.

The first line of our JavaScript code is a function definition; similar to Python's "def" we use the `function` keyword to define a new function named `initialise()`. We declared a variable with `var mapOptions =` and assigned a new JavaScript object to this variable that looks similar to a Python dictionary. We define a location with a latitude-longitude tuple-like object, which we have access to because of Lines 4 to 6, and the object also contains a `"zoom"` level. These options describe our initial map: which area should be displayed and at what zoom level.

Finally, we created a new variable, `map`, and initialized a Google map object, passing in the ID of an HTML element (which we'll explain in more detail in the following section) and the map options we just defined. We then reached the end of our JavaScript code, so we closed the `<script>` tag.

The body of our HTML code

Although our `<body>` section is only a couple of lines, it has some subtleties. The first line opens the `<body>` tag and also defines the `onload` parameter. This parameter takes the name of a JavaScript function that will be called automatically when the page is loaded. Note that the function name (`"initialize"`, in our case, as this is the function we just wrote and want to be run automatically in order to create our map) is enclosed in inverted commas. This might be counterintuitive if you think of Python, in which inverted commas are used mainly for string literals. Think of it as passing the function *name* to the body block but note the fact that we still use the open-close brackets as part of the name.

The next line creates a `<div>` element. Normally, `<div>` does nothing except enclose more HTML, but this doesn't mean that an empty `<div>` block, as we have here, is pointless. Note the ID, `map-canvas`, that we give our `<div>`. This matches the name in our JavaScript code; that is, the JavaScript function will look for an HTML element called `map-canvas` (using `document.getElementById()`) and transform this into Google Maps widget. Therefore, it makes sense to use a `<div>` element as we want an empty element for our JavaScript code to use.

Finally, our `<div>` element also includes some inline CSS. We can define the width and height of our map (which is a requirement of the Google Maps API) using CSS's `height` and `width` attributes. In this case, we defined the map to a constant `height` value of `500` pixels and a `width` value of `80%` of the page. The percentage for the width is useful as the scrolling functionality is often overloaded with the zoom functionality. That is, if the user wants to scroll down on our page using a touchpad or mouse wheel and his or her cursor is over the map, the map will zoom in instead of the page scrolling down. The 20 percent "blank" space on the right-hand side, therefore, provides the user with somewhere to move the mouse to while scrolling. Similarly, for touchscreens, the user would "*pan*" around the map while trying to scroll, but can use this space to put his or her finger while scrolling.

Testing and debugging

We should now be able to run our web app locally and see the embedded Google Map. If your app is not already running, use your terminal to start it up again and navigate to `localhost:5000` in your browser. As we don't store the code for Google Maps locally, this needs to be fetched from Google's servers, so we need our local machine to be online for this to work (similar to fetching the data we needed for our Headlines application).

Debugging JavaScript code is a bit tricky as any errors won't be registered by Flask and will therefore not be seen in your app output. If your web page is blank or does anything unexpected, the first place to look is your browser's developer console. This is a developer's tool that can be found in all the major browsers, normally by pressing *Ctrl* + *Shift* + *C* and navigating to the "**Console**" tab in the window or sidebar that appears. Here, you'll note any JavaScript errors or warnings that your code has triggered, so this tool is invaluable in debugging a web application.

Although the console should report line numbers along with errors, it can sometimes be difficult to track down exactly what is going wrong. JavaScript is a dynamically typed language and is infamous for having some pretty quirky and counterintuitive behavior. If necessary, you can also add JavaScript lines between the `<script>` tags in your HTML that do nothing but log in to the developer tools console. To do this, use the following:

```
console.log("A message");
```

This is similar to a Python `print` statement, and you can pass variables and most objects to see a string representation of them logged to the output. Use the + symbol to concatenate. For example, if you have a variable named "a" and you want to see its value at a specific point in code, you could add the following line:

```
console.log("The value of a is: " + a);
```

For a more sophisticated approach to debugging, take a look at the **Debugger** tab of the developer tools window (or its equivalent in your browser) and play around with setting breakpoints in JavaScript. The developer tools are generally a powerful suite of tools and their full functionality is unfortunately beyond the scope of this book. The following screenshot shows the Mozilla Firefox developer console with a breakpoint set just before the map loads:

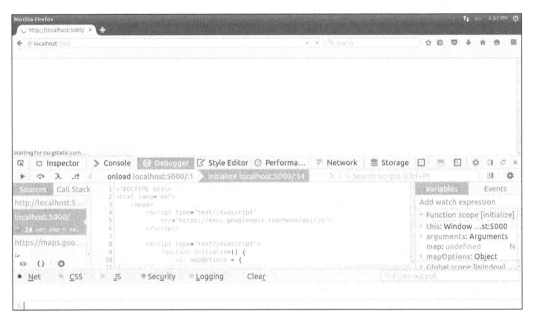

Once all the bugs are squashed (or straight-away if you are meticulous and lucky), you should see a page in your browser containing an embedded Google Map centered on **Grahamstown**, South Africa. Play around with the zoom level and coordinates set by the mapOptions variable in your JavaScript code to get the initial map of your choice. Clicking and holding on the map will allow "panning" or moving around the world. Zooming is done by scrolling with your middle mouse wheel, using your touchpad, or "pinch zooming" on touchscreen. The result should look similar to the following screenshot:

Let's now move on to making our map more interactive and useful.

Making our map interactive

The first functionality we'll add to our app will allow the user to place a marker on the map. This will eventually allow the user to add a crime report by indicating where the crime took place, thus adding to our crowd-sourced database of crimes. We'll implement the marker functionality in JavaScript, as well, using a "listener".

Adding markers

JavaScript is *event-driven*. Actions such as a mouse move or mouse click are events, and we can react to these events by setting up an event listener. The listener simply runs in the background, waiting for a specific event, and then triggers a specified action if it detects the event. We'll set up a listener for a mouse click, and if detected, we'll place a map marker at the location of the mouse when clicked.

Using the Google Map API, this can be achieved in a few lines of code. First, we'll make our `map` variable global. Then, we'll create a `placeMarker()` function that will reference our `map` variable and place a marker on it when called. In our existing `initalise()` function, we'll add a click listener that will call the `placeMarker()` function when triggered.

The full JavaScript code can be seen here with the modified lines highlighted:

```
<script type="text/javascript"
  src="https://maps.googleapis.com/maps/api/js">
</script>

<script type="text/javascript">

  var map;
  function initialize() {
  var mapOptions = {
    center: new google.maps.LatLng(-33.30578381949298,
      26.523442268371582),
    zoom: 15
  };
  map = new google.maps.Map(document.getElementById("map-
    canvas"), mapOptions);
  google.maps.event.addListener(map, 'click',
    function(event){
    placeMarker(event.latLng);
    });
  }

  function placeMarker(location) {
  var marker = new google.maps.Marker({
    position: location,
    map: map
  });
  }
</script>
```

Note specifically the change from `var map = new google.maps.Map` to `map = new google.maps.Map`. We removed the `var` declaration, which means that we assigned our new map to our global `map` variable instead of creating a new local variable.

The next line makes a call to `addListener()`, which might look a little odd. The `addListener()` function takes a `map`, `event`, and `function` to be called when the listener is triggered. As in Python, JavaScript has first-class functions, which means that we can pass functions as arguments to other functions. Unlike Python, we don't need to use the `lambda` keyword to create an anonymous function; we can simply declare the function we want to pass in place of the argument. In this case, we created an anonymous function that takes an `event` argument and in turn calls our `placeMarker()` function, passing it the `latLng` property of `event`. In our case, `event` is the mouse click that is picked up by the listener, and the `latLng` property is the location of the mouse click.

In our `placeMarker()` function, we accepted a location and created a new `Marker` object, placing it at the passed-in location on our map (this is why we made the map global; now we can refer to it in this new function).

In summary, when the page loads, we will add a listener that hangs around in the background, waiting for a click. When a click is detected, the listener makes a call to `placeMarker()`, passing in the coordinates of the click it detected. The `placeMarker()` function then adds a marker at the specified coordinates, meaning that the user sees a marker appear on the map as he or she clicks on the map. Give it a try, using the console and debugger in your browser, as we did before, if things don't go as expected. You should see a new marker placed on the map for every click and be able to generate maps that look similar to the following screenshot:

Using a single marker

Creating a new marker for every click is not ideal. We actually want the user to be able to move the marker with each click instead of creating a new one. Adding more than one crime at a time would be overcomplicated and not overly useful.

To achieve this, create another global `marker` variable under the existing global `map` variable. Then, add a simple condition to the `placeMarker()` function that creates a new marker only if there isn't one already and moves the location of the existing one otherwise.

The full code, again with the modified lines highlighted, is shown as follows. Again, note that we removed `var` from the line where we created a new `marker` variable, thus using the global variable instead of creating a local one. With these changes, each click on the map should move the marker instead of creating a new one. Try it out:

```
<script type="text/javascript"
  src="https://maps.googleapis.com/maps/api/js">
</script>

<script type="text/javascript">

  var map;
  var marker;
  function initialize() {
    var mapOptions = {
    center: new google.maps.LatLng(-33.30578381949298,
     26.523442268371582),
    zoom: 15
    };
    map = new google.maps.Map(document.getElementById("map-
     canvas"), mapOptions);
    google.maps.event.addListener(map, 'click',
     function(event){
      placeMarker(event.latLng);
    });
  }

  function placeMarker(location) {
    if (marker) {
      marker.setPosition(location);
    } else {
     marker = new google.maps.Marker({
      position: location,
      map: map
    });
    }
  }
</script>
```

Adding an input form for new crimes

We want the user to be able to specify more information than simply a location. The next step is to create a form that the user can use to add date, category, and description data to a crime submission. Each of these pieces of information will be stored in the database columns we created in the previous chapter. Creating web forms is a common enough task that there are many frameworks and plugins to help automate as much of the process as possible, as most forms need a pretty frontend, which includes error messages if the user puts in unexpected input, as well as backend logic to process the data and do a more thorough validation to prevent malformed or incorrect data from polluting the database.

However, in the spirit of learning, we'll now create the backend and frontend of a web form from scratch. In our next project, we'll take a look at how to do something similar using various tools to make the process less laborious.

Our goal is to have a number of input fields to the right of our map, which allows the user to specify details about a witnessed or experienced crime and submit it to be included with our existing data. The form should have the following inputs:

- **Category**: A drop-down menu that allows the user to select which category the crime falls into
- **Date**: A calendar that allows the user to easily enter the date and time of the crime
- **Description**: A larger text box that allows the user to describe the crime in free-form text
- **Latitude and Longitude**: Text boxes that are automatically populated based on the location selected using the marker

After filling the preceding fields, the user should be able to click on a **Submit** button and view the crime he or she just submitted appear on the map.

The HTML code for the form

The HTML code needed for our form is very similar to the forms created in our earlier project, but it has some new elements as well, namely `<textarea>` and `<label>` and an input with `type= "date"`. The `<textarea>` element is very similar to the standard text fields we noted before but appears as a larger square to encourage the user to enter more text. Label elements can define a `for` attribute to specify what we are labeling. The text between the opening and closing `label` tags is then shown close to the element to be labeled.

This is useful for our form as we can prompt the user about what data to enter in each field. The date field will provide a nice calendar drop-down menu to select a date. Unfortunately, it's a fairly recent addition to HTML and is not supported in all browsers. In unsupported browsers (including Firefox), this will be identical to a text input, so we'll look at how to handle dates input by the user at the end of this chapter.

Also, note that we put the form inside a `<div>` element to make it easier to style and position on the page (we'll also do this later). The full `<body>` element of our HTML page now looks as follows (note that we added a heading and paragraph above the map, while the form is added below the map). Take a look at the following code:

```
<body onload="initialize()">
  <h1>CrimeMap</h1>
  <p>A map of recent criminal activity in the
  Grahamstown area.</p>
  <div id="map-canvas" style="width:70%;
  height:500px"></div>

  <div id="newcrimeform">
   <h2>Submit new crime</h2>
   <form action="/submitcrime" method="POST">
    <label for="category">Category</label>
    <select name="category" id="category">
     <option value="mugging">Mugging</option>
     <option value="breakin">Break-in</option>
    </select>
    <label for="date">Date</label>
    <input name="date" id="date" type="date">
    <label for="latitude">Latitude</label>
    <input name="latitude" id="latitude"
     type="text">
    <label for="longitude">Longitude</label>
    <input name="longitude" id="longitude"
     type="text">
    <label for="description">Description</label>
    <textarea name="description" id="description"
       placeholder="A brief but detailed
     description of the crime"></textarea>
    <input type="submit" value="Submit">
   </form>
  </div>
</body>
```

Refresh your page to see the form below the map. You'll notice that it looks pretty terrible with different-sized fields and a horizontal layout, as in the following screenshot:

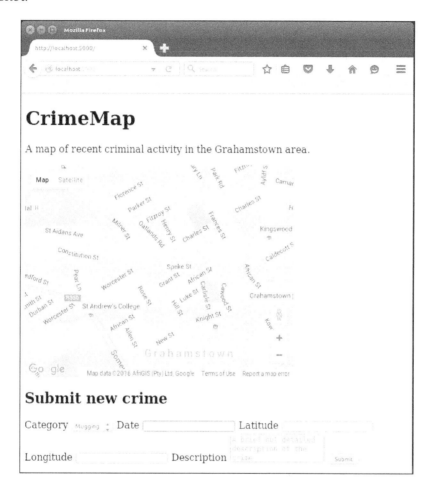

Let's add some CSS to fix this.

Adding external CSS to our web application

To make the form appear to the right of our map, we'll use CSS. We already have some CSS for our map, and we could add more CSS in a similar way. However, refer to our discussion of inline, internal, and external CSS from *Chapter 5, Improving the User Experience of Our Headlines Project*, in the *Adding CSS to our Headlines application* section, and remember that having all CSS in a separate file is best practice. Therefore, we'll create a `style.css` file and consider how to link it to our Flask app.

Creating the CSS file in our directory structure

By default in Flask, our static files should be kept in a directory called `static`. We'll want to keep various kinds of files in here eventually, such as images, JavaScript, and CSS, so we'll create a subdirectory called `css` and create our `style.css` file inside this. Navigate to your project directory in your terminal and run the following to add this directory structure and file to our project:

```
mkdir -p static/css
touch static/css/style.css
```

Adding CSS code

Insert the following CSS code into this new file:

```css
body {
  font-family: sans-serif;
  background: #eee;
}

input, select, textarea {
  display: block;
  color: grey;
  border: 1px solid lightsteelblue;
  line-height: 15px;
  margin: 2px 6px 16px 0px;
  width: 100%;
}

input[type="submit"] {
  padding: 5px 10px 5px 10px;
  color: black;
  background: lightsteelblue;
  border: none;
  box-shadow: 1px 1px 1px #4C6E91;
}

input[type="submit"]:hover {
  background: steelblue;
}

#map-canvas {
  width: 70%;
  height: 500px;
  float: left;
```

```
}

#newcrimeform {
 float: right;
 width: 25%;
}
```

You'll probably notice the similarities with the CSS code that we used for our Headlines project. However, there are still some important points to note:

- We defined the `width` and `height` of any element with the ID of `map-canvas` here (in the second-last block), so we can remove the inline style from our `body.html` file.

- We used CSS's float functionality to display our form to the right of our map instead of below it. The map takes up `70%` of the `width` of the page, and the form takes up `25%` (with the last 5% left so that the map and form have some space between them. Our map floats to the left of the page, while the form floats to the right. Because they take up less than 100% of the width combined, they'll be displayed side by side in the browser.)

Configuring Flask to use CSS

Normally in HTML pages, we can link to external CSS files simply by giving a relative path to the stylesheet. As we're using Flask, we need to configure our application to return the CSS file as a static one. By default, Flask serves files from a directory named `static` in the route of the project, which is why it's important to place the CSS file here, as described earlier. Flask can generate a URL for the CSS file we need to link to using the `url_for` function. In the `home.html` template, add the following line to the top of the `<head>` section:

```
<link type="text/css" rel="stylesheet" href="{{url_for('static',
    filename='css/style.css') }}" />
```

This creates a link between our HTML and CSS. We used attributes to describe the link as being to a `text/css` file and that it is a stylesheet. We then gave its location with `href` using the `url_for()` function.

We also need to add a line of JavaScript code to populate the location input automatically whenever the marker on the map is created or moved. This is achieved by adding the lines highlighted in the following to the `placeMarker()` function:

```
function placeMarker(location) {
 if (marker) {
  marker.setPosition(location);
 } else {
```

```
    marker = new google.maps.Marker({
      position: location,
      map: map
    });
  }
  document.getElementById('latitude').value = location.lat();
  document.getElementById('longitude').value = location.lng();
}
```

These lines simply find the latitude and longitude boxes (identified by their id attribute) and insert the location used to place the marker. When we POST the form to the server, we'll be able to read these values on the backend.

Finally, remove the inline CSS that we added earlier as this functionality is now the responsibility of our external stylesheet. Take a look at the following line in the home.html file:

```
<div id="map-canvas" style="width:70%; height:500px"></div>
```

The preceding line can be modified to instead be as follows:

```
<div id="map-canvas"></div>
```

Viewing the result

Reload the page in your browser to view the result. Remember that CSS and JavaScript are often cached by your browser, so hit *Ctrl + R* for a hard refresh if you see unexpected behavior. If *Ctrl + R* does not work, try hitting *Ctrl + Shift + Delete* and select the **cache** option in the browser's menu and clear the browsing data before refreshing again.

The styled map with the form should look similar to the following screenshot:

Note that clicking on the map now populates the latitude and longitude boxes with the coordinates of the marker.

Publishing the result

We have the form, the map, and some CSS, so now is a good time to push the result to our VPS so that we can see what it looks like on different devices or ask people for feedback.

To push our changes, fire up a terminal, change the directory to the root folder, and run the following:

```
git add crimemap.py
git add templates/home.html
git add static
git commit -m "Map with form and CSS"
git push origin master
```

Then, SSH into your VPS and pull the new code by running the following:

```
cd /var/www/crimemap
git pull origin master
sudo service apache2 reload
```

Visit the IP of your VPS to check whether the page worked and looks right. As usual, look at /var/log/apache2/error.log if anything unexpected happens.

Linking the form to the backend

It's all very well to have a pretty form to accept user input, but at the moment, we're just throwing away any submitted data. Instead of processing input in real time, as we did in our headlines application, we want to capture the input and store it in our database. Let's take a look at how to achieve this.

Setting up the URL to collect POST data

As in our Headlines project, the first step is to set up a URL on our server to which the data can be posted. In the HTML form we created, we set this URL to be /submitcrime, so let's create this as a route in our Flask app. In crimemap.py, add the following function:

```
@app.route("/submitcrime", methods=['POST'])
def submitcrime():
  category = request.form.get("category")
  date = request.form.get("date")
  latitude = float(request.form.get("latitude"))
  longitude = float(request.form.get("longitude"))
  description = request.form.get("description")
  DB.add_crime(category, date, latitude, longitude, description)
  return home()
```

Here, we simply grabbed all the data the user entered and passed it to our database helper. We used the DB.add_crime() function in the preceding code, but this does not yet exist. We need it to really add the new data to our database for our real DBHelper, and we also need a stub of this function for MockDBHelper. Let's take a look at how to add these.

Adding the database methods

In `MockDBHelper.py`, the function is simple. It needs to take the same arguments and then not do anything. Add the following to `mockdbhelper.py`:

```
def add_crime(self, category, date, latitude, longitude,
    description):
    pass
```

The real function needs to be added to `dbhelper.py` and is a bit more involved. It looks:

```
def add_crime(self, category, date, latitude, longitude,
    description):
    connection = self.connect()
    try:
        query = "INSERT INTO crimes (category, date, latitude, \
            longitude, description) \
            VALUES (%s, %s, %s, %s, %s)"
        with connection.cursor() as cursor:
            cursor.execute(query, (category, date, latitude, longitude,
description))
            connection.commit()
    except Exception as e:
        print(e)
    finally:
        connection.close()
```

There is nothing we haven't seen before here. We used placeholder values and only populated them within the `cursor.execute()` statement to avoid SQL injection, and we closed our connection in a `finally` block to make sure it always happens.

Testing the code on the server

Here is another good point to commit all the changes to the repository and do a quick check for bugs. Once the new code runs on your VPS, try adding a crime to the database by visiting your IP address and filling in the form we made. On your VPS, you can check to make sure the data was successfully added by running the following commands. Note that this fires up a live SQL shell — a direct connection to your database that should be used with care. A mistyped command can result in data being irretrievably lost or corrupted. Run the following:

```
mysql -p
<your database password>
use database crimemap
select * from crimes;
```

You'll see that MySQL prints a nice ASCII table that shows a summary of the data in your database, as in the following screenshot (in this case, all the records and columns from the `crimes` table of the `crimemap` database are shown):

```
mysql> select * from crimes;
+----+-----------+-----------+---------------------+----------+--------------+---------------------+
| id | latitude  | longitude | date                | category | description  | updated_at          |
+----+-----------+-----------+---------------------+----------+--------------+---------------------+
| 19 | -33.307438| 26.522497 | 2016-03-03 00:00:00 | mugging  | test 1       | 2016-02-27 04:58:30 |
| 20 | -33.308372| 26.523701 | 2100-01-01 00:00:00 | mugging  | Thought Crime| 2016-02-27 04:58:54 |
+----+-----------+-----------+---------------------+----------+--------------+---------------------+
2 rows in set (0.00 sec)
```

Displaying existing crimes on our map

Now, the user can add new crimes to our crime database, but we want the map to display crimes that are already added as well. To achieve this, whenever the page is loaded, our app needs to make a call to the database to get the latest crime data. We then need to pass this data to our template file, loop through each crime, and place a marker in the correct place on the map.

Now, our data is stored in a MySQL database. We will access it using Python on the server side, and we want to display it using JavaScript on the client side; so, we'll need to spend a bit of time on converting our data to the appropriate format. When we access the data through our Python `pymysql` driver, we will receive it as a tuple. To display the data using JavaScript, we want it in JSON. JSON, you might remember from our Headlines project, is JavaScript Object Notation, a structured data format that JavaScript can easily read and manipulate. As with our previous project, we'll take advantage of the fact that Python dictionaries are very similar to JSON. We'll create a Python dictionary from the tuple we get out of our database, convert this to a JSON string, and pass it to our template, which will use JavaScript to display the data as markers on our map.

Getting data from SQL

We'll start in our `DBHelper` class—adding a method to return the fields we need for each crime in our database. Add the following method to your `dbhelper.py` file:

```python
def get_all_crimes(self):
 connection = self.connect()
 try:
  query = "SELECT latitude, longitude, date, category,
   description FROM crimes;"
  with connection.cursor() as cursor:
   cursor.execute(query)
  named_crimes = []
```

```
    for crime in cursor:
     named_crime = {
       'latitude': crime[0],
       'longitude': crime[1],
       'date': datetime.datetime.strftime(crime[2], '%Y-
         %m-%d'),
       'category': crime[3],
       'description': crime[4]
     }
     named_crimes.append(named_crime)
    return named_crimes
  finally:
   connection.close()
```

Also, add the new `import` we need for the `datetime` module to the top of `dbhelper.py` via the following:

```
import datetime
```

We ignored the `id` and `updated_at` fields as the user is not interested in these using the SELECT operator to choose all our other fields. As we have no WHERE clause, this query will return all the crimes we have in our database. Once we have all the crimes, we could simply return them in their default representation of a tuple of tuples. However, this makes the maintenance of our application difficult. We don't want to have to remember that `latitude` is the first element of our tuple, `longitude` is the second, and so on. This would make developing the JavaScript part of our application a pain, as we'd have to keep referring back to our `DBHelper` to find out how exactly to grab, for example, just the `category` element of our data. If we wanted to make changes to our application in the future, it would probably require the same changes to be made here and in our JavaScript code.

Instead, we will create a dictionary from each of our records and return the dictionaries. This has two advantages: firstly, it's much easier to develop as we can refer to the elements of our data by name instead of by index, and secondly, we can easily convert our dictionary to JSON to be used in our JavaScript code. For most of the items in our dictionary, we will simply use the database column name as a key and the data itself as the value. The exception is the date; our database driver returns this as a Python `datetime` object, but we want to display it as a string for our user, so we will format it as "yyyy-mm-dd" before storing it in our dictionary.

We can add a stub of this method to our `MockDBHelper` so that we can continue to run our code locally without a database. In this case, instead of just returning a blank list, we'll return a mock crime, as well, in the same format that we'd expect from our real `DBHelper`. It's good practice to make any mock classes you create behave similarly to their real equivalents as this can help catch development errors while we're still testing locally.

Add the following function to `mockdbhelper.py`:

```
def get_all_crimes(self):
  return [{ 'latitude': -33.301304,
     'longitude': 26.523355,
     'date': "2000-01-01",
     'category': "mugging",
     'description': "mock description" }]
```

Passing the data to our template

Now that we have the ability to retrieve the data we want from our database by calling a single function, let's look at how we will use it in our main Flask app and pass it on to our template file.

Every time a user visits our home page, we want to get the crime data from the database and pass it to the template in JSON format to be displayed using JavaScript in our user's browser. As most of the hard work is done in our `DBHelper` class, we can keep our `home()` function quite neat. The entire function looks as follows:

```
@app.route("/")
def home():
  crimes = DB.get_all_crimes()
  crimes = json.dumps(crimes)
  return render_template("home.html", crimes=crimes)
```

We will use the `json.dumps()` function, which is the opposite of `json.loads()` that we used in the first project to create a JSON string for our dictionary (the letter "s" in `dumps` stands for "string") and then pass the JSON string on to our template so that it can use it to populate the map.

We also need to add an import for the JSON library. Near the top of `crimemap.py`, add the following line:

```
import json
```

Using the data in our template

Our template now has access to a JSON-formatted list of all the crimes in our database, and we can use this list to display markers on the map — one for each existing crime. We want to use the location data to choose where to place the marker, and then we want to embed `category`, `date`, and `description` as a label for our marker. This means that when the user moves his or her mouse over one of the markers, the information about the crime represented by this marker will be displayed.

We need to add a new function to our JavaScript code in our `home.html` file. Under the `initialize()` function, add the following:

```
function placeCrimes(crimes) {
 for (i=0; i<crimes.length; i++) {
  crime = new google.maps.Marker( {
    position: new google.maps.LatLng(crimes[i].latitude, crimes[i].
longitude),
    map: map,
    title: crimes[i].date + "\n" +
     crimes[i].category + "\n" + crimes[i].description
   }
  );
 }
}
```

This function takes `crimes` an argument, loops through it, and creates a new marker on our map (which we can refer to now as we previously made it a global variable) for each crime in the list. We used the call to `google.maps.Marker()` to create the marker and pass in a dictionary of arguments (in this case, a `google.maps.LatLng()` "position", which we construct from our `latitude` and `longitude` parameters); a reference to our map, which is `map`; and a concatenation of our `date`, `category`, and `description`, separated by new line characters as the `title`.

> **Customizing Google Map markers**
>
> The marker we placed can be customized pretty heavily. The full list of options we can pass in can be seen at `https://developers.google.com/maps/documentation/javascript/reference?hl=en#MarkerOptions`.

All that's left is to make a call to our new function inside our `initialize()` function and pass in the JSON map list that we built in Python. The entire `initialize()` function is shown here with the new section highlighted:

```
function initialize() {
 var mapOptions = {
  center: new google.maps.LatLng(-33.30578381949298,
   26.523442268371582),
  zoom: 15
 };
 map = new google.maps.Map(document.getElementById("map-
  canvas"), mapOptions);
```

```
google.maps.event.addListener(map, 'click', function(event){
  placeMarker(event.latLng);
});
placeCrimes({{crimes | safe}});
}
```

We simply called our `placeCrimes()` function and passed in the crimes. Note that we used the Jinja built-in `safe` function by using the | (pipe) symbol and passing in our `crimes` data. This is necessary as, by default, Jinja escapes most special characters, but we need our JSON string to be interpreted raw with all special characters as is.

However, by using the `safe` function, we tell Jinja that we know that our data is safe and at this stage, this is not necessarily the case. Just because we have no malicious intent, it does not mean that all our data is inherently safe. Remember, most of the pieces of data were submitted by our users, and our data is therefore definitely not safe. We'll take a look at the big security hole we've opened in our app right after we make sure that it works (with normal, expected usage) as intended.

> If you're familiar with *nix shells, | or pipe should be pretty straightforward syntax. If not, think of it as a usual function with input and output. Instead of passing input as parameters in parentheses and using some form of a `return` function to get output, we will instead have our input on the left-hand side of the | symbol and the function name on the right-hand side (in this case, `safe`). The input gets piped through the function, and we are left with the output in place. This syntax can be very useful to chain lots of functions together, as each outer function is simply placed on the right-hand side after another | symbol.

Viewing the results

First, test out the code locally. This will make sure that everything still runs and will possibly catch some more subtle bugs as well. As we are using a mock for our database function, we won't have a lot of confidence that this works until we see it run on the VPS.

Once you run `python crimemap.py` in your terminal and visit `localhost:5000` in your browser, you should see the following:

We can note a single marker with the details we specified in our `MockDBHelper`. In the screenshot, we moved our mouse over the marker to make the `title` appear with all the details of the crime.

Now it's time to `commit` to `git` and push to our VPS. Run the following commands locally from your `crimemap` directory:

```
git add crimemap.py
git add dbhelper.py
git add mockdbhelper.py
git add templates/home.html
git commit -m "add new crimes functionality"
git push origin master
```

Then, SSH to your VPS to pull the new changes:

```
ssh username@123.456.789.123
cd /var/www/crimemap
git pull origin master
sudo service apache2 reload
```

If we visit the IP address of our VPS now, we should see the two crimes we added before we were able to display them. As we used the real DBHelper and our MySQL database for the production site, we should be able to add crimes using the form and see each crime added as a marker to the map in real time. Hopefully, you'll get something similar to the following screenshot:

If things don't work out as expected, as always run the following on your VPS and take a look at the output while visiting the site:

```
tail -f /var/log/apache2/error.log
```

Also, use your browser's debugger by pressing *Ctrl + Shift + C* to catch any JavaScript errors that might have crept in.

Our crime map is now functional and can already be used to start tracking crime in a town and keep people informed. However, we'll still add some finishing touches in the next chapter before moving on to our final project.

Summary

In this chapter, we looked at how to create a mock database in Python so that we could develop our application without needing access to a real database. We also added a Google Maps widget to our application and allowed our users to easily submit a latitude and longitude by clicking on the map while being able to view the locations and descriptions of existing crimes as well.

In the next chapter, we'll look at another injection vulnerability, XSS, and talk about how to protect against it as well as input validation in general.

8
Validating User Input in Our Crime Map Project

Users will always use your application in ways you didn't intend or expect, either out of ignorance or malicious intent. Every bit of input that the user has any control over should be validated to make sure it conforms to what is expected.

We'll polish off our second project by making sure that users can't break it accidentally or through maliciously crafted input.

In this chapter, we will cover the following topics:

- Choosing where to validate
- Trying out an XSS example
- Validating and sanitizing

Choosing where to validate

There are a few choices to make when it comes to validating user input and displaying feedback that helps them fix any mistakes they make. The major choice is *where* to do the validation: in the browser, on the server, or both.

We could do it in JavaScript in the user's browser. The advantages of this approach are that the users will get faster feedback (they don't have to wait to send data to our server, have it validated, and have a response sent back), and it also lightens the load on our server; if we don't use CPU cycles and network bandwidth to validate user data, it means we have lower costs associated with running our server. The disadvantage of this approach is that we have no assurance that the user will not bypass these checks; if the checks are run in the user's browser, then the user has full control over them. This means that data that is validated by client-side checks is still not guaranteed to be what we expect.

We could do it on the server after the user submits the data. The advantages and disadvantages of this approach are the opposite of those described earlier. We use more processing time that we're paying for, but we get extra assurance about the integrity of our checks. On the other hand, the user normally has to wait longer to get feedback about legitimate (not malicious) errors.

The final option is to do both. This gives us the best of all worlds; we can give fast feedback to the user in JavaScript, but then recheck the results on the server side to make sure that nothing got past our client-side checks. The flipside of this is that we end up wasting time on CPU cycles checking legitimate data twice, and we also have to put more effort into development as we have to write validation checks in JavaScript and in Python.

In this project, as we will implement our form management from scratch, we'll just do some very basic checks on the server side and no checking on the client side. In our next project, when we use frameworks to handle user input, we'll discuss how to easily use some more sophisticated validation methods.

Identifying inputs that require validation

We have already noted that not all browsers support the HTML5 `"date"` type input. This means that, as our site stands, some users will possibly type the date of the crime in manually, and this means that we need to be able to deal with the user inputting dates in various formats. Our database expects yyyy-mm-dd (for example, 2015-10-10 for October 10, 2015), but our users will not necessarily conform to this format even if we tell them to. The **Date** field, then, is one of the inputs we would want to validate.

Our **Latitude** and **Longitude** fields are also editable by the user, and therefore the user could enter text or other invalid coordinates in them. We could add validation checks for these, but, as the user should never actually need to edit these values, we'll instead consider how to make them *read only*. We'll add a validation check to make sure that the user has not left them blank, though.

The **Description** is the most obviously dangerous field. The user can freely input text here, and this means that the user has opportunities to *inject* code into our app. This means that instead of filling in a text description, as we'd probably expect, the user can input JavaScript or HTML code here that interferes with the code that we expect to run. Doing so would be an example of a so-called XSS or cross-site scripting attack, and we'll look at some malicious inputs that a user might use here.

Our last input is the **Category**. This might seem perfectly safe as the user has to select it from a drop-down list. However, it's important that the drop-down is merely a convenience, and, actually, a user with some very basic knowledge can use free-form text here as well. This is because the browser uses the information from the form to create a POST request, which it sends to our server. As a POST request is just text that is structured in a certain way and sent over HTTP; there is nothing stopping our tech-savvy users from constructing the POST request without using a web browser (they could use Python or another programming language instead or even some more specialized, but freely available software, such as BURP Suite).

As we can see, all of our inputs need validation in some form or another. Before we take a look at exactly how to go about validating input, let's take a brief look at what a malicious user might do if we decided not to implement validation.

Trying out an XSS example

One of the most sought-after attacks by malicious users is a so-called *persistent* XSS attack. This means that the attacker not only manages to inject code into your web app but this injected code also remains for an extended period of time. Most often, this is achieved by tricking the app into storing the malicious, injected code in a database and then running the code on a page on subsequent visits.

 In the following examples, we will *break* our application, specific inputs to our form. You will need to log in to the database on VPS afterwards to manually clear these inputs that leave our app in a broken state.

As our app currently stands, an attacker could carry out a persistent XSS attack by filing out the **Category**, **Date**, **Latitude**, and **Longitude** fields as usual, and using the following for the **Description** field:

```
</script><script>alert(1);</script>
```

This might look a bit strange, but give it a go. You should see the following:

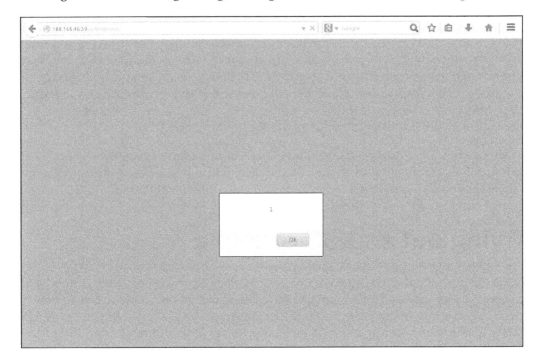

And after you click **OK** on the popup, you'll probably notice a strange excerpt from JavaScript at the top of our page (your value for longitude will be different, depending on where you placed the marker):

```
", "longitude": 26.52799}]); } function placeCrimes(crimes) { for
    (i=0; i
```

Let's look at what happened here. If we look at the full source code of our page, as it got interpreted by our browser, things will make more sense. Right-click on the page and click on **View Page Source** or an equivalent.

The placecrimes() call in the initialize function of our JavaScript code can be seen to now read as follows:

```
placeCrimes([{"latitude": -33.305645, "date": "2015-10-10",
"category": "mugging", "description":
"</script><script>alert(1);</script>", "longitude": 26.52799}]);
```

If your browser uses any form of code highlighting, it'll be easier to see what's happening. The opening `<script>` tag near the beginning of our page is now closed by the description of our first crime, as our browser knows to interpret anything that comes between `<script>` and `</script>` as JavaScript code. As we have `</script>` at the beginning of our `"description"`, the browser closes this section of JavaScript. Immediately after this, a new JavaScript section is opened by `<script>`, which is the next part of our description. Following this, we have `alert(1);`, which simply creates the pop-up box with **1** in it that we noted earlier. This script section is closed again, and the rest of our page is now interpreted as a mess by our browser. We can see the rest of our JSON (`"longitude":` ...) until halfway through our `for` loop is displayed to the user, and the `"<"` symbol from `i<crimes.length` is now interpreted by the browser as another opening tag so that the JavaScript that follows this is hidden again.

To fix our app, wipe all the crime data from your database with the following commands (which you should run on VPS):

```
mysql crimemap -p
<your database password>
delete from crimes;
```

You should see a message about how many crime records were deleted from the `crimes` table, similar to that seen in the following screenshot:

The potential of persistent XSS

It may seem pretty bad that our web application is broken. Worse still, reloading the page is not a solution. As the malicious description is stored in our database, the same issue will appear no matter how many times we reload the page. Even worse, the `"alert(1);"` example is just this—an example to show that the attacker has the freedom to run any code he or she desires. Often, an attacker uses this to trick the user into visiting another (malicious) page, banking on the fact that the user trusts the original page and will, therefore, be more likely trust the content on it. The possibilities are really only limited by our attacker's imagination.

Validating and sanitizing

To prevent the preceding, we've already chosen to inspect the data on the server side and make sure it conforms to our expectation. We still have a few more choices to make, though.

White and blacklisting

We need to create some rules to choose between acceptable inputs and unacceptable inputs, and there are two main ways of doing this. One way is to *blacklist* inputs that look malicious. Using this method, we would create a list of characters that might be used maliciously, such as "<" and ">", and we will reject inputs that contain these characters. The alternative is to use a *whitelist* approach. This is the opposite of blacklisting, in that, instead of choosing which characters we won't allow, we can choose a list of characters that we *will* allow.

It may seem like a nit-picky distinction, but it is important nonetheless. If we go with a blacklist approach, we are more likely to be outsmarted by malicious users who manage to inject code using only characters that we haven't added to our ban list.

On the other hand, using a whitelist approach, we are more likely to frustrate users who want to use characters which we haven't thought to add to the whitelist.

As our app only requires a `"description"` input to be free-text and because our app is localized (in the examples we used, the app is specific to Grahamstown, South Africa, and therefore we will expect our users to only need normal Latin characters and not, for example, Chinese characters), we should be able to employ whitelisting without getting in the way of our users.

Validating versus sanitizing

Next, we have to decide what to do with invalid input. Do we reject it completely and ask the user to try again, or do we just strip away the invalid parts of the user input and keep the rest? Removing or modifying user input (for example, by adding escape characters) is referred to as *sanitizing* the input. The advantage of this approach is that the user is often oblivious to it; if he or she inadvertently includes a special character in the description of the crime and we remove it, it's unlikely to make the rest of the description incomprehensible or worthless. The disadvantage is that if the user does end up relying on too many characters that we have blacklisted, it can corrupt the information to the point of being unusable or even misconstruing what the user intended.

Implementing validation

With all of the preceding in mind, we want to:

- Check the category that the user submits and make sure it is in the list of categories that we expect

- Check the date that the user submits and make sure that we can properly understand it as a date

- Check the latitude and longitude that the user submits and make sure that these are parsable as floating point numbers

- Check the description that the user submits and strip out all characters except for those that are alphanumeric or part of a preselected list of basic punctuation characters

Although we'll silently edit the `description` to remove non-whitelisted characters, we want to reject the entire submission and make the user start again if the other fields aren't as we expect. We, therefore, also want to add a way of displaying custom error messages to the user after he or she submits the form. Let's add a few Python functions to help us with all of this. We'll also restructure some of our code to conform to the *Don't repeat yourself(DRY)* principle.

Validating the category

Previously, when we created the drop-down list for `categories`, we hardcoded the two `categories` we wanted into our template. This is already not ideal as it means that we have to write our more boilerplate code (such as HTML tags) if we ever want to add or edit the `categories`. Now that we also want access the list of `categories` in Python, so that we can validate that the user hasn't sneakily used a category that isn't in our list, it makes sense to restructure it a bit so that we only define our list of `categories` once.

We'll define the list in our Python code and then we can pass it to our template to construct the drop-down list and use the same list for validation when the user submits the form. At the top of `crimemap.py`, along with our other globals, add the following:

```
categories = ['mugging', 'break-in']
```

In the `return` statement of the `home()` function, pass in this list as a named argument. The line should now look similar to this:

```
return render_template("home.html", crimes=crimes,
categories=categories)
```

In `home.html`, change the `<select>` block to use a Jinja `for` loop, as follows:

```
<select name="category" id="category">
    {% for category in categories %}
        <option value="{{category}}">{{category}}</option>
    {% endfor %}
</select>
```

With these small modifications, we have a much easier way to maintain our list of `categories`. We can now also use the new list to validate. As the category is provided by a drop-down list, the average user does not enter an invalid value here, so we don't have to worry too much about providing polite feedback. In this case, we'll just ignore the submission and return to the home page again.

Add the following `if` statement directly below where we loaded the category data into a variable in the `submitcrime()` function:

```
category = request.form.get("category")
if category not in categories:
    return home()
```

If triggered, this `return` would happen before we add anything to the database, and our user's attempted input would be discarded.

Validating the location

As our location data should be populated automatically by the marker that the user places on the map, we want to make these fields `readonly`. This means that our JavaScript will still be able to modify the values as the marker gets used, but the fields will reject input or modification from the user's keyboard. To do this, simply add the `readonly` attribute where we define the form in our `home.html` template. The updated `input` definitions should look as follows:

```
<label for="latitude">Latitude</label>
<input name="latitude" id="latitude" type="text" readonly>
<label for="longitude">Longitude</label>
<input name="longitude" id="longitude" type="text" readonly>
```

As with the drop-down list, though, the `readonly` property is only enforced at a browser level and is easily bypassed. We, therefore, want to add a server-side check as well. To do this, we'll use the Python philosophy of "it is better to ask for forgiveness than permission", or, in other words, assume everything will be OK and deal with the other cases in an `except` block instead of using too many `if` statements.

If we can parse the user's location data into floating point numbers, it's almost definitely safe as it's pretty difficult to do things such as modifying HTML, JavaScript, or SQL code using only numbers. Add the following code around the section of the `submitcrime()` function where we parse the location inputs:

```
try:
    latitude = float(request.form.get("latitude"))
    longitude = float(request.form.get("longitude"))
except ValueError:
    return home()
```

If there's any unexpected text in the `latitude` or `longitude` inputs, `ValueError` will be thrown when we attempt to cast to the float type, and, again, we'll return to the home page before putting any of the potentially dangerous data into our database.

Validating the date

For the `date` input, we could take the same approach as we did for the `category`. Most of the time, the user will select the date from a calendar picker and, therefore, will be unable to input an invalid date. However, as not all browsers support the `date` input type, sometimes, normal users will type out the dates manually, and this may lead to accidental error.

Therefore, in this case, we don't only want to reject invalid input. We want to, as far as possible, work out what the user intended, and if we cannot, we want to display a message to the user to indicate what needs to be fixed.

To allow for a more flexible input, we'll use a Python module called `dateparser`. This module allows us to take even inconsistently formatted dates and convert them into accurate Python `datetime` objects. The first thing we need to do is install it through `pip`. Run the following command locally *and* on VPS:

```
pip install --user dateparser
```

If you haven't used it before, you might like to play around a bit with the possibilities. The following standalone script demonstrates some of the magic that `dateparser` provides:

```
import dateparser
print dateparser.parse("1-jan/15")
print dateparser.parse("1 week and 3 days ago")
print(dateparser.parse("3/4/15")
```

All the preceding strings are correctly parsed into `datetime` objects, except, arguably, the last one, as `dateparser` uses the American format and interprets it to be March 4, 2015, instead of April 3, 2015.

Some more examples as well as other information about the `dateparser` module can be found on PyPI at `https://pypi.python.org/pypi/dateparser`.

Just using this package will solve a lot of our problems as we can now transform invalid inputs into valid ones without any help from the user at all. The slight inconvenience is that we have already set up our database to accept dates to be inserted as strings in the *"yyyy-mm-dd"* format; however, to take advantage of our new `dateparser` module, we'll want to convert the user's input to a `datetime` object. The slightly counterintuitive workaround is to convert the string input we receive from the user to a `datetime` object and then back to a string (which will always be in the correct format) before passing it into our database code to store in MySQL.

First off, add the following helper function to your `crimemap.py` file:

```
def format_date(userdate):
    date = dateparser.parse(userdate)
    try:
        return datetime.datetime.strftime(date, "%Y-%m-%d")
    except TypeError:
        return None
```

Also, add the imports for the `datetime` and `dateparser` modules to the top of `crimemap.py`, as follows:

```
import datetime
import dateparser
```

We'll pass the `date` as input by our user (`userdate`) into this function and parse this using our `dateparser` module. If the date is completely unparsable (for example, "aaaaa"), the `dateparser.parse` function will just return nothing instead of throwing an error. Therefore, we will put the call to `strftime`, which will format the date as a string in the correct format into a `try except` block; if our `date` variable is empty, we'll get a `TypeError`, in which case our helper function will also return `None`.

Now, we need to decide what to do in case we cannot parse the date. Unlike the other validation cases we looked at, in this case, we want to prompt the user with a message saying that we were unable to understand his or her input. To achieve this, we'll add an error message parameter to the `home()` function and pass in a relevant error message from the `submitcrime()` function. Modify the `home()` function to add the parameter and to pass the parameter into our template, as follows:

```
@app.route("/")
def home(error_message=None):
    crimes = DB.get_all_crimes()
    crimes = json.dumps(crimes)
    return render_template("home.html", crimes=crimes,
categories=categories, error_message=error_message)
```

Then, modify the `submitcrime()` function to add some logic to parsing the date input by our user and to pass an error message to our `home()` function if we fail to parse the `date`, as follows:

```
if category not in categories:
    return home()
date = format_date(request.form.get("date"))
if not date:
    return home("Invalid date. Please use yyyy-mm-dd format")
```

We also need to add a section to our template file to display the error message if it exists. We'll add it to the top of the form where it should catch the user's attention via the following code:

```
<div id="newcrimeform">
    <h2>Submit new crime</h2>
    {% if error_message %}
        <div id="error"><p>{{error_message}}</p></div>
    {% endif %}
    <form action="/submitcrime" method="POST">
```

We will add the preceding `if` statement as we'll otherwise see the word "None" appear above our form when the `error_message` variable has its default value of `None`. Also, note that the message itself appears in a `<div>` tag with an ID of error. This allows us to add some CSS to make the error message appear in red. Add the following block to your `style.css` file in your static directory:

```
#error {
    color: red;
}
```

That's it for validating our date. If you have a browser that does not support the `date` input, try creating a new crime and inputting a string that even `dateparser` cannot interpret as a legitimate date to make sure you see the error as expected. It should look something like the following image:

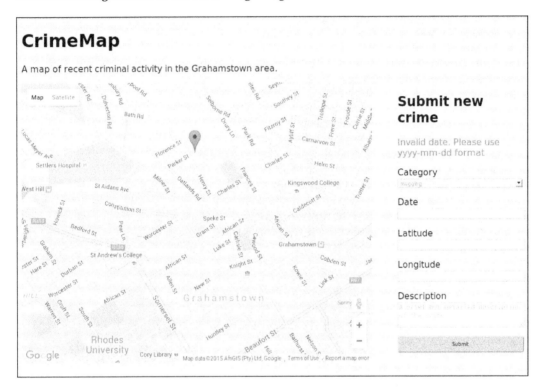

 Flask provides some pretty nifty functionality for message *flashing* — that is, to display optional text to the user at a specific position on the page. This has some more powerful and flexible functionality than the basic example we discussed, and should certainly be considered for similar cases. Information about message flashing in Flask can be found at `http://flask.pocoo.org/docs/0.10/patterns/flashing/`.

Validating the description

We can assume that a user will be able to convey basic information about a crime using only numbers, letters (capital and lowercase), and some basic punctuation marks, so let's create a simple Python function that filters out all characters from a string except the ones we have identified as safe. Add the following `sanitize()` function to your `crimemap.py` file:

```
def sanitize_string(userinput):
    whitelist = string.letters + string.digits + " !?$.,;:-'()&"
    return filter(lambda x: x in whitelist, userinput)
```

Then, add the import for string to the imports section of `crimemap.py`, as follows:

```
import string
```

Our `sanitize_string()` function is quite concise, and uses some of Python's functional programming potential. The `filter` function applies another function repeatedly for each element in a list and builds a new list based on the ones that "pass." In this case, the function that we will pass into `filter()` is a simple `lambda` function that checks whether or not a letter belongs to our `whitelist`. The result of our function is a string similar to the input one, but with all the characters that aren't part of our whitelist removed.

Our whitelist is built from all the letters (uppercase and lowercase), the digits one to nine, and some basic punctuation marks that people may use while typing informal descriptions of events.

To use our new function, simply change the line near the end of the `submitcrime()` function in `crimemap.py` from the following to the subsequent:

```
description = request.form.get("description")
description = sanitize_string(request.form.get("description"))
```

Note that, as our SQL driver mitigates against SQL injection and our `json.dumps()` function escapes double quotation marks, we should be largely safe just by blacklisting characters such as angle brackets, which we used to demonstrate an XSS attack. This would allow more flexibility for our users, but malicious users can be determined and creative in crafting input that will bypass the filters we set up. Refer to `https://www.owasp.org/index.php/XSS_Filter_Evasion_Cheat_Sheet` for some examples. Give the validation changes a go locally first and then, if everything looks good by committing to `git`, push the repo to the remote, and pull it onto VPS. Restart Apache and visit your IP address. Try submitting a crime using `</script>` in the `description`, and you'll notice when you hover the cursor over the marker for this crime that all we've stored is `"script"`. We will strip the slash and the angle brackets, thus ensuring protection against XSS.

We already discussed the pros and cons of blacklisting and whitelisting, but, to emphasise that whitelisting is not a perfect approach, take a look at the post here about mistakes developers often make when whitelisting an input for users' names: `http://www.kalzumeus.com/2010/06/17/falsehoods-programmers-believe-about-names/`

The last change we can make to our `dbhelper.py`, `mockdbhelper.py`, and `crimemap.py` files is to remove the functions we no longer need. When we had a basic database application that was not specific to crimes, we had the `get_all_inputs()`, `add_input()`, and `clear_all()` functions in our `DBHelper` classes and the `add()` and `clear()` functions in our `crimemap.py` file. All of these can be removed.

Summary

We have spent a whole chapter looking at validation, but if you look at the major companies that have faced information security breaches over the last few years, you'll agree that security is worth spending some time on. We looked specifically at cross-site scripting or XSS attacks, but we also discussed some more general points of input validation. This takes us to the end of our second project.

One thing that is notably missing is to work out who added which crimes. If one malicious user adds a bunch of bogus crimes to our database, they could potentially mess up our entire dataset!

In our next project, we'll look at authenticating users through a User Account Control system, which will give us more control over who we let on our site and what they can do.

Building a Waiter Caller App

9

After going through the headlines project, in which you learned the basics of Flask, and the Crimemap project, in which you learned about some more useful Flask features, such as how to use a database and how to write some basic JavaScript code, we're now ready for our most sophisticated project yet! We will build a waiter caller web application that allows restaurant patrons to easily call a waiter to their table. The restaurant manager will easily be able to register for and start using our application without the need to invest in expensive hardware.

We will dive even deeper into the Flask world, taking a look at some Flask extensions to help us with user account control and web forms, and we'll look at how to use template inheritance in Jinja, too. We'll also use the Bootstrap frontend framework so that we don't have to do so much of the HTML and CSS code from scratch.

In contrast with the MySQL database we used for our previous application, we'll take a look at a controversial alternative: MongoDB. MongoDB is a NoSQL database, which means that we don't deal with tables, rows, and columns in it. We'll also discuss exactly what this means.

One of the most difficult tasks for a waiter is to know when a patron needs something. Either the patron complains that they waited for far too long before the waiter came and asked about dessert options, or they complain that the waiter was constantly interrupting conversation in order to ask whether everything was all right. In order to solve this problem, some restaurants install dedicated buttons at each table which, when pressed, notify the waiter that his attention is wanted. However, the cost of specialized hardware and installation is prohibitive for smaller establishments and often just too much hassle for larger ones.

In our modern day and age, nearly all restaurant-goers have smartphones, and we can leverage this fact to provide restaurants with a much more cost-effective solution. When patrons want attention, they will simply visit a short URL on their phone, and the waiters will receive a notification on a centralized screen.

We want the application to allow for multiple, unrelated restaurants to use the same web application, so each should have a private login account for our system. We want it to be easy for the restaurant manager to set up; that is, we as developers should not need to be involved at all when a new restaurant joins the system.

The setup required for our application is as follows:

- The restaurant manager signs up a new account on our web application
- The restaurant manager provides basic information about how many tables the restaurant has
- The web application provides a unique URL for each table
- The restaurant manager prints out these URLs and ensures that the relevant URL is easily accessible from each table

The usage of our application should have the following features:

- The restaurant staff should be able to log into the web application from a centralized screen and see a simple notification page.
- Some patrons would want service and visit the URL relevant to their table on a smartphone, so this should be possible.
- In real time, the waiters should see a notification appear on a centralized screen. The waiter will then acknowledge the notification on the screen and attend to the patrons.
- If more notifications arrive before the first one is acknowledged, the later ones should appear beneath the earlier ones.

Over the next three chapters, we'll implement a Flask application that has all of the preceding features. We'll have a database to store the account information of all the individual restaurants that register to use our application so that we can process patron requests for each of them individually. Patrons will be able to make requests, which will be registered in the database, while the restaurant staff will be able to view current attention requests for their establishment. We'll build a user account control system so that restaurants can have their own password-protected accounts for our application.

To start with, we'll set up a new Flask application, Git repository, and Apache configuration to serve our new project. We'll introduce Twitter's Bootstrap framework as the one we'll use on the frontend. We'll download a basic Bootstrap template as a start for the frontend of our application and make some changes to integrate it into a basic Flask application. Then, we'll set up a user account control system that allows users to register, log in, and log out of our application by supplying an e-mail address and password.

In this chapter, we'll cover the following topics:

- Setting up a new `git` repository
- Using Bootstrap to kick-start our application
- Adding User Account Control to our application

Setting up a new Git repository

As before, we need to create a new `git` repository to host our new project. The first step is to go to log into the web interface of BitBucket or whichever code repository host you are using, select the **Create a new Repository** option, and select the **Git** radio option, taking note of the URL with which it provides you. As the next steps are identical to the previous projects, we will give you only a summary. If you need more fine-grained guidance, refer to the *Installing and using git* section of *Chapter 1, Hello, World!.*

Setting up the new project locally

To set up the local project structure, run the following commands locally:

```
mkdir waitercaller
cd waitercaller
git init
git remote add origin <new-repository-url>
mkdir templates
mkdir static
touch waitercaller.py
touch templates/home.html
touch .gitignore
```

We want to get the minimal running app for this project so that we can iron out any configuration issues before we get started with development. Add the following to your waitercaller.py file:

```
from flask import Flask

app = Flask(__name__)

@app.route("/")
def home():
    return "Under construction"

if __name__ == '__main__':
    app.run(port=5000, debug=True)
```

Then, push the project outline to the repository with the following commands:

```
git add .
git commit -m "Initial commit"
git push origin master
```

Setting up the project on our VPS

On your VPS, run the following commands to clone the repository, and set up Apache2 to serve our new project as the default website:

```
cd /var/www/
git clone <new-repository-url>
cd waitercaller
nano waitercaller.wsgi
```

Add the following code to the .wsgi file we created with the most recent command:

```
import sys
sys.path.insert(0, "/var/www/waitercaller")
from waitercaller import app as application
```

Now, hit *Ctrl + X* and select *Y* when prompted to quit Nano.

Lastly, create the Apache configuration file by running the following:

```
cd /etc/apache2/sites-available
nano waitercaller.conf
```

Add the following configuration data to the `waitercaller.conf` file we just created:

```
<VirtualHost *>

    WSGIScriptAlias / /var/www/waitercaller/waitercaller.wsgi
    WSGIDaemonProcess waitercaller
    <Directory /var/www/waitercaller>
       WSGIProcessGroup waitercaller
       WSGIApplicationGroup %{GLOBAL}
        Order deny,allow
        Allow from all
    </Directory>
</VirtualHost>
```

Quit Nano, saving the new file as before. Now, to disable our `crimemap` project as the default site and enable our new project instead, run the following commands:

```
sudo a2dissite crimemap.conf
sudo a2ensite waitercaller.conf
sudo service apache2 reload
```

Verify that everything worked by visiting the IP address of your VPS in your web browser. You should see the **Under construction** string. Have another look at your configuration and log files if things don't work out as expected.

Using Bootstrap to kick-start our application

In our previous projects, we spent quite a bit of time on frontend work, fiddling around with CSS and HTML, and we didn't even touch on some of the frontend problems that web application developers need to be aware of, such as making sure our content looks good and functions correctly on all devices of all screen sizes running any browser on any operating system. This diversity of browsers and devices as well as the inconsistent way in which each of them implements certain JavaScript, HTML, and CSS functionality is one of the biggest challenges of web development, and there is no silver bullet to solve the problem. However, frontend frameworks such as Bootstrap can take away some of the pain, providing shortcuts for developers to improve their user experience.

Introducing Bootstrap

Bootstrap was developed by Twitter and is released under an open license. It can greatly speed up CSS development as it provides many styles for different HTML layouts and form inputs. It can also provide *responsiveness*; that is, it can allow your website to automatically change the layout of certain elements based on the screen size of your user's device. We'll discuss exactly what this means for us and for this project later in the chapter.

 Bootstrap has faced some criticism, but it still holds its popularity. There are many alternatives with different strengths and weaknesses. As modern web development is a fast-evolving field, there are also many new frameworks that appear regularly. Existing frameworks often get major updates and don't provide backward compatibility to old versions. For important production web applications, current research into what best fits the specific needs of this project is always crucial.

Bootstrap's main offerings are reusable in CSS and JavaScript modules. We'll mainly use it for its CSS components.

Take a look at Bootstrap's homepage at `http://getbootstrap.com/` as well as the subpages at `http://getbootstrap.com/getting-started/#examples` and `http://getbootstrap.com/components/` to get an idea of what Bootstrap provides.

Instead of writing CSS from scratch, Bootstrap allows us to use various inputs, icons, navigation bars, and other often-needed components of a website that look good by default.

Downloading Bootstrap

There are a few ways to install Bootstrap, but keeping in mind that Bootstrap can be thought of as a collection of some JavaScript, CSS, and icon files, we will not do anything too fancy. We can simply download a `.zip` file of the compiled code files and use these files in our local project. We'll include bootstrap in our `git` repository, so there is no need to install it on our VPS as well. Perform the following steps:

1. Head over to `http://getbootstrap.com/getting-started/#download` and select the **Download Bootstrap** option, which should be the compiled and minified version without documentation.

2. Unzip the file you downloaded, and you'll find a single directory called `bootstrap-3.x.x` (here, the repeated letter x represents numbers that indicate which version of Bootstrap is contained). Inside the directory, there will be some subdirectories, probably `js`, `css`, and `fonts`.

3. Copy the `js`, `css`, and `fonts` directories to the `static` directory of the `waitercaller` project. Your project should now have the following structure:

```
waitercaller/
templates
    home.html
static
    css/
    fonts/
    js
.gitignore
waitercaller.py
```

Because of the regular Bootstrap updates, we included a complete copy of the code for Bootstrap 3.3.5 in the accompanying code bundle (the latest version during the writing of this book). While the latest version is probably better, it might not be compatible with the examples we give. You can choose to test the waters with the version we provide, knowing that the examples should work as expected, or jump in at the deep end and, if necessary, try to work out how to adapt the examples to the newer Bootstrap code.

Bootstrap templates

Bootstrap strongly encourages users to build customized frontend pages instead of simply using existing templates. You've probably noticed a lot of modern web pages look very similar; this is because frontend designing is difficult, and people like taking shortcuts. As this book focuses on Flask development, we'll also take a bit of a frontend shortcut and start with one of the example template files that Bootstrap provides. The template file we'll work with can be seen at `http://getbootstrap.com/examples/jumbotron/`, and the adaptation for our project can be found in the accompanying code bundle for this chapter at `tempates/home.html`. You can note from the similarity of the two files that we didn't have to do too much work to get a basic web page that also looks good.

Copy the code from the `templates/home.html` file in the code bundle to the same place in your own project directory that we created earlier. If you included all the Bootstrap files properly in your `static` folder, opening this new file directly in your web browser will result in a page that looks similar to the following screenshot. (Note that at this stage, we still use pure HTML and none of the Jinja functionality, so you can just open the file locally in your web browser instead of serving it from a Flask application.):

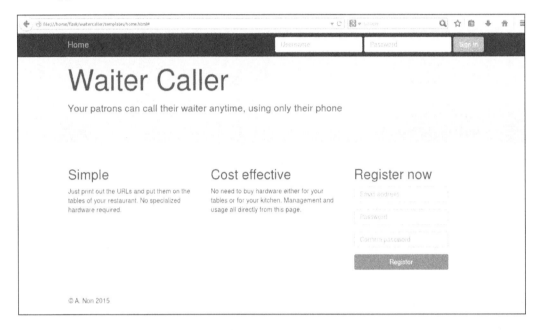

We can note the advantages of the styling of inputs, headers, the navigation bar, and Jumbotron (the gray bar near the top with the oversized **Waiter Caller** text in it) that we can achieve with very little code. However, perhaps the most significant time-saving element of using Bootstrap is the *responsiveness* that our site has. Bootstrap is based on a grid layout, which means that different elements of the grid can rearrange themselves to better fit on any device. Note this part of HTML from the template:

```
<div class="row">
  <div class="col-md-4">
    <h2>Simple</h2>
```

A `"row"` has space for 12 columns. Our three main content elements below the Jumbotron each take up four columns, thus filling the row (*4 x 3 = 12*). We specified this using the `class="col-md-4"` attribute. Think of this as a medium (`md`) column of size four. You can read more about how the grid system works and take a look at some examples at `http://getbootstrap.com/css/`.

There's also some code that doesn't look used in the preceding screenshot, similar to this:

```
<button type="button" class="navbar-toggle collapsed" data-
    toggle="collapse" data-target="#navbar" aria-expanded="false"
    aria-controls="navbar">
```

The two preceding excerpts are perhaps the most important components in making our web application responsive. To understand what this means, resize your browser window while the page is open. This simulates how our page will be seen on smaller devices, such as phones and tablets. It should look similar to the following screenshot:

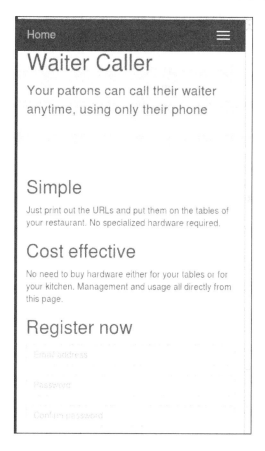

We can note that our three main content elements that used the Bootstrap grid functionality are now arranged beneath each other instead of side by side. This is ideal for smaller devices in which users are more used to scrolling down than to looking for more content on the side. Our navigation bar has also become more concise with the login inputs now hidden.

These can be revealed by selecting the *hamburger* icon in the upper right-hand corner; this is a controversial, but highly prevalent, element in web development. Most users instinctively know that they can touch the icon to get some form of menu or expansion, but there are many criticisms of using this technique. For now, we'll just accept this as normal practice and not go into the problems behind it. It's definitely better than trying to display exactly the same content no matter the screen size and having our users zoom into the page section by section, depending on which part they need to see.

Adding user account control to our application

For user account control, a user is expected to log in and authenticate using a password. For example, when you log in to your Webmail account, you enter your password upon visiting the page. Thereafter, all your actions are taken as authenticated; that is, you do not have to enter your password again when you send an e-mail. The Webmail client *remembers* that you are logged in, and you are therefore allowed to complete certain actions.

However, HTTP is a stateless protocol, which means that we have no direct way of knowing that the user who logged in is the same user who made the request to send an e-mail. As a workaround for this problem, we will give the user a cookie when he or she logs in initially, and the user's browser will then send this cookie to us with *every* subsequent request. We'll use our database to keep track of which users are currently logged in. This allows us to authenticate the user for every request without requesting the user's password multiple times.

We could implement this from scratch using Flask cookies in a similar way to what we saw in our Headlines project. However, there are numerous steps that we would need to implement, such as selecting which pages in our application require authentication and ensuring that the cookie is secure, and be involved in deciding what information to store in the cookie.

Instead, we'll go up one level of abstraction and use the `Flask-Login` extension.

Introducing Flask-Login

`Flask-Login` is a Flask extension that implements the groundwork required for all user account control systems. To use this, we need to install it through `pip` and then create a user class that follows a specific pattern. You can find a summary of `Flask-Login` as well as comprehensive documentation at `https://flask-login.readthedocs.org/en/latest/`.

Installing and importing Flask-Login

To install `Flask-Login`, run the following command:

```
pip install --user flask-login
```

As with all the Python modules we install, remember to do this both locally and on your VPS.

To begin with, we'll add the most basic login functionality possible. Our application will display **You are logged in** for users who have authenticated, but users who do not enter a correct password will not be able to see the message.

Using Flask extensions

When we install Flask extensions, we can automatically access them through the `flask.ext` path. The first class we'll use from the `Flask-Login` extension is the so-called `LoginManager` class. We'll also use the `@login_required` decorator to specify which routes are restricted to users who are logged in. Add the following imports to your `waitercaller.py` file:

```
from flask.ext.login import LoginManager
from flask.ext.login import login_required
```

Now, we need to connect the extension to our Flask app. In a pattern that will become familiar as we use more Flask extensions, add the following line to `waitercaller.py` directly below the place where you create the `app` variable:

```
app = Flask(__name__)
login_manager = LoginManager(app)
```

The `LoginManager` class we instantiated now has a reference to our application. We'll use this new `LoginManager` class to—you guessed it—manage logins for our application.

Adding a restricted route

Now, let's add a route to our application at `/account` and make sure that only authenticated users can view this page. The easy part of this step is to make sure that *non* authenticated users *can't* see the page, so we'll start with this.

First, we want our application to render our Bootstrap template by default. Add the following route to the `waitercaller.py` file:

```
@app.route("/")
def home():
    return render_template("home.html")
```

Now, we'll add a restricted route that users who aren't logged in can't see. Add the following function to `waitercaller.py`:

```
@app.route("/account")
@login_required
def account():
    return "You are logged in"
```

Note that we're using the `@login_required` decorator. Similarly to the `@app.route` decorator, this is a function that takes the function below it as input and returns a modified function. In this case, instead of the routing magic, it'll verify that the user is logged in, and if not, it'll redirect the user to an **Unauthorized** page instead of returning the content we specified in the `return` statement. It's important that the `@app.route` decorator is first and the `@login_required` one is below it, as in the preceding example.

You've probably seen **404 page not found** errors sometimes while browsing the Web. While **404** is especially infamous, there are many error codes that are part of the HTTP specification. Different browsers may show different default error messages when these are received, and it's also possible to define custom error pages to be shown when the specified errors are hit.

As we haven't set up any of the login logic yet, no user should be able to authenticate and view the new route we created. Start your Flask application locally and try to visit the account route at `localhost:5000/account`. If all went well, you should see an unauthorized error message similar to the following screenshot:

Authenticating a user

The Internet can be a dark and scary place. This is why you need to put passwords into many web applications; the password proves that you are who you claim to be. By telling us something that only you know, the web application knows you are "you" and not an imposter.

The simplest way to implement a password checking system would be to store passwords associated with usernames in a database. When the user logs in, you need to first verify that the username exists, and if it does, you need to verify that the password the user just gave matches the one that he or she used when registering.

In practice, this is a terrible idea. Databases may be accessed by any number of people, including employees of the company that runs the web application and, potentially, hackers. Instead, we'll eventually store a cryptographic hash of the user's password; however for now, to make sure our login system works, we'll work with plaintext passwords.

We'll set up a mock database that is very similar to the one we used in our Crime Map project and check whether we can allow a mock user to view our account page if, and only if, the correct password is entered.

Creating a user class

As we are using the Flask-Login module, we need to create a User class that conforms to a strict format. Flask-Login is flexible enough to allow some more advanced login functionality, such as distinguishing between *active* and *nonactive* accounts as well as anonymous users. We won't use these features, but we need to create a User class that can work with Flask-Login, so we'll have some methods that look redundant.

Create a new file called user.py in your waitercaller directory. Add the following code to it:

```
class User:
    def __init__(self, email):
        self.email = email

    def get_id(self):
        return self.email

    def is_active(self):
        return True

    def is_anonymous(self):
        return False

    def is_authenticated(self):
        return True
```

`Flask-Login` requires that we implement a `get_id()` method in our `User` class that returns a unique identifier for the user. We'll be using the user's e-mail address for this, so in the `get_id()` function we can simply return that.

We'll regard all our users as having active accounts; so, in this method, which is also required, we'll simply return `True`. The opposite goes for the `is_anonymous()` function; while this is also required, we won't deal with the concept of anonymous logins in our application, so we'll always return `False`.

The last function may look a bit odd; we'll always return `True` for `is_authenticated()`. This is because we only create the user object when the correct username and password combination is entered, so if the user object exists, it'll be authenticated.

Mocking our database for users

We'll create a `MockDBHelper` class again and also create a configuration file to indicate that this should be used locally when we test our application and don't have access to the database. It needs to have a function that takes a username and password and checks whether these exist in the database and are associated with each other.

First, create a file called `mockdbhelper.py` in your `waitercaller` directory and add the following code:

```
MOCK_USERS = {'test@example.com': '123456'}

class MockDBHelper:

    def get_user(self, email):
        if email in MOCK_USERS:
            return MOCK_USERS[email]
        return None
```

At the top, we have a dictionary that acts as the database storage. We have a single `get_user()` method that checks whether a user exists in our database and returns the password if it does.

Now, create a `config.py` file in the `waitercaller` directory and add the single line as follows:

```
test = True
```

As in our last project, this file will let our application know whether it is running in our test (local) environment or in our production (VPS) one. Unlike our previous project, we'll add other information into this file later that doesn't involve the database, which is why we'll call it `config.py` instead of `dbconfig.py`. We don't want to check this file into our `git` repository as it'll be different on our VPS and will also contain sensitive database credentials that we don't want to store; so, create a `.gitignore` file in your `waitercaller` directory with the following lines:

```
config.py
*.pyc
```

Logging in a user

Our template already has a login form set up that allows a user to enter an e-mail and a password. We'll now set up functionality that allows us to enter and check the input into this form against our mock database. If we enter an e-mail and password that exist in our mock database, we'll log the user in and allow access to our `/account` route. If not, we'll just redirect back to the home page (we'll look at displaying feedback to a user who inputs invalid information in the next chapter in the *Adding user feedback using WTForms* section).

Adding imports and configuration

We need to import the `login_user` function that is part of the `Flask-Login` extension as well as our new `User` class code and database helper. Add the following lines to your imports in `waitercaller.py`:

```
from flask.ext.login import login_user

from mockdbhelper import MockDBHelper as DBHelper
from user import User
```

As we don't have a database helper except for our mock one at the moment, we'll always import the mock one. Later, we'll use the value in `config.py` to decide which database helper to `import` — the real or mock one — as we did in our previous project.

We also need to create a `DBHelper` global class so that our application code can easily talk to our database. Add the following line beneath the import section of `waitercaller.py`:

```
DB = DBHelper()
```

Finally, we also need to configure a secret key for our application. This is used to cryptographically sign the session information cookies that `Flask-Login` hands out to our users when they log in. Signing the cookies prevents our users from editing them manually, which helps prevent fraudulent logins. For this step, you should create a long and secure secret key; you will never have to remember it, so don't think about it as you would about a password or passphrase. Although randomly mashing your keyboard should be sufficient, humans are generally terrible at creating unbiased randomness, so you could also use the following command to create a random string using `/dev/urandom` (changing `100` to the number of characters you want) via the following:

```
cat /dev/urandom | base64 | head -c 100 ; echo
```

Once you have a long random string of characters, add the following line to your `waitercaller.py` file under the place where you declared the `app` variable, substituting the random characters for your own:

```
app.secret_key = 'tPXJY3X37Qybz4QykV+hOyUxVQeEXf1Ao2C8upz+fGQXKsM'
```

Adding the login functionality

There are two main parts of logging a user in to consider. The first is when the user enters an e-mail address and password to authenticate, and the second is when the user does so by sending the required cookie—that is, he or she is still in the same browser *session* as when a successful login was completed.

Writing the login function

We already created the stub of our login route for the first case, so now, we will flesh that out a bit to check the input information against our database and use `Flask-Login` to log the user in if the e-mail and password match.

We'll also introduce a cleaner way of calling one Flask route from a separate one. Add the following lines to the imports section of `waitercaller.py`:

```
from flask import redirect
from flask import url_for
```

The first takes a URL and creates a response for a route that simply redirects the user to the URL specified. The second builds a URL from a function name. In Flask applications, you'll often see these two functions used together, as in the following example.

Write the login function in `waitercaller.py` to match what follows through this code:

```
@app.route("/login", methods=["POST"])
def login():
    email = request.form.get("email")
    password = request.form.get("password")
    user_password = DB.get_user(email)
    if user_password and user_password == password:
        user = User(email)
        login_user(user)
        return redirect(url_for('account'))
    return home()
```

We also need to add `import` for the `request` library. Add the following line to the `import` section of `waitercaller.py`:

```
from flask import request
```

We'll load the user's input into `email` and `password` variables and then load the stored password into a `user_password` variable. The `if` statement is verbose as we explicitly verified that a password was returned (that is, we verified that the user exists) and that the password was correct, even though the second condition implies the first. Later on, we'll talk about the trade-off of differentiating between the two conditions when giving feedback to our user.

If everything is valid, we will create a `User` object from the e-mail address, now using the e-mail address as the unique identifier required by Flask login. We will then pass our `User` object to the `Flask-Login` module's `login_user()` function so that it can handle the authentication magic. If the login is successful, we will redirect the user to the account page. As the user is now logged in, this will return the `"You are logged in"` string instead of the `"Unauthorized"` error we got before.

Note that we will create a URL for our account page using the `url_for()` function. We will pass the result of this into the `redirect()` function so that the user is taken from the `/login` route to the `/account` one. This is preferable to simply using the following:

```
return account()
```

Our intention is more explicit, and the user will see the correct URL in the browser (that is, both will take the user to the `/account` page), but if we don't use the `redirect()` function, `/login` will still be displayed in the browser even on the `/account` page.

Creating the load_user function

If the user has already logged in, their browser will send us information through the cookie that `Flask-Login` gave them when we called the `login_user` function. This cookie contains a reference to the unique identifier we specified when we created our `User` object—in our case, the e-mail address.

`Flask-Login` has an existing function that we called `user_loader`, which will handle this for us; we just need to use it as a decorator for our own function that checks the database to make sure the user exists and creates a `User` object from the identifier we are given.

Add the following function to your `waitercaller.py` file:

```
@login_manager.user_loader
def load_user(user_id):
    user_password = DB.get_user(user_id)
    if user_password:
        return User(user_id)
```

The decorator indicates to `Flask-Login` that this is the function we want to use to handle users who already have a cookie assigned, and it'll pass the `user_id` variable from the cookie to this function whenever a user visits our site, which already has one. Similarly to what we did before, we will check whether the user is in our database (`user_password` will be blank if `user_id` is invalid), and if it is, we will recreate the `User` object. We'll never explicitly call this function or use the result as it'll only be used by the `Flask-Login` code, but our application will throw an error if a user who is given a cookie by our `login()` function visits the site and `Flask-Login` can't find an implementation for this `user_loader()` function.

It might seem unnecessary to check the database in this step considering we gave the user a supposedly tamper-proof token that proves that he or she is a valid user, but it is in fact necessary as the database may have been updated since the user last logged in. If we make the user's session token valid for a long time (recall that in our Headlines project, we made the cookies last for a year), there is the possibility that the user's account will have been modified or deleted since the cookie was assigned.

Checking the login functionality

It's time to give our new login functionality a try! Fire up the `waitercaller.py` file locally and visit `localhost:5000` in your web browser. Type in the e-mail ID `test@example.com` and password `123456` from our mock database and hit the login button. You should be redirected to `http://localhost:5000/account` and view the **You are logged in** message.

Close your browser and reopen it, this time visiting `localhost:5000/account` directly. As we didn't tell `Flask-Login` to remember users, you should now see the **Unauthorized** error again.

Because of the nature of our application, we would expect most users to want to stay logged in so that the restaurant staff can simply open the page in the morning and use the functionality straightaway. `Flask-Login` makes this change very straightforward. Simply change the line of your `login()` function that reads the following:

```
login_user(user)
```

Your new `login()` function should now read:

```
login_user(user, remember=True)
```

Now, if you repeat the preceding steps, you should view the **You are logged in** message as shown in the following screenshot, even after restarting your browser:

Now that we can log a user in, let's take a look at how we can allow the user to log out as well.

Logging out a user

`Flask-Login` provides a logout function that works straight out of the box. All we have to do is link it up to a route. Add the following route to your `waitercaller.py` file:

```
@app.route("/logout")
def logout():
    logout_user()
    return redirect(url_for("home"))
```

Then, add the `import` for the `logout_user()` function to the imports section of `waitercaller.py`:

```
from flask.ext.login import logout_user
```

Note here that there's no need to pass the `User` object to `Flask-Login` for this call; the `logout()` function simply removes the session cookie from the user's browser. Once the user is logged out, we can redirect them back to the home page.

Visit `localhost:5000/logout` in your browser and then attempt to visit `localhost:5000/account` again. You should see the **Unauthorized** error again as the `test@example.com` user got logged out.

Registering a user

It's great that we can log users in, but at the moment we can only do so with the mock user that we hardcoded into our database. We need to be able to add new users to our database when the registration form is filled out. We'll still do all of this through our mock database, so every time our application is restarted, all the users will be lost (they will only be saved in the local Python dictionary variable, which is lost when the application is terminated).

We mentioned that storing the users' passwords was a very bad idea; so first, we'll take a brief look at how cryptographic hashing works and how we can manage passwords more securely.

Managing passwords with cryptographic hashes

Instead of storing the password, we want to store something that is *derived from* the password. When the user registers and gives us a password, we'll run some modification on it and store the result of the modification instead. Then, the next time the user visits our site and uses the password to log in, we can run the same modification on the input password and verify that the result matches what we stored.

The catch is that we want our modification to be nonreversible; that is, someone who has access to the modified password should not be able to deduce the original.

Enter hash functions. These little pieces of mathematical wizardry take a string as input and return a (big) number as output. The same string input will always result in the same output, but it is almost impossible for two different inputs to produce the same output. Hash functions are so-called *one-way* functions as it is provably impossible to deduce the input if you only have the output.

Password storage and management is a big topic that we can only touch on in this project. For more information on most things regarding information security, www.owasp.org is a good resource. Their comprehensive guide to storing passwords securely can be found at https://www.owasp.org/index.php/Password_Storage_Cheat_Sheet.

Python hashlib

Let's take a look at how to use hash functions in Python. Run the following in a Python shell:

```
import hashlib
hashlib.sha512('123456').hexdigest()
```

As output, you should see the hash **ba3253876aed6bc22d4a6ff53 d8406c6ad864195ed144ab5c87621b6c233b548baeae6956df346ec8c17f5ea 10f35ee3cbc514797ed7ddd3145464e2a0bab413**, as shown in the following screenshot:

```
Python 2.7.6 (default, Mar 22 2014, 22:59:56)
[GCC 4.8.2] on linux2
Type "help", "copyright", "credits" or "license" for more in
formation.
>>> import hashlib
>>> hashlib.sha512('123456').hexdigest()
'ba3253876aed6bc22d4a6ff53d8406c6ad864195ed144ab5c87621b6c23
3b548baeae6956df346ec8c17f5ea10f35ee3cbc514797ed7ddd3145464e
2a0bab413'
>>> _
```

The random-looking string of hexadecimal characters is the sha512 hash of the '123456' string, and this is what we will store in our database. Every time the user enters the plaintext password, we'll run it through the hash function and verify that the two hashes meet up. If an attacker or employee sees the hash in the database, they cannot masquerade as the user because they cannot deduce '123456' from the hash.

Reversing hashes

Actually, the heading of this section isn't entirely true. While there is no way to *reverse* a hash and write a function that takes the preceding hexadecimal string as input and produces '123456' as output, people can be pretty determined. The hacker may still try every possible likely input and run it through the same hash function and keep doing this until the hashes match up. When the hacker comes across an input that produces **ba3253876aed6bc22d4a6ff53d8406c6ad864195ed144ab5c87621b6c233b548 baeae6956df346ec8c17f5ea10f35ee3cbc514797ed7ddd3145464e2a0bab413** as an output, he has effectively cracked the password.

However, hashing functions tend to need a lot of processing power, so it is not practical to run through large amounts of input (known as *brute forcing*). People have also created so-called rainbow tables with all common inputs precomputed and stored in a database so that the results can be found instantly. This is a classic *space-time* trade-off that is so often seen in computer science. If we compute hashes for all possible inputs, it will take a long time; if we want to compute every possible combination in advance so that we can look up the results instantly, we need a lot of storage space.

If you go to a hash reversal website, such as `http://md5decrypt.net/en/Sha512/`, and input the exact hex string you noted here, it'll tell you that the decrypted version is **123456**.

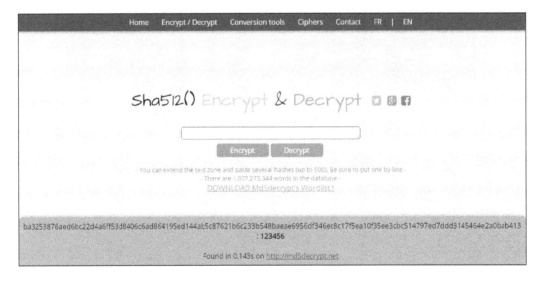

It didn't actually try every possible combination of inputs in the claimed **0.143** seconds, but it stored the answer from a previous time when the hash was computed. Such sites have a large database containing mappings and plaintext strings along with their hashed equivalents.

If you hash a string such as `b^78asdflkjwe@#xx...&AFs[--l` and paste the resulting hash into the md5decrypt website, you'll note that the string is not common enough for this particular site to have precomputed, and instead of getting the plain text back again, you'll get a screen that looks similar to the following screenshot:

We want all of the passwords we store to be complicated enough to not exist in precomputed hash tables. However, our users are more likely to choose passwords that are common enough that they *have* been precomputed. The solution is to add what is known as *salt* to our passwords before we store them.

Salting passwords

As users tend to use weak passwords, such as `123456`, that quite likely exist in precomputed hash tables, we want to do our users a favor and add some random value to their passwords when we store them. This makes it even more difficult for a malicious attacker who has access to the stored hash to gain the user's private password, even though we will store the random value we used with the password. This is known as *salting* the password; similarly to salting food, it is easy for us to add some salt to the password, but removing the salt is hopefully impossible.

In summary, we want to:

- Accept a plaintext password from the user at registration time
- Add some random value (salt) to this password to strengthen it
- Hash the concatenation of the password and salt
- Store the hash and salt

When the user logs in, we need to:

- Take the plaintext password from the user
- Find the stored salt in our database and add it to the user's input
- Hash the concatenation of the password and salt
- Verify that the result matches what we previously stored

Implementing secure password storage in Python

To implement the preceding, we'll create a very small `PasswordHelper` class that will take care of the hashing and generation of random salts. Although this is very little code, when we use the standard `hashlib`, `os`, and `base64` Python libraries, it is good practice to abstract all the cryptography logic to its own class. That way, if we change how we implement password management, we can make most of our changes to this new class and not have to touch the main application code.

We also need to make some changes to our `login()` function, flesh out our `registration()` function, and create a new method for our database helper code that will add a new user to our mock database.

Creating the PasswordHelper class

Let's start with `PasswordHelper`. Create a file called `passwordhelper.py` in your `waitercaller` directory and add the following code to it:

```
import hashlib
import os
import base64

class PasswordHelper:

    def get_hash(self, plain):
        return hashlib.sha512(plain).hexdigest()

    def get_salt(self):
        return base64.b64encode(os.urandom(20))

    def validate_password(self, plain, salt, expected):
        return self.get_hash(plain + salt) == expected
```

The first two methods are used when a user registers for the first time and can be explained as follows:

- The get_hash() method is just a wrapper of the sha512 hash function that we looked at earlier. We'll use this to create the final hash that we will store in our database.

- The get_salt() method uses os.urandom() to generate a cryptographically secure random string. We will encode this as a base64 string as the random string may contain any bytes, some of which we may have issues with storing in our database.

The validate_password() method is used when the user logs in and gives us the original plaintext password again. We'll pass in what the user gave us (the plain parameter), the salt that we stored when they registered, and verify that hashing the two produces the same hash that we stored (the expected parameter).

Updating our database code

We now need to store a password and salt associated with each user; we can't use the simple e-mail and password dictionary that we had before. Instead, for our mock database, we'll use a list of dictionaries, with every piece of information we need to store having a key and value.

We'll also update the code in mockdbhelper.py to read as follows:

```
MOCK_USERS = [{"email": "test@example.com", "salt":
  "8Fb23mMNHD5Zb8pr2qWA3PE9bH0=", "hashed":
  "1736f83698df3f8153c1fbd6ce2840f8aace4f200771a46672635374073cc876c
  "f0aa6a31f780e576578f791b5555b50df46303f0c3a7f2d21f91aa1429ac22e"}]


class MockDBHelper:
    def get_user(self, email):
        user = [x for x in MOCK_USERS if x.get("email") == email]
        if user:
            return user[0]
        return None

    def add_user(self, email, salt, hashed):
MOCK_USERS.append({"email": email, "salt": salt, "hashed":hashed})
```

Our mock user still has the password `123456`, but a potential attacker can no longer work this out by looking up the hash in a rainbow table. We also created the `add_user()` function, which takes the `email`, `salt`, and `hashed` password for a new user and stores a record of this. Our `get_user()` method now needs to loop through all the mock users to find out whether any match the input e-mail address. This is inefficient but will be handled more efficiently by our database, and as we will never have hundreds of mock users, we don't need to worry about this.

Updating our application code

In our main `waitercaller.py` file, we need to add another `import` for our password helper and instantiate a global instance of our password helper class so that we can use it in our `register()` and `login()` functions. We also need to modify our `login()` function to account for the new database model and flesh out our `register()` function to perform some validation and call the database code to add a new user.

Add the following line to the imports section of `waitercaller.py`:

```
from passwordhelper import PasswordHelper
```

Then, add the following near the place where you created the `DBHelper()` object:

```
PH = PasswordHelper()
```

Now, modify the `login()` function to read as follows:

```
@app.route("/login", methods=["POST"])
def login():
    email = request.form.get("email")
    password = request.form.get("password")
    stored_user = DB.get_user(email)
    if stored_user and PH.validate_password(password,
      stored_user['salt'], stored_user['hashed']):

        user = User(email)
        login_user(user, remember=True)
        return redirect(url_for('account'))
    return home()
```

The only real change is in the `if` statement, in which we will now use the password helper to validate the password using the salt and user-provided password. We will also change the variable name of the user to `stored_user` as this is now a dictionary instead of just the password value it used to be.

Finally, we need to build the `register()` function. This will use the password and database helper to create a new salted and hashed password and store this along with the user's e-mail address in our database.

Add a `/register` route and associated function to the `waitercaller.py` file with the following code:

```
@app.route("/register", methods=["POST"])
def register():
    email = request.form.get("email")
    pw1 = request.form.get("password")
    pw2 = request.form.get("password2")
    if not pw1 == pw2:
        return redirect(url_for('home'))
    if DB.get_user(email):
        return redirect(url_for('home'))
    salt = PH.get_salt()
    hashed = PH.get_hash(pw1 + salt)
    DB.add_user(email, salt, hashed)
    return redirect(url_for('home'))
```

We asked the user to input their password twice on our registration form as it's easy for users to make a typo when they register and then not be able to access their account (as they registered with a different password from the one they meant to). Therefore, in this step, we can confirm that the two passwords entered by the user are the same.

We also verified that the user doesn't already exist as each user needs to use a unique e-mail address.

Finally, we generated a salt, created a hash from the password and salt, and stored this in our database. Then, we redirected the user back to homepage, testing our registration functionality.

It's time to give the application a test run again. Close your browser and restart the application locally. Visit the homepage and register an account by choosing an e-mail and password. When you get redirected to the homepage after registration, log in using the same username and password you just registered with. If all went well, you'll see the **You are logged in** message. Again, visit `http://localhost:5000/logout` in order to log out.

Summary

In this chapter, we looked at how to use Bootstrap to make our application look good out of the box and to be responsive based on our user's screen size. We got a basic User Account Control system up and running, and we can register users, log users in, and log them out again.

We also spent some time looking at how to securely store passwords using cryptographic hash functions and salts.

In the next chapter, we'll build out the functionality of our application, which we discussed in the project outline at the start of this chapter. We'll also look at an easier way to create the forms that our visitors will use to interact with our application.

10
Template Inheritance and WTForms in Waiter Caller Project

In the previous chapter, we created a rudimentary user account system. However, we only made a very simple route access controlled—the one that simply showed the string "You are logged in". In this chapter, we'll add some more of the desired functionality, and allow logged-in users to add restaurant tables, see the URLs associated with these tables, and view attention requests from customers. One of the problems we'll come across is that of wanting to reuse the same elements for different pages of our application. You'll see how to solve this problem without code duplication by using Jinja's inheritance system. As mentioned in the previous chapter, we do not communicate very well with our user when mistakes, such as entering an incorrect password, are made. To address this, we'll take a look at another Flask extension, WTForms, and see how it can simplify creating and validating forms.

In this chapter, we'll cover the following topics:

- Adding account and dashboard pages to our application
- Shortening URLs using the bitly API
- Adding functionality for handling attention requests
- Adding user feedback through WTForms

Adding the Account and Dashboard pages

We want to add two new pages to our application: 'Dashboard', where all requests from the patrons of a particular restaurant can be seen, and 'Account', where the restaurants can manage their tables and view the URLs that they need to make available on the tables.

We could simply create two new `.html` files in our `templates` directory and write the HTML from scratch. But we'll soon find that we need many of the same elements from our home page (at the very least, the parts that include and configure Bootstrap). Then we'll be tempted to just copy and paste the HTML from the home page and start working on our new page from there.

Introducing Jinja templates

Copying and pasting code is usually a sign that something is wrong. In application code, it means that you haven't modularized your code well, and you need to create some more classes and probably add a couple of `import` statements to include the reused code wherever it is needed. Using Jinja, we can follow a very similar pattern, by using *template inheritance*. We'll first split our home page into two separate template files, `base.html` and `home.html`, with all the elements that we want to reuse in the base file. We can then have all three of our other pages (Home, Account, and Dashboard) inherit from the *base template*, and only write the code that differs across the three.

Jinja handles inheritance by using the concept of *blocks*. Each parent template can have named blocks, and a child that extends a parent can fill in these blocks with its own custom content. The Jinja inheritance system is quite powerful, and accounts for nested blocks and overwriting existing blocks. However, we're only going to scratch the surface of its functionality. We'll have our base template contain all the reusable code, and it'll contain one blank block named `content` and one named `navbar`. Each of our three pages will extend from the base template, providing their own version of the content block (for the main page content) and the navigation bar. We'll need to make the navigation bar dynamic, because the **Login** fields of the bar at the top of the page will only appear if the user isn't logged in.

Creating the base template

Create a new file called `base.html` in your `templates` directory, and insert the following code:

```html
<!DOCTYPE html>
<html lang="en">
  <head>
    <meta charset="utf-8">
    <meta http-equiv="X-UA-Compatible" content="IE=edge">
    <meta name="viewport" content="width=device-width,
    initial-scale=1">

    <title>Waiter Caller</title>

    <!-- Bootstrap core CSS -->
    <link href="../static/css/bootstrap.min.css" rel="stylesheet">

    <!-- HTML5 shim and Respond.js for IE8 support of HTML5
    elements and media queries -->
    <!--[if lt IE 9]>
      <script src="https://oss.maxcdn.com/html5shiv/3.7.2/
      html5shiv.min.js"></script>
      <script src="https://oss.maxcdn.com/respond/1.4.2/
      respond.min.js"></script>
    <![endif]-->

  </head>
  <body>

    {% block navbar %}
    <nav class="navbar navbar-inverse navbar-fixed-top">
      <div class="container">
        <div class="navbar-header">
          <a class="navbar-brand" href="/dashboard">Dashboard</a>
          <a class="navbar-brand" href="/account">Account</a>
        </div>
      </div>
    </nav>
    {% endblock %}

    {% block content %}
    {% endblock %}
```

```
      <div class="container">

        <hr>
        <footer>
          <p>&copy; A. Non 2015</p>
        </footer>
      </div>
    <!-- Bootstrap core JavaScript
      ================================================== -->
      <!-- Placed at the end of the document so the pages load faster
      -->
      <script   src="https://ajax.googleapis.com/ajax/libs/
        jquery/1.11.3/jquery.min.js"></script>
      <script src="../static/js/bootstrap.min.js"></script>
    </body>
  </html>
```

In the preceding code, we have all our header and our page footer code—elements that will be common across all our pages—in one file. We define two blocks, using the Jinja syntax, which is similar to the other Jinja statements that we have seen, namely:

```
{% block content %}
{% endblock %}
```

And

```
{% block navbar %}
[...]
{% endblock %}
```

In this example, content and navbar are the names of our blocks, and we can choose these freely, while block and endblock are Jinja keywords, and the {% %} symbols are used to indicate the Jinja statements as in earlier examples. This is in itself a completely valid Jinja template; even though the content block is empty, we can render the template directly from our Flask app, and we would see a page that simply pretended that the content block didn't exist.

We can also extend this template, though; that is, we can create children using it as the parent. Children have the option of *overwriting* any of the specified blocks simply by declaring them again. We declared navbar as a block as our home page will use the navigation bar that we wrote earlier—the one that includes a login form. Once logged in, however, our pages for dashboard and account will have exactly the same navigation bar—the one we define in our base template.

Creating the dashboard template

Our dashboard page will eventually show all customers' requests for service so that a waiter can easily see which tables need attention. For now though, we'll just create an outline of the page. Create a new file in your `templates` directory called `dashboard.html`, and add the following code:

```
{% extends "base.html" %}

{% block content %}
    <div class="jumbotron">
      <div class="container">
        <h1>Dashboard</h1>
        <p>View all patron requests below</p>
      </div>
    </div>

    <div class="container">
      <div class="row">
        <div class="col-md-12">
          <h2>Requests</h2>
          <p>All your customers are currently satisfied - no
          requests</p>
        </div>
      </div>
    </div>
{% endblock %}
```

The most important line in the preceding code snippet is the first one—we use the Jinja `extends` keyword to indicate that this template should inherit all the code contained in another template. The keyword is followed by the filename of the template to inherit from, contained within inverted commas.

Following that, we simply create the content block in exactly the same way we did in our base template. This time, instead of leaving it blank, we add some HTML to be displayed on our dashboard page.

Creating the account template

The account page will be the one where the user can add new tables, delete tables, or get the URL for the existing tables. Again, as we do not yet have any application code to represent a table, we'll just create an outline of the page. Create a file called `account.html` in your `templates` directory, and add the following code:

```
{% extends "base.html" %}

{% block content %}
    <div class="jumbotron">
```

```
      <div class="container">
        <h1>Account</h1>
        <p>Manage tables and get URLs</p>
      </div>
    </div>

    <div class="container">
      <div class="row">
        <div class="col-md-12">
          <h2>Tables</h2>

        </div>
      </div>
    </div>
  {% endblock %}
```

Creating the home template

The home.html template contains the entire code specific to our home page, and which isn't part of the base template. The code can be seen in the code bundle as templates/home_1.html, but is not included here as it is too long. Have a look at it and see how we define a new navbar block which contains the login form, and which overrides the default one provided in the base template. Similarly, it defines the content block, which replaces the empty content block that we defined in our base template. The end result hasn't changed — we'll still see exactly the same home page, but now the code is split between the base.html and home.html files, allowing us to reuse large parts of it for the new pages that we created previously.

Adding the routing code

We need our Python code to return the new template files when /account and /dashboard are visited. Add the dashboard() function to your waitercaller.py file, and modify the account function() to read as follows:

```python
@app.route("/dashboard")
@login_required
def dashboard():
    return render_template("dashboard.html")

@app.route("/account")
@login_required
def account():
    return render_template("account.html")
```

Give the new pages a go! Start the application locally as before, by running:

```
python waitercaller.py
```

Navigate to `http://localhost:5000` to see the home page. Log in using the form, and now, instead of the bare message we had before, you should see a nicer looking skeleton of the **Account** page, as seen in the following image:

Click on the **Dashboard** link in the navigation bar at the top, and you should see the skeleton for that page, too, as seen in the following image:

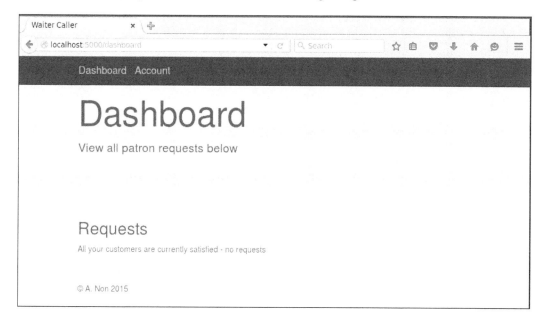

Creating restaurant tables

Now we need to introduce the concept of a *table* to our application, and be able to represent this both in our database and in our application code. A table should have the following attributes:

- An ID number that uniquely identifies that table across all users of our app
- A name that is user-definable and unique within a specific user's tables
- An owner so that we will know to which user a table belongs

If we were following an **Object Oriented Programming** style religiously, we would create a `Table` class which had these properties. We would then also create a bunch of other classes for everything in our application. Following this approach, we would also create methods to serialize each of our objects into something that can be stored in our database, and more methods to *deserialize* them from the database back to objects.

For the sake of brevity, and because our model is simple enough, we'll be taking a shortcut that is sure to offend some, and simply use Python dictionaries to represent most of our objects. We'll see when we add MongoDB to our application that these dictionaries will be trivial to write to and read from the database.

Writing the restaurant table code

Let's have a brief look at what our tables need to do. First, the user of our app will need to be able to add and remove new tables on the `account` page—both initially when an account is registered and later if changes need to be made. Secondly, the user should be able to view the URL associated with each table, so that these URLs can be printed and made available at the physical tables. When a new table is added, we'll need to create a mock database.

We'll start by providing our users with an input box on the `account` page, where they can input the name or number of a new table in order to create it. When a new table is created, we'll create a unique ID number and use that to create a new URL. We'll then use the bitly API to create a shortened version of the URL—one that our users' patrons will be able to type into a smartphone more easily. We'll then store the table name, ID, and shortened URL in our mock database.

Adding the create table form

In the `account.html` template, add the following directly beneath the line `<h2>Tables</h2>`:

```
<h2>Add new table</h2>
<form class="form-inline" action="/account/createtable"
method="POST">
```

```
    <input type="text" name="tablenumber"
    placeholder="Table number or name" class="form-control">
    <input type="submit" value="Create" class="btn btn-primary">
</form>
```

This is a very basic form with a single input for a new table name and a button to submit the form. If you load the application and navigate to the **Account** page, you should now see something like the following image:

Adding the create table route

Creating a table backend is not too complicated, but it has subtleties that are important to understand. First, our users can give the table any name they want. For most users, these names will probably just be incrementing numbers starting from 1 and ending at the number of tables in the restaurant, as this is a common way for restaurants to name their tables. Because many restaurant managers will be using our application, we can't assume that these names will be unique across all accounts. Most users of our application will probably have a table called 1. Therefore, when a restaurant patron indicates that he or she is at Table 1 and wants service, we have to be able to pick the correct Table 1 from potentially many restaurants. To solve this, each table in our database will have a unique ID that we'll use for table identification in the URLs, but we'll display the user-chosen name (for example, 1) on the **Account** page to allow our users to easily manage their personal list of tables.

When we insert a new item into our database, we'll get the unique ID of that item. But, because we want to use the ID as part of the URL, we get into a sort of chicken-or-egg-first situation where we need to insert the table into the database in order to get the ID, but we also need the ID in order to create the URL before we can properly insert the table into the database.

To solve this problem, we have to insert a half-created table into our database to get the ID, then use the ID to create the URL, and then update the table we just created to associate it with the URL.

Add the following route to your `waitercaller.py` file which does this (or rather, will do this once we've created the required functions in our database code):

```
@app.route("/account/createtable", methods=["POST"])
@login_required
def account_createtable():
    tablename = request.form.get("tablenumber")
    tableid = DB.add_table(tablename, current_user.get_id())
    new_url = config.base_url + "newrequest/" + tableid
    DB.update_table(tableid, new_url)
    return redirect(url_for('account'))
```

Note that we structure all the functionality of our application that is related to our account page under a `sub-route` /account/. We preface the function name for routes that belong to the account with `account_`. This helps us have clearer sections in our application code, which can become messy and unmaintainable as we add more and more routes.

We have to associate each table with an owner, so we use the `FlaskLogin current_user` functionality to get the currently logged-in user's ID. We're also going to use our `config.py` file to define the base URL to be associated with the tables.

Add the following imports to `waitercaller.py` in order to use the `current_user` functionality and access our `config`:

```
from flask.ext.login import current_user
import config
```

Add the following to the `config.py` file (remember, this isn't part of the Git repository, so this value is only used for local development):

```
base_url = "http://127.0.0.1:5000/"
```

The preceding URL is exactly equivalent to `localhost:5000` that we've been using, as `127.0.0.1` is a special IP address that always points back to your own machine. However, we'll use an IP address in our `config` instead of `localhost` to maintain compatibility with the Bitly API that we'll use in the next section, *Shortening URL's using the bitly API,* of this chapter.

Adding the create table database code

The mock database code for our tables is similar to that for our users and passwords. Create the following list of dictionaries at the top of the `mockdbhelper.py` file to store your tables:

```
MOCK_TABLES = [{"_id": "1", "number": "1", "owner":
"test@example.com","url": "mockurl"}]
```

The preceding code also creates a single table, 1, and assigns it to our mock user. Note that 1, which is the value of the _id key, is the ID number that, for our production system, will be unique across all user accounts. The 1 that is the value of the number key is the user-chosen value that might be duplicated across different users of our system. Because we only have one test user, we'll simplify our mock code, and always use the same value for both the unique ID and the user-chosen number.

For our mock database, adding a table is simply appending a new dictionary that represents a table to our list of existing mock tables. Add the following method to the mockdbhelper.py file:

```
def add_table(self, number, owner):
    MOCK_TABLES.append({"_id": number, "number": number, "owner":
    owner})
    return number
```

We return number from this function, which is the mock ID. In our test code, this is the same value that was input to this function. In our real code, this number will be the generated ID, and will be different from the input.

Finally, we need to add the update_table() method that will allow us to associate a URL with a table. Add the following method to mockdbhelper.py:

```
def update_table(self, _id, url):
    for table in MOCK_TABLES:
        if table.get("_id") == _id:
            table["url"] = url
            break
```

Our application code gives the preceding method both the table ID generated by the add_table() method and the URL to associate with the table. The update_table() method then finds the correct table and associates the URL with the table. Again, the for loop through a list might look inefficient as opposed to using a dictionary, but it's important for our mock database code to use the same ideas as the real database code that we'll write in the next chapter. As our real database will store a collection of tables, our mock code emulates this by storing them in a list.

Adding the view table database code

We now have the functionality for adding new tables in place, but we can't see them yet. We want all the existing tables to be listed on the account page so that we can see which tables exist, have the ability to delete them, and view their URLs.

Adding the following method to `mockdbhelper.py` will allow us to access the existing tables of a specific user:

```
def get_tables(self, owner_id):
    return MOCK_TABLES
```

Again, we simplify and have our test code ignore the `owner_id` argument and return all the tables (as we only have one test user). However, it's important that our mock methods take the same inputs and outputs as our real methods will, as we don't want our application code to be aware of whether it is running production or test code.

Modifying the account route to pass table data

We should get the latest information about the tables from the database and display these tables to the user each time our account page is loaded. Modify the `/account` route in `waitercaller.py` to look as follows:

```
@app.route("/account")
@login_required
def account():
    tables = DB.get_tables(current_user.get_id())
    return render_template("account.html", tables=tables)
```

This preceding method now gets the tables from the database and passes the data through to the template.

Modifying the template to show the tables

Our template now has access to the table data, so all we need to do is to loop through each table and display the relevant information. The terminology used could get a bit confusing at this point, as we will use an HTML table to display information about our virtual restaurant tables, even though the uses of the word table are unrelated. HTML tables are a way to display tabulated data, which in our case is data about the restaurant tables.

In the `account.html` file, add the following code beneath the line `<h2>tables</h2>`:

```
<table class="table table-striped">
  <tr>
    <th>No.</th>
    <th>URL</th>
    <th>Delete</th>
  </tr>
  {% for table in tables %}
    <form class="form-inline" action="/account/deletetable">
```

```
    <tr>
      <td>{{table.number}}</td>
      <td>{{table.url}}</td>
      <td><input type="submit" value="Delete"
      class="form-control"></td>
      <input type="text" name="tableid"
      value="{{table._id}}" hidden>
    </tr>
  </form>
  {% endfor %}
</table>
```

The preceding code creates a simple table of tables, displaying the table number (user chosen), the URL, and a delete button for each table. Each table is, in fact, a form that submits a request to delete that specific table. In order to do this, we also use a hidden input containing the unique ID of each table. This ID is passed along with the delete request so that our application code knows which table to delete from the database.

Adding the delete table route to our backend code

Add the following route to your waitercaller.py file, which simply accepts the table ID that needs to be deleted and then asks the database to delete it:

```
@app.route("/account/deletetable")
@login_required
def account_deletetable():
  tableid = request.args.get("tableid")
  DB.delete_table(tableid)
  return redirect(url_for('account'))
```

Create the following method in mockdbhelper.py, which accepts a table ID and deletes that table:

```
def delete_table(self, table_id):
    for i, table in enumerate(MOCK_TABLES):
        if table.get("_id") == table_id:
            del MOCK_TABLES[i]
          break
```

Similar to the update code that we wrote earlier, it's necessary to loop through the mock tables to find the one with the correct ID before we can delete it.

Testing the restaurant table code

We've added quite a lot of code to our application. Since a lot of the different sections of code that we've added depend on each other, it has been difficult to actually run the code while writing it. However, now we have the functionality to create, view, and delete tables, so we can now give our application another test run. Fire up the application, log in, and navigate to the **Account** page. You should see the single mock table and be able to add more using the create table form. Play around by adding new tables and deleting the existing ones. When you add tables, they should get a URL associated with them based on their number (remember that for our production application, this number will be a long unique identifier instead of simply the number that we choose for our table). The interface should look like the following image:

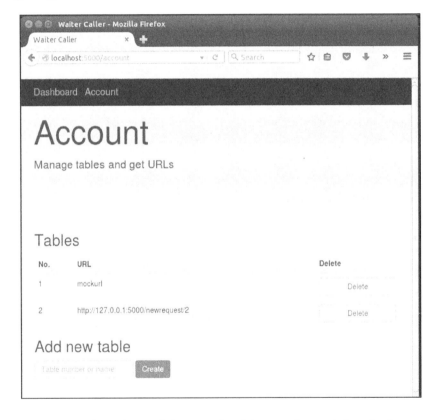

Also take another look at the mobile view for this page by resizing the browser window, making it narrow enough to trigger the layout switch. Note that because we've used Bootstrap's responsive layout features, the **Delete** buttons shunt up closer to the URLs and the **Create** button moves beneath the text input, as in the following image:

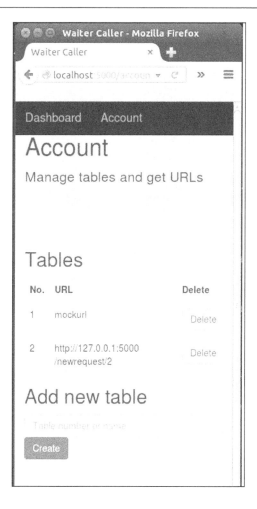

This might not look quite as good as the full-sized view, but it'll certainly be helpful to our visitors who want to use our site from their phones, as they won't need to worry about zooming in or scrolling sideways to access all the functionality of our site.

Shortening URLs using the bitly API

Our users will not want to type in the long URLs that we currently provide for calling a waiter to their table. We'll now look at using the bitly API to create shorter equivalents of the URLs that we've already created. The shorter URLs, which can be typed into address bars (especially on mobile devices) more easily, will then be shown as being associated with the corresponding tables instead of the longer ones we have now.

Introducing Bitly

The premise behind Bitly — and many similar services — is simple. Given a URL of arbitrary length, the service returns a shorter URL of the form `bit.ly/XySDj72`. Bitly and similar services normally have very short root domains (`bit.ly` is five letters), and they simply maintain a database that links the short URLs they create to the longer ones input by the users. Because they use a combination of lower- and uppercase characters as well as digits to create the shortened URLs, there is no shortage of combinations to use, even while keeping the total length of the URL very short.

Using the bitly API

As with the other APIs that we have used, bitly is free to use within certain limitations, but requires registration in order to get an API token. The bitly API is accessed over HTTPS and returns JSON responses (similar to what we've seen before). To interface with the API, we'll use a few lines of Python along with the `urllib2` and `json` standard libraries.

Getting a bitly oauth token

At the time of writing, bitly offers two ways of authenticating with their API. The first is to use an API token given to you when you register. The second way is to use an oauth token. As API tokens are being deprecated by bitly, we'll be using an oauth token.

The first step is to register an account on `bitly.com` and confirm your e-mail address. Simply head over to `bitly.com`, hit the **Sign up** button, and give a username, e-mail address and password. Click the confirmation link that they send to the provided e-mail, and sign in to your bitly account.

To register for an oauth token, go to `https://bitly.com/a/oauth_apps` and enter your password again when prompted. You should now see your new oauth token displayed on the screen. Copy this, as we'll need it in the Python code that we're about to write. It should look something like this:
`ad922578a7a1c6065a3bb91bd62b02e52199afdb`

Creating the bitlyhelper file

Following the pattern we've used throughout the building of this web application, we'll create a `BitlyHelper` class to shorten the URLs. Again, this is good practice, as it allows us to easily replace just this module with another link shortening service if we ever need to. Create a file named `bitlyhelper.py` in your `waitercaller` directory and add the following code, substituting your bitly oauth token as appropriate. The token in the following snippet is valid for this Waiter Caller application. You should substitute the token that you received by following the steps outlined above.

```python
import urllib2
import json

TOKEN = "cc922578a7a1c6065a2aa91bc62b02e41a99afdb"
ROOT_URL = "https://api-ssl.bitly.com"
SHORTEN = "/v3/shorten?access_token={}&longUrl={}"

class BitlyHelper:

    def shorten_url(self, longurl):
        try:
            url = ROOT_URL + SHORTEN.format(TOKEN, longurl)
            response = urllib2.urlopen(url).read()
            jr = json.loads(response)
            return jr['data']['url']
        except Exception as e:
            print e
```

This class, `BitlyHelper`, provides a single method that takes in a long URL and returns a short one. There should be nothing about the last code snippet that is difficult to understand, as it only uses the ideas we've already seen while using JSON-based APIs over HTTP.

Using the bitly module

To use our bitly code, we simply need to create a `BitlyHelper` object in our main application code, and then use it to create a short URL every time a new restaurant table is created. Modify the globals section of `waitercaller.py` as follows:

```python
DB = DBHelper()
PH = PasswordHelper()
BH = BitlyHelper()
```

And add the import for `BitlyHelper()` to the imports section of `waitercaller.py`:

```
from bitlyhelper import BitlyHelper
```

Now modify the `createtable` method to read as follows:

```
@app.route("/account/createtable", methods=["POST"])
@login_required
def account_createtable():
  tablename = request.form.get("tablenumber")
  tableid = DB.add_table(tablename, current_user.get_id())
  new_url = BH.shorten_url(config.base_url + "newrequest/" +
  tableid)

  DB.update_table(tableid, new_url)
  return redirect(url_for('account'))
```

Fire up the app and go to the account page again. Create a new table, and you should see that the URL of the new table is a bitly URL. If you visit this URL in the browser, you'll see that it automatically redirects to something like `http://127.0.0.1/newrequest/2` (which, in turn, should throw a server error at this point).

Now that we can associate a short URL with every new table created, we need to add the idea of a *request* to our application, so that when our users' patrons visit these URLs, we notify the restaurant of the request for attention.

Adding functionality to handle attention requests

We need to deal with two aspects of attention requests. The first, as discussed earlier, is to create new requests when a user visits a URL. The second is to allow the waiters of the restaurant to view these requests and mark them as resolved.

Writing the attention request code

When a user visits a URL, we should create an attention request and store it in the database. This attention request should contain:

- The time the request was made
- The table from which the request was made

As before, we'll just use a Python dictionary to represent the *attention request object*. We need to have our application code create new attention requests and allow these requests to be added, retrieved, and deleted from the database.

Adding the attention request route

Add the following route to `waitercaller.py`:

```
@app.route("/newrequest/<tid>")
def new_request(tid):
  DB.add_request(tid, datetime.datetime.now())
  return "Your request has been logged and a waiter will be with
  you shortly"
```

This route matches a dynamic table ID. Since our URLs use the globally unique table ID and not the user-chosen table number, we don't need to worry about which restaurant owns the table. We tell our database to create a new request, which contains the table ID and the current time. We then display a message to the patron, notifying him or her that the request was successfully made. Note that this is the only route for the application that our users' patrons will use. The rest of the routes are all intended to be used only by the restaurant managers or waiters themselves.

We also need the Python `datetime` module to get the current time. Add the following line to your imports section in `waitercaller.py`:

```
import datetime
```

Adding the attention request database code

The database code for the attention requests uses the same ideas as the code we recently added for dealing with restaurant tables. Add the following global at the top of `mockdbhelper.py`:

```
MOCK_REQUESTS = [{"_id": "1", "table_number": "1","table_id": "1",
  "time": datetime.datetime.now()}]
```

The preceding global creates a single mock attention request for table number 1 (an existing mock table) and sets the time of the request to be the time when we started the `waitercaller` app by running:

python waitercaller.py

Whenever we make changes to our app during development, the server restarts, and this time will also be updated to the current time whenever this happens.

We also need to add the import for the `datetime` module to the top of the `dbconfig.py` file:

```
import datetime
```

For the actual `add_request()` method, it is again important to distinguish between the table number (user chosen) and the table ID (globally unique across all our users). The URL used for creating the request made use of the globally unique ID, but the waiters will want to see the human readable table name next to the request notification. At the time of adding a request, we therefore find the table number associated with the table ID and include that as part of the stored request.

Add the following method to `mockdbhelper.py`:

```
def add_table(self, number, owner):
    MOCK_TABLES.append(
        {"_id": str(number), "number": number, "owner":
        owner})
    return number
```

Again, we use `table_id` as the unique ID for our dictionary that represents a request. As before, when we add a real database, we will generate a new request ID here, which will not be the same as our table ID.

Add the get and delete methods for attention requests

While we are editing the database code, add the following methods as well:

```
def get_requests(self, owner_id):
    return MOCK_REQUESTS

def delete_request(self, request_id):
    for i, request [...]
        if requests [...]
            del MOCK_REQUESTS[i]
            break
```

The first method gets all attention requests for a specific user and will be used to populate our dashboard page with all the unresolved requests that require attention from waiters. The second deletes a specific request and will be used (also from the dashboard page) when waiters mark a request as resolved.

 If our Waiter Caller application aimed to provide more advanced functionality, we might add a property to requests to mark them as resolved, instead of deleting them outright. If we wanted to provide an analysis on how many requests were being made, how long they took on an average to be resolved, and so on, then keeping the resolved requests would be essential. For our simple implementation, resolved requests are of no further use, and we simply delete them.

Modifying the dashboard route to use attention requests

When the restaurant manager or waiter opens the dashboard of the app, they should see all current attention requests along with the time when the request was made (so that the patrons who have been waiting for longer can be prioritized). We have the time the request was logged, so we'll calculate the time elapsed since the request was made.

Modify the `dashboard()` route in `waitercaller.py` to read as follows:

```
@app.route("/dashboard")
@login_required
def dashboard():
    now = datetime.datetime.now()
    requests = DB.get_requests(current_user.get_id())
    for req in requests:
        deltaseconds = (now - req['time']).seconds
        req['wait_minutes'] = "{}.{}".format((deltaseconds/60),
            str(deltaseconds % 60).zfill(2))
    return render_template("dashboard.html", requests=requests)
```

The modified `dashboard()` route grabs all the attention requests that belong to the currently logged in user, using `current_user.get_id()` as before. We calculate a *delta time* for each request (the current time minus the request time) and add this as an attribute for each request in our requests list. Then we pass the updated list through to the template.

Modifying the template code to display attention requests

We want our dashboard code to check if any attention requests exist and then to display each of these in a way similar to the way the tables are displayed on the account page. Every attention request should have a **Resolve** button to allow the waiter to indicate that he has dealt with the request.

If no attention requests exist, we should display the same message we had displayed on the dashboard page previously, indicating that all the patrons are currently satisfied.

Add the following code to the body of `dashboard.html`, removing the placeholder statement that we added previously:

```
<h2>Requests</h2>
{% if requests %}
  <table class="table table-striped">
    <tr>
      <th>No.</th>
      <th>Wait</th>
      <th>Resolve</th>
    </tr>
    {% for request in requests %}
      <tr>
        <form class="form-inline" action="/dashboard/resolve">
          <td>{{request.table_number}}</td>
          <td>{{request.wait_minutes}}</td>
          <input type="text" name="request_id"
          value="{{request._id}}" hidden>
          <td><input type="submit" value="Resolve"
          class="btn btn-primary"></td>
        </form>
      </tr>
    {% endfor %}
  </table>
{% else %}
  <p>All your customers are currently satisfied - no requests</p>
{% endif %}
```

The preceding code is very similar to the table code we saw for the `accounts` template. Instead of the **Delete** button, we have a **Resolve** button, which similarly uses a hidden text input containing the request ID to resolve the correct attention request.

Adding the resolve request application code

Let's add the application code to handle resolving requests. Similar to the way we used the sub-route `/account` for all our account functionality, we use `/dashboard` in the form discussed earlier. Add the following route to `waitercaller.py`:

```
@app.route("/dashboard/resolve")
@login_required
def dashboard_resolve():
  request_id = request.args.get("request_id")
  DB.delete_request(request_id)
  return redirect(url_for('dashboard'))
```

We've already added the database code to remove an attention request, so here we simply need to call that code with the correct request ID, which we have from the hidden field in our template.

With that, most of the functionality of our application should be testable. Let's try it out!

Testing the attention request code

Fire up the app, and test out all the new functionality. First, navigate to the **Account** page and then, in a new tab, navigate to the URL listed for the test table (or add a new table and use the new URL to retest the earlier code as well). You should see the '**Your request has been logged and a waiter will be with you shortly**' message as in the following image:

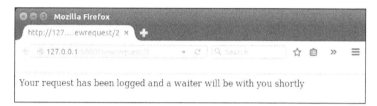

Now go back to the application and navigate to the **Dashboard** page. You should see the mock request as well as the new request you just created by visiting the URL, as seen in the following screenshot:

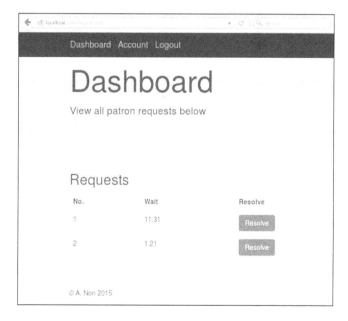

Refresh the page and note that the values in the '**Wait**' column get incremented appropriately (every refresh will recalculate the deltas in the application code).

Auto-refreshing the dashboard page

The waiters will not want to constantly refresh the dashboard in order to check for new requests and to update the wait times on the existing one. We'll add a meta HTML tag to tell the browser that the page should be refreshed at regular intervals. We'll add a generic placeholder for meta tags in our base template and then override it with the refresh tag in our `dashboard.html` template.

In the `dashboard.html` file, add a Jinja block that contains the meta HTML tag above the content block:

```
{% extends "base.html" %}
{% block metarefresh %} <meta http-equiv="refresh" content="10" > {%
endblock %}

{% block content %}
```

Meta HTML tags indicate messages that don't directly relate to the content that we are serving. They can also be used to add information about the author of a page or to give a list of keywords that search engines may use while indexing the page. In our case, we're specifying a meta tag that asks the browser to refresh every ten seconds.

In the `base.html` file, create an equivalent empty placeholder:

```
{% block metarefresh %} {% endblock %}

<title>Waiter Caller</title>
```

Now open the app in your browser again and navigate to the dashboard page. Every 10 seconds, you should see the page refresh and the wait times update. If you create new attention requests, you'll see these appear after the automatic refresh as well.

Adding user feedback with WTForms

We now have a web application that is largely functional, but still fails to provide the user with helpful feedback, especially when it comes to submitting web forms. Let's look at how to make our application more intuitive by providing feedback when the user succeeds or fails to complete various actions.

To make our life easier, we'll use another Flask add-on, WTForms, which lets us validate inputs by using prespecified patterns or by creating our own. We'll use WTForms to implement all our web forms, namely:

- The registration form
- The sign-in form
- The create table form

Introducing WTForms

You might have noticed that creating the registration form for new users to sign up for our web app was a bit cumbersome. We had to create the HTML form in our template file and then fetch all the input data when the form was submitted in our Python backend code. In order to do this, we had to use the same strings, such as `email` and `password`, in our HTML code (for the `name` attribute) and in our Python code (to load the data from the various fields into variables). These strings, `email` and `password`, are examples of what are sometimes called *magic strings*. It might seem obvious to us, while creating the application, that the strings have to be the same in both the files, but to another developer who might need to maintain the application in the future, or even to our future selves, this implicit link might be a lot less obvious and more confusing.

Furthermore, we had to use a fairly ugly `if` statement in our application code to make sure that the passwords matched. It turns out that we want to do much more validation on user input than just checking that the passwords match. We probably want to also validate that the e-mail address looks like an e-mail address, that the password isn't too short, and possibly more besides. As our user-input forms get longer, and the validation rules get more complicated, we can see that our application code would quickly get pretty messy if we carried on developing forms as we have been doing so far.

Finally, as mentioned earlier, our forms failed to provide the user with helpful feedback when things went wrong.

WTForms solves all of these problems in a simple and intuitive way. We'll soon explain how to create Python classes to represent forms. These classes will contain validation rules, field types, field names, and feedback messages, all in the same place. Our Jinja templates and our application code can then use the *same object* to render the form (when the user views the page) and to process the input (when the user submits the form). Using WTForms therefore allows us to keep our code cleaner and to speed up development. We'll take a quick look at installing WTForms for Flask, before diving into how we can use it for improving our application.

Note that WTForms is a general Python web development add-on that works with many different Python web development frameworks (such as Flask, Django, and others) and template managers (such as Jinja2, Mako, and others). We'll install a Flask-specific extension that will install WTForms and make it easy to interface with our Flask application.

Installing Flask-WTF

We need to install the WTForms add-on for Flask. This is done in the same way as our previous extensions. Simply run the following command (as always, remembering to do it both locally and on your VPS):

```
pip install --user Flask-WTF
```

Creating the registration form

Now let's take a look at building forms. We'll be building a few forms, so we'll create a new Python file in our project to hold all of these. In your `waitercaller` directory, create a file called `forms.py` and add the following code:

```
from flask_wtf import Form
from wtforms import PasswordField
from wtforms import SubmitField
from wtforms.fields.html5 import EmailField
from wtforms import validators

class RegistrationForm(Form):
    email = EmailField('email',
    validators=[validators.DataRequired(), validators.Email()])
    password = PasswordField('password',
    validators=[validators.DataRequired(),
    validators.Length(min=8, message="Please choose a password
    of at least 8 characters")])
    password2 = PasswordField('password2',
    validators=[validators.DataRequired(),
    validators.EqualTo('password', message='Passwords must
    match')])
    submit = SubmitField('submit', [validators.DataRequired()])
```

The class, `RegistrationForm`, inherits from `Form`, a generic form object that we find inside the `flask_wtf` extension. Everything else is from the `wtforms` module directly (and not from the Flask-specific extension). The form is built from a number of different fields—in our case, an `EmailField`, two `PasswordFields`, and a `Submit` field. All of these will be rendered as their HTML equivalents in our template. We assign each of these desired fields to variables.

We'll use these variables to render the fields and to retrieve data from the fields. Each time we create a field, we pass in some arguments. The first is a string argument to name the form. The second argument is a list of Validators. **Validators** are sets of rules that we can use to differentiate between valid input and invalid input. WTForms provides all the validators that we need, but it's also easy to write custom validators. We use the following validators:

- `DataRequired`: This simply means that if the field is left blank, the form is invalid for all fields.

- `Email`: This uses a regular expression to ensure that the e-mail address is made up of alphanumeric characters, and has an @ symbol and a full-stop in their appropriate places. (Fun fact: this is a surprisingly complicated problem! See `http://www.regular-expressions.info/email.html`.)

- `EqualTo`: This ensures that the data entered in the field is the same as the data entered into another field.

- `Length`: This validator takes optional min and max arguments to define the number of characters the data should contain. We set this to a minimum of 8 to ensure that our users don't pick very weak passwords.

Recall our discussion of the trade-offs between backend and frontend validation and note that these are all backend validation methods, completed server-side. Therefore, it is still worthwhile to add the `Email` validator even if the user's browser supports HTML5; the fact that it is an `email` field will prevent the user from submitting an invalid e-mail address (using a frontend validation check).

Another thing about validators is that we can add a message argument for each validator — not just for each field — and each field can have more than one validator. We'll see later how to display this message to the user if that specific validation check fails.

It's important to note that the variable names you choose for each form field (`email`, `password`, and `password2` in the registration form that we created previously) are more important than most variable names because the `name` and `id` attributes for the final HTML field will be taken from the variable names.

Rendering the registration form

The next step is to use our form object for rendering an empty registration form when a user loads our home page. To do this, we have to modify both our application code (to create an instance of the registration form class and pass it to the template) and our frontend code (to render our fields from the variables of the class, instead of hardcoding them in HTML).

Updating the application code

In our `waitercaller.py` file, we need to import the form we created, instantiate it, and pass it to our template.

Add an import for our registration form:

```
from forms import RegistrationForm
```

Now instantiate the form in our `home()` function and pass the form on to the template. The final `home()` function should read as follows:

```
@app.route("/")
def home():
  registrationform = RegistrationForm()
  return render_template("home.html",
  registrationform=registrationform)
```

Updating the template code

Now that our template has access to an instantiated `RegistrationForm` object, we can use Jinja to render the fields of our form. Update the registration form in `home.html` to read as follows:

```
<h2>Register now</h2>
<form class="form-horizontal" action="/register" method="POST">
  {{ registrationform.csrf_token }}
    <div class="form-group">
      <div class="col-sm-9">
        {{ registrationform.email(class="form-control",
        placeholder="Email Address" )}}
      </div>
    </div>
    <div class="form-group">
      <div class="col-sm-9">
        {{ registrationform.password(class="form-control",
        placeholder="Password" )}}
      </div>
    </div>
    <div class="form-group">
      <div class="col-sm-9">
        {{ registrationform.password2(class="form-control",
        placeholder="Confirm Password" )}}
      </div>
    </div>
    <div class="form-group">
```

```
        <div class="col-sm-9">
          {{ registrationform.submit(class="btn btn-primary
          btn-block")}}
        </div>
      </div>
    </form>
```

The Bootstrap boilerplate (the div tags specifying Bootstrap classes) remains unchanged, but now, instead of creating input fields in HTML, we call functions belonging to our `registrationform` variable that was passed in from the `home()` route. Each variable that we declared in our `RegistrationForm` class (`email`, `password`, `password2`, and `submit`) is available as a function to which we can pass additional HTML attributes as arguments. The `name` and `id` attributes will be set automatically based on the variable names we provided when we wrote the form, and we can add further attributes, such as `class` and `placeholder` by passing them in here. As before, we use `'form-control'` as the class of our inputs, and also specify the `'placeholder'` values to prompt the user to input information.

We also render the `csrf_token` field at the beginning of the new code. This is a very useful security default that WTForms provides. One of the more common web application vulnerabilities is called **Cross Site Request Forgery** (**CSRF**). Although a detailed description of this vulnerability falls outside the scope of this book, in short, it exploits the fact that cookies are implemented at the browser level rather than at a web page level. Because cookies are used for authentication, if you log into your one site that is vulnerable to CSRF, and then in a new tab, navigate to a malicious site that can exploit a CSRF vulnerability, the malicious site can carry out actions on the vulnerable site on your behalf. This is achieved by sending across the legitimate cookie (that you created when you logged into the vulnerable site), along with an action that requires authentication. In the worst case scenario, the vulnerable site is your online banking, and the malicious site carries out financial transactions on your behalf, without your knowledge, using the CSRF vulnerability. The CSRF token mitigates against this vulnerability by adding a hidden field to every form with a cryptographically secure set of randomly generated characters. Because the malicious site cannot access this hidden field (even though it can access our cookies), we know that a POST request that includes these characters originates from our site, and not a malicious third-party one. If you find this level of web application security interesting, read more about the CSRF vulnerability on the **Open Web Application Security Project** (**OWASP**) website (`https://www.owasp.org/index.php/Cross-Site_Request_Forgery_(CSRF)`). Either way, you should always include the CSRF field in all forms—in fact, the validation step will fail if you omit it.

Testing the new form

Because we used the same Id and name attributes for our form as we did before, our application code for handling the processing of data when the form is submitted will still work. Therefore, fire up the application and make sure that everything is still working at this point. If all has gone well, the home page of the application will look identical to when we last tested our application. You should also be able to use your browser's 'view source' function to check that the various form fields were converted into various HTML input types as expected.

Using WTForms in our application code

The next step is to update our application code to use WTForms for catching data that has been input through the form. Now, instead of having to remember which "name" attributes we used, we can simply instantiate a new `RegistrationForm` object and populate it from the post data received backend. We can also easily run all our validation rules and get a list of errors for each field.

In `waitercaller.py`, modify the `register()` function to read as follows:

```
@app.route("/register", methods=["POST"])
def register():
  form = RegistrationForm(request.form)
  if form.validate():
    if DB.get_user(form.email.data):
      form.email.errors.append("Email address already registered")
      return render_template('home.html', registrationform=form)
    salt = PH.get_salt()
    hashed = PH.get_hash(form.password2.data + salt)
    DB.add_user(form.email.data, salt, hashed)
    return redirect(url_for("home"))
  return render_template("home.html", registrationform=form)
```

In the preceding code, the first change is the first line of the function. We instantiate a new `RegistrationForm` and populate it by passing in the `request.form` object, from which we previously pulled each field individually. As mentioned before, it's great that we don't have to hardcode the field names now! We can instead access the user's input data through the forms properties, such as `form.email.data`.

The second line is also a big change. We can call `form.validate()` to run all our validation rules, and this will return `True` only if all the rules pass, else it will populate the form object with all the relevant failure messages. The last line of the function, therefore, will only get called if there are validation errors. In this case, we now re-render our home page template, passing across a fresh copy of the form (which now has a reference to the errors. We'll see how to display these in the next step).

If the e-mail address is found in our database, we now append an error message to the error messages for the e-mail field and re-render the template to pass this error back to the frontend.

Note that previously, our three return options were all simply redirected to the home page, made using the Flask `redirect()` function. Now we have replaced them all with `render_template()` calls, as we need to pass the new form (with the error messages added) along to the frontend.

Displaying errors to our user

The final step for our new registration form is to display any errors to the user so that the user can fix them and resubmit the form. To do this, we'll add some Jinja `if` statements to our template to check if any errors exist in the form object and display them if they do. Then we'll add some CSS to make these errors appear in red. Finally, we'll look at how we could do all of this more concisely (which we'd definitely want if we had more and larger forms).

Displaying the errors in our template

All we need to do to display the errors is add an `if` statement above each of our input fields, checking if there are any errors to display for that field (remember WTForms automatically populates the error lists for our form object when we run the `validate()` method). If we find errors to display for that field, we need to loop through all of them and display each one. Although, in our case, each field can only have a single error, remember that we can add more than one validator to each field, so it's definitely possible to have forms which have several errors for each field. We don't want the user to have to fix one error and resubmit, only to find out that there are still others—instead, the user would want to be informed of all errors after a single submission of the form.

Modify the registration form in `home.html` to read as follows:

```
<div class="form-group">
  <div class="col-sm-9">
    {% if registrationform.email.errors %}
      <ul class="errors">{% for error in
      registrationform.email.errors %}<li>{{ error }}</li>
      {% endfor %}</ul>
    {% endif %}

    {{ registrationform.email(class="form-control",
    placeholder="Email Address" )}}
  </div>
</div>
<div class="form-group">
```

```
<div class="col-sm-9">
  {% if registrationform.password.errors %}
    <ul class="errors">{% for error in
    registrationform.password.errors %}<li>
    {{ error }}</li>{% endfor %}</ul>
  {% endif %}

  {{ registrationform.password(class="form-control",
  placeholder="Password" )}}
</div>
</div>
<div class="form-group">
  <div class="col-sm-9">
    {% if registrationform.password2.errors %}
      <ul class="errors">{% for error in
      registrationform.password2.errors %}<li>
      {{ error }}</li>{% endfor %}</ul>
    {% endif %}

    {{ registrationform.password2(class="form-control",
    placeholder="Confirm Password" )}}
  </div>
</div>
```

Note that we display our errors by building a list (within the `<ul>` tags), and that we assign these lists the class attribute of `errors`. We don't have any CSS code yet to define what error lists should look like, so let's fix that quickly.

Adding CSS for the errors

The CSS code for the errors is the only custom CSS code we'll be using in the project (the rest of our CSS is all free with Bootstrap). Therefore, it's fine to add our CSS directly into the `base.html` template file (we'll use it in our other templates as well), instead of creating a new external CSS file or editing the Bootstrap files.

If you're curious, take a look at the `bootstrap.min.css` file inside the `static/css` directory and note that it's quite difficult to read and modify (it's all in a single line!). The reason for this is to make the page load faster—every space and newline character makes the file a little bit bigger, which means our users' browsers would take longer to download the CSS file that is needed to display the web page. This is why large CSS and JavaScript libraries (such as the Bootstrap ones) come with a *minified* version (this is what the 'min' in `bootstrap.min.css` stands for). If we wanted to add our new CSS code to the Bootstrap file, we'd probably add it to the non-minified version and then re-minify it to create the minified one that we'd use in production.

Add the following style between the `<head>` tags of the `base.html` file:

```
<style type="text/css">
  ul.errors {
    list-style-type: none;
    padding: 0;
    color: red;
  }
</style>
```

The first line in the preceding styling code means that it should only apply to `<ul>` elements which have a class of errors (that is, the feedback messages we just added to our home page). The next three lines remove the bullet point that lists use by default, remove the indent that lists use by default, and set the font color to red.

Testing the final registration form

Our registration form is now finished. It now uses WTForms, so it is cleaner and easier to maintain, and we don't have to rely on a developer knowing that the HTML `name` attribute has to match up with the Python code. Let's have a look to make sure everything still works and that our new error messages are displayed when we expect them to be and are not shown when we don't want them.

Run your application again and try to register a new account. Try out various combinations of errors, such as using an already registered e-mail address (remember that our test database is cleared every time we restart the application), using a password that is too short, using non-matching strings for the two `password` fields, or using an invalid e-mail address. If all has gone according to plan, your form with errors should look similar to the one below:

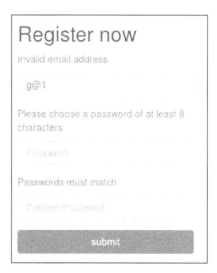

There are a couple of interesting things to note about the last image. First, note that the e-mail address g@1 is taken to be valid by the HTML5 input box (frontend validation), but not by the `Email()` validator (backend validation). This is why I could submit the form even though I'm using a browser that supports the HTML5 e-mail field, and was only told that the e-mail address was invalid after the data went to the backend. Second, note that after the form was submitted, the e-mail address was repopulated automatically, while the password fields are now blank. This is a useful default of most browsers. We are likely to want to submit similar information the second time round, after fixing the errors, but for security reasons, we always want to get rid of passwords as quickly as possible.

Note the '**Invalid email address**.' message in the preceding image. In our `forms.py` file, we only specified the error message for the case when the password was too short, but WTForms provides default messages for its built-in validators. Similarly, if you leave the password field blank, you'll see the message '**This field is required**' — another useful default that we did not have to write.

That's most of the heavy lifting done for form validation and user feedback. Now that you have a good conceptual grasp of how everything works, we'll go over it quickly once:

- Displaying feedback when the user's registration is successful (at the moment, we rather pessimistically only seem to be confirmed with failure, but the user will want to know that an account has been successfully registered if everything goes well).

- Moving our login form to WTForms and adding feedback for when users fail to log in.

- Moving our 'new table' form to WTForms and adding feedback where necessary.

Adding a successful registration notification

Normally, we would show the user a new page after a successful registration, thanking them for registering and informing them that everything has been successful (see the next chapter for a more complete list of things we could improve on if we were writing this application for a production environment instead of using it as an educational project). To keep our application to as few pages as possible, and to prevent this book from growing too long, we'll show the user a JavaScript popup box instead. Generally, when creating user interfaces, we want to avoid as many popups as possible, as users find them irritating. However, they are occasionally necessary, so using one here will help keep our application simple and give us an opportunity to learn a bit more JavaScript.

JavaScript is event-based. This means that we can write code that is triggered by user actions (such as a mouse click) or other events such as an 'onload' event, which is triggered when a specific resource loads in the user's browser. Previously, in our Crime Map project, we used this to initialize the JavaScript Google Map widget after the <body> tag had loaded. Now we'll do something similar, but use this to display a JavaScript alert box instead. We'll also make our message dynamic and pass it to the frontend from the backend code.

Passing the message from the application code

The backend change for this is easy. Simply change the register() function to pass in the appropriate message if we process all the input data without any errors. In waitercaller.py, update the register() function to read as follows:

```
hashed = PH.get_hash(form.password2.data + salt)
DB.add_user(form.email.data, salt, hashed)
return render_template("home.html", registrationform=form,
onloadmessage="Registration successful. Please log in.")

return render_template("home.html", registrationform=form)
```

Using the message in the template code

The change is slightly trickier to implement in our template because we don't actually have access to the <body> tag (where we want to specify the JavaScript alert) in our home.html template. Instead, our <body> is defined in our base.html skeleton template from which all our other templates inherit.

To modify the <body> tag only in our home.html template, we need to make the <body> tag appear within an inheritable Jinja block, similar to our content block. To do this, we need to make changes to our base.html template and to our home.html template.

In base.html, make the following change where the <body> tag is created:

```
</head>
{% block bodytag %}

<body>
{% endblock %}
```

Now the `<body>` tag can be overwritten by child templates, as it appears inside a configurable block. In `home.html`, we'll overwrite the `<body>` block directly after the first line, if an alert message is specified. Remember that if this message is not specified, the `home.html` template will simply inherit the default `<body>` tag from the `base.html` template. In `home.html`, add the following code directly after the first line:

```
{% block bodytag %}
  <body {% if onloadmessage %} onload="alert('{{onloadmessage}}');" {%
endif %}>
{% endblock %}
```

The only slightly tricky part is matching up all the quotation marks and brackets in the `onload` attribute. The entire `alert` function (the JavaScript we want to run) should appear within double quotation marks. The string inside the `alert` function (the message that is actually displayed to the user) should be inside single quotation marks. Finally, the `onloadmessage` variable should be inside double braces, so that we get the contents of the variable rather than the string of the variable name.

Now, after a successful registration, the user will see an alert confirming that everything went well and that a login is possible, as seen in the following image. It would be better to add a new page to properly inform the user of the successful registration, but to keep our app simple (and so we could introduce the onload functionality, which is generally useful), we opted for a slightly messier way of communicating this.

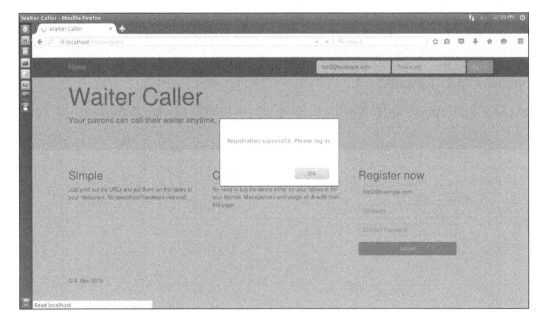

Modifying the login form

The changes necessary to move the login form to WTForms are very similar to the changes we made for the registration form, so we'll provide the code with minimal discussion. Refer to the code bundle if you are unsure where to insert the code or make changes.

Creating the new LoginForm in the application code

In forms.py, add the LoginForm class:

```
class LoginForm(Form):
    loginemail = EmailField('email',
    validators=[validators.DataRequired(), validators.Email()])
    loginpassword = PasswordField('password',
    validators=[validators.
    DataRequired(message="Password field is required")])
    submit = SubmitField('submit', [validators.DataRequired()])
```

Here we specify a custom message for the password field's DataRequired validator, as the error messages won't align with the fields as nicely as they did for the registration form. We also use the variable names loginemail and loginpassword, as these will become the HTML element id and name attributes, and it's preferable that they don't get overridden by the login and password fields in the registration form on the same page.

In waitercaller.py, add the import for the login form:

```
from forms import LoginForm
```

And rewrite the login() function as follows:

```
@app.route("/login", methods=["POST"])
def login():
    form = LoginForm(request.form)
    if form.validate():
        stored_user = DB.get_user(form.loginemail.data)
        if stored_user and
        PH.validate_password(form.loginpassword.data,
        stored_user['salt'], stored_user['hashed']):
            user = User(form.loginemail.data)
            login_user(user, remember=True)
            return redirect(url_for('account'))
        form.loginemail.errors.append("Email or password invalid")
    return render_template("home.html", loginform=form,
    registrationform=RegistrationForm())
```

It may seem that the "**Email or password invalid**" error is quite vague and could be more specific. It's true that the user may find it helpful to know where the mistake lies, as many people use many different e-mail addresses and different passwords. Thus, it would be convenient to know whether you, as a user, have entered the wrong e-mail and need to try to remember which e-mail address you signed up for, or if you have the correct e-mail address and have misremembered your anniversary or date of birth or whatever mnemonic you use to remember your password. However, the convenience is offset by yet another security issue. If we display "**Invalid password**" when the user enters a correct e-mail address but the incorrect password, this would allow a malicious attacker to try a large list of e-mail addresses against our website, and slowly build up a list of e-mail addresses that belong to our users. The attacker could then target these users in a phishing attack by using the knowledge that these users are our customers. This is yet another case that shows how developers have to be constantly vigilant against what information they might be allowing an attacker to infer, even if it's not directly provided.

The last backend changes that we need to make are to initialize and pass in a new `LoginForm` object whenever we render the `home.html` template. These changes have to be made:

- Once in the `home()` function
- Three times in the `register()` function

Change the `home()` function to read as follows:

```
@app.route("/")
def home():
  return render_template("home.html",
  loginform=LoginForm(), registrationform=RegistrationForm())
```

Change the last two lines of the `register()` function to:

```
  return render_template("home.html", loginform=LoginForm(),
  registrationform=form, onloadmessage="Registration successful.
  Please log in.")
  return render_template("home.html", loginform=LoginForm(),
  registrationform=form)
```

And the `return` statement in the middle of the `register()` function to:

```
  return render_template("home.html", loginform=LoginForm(),
  registrationform=form)
```

Using the new LoginForm in the template

For the template changes, `home.html` should now use the following `login` form:

```
<form class="navbar-form navbar-right" action="/login"
method="POST">
  {% if loginform.errors %}
    <ul class="errors">
      {% for field_name, field_errors in loginform.errors|dictsort
      if field_errors %}
        {% for error in field_errors %}
          <li>{{ error }}</li>
        {% endfor %}
      {% endfor %}
    </ul>
  {% endif %}
  {{ loginform.csrf_token}}
  <div class="form-group">
    {{ loginform.email(class="form-control", placeholder="Email
    Address")}}
  </div>
  <div class="form-group">
    {{ loginform.password(class="form-control",
    placeholder="Password")}}
  </div>
  <div class="form-group">
    {{ loginform.submit(value="Sign in",
    class="btn btn-success")}}
  </div>
</form>
```

Instead of displaying the errors above each field, as we did for the registration form, we'll just display all the errors above the login form. To do this, we can use the `loginform.errors` property, which is a dictionary mapping of each field to a list of its errors. The error displaying code is therefore slightly more verbose, as it has to loop through all the keys and values of this dictionary, and we use the `convenient` |`dictsort` Jinja notation to sort the dictionary before displaying the errors.

Modifying the create table form

The last form change we need to make is to the create table form, for when an already logged-in user adds a new restaurant table to his or her account. The new form to be added to forms.py looks like this:

```
class CreateTableForm(Form):
  tablenumber = TextField('tablenumber',
    validators=[validators.DataRequired()])
  submit = SubmitField('createtablesubmit',
    validators=[validators.DataRequired()])
```

This requires a new import in forms.py as well:

```
from wtforms import TextField
```

In waitercaller.py, we need to import the new form with:

```
from forms import CreateTableForm
```

Update the account_createtable() function to:

```
@app.route("/account/createtable", methods=["POST"])
@login_required
def account_createtable():
  form = CreateTableForm(request.form)
  if form.validate():
    tableid = DB.add_table(form.tablenumber.data,
      current_user.get_id())
    new_url = BH.shorten_url(config.base_url + "newrequest/" +
      tableid)
    DB.update_table(tableid, new_url)
    return redirect(url_for('account'))

  return render_template("account.html", createtableform=form,
    tables=DB.get_tables(current_user.get_id()))
```

And the account() route to:

```
@app.route("/account")
@login_required
def account():
    tables = DB.get_tables(current_user.get_id())
    return render_template("account.html",
      createtableform=CreateTableForm(), tables=tables)
```

Finally, the form in the `account.html` template should be changed to:

```
<form class="form-inline" action="/account/createtable"
method="POST">
  <div class="form-group">
    {% if createtableform.tablenumber.errors %}
      <ul class="errors">
        {% for error in createtableform.tablenumber.errors %}
          <li>{{error}}</li>
        {% endfor %}
      </ul>
    {% endif %}
    {{ createtableform.csrf_token}}
    {{ createtableform.tablenumber(class="form-control",
      placeholder="Table number or name")}}
    {{ createtableform.submit(value="Create",
      class="btn btn-primary") }}
  </div>
</form>
```

At the moment, if the user leaves the field blank and hits the **Create** button, we can only ever have a single error displayed on the `create table` form, that is, '**This field is required**', which we can see in the following screenshot:

With this in mind, it is debatable whether the for loop should loop through all the error messages. On the one hand, it is bad to 'future proof' too much, as you are left with a code base that contains a lot of unnecessary code that is over complicated. On the other hand, we may well add more error messages to the WTForm (such as if the user tries to create a table with a number that already exists), and therefore, it is arguably worthwhile to add the for loop.

The one form left that we have not converted to WTForms is the `delete table` form. As this is only a single **Submit** button, it is left as an exercise (the CSRF protection would still be a worthwhile gain in moving this form to WTForms.).

Summary

We've fleshed out our application's functionality, and it's now a lot more powerful. We added **Dashboard** and **Account** pages, and wrote all the application code, database code, and frontend code to handle our requirements.

We looked at Jinja templates as a way to avoid duplicating the frontend code, and we also looked at how to use the bitly API to shorten links.

We then added WTForms, and saw how this could make our user feedback easier, our forms easier to validate, and our web application more secure. Our users are now kept up-to-date with information about their registration, login, and usage of the application.

In the next chapter, we'll add a real database to our code and then work on some finishing touches.

11
Using MongoDB with Our Waiter Caller Project

Our web application now has nearly all of its functionality. If we plan to monetize this application, now would be the time where we'd demo it to potential customers. Even though their data (such as their account name and virtual table data) would be lost every time we had to restart our server, this data is trivial enough to make a full demo of the application feasible.

In this chapter, we will add a proper database for use in production. We'll use MongoDB—a slightly controversial NoSQL database management system that has become extremely popular, arguably largely because of its simplicity. We'll take a look at how to install in on our VPS, configure it correctly, and access it using a Python driver. Then, we'll implement the full `DBHelper` class to replace `MockDBHelper`, which we use for testing. To end off, we'll look at adding indices to MongoDB and a favicon to our application.

In this chapter, we'll cover the following topics:

- Introducing MongoDB
- Installing MongoDB
- Using the MongoDB shell
- Introducing PyMongo
- Adding some finishing touches

Introducing MongoDB

MongoDB is a NoSQL database. This means that unlike the MySQL database we used for our Crime Map project, it is not organized into tables, rows, and columns; instead, it is organized into collections, documents, and fields. While it can be useful to think of these new terms as a sort of translation from those we use for relational databases, the concepts do not perfectly translate. If you have a background in relational databases, a useful and more complete reference to these translations can be found on the official MongoDB website at `https://docs.mongodb.org/manual/reference/sql-comparison/`.

MongoDB's structure is much more flexible than that of a SQL database—not all of our data has to confirm to a specific schema, and this can save development time. For our Crime Map project, we had to spend time up front looking at our data and deciding how to represent it in a database. We then had to set up a bunch of fields, specifying the data type, length, and other constraints. MongoDB, by contrast, requires none of this. It's more flexible than an RDBMS, and it uses documents to represent the data. Documents are essentially bits of JSON data similar to the data we pulled from the APIs we used. This means that we can easily add or remove fields as necessary, and we do not need to specify data types for our fields.

The downside of this is that by not being forced to be structured and consistent, it's easy for us to get lazy and fall into bad practices of mixing different data types in a single field and allowing invalid data to pollute our database. In short, MongoDB gives us more freedom, but in doing so, it shifts some of the responsibility for being clean and consistent onto our shoulders.

Installing MongoDB

MongoDB can be found in the Ubuntu software repositories, but as updates are frequent and the repository versions tend to lag behind, it's highly recommended to install it from the official Mongo package directly.

We'll go through how to do this step by step here, but as the installation procedures may change, it's advisable to get an updated version of the required URLs and steps from the official installation guide available at `https://docs.mongodb.org/manual/tutorial/install-mongodb-on-ubuntu/`.

The first thing we need to do is import MongoDB's public key so that the installation can be authenticated. On your VPS only (as before, we will not install a database server on our development machine), run the following:

```
sudo apt-key adv --keyserver hkp://keyserver.ubuntu.com:80
--recv EA312927
```

Now that we have the key, we can use the following command to add a link to the MongoDB package to our software sources. Note that this command is specific to Ubuntu 14.04 "Trusty", which, at the time of writing, is the latest long-term support Ubuntu version. If your VPS runs a different version of Ubuntu, make sure you get the correct command from the MongoDB documentation link provided earlier. To discover which version of Ubuntu you have, run `lsb_release -a` in your terminal and examine the output for a version number and name:

```
echo "deb http://repo.mongodb.org/apt/ubuntu trusty/mongodb-org/3.2
multiverse" | sudo tee /etc/apt/sources.list.d/mongodb-org-3.2.list
```

Now, we simply need to update our source lists by running:

```
sudo apt-get update
```

Finally, do the actual installation by running the following command:

```
sudo apt-get install -y mongodb-org
```

The preceding command will install MongoDB with some sensible defaults and start the server. It'll also configure it in such a way that the server will start up automatically if you reboot your VPS.

Using the MongoDB shell

Similarly to what we discussed with MySQL, MongoDB comes with a simple shell. This is ideal to run quick, one-off commands and get used to the syntax. Let's run through the basic CRUD operations to get familiar with how MongoDB works.

As in our previous project, once we introduce MongoDB, we'll move to using it only through Python code; however, to start out, we'll write commands directly in the shell. This means there will be some slight differences in syntax, but as nearly everything is JSON based, these differences shouldn't be a problem.

Starting the MongoDB shell

To start the MongoDB shell, run the following command on your VPS:

```
mongo
```

This will start the interactive MongoDB shell as in the following image, which you can exit at any time by pressing *Ctrl + C* or by typing `exit` into the shell and pressing *Enter*.

Running commands in the MongoDB shell

As with MySQL, the top-level concept in MongoDB is a database. By default, this will connect to a database named `test`. We can change databases using the `use` command. Run the following command in the shell:

```
use sandbox
```

You should see the output "**Switched to db sandbox**". This is where we can note the first big difference between MySQL and MongoDB. With MySQL, we would first have had to create the database. This is a common pattern we'll see with MongoDB; if you reference a database, collection, or field that doesn't exist, it'll be automatically created for you.

Creating data with MongoDB

Now, let's create a collection (similar to a table in our MySQL database from the Crime Map project) and add a document (as with a row from a table in our MySQL database) to it. Run the following in the MongoDB shell:

```
db.people.insert({"name":"John Smith", "age": 35})
```

In the preceding command, `db` refers to the current database. Directly after, `people` refers to the collection called of this name. As it doesn't exist, it'll get created as we attempt to use it. Following this is `insert`, which means we want to add something to the database. We will pass as an argument (inside round the brackets), which is a JSON structure. In our case, we represented a person with a JSON object containing the person's name and age. Note that everything is in quotation marks except for the value of the `age` field; again, unlike MySQL, we don't have to specify the types for this data. MongoDB will store the name as a string and the age as an integer, but it applies no restrictions to these fields.

Add another person to the database to make the next operations that we will try out more meaningful. Run the following:

```
db.people.insert({"name":"Mary Jones"})
```

Reading data with MongoDB

Instead of the SQL concept of a SELECT statement, MongoDB uses a find() command. Similarly to SQL, we can specify the criteria to search for in data and also choose which fields we want the database to return. Run the following command:

```
db.people.find()
```

This is the most basic version of the find operation. It'll simply *find* or *retrieve* all the data and all its fields from the people collection. You should see MongoDB output all the information about both the people we just added. You'll note that each person also has an ObjectId field added; MongoDB adds unique identifier fields to each of our documents automatically, and these ID fields are also automatically indexed.

We can also use find with a single argument. The argument specifies criteria, and MongoDB only returns documents that match. Run the following command:

```
db.people.find({"name":"John Smith"})
```

This will return all the fields from all the records if the name matches John Smith, so you should see a single result returned and printed to the shell, as in the screenshot that follows:

```
> db.people.find({"name":"John Smith"})
{ "_id" : ObjectId("56d5e9a1bf738a9a34175181"), "name" : "Jo
hn Smith", "age" : 35 }
>
```

Finally, if we don't want all the fields returned, we can run the find command and pass in a second argument to specify which fields we want. Run the following command, and you should see results as in the following screenshot:

```
db.people.find({"name":"John Smith"}, {"age":1})
```

```
> db.people.find({"name":"John Smith"}, {"age":1})
{ "_id" : ObjectId("56d5e9a1bf738a9a34175181"), "age" : 35 }
> _
```

The first argument says we're only interested in people who are called "John Smith". The second argument says we're only interested in their age. Here, 1 is a flag that says we want this field. We could instead use 0 to say that we're not interested in a field, in which case, all the fields will be returned except this one.

Note that even though we said we were only interested in the age field, the preceding command returned the _id field as well. The _id field is always returned unless explicitly excluded. For example, we could run the following:

```
db.people.find({"name":"John Smith"}, {"age":1, "_id": 0})
```

This will return only John's age and nothing else. Also, note that the key for the _id field is _id and not id; this is to prevent a conflict with the id keyword in many programming languages, including Python.

Each of our examples used very basic JSON objects with only a single value, but we can specify multiple values for each argument. Consider the difference between the following commands:

```
db.people.find({"name":"John Smith", "age":1})
db.people.find({"name":"John Smith"}, {"age":1})
```

The first command uses find with a single argument that returns all records for all the people with the name John Smith and aged 1. The second command uses find with two arguments and returns the age field (and _id field) of all the people with the name John Smith.

A final difference to note from MySQL is that there is no need to commit new data. Once we run the insert statement, the data will be in the database until we remove it.

Updating data with MongoDB

Updating existing records is slightly more complicated. MongoDB provides an update method, which can be called in the same way as insert and find. It also takes two arguments—the first specifying the criteria to find the document we want to update, and the second providing a new document to replace it with. Run the following command:

```
db.people.update({"name":"John Smith"},
{"name":"John Smith", "age":43})
```

This finds the person with the name John Smith, and replaces him with a new person, also with the name John Smith and aged 43. If there are a lot of fields and we only want to change a single one, it is tedious and wasteful to recreate all the old fields. Therefore, we can use MongoDB's $set keyword instead, which will only replace the specified fields inside a document instead of replacing the whole document. Run the following command:

```
db.people.update({"name":"John Smith"}, {$set: {"age":35}})
```

This updates John's age back to 35 again, which is probably a relief to him. Instead of having to overwrite the whole document, here we only changed the age field. We did this using the $set keyword in the second argument. Note that the update function still takes two arguments and the second one now has a nested JSON structure—the out JSON object has $set as the key and another JSON object as a value. The inner JSON object specifies the updates that we want to make.

Deleting data with MongoDB

Deleting data is as easy as finding it. We will simply use the remove function instead of find and then specify the matching criteria in a single argument, just as we would with find. Run the following command to delete John from our database:

```
db.people.remove({"name":"John Smith"})
```

You will see a confirmation that one record was deleted, as shown in the following image:

```
> db.people.remove({"name":"John Smith"})
WriteResult({ "nRemoved" : 1 })
>
```

You can also check that John is deleted by running the following:

```
db.people.find()
```

Now, only Mary will be returned, as in the following image:

```
> db.people.find()
{ "_id" : ObjectId("56d5ec656167126b1233848c"), "name" : "Mary Jones" }
>
```

To remove all the documents from a collection, we can pass in an empty argument. Run the following command to remove all the remaining people:

```
db.people.remove({})
```

Here, {} specifies an empty criteria condition and therefore matches all the documents. Check that our `people` collection is empty by running the `find` command again, as follows:

```
db.people.find()
```

You'll see no output, as shown in the following screenshot (with the earlier examples included for context), because our `people` collection is now empty:

```
> db.people.remove({"name":"John Smith"})
WriteResult({ "nRemoved" : 1 })
> db.people.find()
{ "_id" : ObjectId("56d5ec656167126b1233848c"), "name" : "Ma
ry Jones" }
> db.people.remove({})
WriteResult({ "nRemoved" : 1 })
> db.people.find()
> _
```

Now that we looked at the basics of MongoDB, let's take a look at how to run similar commands using Python instead of operating through the shell.

Introducing PyMongo

PyMongo is a library that implements drivers for MongoDB and will allow us to execute commands on our database from our application code. As usual, install it through pip using the following command (note that, similarly to MongoDB, you only need to install this library on the server):

```
pip install --user pymongo
```

Now, we can import this library into our application and build our real `DBHelper` class, implementing all the methods we used in our `MockDBHelper` class.

Writing the DBHelper class

The last class that we need is the `DBHelper` class, which will contain all the functions that are required for our application code to talk to our database. This class will use the `pymongo` library we just installed in order to run MongoDB commands. Create a file named `dbhelper.py` in the `waiter` directory and add the following code:

```
import pymongo

DATABASE = "waitercaller"
```

```
class DBHelper:

  def __init__(self):
    client = pymongo.MongoClient()
    self.db = client[DATABASE]
```

This code imports the `pymongo` library, and in the constructor, it creates a client—a Python object that will let us run the CRUD operations we tried out earlier on our database. We defined the name of our database as a global one, and in the second line of our constructor, we connected to the specified database using `client`.

Adding the user methods

For user management, we need the same two functions we had in our mock class. The first is to get a user out of the database (in order to log this user in) and the second is to add new users to the database (in order to register new users). Add the following two methods to the `DBHelper` class:

```
    def get_user(self, email):
        return self.db.users.find_one({"email": email})

    def add_user(self, email, salt, hashed):
        self.db.users.insert({"email": email, "salt": salt,
        "hashed": hashed})
```

For the first method, we used PyMongo's `find_one()` function. This is similar to the `find()` method we used in the MongoDB shell but returns only a single match instead of all the matching results. As we only allow one registration per e-mail address, there will always be either one or zero matches. Using `find()` instead of `find_one()` here would also work, but we would get back a Python generator that produces a single or zero element. Using `find_one()`, we will get back either a single user result or none, which is exactly what our login code needs.

For the `add_user()` method, we used `insert()` exactly as we discussed when playing with the MongoDB shell and inserted a new document containing the e-mail address, salt, and salted hash of the password.

Adding the table methods

We need methods to handle the following cases for the virtual tables that our users will create:

*   One to add new tables
*   One to update tables (so that we can add the shortened bitly URL)

- One to get all the tables (so that we can display them in the **Account** page)

- One to get a single table (so that we can add the local table number to our requests)

- One to delete a table

This is a nice set of methods as it demonstrates all four of the CRUD database operations. Add the following code to the `DBHelper` class:

```
def add_table(self, number, owner):
    new_id = self.db.tables.insert({"number": number, "owner":
    owner})
    return new_id

def update_table(self, _id, url):
    self.db.tables.update({"_id": _id}, {"$set": {"url": url}})

def get_tables(self, owner_id):
    return list(self.db.tables.find({"owner": owner_id}))

def get_table(self, table_id):
    return self.db.tables.find_one({"_id": ObjectId(table_id)})

def delete_table(self, table_id):
    self.db.tables.remove({"_id": ObjectId(table_id)})
```

For the `add_table()` method, MongoDB will assign a unique identifier every time we insert a table. This gives us true multiuser support. Our mock code used the user-chosen table number as a unique identifier and would break with multiple users when two or more users chose the same table number. In the `add_table()` method, we returned this unique identifier to the application code, which can then be used to build the URL that's needed to make new requests for this specific table.

The `update_table()` method uses the `insert()` function that we discussed earlier. As in our previous example, we used the `$set` keyword to keep our original data intact, and only edited a specific field (instead of overwriting the entire document).

> Note that unlike in the MongoDB shell example, we now need quotation marks around `$set`; this makes it syntactically legal Python code (all the keys of a dictionary have to be strings), and PyMongo takes care of the magic in the background to convert our Python dictionaries into MongoDB commands and objects.

The `get_tables()` function used the `find()` function instead of the `find_one()` function that we used for the user code. This caused PyMongo to return a Python generator that can produce all the data that matched the *find* criteria. As we assumed that we'll always be able to load all the tables into memory, we converted this generator to a list, which we then passed to our template.

The `get_table()` function is used in cases when we only have access to the table ID and need to get other information about the table. This is exactly the scenario when we processed requests; the URL of the request contained the table's unique ID but wanted to add the table number to the **Dashboard** page. The unique identifiers that MongoDB generated are actually objects rather than simple strings, but we had just the string from our URL. Therefore, we created `ObjectId` and passed in the string before using this ID to query the database. `ObjectId` can be imported from the `bson` library, which was installed automatically. This means we also need to add another import statement. Add the following line to the top of the `dbhelper.py` file:

```
from bson.objectid import ObjectId
```

Finally, the `delete_table()` method used the `remove()` function exactly as we did before. Here, we removed a table by its unique identifier, so again, we created an `ObjectId` object from the string we had before passing it to the database.

Adding the request methods

We have to add the last three methods to the `DBHelper` class to deal with the attention requests. We need to:

- Add a request when a patron visits the provided URL
- Get all the requests for a specific user to display on the **Dashboard** page
- Delete requests from the database when the user hits the **Resolve** button

Add the following methods to the `dbhelper.py` file:

```python
def add_request(self, table_id, time):
    table = self.get_table(table_id)
    self.db.requests.insert({"owner": table['owner'],
    "table_number": table['number'],
    "table_id": table_id, "time": time})

def get_requests(self, owner_id):
    return list(self.db.requests.find({"owner": owner_id}))

def delete_request(self, request_id):
    self.db.requests.remove({"_id": ObjectId(request_id)})
```

Changing the application code

Now that we have a real `DBHelper` class, we need to conditionally import it based on which environment we're in. Change the import for the `MockDBHelper` class in the `waitercaller.py` file to read, as follows:

```
if config.test
    from mockdbhelper import MockDBHelper as DBHelper
else:
    from dbhelper import DBHelper
```

Ensure that the preceding four lines are added beneath the `config` import.

Also, our `DBHelper` class deals mainly with many instances of `ObjectId`, while our `MockDBHelper` class uses strings. We therefore need a small change to our `account_createtable()` function to cast `ObjectId` to a string. Take a look at the line in `waitercaller.py` that reads the following:

```
new_url = BH.shorten_url(config.base_url +
"newrequest/" + tableid)
```

Now, change this to the following:

```
new_url = BH.shorten_url(config.base_url +
"newrequest/" + str(tableid))
```

This will ensure that `tableid` is always a string before we concatenate it to our URL.

The last code changes we need for our production is a different `config` file to specify the correct `base_url` for our VPS and to indicate that the `MockDBHelper` class should not be used. As we don't check our `config` file into our `git` repository, we'll need to create this directly on the VPS.

Testing our application in production

Our application should now be fully functional once we add the preceding code! As with the database section of our Crime Map application, this bit is the most delicate as we haven't been able to test the `DBHelper` code locally, and we'll have to debug it directly on the VPS. However, we're confident, from our `MockDBHelper` class, that all our application logic is working, and if the new database code holds up, everything else should go as expected. Let's push our code to the server and test it out.

Locally, run the following commands in your `waitercaller` directory:

```
git add .
git commit -m "DBHelper code"
git push origin master
```

On your VPS, change to the `WaiterCaller` directory, pull the new code, and restart Apache, as follows:

```
cd /var/www/waitercaller
git pull origin master
```

Now, create the production `config` file using nano by running the following command:

```
nano config.py
```

Type the following into the new `config.py` file, substituting the IP address in `base_url` with the IP address of your VPS.

```
test = False
base_url = "http://123.456.789.123/
```

Then, save and quit the file by hitting *Ctrl + X* and entering *Y* when prompted.

Now, run the following command to reload Apache with the new code:

```
sudo service apache2 reload
```

Visit the IP address of your VPS in your local browser and do a run-through of all the functionality to make sure everything works as expected. This includes attempting to sign up with invalid data, signing up, attempting to log in with invalid data, logging in, creating a table, creating a request, viewing the dashboard, waiting for the dashboard to refresh, resolving a request, and more. For a full test, all the actions should be completed several times in varying combinations.

You'll probably understand how tedious this gets even for our relatively simple application. For more complicated applications, it is well worth the effort to create automatic tests—code that imitates what a user would do on the site but also has built-in expectations of what should happen at each step. Tools such as Selenium (`www.seleniumhq.org`) come in very useful to build such tests.

> As always, if anything goes wrong or you get the dreaded "500: Internal Server Error", check the Apache error file at `/etc/log/apache2/error.log` for hints.

Adding some finishing touches

To end off, we'll add a couple of indices to our database to improve efficiency and prevent multiple requests from being open for a single table. After this, we'll add a favicon to personalize our web application.

Adding indices to MongoDB

Database indices are used to increase efficiency. Normally, to find a subset of documents in our database that match certain criteria (that is, whenever we use the MongoDB `find()` method), the database engine has to examine each record and add the ones that match the returned result. If we add an index to a specific field, the database will store more metadata, which can be thought about as storing a sorted copy of this field. To find out whether `john@example.com` appears in a sorted list is much more efficient than checking whether it appears in an unsorted list. However, the indices do take up additional storage space, so choosing where to add indices is a classic *space-time tradeoff* that's seen everywhere in computer science. MongoDB can also use indices to place some constraints on a field. In our case, we'll use a *unique* index, which prevents a new document from being added to the database if the value for the indexed field already appears in another document in this collection.

We'll add two indices to MongoDB. We'll add an index on the `email` field of our `users` collection as we will use this field to find users on login, and we want the lookups to be as fast as possible. We also want to ensure at a database level that each e-mail address is unique. We already have two checks for this: the HTML5 field does a frontend check, and our application code does a backend check. Even though a database check may seem unnecessary, it takes little effort to set up and follows the good principles of baked-in security (in which checks aren't just tacked on as an afterthought, but all data is validated as often as possible instead), and the principle that each *layer* of an application (the frontend, application layer, and database layer in our case) shouldn't blindly trust the data that is passed from a higher layer.

We'll also add a unique index on the `table_id` field for a requests collection. This will prevent a single impatient table from spamming the dashboard with multiple requests by refreshing the page that creates a new request. It's also useful because our requests are created using GET requests, which can easily be duplicated (by a browser preloading a page or a social network scraping the links a user visits to find out more about them). By ensuring that each request's `table_id` is unique, we can prevent both of these issues.

Where do we add indices?

When we built our MySQL database, we had a setup script that ran independently of our Crime Map web application. This setup script built the skeleton of the database, and we wrote it in Python so that we could easily run it again if we ever needed to migrate to a new server or to reinstall our database.

As MongoDB is so much more flexible, we didn't need a setup script. We can start our application off on a new server, and — as long as we install MongoDB — the database will recreate itself from scratch as new data is added or the old data is restored from a backup.

The lack of a setup script does mean that we don't really have a good place to add indices to our database. If we add the indices through the MongoDB shell, it means that someone has to remember to add them again if the application needs to migrate to a new server. Therefore, we'll create an independent Python script just to make the indices. On your local machine, create a Python file in the `waitercaller` directory and call it `create_mongo_indices.py`. Add the following code:

```
import pymongo
client = pymongo.MongoClient()
c = client['waitercaller']
print c.users.create_index("email", unique=True)
print c.requests.create_index("table_id", unique=True)
```

The connection code is the same that we used before, and the code used to create indices is simple enough. We called the `create_index()` method on the collection we want to create an index on and then passed in the field name to use to create the index. In our case, we also passed in the `unique=True` flag to specify that the indices should also have a unique constraint added to them.

Now, we need to make a small change to our application so that it can deal with the case of a new request being made when an identical request is already open. In the `dbhelper.py` file, update the `add_request()` method to the following:

```
def add_request(self, table_id, time):
    table = self.get_table(table_id)
    try:
        self.db.requests.insert({"owner": table['owner'],
        "table_number": table['number'], "table_id": table_id,
        "time": time})
        return True
    except pymongo.errors.DuplicateKeyError:
        return False
```

If we try to insert a request into our database with a duplicate `table_id` field, `DuplicateKeyError` will be thrown. In the updated code, we will catch this error and return `False` to indicate that the request wasn't successfully created. We will also now return `True` when the request is successful. To take advantage of this information in the application code, we also need to update the `new_request()` method. Edit the method so that it looks similar to this:

```
@app.route("/newrequest/<tid>")
def new_request(tid):
    if DB.add_request(tid, datetime.datetime.now()):
        return "Your request has been logged and a waiter will
        be with you shortly"
    return "There is already a request pending for this table.
    Please be patient, a waiter will be there ASAP"
```

Now, we will check whether the new request was successfully created or whether an existing one blocked it. In the latter case, we will return a different message, requesting patience from the patron.

To test the new functionality, add the new and modified files to Git (`waitercaller.py`, `dbhelper.py`, `create_mongo_indices.py`), commit, and then push them. On your VPS, pull in the new changes, restart Apache, and run the following:

```
python create_mongo_indices.py
```

To create the indices we discussed before, run some tests again in your browser to make sure nothing broke and to verify that you get the new message displayed when you visit the same attention request URL repeatedly without resolving the request, as in the screenshot that follows:

You may find that, due to your browser pre-fetching pages, attention requests get made automatically when you first create tables through the account page. If you see the message as displayed in the above image when you don't expect to, resolve any open requests on the dashboard page, and visit the newrequest URL again.

Adding a favicon

The last thing we'll add to our application is a favicon. *Favicons* are the small images that most browsers display in the tab bar when a page is open and on the bookmarks bar if a user bookmarks a site. They add a friendly touch to the site and help a user identify a site more quickly.

The tricky part about favicons is that they have to be really small. It's customary to use a 16x16 pixel image as a favicon—which doesn't leave that much room for creativity. There are some nice websites to help you create the perfect favicon for your website. One such site is `favicon.cc`, which allows you to create a favicon from scratch (giving you 16x16 blank pixels to start), or it can import an image. Using the import functionality, you can use a bigger image that `favicon.cc` attempts to reduce to 16x16 pixels—this has mixed results and generally works better with simpler images. An example favicon is included in the code bundle in the static directory, and an enlarged version of it is shown in the following image:

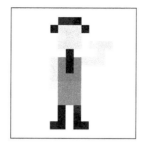

Once you have an icon (you can use the one provided in the code bundle), it's easy to tell Flask to serve it along with the rest of the page. Make sure your icon is called `favicon.ico` (the standard extension for icon files is `.ico`) and put it in the `waitercaller/static` directory. Then, add the following line to the `<head>` section of the `base.html` template:

```
<link rel="shortcut icon" href="{{ url_for('static',
filename='favicon.ico') }}">
```

This creates a link to the `favicon.ico` file using Jinja's `url_for` function to generate the full URL needed to be directed to the static directory, which is simply converted to the plain HTML (which you can see by hitting **View source** in your browser). Take a look at the following:

```
<link rel="shortcut icon" href="/static/favicon.ico">
```

Now, if you reload the page again, you will see the favicon in the tab heading, and if you bookmark the page, you'll view the icon in the bookmarks toolbar of your browser as well, as seen in the following screenshot:

That's it for our last project. Of course, no web application is ever truly complete, and there are countless improvements to make and features to add. By this stage in the book, you will have more than enough knowledge to start adding your own changes and bringing your original ideas into creation, either as extensions to the projects we walked through in this book or from scratch, as brand-new web applications.

Summary

In this chapter, we completed our Waiter Caller web application. We installed MongoDB on our server, learned how to use it through the shell, and then installed PyMongo. Using PyMongo, we created a new database helper class to allow our application code to run operations on the new database.

Finally, we added a favicon to make our web application friendlier and more aesthetically pleasing to users.

In the next and final chapter, we'll take a look at what could still be added to our application to improve usability and security and end with some pointers on where to look next to continue learning about Flask and web development through Python.

A Sneak Peek into the Future

We covered quite a variety of topics in this book, and we walked through the building of three functional and useful web applications. However, books, by nature, are of a finite length, while the world of web development tends towards the infinite, so we couldn't add everything. In this final chapter, we'll take a whistle-stop tour around the technologies that we weren't able to cover in detail. We'll start with looking at technologies that could be used directly to expand or improve the projects we created in this book. Then, we'll look at some more advanced Flask features that we didn't need to use in our projects but which will almost certainly be useful in other projects. Finally, we'll have a brief discussion of the technologies that are useful for web development in general but are not specific to either the projects we built here or to Flask.

Expanding the projects

The projects we built are all functional, but they are not quite ready for heavy, real-time use. If they were to be built out to handle thousands of users or were commercial applications, they would need a few more features. These are discussed in the following sections.

Adding a domain name

We accessed all of our projects using the IP address of our VPS. You're almost certainly used to visiting web applications using domain names rather than IP addresses. When you use a domain name, such as `http://google.com`, your browser first sends off a request to a DNS server to find out what the IP address associated with this domain is. DNS servers are similar to huge automatic telephone books that exist solely to translate the domain names that humans find easier to remember (such as `http://google.com`) in than the IP addresses that organize the Internet (for example, 123.456.789.123).

To use a domain name instead of the IP address, you need to purchase one from a registrar. Often your **Internet Service Provider (ISP)** can assist you with purchasing a domain name (such as `yourname.com`). Domain names are normally fairly inexpensive, and you can get them for as little as a few dollars a year.

Once you purchase a domain name, you need to set up the DNS settings correctly. Most ISPs have an online control panel where you can do this yourself, but you may have to contact them to assist you. Your domain needs to point to your VPS. To do this, you create an "A" type DNS record that maps the domain to your IP.

Once your domain name points at your server, you can configure Apache to recognize it by using it instead of our `example.com` placeholder that we put in the Apache configuration files, such as `/etc/apache2/sites-available/waitercaller.conf`.

Changes to domain names also take a while to propagate — that is, the major DNS servers of the world need to be updated so that when someone visits your domain name, the DNS server can redirect them to your IP address. DNS propagation can take hours.

Adding HTTPS

You've probably noticed that banks, large corporations such as Google and Microsoft, and an ever-growing number of other companies, have their websites automatically redirect to an **HTTPS** version. The "S" stands for *secure*, so the full acronym becomes **Hyper Text Transport Protocol Secure**. Whenever you see HTTPS in your browser's navigation bar (normally with a green padlock next to it) it means that all traffic flowing between you and the server is encrypted. This prevents so-called *man in the middle attacks*, where a malicious person between you and the server can view or modify the content that you and the server exchange.

Until recently, this encryption was achieved by the site owner by purchasing an expensive certificate from **Certificate Authority (CA)**. CA's job is to act as a trusted third party between you and the server, issuing a signed certificate to the owner of a site. This certificate can be used to set up an encrypted channel between the client and the server. Because of the prohibitive cost, HTTPS was only used where security was absolutely necessary (for example, in online banking) and by companies such as Google who could afford the high fees. With everyone beginning to realize that the trust-based model of World Wide Web is inherently flawed, HTTPS is becoming more and more popular even for small blogs and personal websites. Companies such as Let's Encrypt (`https://letsencrypt.org`) are now offering certificates for free and these certificates can easily be installed and configured to work with popular web servers, such as Apache.

For our final project, as we are handling sensitive data (specifically passwords), using HTTPS is a must for nontrivial usage of our application, and it's also desirable for our other two projects (HTTPS is always better than HTTP). Although the process of setting up certificates to work with your web server is far simpler now than it was a couple of years ago, a full walk-through of how to set up Apache2 to play with a CA certificate is beyond the scope of this book.

However, if you only take the time to learn about one of the technologies mentioned in this chapter, then it should be this one. Here is a link to a very simple Digital Ocean tutorial that shows you how to set up the certificate on Ubuntu 14.04 to work with Apache2 (the exact configuration we used in this book):

```
https://www.digitalocean.com/community/tutorials/how-to-secure-
apache-with-let-s-encrypt-on-ubuntu-14-04
```

E-mail confirmation for new registrations

You probably noted in our third project that our registration process was a little bit unusual. The normal way for new users to register on a site is as follows:

1. User fills out registration form and submits it.
2. Server saves the data in the database.
3. Server generates a unique and secure token and stores the token associated with the registration, which it marks as incomplete.
4. Server e-mails the token to the user in the form of a URL and requests that the user click on the URL to confirm the account.
5. User clicks on URL with the unique token.
6. Server finds an incomplete registration associated with this token and marks the registration as confirmed.

The preceding process is in order to prove that the user gave us a real e-mail address to which he or she has access. Of course, the user does not want to wait for someone to manually send an e-mail, so the confirmation e-mail has to be sent automatically. This leads to a few complications, including the need to set up a mail server and the fact that the automatic confirmation e-mail we send may well end up in the user's spam folder, leading to frustration all round. Another option is to use an *E-mail as a service* platform, such as Amazon's **Simple E-mail Service** (**SES**). However, these are not usually free.

Once the user has a confirmed e-mail account, we can also use it to allow the user to reset a forgotten password. Again, this would involve sending an automatic e-mail to users who wanted to reset their password. The e-mail would again contain a secure unique token in a URL that the user would click on to prove that he or she really did make the password reset request. We would then allow the user to type in a new password and update the database with the new (hashed and salted) password. Note that we can't and shouldn't send the user his or her own password because we store only the salted and hashed version of the password; we have no way of discovering the forgotten one.

The complete user account system with automatic e-mail confirmations and the "forgot your password" functionality is fairly complex. We could set it up using nothing but Python and Flask and an e-mail server, but in the next section, we'll also discuss some more Flask extensions that could make this process easier.

Google Analytics

If we run any of the web applications commercially, we'll probably be interested in how many people actually use them. This would help us in deciding how (and whether) to monetize our applications and provide other useful insights.

The most common way to achieve this is through Google Analytics. This is a service from Google to track not only how many people visit your site but also how long they spend on it, how they found it, their country, information about the device they use for web browsing, and many other insightful statistics. Google Analytics is free, and to get started with using it, you need to simply create an account on `https://analytics.google.com` (or use your existing Google account). After filling in some information about your site, you'll be given a short snippet of JavaScript. This JavaScript code contains a unique tracking ID assigned to your site. You need to add the JavaScript code to your site, and whenever anyone visits the site, the JavaScript code will be loaded into their web browser and will send information about them to Google, which will then use the unique ID to associate the information with you. On the Google Analytics dashboard, you can then see graphs of the number of visitors, the length of their visits, and many more pieces of information.

In the case of our waiter-caller project, we'd add the JavaScript at the end of the `base.html` file along with the Bootstrap JavaScript code.

Scalability

The best problem to have as a web application creator is having made an application that is too popular. If lots of people are visiting your application, it means that you created something good (and you can possible start charging people money for it). Our little VPS will not handle a lot of traffic. If thousands of people visit the site simultaneously, we'll run out of network bandwidth, processing capacity, memory, and disk space very quickly.

A complete discussion on creating scalable web applications would be a book all on its own. However, some of the steps we would need to take would be:

- **Run the database on a dedicated machine**: At the moment, we run our web server and database on the same physical machine. For a larger web application, the database would have its own dedicated machine so that heavy database use (for instance, many restaurant patrons creating new requests) wouldn't have a negative impact on the people who just wanted to browse our home page. Normally, the database machine would have lots of disk space and memory, while the machine running the web server would focus more on having high bandwidth availability and processing power.

- **Run a load balancer**: If we have a lot of visitors, one machine will not be able to keep up with the load no matter how big and powerful the machine is. We would therefore run several duplicate web server machines. The problem would then be to evenly distribute new visitors among all the different machines. To solve this, we would use something called a *load balancer*, which is responsible for nothing but accepting the initial request from the user (that is, when the user visits your homepage) and assigning this user to one of the replica web servers.

As we grow bigger, the situation would grow more and more complicated, and we would add replica database machines as well. A popular site requires full-time maintenance, often by a team of people, because hardware fails, malicious users exist, and updates (which are necessary to mitigate attacks by malicious users) tend to break the compatibility between software. On the bright side, if any web applications were to grow popular enough to warrant the preceding, the application would probably also generate enough revenue to make all the issues discussed an "SEP", or somebody else's problem. That is, we could hire a system's administrator, a database administrator, and a chief security officer, tell them to sort it out, and spend the rest of our days on ocean cruises. On this note, let's take a look at some Flask-specific expansions to our knowledge.

Expanding your Flask knowledge

You might expect that Flask, being a micro framework, could be covered in its entirety in a single book. However, there are some potentially very useful parts of Flask that we didn't need for any of our three projects. We'll briefly outline these here.

VirtualEnv

The first library worth mentioning is not actually Flask-specific, and if you've spent some time on Python development before, you will almost certainly come across it. `VirtualEnv` is a Python library that creates a virtual Python environment on your machine. It can be used in conjunction with Flask either only on your development machine or both on your development machine and server. Its main purpose is to isolate your entire Python environment into a virtual one, including all the Python modules that you use. This has two major benefits. The first is that sometimes you need to run two different Python projects on the same machine, but each project requires a different version of the same library. Using `VirtualEnv`, each project would have its own virtualized version of the Python setup, so it becomes trivial to install two different version of the same library. The second advantage is that your environment becomes more portable, and in theory, it is easy to migrate an application running in a `VirtualEnv` environment to another machine that has `VirtualEnv` installed.

The `VirtualEnv` environment is widely used for Python development, especially for Flask. My decision to not include it in the main body of the book proved highly controversial with the reviewers, many of whom felt that the book was incomplete without it. I decided not to include it for two reasons. The first is that while I was learning Flask, I read many tutorials and examples, which included VirtualEnv. I always found the extra work needed for the setup and explanation of `VirtualEnv` and virtual environments in general to be distracting from the main content of the tutorial (namely, using Flask). The second reason is that I still often do not use it in the Flask projects I build today. If you're not running old software that depends on a particular version of a particular library, then installing useful Python libraries system-wide so that they can be used by all your Python applications is convenient. Also, sometimes, VirtualEnv can just become a mission without providing any value.

Of course, you may already have your own opinion on VirtualEnv, in which case you're welcome to go along with it. There's nothing stopping anyone from building any of the projects in this book in a `VirtualEnv` environment if they have a little experience. If you have not used it before, it's well worth looking at. You can install it through pip and try it out to take a look at exactly what it does and whether it can be of use in your particular scenario. You can read more about it and how to use it here:

`http://docs.python-guide.org/en/latest/dev/virtualenvs/`

Flask Blueprints

Perhaps the biggest feature of Flask that we haven't mentioned in this book is Flask Blueprints. You must have noted after building three Flask applications that certain patterns crop up time and again. Repeated code is bad code even over a number of different applications; if you find a better way to do something or need to make some changes for an update, you don't want to make the same change across several applications.

Blueprints provide a way to specify patterns for a Flask application. If you have several applications that use the same code to return templates or connect to a database, you can rather write this common code in a blueprint and then have all the applications register the blueprint.

You can read more about Flask Blueprints, take a look at examples, and learn how to get started with using them at `http://flask.pocoo.org/docs/0.10/blueprints/`.

Flask extensions

We looked at quite a few different Flask extensions over the course of our three projects. However, because of the educational focus of the book, we chose to write some code from scratch that may be better off using existing extensions. (Generally when developing, we want to avoid reinventing the wheel. If someone else has already put thought into solving a problem and provided a well-developed and well-maintained solution, it's better to use their offerings than to try and create our own.) Of special interest are the extensions we could use to make our user account system simpler and more powerful and those that offer us a more abstract way to talk to our database.

Flask-SQLAlchemy

Another controversial decision in this book was of not introducing the Flask-SQLAlchemy extension along with MySQL. SQLAlchemy provides a SQL toolkit and ORM to make it easier and more secure to interact with SQL databases from a Python environment. ORM provides another layer of abstraction between the web application and database. Instead of having to write the SQL code directly, one can make calls to a database using Python objects, which ORM will then translate to and from SQL. This makes the database easier to write and maintain and also more secure (ORM is normally very good at mitigating against any potential SQL injection vulnerabilities). The reasons to omit it were similar to the reasons to omit VirtualEnv — when learning, too many layers of abstraction can do more harm than good, and it's always advantageous to have first-hand experience with the problems that tools solve before blindly using the tools directly.

For any Flask application that uses a MySQL database, such as our Crime Map project, it is highly recommendable to use ORM, as with most Flask extensions. Flask-SQLAlchemy is just a wrapper for an existing non-Flask-specific library. You can find out more about SQLAlchemy at `http://www.sqlalchemy.org/` and a comprehensive guide to Flask-SQLAlchemy, including common usage patterns, here:

`http://flask.pocoo.org/docs/0.10/patterns/sqlalchemy/`

Flask MongoDB extensions

There are several Flask extensions that are intended to make interfacing with MongoDB easier. As MongoDB is relatively new, none of these has reached quite the maturity or is in as wide use as SQLAlchemy; therefore, if you intend to use one of them, it is recommended that you examine each to decide which one best suits your needs.

Flask-MongoAlchemy

Perhaps the most similar to SQLAlchemy (and not just by name) is Flask-MongoAlchemy. Similarly to SQLAlchemy, MongoAlchemy is not Flask-specific. You can read more about the main project here at `http://www.mongoalchemy.org`. Flask-MongoAlchemy is a Flask wrapper for MongoAlchemy, which you can read more about here:

`http://pythonhosted.org/Flask-MongoAlchemy`

Flask-PyMongo

A thinner wrapper to MongoDB that is closer to using PyMongo directly as we did in our third project is Flask-PyMongo. Unlike MongoAlchemy, this does not provide an ORM equivalent; instead, it simply provides a way of connecting to MongoDB through PyMongo using syntax that is more consistent with the way Flask usually handles external resources. You can have a quick introduction to Flask-PyMongo on its GitHub page here:

`https://github.com/dcrosta/flask-pymongo`

Flask-MongoEngine

Yet another solution to using Flask in conjunction with MongoDB is MongoEngine (`http://mongoengine.org`). This is notable because it integrates with WTForms and Flask-Security, which we'll discuss in the following sections. You can read more about the Flask-specific extension for Mongo Engine at `https://pypi.python.org/pypi/flask-mongoengine`.

Flask-Mail

If we wanted to implement an automatic e-mail sending solution, such as that described earlier in this chapter, a helpful extension would be Flask-Mail. This allows you to easily send e-mails from your Flask application along with handling attachments and bulk mailing. As mentioned before, these days, it's worthwhile to consider using a third-party service such as Amazon's SES instead of sending e-mails yourself. You can read more about Flask-Mail at `http://pythonhosted.org/Flask-Mail`.

Flask-Security

The final extension we'll talk about is Flask-Security. This extension is notable because a large part of it is actually built by combining other Flask extensions. In some ways, it departs from the Flask philosophy of doing as little as possible to be useful and allowing the user full freedom for custom implementations. It assumes that you are using one of the database frameworks we described, and it pulls together functionality from Flask-Login, WTForms, Flask-Mail, and other extensions to attempt to make building user account control systems as straightforward as possible. If we used this, we would have had a centralized way of handling registering accounts, logging in accounts, encrypting passwords, and sending e-mails instead of having to implement each part of the login system separately. You can read more about Flask-Security here:

```
https://pythonhosted.org/Flask-Security
```

Other Flask extensions

There are many Flask extensions, and we've only highlighted the ones that we think would be generally applicable in many web development scenarios here. Of course, when you develop a unique web application, you'll have much more specific needs, and chances are that someone has already had a similar need and created a solution. You can find an extensive (but not complete) list of Flask extensions here:

```
http://flask.pocoo.org/extensions
```

Expanding your web development knowledge

In this book, we focused on backend development—that done through Python or Flask. A large part of developing web applications is building a frontend that is powerful, aesthetically pleasing, and intuitive to use. Although we provided a solid grounding in HTML, CSS, and JavaScript, each of these topics is big enough for its own book, and many such books exist.

JavaScript is perhaps the most important of the three. Known as the "language of the web", it has gained steadily in popularity over the last few years (although, as with all languages, it has its fair share of critics). There are many frameworks for building JavaScript-intensive web applications (so many, in fact, that their sheer number and the frequency of new ones being released has become a topic of humor among developers). We introduced Bootstrap in this book, which includes basic JavaScript components, but for more heavily interactive applications, there exist larger frameworks. Three of the more popular frontend frameworks include AngularJS (built by Google), React.js (built by Facebook), and Ember.js (sponsored by a variety of corporations, including Yahoo!). Learning any of these frameworks or one of the many others will definitely help you build larger and more complicated web applications with richer frontends.

JavaScript is also no longer limited to the frontend, and many modern web applications are built using JavaScript on the server side as well. A common way to achieve this is through Node.js, which could have fully replaced Python and Flask in any of the projects we built.

HTML5 and CSS3 have grown far more powerful than the older technologies they evolved from. Earlier, there was a clear division of labor, with HTML for content, CSS for styling, and JavaScript for actions. Now, there is far more overlap between the capabilities of the three technologies, and some impressive and interactive applications are built using only HTML5 and CSS3 without the normal addition of JavaScript.

Summary

In this appendix, we looked forwards and pointed out some key areas and resources that will help you move beyond what was covered in detail in this book. We covered these areas in three topics: the projects we worked on in this book, the Flask resources that we didn't use, and web development in general.

This brings us to the end. However, the world of technology is so vast and so rapidly moving that, hopefully, this is more of a beginning than an end. As you continue your adventures, learning more about life, Python, and web development, I hope that some of the ideas presented in this book stay with you.

Module 2

Flask Framework Cookbook

Over 80 hands-on recipes to help you create small-to-large web applications using Flask

1
Flask Configurations

This introductory chapter will help you to understand the different ways Flask can be configured to suit various needs as per the demands of the project.

In this chapter, we will cover the following recipes:

- ► Environment setup with virtualenv
- ► Handling basic configurations
- ► Class-based settings
- ► Organization of static files
- ► Being deployment specific with instance folders
- ► Composition of views and models
- ► Creating a modular web app with blueprints
- ► Making a Flask app installable using setuptools

Introduction

"Flask is a microframework for Python based on Werkzeug, Jinja2 and good intentions."

Flask official documentation

Why micro? Does it mean that Flask is lacking in functionality or that your complete web application has to mandatorily go inside one file? Not really! It simply refers to the fact that Flask aims at keeping the core of the framework small but highly extensible. This makes writing applications or extensions very easy and flexible and gives developers the power to choose the configurations they want for their application, without imposing any restrictions on the choice of database, templating engine, and so on. In this chapter, you will learn some ways to set up and configure Flask.

Getting started with Flask hardly takes 2 minutes. Setting up a simple Hello World application is as easy as baking a pie:

```
from flask import Flask
app = Flask(__name__)

@app.route('/')
def hello_world():
    return 'Hello to the World of Flask!'

if __name__ == '__main__':
    app.run()
```

Now, Flask needs to be installed; this can be done simply via `pip`:

$ pip install Flask

The preceding snippet is a complete Flask-based web application. Here, an instance of the imported `Flask` class is a **Web Server Gateway Interface** (**WSGI**) (`http://legacy.python.org/dev/peps/pep-0333/`) application. So, `app` in this code becomes our WSGI application, and as this is a standalone module, we set the `__name__` string as `'__main__'`. If we save this in a file with the name `app.py`, then the application can simply be run using the following command:

$ python app.py
  * Running on http://127.0.0.1:5000/

Now, if we just head over to our browser and type `http://127.0.0.1:5000/`, we can see our application running.

 Never save your application file as `flask.py`; if you do so, it will conflict with Flask itself while importing.

Environment setup with virtualenv

Flask can be installed using `pip` or `easy_install` globally, but we should always prefer to set up our application environment using `virtualenv`. This prevents the global Python installation from getting affected by our custom installation by creating a separate environment for our application. This separate environment is helpful because you can have multiple versions of the same library being used for multiple applications, or some packages might have different versions of the same libraries as dependencies. `virtualenv` manages this in separate environments and does not let a wrong version of any library affect any application.

How to do it...

We will first install `virtualenv` using `pip` and then create a new environment with the name `my_flask_env` inside the folder in which we ran the first command. This will create a new folder with the same name:

```
$ pip install virtualenv
$ virtualenv my_flask_env
```

Now, from inside the `my_flask_env` folder, we will run the following commands:

```
$ cd my_flask_env
$ source bin/activate
$ pip install flask
```

This will activate our environment and install Flask inside it. Now, we can do anything with our application within this environment, without affecting any other Python environment.

How it works...

Until now, we have used `pip install flask` multiple times. As the name suggests, the command refers to the installation of Flask just like any Python package. If we look a bit deeper into the process of installing Flask via `pip`, we will see that a number of packages are installed. The following is a summary of the package installation process of Flask:

```
$ pip install -U flask
Downloading/unpacking flask
.........
.........
Many more lines........
.........
Successfully installed flask Werkzeug Jinja2 itsdangerous markupsafe
Cleaning up...
```

> In the preceding command, `-U` refers to the installation with upgrades. This will overwrite the existing installation (if any) with the latest released versions.

If we notice carefully, there are five packages installed in total, namely `flask`, `Werkzeug`, `Jinja2`, `itsdangerous`, and `markupsafe`. These are the packages on which Flask depends, and it will not work if any of them are missing.

There's more...

To make our lives easier, we can use `virtualenvwrapper`, which, as the name suggests, is a wrapper written over `virtualenv` and makes the handling of multiple `virtualenv` easier.

> Remember that the installation of `virtualenvwrapper` should be done at a global level. So, deactivate any `virtualenv` that might still be active. To deactivate it, just use the following command:
>
> `$ deactivate`
>
> Also, it is possible that you might not be able to install the package at a global level because of permission issues. Switch to superuser or use `sudo` in this case.

You can install `virtualenvwrapper` using the following commands:

```
$ pip install virtualenvwrapper
$ export WORKON_HOME=~/workspace
$ source /usr/local/bin/virtualenvwrapper.sh
```

In the preceding code, we installed `virtualenvwrapper`, created a new environment variable with the name `WORKON_HOME`, and provided it with a path, which will act as the home for all our virtual environments created using `virtualenvwrapper`. To install Flask, use the following commands:

```
$ mkvirtualenv flask
$ pip install flask
```

To deactivate a `virtualenv`, we can just run the following command:

```
$ deactivate
```

To activate an existing `virtualenv` using `virtualenvwrapper`, we can run the following command:

```
$ workon flask
```

See also

References and installation links are as follows:

- https://pypi.python.org/pypi/virtualenv
- https://pypi.python.org/pypi/virtualenvwrapper
- https://pypi.python.org/pypi/Flask
- https://pypi.python.org/pypi/Werkzeug

- ▸ `https://pypi.python.org/pypi/Jinja2`
- ▸ `https://pypi.python.org/pypi/itsdangerous`
- ▸ `https://pypi.python.org/pypi/MarkupSafe`

Handling basic configurations

The first thing that comes to mind is configuring a Flask application as per the need. In this recipe, we will try to understand the different ways in which Flask configurations can be done.

Getting ready

In Flask, a configuration is done on an attribute named `config` of the `Flask` object. The `config` attribute is a subclass of the dictionary data type, and we can modify it just like any dictionary.

How to do it...

For instance, to run our application in the debug mode, we can write the following:

```
app = Flask(__name__)
app.config['DEBUG'] = True
```

> The debug Boolean can also be set at the `Flask` object level rather than at the `config` level:
>
> ```
> app.debug = True
> ```
>
> Alternatively, we can use this line of code:
>
> ```
> app.run(debug=True)
> ```
>
> Enabling the debug mode will make the server reload itself in the case of any code changes, and it also provides the very helpful `Werkzeug` debugger when something goes wrong.

There are a bunch of configuration values provided by Flask. We will come across them in the relevant recipes.

As the application grows larger, there originates a need to manage the application's configuration in a separate file as shown here. Being specific to machine-based setups in most cases will most probably not be a part of the version-control system. For this, Flask provides us with multiple ways to fetch configurations. The most frequently used ones are discussed here:

- ▸ From a Python configuration file (`*.cfg`), the configuration can be fetched using:
  ```
  app.config.from_pyfile('myconfig.cfg')
  ```

▶ From an object, the configuration can be fetched using:

```
app.config.from_object('myapplication.default_settings')
```

Alternatively, we can also use:

```
app.config.from_object(__name__) #To load from same file
```

▶ From the environment variable, the configuration can be fetched using:

```
app.config.from_envvar('PATH_TO_CONFIG_FILE')
```

How it works...

Flask is intelligent enough to pick up only those configuration variables that are written in uppercase. This allows us to define any local variables in our configuration files/objects and leave the rest to Flask.

The best practice to use configurations is to have a bunch of default settings in `app.py` or via any object in our application itself and then override the same by loading it from the configuration file. So, the code will look like this:

```
app = Flask(__name__)
DEBUG = True
TESTING = True
app.config.from_object(__name__)
app.config.from_pyfile('/path/to/config/file')
```

Class-based settings

An interesting way of laying out configurations for different deployment modes, such as production, testing, staging, and so on, can be cleanly done using the inheritance pattern of classes. As the project gets bigger, you can have different deployment modes such as development, staging, production, and so on, where each mode can have several different configuration settings, and some settings will remain the same.

How to do it...

We can have a default setting base class, and other classes can inherit this base class and override or add deployment-specific configuration variables.

The following is an example of our default setting base class:

```python
class BaseConfig(object):
    'Base config class'
    SECRET_KEY = 'A random secret key'
    DEBUG = True
    TESTING = False
    NEW_CONFIG_VARIABLE = 'my value'

class ProductionConfig(BaseConfig):
    'Production specific config'
    DEBUG = False
    SECRET_KEY = open('/path/to/secret/file').read()

class StagingConfig(BaseConfig):
    'Staging specific config'
    DEBUG = True

class DevelopmentConfig(BaseConfig):
    'Development environment specific config'
    DEBUG = True
    TESTING = True
    SECRET_KEY = 'Another random secret key'
```

 The secret key is stored in a separate file because, for security concerns, it should not be a part of your version-control system. This should be kept in the local filesystem on the machine itself, whether it is your personal machine or a server.

How it works...

Now, we can use any of the preceding classes while loading the application's configuration via `from_object()`. Let's say that we save the preceding class-based configuration in a file named `configuration.py`:

```python
app.config.from_object('configuration.DevelopmentConfig')
```

So, overall, this makes the management of configurations for different deployment environments flexible and easier.

Downloading the example code

You can download the example code files for all Packt books you have purchased from your account at `http://www.packtpub.com`. If you purchased this book elsewhere, you can visit `http://www.packtpub.com/support` and register to have the files e-mailed directly to you.

Organization of static files

Organizing static files such as JavaScript, stylesheets, images, and so on efficiently is always a matter of concern for all web frameworks.

How to do it...

Flask recommends a specific way to organize static files in our application:

```
my_app/
    - app.py
    - config.py
    - __init__.py
    - static/
        - css/
        - js/
        - images/
            - logo.png
```

While rendering them in templates (say, the `logo.png` file), we can refer to the static files using the following line of code:

```
<img src='/static/images/logo.png'>
```

How it works...

If there exists a folder named `static` at the application's root level, that is, at the same level as `app.py`, then Flask will automatically read the contents of the folder without any extra configuration.

There's more...

Alternatively, we can provide a parameter named `static_folder` to the application object while defining the application in `app.py`:

```
app = Flask(__name__, static_folder='/path/to/static/folder')
```

In the `img src` path in the *How to do it...* section, `static` refers to the value of `static_url_path` on the application object. This can be modified as follows:

```
app = Flask(
    __name__, static_url_path='/differentstatic',
    static_folder='/path/to/static/folder'
)
```

Now, to render the static file, we will use the following:

```
<img src='/differentstatic/logo.png'>
```

 It is always a good practice to use `url_for` to create the URLs for static files rather than explicitly define them:
```
<img src='{{ url_for('static', filename="logo.png")
}}'>
```
We will see more of this in the upcoming chapters.

Being deployment specific with instance folders

Flask provides yet another way of configuration where we can efficiently manage deployment-specific parts. Instance folders allow us to segregate deployment-specific files from our version-controlled application. We know that configuration files can be separate for different deployment environments such as development and production, but there are many more files such as database files, session files, cache files, and other runtime files. So, we can say that an instance folder is like a holder bin for these kinds of files.

How to do it...

By default, the instance folder is picked up from the application automatically if we have a folder named `instance` in our application at the application level:

```
my_app/
    - app.py
    - instance/
        - config.cfg
```

We can also explicitly define the absolute path of the instance folder using the `instance_path` parameter on our application object:

```
app = Flask(
    __name__, instance_path='/absolute/path/to/instance/folder'
)
```

To load the configuration file from the instance folder, we will use the `instance_relative_config` parameter on the application object:

```
app = Flask(__name__, instance_relative_config=True)
```

This tells the application to load the configuration file from the instance folder. The following example shows how this will work:

```
app = Flask(
    __name__, instance_path='path/to/instance/folder',
    instance_relative_config=True
)
app.config.from_pyfile('config.cfg', silent=True)
```

How it works...

In the preceding code, first, the instance folder is loaded from the given path, and then, the configuration file is loaded from the file named `config.cfg` in the given instance folder. Here, `silent=True` is optional and used to suppress the error in case `config.cfg` is not found in the instance folder. If `silent=True` is not given and the file is not found, then the application will fail, giving the following error:

```
IOError: [Errno 2] Unable to load configuration file (No such file or
    directory): '/absolute/path/to/config/file'
```

> It might seem that loading the configuration from the instance folder using `instance_relative_config` is redundant work and can be moved to one of the configuration methods. However, the beauty of this process lies in the fact that the instance folder concept is completely independent of configuration, and `instance_relative_config` just compliments the configuration object.

Composition of views and models

As we go big, we might want to structure our application in a modular manner. We will do this by restructuring our Hello World application.

How to do it...

1. First, create a new folder in our application and move all our files inside this new folder.

2. Then, create `__init__.py` in our folders, which are to be used as modules.

3. After that, create a new file called `run.py` in the topmost folder. As the name implies, this file will be used to run the application.

4. Finally, create separate folders to act as modules.

Refer to the following file structure for a better understanding:

```
flask_app/
    - run.py
    - my_app/
        - __init__.py
        - hello/
            - __init__.py
            - models.py
            - views.py
```

First, the `flask_app/run.py` file will look something like the following lines of code:

```
from my_app import app
app.run(debug=True)
```

Then, the `flask_app/my_app/__init__.py` file will look something like the following lines of code:

```
from flask import Flask
app = Flask(__name__)

import my_app.hello.views
```

Then, we will have an empty file just to make the enclosing folder a Python package, `flask_app/my_app/hello/__init__.py`:

```
# No content.
# We need this file just to make this folder a python module.
```

The models file, `flask_app/my_app/hello/models.py`, has a non-persistent key-value store:

```
MESSAGES = {
    'default': 'Hello to the World of Flask!',
}
```

Finally, the following is the views file, `flask_app/my_app/hello/views.py`. Here, we fetch the message corresponding to the key that is asked for and also have a provision to create or update a message:

```
from my_app import app
from my_app.hello.models import MESSAGES

@app.route('/')
@app.route('/hello')
def hello_world():
```

```
        return MESSAGES['default']


@app.route('/show/<key>')
def get_message(key):
    return MESSAGES.get(key) or "%s not found!" % key


@app.route('/add/<key>/<message>')
def add_or_update_message(key, message):
    MESSAGES[key] = message
    return "%s Added/Updated" % key
```

 Remember that the preceding code is nowhere near production-ready. It is just for demonstration and to make things understandable for new users of Flask.

How it works...

We can see that we have a circular import between my_app/__init__.py and my_app/ hello/views.py, where, in the former, we import views from the latter, and in the latter, we import the app from the former. So, this actually makes the two modules depend on each other, but here, it is actually fine as we won't be using views in my_app/__init__.py. We do the import of views at the bottom of the file so that they are not used anyway.

We have used a very simple non-persistent in-memory key-value store for the demonstration of the model layout structure. It is true that we could have written the dictionary for the MESSAGES hash map in views.py itself, but it's best practice to keep the model and view layers separate.

So, we can run this app using just run.py:

```
$ python run.py
* Running on http://127.0.0.1:5000/
* Restarting with reloader
```

 The reloader indicates that the application is being run in the debug mode, and the application will reload whenever a change is made in the code.

Now, we can see that we have already defined a default message in `MESSAGES`. We can view this message by opening `http://127.0.0.1:5000/show/default`. To add a new message, we can type `http://127.0.0.1:5000/add/great/Flask%20is%20 greatgreat!!`. This will update the `MESSAGES` key-value store to look like the following:

```
MESSAGES = {
    'default': 'Hello to the World of Flask!',
    'great': 'Flask is great!!',
}
```

Now, if we open the link `http://127.0.0.1:5000/show/great` in a browser, we will see our message, which, otherwise, would have appeared as a not-found message.

See also

▶ The next recipe, *Creating a modular web app with blueprints*, provides a much better way of organizing your Flask applications and is a readymade solution to circular imports.

Creating a modular web app with blueprints

A **blueprint** is a concept in Flask that helps make large applications really modular. They keep application dispatching simple by providing a central place to register all the components in the application. A blueprint looks like an application object but is not an application. It looks like a pluggable application or a smaller part of a bigger application, but it is not so. A blueprint is actually a set of operations that can be registered on an application and represents how to construct or build an application.

Getting ready

We will take the application from the previous recipe, *Composition of views and models*, as a reference and modify it to work using blueprints.

How to do it...

The following is an example of a simple Hello World application using blueprints. It will work in a manner similar to the previous recipe but is much more modular and extensible.

First, we will start with the `flask_app/my_app/__init__.py` file:

```
from flask import Flask
from my_app.hello.views import hello

app = Flask(__name__)
app.register_blueprint(hello)
```

Next, the views file, `my_app/hello/views.py`, will look like the following lines of code:

```
from flask import Blueprint
from my_app.hello.models import MESSAGES

hello = Blueprint('hello', __name__)


@hello.route('/')
@hello.route('/hello')
def hello_world():
    return MESSAGES['default']


@hello.route('/show/<key>')
def get_message(key):
    return MESSAGES.get(key) or "%s not found!" % key


@hello.route('/add/<key>/<message>')
def add_or_update_message(key, message):
    MESSAGES[key] = message
    return "%s Added/Updated" % key
```

We have defined a blueprint in the `flask_app/my_app/hello/views.py` file. We don't need the application object anymore here, and our complete routing is defined on a blueprint named `hello`. Instead of `@app.route`, we used `@hello.route`. The same blueprint is imported in `flask_app/my_app/__init__.py` and registered on the application object.

We can create any number of blueprints in our application and do most of the activities that we would do with our application, such as providing different template paths or different static paths. We can even have different URL prefixes or subdomains for our blueprints.

How it works...

This application will work in exactly the same way as the last application. The only difference is in the way the code is organized.

See also

▶   The previous recipe, *Composition of views and models*, is useful to get a background on how this recipe is useful.

Making a Flask app installable using setuptools

So, we have a Flask application now, but how do we install it just like any Python package? It is possible that any other application depends on our application or our application is in fact an extension for Flask and would need to be installed in a Python environment so that it can be used by other applications.

How to do it...

Installing a Flask app can be achieved very easily using the `setuptools` library of Python. We will have to create a file called `setup.py` in our application's folder and configure it to run a setup script for our application. It will take care of any dependencies, descriptions, loading test packages, and so on.

The following is an example of a simple `setup.py` script for our Hello World application:

```python
#!/usr/bin/env python
# -*- coding: UTF-8 -*-
import os
from setuptools import setup

setup(
    name = 'my_app',
    version='1.0',
    license='GNU General Public License v3',
    author='Shalabh Aggarwal',
    author_email='contact@shalabhaggarwal.com',
    description='Hello world application for Flask',
    packages=['my_app'],
    platforms='any',
    install_requires=[
        'flask',
    ],
    classifiers=[
        'Development Status :: 4 - Beta',
        'Environment :: Web Environment',
        'Intended Audience :: Developers',
        'License :: OSI Approved :: GNU General Public License v3',
        'Operating System :: OS Independent',
```

```
          'Programming Language :: Python',
          'Topic :: Internet :: WWW/HTTP :: Dynamic Content',
          'Topic :: Software Development :: Libraries :: Python Modules'
      ],
  )
```

How it works...

In the preceding script, most of the configuration is self-explanatory. The classifiers are used when we make this application available on PyPI. These will help other users search the application using these classifiers.

Now, we can just run this file with the `install` keyword as shown here:

$ python setup.py install

This will install this application along with all its dependencies mentioned in `install_requires`, that is, Flask and all the dependencies of Flask as well. Then, this app can be used just like any Python package in our Python environment.

See also

> ▸ The list of valid trove classifiers can be found at `https://pypi.python.org/pypi?%3Aaction=list_classifiers`

2

Templating with Jinja2

This chapter will cover the basics of Jinja2 templating from the perspective of Flask; we will also learn how to make applications with modular and extensible templates.

In this chapter, we will cover the following recipes:

- ► Bootstrap layout
- ► Block composition and layout inheritance
- ► Creating a custom context processor
- ► Creating a custom Jinja2 filter
- ► Creating a custom macro for forms
- ► Advanced date and time formatting

Introduction

In Flask, we can write a complete web application without the need of any third-party templating engine. For example, have a look at the following code; this is a simple Hello World application with a bit of HTML styling included:

```
from flask import Flask
app = Flask(__name__)

@app.route('/')
@app.route('/hello')
@app.route('/hello/<user>')
def hello_world(user=None):
    user = user or 'Shalabh'
    return '''
<html>
```

```
    <head>
      <title>Flask Framework Cookbook</title>

    </head>
      <body>
        <h1>Hello %s!</h1>
        <p>Welcome to the world of Flask!</p>
      </body>
  </html>''' % user

if __name__ == '__main__':
    app.run()
```

Is the preceding pattern of writing the application feasible in the case of large applications that involve thousands of lines of HTML, JS, and CSS code? Obviously not!

Here, templating saves us because we can structure our view code by keeping our templates separate. Flask provides default support for Jinja2, although we can use any templating engine as suited. Furthermore, Jinja2 provides many additional features that make our templates very powerful and modular.

Bootstrap layout

Most of the applications in Flask follow a specific pattern to lay out templates. In this recipe, we will talk about the recommended way of structuring the layout of templates in a Flask application.

Getting ready

By default, Flask expects the templates to be placed inside a folder named `templates` at the application root level. If this folder is present, then Flask will automatically read the contents by making the contents of this folder available for use with the `render_template()` method, which we will use extensively throughout this book.

How to do it...

Let's demonstrate this with a small application. This application is very similar to the one we developed in *Chapter 1, Flask Configurations*. The first thing to do is add a new folder named `templates` under `my_app`. The application structure will now look like the following lines of code:

```
flask_app/
    - run.py
```

```
my_app/
    - __init__.py
    - hello/
        - __init__.py
        - views.py
    - templates
```

We need to make some changes to the application. The `hello_world` method in the views file, `my_app/hello/views.py`, will look like the following lines of code:

```
from flask import render_template, request

@hello.route('/')
@hello.route('/hello')
def hello_world():
    user = request.args.get('user', 'Shalabh')
    return render_template('index.html', user=user)
```

In the preceding method, we look for a URL query argument, `user`. If it is found, we use it, and if not, we use the default argument, `Shalabh`. Then, this value is passed to the context of the template to be rendered, that is, `index.html`, and the resulting template is rendered.

To start with, the `my_app/templates/index.html` template can be simply put as:

```
<html>
  <head>
    <title>Flask Framework Cookbook</title>
  </head>
  <body>
    <h1>Hello {{ user }}!</h1>
    <p>Welcome to the world of Flask!</p>
  </body>
</html>
```

How it works...

Now, if we open the URL, `http://127.0.0.1:5000/hello`, in a browser, we will see a response, as shown in the following screenshot:

We can also pass a URL argument with the `user` key as `http://127.0.0.1:5000/hello?user=John`; we will see the following response:

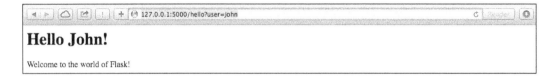

As we can see in `views.py`, the argument passed in the URL is fetched from the `request` object using `request.args.get('user')` and passed to the context of the template being rendered using `render_template`. The argument is then parsed using the Jinja2 placeholder, `{{ user }}`, to fetch the contents from the current value of the `user` variable from the template context. This placeholder evaluates all the expressions that are placed inside it, depending on the template context.

See also

> ▸ The Jinja2 documentation can be found at `http://jinja.pocoo.org/`. This comes in handy when writing templates.

Block composition and layout inheritance

Usually, any web application will have a number of web pages that will be different from each other. Code blocks such as headers and footers will be the same in almost all the pages throughout the site. Likewise, the menu also remains the same. In fact, usually, just the center container block changes, and the rest usually remains the same. For this, Jinja2 provides a great way of inheritance among templates.

It's a good practice to have a base template where we can structure the basic layout of the site along with the header and footer.

Getting ready

In this recipe, we will try to create a small application where we will have a home page and a product page (such as the ones we see on e-commerce stores). We will use the **Bootstrap** framework to give a minimalistic design to our templates. Bootstrap can be downloaded from `http://getbootstrap.com/`.

Here, we have a hardcoded data store for a few products placed in the `models.py` file. These are read in `views.py` and sent over to the template as template context variables via the `render_template()` method. The rest of the parsing and display is handled by the templating language, which, in our case, is Jinja2.

How to do it...

Have a look at the following layout:

```
flask_app/
    - run.py
    my_app/
        - __init__.py
        - product/
            - __init__.py
            - views.py
            - models.py
        - templates/
            - base.html
            - home.html
            - product.html
        - static/
            - js/
                - bootstrap.min.js
            - css/
                - bootstrap.min.css
                - main.css
```

In the preceding layout, `static/css/bootstrap.min.css` and `static/js/bootstrap.min.js` are standard files and can be downloaded from the Bootstrap website mentioned in the *Getting ready* section. The `run.py` file remains the same as always. The rest of the application is explained here. First, we will define our models, `my_app/product/models.py`. In this chapter, we will work on a simple non-persistent key-value store. We will start with a few hardcoded product records made well in advance:

```python
PRODUCTS = {
    'iphone': {
        'name': 'iPhone 5S',
        'category': 'Phones',
        'price': 699,
    },
    'galaxy': {
        'name': 'Samsung Galaxy 5',
        'category': 'Phones',
        'price': 649,
    },
    'ipad-air': {
        'name': 'iPad Air',
        'category': 'Tablets',
        'price': 649,
```

```
    },
    'ipad-mini': {
        'name': 'iPad Mini',
        'category': 'Tablets',
        'price': 549
    }
}
```

Next comes the views, that is, `my_app/product/views.py`. Here, we will follow the blueprint style to write the application:

```python
from werkzeug import abort
from flask import render_template
from flask import Blueprint
from my_app.product.models import PRODUCTS


product_blueprint = Blueprint('product', __name__)

@product_blueprint.route('/')
@product_blueprint.route('/home')
def home():
    return render_template('home.html', products=PRODUCTS)


@product_blueprint.route('/product/<key>')
def product(key):
    product = PRODUCTS.get(key)
    if not product:
        abort(404)
    return render_template('product.html', product=product)
```

The name of the blueprint, `product`, that is passed in the `Blueprint` constructor will be appended to the endpoints defined in this blueprint. Have a look at the `base.html` code for clarity.

> The `abort()` method comes in handy when you want to abort a request with a specific error message. Flask provides basic error message pages that can be customized as needed. We will see them in the *Creating custom 404 and 500 handlers* recipe in *Chapter 4, Working with Views*.

The application's configuration file, `my_app/__init__.py`, will now look like the following lines of code:

```
from flask import Flask
from my_app.product.views import product_blueprint

app = Flask(__name__)
app.register_blueprint(product_blueprint)
```

Apart from the CSS code provided by Bootstrap, we have a bit of custom CSS code in `my_app/static/css/main.css`:

```css
body {
  padding-top: 50px;
}
.top-pad {
  padding: 40px 15px;
  text-align: center;
}
```

Coming down to templates, the first template acts as the base for all templates. This can aptly be named as `base.html` and placed at `my_app/templates/base.html`:

```html
<!DOCTYPE html>
<html lang="en">
  <head>
    <meta charset="utf-8">
    <meta http-equiv="X-UA-Compatible" content="IE=edge">
    <meta name="viewport" content="width=device-width, initial-
      scale=1">
    <title>Flask Framework Cookbook</title>
    <link href="{{ url_for('static',
      filename='css/bootstrap.min.css') }}" rel="stylesheet">
    <link href="{{ url_for('static', filename='css/main.css') }}"
      rel="stylesheet">
  </head>
  <body>
    <div class="navbar navbar-inverse navbar-fixed-top"
      role="navigation">
      <div class="container">
        <div class="navbar-header">
          <a class="navbar-brand" href="{{ url_for('product.home')
            }}">Flask Cookbook</a>
        </div>
      </div>
    </div>
```

```
        <div class="container">
          {% block container %}{% endblock %}
        </div>

        <!-- jQuery (necessary for Bootstrap's JavaScript plugins) -->
        <script src="https://ajax.googleapis.com/ajax/libs/jquery/
          2.0.0/jquery.min.js"></script>
        <script src="{{ url_for('static', filename='js/
          bootstrap.min.js') }}"></script>
      </body>
    </html>
```

Most of the preceding code is normal HTML and Jinja2 evaluation placeholders, which were introduced in the previous chapter. An important point to note is how the `url_for()` method is used for blueprint URLs. The blueprint name is appended to all the endpoints. This becomes very useful when we have multiple blueprints inside one application, and some of them can have similar-looking URLs.

In the home page, `my_app/templates/home.html`, we iterate over all the products and show them:

```
{% extends 'base.html' %}

{% block container %}
  <div class="top-pad">
    {% for id, product in products.iteritems() %}
      <div class="well">
        <h2>
          <a href="{{ url_for('product.product', key=id) }}">{{
            product['name'] }}</a>
          <small>$ {{ product['price'] }}</small>
        </h2>
      </div>
    {% endfor %}
  </div>
{% endblock %}
```

The individual product page, `my_app/templates/product.html`, looks like the following lines of code:

```
{% extends 'home.html' %}

{% block container %}
  <div class="top-pad">
    <h1>{{ product['name'] }}
      <small>{{ product['category'] }}</small>
```

```
    </h1>
    <h3>$ {{ product['price'] }}</h3>
  </div>
{% endblock %}
```

How it works...

In the preceding template structure, we saw that there is an inheritance pattern being followed. The base.html file acted as the base template for all other templates. The home.html file inherited from base.html, and product.html inherited from home.html. In product. html, we also saw that we overwrote the container block, which was first populated in home.html. On running this app, we will see the output as shown in the following screenshots:

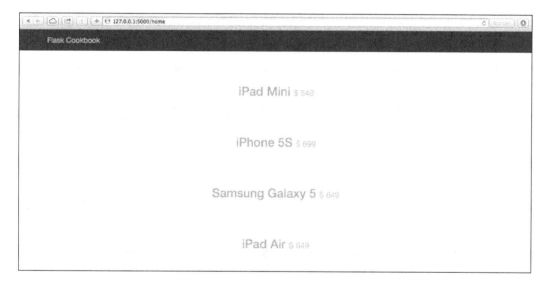

The preceding screenshot shows how the home page will look. Note the URL in the browser. This is how the product page will look:

▶ Check out the *Creating a custom context processor* and *Creating a custom Jinja2 filter* recipes, which extend this application

Creating a custom context processor

Sometimes, we might want to calculate or process a value directly in the templates. Jinja2 maintains a notion that the processing of logic should be handled in views and not in templates, and thus, it keeps the templates clean. A context processor becomes a handy tool in this case. We can pass our values to a method; this will then be processed in a Python method, and our resultant value will be returned. Therefore, we are essentially just adding a function to the template context (thanks to Python for allowing us to pass around functions just like any other object).

How to do it...

Let's say we want to show the descriptive name of the product in the format `Category / Product-name`:

```
@product_blueprint.context_processor:
def some_processor():
    def full_name(product):
        return '{0} / {1}'.format(product['category'],
            product['name'])
    return {'full_name': full_name}
```

A context is simply a dictionary that can be modified to add or remove values. Any method decorated with `@product_blueprint.context_processor` should return a dictionary that updates the actual context.

We can use the preceding context processor as follows:

```
{{ full_name(product) }}
```

We can add this to our app for the product listing (in the `flask_app/my_app/templates/product.html` file) in the following manner:

```
{% extends 'home.html' %}

{% block container %}
  <div class="top-pad">
    <h4>{{ full_name(product) }}</h4>
    <h1>{{ product['name'] }}
```

```
        <small>{{ product['category'] }}</small>
    </h1>
    <h3>$ {{ product['price'] }}</h3>
  </div>
{% endblock %}
```

The resulting parsed HTML page will look like the following screenshot:

See also

▶ Have a look at the *Block composition and layout inheritance* recipe to understand the context of this recipe

Creating a custom Jinja2 filter

After looking at the previous recipe, experienced developers might think that it was stupid to use a context processor to create a descriptive product name. We can simply write a filter to get the same result; this will make things much cleaner. A filter can be written to display the descriptive name of the product as shown here:

```
@product_blueprint.template_filter('full_name')
def full_name_filter(product):
    return '{0} / {1}'.format(product['category'],
      product['name'])
```

This can be used as follows:

```
{{ product|full_name }}
```

The preceding code will yield a similar result as it did in the previous recipe.

How to do it...

To take things to a higher level, let's create a filter to format the currency based on the current local language:

```
import ccy
from flask import request

@app.template_filter('format_currency')
def format_currency_filter(amount):
    currency_code = ccy.countryccy(request.accept_languages.best[-
      2:])
    return '{0} {1}'.format(currency_code, amount)
```

 The `request.accept_languages` list might now work in cases where a request does not have the `ACCEPT-LANGUAGES` header.

The preceding snippet will require the installation of a new package, `ccy`:

```
$ pip install ccy
```

The filter created here takes the language that best matches the current browser locale (which, in my case, is **en-US**), takes the last two characters from the locale string, and then gets the currency as per the ISO country code that is represented by the last two characters.

How it works...

The filter can be used in our template for the product as shown:

```
<h3>{{ product['price']|format_currency }}</h3>
```

It will yield the result shown in the following screenshot:

See also

▸ Check out the *Block composition and layout inheritance* recipe to understand the context of this recipe

Creating a custom macro for forms

Macros allow us to write reusable pieces of HTML blocks. They are analogous to functions in regular programming languages. We can pass arguments to macros like we do to functions in Python and then use them to process the HTML block. Macros can be called any number of times, and the output will vary as per the logic inside them.

Getting ready

Working with macros in Jinja2 is a very common topic and has a lot of use cases. Here, we will just see how a macro can be created and then used after importing.

How to do it...

One of the most redundant pieces of code in HTML is defining input fields in forms. Most of the fields have similar code with some modifications of style and so on. The following is a macro that creates input fields when called. The best practice is to create the macro in a separate file for better reuseability, for example, `_helpers.html`:

```
{% macro render_field(name, class='', value='', type='text') -%}
    <input type="{{ type }}" name="{{ name }}" class="{{ class }}"
        value="{{ value }}"/>
{%- endmacro %}
```

 The minus sign (-) before/after % will strip the whitespaces after and before these blocks and make the HTML code cleaner to read.

Now, this macro should be imported in the file to be used:

```
{% from '_helpers.jinja' import render_field %}
```

Then, it can simply be called using the following:

```
<fieldset>
    {{ render_field('username', 'icon-user') }}
    {{ render_field('password', 'icon-key', type='password') }}
</fieldset>
```

It is always a good practice to define macros in a different file so as to keep the code clean and increase code readability. If a private macro that cannot be accessed out of the current file is needed, then name the macro with an underscore preceding the name.

Advanced date and time formatting

Date and time formatting is a painful thing to handle in web applications. Handling them at the level of Python, using the `datetime` library increases the overhead and is pretty complex when it comes to handling time zones correctly. We should standardize the timestamps to UTC when stored in the database, but then, the timestamps need to be processed every time they need to be presented to the users worldwide.

It is a smart thing to defer this processing to the client side, that is, the browser. The browser always knows the current time zone of the user and will be able to do the date and time manipulation correctly. Also, this takes off the necessary overhead from our application servers. We will use **Moment.js** for this purpose.

Getting ready

Just like any JS library, Moment.js can be included in our app in the following manner. We will just have to place the JS file, `moment.min.js`, in the `static/js` folder. This can then be used in our HTML file by adding the following statement along with other JS libraries:

```
<script src="/static/js/moment.min.js"></script>
```

The basic usage of Moment.js is shown in the following code. This can be done in the browser console for JavaScript:

```
>>> moment().calendar();
"Today at 4:49 PM"
>>> moment().endOf('day').fromNow();
"in 7 hours"
>>> moment().format('LLLL');
"Tuesday, April 15 2014 4:55 PM"
```

How to do it...

To use Moment.js in our application, the best way will be to write a wrapper in Python and use it via `jinja2` environment variables. Refer to `http://runnable.com/UqGXnKwTGpQgAA07/dates-and-times-in-flask-for-python` for more information:

```
from jinja2 import Markup

class momentjs(object):
    def __init__(self, timestamp):
```

```
        self.timestamp = timestamp

    # Wrapper to call moment.js method
    def render(self, format):
        return Markup("<script>\ndocument.write(moment(\"%s\").%s)
            ;\n</script>" % (self.timestamp.strftime("%Y-%m-
            %dT%H:%M:%S"), format))

    # Format time
    def format(self, fmt):
        return self.render("format(\"%s\")" % fmt)

    def calendar(self):
        return self.render("calendar()")

    def fromNow(self):
        return self.render("fromNow()")
```

We can add as many Moment.js methods as we want to parse to the preceding class as and when needed. Now, in our `app.py` file, we can set this created class to the `jinja` environment variables:

```
# Set jinja template global
app.jinja_env.globals['momentjs'] = momentjs
```

We can use it in templates as follows:

```
<p>Current time: {{ momentjs(timestamp).calendar() }}</p>
<br/>
<p>Time: {{momentjs(timestamp).format('YYYY-MM-DD HH:mm:ss')}}</p>
<br/>
<p>From now: {{momentjs(timestamp).fromNow()}}</p>
```

See more

 ▸   Read more about the Moment.js library at `http://momentjs.com/`

3
Data Modeling in Flask

This chapter covers one of the most important parts of any application, that is, the interaction with database systems. This chapter will take us through how Flask can connect to database systems, define models, and query the databases for retrieval and feeding of data.

In this chapter, we will cover the following recipes:

- ▸ Creating a SQLAlchemy DB instance
- ▸ Creating a basic product model
- ▸ Creating a relational category model
- ▸ Database migration using Alembic and Flask-Migrate
- ▸ Model data indexing with Redis
- ▸ Opting the NoSQL way with MongoDB

Introduction

Flask has been designed to be flexible enough to support any database. The simplest way would be to use the direct sqlite3 package, which is a DB-API 2.0 interface and does not actually give an ORM. Here, we will use SQL queries to talk with the database. This approach is not suggested for large projects as it can eventually become a nightmare to maintain the application. Also, with this approach, the models are virtually non-existent and everything happens in the view functions, where we write queries to interact with the DB.

In this chapter, we will talk about creating an ORM layer for our Flask applications with SQLAlchemy for relational database systems, which is recommended and widely used for applications of any size. Also, we will have a glance over how to write a Flask app with the NoSQL database system.

ORM refers to Object Relational Mapping/Modeling and implies how our application's data models store and deal with data at a conceptual level. A powerful ORM makes designing and querying business logic easy and streamlined.

Creating a SQLAlchemy DB instance

SQLAlchemy is a Python SQL toolkit and provides an ORM that gives the flexibility and power of SQL with the feel of Python's object-oriented nature.

Getting ready

Flask-SQLAlchemy is the extension that provides the SQLAlchemy interface for Flask.

This extension can be simply installed using `pip` as follows:

```
$ pip install flask-sqlalchemy
```

The first thing to keep in mind with Flask-SQLAlchemy is the application config parameter that tells SQLAlchemy about the location of the database to be used:

```
app.config['SQLALCHEMY_DATABASE_URI'] = os.environ('DATABASE_URI')
```

This `SQLALCHEMY_DATABASE_URI` is a combination of the database protocol, any authentication needed, and also the name of the database. In the case of SQLite, this would look something like the following:

```
sqlite:////tmp/test.db
```

In the case of PostgreSQL, it would look like the following:

```
postgresql://yourusername:yourpassword@localhost/yournewdb.
```

This extension then provides a class named `Model` that helps in defining models for our application. Read more about database URLs at `http://docs.sqlalchemy.org/en/rel_0_9/core/engines.html#database-urls`.

For all database systems other than SQLite, separate libraries are needed. For example, for using PostgreSQL, you would need **psycopg2**.

How to do it...

Let's demonstrate this with a small application. We will build over this application in the next few recipes. Here, we will just see how to create a `db` instance and some basic DB commands. The file's structure would look as follows:

```
flask_catalog/
    - run.py
    my_app/
        - __init__.py
```

First, we start with `flask_app/run.py`. It is the usual run file that we have read about up to now in this book:

```
from my_app import app
app.run(debug=True)
```

Then we configure our application configuration file, that is, `flask_app/my_app/__init__.py`.

```
from flask import Flask
from flask.ext.sqlalchemy import SQLAlchemy

app = Flask(__name__)
app.config['SQLALCHEMY_DATABASE_URI'] = 'sqlite:////tmp/test.db'
db = SQLAlchemy(app)
```

Here, we configure our application to point `SQLALCHEMY_DATABASE_URI` to a specific location. Then, we create an object of `SQLAlchemy` with the name `db`. As the name suggests, this is the object that will handle all our ORM-related activities. As mentioned earlier, this object has a class named `Model`, which provides the base for creating models in Flask. Any class can just subclass or inherit the `Model` class to create models, which will act as database tables.

Now, if we open the URL `http://127.0.0.1:5000` in a browser, we will actually see nothing. This is because there is nothing in the application.

There's more...

Sometimes, you might want a single SQLAlchemy `db` instance to be used across multiple applications or create an application dynamically. In such cases, we might not prefer to bind our `db` instance to a single application. Here, we will have to work with application contexts to achieve the desired outcome.

In this case, we will register our application with SQLAlchemy differently, as follows:

```
from flask import Flask
from flask.ext.sqlalchemy import SQLAlchemy

db = SQLAlchemy()

def create_app():
    app = Flask(__name__)
    db.init_app(app)
    return app
```

 The preceding approach can be taken up while initializing the `app` with any Flask extension and is very common when dealing with real-life applications.

Now, all the operations that were earlier possible globally with the `db` instance will now require a Flask application context at all times:

```
Flask application context
>>> from my_app import create_app
>>> app = create_app()
>>> app.test_request_context().push()
>>> # Do whatever needs to be done
>>> app.test_request_context().pop()
Or we can use context manager
with app():
    # We have flask application context now till we are inside the
with block
```

See also

▶ The next couple of recipes will extend the current application to make a complete application, which will help us understand the ORM layer better

Creating a basic product model

In this recipe, we will create an application that will help us store products to be displayed on the catalog section of a website. It should be possible to add products to the catalog and delete them as and when required. As we saw in previous chapters, this is possible to do using non-persistent storage as well. But, here we will store data in a database to have persistent storage.

How to do it...

The new directory layout will look as follows:

```
flask_catalog/
    - run.py
    my_app/
        - __init__.py
        catalog/
            - __init__.py
            - views.py
            - models.py
```

First of all, we will start by modifying our application configuration file, that is, `flask_catalog/my_app/__init__.py`:

```
from flask import Flask
from flask.ext.sqlalchemy import SQLAlchemy

app = Flask(__name__)
app.config['SQLALCHEMY_DATABASE_URI'] = 'sqlite:////tmp/test.db'
db = SQLAlchemy(app)

from my_app.catalog.views import catalog
app.register_blueprint(catalog)

db.create_all()
```

The last statement in the file is `db.create_all()`, which tells the application to create all the tables in the database specified. So, as soon as the application runs, all the tables will be created if they are not already there. Now is the time to create models that are placed in `flask_catalog/my_app/catalog/models.py`:

```
from my_app import db

class Product(db.Model):
    id = db.Column(db.Integer, primary_key=True)
    name = db.Column(db.String(255))
    price = db.Column(db.Float)

    def __init__(self, name, price):
        self.name = name
        self.price = price

    def __repr__(self):
        return '<Product %d>' % self.id
```

In this file, we have created a model named `Product` that has three fields, namely `id`, `name`, and `price`. The `id` field is a self-generated field in the database that will store the ID of the record and is the primary key. `name` is a field of type string and `price` is of type float.

Now, we add a new file for views, which is `flask_catalog/my_app/catalog/views.py`. In this file, we have multiple view methods that control how we deal with the product model and the web application in general:

```python
from flask import request, jsonify, Blueprint
from my_app import app, db
from my_app.catalog.models import Product

catalog = Blueprint('catalog', __name__)

@catalog.route('/')
@catalog.route('/home')
def home():
    return "Welcome to the Catalog Home."
```

This method handles how the home page or the application landing page looks or responds to the users. You would most probably use a template for rendering this in your applications. We will cover this a bit later. Have a look at the following code:

```python
@catalog.route('/product/<id>')
def product(id):
    product = Product.query.get_or_404(id)
    return 'Product - %s, $%s' % (product.name, product.price)
```

This method controls the output to be shown when a user looks up a specific product using its ID. We filter for the product using the ID and then return its information if the product is found; if not, we abort with a 404 error. Consider the following code:

```python
@catalog.route('/products')
def products():
    products = Product.query.all()
    res = {}
    for product in products:
        res[product.id] = {
            'name': product.name,
            'price': str(product.price)
        }
    return jsonify(res)
```

This method returns the list of all products in the database in JSON format. Consider the following code:

```
@catalog.route('/product-create', methods=['POST',])
def create_product():
    name = request.form.get('name')
    price = request.form.get('price')
    product = Product(name, price)
    db.session.add(product)
    db.session.commit()
    return 'Product created.'
```

This method controls the creation of a product in the database. We first get the information from a request and then create a `Product` instance from this information. Then, we add this `Product` instance to the database session and finally commit to save the record to the database.

How it works...

In the beginning, the database is empty and has no product. This can be confirmed by opening `http://127.0.0.1:5000/products` in a browser. This would result in an empty page with just {}.

Now, first we would want to create a product. For this, we need to send a POST request, which can be sent from the Python prompt using the `requests` library easily:

```
>>> import requests
>>> requests.post('http://127.0.0.1:5000/product-create',
  data={'name': 'iPhone 5S', 'price': '549.0'})
```

To confirm whether the product is in the database now, we can open `http://127.0.0.1:5000/products` in the browser again. This time, it would show a JSON dump of the product details.

See also

▶ The next recipe, *Creating a relational category model*, demonstrates the relational aspect of tables

Creating a relational category model

In our previous recipe, we created a simple product model that had a couple of fields. However, in practice, applications are much more complex and have various relationships among their tables. These relationships can be one-to-one, one-to-many, many-to-one, or many-to-many. We will try to understand some of them in this recipe with the help of an example.

How to do it...

Let's say we want to have product categories where each category can have multiple products, but each product should have at least one category. Let's do this by modifying some files from the preceding application. We will make modifications to both models and views. In models, we will add a `Category` model, and in views, we will add new methods to handle category-related calls and also modify the existing methods to accommodate the newly added feature.

First, we will modify our `models.py` file to add the `Category` model and some modifications to the `Product` model:

```
from my_app import db

class Product(db.Model):
    id = db.Column(db.Integer, primary_key=True)
    name = db.Column(db.String(255))
    price = db.Column(db.Float)
    category_id = db.Column(db.Integer,
      db.ForeignKey('category.id'))
    category = db.relationship(
        'Category', backref=db.backref('products', lazy='dynamic')
    )

    def __init__(self, name, price, category):
        self.name = name
        self.price = price
        self.category = category

    def __repr__(self):
        return '<Product %d>' % self.id
```

In the preceding `Product` model, notice the newly added fields for `category_id` and `category`. The `category_id` field is the foreign key to the `Category` model, and `category` represents the relationship table. As evident from the definitions themselves, one of them is a relationship, and the other uses this relationship to store the foreign key value in the database. This is a simple many-to-one relationship from product to category. Also, notice the `backref` argument in the `category` field; this argument allows us to access products from the `Category` model by writing something as simple as `category.products` in our views. This acts like the one-to-many relationship from the other end. Consider the following code:

```
class Category(db.Model):
    id = db.Column(db.Integer, primary_key=True)
    name = db.Column(db.String(100))

    def __init__(self, name):
        self.name = name

    def __repr__(self):
        return '<Category %d>' % self.id
```

The preceding code is the `Category` model, which has just one field called `name`.

Now, we will modify our `views.py` file to accommodate the changes in our models:

```
from my_app.catalog.models import Product, Category

@catalog.route('/products')
def products():
    products = Product.query.all()
    res = {}
    for product in products:
        res[product.id] = {
            'name': product.name,
            'price': product.price,
            'category': product.category.name
        }
    return jsonify(res)
```

Here, we have just one change where we are sending the category name and the product's JSON data is being generated to be returned. Consider the following code:

```
@catalog.route('/product-create', methods=['POST',])
def create_product():
    name = request.form.get('name')
    price = request.form.get('price')
    categ_name = request.form.get('category')
    category = Category.query.filter_by(name=categ_name).first()
    if not category:
        category = Category(categ_name)
    product = Product(name, price, category)
    db.session.add(product)
    db.session.commit()
    return 'Product created.'
```

Check out how we are looking for the category before creating the product. We will first search for an existing category with the category name in the request. If an existing category is found, we will use it for product creation; otherwise, we will create a new category. Consider the following code:

```
@catalog.route('/category-create', methods=['POST',])
def create_category():
    name = request.form.get('name')
    category = Category(name)
    db.session.add(category)
    db.session.commit()
    return 'Category created.'
```

The preceding code is a relatively simple method for creating a category using the name provided in the request. Consider the following code:

```
@catalog.route('/categories')
def categories():
    categories = Category.query.all()
    res = {}
    for category in categories:
        res[category.id] = {
            'name': category.name
        }
        for product in category.products:
            res[category.id]['products'] = {
                'id': product.id,
                'name': product.name,
                'price': product.price
            }
    return jsonify(res)
```

The preceding method does a bit of tricky stuff. Here, we fetched all the categories from the database, and then for each category, we fetched all the products and then returned all the data as a JSON dump.

See also

▶ Read through the *Creating a basic product model* recipe to understand the context of this recipe and how this recipe works for a browser

Database migration using Alembic and Flask-Migrate

Now, let's say we want to update our models to have a new field called `company` in our `Product` model. One way is to drop the database and then create a new one using `db.drop_all()` and `db.create_all()`. However, this approach cannot be followed for applications in production or even in staging. We would want to migrate our database to match the newly updated model with all the data intact.

For this, we have **Alembic**, which is a Python-based tool to manage database migrations and uses SQLAlchemy as the underlying engine. Alembic provides automatic migrations to a great extent with some limitations (of course, we cannot expect any tool to be seamless). To act as the icing on the cake, we have a Flask extension called **Flask-Migrate**, which eases the process of migrations even more.

Getting ready

First of all, we will install Flask-Migrate:

```
$ pip install Flask-Migrate
```

This will also install Flask-Script and Alembic, among some other dependencies. Flask-Script powers Flask-Migrate to provide some easy-to-use command-line arguments, which provide a good level of abstraction to the users and hide all the complex stuff (which are actually not very difficult to customize if needed).

How to do it...

To enable migrations, we will need to modify our app definition a bit.

The following code shows what such a config looks like if we modify the code for our catalog application.

The following lines of code show how `my_app/__init__.py` looks:

```
from flask import Flask
from flask.ext.sqlalchemy import SQLAlchemy
from flask.ext.script import Manager
from flask.ext.migrate import Migrate, MigrateCommand

app = Flask(__name__)
app.config['SQLALCHEMY_DATABASE_URI'] = 'sqlite:////tmp/test.db'
db = SQLAlchemy(app)
migrate = Migrate(app, db)

manager = Manager(app)
manager.add_command('db', MigrateCommand)

import my_app.catalog.views

db.create_all()
```

Also, we will have to make a small change in `run.py`:

```
from my_app import manager
manager.run()
```

This change in `run.py` is because now we are using the Flask script manager to handle the running of our application. The script manager also provides extra command-line arguments as specified. In this example, we will have `db` as a command-line argument.

If we pass `--help` to `run.py` while running it as a script, the terminal will show all the available options, as shown in the following screenshot:

```
(mydev)Shalabh-Aggarwals-MacBook-Pro-2:flask_catalog shalabhaggarwal$ python run.py --help
usage: run.py [-h] {shell,db,runserver} ...

positional arguments:
  {shell,db,runserver}
    shell               Runs a Python shell inside Flask application context.
    db                  Perform database migrations
    runserver           Runs the Flask development server i.e. app.run()

optional arguments:
  -h, --help            show this help message and exit
```

Now, to run the application, we will have to run the following:

```
$ python run.py runserver
```

To initialize migrations, we have to run the `init` command:

```
$ python run.py db init
```

After we make changes to models, we have to call the `migrate` command:

```
$ python run.py db migrate
```

To make the changes reflect on the database, we will call the `upgrade` command:

```
$ python run.py db upgrade
```

How it works...

Now, let's say we modify the model of our `product` table to add a new field called `company` as shown here:

```
class Product(db.Model):
    # ...
    # Same product model as last recipe
    # ...
    company = db.Column(db.String(100))
```

The result of `migrate` will be something like the following snippet:

```
$ python run.py db migrate

INFO  [alembic.migration] Context impl SQLiteImpl.

INFO  [alembic.migration] Will assume non-transactional DDL.

INFO  [alembic.autogenerate.compare] Detected added column
  'product.company'   Generating <path/to/application>/
  flask_catalog/migrations/versions/2c08f71f9253_.py ... done
```

In the preceding code, we can see that Alembic compares the new model with the database table and detects a newly added column for `company` in the `product` table (created by the `Product` model).

Similarly, the output of `upgrade` will be something like the following snippet:

```
$ python run.py db upgrade

INFO  [alembic.migration] Context impl SQLiteImpl.

INFO  [alembic.migration] Will assume non-transactional DDL.

INFO  [alembic.migration] Running upgrade None -> 2c08f71f9253, empty
  message
```

Here, Alembic performs the upgrade of the database for the migration detected earlier. We can see a hex code in the preceding output. This represents the revision of the migration performed. This is for internal use by Alembic to track the changes to database tables.

See also

▶ Check out the *Creating a basic product model* recipe to understand the context of this recipe

Model data indexing with Redis

There might be some features that we want to implement but do not want to have a persistent storage for them. So, we would like to have these stored in a cache-like storage for a short period of time and then hide them, for example, showing a list of the recently visited products to the visitors on the website.

Getting ready

We will do this with the help of **Redis**, which can be installed using the following command:

```
$ pip install redis
```

Make sure that you run the Redis server for the connection to happen. To install and run a Redis server, refer to http://redis.io/topics/quickstart.

Then, we need to have the connection open to Redis. This can be done by adding the following lines of code to my_app/__init__.py:

```
from redis import Redis
redis = Redis()
```

We can do this in our application file, where we will define the app, or in the views file, where we will use it. It is preferred that you do this in the application file because then the connection will be open throughout the application, and the redis object can be used by just importing it where needed.

How to do it...

We will maintain a set in Redis that will store the recently visited products. This will be populated whenever we visit a product. The entry will expire after 10 minutes. This change goes in views.py:

```
from my_app import redis

@catalog.route('/product/<id>')
def product(id):
    product = Product.query.get_or_404(id)
    product_key = 'product-%s' % product.id
    redis.set(product_key, product.name)
    redis.expire(product_key, 600)
    return 'Product - %s, $%s' % (product.name, product.price)
```

It is a good practice to fetch the `expire` time, that is, `600`, from a configuration value. This can be set on the application object in `my_app/__init__.py`, and then can be fetched from here.

In the preceding method, note the `set()` and `expire()` methods on the `redis` object. First, we set the product ID using the `product_key` value in the Redis store. Then, we set the `expire` time of the key to `600` seconds.

Now, we will look for the keys that are still alive in the cache and then fetch the products corresponding to these keys and return them:

```
@catalog.route('/recent-products')
def recent_products():
    keys_alive = redis.keys('product-*')
    products = [redis.get(k) for k in keys_alive]
    return jsonify({'products': products})
```

How it works...

An entry is added to the store whenever a user visits a product, and the entry is kept there for 600 seconds (10 minutes). Now, this product will be listed in the recent products list for the next 10 minutes unless it is visited again, which will reset the time to 10 minutes again.

Opting the NoSQL way with MongoDB

Sometimes, the data to be used in the application we are building might not be structured at all, can be semi-structured, or can be data whose schema changes over time. In such cases, we would refrain from using an RDBMS, as it adds to the pain and is difficult to understand and maintain. For such cases, we might want to use a **NoSQL** database.

Also, as a result of fast and quick development in the currently prevalent development environment, it is not always possible to design the perfect schema the first time. NoSQL provides the flexibility to modify the schema without much of a hassle.

In production environments, the database usually grows to a huge size in a short period of time. This drastically affects the performance of the overall system. Vertical- and horizontal-scaling techniques are available as well, but they can be very costly at times. In such cases, a NoSQL database can be considered, as it is designed from scratch for similar purposes. The ability of NoSQL databases to run on large multiple clusters and handle huge volumes of data generated with high velocity makes them a good choice when looking to handle scaling issues with traditional RDBMS.

Here, we will use **MongoDB** to understand how to integrate NoSQL with Flask.

Getting ready

There are many extensions available to use Flask with MongoDB. We will use Flask-MongoEngine as it provides a good level of abstraction, which makes it easier to understand. It can be installed using the following command:

```
$ pip install flask-mongoengine
```

Remember to run the MongoDB server for the connection to happen. For more details on installing and running MongoDB, refer to http://docs.mongodb.org/manual/installation/.

How to do it...

The following is an application that is a rewrite of our catalog application using MongoDB. The first change comes to our configuration file, my_app/__init__.py:

```python
from flask import Flask
from flask.ext.mongoengine import MongoEngine
from redis import Redis


app = Flask(__name__)
app.config['MONGODB_SETTINGS'] = {'DB': 'my_catalog'}
app.debug = True
db = MongoEngine(app)

redis = Redis()

from my_app.catalog.views import catalog
app.register_blueprint(catalog)
```

 Note that instead of the usual SQLAlchemy-centric settings, we now have MONGODB_SETTINGS. Here, we just specify the name of the database to use. First, we will have to manually create this database in MongoDB using the command line:

```
>>> mongo
MongoDB shell version: 2.6.4
> use my_catalog
switched to db my_catalog
```

Next, we will create a `Product` model using MongoDB fields. This happens as usual in the models file, `flask_catalog/my_app/catalog/models.py`:

```
import datetime
from my_app import db


class Product(db.Document):
    created_at = db.DateTimeField(
        default=datetime.datetime.now, required=True
    )
    key = db.StringField(max_length=255, required=True)
    name = db.StringField(max_length=255, required=True)
    price = db.DecimalField()

    def __repr__(self):
        return '<Product %r>' % self.id
```

 Note the MongoDB fields used to create the model and their similarity with the SQLAlchemy fields used in the previous recipes. Here, instead of an ID field, we have `created_at`, which stores the timestamp in which the record was created.

The following is the views file, namely `flask_catalog/my_app/catalog/views.py`:

```
from decimal import Decimal
from flask import request, Blueprint, jsonify
from my_app.catalog.models import Product

catalog = Blueprint('catalog', __name__)

@catalog.route('/')
@catalog.route('/home')
def home():
    return "Welcome to the Catalog Home."

@catalog.route('/product/<key>')
def product(key):
    product = Product.objects.get_or_404(key=key)
    return 'Product - %s, $%s' % (product.name, product.price)

@catalog.route('/products')
def products():
    products = Product.objects.all()
```

```
    res = {}
    for product in products:
        res[product.key] = {
            'name': product.name,
            'price': str(product.price),
        }
    return jsonify(res)

@catalog.route('/product-create', methods=['POST',])
def create_product():
    name = request.form.get('name')
    key = request.form.get('key')
    price = request.form.get('price')
    product = Product(
        name=name,
        key=key,
        price=Decimal(price)
    )
    product.save()
    return 'Product created.'
```

You will notice it is very similar to the views created for the SQLAlchemy-based models. There are just a few differences in the methods that are called from the MongoEngine extension; they should be easy to understand.

See also

▸ Check out the *Creating a basic product model* recipe to understand how this application works

4
Working with Views

For any web application, it is very important to control how you interact with web requests and the proper responses to be catered for these requests. This chapter takes us through the various methods of handling the requests properly and designing them in the best way.

In this chapter, we will cover the following recipes:

- ▸ Writing function-based views and URL routes
- ▸ Class-based views
- ▸ URL routing and product-based pagination
- ▸ Rendering to templates
- ▸ Dealing with XHR requests
- ▸ Decorator to handle requests beautifully
- ▸ Creating custom 404 and 500 handlers
- ▸ Flashing messages for better user feedback
- ▸ SQL-based searching

Introduction

Flask offers several ways of designing and laying out the URL routing for our applications. Also, it gives us the flexibility to keep the architecture of our views as simple as just functions to a more complex but extensible class-based layout (which can be inherited and modified as needed). In earlier versions, Flask just had function-based views. However, later, in version 0.7, inspired by Django, Flask introduced the concept of pluggable views, which allows us to have classes and then write methods in these classes. This also makes the process of building a RESTful API pretty simple. Also, we can always go a level deeper into Werkzeug and use the more flexible but slightly more complex concept of URL maps. In fact, large applications and frameworks prefer using URL maps.

Writing function-based views and URL routes

This is the simplest way of writing views and URL routes in Flask. We can just write a method and decorate it with the endpoint.

Getting ready

To understand this recipe, we can start with any Flask application. The app can be a new, empty, or any complex app. We just need to understand the methods outlined in this recipe.

How to do it...

The following are the three most widely used, different kinds of requests, demonstrated with short examples.

A simple GET request

Consider the following code:

```
@app.route('/a-get-request')
def get_request():
    bar = request.args.get('foo', 'bar')
    return 'A simple Flask request where foo is %s' % bar
```

This is a simple example of what a GET request looks like. Here, we just check whether the URL query has an argument called `foo`. If yes, we display this in the response; otherwise, the default is `bar`.

A simple POST request

Consider the following code:

```
@app.route('/a-post-request', methods=['POST'])
def post_request():
    bar = request.form.get('foo', 'bar')
    return 'A simple Flask request where foo is %s' % bar
```

This is similar to the GET request but with a few differences, that is, the route now contains an extra argument called `methods`. Also, instead of `request.args`, we now use `request.form`, as POST assumes that the data is submitted in a form manner.

 Is it really necessary to write GET and POST in separate methods? No!

A simple GET/POST request

Consider the following code:

```
@app.route('/a-request', methods=['GET', 'POST'])
def some_request():
    if request.method == 'GET':
        bar = request.args.get('foo', 'bar')
    else:
        bar = request.form.get('foo', 'bar')
    return 'A simple Flask request where foo is %s' % bar
```

Here, we can see that we have amalgamated the first two methods into one, and now, both GET and POST are handled by one view function.

How it works...

Let's try to understand how the preceding methods work.

By default, any Flask view function supports only GET requests. In order to support or handle any other kind of request, we have to specifically tell our `route()` decorator about the methods we want to support. This is exactly what we did in our last two methods for POST and GET/POST.

For GET requests, the `request` object will look for `args`, that is, `request.args.get()`, and for POST, it will look for `form`, that is, `request.form.get()`.

Also, if we try to make a GET request to a method that supports only POST, the request will fail with a 405 HTTP error. The same holds true for all the methods. See the following screenshot:

There's more...

Sometimes, we might want to have a URL map kind of a pattern, where we prefer to define all the URL rules with endpoints at a single place rather than them being scattered all around the application. For this, we will need to define our methods without the `route()` decorator and define the route on our application object as shown here:

```
def get_request():

    bar = request.args.get('foo', 'bar')
```

```
        return 'A simple Flask request where foo is %s' % bar

app = Flask(__name__)
app.add_url_rule('/a-get-request', view_func=get_request)
```

Make sure that you give the correct relative path to the method assigned to `view_func`.

Class-based views

Flask introduced the concept of pluggable views in version 0.7; this added a lot of flexibility to the existing implementation. We can write views in the form of classes; these views can be written in a generic fashion and allow for an easy and understandable inheritance.

Getting ready

Refer to the previous recipe, *Writing function-based views and URL routes*, to understand the basic function-based views first.

How to do it...

Flask provides a class named `View`, which can be inherited to add our custom behavior.

The following is an example of a simple GET request:

```
from flask.views import View

class GetRequest(View):

    def dispatch_request(self):
        bar = request.args.get('foo', 'bar')
        return 'A simple Flask request where foo is %s' % bar

app.add_url_rule(
    '/a-get-request', view_func=GetRequest.as_view('get_request')
)
```

To accommodate both the GET and POST requests, we can write the following code:

```
from flask.views import View

class GetPostRequest(View):
    methods = ['GET', 'POST']

    def dispatch_request(self):
        if request.method == 'GET':
```

```
                bar = request.args.get('foo', 'bar')
            if request.method == 'POST':
                bar = request.form.get('foo', 'bar')
            return 'A simple Flask request where foo is %s' % bar

    app.add_url_rule(
        '/a-request',
        view_func=GetPostRequest.as_view('a_request')
    )
```

How it works...

We know that by default, any Flask view function supports only GET requests. The same applies in the case of class-based views. In order to support or handle any other kind of request, we have to specifically tell our class, via a class attribute called `methods`, about the HTTP methods we want to support. This is exactly what we did in our previous example of GET/POST requests.

For GET requests, the `request` object will look for `args`, that is, `request.args.get()`, and for POST, it will look for `form`, that is, `request.form.get()`.

Also, if we try to make a GET request to a method that supports only POST, the request will fail with a 405 HTTP error. The same holds true for all the methods.

There's more...

Now, many of us might be thinking that is it not possible to just declare GET and POST methods inside a `View` class and let Flask handle the rest of the stuff. The answer to this question is `MethodView`. Let's write our previous snippet using `MethodView`:

```
from flask.views import MethodView
class GetPostRequest(MethodView):

    def get(self):
        bar = request.args.get('foo', 'bar')
        return 'A simple Flask request where foo is %s' % bar

    def post(self):
        bar = request.form.get('foo', 'bar')
        return 'A simple Flask request where foo is %s' % bar

app.add_url_rule(
    '/a-request',
    view_func=GetPostRequest.as_view('a_request')
)
```

> ▸ Refer to the previous recipe, *Writing function-based views and URL routes*, to understand the contrast between class- and function-based views

URL routing and product-based pagination

At times, we might have to parse the various parts of a URL in different parts. For example, our URL can have an integer part, a string part, a string part of specific length, slashes in the URL, and so on. We can parse all these combinations in our URLs using URL converters. In this recipe, we will see how to do this. Also, we will learn how to implement pagination using the Flask-SQLAlchemy extension.

Getting ready

We have already seen several instances of basic URL converters. In this recipe, we will look at some advanced URL converters and learn how to use them.

How to do it...

Let's say we have a URL route defined as follows:

```
@app.route('/test/<name>')
def get_name(name):
    return name
```

Here, `http://127.0.0.1:5000/test/Shalabh` will result in `Shalabh` being parsed and passed in the `name` argument of the `get_name` method. This is a unicode or string converter, which is the default one and need not be specified explicitly.

We can also have strings with specific lengths. Let's say we want to parse a URL that can contain a country code or currency code. Country codes are usually two characters long and currency codes are three characters long. This can be done as follows:

```
@app.route('/test/<string(minlength=2,maxlength=3):code>')
def get_name(code):
    return code
```

This will match both US and USD in the URL, that is, `http://127.0.0.1:5000/test/USD` and `http://127.0.0.1:5000/test/US` will be treated similarly. We can also match the exact length using the `length` parameter instead of `minlength` and `maxlength`.

We can also parse integer values in a similar fashion:

```
@app.route('/test/<int:age>')
def get_age(age):
    return str(age)
```

We can also specify the minimum and maximum values that can be accepted. For example, we can have `@app.route('/test/<int(min=18,max=99):age>')`. We can also parse float values using `float` in place of `int` in the preceding example.

Sometimes, we might want to escape slashes in our URLs or parse URLs with some filesystem path or another URL's path. This can be done as follows:

```
@app.route('/test/<path:file>/end')
def get_file(file):
    return file
```

This will catch something like `http://127.0.0.1:5000/test/usr/local/app/settings.py/end` and identify `usr/local/app/settings.py` as the file argument to be passed to the method.

Adding pagination to applications

In the *Creating a basic product model* recipe in *Chapter 3*, *Data Modeling in Flask*, we created a handler to list out all the products in our database. If we have thousands of products, then generating the list of all these products in one go can take a lot of time. Also, if we have to render these products on a template, then we would not want to show more than 10-20 products on a page in one go. Pagination proves to be of great help in building great applications.

Let's modify the `products()` method to list products to support pagination:

```
@catalog.route('/products')
@catalog.route('/products/<int:page>')
def products(page=1):
    products = Product.query.paginate(page, 10).items
    res = {}
    for product in products:
        res[product.id] = {
            'name': product.name,
            'price': product.price,
            'category': product.category.name
        }
    return jsonify(res)
```

In the preceding handler, we added a new URL route that adds a `page` parameter to the URL. Now, `http://127.0.0.1:5000/products` will be the same as `http://127.0.0.1:5000/products/1`, and both will return the list of the first 10 products from the DB. Then, `http://127.0.0.1:5000/products/2` will return the next 10 products and so on.

The `paginate()` method takes three arguments and returns an object of the `Pagination` class. These three arguments are:

- ▶ page: This is the current page to be listed.
- ▶ per_page: This is the number of items to be listed per page.
- ▶ error_out: If no items are found for the page, then this aborts with a 404 error. To prevent this behavior, set this parameter to `False`, and then, it will just return an empty list.

See also

- ▶ The *Creating a basic product model* recipe in *Chapter 3, Data Modeling in Flask*, to understand the context of this recipe for pagination

Rendering to templates

After writing the views, we will surely want to render the content on a template and get information from the underlying database.

Getting ready

To render to templates, we will use Jinja2 as the templating language. Refer to *Chapter 2, Templating with Jinja2*, to understand templating in depth.

How to do it...

We will again work in reference to our existing catalog application from the previous recipe. We will now modify our views to render templates and then display data from the database in these templates.

The following is the modified `views.py` code and the templates. The complete app can be downloaded from the code bundle provided with this book.

We will start by modifying our views, that is, `flask_catalog_template/my_app/catalog/views.py`, to render templates on specific handlers:

```
from flask import render_template


@catalog.route('/')
@catalog.route('/home')
def home():
    return render_template('home.html')
```

Notice the `render_template()` method. This method will render `home.html` when the home handler is called. Consider the following code:

```
@catalog.route('/product/<id>')
def product(id):
    product = Product.query.get_or_404(id)
    return render_template('product.html', product=product)
```

Here, the `product.html` template will be rendered with the `product` object in the template context. Consider the following code:

```
@catalog.route('/products')
@catalog.route('/products/<int:page>')
def products(page=1):
    products = Product.query.paginate(page, 10)
    return render_template('products.html', products=products)
```

Here, the `products.html` template will be rendered with the list of paginated `product` objects in the context. Consider the following code:

```
@catalog.route('/product-create', methods=['POST',])
def create_product():
    # … Same code as before …
    return render_template('product.html', product=product)
```

As we can see in the preceding code, in this case, the template corresponding to the newly created product will be rendered. This can also be done using `redirect()`, but we will cover this at a later stage. Have a look at the following code:

```
@catalog.route('/category-create', methods=['POST',])
def create_category():
    # … Same code as before …
    return render_template('category.html', category=category)


@catalog.route('/category/<id>')
def category(id):
```

```
        category = Category.query.get_or_404(id)
        return render_template('category.html', category=category)


    @catalog.route('/categories')
    def categories():
        categories = Category.query.all()
        return render_template('categories.html',
            categories=categories)
```

All the three handlers in the preceding code work in a similar way as discussed earlier with regard to rendering the product-related templates.

The following are all the templates created and rendered as a part of the application. To understand how these templates are written and how they work, refer to *Chapter 2, Templating with Jinja2*.

The `flask_catalog_template/my_app/templates/home.html` file looks as follows:

```
    {% extends 'base.html' %}

    {% block container %}
      <h1>Welcome to the Catalog Home</h1>
      <a href="{{ url_for('catalog.products') }}">Click here to see
        the catalog</a>
    {% endblock %}
```

The `flask_catalog_template/my_app/templates/product.html` file looks as follows:

```
    {% extends 'home.html' %}

    {% block container %}
      <div class="top-pad">
        <h1>{{ product.name }}<small> {{ product.category.name
          }}</small></h1>
        <h4>{{ product.company }}</h4>
        <h3>{{ product.price }}</h3>
      </div>
    {% endblock %}
```

The `flask_catalog_template/my_app/templates/products.html` file looks as follows:

```
    {% extends 'home.html' %}

    {% block container %}
```

```
    <div class="top-pad">
      {% for product in products.items %}
        <div class="well">
          <h2>
            <a href="{{ url_for('catalog.product', id=product.id)
              }}">{{ product.name }}</a>
            <small>$ {{ product.price }}</small>
          </h2>
        </div>
      {% endfor %}
      {% if products.has_prev %}
        <a href="{{ url_for('catalog.products',
          page=products.prev_num) }}">
          {{"<< Previous Page"}}
        </a>
      {% else %}
        {{"<< Previous Page"}}
      {% endif %} |
      {% if products.has_next %}
        <a href="{{ url_for('catalog.products',
          page=products.next_num) }}">
          {{"Next page >>"}}
        </a>
      {% else %}
        {{"Next page >>"}}
      {% endif %}
    </div>
  {% endblock %}
```

The `flask_catalog_template/my_app/templates/category.html` file looks as follows:

```
{% extends 'home.html' %}

{% block container %}
  <div class="top-pad">
    <h2>{{ category.name }}</h2>
    <div class="well">
      {% for product in category.products %}
        <h3>
          <a href="{{ url_for('catalog.product', id=product.id) }}">{{
  product.name }}</a>
          <small>$ {{ product.price }}</small>
        </h3>
```

```
        {% endfor %}
      </div>
    </div>
  {% endblock %}
```

The `flask_catalog_template/my_app/templates/categories.html` file looks as follows:

```
{% extends 'home.html' %}

{% block container %}
  <div class="top-pad">
    {% for category in categories %}
    <a href="{{ url_for('catalog.category', id=category.id) }}">
      <h2>{{ category.name }}</h2>
    </a>
    {% endfor %}
  </div>
{% endblock %}
```

How it works...

Our view methods have a `render_template` method call at the end. This means that after the successful completion of the method operations, we will render a template with some parameters added to the context.

 Note how pagination has been implemented in the `products.html` file. It can be further improved to show the page numbers as well between the two links for navigation. I suggest that you try this out on your own.

See also

▶ Refer to the *URL routing and product-based pagination* recipe, to understand pagination and the rest of the application used in this recipe

Dealing with XHR requests

Asynchronous JavaScript XMLHttpRequest (**XHR**), commonly known as **Ajax**, has become an important part of web applications over the last few years. With the advent of one-page applications and JavaScript application frameworks such as **AngularJS**, **BackboneJS**, and more, this technique of web development has risen exponentially.

Getting ready

Flask provides an easy way to handle the XHR requests in the view handlers. We can even have common methods for normal web requests and XHRs. We can just look for a flag on our `request` object to determine the type of call and act accordingly.

We will update the catalog application from the previous recipe to have a feature that will demonstrate XHR requests.

How to do it...

The Flask `request` object has a flag called `is_xhr`, which tells us whether the request made is an XHR request or a simple web request. Usually, when we have an XHR request, the caller expects the result to be in the JSON format, which can then be used to render content at the correct place on the web page without reloading the page.

So, let's say we have an Ajax call to fetch the number of products in the database on the home page. One way to fetch the products is to send the count of products along with the `render_template()` context. Another way is to send this information over as the response to an Ajax call. We will implement the latter to understand how Flask handles XHR:

```python
from flask import request, render_template, jsonify


@catalog.route('/')
@catalog.route('/home')
def home():
    if request.is_xhr:
        products = Product.query.all()
        return jsonify({
            'count': len(products)
        })
    return render_template('home.html')
```

This design of handling XHR and regular requests together in one method can become a bit bloated, as the application grows large and different logic handling has to be done in the case of XHR in comparison to regular requests.

In such cases, these two types of requests can be separated into different methods where the handling of XHR is done separately from regular requests. This can even be extended to have different blueprints to make URL handling even cleaner.

In the preceding method, we first checked whether this is an XHR. If it is, we return the JSON data; otherwise, we just render `home.html` as we have done until now. First, modify `flask_catalog_template/my_app/templates/base.html` to a block for `scripts`. This empty block, which is shown here, can be placed after the line where the BootstrapJS script is included:

```
{% block scripts %}

{% endblock %}
```

Next, we have `flask_catalog_template/my_app/templates/home.html`, where we send an Ajax call to the `home()` handler, which checks whether the request is an XHR request. If it is, it fetches the count of products from the database and returns it as a JSON object. Check the code inside the `scripts` block:

```
{% extends 'base.html' %}

{% block container %}
  <h1>Welcome to the Catalog Home</h1>
  <a href="{{ url_for('catalog.products') }}" id="catalog_link">
    Click here to see the catalog
  </a>
{% endblock %}

{% block scripts %}
<script>
$(document).ready(function(){
  $.getJSON("/home", function(data) {
    $('#catalog_link').append('<span class="badge">' + data.count
      + '</span>');
  });
});
</script>
{% endblock %}
```

How it works...

Now, our home page contains a badge, which shows the number of products in the database. This badge will load only after the whole page has loaded. The difference in the loading of the badge and the other content on the page will be notable when the database has a considerably huge number of products.

The following screenshot shows how the home page looks now:

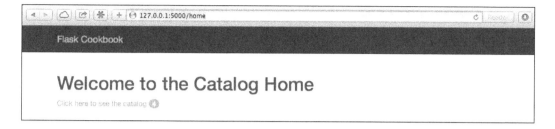

Decorator to handle requests beautifully

Some of us might think that checking whether a request is XHR or not every time kills code readability. To solve this, we have an easy solution. We can just write a simple decorator that will handle this redundant code for us.

Getting ready

In this recipe, we will be writing a decorator. For some of the beginners in Python, this might seem like alien territory. In this case, read `http://legacy.python.org/dev/peps/pep-0318/` for a better understanding of decorators.

How to do it...

The following is the decorator method that we have written for this recipe:

```
from functools import wraps

def template_or_json(template=None):
    """"Return a dict from your view and this will either
    pass it to a template or render json. Use like:

    @template_or_json('template.html')
    """
    def decorated(f):
        @wraps(f)
        def decorated_fn(*args, **kwargs):
            ctx = f(*args, **kwargs)
            if request.is_xhr or not template:
                return jsonify(ctx)
            else:
                return render_template(template, **ctx)
        return decorated_fn
    return decorated
```

This decorator simply does what we have done in the previous recipe to handle XHR, that is, checking whether our request is XHR and based on the outcome, either rendering the template or returning JSON data.

Now, let's apply this decorator to our `home()` method, which handled the XHR call in the previous recipe:

```
@app.route('/')
@app.route('/home')
@template_or_json('home.html')
def home():
    products = Product.query.all()
    return {'count': len(products)}
```

See also

▸ Refer to the *Dealing with XHR requests* recipe to understand how this recipe changes the coding pattern

▸ The reference for this recipe comes from `http://justindonato.com/notebook/template-or-json-decorator-for-flask.html`

Creating custom 404 and 500 handlers

Every application throws errors to users at some point of time. These errors can be due to the user typing a wrong URL (404), application overload (500), or something forbidden for a certain user to access (403). A good application handles these errors in an interactive way instead of showing an ugly white page, which makes no sense to most users. Flask provides an easy-to-use decorator to handle these errors.

Getting ready

The Flask `app` object has a method called `errorhandler()`, which enables us to handle our application's errors in a much more beautiful and efficient manner.

How to do it...

Consider the following code snippet:

```
@app.errorhandler(404)
def page_not_found(e):
    return render_template('404.html'), 404
```

Here, we have created a method that is decorated with `errorhandler()` and renders the `404.html` template whenever the **404 Not Found** error occurs.

The following lines of code represent the `flask_catalog_template/my_app/templates/404.html` template, which is rendered in the case of 404 errors:

```
{% extends 'home.html' %}

{% block container %}
  <div class="top-pad">
    <h3>Hola Friend! Looks like in your quest you have reached a
      location which does not exist yet.</h3>
    <h4>To continue, either check your map location (URL) or go
      back <a href="{{ url_for('catalog.home') }}">home</a></h4>
  </div>
{% endblock %}
```

How it works...

So, now, if we open a wrong URL, say `http://127.0.0.1:5000/i-am-lost`, then we will get what is shown in the following screenshot:

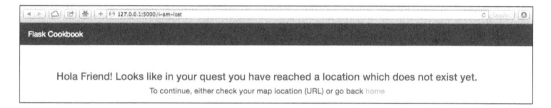

Similarly, we can add more error handlers for other error codes too.

There's more...

It is also possible to create custom errors as per the application requirements and bind them to error codes and custom error screens. This can be done as follows:

```
class MyCustom404(Exception):
    pass

@app.errorhandler(MyCustom404)
def special_page_not_found(error):
    return render_template("errors/custom_404.html"), 404
```

Flashing messages for better user feedback

An important part of all good web applications is to give users feedback about various activities. For example, when a user creates a product and is redirected to the newly created product, then it is a good practice to tell the user that the product has been created.

Getting ready

We will be adding the flash messages functionality to our existing catalog application. We also have to make sure that we add a secret key to the application, because the session depends on the secret key, and in the absence of the secret key, the application will error out while flashing.

How to do it...

To demonstrate the flashing of messages, we will flash messages on the creation of products. First, we will add a secret key to our app configuration in `flask_catalog_template/my_app/__init__.py`:

```
app.secret_key = 'some_random_key'
```

Now, we will modify our `create_product()` handler in `flask_catalog_template/my_app/catalog/views.py` to flash a message to the user about the product's creation. Also, a small change has been made to this handler where now, it will be possible to create the product from a web interface using a form:

```
from flask import flash

@catalog.route('/product-create', methods=['GET', 'POST'])
def create_product():
    if request.method == 'POST':
        name = request.form.get('name')
        price = request.form.get('price')
        categ_name = request.form.get('category')
        category = Category.query.filter_by
          (name=categ_name).first()
        if not category:
            category = Category(categ_name)
        product = Product(name, price, category)
        db.session.add(product)
        db.session.commit()
        flash('The product %s has been created' % name, 'success')
        return redirect(url_for('catalog.product', id=product.id))
    return render_template('product-create.html')
```

In the preceding method, we first checked whether the request type is POST. If yes, then we proceed to product creation as always or render the page with a form to create a new product. Also, notice the `flash` statement that will alert the user on the successful creation of a product. The first argument to `flash()` is the message to be displayed, and the second is the category of the message. We can use any identifier as suited in the message category. This can be used later to determine the type of alert message to be shown.

A new template is added; it holds the code for the product form. The path of the template will be `flask_catalog_template/my_app/templates/product-create.html`:

```html
{% extends 'home.html' %}

{% block container %}
  <div class="top-pad">
    <form
        class="form-horizontal"
        method="POST"
        action="{{ url_for('catalog.create_product') }}"
        role="form">
      <div class="form-group">
        <label for="name" class="col-sm-2 control-
          label">Name</label>
        <div class="col-sm-10">
          <input type="text" class="form-control" id="name"
            name="name">
        </div>
      </div>
      <div class="form-group">
        <label for="price" class="col-sm-2 control-
          label">Price</label>
        <div class="col-sm-10">
          <input type="number" class="form-control" id="price"
            name="price">
        </div>
      </div>
      <div class="form-group">
        <label for="category" class="col-sm-2 control-
          label">Category</label>
        <div class="col-sm-10">
          <input type="text" class="form-control" id="category"
            name="category">
        </div>
      </div>
      <button type="submit" class="btn btn-
        default">Submit</button>
    </form>
  </div>
{% endblock %}
```

We will also modify our base template, that is, `flask_catalog_template/my_app/templates/base.html`, to accommodate flashed messages. Just add the following lines of code inside the `<div>` container before the `container` block:

```
<br/>
<div>
  {% for category, message in get_flashed_messages
    (with_categories=true) %}
    <div class="alert alert-{{category}} alert-dismissable">
      <button type="button" class="close" data-dismiss="alert"
        aria-hidden="true">&times;</button>
      {{ message }}
    </div>
  {% endfor %}
</div>
```

 Notice that in the `<div>` container, we have added a mechanism to show a flashed message that fetches the flashed messages in the template using `get_flashed_messages()`.

How it works...

A form, like the one shown in the following screenshot, will show up when you navigate to `http://127.0.0.1:5000/product-create`:

Fill up the form and click on **Submit**. This will lead to the usual product page with an alert message at the top:

Flask Cookbook

The product iPhone 6 has been created

iPhone 6 Phones

749.0

SQL-based searching

In any web application, it is important to be able to search the database for records based on some criteria. In this recipe, we will go through how to implement basic SQL-based searching in SQLAlchemy. The same principle can be used to search any other database system.

Getting ready

We have been implementing some level of search in our catalog application from the beginning. Whenever we show the product page, we search for a specific product using its ID. We will now take it to a more advanced level and search on the basis of name and category.

How to do it...

The following is a method that searches in our catalog application for name, price, company, and category. We can search for any one or multiple criterion (except for the search on category, which can only be searched alone). Notice that we have different expressions for different values. For a float value in price, we can search for equality, while in the case of a string, we can search using `like`. Also, carefully note how `join` is implemented in the case of category search. Place this method in the views file, that is, `flask_catalog_template/my_app/catalog/views.py`:

```
from sqlalchemy.orm.util import join

@catalog.route('/product-search')
@catalog.route('/product-search/<int:page>')
def product_search(page=1):
```

```
name = request.args.get('name')
price = request.args.get('price')
company = request.args.get('company')
category = request.args.get('category')
products = Product.query
if name:
    products = products.filter(Product.name.like('%' + name +
        '%'))
if price:
    products = products.filter(Product.price == price)
if company:
    products = products.filter(Product.company.like('%' +
        company + '%'))
if category:
    products = products.select_from(join(Product,
        Category)).filter(
            Category.name.like('%' + category + '%')
        )
return render_template(
    'products.html', products=products.paginate(page, 10)
)
```

How it works...

We can search for products by entering a URL, for example `http://127.0.0.1:5000/product-search?name=iPhone`. This will search for products with the name `iPhone` and list out the results on the `products.html` template. Similarly, we can search for price and/or company or category as needed. Try various combinations by yourself for a better understanding.

 We have used the same product list page to render our search results. It will be interesting to implement the search using Ajax. I will leave this to you to implement yourselves!

5
Webforms with WTForms

Form handling is an integral part of any web application. There can be innumerable cases that make the presence of forms in any web app very important. Some cases can be where users need to log in or submit some data or cases where applications might require input from users. As important as the forms are, their validation holds equal importance, if not more. Presenting this information to users in an interactive fashion adds a lot of value to the application.

In this chapter, we will cover the following recipes:

- ▸ SQLAlchemy model data as form representation
- ▸ Validating fields on the server side
- ▸ Creating a common forms set
- ▸ Creating custom fields and validation
- ▸ Creating a custom widget
- ▸ Uploading files via forms
- ▸ Cross-site Request Forgery protection

Introduction

There are various ways in which we can design and implement forms in a web application. With the advent of Web 2.0, form validation and communicating correct messages to the user has become very important. Client-side validations can be implemented at the frontend using JavaScript and HTML5. Server-side validations have a more important role in adding security to the application rather than being interactive. Server-side validations prevent any incorrect data from going through to the database and, hence, curb frauds and attacks.

WTForms provides a lot of fields with server-side validation by default and, hence, increases the development speed and decreases the overall effort. It also provides the flexibility to write custom validations and custom fields as needed.

We will use a Flask extension for this chapter. This extension is called Flask-WTF (`https://flask-wtf.readthedocs.org/en/latest/`); it provides a small integration between WTForms and Flask and takes care of important and simple stuff that we would have to otherwise reinvent in order to make our application secure and effective. We can install it using the following command:

```
$ pip install Flask-WTF
```

SQLAlchemy model data as form representation

First, let's build a form using a SQLAlchemy model. We will take the product model from our catalog application and add the functionality to create products from the frontend using a webform.

Getting ready

We will use our catalog application from *Chapter 4, Working with Views*. We will develop a form for the `Product` model.

How to do it...

To remind you, the `Product` model looks like the following lines of code in the `models.py` file:

```python
class Product(db.Model):
    id = db.Column(db.Integer, primary_key=True)
    name = db.Column(db.String(255))
    price = db.Column(db.Float)
    category_id = db.Column(db.Integer,
      db.ForeignKey('category.id'))
    category = db.relationship(
        'Category', backref=db.backref('products', lazy='dynamic')
    )
    company = db.Column(db.String(100))
```

First, we will create a `ProductForm` class; this will subclass the `Form` class, which is provided by `flask_wtf`, to represent the fields needed on a webform:

```
from flask_wtf import Form
from wtforms import TextField, DecimalField, SelectField

class ProductForm(Form):
    name = TextField('Name')
    price = DecimalField('Price')
    category = SelectField('Category', coerce=int)
```

We import `Form` from the `flask-wtf` extension. Everything else like `fields` and `validators` are imported from `wtforms` directly. The `Name` field is of type `TextField`, as it requires text data, while `Price` is of type `DecimalField`, which will parse the data to Python's `Decimal` datatype. We have kept `Category` as type `SelectField`, which means that we can choose only from the previously created categories while creating a product.

> Note that we have a parameter called `coerce` in the field definition for `Category` (which is a selection list); this means that the incoming data from the HTML form will be coerced into an integer value before validation or any other processing. Here, coercing simply means converting the value provided in a specific datatype to a different datatype.

The `create_product()` handler in `views.py` should now accommodate the form created earlier:

```
from my_app.catalog.models import ProductForm

@catalog.route('/product-create', methods=['GET', 'POST'])
def create_product():
    form = ProductForm(request.form, csrf_enabled=False)

    categories = [(c.id, c.name) for c in Category.query.all()]
    form.category.choices = categories

    if request.method == 'POST':
        name = request.form.get('name')
        price = request.form.get('price')
        category = Category.query.get_or_404(
            request.form.get('category')
        )
```

```
      product = Product(name, price, category)
      db.session.add(product)
      db.session.commit()
      flash('The product %s has been created' % name, 'success')
      return redirect(url_for('catalog.product', id=product.id))
   return render_template('product-create.html', form=form)
```

The `create_product()` method accepts values from a form on a POST request. This method will render an empty form with the prefilled choices in the `Category` field on a GET request. On the POST request, the form data will be used to create a new product, and when the creation of the product is completed, the newly created product's page will be displayed.

 You will notice that while creating the `form` object as `form = ProductForm(request.form, csrf_enabled=False)`, we set `csrf_enabled` to `False`. CSRF is an important part of any secure web application. We will talk about it in detail in the *Cross-site Request Forgery protection* recipe of this chapter.

The `templates/product-create.html` template also needs some modification too. The `form` objects created by WTForms provide an easy way to create HTML forms and keep the code readable:

```
{% extends 'home.html' %}

{% block container %}
  <div class="top-pad">
    <form method="POST" action="{{
      url_for('catalog.create_product') }}" role="form">
      <div class="form-group">{{ form.name.label }}: {{
        form.name() }}</div>
      <div class="form-group">{{ form.price.label }}: {{
        form.price() }}</div>
      <div class="form-group">{{ form.category.label }}: {{
        form.category() }}</div>
      <button type="submit" class="btn btn-
        default">Submit</button>
    </form>
  </div>
{% endblock %}
```

How it works...

On a GET request, that is, on opening `http://127.0.0.1:5000/product-create`, we will see a form similar to the one shown in the following screenshot:

You can fill in this form to create a new product.

See also

▶ The *Validating fields on the server side* recipe to understand how to validate the fields we just learned to create

Validating fields on the server side

We have forms and fields, but we need to validate them in order to make sure that only the correct data goes through to the database and errors are handled beforehand rather than corrupting the database. These validations can also prevent the application against **cross-site scripting** (**XSS**) and CSRF attacks. WTForms provides a whole lot of field types that themselves have validations written for them by default. Apart from these, there are a bunch of validators that can be used on the basis of choice and need. We will use a few of them to understand this concept further.

How to do it...

It is pretty easy to add validations to our WTForm fields. We just need to pass a `validators` parameter, which accepts a list of validators to be implemented. Each of the validators can have their own arguments, which enable us to control the validations to a great extent.

Let's modify our `ProductForm` class to have validations:

```
from decimal import Decimal
from wtforms.validators import InputRequired, NumberRange

class ProductForm(Form):
    name = TextField('Name', validators=[InputRequired()])
    price = DecimalField('Price', validators=[
        InputRequired(), NumberRange(min=Decimal('0.0'))
    ])
    category = SelectField(
        'Category', validators=[InputRequired()], coerce=int
    )
```

Here, we have the `InputRequired` validator on many fields; this means that these fields are required, and the form will not be submitted unless we have a value for these fields.

The `Price` field has an additional validator `NumberRange` with a `min` parameter set to 0. This implies that we cannot have a value less than 0 as the price of a product. To complement these changes, we will have to modify our `create_product()` method a bit:

```
@catalog.route('/product-create', methods=['GET', 'POST'])
def create_product():
    form = ProductForm(request.form, csrf_enabled=False)

    categories = [(c.id, c.name) for c in Category.query.all()]
    form.category.choices = categories

    if request.method == 'POST' and form.validate():
        name = form.name.data
        price = form.price.data
        category = Category.query.get_or_404(
            form.category.data
        )
        product = Product(name, price, category)
        db.session.add(product)
        db.session.commit()
        flash('The product %s has been created' % name, 'success')
        return redirect(url_for('product', id=product.id))

    if form.errors:
        flash(form.errors, 'danger')

    return render_template('product-create.html', form=form)
```

The flashing of `form.errors` will just display the errors in the form of a JSON object. This can be formatted to be shown in a pleasing format to the user. This is left for the users to try by themselves.

Here, we modified our `create_product()` method to validate the form for the input values and to check for the request method type. On a POST request, the form data will be validated first. If the validation fails for some reason, the same page will be rendered again, with error messages flashed on it. If the validation succeeds and the creation of the product is completed, the newly created product's page will be displayed.

How it works...

Now, try to submit the form without any field filled in, that is, an empty form. An alert message with an error will be shown as follows:

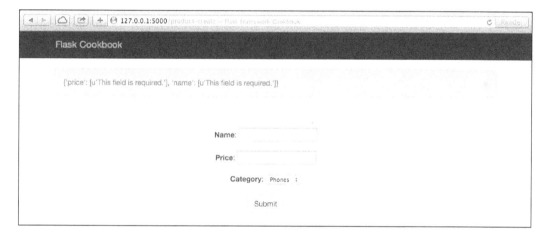

Try different combinations of form submission, which will violate the defined validators, and see the different error messages that come up.

There's more...

We can replace the processes of checking for the method type being a POST or PUT request and form validation with one step using `validate_on_submit`. So, the original code is:

```
if request.method == 'POST' and form.validate():
```

This can be replaced by:

```
if form.validate_on_submit():
```

See also

▸ Refer to the previous recipe, *SQLAlchemy model data as form representation*, to understand basic form creation using WTForms

Creating a common forms set

An application can have loads of forms, depending on the design and purpose. Many of these forms will have common fields with common validators. Many of us might think, "Why not have common forms parts and then reuse them as and when needed?" This is very much possible with the class structure for forms' definition provided by WTForms.

How to do it...

In our catalog application, we can have two forms, one each for the `Product` and `Category` models. These forms will have a common field called `Name`. We can create a common form for this field, and then, the separate forms for the `Product` and `Category` models can use this form instead of having a `Name` field in each of them. This can be done as follows:

```
class NameForm(Form):
    name = TextField('Name', validators=[InputRequired()])


class ProductForm(NameForm):
    price = DecimalField('Price', validators=[
        InputRequired(), NumberRange(min=Decimal('0.0'))
    ])
    category = SelectField(
        'Category', validators=[InputRequired()], coerce=int
    )
    company = TextField('Company', validators=[Optional()])



class CategoryForm(NameForm):
    pass
```

We created a common form called `NameForm`, and the other forms, `ProductForm` and `CategoryForm`, inherit from this form to have a field called `Name` by default. Then, we can add more fields as needed.

We can modify the `category_create()` method to use `CategoryForm` to create categories:

```
@catalog.route('/category-create', methods=['GET', 'POST'])
def create_category():
    form = CategoryForm(request.form, csrf_enabled=False)

    if form.validate_on_submit():
        name = form.name.data
        category = Category(name)
        db.session.add(category)
        db.session.commit()
        flash('The category %s has been created' % name,
          'success')
        return redirect(url_for('catalog.category',
          id=category.id))

    if form.errors:
        flash(form.errors)

    return render_template('category-create.html', form=form)
```

A new template `templates/category-create.html` also needs to be added for category creation:

```
{% extends 'home.html' %}

{% block container %}
  <div class="top-pad">
    <form method="POST" action="{{
      url_for('catalog.create_category') }}" role="form">
      <div class="form-group">{{ form.name.label }}: {{
        form.name() }}</div>
      <button type="submit" class="btn btn-
        default">Submit</button>
    </form>
  </div>
{% endblock %}
```

How it works...

The newly created category form will look like the following screenshot:

Name:

Submit

 This is a very small example of how a common forms set can be implemented. The actual benefits of this approach can be seen in e-commerce applications, where we can have common address forms, and then, they can be expanded to have separate billing and shipment addresses.

Creating custom fields and validation

Apart from providing a bunch of fields and validations, Flask also provides the flexibility to create custom fields and validations. Sometimes, we might need to parse some form of data that cannot be processed using the available current fields. In such cases, we can implement our own fields.

How to do it...

In our catalog application, we used `SelectField` for the category, and we populated the values for this field in our `create_product()` method on a GET request. It would be much more convenient if we did not bother about this and the population of this field was taken care of by itself. Let's implement a custom field for this in `models.py`:

```
class CategoryField(SelectField):

    def iter_choices(self):
        categories = [(c.id, c.name) for c in
          Category.query.all()]
        for value, label in categories:
```

```
              yield (value, label, self.coerce(value) == self.data)

    def pre_validate(self, form):
        for v, _ in [(c.id, c.name) for c in
          Category.query.all()]:
            if self.data == v:
                break
        else:
            raise ValueError(self.gettext('Not a valid choice'))

class ProductForm(NameForm):
    price = DecimalField('Price', validators=[
        InputRequired(), NumberRange(min=Decimal('0.0'))
    ])
    category = CategoryField(
        'Category', validators=[InputRequired()], coerce=int
    )
```

`SelectField` implements a method called `iter_choices()`, which populates the values to the form using the list of values provided to the `choices` parameter. We overwrote the `iter_choices()` method to get the values of categories directly from the database, and this eliminates the need to populate this field every time we need to use this form.

> The behavior created by `CategoryField` here can also be achieved using `QuerySelectField`. Refer to `http://wtforms.readthedocs.org/en/latest/ext.html#wtforms.ext.sqlalchemy.fields.QuerySelectField` for more information.

Due to the changes described in this section, our `create_product()` method in `views.py` will have to be modified. For this, just remove the following two statements that populated the categories in the form:

```
categories = [(c.id, c.name) for c in Category.query.all()]
form.category.choices = categories
```

How it works...

There will not be any visual effect on the application. The only change will be in the way the categories are populated in the form, as explained in the previous section.

There's more...

We just saw how to write custom fields. Similarly, we can write custom validations too. Let's assume that we do not want to allow duplicate categories. We can implement this in our models easily, but let's do this using a custom validator on our form:

```python
from wtforms.validators import import ValidationError

def check_duplicate_category(case_sensitive=True):
    def _check_duplicate(form, field):
        if case_sensitive:
            res = Category.query.filter(
                Category.name.like('%' + field.data + '%')
            ).first()
        else:
            res = Category.query.filter(
                Category.name.ilike('%' + field.data + '%')
            ).first()
        if res:
            raise ValidationError(
                'Category named %s already exists' % field.data
            )
    return _check_duplicate

class CategoryForm(NameForm):
    name = TextField('Name', validators=[
        InputRequired(), check_duplicate_category()
    ])
```

So, we created our validator in a factory style, where we can get separate validation results based on whether we want a case-sensitive comparison or not. We can even write a class-based design, which makes the validator much more generic and flexible, but I will leave that for the readers to explore.

Creating a custom widget

Just like we can create custom fields and validators, we can also create custom widgets. These widgets allow us to control how our fields will look like at the frontend. Each field type has a widget associated with it. WTForms, by itself, provides a lot of basic and HTML5 widgets. To understand how to write a custom widget, we will convert our custom selection field for category into a radio field. I agree with many who would argue that we can directly use the radio field provided by WTForms. Here, we are just trying to understand how to do it ourselves.

The widgets provided by default by WTForms can be found at `https://wtforms.readthedocs.org/en/latest/widgets.html`.

How to do it...

In our previous recipe, we created `CategoryField`. This field used the `Select` widget, which was provided by the `Select` superclass. Let's replace the `Select` widget with a radio input:

```
from wtforms.widgets import html_params, Select, HTMLString

class CustomCategoryInput(Select):

    def __call__(self, field, **kwargs):
        kwargs.setdefault('id', field.id)
        html = []
        for val, label, selected in field.iter_choices():
            html.append(
                '<input type="radio" %s> %s' % (
                    html_params(
                        name=field.name, value=val,
                        checked=selected, **kwargs
                    ), label
                )
            )
        return HTMLString(' '.join(html))

class CategoryField(SelectField):
    widget = CustomCategoryInput()

    # Rest of the code remains same as in last recipe Creating
      custom field and validation
```

Here, we added a class attribute called `widget` in our `CategoryField` class. This widget points to `CustomCategoryInput`, which takes care of HTML code generation for the field to be rendered. This class has a `__call__` method, which is overwritten to return radio inputs corresponding to the values provided by the `iter_choices()` method of `CategoryField`.

How it works...

When you open the product-creation page `http://127.0.0.1:5000/product-create`, it will look like the following screenshot:

See also

▶ The previous recipe, *Creating custom fields and validation*, to understand more about the level of customization that can be done to the components of WTForms

Uploading files via forms

Uploading files via forms and doing it properly is usually a matter of concern for many web frameworks. Flask and WTForms handle this for us in a simple and streamlined manner.

How to do it...

First, we will start with the configuration bit. We need to provide a parameter to our application configuration, that is, UPLOAD_FOLDER. This parameter tells Flask about the location where our uploaded files will be stored. We will implement a feature to store product images.

One way to store product images can be to store images in a binary type field in our database, but this method is highly inefficient and never recommended in any application. We should always store images and other uploads in the filesystem and store their location in the database using a string field.

Add the following statements to the configuration in `my_app/__init__.py`:

```
import os

ALLOWED_EXTENSIONS = set(['txt', 'pdf', 'png', 'jpg', 'jpeg', 'gif'])

app.config['UPLOAD_FOLDER'] = os.path.realpath('.') +
    '/my_app/static/uploads'
```

> Note the `app.config['UPLOAD_FOLDER']` statement where we store the images inside a subfolder in the `static` folder itself. This will make the process of rendering images easier. Also note the `ALLOWED_EXTENSIONS` statement that is used to make sure that only files of a specific format go through. The list here is actually for demonstration purposes only, and for image types, we can filter this list even more.

In the models file, that is, `my_app/catalog/models.py`, add the following highlighted statements in their designated places:

```
from wtforms import FileField

class Product(db.Model):
    image_path = db.Column(db.String(255))

    def __init__(self, name, price, category, image_path):
        self.image_path = image_path

class ProductForm(NameForm):
    image = FileField('Product Image')
```

Check `FileField` for `image` in `ProductForm` and the field for `image_path` in the `Product` model. This is in line with what we discussed earlier about storing files on the filesystem and storing their path in the DB.

Now, we can modify the `create_product()` method to save the file in `my_app/catalog/views.py`:

```
import os
from werkzeug import secure_filename
from my_app import ALLOWED_EXTENSIONS

def allowed_file(filename):
    return '.' in filename and \
```

```
                    filename.lower().rsplit('.', 1)[1] in
                        ALLOWED_EXTENSIONS


    @catalog.route('/product-create', methods=['GET', 'POST'])
    def create_product():
        form = ProductForm(request.form, csrf_enabled=False)

        if form.validate_on_submit():
            name = form.name.data
            price = form.price.data
            category = Category.query.get_or_404(
                form.category.data
            )
            image = request.files['image']
            filename = ''
            if image and allowed_file(image.filename):
                filename = secure_filename(image.filename)
                image.save(os.path.join(app.config['UPLOAD_FOLDER'],
                    filename))
            product = Product(name, price, category, filename)
            db.session.add(product)
            db.session.commit()
            flash('The product %s has been created' % name, 'success')
            return redirect(url_for('catalog.product', id=product.id))

        if form.errors:
            flash(form.errors, 'danger')

        return render_template('product-create.html', form=form)
```

We need to add the new field to the product-create form in template templates/
product-create.html. Modify the form tag definition to include the enctype parameter,
and add the field for the image before the **Submit** button (or wherever you feel it is necessary
inside the form):

```
<form method="POST"
    action="{{ url_for('create_product') }}"
    role="form"
    enctype="multipart/form-data">
<!-- The other field definitions as always -->
<div class="form-
  group">{{ form.image.label }}: {{
  form.image(style='display:inline;') }}</div>
```

The form should have the enctype="multipart/form-data" statement to tell the
application that the form input will have multipart data.

Rendering the image is very easy as we are storing the files in the `static` folder. Just add the `img` tag wherever the image needs to be displayed in `templates/product.html`:

```
<img src="{{ url_for('static', filename='uploads/' +
  product.image_path) }}"/>
```

How it works...

The field to upload the image will look something like the following screenshot:

After the creation of the product, the image will be displayed as shown in the following screenshot:

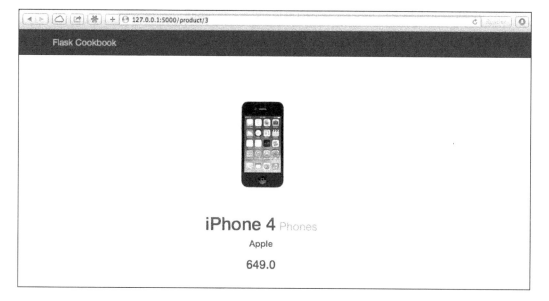

Cross-site Request Forgery protection

In the first recipe of this chapter, we learned that CSRF is an important part of webform security. We will talk about it in detail now. CSRF stands for Cross-Site Request Forgery, which basically means that someone can hack into the request that carries a cookie and use this to trigger some destructive action. We won't be discussing CSRF in detail here, as ample resources are available on the Internet to learn about this. We will talk about how WTForms will help us in preventing CSRF. Flask does not provide any security from CSRF by default, as this has to be handled at the form validation level, which is not provided by Flask. However, this is done by the Flask-WTF extension for us.

 More about CSRF can be read at `http://en.wikipedia.org/wiki/Cross-site_request_forgery`.

How to do it...

Flask-WTF, by default, provides a form that is CSRF protected. If we have a look at the recipes so far, we will notice that we have explicitly told our form to *not be CSRF protected*. We just have to remove the corresponding statement to enable CSRF.

So, `form = ProductForm(request.form, csrf_enabled=False)` will become `form = ProductForm(request.form)`.

Some configuration bits also need to be done in our application:

```
app.config['WTF_CSRF_SECRET_KEY'] = 'random key for form'
```

By default, the CSRF key is the same as our application's secret key.

With CSRF enabled, we will have to provide an additional field in our forms; this is a hidden field and contains the CSRF token. WTForms takes care of the hidden field for us, and we just have to add `{{ form.csrf_token }}` to our form:

```
<form method="POST" action="/some-action-like-create-product">
    {{ form.csrf_token }}
</form>
```

That was easy! Now, this is not the only type of form submission that we do. We also submit AJAX form posts; this actually happens a lot more than normal forms with the advent of JS-based web applications, which are replacing traditional web applications.

For this, we have added an additional step in our application's configuration:

```
from flask_wtf.csrf import CsrfProtect

#
# Add configurations
#
CsrfProtect(app)
```

The preceding configuration will allow us to access the CSRF token using `{{ csrf_token() }}` anywhere in our templates. Now, there are two ways to add a CSRF token to AJAX POST requests.

One way is to fetch the CSRF token in our `script` tag and use it in the POST request:

```
<script type="text/javascript">
    var csrfToken = "{{ csrf_token() }}";
</script>
```

Another way is to render the token in a `meta` tag and use it whenever required:

```
<meta name="csrf-token" content="{{ csrf_token() }}"/>
```

The difference between both is that the first approach might have to be repeated at multiple places depending on the number of `script` tags in the application.

Now, to add the CSRF token to AJAX POST, we have to add the `X-CSRFToken` attribute to it. This attribute's value can be taken from any of the two approaches stated earlier. We will take the second one as our example:

```
var csrfToken = $('meta[name="csrf-token"]').attr('content');

$.ajaxSetup({
    beforeSend: function(xhr, settings) {
        if (!/^(GET|HEAD|OPTIONS|TRACE)$/i.test(settings.type)) {
            xhr.setRequestHeader("X-CSRFToken", csrftoken)
        }
    }
})
```

This will make sure that a CSRF token is added to all the AJAX POST requests that go out.

How it works...

The following screenshot shows what the CSRF token added by WTForms in our form looks like:

The token is completely random and different for all the requests. There are multiple ways of implementing CSRF-token generation, but this is out of the scope of this book, although I would encourage users to take a look at some implementations to understand how it's done.

6
Authenticating in Flask

Authentication is an important part of any application, be it web-based, desktop, or mobile. Each kind of application has certain best practices of handling user authentication. In web-based applications, especially SaaS-based applications, this process is of utmost importance, as it acts as the thin red line between the application being secure and unsecure.

In this chapter, we will cover the following recipes:

- Simple session-based authentication
- Authenticating using the Flask-Login extension
- Using OpenID for authentication
- Using Facebook for authentication
- Using Google for authentication
- Using Twitter for authentication

Introduction

To keep things simple and flexible, Flask, by default, does not provide a mechanism for authentication. It always has to be implemented by us, the developers, as per our and the application's requirements.

Authenticating users for your application can be done in multiple ways. It can be done using a simple session-based implementation or a more secure approach using the Flask-Login extension. We can also implement authentication by integrating with popular third-party services such as OpenID or social logins such as Facebook, Google, and so on. In this chapter, we will go through all of these methods.

Simple session-based authentication

In session-based authentication, when the user logs in for the first time, the user details are set in the session of the application's server side and stored in a cookie on the browser. After that, when the user opens the application, the details stored in the cookie are used to check against the session, and the user is automatically logged in if the session is alive.

 SECRET_KEY should always be specified in your application's configuration; otherwise, the data stored in the cookie as well as the session on the server side will be in plain text, which is highly unsecure.

We will implement a simple mechanism to do this ourselves.

 The implementation done in this recipe is only to explain how authentication basically works at a lower level. This approach should *not* be adopted in any production-level application.

Getting ready

We can start with a Flask app configuration as seen in *Chapter 5, Webforms with WTForms*. The application's configuration will be done to use the SQLAlchemy and WTForms extensions (refer to the previous chapter for details).

How to do it...

Before we start with the authentication, we need to have a model to store the user details. We will first create the models and forms in `flask_authentication/my_app/auth/models.py`:

```python
from werkzeug.security import generate_password_hash,
  check_password_hash
from flask_wtf import Form
from wtforms import TextField, PasswordField
from wtforms.validators import InputRequired, EqualTo
from my_app import db


class User(db.Model):
    id = db.Column(db.Integer, primary_key=True)
    username = db.Column(db.String(100))
    pwdhash = db.Column(db.String())

    def __init__(self, username, password):
```

```
        self.username = username
        self.pwdhash = generate_password_hash(password)

    def check_password(self, password):
        return check_password_hash(self.pwdhash, password)
```

The preceding code is the User model, which has two fields: username and pwdhash. The username field works as its name suggests. The pwdhash field stores the salted hash of the password, because it is not recommended that you store passwords directly in databases.

Then, we will create two forms: one for user registration and the other for login. In RegistrationForm, we will create two fields of type PasswordField, just like any other website's registration; this is to make sure that the user enters the same password in both fields:

```
class RegistrationForm(Form):
    username = TextField('Username', [InputRequired()])
    password = PasswordField(
        'Password', [
            InputRequired(), EqualTo('confirm', message='Passwords
                must match')
        ]
    )
    confirm = PasswordField('Confirm Password', [InputRequired()])

class LoginForm(Form):
    username = TextField('Username', [InputRequired()])
    password = PasswordField('Password', [InputRequired()])
```

Then, we will create views in flask_authentication/my_app/auth/views.py to handle the user requests for registration and login:

```
from flask import request, render_template, flash, redirect,
  url_for, \
    session, Blueprint
from my_app import app, db
from my_app.auth.models import User, RegistrationForm, LoginForm

auth = Blueprint('auth', __name__)

@auth.route('/')
@auth.route('/home')
def home():
    return render_template('home.html')

@auth.route('/register', methods=['GET', 'POST'])
def register():
```

```
    if session.get('username'):
        flash('Your are already logged in.', 'info')
        return redirect(url_for('auth.home'))

    form = RegistrationForm(request.form)

    if request.method == 'POST' and form.validate():
        username = request.form.get('username')
        password = request.form.get('password')
        existing_username =
          User.query.filter_by(username=username).first()
        if existing_username:
            flash(
                'This username has been already taken. Try another
                  one.',
                'warning'
            )
            return render_template('register.html', form=form)
        user = User(username, password)
        db.session.add(user)
        db.session.commit()
        flash('You are now registered. Please login.', 'success')
        return redirect(url_for('a
    if form.errors:
        flash(form.errors, 'danger')

    return render_template('register.html', form=form)
```

The preceding method handles user registration. On a GET request, the registration form is shown to the user; this form asks for the username and password. Then, the username is checked for its uniqueness after the form validation is complete. If the username is not unique, the user is asked to choose a new username; otherwise, a new user is created in the database and redirected to the login page, which is handled as shown in the following code:

```
@auth.route('/login', methods=['GET', 'POST'])
def login():
    form = LoginForm(request.form)

    if request.method == 'POST' and form.validate():
        username = request.form.get('username')
        password = request.form.get('password')
```

```
        existing_user =
          User.query.filter_by(username=username).first()

        if not (existing_user and existing_user.check_password
          (password)):
            flash('Invalid username or password. Please try
              again.', 'danger')
            return render_template('login.html', form=form)

        session['username'] = username
        flash('You have successfully logged in.', 'success')
        return redirect(url_for('auth.home'))

    if form.errors:
        flash(form.errors, 'danger')

    return render_template('login.html', form=form)
```

The preceding method handles the user login. After the form validation, we first check if the username exists in the database. If not, we ask the user to enter the correct username. Similarly, we check if the password is correct. If not, we ask the user for the correct password. If all the checks pass, the session is populated with a `username` key, which holds the username of the user. The presence of this key on the session indicates that the user is logged in. Consider the following code:

```
@auth.route('/logout')
def logout():
    if 'username' in session:
        session.pop('username')
        flash('You have successfully logged out.', 'success')

    return redirect(url_for('auth.home'))
```

The preceding method becomes self-implied after we understand the `login()` method. Here, we just popped out the `username` key from the session, and the user got logged out automatically.

Then, we will create the templates that are rendered by the `register()` and `login()` handlers for the registration and login, respectively, created earlier.

The `flask_authentication/my_app/templates/base.html` template remains almost the same as it was in *Chapter 5*, *Webforms with WTForms*. The only change will be with the routing where `catalog` will be replaced by `auth`.

First, we will have a simple home page `flask_authentication/my_app/templates/home.html`, which reflects if the user is logged in or not and shows links for registration and login if the user is not logged in:

```
{% extends 'base.html' %}

{% block container %}
  <h1>Welcome to the Authentication Demo</h1>
  {% if session.username %}
    <h3>Hey {{ session.username }}!!</h3>
    <a href="{{ url_for('auth.logout') }}">Click here to
      logout</a>
  {% else %}
  Click here to <a href="{{ url_for('auth.login') }}">login</a> or
      <a href="{{ url_for('auth.register') }}">register</a>
  {% endif %}
{% endblock %}
```

Then, we will create a registration page, `flask_authentication/my_app/templates/register.html`:

```
{% extends 'home.html' %}

{% block container %}
  <div class="top-pad">
    <form
        method="POST"
        action="{{ url_for('auth.register') }}"
        role="form">
      {{ form.csrf_token }}
      <div class="form-group">{{ form.username.label }}: {{
        form.username() }}</div>
      <div class="form-group">{{ form.password.label }}: {{
        form.password() }}</div>
      <div class="form-group">{{ form.confirm.label }}: {{
        form.confirm() }}</div>
      <button type="submit" class="btn btn-default">
        Submit</button>
    </form>
  </div>
{% endblock %}
```

Finally, we will create a simple login page, `flask_authentication/my_app/templates/login.html`:

```
{% extends 'home.html' %}

{% block container %}
  <div class="top-pad">
    <form
        method="POST"
        action="{{ url_for('auth.login') }}"
        role="form">
      {{ form.csrf_token }}
      <div class="form-group">{{ form.username.label }}: {{
        form.username() }}</div>
      <div class="form-group">{{ form.password.label }}: {{
        form.password() }}</div>
      <button type="submit" class="btn btn-default">
        Submit</button>
    </form>
  </div>
{% endblock %}
```

How it works...

How this application works is demonstrated with the help of the screenshots in this section.

The first screenshot is the home page that comes up on opening `http://127.0.0.1:5000/home`:

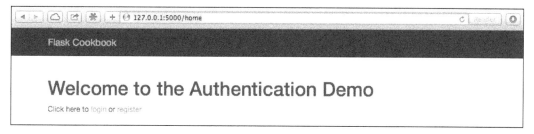

This is the home page visible to a user that is not logged in

The registration page that comes up on opening `http://127.0.0.1:5000/register` looks like the following screenshot:

The registration form

After the registration, the login page will be shown on opening `http://127.0.0.1:5000/login`:

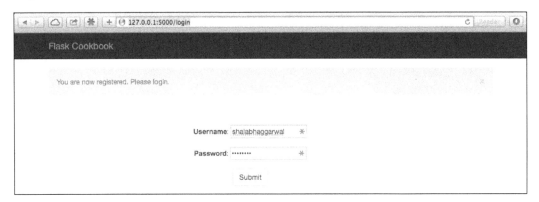

The login page rendered after successful registration

Finally, the home page is shown to the logged-in user at `http://127.0.0.1:5000/home`:

Home page as shown to a logged-in user

▸ The next recipe, *Authenticating using the Flask-Login extension*, which covers a much secure and production-ready method of performing user authentication

Authenticating using the Flask-Login extension

In our previous recipe, we learned how to implement session-based authentication ourselves. Flask-Login is a popular extension that handles a lot of stuff for us in a very good way, saving us from reinventing the wheel all over again. It also does not bind us to any specific database or limit us to any specific fields/methods for authentication. It can also handle the *Remember me* feature, account recovery features, and so on.

Getting ready

We can modify the application created in the previous recipe to accommodate the changes to be done by the Flask-Login extension.

Before that, we have to install the extension itself:

```
$ pip install Flask-Login
```

How to do it...

To use Flask-Login, we have to first modify our application's configuration, which is in `flask_authentication/my_app/__init__.py`:

```python
from flask.ext.login import LoginManager

#
# Do other application config
#

login_manager = LoginManager()
login_manager.init_app(app)
login_manager.login_view = 'login'
```

After importing the `LoginManager` class from the extension, we will create an object of this class. Then, we can configure the `app` object for use with `LoginManager` using `init_app()`. Then, we will have multiple configurations that can be done on our `login_manager` object as per our needs. Here, I have just demonstrated one basic and compulsory configuration, that is, `login_view`, which points to the view handler for our login requests. Further, we can even configure the messages to be shown to the users, how long our session will last, the app to handle logins using request headers, and so on. Refer to the Flask-Login documentation at `https://flask-login.readthedocs.org/en/latest/#customizing-the-login-process` for more details.

Flask-Login calls for some additional methods to be added to our `User` model/class:

```
def is_authenticated(self):
    return True


def is_active(self):
    return True


def is_anonymous(self):
    return False


def get_id(self):
    return unicode(self.id)
```

In the preceding code, we added four methods, which are explained as follows:

- `is_authenticated()`: This method usually returns `True`. This should return `False` only in cases where we do not want a user to be authenticated.

- `is_active()`: This method usually returns `True`. This should return `False` only in cases where we have blocked or banned a user.

- `is_anonymous()`: This method is used to indicate a user who is not supposed to be logged in to the system and should access the application as anonymous. This should usually return `False` for regular logged-in users.

- `get_id()`: This method represents the unique ID used to identify the user. This should be a unicode value.

Next, we have to make changes to our views in `my_app/views.py`:

```
from flask import g
from flask.ext.login import current_user, login_user, \
    logout_user, login_required
from my_app import login_manager


@login_manager.user_loader
def load_user(id):
```

```
        return User.query.get(int(id))

    @auth.before_request
    def get_current_user():
        g.user = current_user
```

In the preceding method, the `@auth.before_request` decorator implies that this method will be called before the view function whenever a request is received. Here, we have memoized our logged-in user:

```
    @auth.route('/login', methods=['GET', 'POST'])
    def login():
        if current_user.is_authenticated():
            flash('You are already logged in.')
            return redirect(url_for('auth.home'))

            # Same block of code as from last recipe Simple session
              based authentication
            # Next replace the statement session['username'] =
              username by the one below
            login_user(existing_user)
            flash('You have successfully logged in.', 'success')
            return redirect(url_for('auth.home'))

        if form.errors:
            flash(form.errors, 'danger')

        return render_template('login.html', form=form)

    @auth.route('/logout')
    @login_required
    def logout():
        logout_user()
        return redirect(url_for('home'))
```

Notice that now, in `login()`, we checked if the `current_user` is authenticated before doing anything else. Here, `current_user` is a proxy to represent the object for the currently logged-in `User` record. Then, after all the validations and checks are done, the user is logged in using the `login_user()` method. This method accepts the user object and handles all the session-related activities to be done to log in a user.

Now, coming on to the `logout()` method, we first saw that there is a decorator added for `login_required()`. This decorator makes sure that the user is logged in before this method is executed. It can be used for any view method in our application. To log a user out, we just have to call `logout_user()`, which will clean up the session for the currently logged-in user and, in turn, log the user out of the application.

As we do not handle sessions ourselves, there will be a minor change in the templates too. This happens whenever we want to check if the user is logged in and there is some content to be shown based on this choice:

```
{% if current_user.is_authenticated() %}
...do something...
{% endif %}
```

How it works...

The demonstration in this recipe works exactly as it did in the previous recipe, *Simple session-based authentication*. Only the implementation differs, but the end result remains the same.

There's more...

The Flask-Login extension makes the implementation of the *Remember me* feature pretty simple. To do this, we just have to pass `remember=True` to the `login_user()` method. This will save a cookie on the user's computer, and Flask-Login will automatically use the same to log the user in automatically if the session is active. Readers should try implementing this on their own.

See also

- ▸ The previous recipe, *Simple session-based authentication*, to understand the complete working of this recipe.
- ▸ Flask provides a special object called `g`. You can read more about this at `http://flask.pocoo.org/docs/0.10/api/#flask.g`.

Using OpenID for authentication

OpenID allows us to use an existing account to sign in to multiple websites without the need to create new passwords for each website. Thus, this eliminates the need to share personal information with all the websites. There are certain cooperating sites (also known as **relying parties**) that authenticate user logins, and thousands of sites accept OpenID as an authentication mechanism. OpenID also allows you to control which information can be shared with the websites you visit and register with. Read more about OpenID and relying parties at `http://en.wikipedia.org/wiki/OpenID`.

Flask has an extension called **Flask-OpenID**, which makes the use and integration of OpenID with our application very simple and easy. This extension depends on the **python-openid** library. To install this, we can simply use the following command:

```
$ pip install Flask-OpenID
```

We will build over the application from the *Authenticating using the Flask-Login extension* recipe.

How to do it...

We will first start with our configuration in `flask_authentication/my_app/__init__.py`:

```
from flask.ext.openid import OpenID

#
# Do other application config
#

oid = OpenID(app, 'openid-store')
```

First, we imported the `OpenID` class from the Flask extension. Then, we instantiated the class using our `app` object and created an object called `oid`. The second argument to `OpenID` while creating the `oid` object is the path to the store, which will store the OpenID information for the authentication process.

 Here, we used a path to a folder on the filesystem, but this can be configured to use your own store, which can be a relational database or a NoSQL document.

As we are integrating OpenID with our existing application keeping the existing functionality intact, we will use our existing `username` field to store the unique identifier received from OpenID, which can be `email` or `nickname`. This calls for the addition of a new form to our application to accept the OpenID URL:

```
class OpenIDForm(Form):
    openid = TextField('OpenID', [InputRequired()])
```

The major chunk of changes will be to our views, that is, `flask_authentication/my_app/auth/views.py`:

```python
from my_app import oid
from my_app.auth.models import OpenIDForm


@auth.route('/login', methods=['GET', 'POST'])
@oid.loginhandler
def login():
    if g.user is not None and current_user.is_authenticated():
        flash('You are already logged in.', 'info')
        return redirect(url_for('home'))

    form = LoginForm(request.form)
    openid_form = OpenIDForm(request.form)

    if request.method == 'POST':
        if request.form.has_key('openid'):
            openid_form.validate()
            if openid_form.errors:
                flash(openid_form.errors, 'danger')
                return render_template(
                    'login.html', form=form,
                    openid_form=openid_form
                )
            openid = request.form.get('openid')
            return oid.try_login(openid, ask_for=['email',
                'nickname'])
        else:
            form.validate()
            if form.errors:
                flash(form.errors, 'danger')
                return render_template(
                    'login.html', form=form,
                    openid_form=openid_form
                )
            username = request.form.get('username')
            password = request.form.get('password')
            existing_user = User.query.filter_by
              (username=username).first()

            if not (existing_user and
              existing_user.check_password(password)):
                flash(
```

```
                          'Invalid username or password. Please try
                            again.',
                          'danger'
                      )
                      return render_template('login.html', form=form)

              login_user(existing_user)
              flash('You have successfully logged in.', 'success')
              return redirect(url_for('auth.home'))

          if form.errors:
              flash(form.errors, 'danger')

          return render_template('login.html', form=form,
            openid_form=openid_form)
```

In the preceding method, we first checked if the current user is authenticated. If yes, then we redirect the user to the home page. Otherwise, if the request method is POST, then we first check if we have an `openid` field in our form. If there is such a field, we validate the `OpenIDForm`, and upon successful validation, we call `oid.try_login()`, which takes the OpenID URL and the fields to be fetched from the OpenID provider as the inputs. If the form does not have an `openid` field, then it is our regular form for a traditional login, and we follow the same process as we did in the previous recipe. Consider the following code:

```
@oid.after_login
def after_login(resp):
    username = resp.nickname or resp.email
    if not username:
        flash('Invalid login. Please try again.', 'danger')
        return redirect(url_for('auth.login'))
    user = User.query.filter_by(username=username).first()
    if user is None:
        user = User(username, '')
        db.session.add(user)
        db.session.commit()
    login_user(user)
    return redirect(url_for('auth.home'))
```

This method is called after OpenID's `try_login()` method receives a response from the provider. All this happens asynchronously. First, we tried to fetch the `nickname` or `email` from the provider. If none of the two are found, then this login is invalid. Then, we checked for an existing user with the `nickname` or `email` by matching in the `username` field. If a user is found, we log the user in; otherwise, we create a new user and then log in.

This also calls for a small change in our `templates/login.html` template to accommodate `OpenIDForm`:

```
{% extends 'home.html' %}

{% block container %}
  <div class="top-pad">
    <ul class="nav nav-tabs">
      <li class="active"><a href="#simple-form" data-
        toggle="tab">Old Style Login</a></li>
      <li><a href="#openid-form" data-toggle="tab">OpenID</a></li>
    </ul>
    <div class="tab-content">
      <div class="tab-pane active" id="simple-form">
        <form
            method="POST"
            action="{{ url_for('auth.login') }}"
            role="form">
          {{ form.csrf_token }}
          <div class="form-group">{{ form.username.label }}: {{
            form.username() }}</div>
          <div class="form-group">{{ form.password.label }}: {{
            form.password() }}</div>
          <button type="submit" class="btn btn-
            default">Submit</button>
        </form>
      </div>
      <div class="tab-pane" id="openid-form">
        <form
            method="POST"
            action="{{ url_for('auth.login') }}"
            role="form">
          {{ openid_form.csrf_token }}
          <div class="form-group">{{ openid_form.openid.label }}:
            {{ openid_form.openid() }}</div>
          <button type="submit" class="btn btn-
            default">Submit</button>
        </form>
      </div>
    </div>
  </div>
{% endblock %}
```

In this code, we created a tabbed structure where the first tab is our conventional login and the second tab corresponds to the OpenID login.

How it works...

The tabbed page for login will look like the following screenshot:

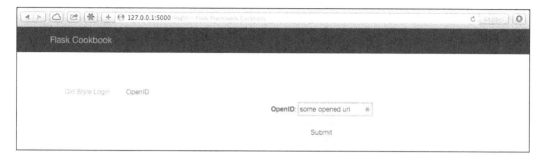

We have to enter an OpenID URL, and the rest of the process will work according to the provider.

Using Facebook for authentication

We have seen that many websites provide an option to log in to their website using third-party authentications such as Facebook, Google, Twitter, LinkedIn, and so on. This has been made possible by OAuth, which is an open standard for authorization. It allows the client site to use an access token to access the protected information/resources provided by the resource server. In this recipe, we will see how to implement OAuth-based authorization via Facebook. In the recipes to follow, we will do the same using other providers.

Getting started

First, we will start by installing the Flask-OAuth extension and its dependencies:

```
$ pip install Flask-OAuth
```

Next, we have to register for a Facebook application that will be used for login. Although the process for registration with the Facebook app is pretty straightforward and self-explanatory, we are only concerned with the **App ID**, **App Secret**, and **Site URL** options. The following screenshot should help you in understanding this. More details can be found on the Facebook developer pages at `https://developers.facebook.com/`.

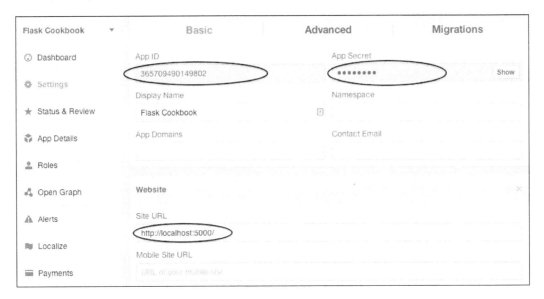

How to do it...

As always, we will first start with the configuration part in `my_app/__init__.py`:

```
from flask_oauth import OAuth

oauth = OAuth()

facebook = oauth.remote_app('facebook',
    base_url='https://graph.facebook.com/',
    request_token_url=None,
    access_token_url='/oauth/access_token',
    authorize_url='https://www.facebook.com/dialog/oauth',
    consumer_key='FACEBOOK_APP_ID',
    consumer_secret='FACEBOOK_APP_SECRET',
    request_token_params={'scope': 'email'}
)
```

In the previous code snippet, we registered a remote Facebook application with our application for authentication. All the parameters passed in `remote_app()` will remain the same for all the Facebook remote apps except `consumer_key` and `consumer_secret`, which actually correspond to the **App ID** and **App Secret** options, respectively, of our Facebook application.

Next, we will modify our views, that is, `my_app/auth/views.py`:

```python
from my_app import facebook


@auth.route('/facebook-login')
def facebook_login():
    return facebook.authorize(
        callback=url_for(
            'auth.facebook_authorized',
            next=request.args.get('next') or request.referrer or
                None,
            _external=True
        ))
```

The previous method calls the `authorize()` method of the `OAuth` instance with a callback URL to which the response received from Facebook should be passed for further action.

 The `_external=True` statement here implies that the URL can be external to the application.

Consider the following code:

```python
@auth.route('/facebook-login/authorized')
@facebook.authorized_handler
def facebook_authorized(resp):
    if resp is None:
        return 'Access denied: reason=%s error=%s' % (
            request.args['error_reason'],
            request.args['error_description']
        )
    session['facebook_oauth_token'] = (resp['access_token'], '')
    me = facebook.get('/me')
    user = User.query.filter_by(username=me.data['email']).first()
    if not user:
        user = User(me.data['email'], '')
```

```
            db.session.add(user)
            db.session.commit()

        login_user(user)
        flash(
            'Logged in as id=%s name=%s' % (me.data['id'],
              me.data['name']),
            'success'
        )
        return redirect(request.args.get('next'))
```

The previous method handles the response received from Facebook and logs the user in, if the user with the same e-mail address already exists; otherwise, it creates a new user and then logs the user in. Consider the following code:

```
@facebook.tokengetter
def get_facebook_oauth_token():
    return session.get('facebook_oauth_token')
```

This method just fetches the token that is stored in the session for the current user.

Finally, we will modify our login template to allow the Facebook login. First, we add a tab for social logins:

```
        <ul class="nav nav-tabs">
            <li class="active"><a href="#simple-form" data-toggle="tab">Old
Style Login</a></li>
            <li><a href="#openid-form" data-toggle="tab">OpenID</a></li>
            <li><a href="#social-logins" data-toggle="tab">Social Logins</
a></li>
        </ul>
```

This is followed by adding the contents for the newly added **Social** logins tab:

```
        <div class="tab-pane" id="social-logins">
            <a href="{{ url_for('auth.facebook_login',
              next=url_for('auth.home')) }}">Login via Facebook</a>
        </div>
```

So, we just added a new tab to allow social logins. Right now, we have just one for Facebook here. More will be added in the recipes to follow. Also, we just have a simple link right now; we can always add styles and buttons as needed.

How it works...

The login page has a new tab that provides an option to the user to log in using social logins:

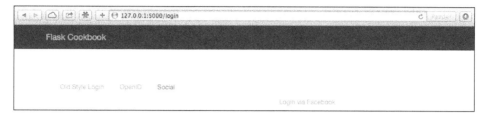

When we click on the **Login via Facebook** link, the application will be taken to Facebook and will ask for user login and permission. Once the permission is granted, the user will be logged in to the application.

Using Google for authentication

Just like we did for Facebook, we can integrate our application to enable login using Google.

Getting ready

We will start by building over the last recipe. It is easy to just implement Google authentication by leaving out the Facebook auth (by leaving out the Facebook-specific parts).

Now, we have to create a project from the Google developer console (`https://console.developers.google.com`). Then, we have to create a client ID for the web application; this ID will provide the credentials needed for OAuth to work. The following screenshot should help:

How to do it...

As always, we will first start with the configuration part in `my_app/__init__.py`:

```python
from flask_oauth import OAuth

oauth = OAuth()

google = oauth.remote_app('google',
    base_url='https://www.google.com/accounts/',
    authorize_url='https://accounts.google.com/o/oauth2/auth',
    request_token_url=None,
    request_token_params={
        'scope': 'https://www.googleapis.com/auth/userinfo.email',
        'response_type': 'code'
    },
    access_token_url='https://accounts.google.com/o/oauth2/token',
    access_token_method='POST',
    access_token_params={'grant_type': 'authorization_code'},
    consumer_key='GOOGLE_CLIENT_ID',
    consumer_secret='GOOGLE_CLIENT_SECRET'
)
```

In the preceding code, we registered a remote Google application with our application for authentication. All the parameters passed in `remote_app()` will remain the same for all the Google remote apps except `consumer_key` and `consumer_secret`, which actually correspond to the **Client ID** and **Client secret** options, respectively, of our Google project.

Next, we will modify our views, that is, `my_app/auth/views.py`:

```python
import requests
from my_app import google

GOOGLE_OAUTH2_USERINFO_URL =
  'https://www.googleapis.com/oauth2/v1/userinfo'

@auth.route('/google-login')
def google_login():
    return google.authorize(
        callback=url_for('auth.google_authorized',
          _external=True))
```

The preceding method calls the `authorize()` method of the `OAuth` instance with a callback URL to which the response received from Google should be passed for further action. Consider the following code:

```
@auth.route('/oauth2callback')
@google.authorized_handler
def google_authorized(resp):
    if resp is None:
        return 'Access denied: reason=%s error=%s' % (
            request.args['error_reason'],
            request.args['error_description']
        )
    session['google_oauth_token'] = (resp['access_token'], '')
    userinfo = requests.get(GOOGLE_OAUTH2_USERINFO_URL,
        params=dict(
            access_token=resp['access_token'],
    )).json()

    user = User.query.filter_by(username=userinfo
        ['email']).first()
    if not user:
        user = User(userinfo['email'], '')
        db.session.add(user)
        db.session.commit()

    login_user(user)
    flash(
        'Logged in as id=%s name=%s' % (userinfo['id'],
            userinfo['name']),
        'success'
    )
    return redirect(url_for('auth.home'))
```

The preceding method handles the response received from Google and logs the user in if a user with the same e-mail address already exists; otherwise, it creates a new user and then logs the user in. An important point to note here is that the route URL of this method is the same as the redirect URL set in our Google client settings (see the _Getting ready_ section of this recipe). Consider the following code:

```
@google.tokengetter
def get_google_oauth_token():
    return session.get('google_oauth_token')
```

This method just fetches the token that is stored in the session for the current user. Finally, we will modify our login template to allow the Google login:

```
<a href="{{ url_for('auth.google_login') }}">Login via Google</a>
```

How it works...

The Google login works in a manner similar to how the Facebook login from the previous recipe works.

Using Twitter for authentication

OAuth was actually born while writing the OpenID API for Twitter. In this recipe, we will integrate Twitter login with our application.

Getting ready

We will continue by building over the *Using Google for authentication* recipe. It is easy to just implement Twitter auth by leaving out specific parts from Facebook and/or Google authentication.

Now, we have to create an application from the Twitter **Application Management** page (https://apps.twitter.com/). It will automatically create **API key** and **API secret** for us to use. Have a look at the following screenshot:

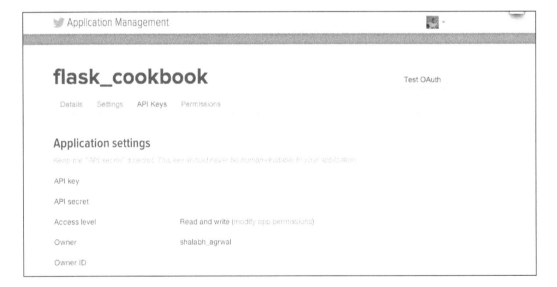

How to do it...

As always, we will first start with the configuration part in `my_app/__init__.py`:

```python
from flask_oauth import OAuth

oauth = OAuth()

twitter = oauth.remote_app('twitter',
    base_url='https://api.twitter.com/1.1/',
    request_token_url='https://api.twitter.com/oauth/request_token',
    access_token_url='https://api.twitter.com/oauth/access_token',
    authorize_url='https://api.twitter.com/oauth/authenticate',
    consumer_key='Twitter API Key',
    consumer_secret='Twitter API Secret'
)
```

In the preceding code, we registered a remote Twitter application with our application for authentication. All the parameters passed in `remote_app()` will remain the same for all Twitter remote apps except `consumer_key` and `consumer_secret`, which actually correspond to the **API key** and **API secret** options, respectively, of our Twitter application.

Next, we will modify our views, that is, `my_app/auth/views.py`:

```python
from my_app import twitter

@auth.route('/twitter-login')
def twitter_login():
    return twitter.authorize(
        callback=url_for(
            'auth.twitter_authorized',
            next=request.args.get('next') or request.referrer or
                None,
            _external=True
        ))
```

The preceding method calls the `authorize()` method of the `OAuth` instance with a callback URL to which the response received from Twitter should be passed for further action. Consider the following code:

```python
@auth.route('/twitter-login/authorized')
@twitter.authorized_handler
def twitter_authorized(resp):
    if resp is None:
        return 'Access denied: reason=%s error=%s' % (
            request.args['error_reason'],
```

```
            request.args['error_description']
        )
    session['twitter_oauth_token'] = resp['oauth_token'] + \
            resp['oauth_token_secret']

    user = User.query.filter_by(username=resp
        ['screen_name']).first()
    if not user:
        user = User(resp['screen_name'], '')
        db.session.add(user)
        db.session.commit()

    login_user(user)
    flash('Logged in as twitter handle=%s' % resp['screen_name'])
    return redirect(request.args.get('next'))
```

The preceding method handles the response received from Twitter and logs the user in if a user with same Twitter screen name (also known as a Twitter handle) already exists; otherwise, it creates a new user and then logs the user in. Consider the following code:

```
@twitter.tokengetter
def get_twitter_oauth_token():
    return session.get('twitter_oauth_token')
```

This method just fetches the token that is stored in the session for the current user. Finally, we will modify our login template to allow the Twitter login:

```
<a href="{{ url_for('auth.twitter_login',
    next=url_for('auth.home')) }}">Login via Twitter</a>
```

This recipe works in a manner similar to how the Facebook and Google logins from the previous recipes work.

> Similarly, we can integrate LinkedIn, GitHub, and scores of other third-party providers that provide support for login and authentication using OAuth. I will leave it to you to implement many more integrations on your own. The following links have been added for quick reference:
>
> ▶ **LinkedIn**: https://developer.linkedin.com/documents/authentication
>
> ▶ **GitHub**: https://developer.github.com/v3/oauth/

7
RESTful API Building

An API, or Application Programming Interface, can be summarized as a developer's interface to the application. Just like end users have a visible frontend user interface to work on and talk to the application, developers also need a user interface to the application. REST, or REpresentational State Transfer, is not a protocol or a standard. It is just a software architectural style or a set of constraints defined for writing applications and aims at simplifying the interfaces within and outside the application. When web service APIs are written in a way to adhere to the REST constraints, then they are known as RESTful APIs. Being RESTful keeps the API decoupled from the internal application details. This results in ease of scalability and keeps things simple. The uniform interface ensures that each and every request is documented.

 It is a topic of debate whether REST is better or SOAP is. It actually is a subjective question as it depends on what needs to be done. Each has its own benefits and should be chosen as per the needs of the application.

In this chapter, we will cover the following recipes:

- Creating a class-based REST interface
- Creating an extension-based REST interface
- Creating a SQLAlchemy-independent REST API
- A complete REST API example

Introduction

As the name suggests, **REpresentational State Transfer** (**REST**) calls for segregating your API into logical resources, which can be accessed and manipulated using HTTP requests, where each request consists of a method out of GET, POST, PUT, PATCH, and DELETE (there can be more, but these are the ones used the most). Each of these methods has a specific meaning. One of the key implied principles of REST is that the logical grouping of resources should be easily understandable and, hence, provide simplicity along with portability.

Up until now in this book, we have used a resource called Product. Let's see how we can logically map our API calls to the resource segregation:

- ▶ `GET /products/1`: This gets the product with ID 1
- ▶ `GET /products`: This gets the list of products
- ▶ `POST /products`: This creates a new product
- ▶ `PUT /products/1`: This updates the product with ID 1
- ▶ `PATCH /products/1`: This partially updates the product with ID 1
- ▶ `DELETE /products/1`: This deletes the product with ID 1

Creating a class-based REST interface

We saw how class-based views work in Flask using the concept of pluggable views in the *Class-based views* recipe in *Chapter 4, Working with Views*. We will now see how we can use the same concept to create views, which will provide a REST interface to our application.

Getting ready

Let's take a simple view that will handle the REST style calls to our `Product` model.

How to do it...

We have to simply modify our views for product handling to extend the `MethodView` class:

```
from flask.views import MethodView

class ProductView(MethodView):

    def get(self, id=None, page=1):
        if not id:
            products = Product.query.paginate(page, 10).items
            res = {}
```

```
        for product in products:
            res[product.id] = {
                'name': product.name,
                'price': product.price,
                'category': product.category.name
            }
    else:
        product = Product.query.filter_by(id=id).first()
        if not product:
            abort(404)
        res = json.dumps({
            'name': product.name,
            'price': product.price,
            'category': product.category.name
        })
    return res
```

The preceding `get()` method searches for the product and sends back a JSON result.

Similarly, we can write the `post()`, `put()`, and `delete()` methods too:

```
def post(self):
    # Create a new product.
    # Return the ID/object of newly created product.
    return

def put(self, id):
    # Update the product corresponding provided id.
    # Return the JSON corresponding updated product.
    return

def delete(self, id):
    # Delete the product corresponding provided id.
    # Return success or error message.
    return
```

Many of us would wonder why we have no routing here. To include routing, we have to do the following:

```
product_view =  ProductView.as_view('product_view')
app.add_url_rule('/products/', view_func=product_view,
    methods=['GET', 'POST'])
app.add_url_rule('/products/<int:id>', view_func=product_view,
    methods=['GET', 'PUT', 'DELETE'])
```

The first statement here converts the class to an actual view function internally that can be used with the routing system. The next two statements are the URL rules corresponding to the calls that can be made.

How it works...

The `MethodView` class identified the type of HTTP method in the request sent and converted the name to lowercase. Then, it matched this to the methods defined in the class and called the matched method. So, if we make a GET call to `ProductView`, it will automatically be mapped to the `get()` method and processed accordingly.

There's more...

We can also use a Flask extension for this called Flask-Classy (`https://pythonhosted.org/Flask-Classy/`). This will handle the classes and routing automatically to a great extent and make life easier. We won't be discussing this here though, but it's an extension that is definitely worth exploring.

Creating an extension-based REST interface

In the previous recipe, *Creating a class-based REST interface*, we saw how to create a REST interface using pluggable views. Here, we will use a Flask extension, Flask-Restless, developed completely from the point of view of building REST interfaces. It provides a simple generation of RESTful APIs for database models defined using SQLAlchemy. These generated APIs send and receive messages in the JSON format.

Getting ready

First, we need to install the Flask-Restless extension:

```
$ pip install Flask-Restless
```

We will build over our application from the *SQL-based searching* recipe of *Chapter 4, Working with Views*, to include a RESTful API interface.

It is advisable that you read *Chapter 4, Working with Views*, before moving ahead if the concepts of views and handlers are not clear.

How to do it...

Adding a RESTful API interface to a SQLAlchemy model is very easy with the use of Flask-Restless. First, we need to add the REST API manager provided by this extension to our application config and create an instance of it using the `app` object:

```
from flask.ext.restless import APIManager

manager = APIManager(app, flask_sqlalchemy_db=db)
```

After this, we need to enable API creation on our models using the `manager` instance. For this, we can just add the following lines of code to `views.py`:

```
from my_app import manager

manager.create_api(Product, methods=['GET', 'POST', 'DELETE'])
manager.create_api(Category, methods=['GET', 'POST', 'DELETE'])
```

This will create RESTful APIs with the `GET`, `POST`, and `DELETE` methods on our models for `Product` and `Category`. By default, only the `GET` method is provided if the `methods` argument is missed out.

How it works...

To test and see how this works, we can send some `requests` using the Python shell using the requests library:

```
>>> import requests
>>> import json
>>> res = requests.get('http://127.0.0.1:5000/api/category')
>>> res.json()
{u'total_pages': 0, u'objects': [], u'num_results': 0, u'page': 1}
```

We made a GET request to fetch a list of categories, but right now, there is no record for it. Let's look for the products now:

```
>>> res = requests.get('http://127.0.0.1:5000/api/product')
>>> res.json()
{u'total_pages': 0, u'objects': [], u'num_results': 0, u'page': 1}
```

We made a GET request to fetch the list of products, but there is no record for it. Let's create a new product now:

```
>>> d = {'name': u'iPhone', 'price': 549.00, 'category':
{'name':'Phones'}}
>>> res = requests.post('http://127.0.0.1:5000/api/product', data=json.
dumps(d), headers={'Content-Type': 'application/json'})
>>> res.json()
{u'category': {u'id': 1, u'name': u'Phones'}, u'name': u'iPhone',
u'company': u'', u'price': 549.0, u'category_id': 1, u'id': 2, u'image_
path': u''}
```

We sent a POST request to create a product with some data. Notice the `headers` argument in the request. Each POST request sent in Flask-Restless should have this header. Now, we should look for the list of products again:

```
>>> res = requests.get('http://127.0.0.1:5000/api/product')
>>> res.json()
{u'total_pages': 1, u'objects': [{u'category': {u'id': 1, u'name':
u'Phones'}, u'name': u'iPhone', u'company': u'', u'price': 549.0,
u'category_id': 1, u'id': 1, u'image_path': u''}], u'num_results': 1,
u'page': 1}
```

If we look for the products again via a GET request, we can see that we have a newly created product in the database now.

Also notice that the results are already paginated by default; this is one of the signs of a good API design.

There's more...

This automatic creation of a RESTful API interface is cool, but every application needs some customizations, validations, and handling of requests as per the application business logic. This is made possible using request `preprocessors` and `postprocessors`. As evident by the names, `preprocessors` are the methods that will run before the request is processed, and `postprocessors` run after the request is processed and before the response is sent by the application. These are defined in `create_api()` as maps of the request type (GET, POST, and so on) and the list of methods to act as `preprocessors` or `postprocessors` on the specified request:

```
manager.create_api(
    Product,
    methods=['GET', 'POST', 'DELETE'],
    preprocessors={
        'GET_SINGLE': ['a_preprocessor_for_single_get'],
        'GET_MANY': ['another_preprocessor_for_many_get'],
```

```
        'POST': ['a_preprocessor_for_post']
    },
    postprocessors={
        'DELETE': ['a_postprocessor_for_delete']
    }
)
```

The GET, PUT, and PATCH requests can be called for single or multiple records; hence, they have two variants each. For example, in the preceding code, we have `GET_SINGLE` and `GET_MANY` for GET requests. The preprocessors and postprocessors for each of the request type accept different arguments and act upon them without returning any return value. Refer to the Flask-Restless documentation at `https://flask-restless.readthedocs.org/en/latest/` at for more details.

Creating a SQLAlchemy-independent REST API

In the previous recipe, *Creating an extension-based REST interface*, we saw how to create a REST API interface using an extension that was dependent on SQLAlchemy. Now, we will use an extension called Flask-Restful, which is written over Flask pluggable views and is independent of ORM.

Getting ready

First, we will start with the installation of the extension:

$ pip install Flask-Restful

We will modify the catalog application from the previous recipe to add a REST interface using this extension.

How to do it...

As always, we will start with changes to our application's configuration, which will look something like the following lines of code:

```
from flask.ext.restful import Api

api = Api(app)
```

Here, `app` is our Flask application object/instance.

Next, we will create our API inside the `views.py` file. Here, we will just try to understand how to lay out the skeleton of the API. Actual methods and handlers will be covered in the *A complete REST API example* recipe:

```python
from flask.ext.restful import Resource
from my_app import api


class ProductApi(Resource):

    def get(self, id=None):
        # Return product data
        return 'This is a GET response'

    def post(self):
        # Create a new product
        return 'This is a POST response'

    def put(self, id):
        # Update the product with given id
        return 'This is a PUT response'

    def delete(self, id):
        # Delete the product with given id
        return 'This is a DELETE response'
```

The preceding API structure is self-explanatory. Consider the following code:

```python
api.add_resource(
    ProductApi,
    '/api/product',
    '/api/product/<int:id>'
)
```

Here, we created the routing for `ProductApi`, and we can specify multiple routes as needed.

How it works...

We will see how this will work on the Python shell using the `requests` library just like we did in the previous recipe:

```
>>> import requests
>>> res = requests.get('http://127.0.0.1:5000/api/product')
>>> res.json()
u'This is a GET response'
>>> res = requests.post('http://127.0.0.1:5000/api/product')
```

```
u'This is a POST response'
>>> res = requests.put('http://127.0.0.1:5000/api/product/1')
u'This is a PUT response'
>>> res = requests.delete('http://127.0.0.1:5000/api/product/1')
u'This is a DELETE response'
```

In the preceding snippet, we saw that all our requests are properly routed to the respective methods; this is evident from the response received.

See also

▶ Make sure you read the next recipe, *A complete REST API example*, to see the API skeleton from this recipe coming to life

A complete REST API example

In this recipe, we will convert the API structure created in the previous recipe, *Creating a SQLAlchemy-independent REST API*, into a full-fledged RESTful API interface.

Getting ready

We will take the API skeleton from the previous recipe as the base to create a complete functional SQLAlchemy-independent RESTful API. Although we will use SQLAlchemy as the ORM for demonstration, this recipe can be written in a similar fashion for any ORM or underlying database.

How to do it...

The following lines of code are the complete RESTful API for the `Product` model. These code snippets will go into the `views.py` file:

```
from flask.ext.restful import reqparse

parser = reqparse.RequestParser()
parser.add_argument('name', type=str)
parser.add_argument('price', type=float)
parser.add_argument('category', type=dict)
```

In the preceding snippet, we created `parser` for the arguments that we expected to have in our requests for POST and PUT. The request expects each of the argument to have a value. If a value is missing for any argument, then `None` is used as the value. Consider the following code:

```
class ProductApi(Resource):

    def get(self, id=None, page=1):
        if not id:
            products = Product.query.paginate(page, 10).items
        else:
            products = [Product.query.get(id)]
        if not products:
            abort(404)
        res = {}
        for product in products:
            res[product.id] = {
                'name': product.name,
                'price': product.price,
                'category': product.category.name
            }
        return json.dumps(res)
```

The preceding `get()` method corresponds to GET requests and returns a paginated list of products if no `id` is passed; otherwise, it returns the corresponding product. Consider the following code:

```
    def post(self):
        args = parser.parse_args()
        name = args['name']
        price = args['price']
        categ_name = args['category']['name']
        category = Category.query.filter_by
          (name=categ_name).first()
        if not category:
            category = Category(categ_name)
        product = Product(name, price, category)
        db.session.add(product)
        db.session.commit()
        res = {}
        res[product.id] = {
            'name': product.name,
            'price': product.price,
            'category': product.category.name,
        }
        return json.dumps(res)
```

The preceding `post()` method will lead to the creation of a new product by making a POST request. Consider the following code:

```
def put(self, id):
    args = parser.parse_args()
    name = args['name']
    price = args['price']
    categ_name = args['category']['name']
    category = Category.query.filter_by
        (name=categ_name).first()
    Product.query.filter_by(id=id).update({
        'name': name,
        'price': price,
        'category_id': category.id,
    })
    db.session.commit()
    product = Product.query.get_or_404(id)
    res = {}
    res[product.id] = {
        'name': product.name,
        'price': product.price,
        'category': product.category.name,
    }
    return json.dumps(res)
```

In the preceding code, we updated an existing product using a PUT request. Here, we should provide all the arguments even if we intend to change a few of them. This is because of the conventional way in which PUT has been defined to work. If we want to have a request where we intend to pass only those arguments that we intend to update, then we should use a PATCH request. Consider the following code:

```
def delete(self, id):
    product = Product.query.filter_by(id=id)
    product.delete()
    db.session.commit()
    return json.dumps({'response': 'Success'})
```

Last but not least, we have the DELETE request, which will simply delete the product that matches the `id` passed. Consider the following code:

```
api.add_resource(
    ProductApi,
    '/api/product',
    '/api/product/<int:id>',
    '/api/product/<int:id>/<int:page>'
)
```

The preceding code is the definition of all the possible routes our API can accommodate.

See also

▸ The API works in a manner similar to what was shown in the *Creating an extension-based REST interface* recipe

 An important facet of REST APIs is token-based authentication to allow only limited and authenticated users to be able to use and make calls to the API. I will urge you to explore this on your own. We covered the basics of user authentication in *Chapter 6, Authenticating in Flask*, which will serve as the base for this concept.

8
Admin Interface for Flask Apps

Every application needs an interface that provides special privileges to some users and can be used to maintain and upgrade the application resources. For example, we can have an interface in an e-commerce application; this interface will allow some special users to create categories, products, and so on. Some users might have permissions to handle other users who shop on the website and deal with their account information and so on. Similarly, there can be many cases where we will need to isolate an interface of our application from normal users.

In this chapter, we will cover the following recipes:

- ▸ Creating a simple CRUD interface
- ▸ Using the Flask-Admin extension
- ▸ Registering models with Flask-Admin
- ▸ Creating custom forms and actions
- ▸ WYSIWYG for textarea integration
- ▸ Creating user roles

Introduction

As opposed to the much popular Python-based web framework, Django, Flask does not provide an admin interface by default. Although this can be seen as a shortcoming by many, this gives the developers the flexibility to create the admin interface as per their requirements and have complete control over the application.

We can opt to write an admin interface for our application from scratch or use an extension of Flask, which does most of the work for us and gives us the option to customize the logic as needed. One very popular extension for creating admin interfaces in Flask is Flask-Admin (`https://pypi.python.org/pypi/Flask-Admin`), which is inspired by the Django admin but is implemented in a way that the developer has complete control over the look, feel, and functionality of the application. In this chapter, we will start with the creation of an admin interface on our own and then move onto using the Flask-Admin extension and fine-tuning it as needed.

Creating a simple CRUD interface

CRUD refers to **Create**, **Read**, **Update**, and **Delete**. A basic necessity of having an admin interface is to have the ability to create, modify, or delete the records/resources from the application as and when needed. We will create a simple admin interface that will allow the admin users to perform these operations on the records that other normal users generally can't.

Getting ready

We will start with our authentication application from the *Authenticating using the Flask-Login extension* recipe in *Chapter 6, Authenticating in Flask*, and add admin authentication and an interface for admins to the same, to allow only the admin users to create, update, and delete user records. Here, in this recipe, I will cover some specific parts that are needed to understand the concepts. For the complete application, refer to the code samples available with the book.

How to do it...

We will start with our models by adding a new field called `admin` to the `User` model in `models.py`. This field will help in identifying whether the user is an admin or not:

```
from wtforms import BooleanField

class User(db.Model):
    id = db.Column(db.Integer, primary_key=True)
    username = db.Column(db.String(60))
    pwdhash = db.Column(db.String())
    admin = db.Column(db.Boolean())

    def __init__(self, username, password, admin=False):
        self.username = username
        self.pwdhash = generate_password_hash(password)
```

```
        self.admin = admin

    def is_admin(self):
        return self.admin
```

The preceding method simply returns the value of the admin field. This can have a custom implementation as per your needs. Consider the following code:

```
class AdminUserCreateForm(Form):
    username = TextField('Username', [InputRequired()])
    password = PasswordField('Password', [InputRequired()])
    admin = BooleanField('Is Admin ?')


class AdminUserUpdateForm(Form):
    username = TextField('Username', [InputRequired()])
    admin = BooleanField('Is Admin ?')
```

Also, we created two forms that will be used by our admin views.

Now, we will modify our views in views.py to implement the admin interface:

```
from functools import wraps
from my_app.auth.models import AdminUserCreateForm,
AdminUserUpdateForm

def admin_login_required(func):
    @wraps(func)
    def decorated_view(*args, **kwargs):
        if not current_user.is_admin():
            return abort(403)
        return func(*args, **kwargs)
    return decorated_view
```

The preceding code is the admin_login_required decorator that works just like the login_required decorator. The difference is that it needs to be implemented along with login_required, and it checks if the currently logged-in user is an admin.

The following are all the handlers that we will need to create a simple admin interface. Note the usage of the @admin_login_required decorator. Everything else is pretty much standard as we learned in the previous chapters of this book, which focused on views and authentication handling:

```
@auth.route('/admin')
@login_required
@admin_login_required
```

```python
def home_admin():
    return render_template('admin-home.html')


@auth.route('/admin/users-list')
@login_required
@admin_login_required
def users_list_admin():
    users = User.query.all()
    return render_template('users-list-admin.html', users=users)


@auth.route('/admin/create-user', methods=['GET', 'POST'])
@login_required
@admin_login_required
def user_create_admin():
    form = AdminUserCreateForm(request.form)

    if form.validate():
        username = form.username.data
        password = form.password.data
        admin = form.admin.data
        existing_username = User.query.filter_by
          (username=username).first()
        if existing_username:
            flash(
                'This username has been already taken. Try another
one.',
                'warning'
            )
            return render_template('register.html', form=form)
        user = User(username, password, admin)
        db.session.add(user)
        db.session.commit()
        flash('New User Created.', 'info')
        return redirect(url_for('auth.users_list_admin'))

    if form.errors:
        flash(form.errors, 'danger')

    return render_template('user-create-admin.html', form=form)
```

The preceding method allows admin users to create new users in the system. This works in a manner pretty similar to the `register()` method but allows the admins to set the `admin` flag on the users. Consider the following code:

```
@auth.route('/admin/update-user/<id>', methods=['GET', 'POST'])
@login_required
@admin_login_required
def user_update_admin(id):
    user = User.query.get(id)
    form = AdminUserUpdateForm(
        request.form,
        username=user.username,
        admin=user.admin
    )

    if form.validate():
        username = form.username.data
        admin = form.admin.data

        User.query.filter_by(id=id).update({
            'username': username,
            'admin': admin,
        })

        db.session.commit()
        flash('User Updated.', 'info')
        return redirect(url_for('auth.users_list_admin'))

    if form.errors:
        flash(form.errors, 'danger')

    return render_template('user-update-admin.html', form=form,
        user=user)
```

The preceding method allows the admin users to update the records of other users. However, as per the best practices of writing web applications, we do not allow the admins to simply view and change the passwords of any user. In most cases, the provision to change passwords should rest with the user who owns the account. Admins, though, can have the provision to update the password in some cases, but still, it should never be possible for them to see the passwords set by the user earlier. This is the topic for discussion in the *Creating custom forms and actions* recipe. Consider the following code:

```
@auth.route('/admin/delete-user/<id>')
@login_required
@admin_login_required
```

```
def user_delete_admin(id):
    user = User.query.get(id)
    user.delete()

    db.session.commit()
    flash('User Deleted.')
    return redirect(url_for('auth.users_list_admin'))
```

The `user_delete_admin()` method should actually be implemented on a POST request. This is left to the readers to implement by themselves.

Followed by models and views, we will create some templates to complement them. It might have been evident to many of us from the code of the views itself that we need to add four new templates, namely, `admin-home.html`, `user-create-admin.html`, `user-update-admin.html`, and `users-list-admin.html`. How these work is shown in the next section. Readers should now be able to implement these templates by themselves, but for reference, the code is always available with the samples provided with the book.

How it works...

To start with, we added a menu item to the application; this provides a direct link to the admin home page, which will look like the following screenshot:

The menu item named Admin

A user must be logged in as admin to access this page and other admin-related pages. If a user is not logged in as admin, then the application will show an error, as shown in the following screenshot:

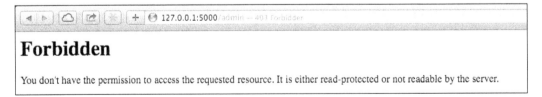

To a logged-in admin user, the admin home page will look as follows:

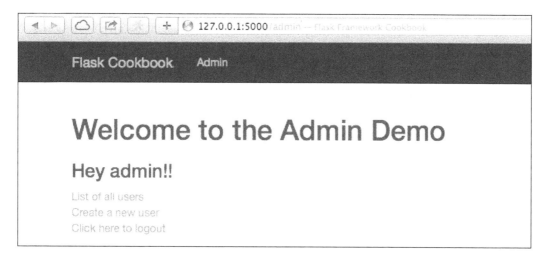

From here, the admin can see the list of users on a system or create a new user. The options to edit or delete the users will be available in the user list page itself.

 To set a user as the first admin, create a new user from the terminal using SQLAlchemy with the admin flag set to `True`.

Using the Flask-Admin extension

Flask-Admin is an available extension that helps in the creation of admin interfaces for our application in a simpler and faster way. All the subsequent recipes in this chapter will focus on using and extending this extension.

Getting ready

First, we need to install the Flask-Admin extension:

```
$ pip install Flask-Admin
```

We will extend our application from the first recipe and keep building over the same.

How to do it...

Adding a simple admin interface to any Flask application using the Flask-Admin extension is just a matter of a couple of statements.

We just need to add the following lines to our application's configuration:

```
from flask.ext.admin import Admin

app = Flask(__name__)

# Add any other application configuration

admin = Admin(app)
```

Just initializing an application with the `Admin` class from the Flask-Admin extension will put up a basic admin page, as shown in the following screenshot:

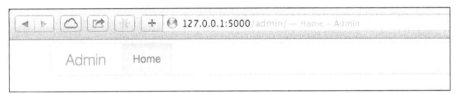

The admin page as created by Flask-Admin

Notice the URL in the screenshot, which is `http://127.0.0.1:5000/admin/`. We can also add our own views to it; this is as simple as adding a new class as a new view that inherits from the `BaseView` class:

```
from flask.ext.admin import BaseView, expose

class HelloView(BaseView):
    @expose('/')
    def index(self):
        return self.render('some-template.html')
```

After this, we will need to add this view to our `admin` object in the Flask configuration:

```
import my_app.auth.views as views

admin.add_view(views.HelloView(name='Hello'))
```

This will make the admin page look like the following screenshot:

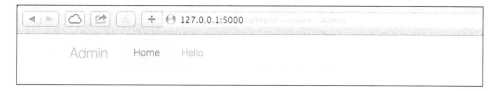

One thing to notice here is that this page does not have any authentication or authorization logic implemented by default, and it will be accessible to all. The reason for this is that Flask-Admin does not make any assumptions about the authentication system in place. As we are using Flask-Login for our applications, we can add a method named `is_accessible()` to our `HelloView` class:

```
def is_accessible(self):
    return current_user.is_authenticated() and
      current_user.is_admin()
```

There's more...

After implementing the preceding code, there is still an admin view that won't be completely user protected and will be publicly available. This will be the admin home page. To make this available only to the admins, we have to inherit from `AdminIndexView` and implement `is_accessible()`:

```
from flask.ext.admin import AdminIndexView

class MyAdminIndexView(AdminIndexView):
    def is_accessible(self):
        return current_user.is_authenticated() and
          current_user.is_admin()
```

Then, just pass this view to the `admin` object in the application's configuration as `index_view`, and we are done:

```
admin = Admin(app, index_view=views.MyAdminIndexView())
```

This approach makes all our admin views accessible only to the admin users. We can also implement any permission or conditional access rules in `is_accessible()` as and when required.

Registering models with Flask-Admin

In the last recipe, we saw how to get started with the Flask-Admin extension to create admin interfaces/views to our application. In this recipe, we will see how to implement admin views for our existing models with the facilities to perform CRUD operations.

Getting ready

We will extend our application from the last recipe to include an admin interface for the `User` model.

How to do it...

Again, with Flask-Admin, registering a model with the admin interface is very easy. We just need to add a single line of code to get this:

```
from flask.ext.admin.contrib.sqla import ModelView

# Other admin configuration as shown in last recipe
admin.add_view(ModelView(views.User, db.session))
```

Here, in the first line, we imported `ModelView` from `flask.ext.admin.contrib.sqla`, which is provided by Flask-Admin to integrate SQLAlchemy models. This will create a new admin view for the `User` model; the view will look like the following screenshot:

Looking at the preceding screenshot, most of us will agree that showing the password hash to any user, be it admin or a normal user, does not make sense. Also, the default model-creation mechanism provided by Flask-Admin will fail for our `User` creation, because we have an `__init__()` method in our `User` model; this method expects values for the three fields, while the model-creation logic implemented in Flask-Admin is very generic and does not provide any value during model creation.

Now, we will customize the default behavior of Flask-Admin to something of our own where we fix the `User` creation mechanism and hide the password hash from the views:

```
class UserAdminView(ModelView):
    column_searchable_list = ('username',)
    column_sortable_list = ('username', 'admin')
    column_exclude_list = ('pwdhash',)
    form_excluded_columns = ('pwdhash',)
    form_edit_rules = ('username', 'admin')

    def is_accessible(self):
        return current_user.is_authenticated() and
          current_user.is_admin()
```

The preceding code shows some rules and settings that our admin view for `User` will follow. These are self-explanatory. A couple of them, `column_exclude_list` and `form_excluded_columns`, might seem a bit confusing. The former will exclude the columns mentioned from the admin view itself and refrain from using these columns in search, creation, and other CRUD operations. The latter will prevent the fields mentioned from being shown on the form for CRUD operations. Consider the following code:

```
def scaffold_form(self):
    form_class = super(UserAdminView, self).scaffold_form()
    form_class.password = PasswordField('Password')
    return form_class
```

The preceding method overrides the creation of the form from the model and adds a password field, which will be used in place of the password hash. Consider the following application:

```
def create_model(self, form):
    model = self.model(
        form.username.data, form.password.data,
          form.admin.data
    )
    form.populate_obj(model)
    self.session.add(model)
    self._on_model_change(form, model, True)
    self.session.commit()
```

The preceding method overrides the model-creation logic to suit our application.

To add this model to the `admin` object in the application config, we will write the following:

```
admin.add_view(views.UserAdminView(views.User, db.session))
```

Notice the `self._on_model_change(form, model, True)` statement. Here, `True`, the last parameter, signifies that the call is for the creation of a new record.

The admin interface for the `User` model will now look like the following screenshot:

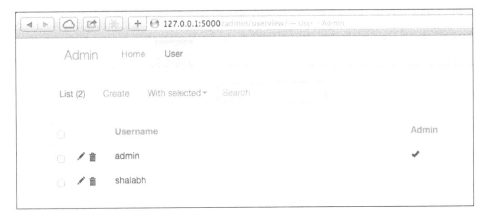

We have a search box here, and no password hash is visible. There are changes to user creation and edit views too. I urge you to run the application to see for yourselves.

Creating custom forms and actions

In this recipe, we will create some custom forms using the forms provided by Flask-Admin. Also, we will create a custom action using the custom form.

Getting ready

In the last recipe, we saw that the edit form view for the `User` record update had no option to update the password for the user. The form looked like the following screenshot:

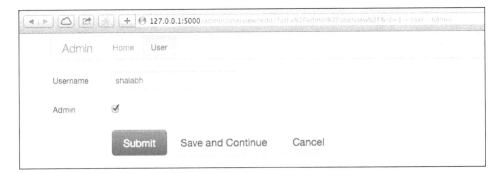

In this recipe, we will customize this form to allow administrators to update the password for any user.

How to do it...

The implementation of this feature will just require changes to `views.py`. First, we will start by importing `rules` from the Flask-Admin forms:

```
from flask.ext.admin.form import rules
```

In the last recipe, we had `form_edit_rules`, which had just two fields, that is, `username` and `admin` as a list. This denoted the fields that will be available for editing to the admin user on the `User` model update view.

Updating the password is not a simple affair of just adding one more field to the list of `form_edit_rules`, because we do not store cleartext passwords. We store password hashes instead, which cannot be edited directly by users. We need to input the password from the user and then convert it to a hash while storing. We will see how to do this in the following code:

```
form_edit_rules = (
    'username', 'admin',
    rules.Header('Reset Password'),
    'new_password', 'confirm'
)
form_create_rules = (
    'username', 'admin', 'notes', 'password'
)
```

The preceding piece of code signifies that we now have a header in our form; this header separates the password reset section from the rest of the section. Then, we will add two new fields, `new_password` and `confirm`, which will help us safely change the password:

```
def scaffold_form(self):
    form_class = super(UserAdminView, self).scaffold_form()
    form_class.password = PasswordField('Password')
    form_class.new_password = PasswordField('New Password')
    form_class.confirm = PasswordField('Confirm New Password')
    return form_class
```

This also calls for a change to the `scaffold_form()` method so that the two new fields become valid when the form renders.

Finally, we will implement the `update_model()` method, which is called when we try to update the record:

```
def update_model(self, form, model):
    form.populate_obj(model)
    if form.new_password.data:
        if form.new_password.data != form.confirm.data:
            flash('Passwords must match')
            return
        model.pwdhash = generate_password_hash
            (form.new_password.data)
    self.session.add(model)
    self._on_model_change(form, model, False)
    self.session.commit()
```

In the preceding code, we will first make sure that the password entered in both the fields is the same. If yes, we will proceed with resetting the password along with any other change.

Notice the `self._on_model_change(form, model, False)` statement. Here, `False`, as the last parameter, signifies that the call is not for the creation of a new record. This is also used in the last recipe, where we created the user. In that case, the last parameter was set to `True`.

How it works...

The user update form will now look like the following screenshot:

Here, if we enter the same password in both the password fields, the user password will be updated.

WYSIWYG for textarea integration

As users of websites, we all know that writing beautiful and formatted text using the normal textarea fields is a nightmare. There are plugins that make our life easier and turn simple textareas into **What you see is what you get** (**WYSIWYG**) editors. One such editor is **CKEditor**. It is open source, provides good flexibility, and has huge community support. Also, it is customizable and allows users to build add-ons as needed.

Getting ready

We start by adding a new textarea field to our `User` model for notes and then integrating this field with CKEditor to write formatted text. This will include the addition of a JavaScript library and a CSS class to a normal textarea field to convert it into a CKEditor-compatible textarea field.

How to do it...

First, we will add the `notes` field to the `User` model, which will then look as follows:

```
class User(db.Model):
    id = db.Column(db.Integer, primary_key=True)
    username = db.Column(db.String(60))
    pwdhash = db.Column(db.String())
    admin = db.Column(db.Boolean())
    notes = db.Column(db.UnicodeText)

    def __init__(self, username, password, admin=False, notes=''):
        self.username = username
        self.pwdhash = generate_password_hash(password)
        self.admin = admin
        self.notes = notes
```

After this, we will create a custom `wtform` widget and field for a CKEditor textarea field:

```
from wtforms import widgets, TextAreaField

class CKTextAreaWidget(widgets.TextArea):
    def __call__(self, field, **kwargs):
        kwargs.setdefault('class_', 'ckeditor')
        return super(CKTextAreaWidget, self).__call__(field,
          **kwargs)
```

In the custom widget in the preceding code, we added a `ckeditor` class to our `TextArea` widget. For more insights into the WTForm widgets, refer to the *Creating a custom widget* recipe in *Chapter 5, Webforms with WTForms*. Consider the following code:

```
class CKTextAreaField(TextAreaField):
    widget = CKTextAreaWidget()
```

In the custom field in the preceding code, we set the widget to `CKTextAreaWidget`, and when this field is rendered, the CSS class `ckeditor` will be added to it.

Next, we need to modify our form rules in the `UserAdminView` class, where we specify the template to be used for the create and edit forms. We will also override the normal `TextAreaField` with `CKTextAreaField` for `notes`:

```
form_overrides = dict(notes=CKTextAreaField)

create_template = 'edit.html'
edit_template = 'edit.html'
```

In the preceding code block, `form_overrides` enables the overriding of a normal textarea field with the CKEditor textarea field.

The last part in this recipe is the `templates/edit.html` template mentioned earlier:

```
{% extends 'admin/model/edit.html' %}

{% block tail %}
    {{ super() }}
    <script src="http://cdnjs.cloudflare.com/ajax/
      libs/ckeditor/4.0.1/ckeditor.js"></script>
{% endblock %}
```

Here, we extended the default `edit.html` file provided by Flask-Admin and added the CKEditor JS file so that our `ckeditor` class on `CKTextAreaField` works.

How it works...

After we have done all the changes, the user create form will look like the following screenshot. Notice the **Notes** field in particular.

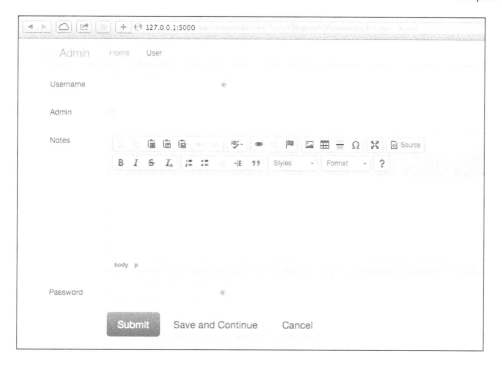

Here, anything entered in the **Notes** field will be automatically formatted in HTML while saving and can be used anywhere later for display purposes.

See also

▶ This recipe is inspired from the gist by the author of Flask-Admin. The gist can be found at `https://gist.github.com/mrjoes/5189850`.

Creating user roles

Until now, we saw how a view that is accessible to a certain set of admin users can be created easily using the `is_accessible()` method. This can be extended to have different kinds of scenarios where specific users will be able to view specific views. There is another way of implementing user roles at a much more granular level in a model where the roles determine whether a user can perform all, some, or any of the CRUD operations.

Getting ready

In this recipe, we will see a basic way of creating user roles, where an admin user can only perform actions they are entitled to.

 Remember that this is just one way of implementing user roles. There are many better ways of doing this, but this one seems to be the best one to demonstrate the concept of creating user roles.

One such method will be to create user groups and assign roles to the groups rather than individual users. Another method can be the complex policy-based user roles, which will include defining the roles according to complex business logic. This approach is usually employed by business systems such as ERP, CRM, and so on.

How to do it...

First, we will add a field named `roles` to the `User` model, which will then look as follows:

```
class User(db.Model):
    id = db.Column(db.Integer, primary_key=True)
    username = db.Column(db.String(60))
    pwdhash = db.Column(db.String())
    admin = db.Column(db.Boolean())
    notes = db.Column(db.UnicodeText)
    roles = db.Column(db.String(4))

    def __init__(self, username, password, admin=False, notes='',
      roles='R'):
        self.username = username
        self.pwdhash = generate_password_hash(password)
        self.admin = admin
        self.notes = notes
        self.roles = self.admin and self.roles or ''
```

Here, we added a new field, `roles`, which is a string field of length 4. We assumed that the only entries that are possible in this field are any combinations of C, R, U, and D. A user with the `roles` value as CRUD will have the permission to perform all the actions, while any missing permission will disallow the user from performing that action. Note that read permission is always implied to any admin user, whether specified or not.

Next, we need to make some changes to the `UserAdminView` class:

```
from flask.ext.admin.actions import ActionsMixin

class UserAdminView(ModelView, ActionsMixin):

    form_edit_rules = (
        'username', 'admin', 'roles', 'notes',
        rules.Header('Reset Password'),
        'new_password', 'confirm'
    )
    form_create_rules = (
        'username', 'admin', 'roles', 'notes', 'password'
    )
```

In the preceding code, we just added the `roles` field to our create and edit forms. We also inherited from a class called `ActionsMixin`. This is needed to handle the mass update actions such as mass deletion. Consider the following code:

```
def create_model(self, form):
    if 'C' not in current_user.roles:
        flash('You are not allowed to create users.',
            'warning')
        return
    model = self.model(
        form.username.data, form.password.data,
        form.admin.data,
        form.notes.data
    )
    form.populate_obj(model)
    self.session.add(model)
    self._on_model_change(form, model, True)
    self.session.commit()
```

In this method, we first checked if the `roles` field on `current_user` has the permission to create records (denoted by C). If not, we show an error message and return from the method. Consider the following code:

```
def update_model(self, form, model):
    if 'U' not in current_user.roles:
        flash('You are not allowed to edit users.', 'warning')
        return
    form.populate_obj(model)
    if form.new_password.data:
        if form.new_password.data != form.confirm.data:
            flash('Passwords must match')
```

```
        return
    model.pwdhash = generate_password_hash
        (form.new_password.data)
self.session.add(model)
self._on_model_change(form, model, False)
self.session.commit()
```

In this method, we first checked if the `roles` field on `current_user` has the permission to update records (denoted by `U`). If not, show an error message and return from the method. Consider the following code:

```
def delete_model(self, model):
    if 'D' not in current_user.roles:
        flash('You are not allowed to delete users.',
          'warning')
        return
    super(UserAdminView, self).delete_model(model)
```

Similarly, here we checked if `current_user` is allowed to delete records. Consider the following code:

```
def is_action_allowed(self, name):
    if name == 'delete' and 'D' not in current_user.roles:
        flash('You are not allowed to delete users.',
          'warning')
        return False
    return True
```

In the preceding method, we checked if the action is `delete` and if `current_user` is allowed to delete. If not, then flash the error message and return a `False` value. This method can be extended to handle any custom-written actions too.

How it works...

This recipe works in a manner very similar to how our application has been working until now, except the fact that now, users with designated roles will be able to perform specified operations. Otherwise, error messages will be displayed.

The user list will now look like the following screenshot:

To test the rest of the functionality, such as creating new users (both normal and admin), deleting users, updating user records, and so on, I urge you to try it for yourselves.

9
Internationalization and Localization

Web applications usually are not limited to one geographical region or to serving people from one linguistic domain. For example, a web application intended for users in Europe will be expected to support other European languages such as German, French, Italian, Spanish, and so on, apart from English. This chapter will cover the basics of how to enable support for multiple languages in a Flask application.

In this chapter, we will cover the following recipes:

- Adding a new language
- Lazy evaluation and the gettext/ngettext functions
- Global language-switching action

Introduction

Adding support for a second language in any web application is a tricky affair. It increases a bit of overhead every time some change is made to the application, and this increases with the number of languages. There can be a number of things that need to be taken care of, apart from just changing the text as per the language. Some of the major ones are currency, number, time and date formatting, and so on.

Flask-Babel, an extension that adds i18n and l10n support to any Flask application, provides some tools and techniques to make this process simpler and easy to implement.

 i18n stands for internationalization, and similarly, l10n stands for localization.

In this chapter, we will be using this extension extensively to understand the concepts mentioned.

Adding a new language

By default, English is the language for applications built in Flask (and almost all web frameworks). We will add a second language to our application and add some translations for the display strings used in the application. The language displayed to the user will vary depending on the current language set in the browser.

Getting ready

We will start with the installation of the Flask-Babel extension:

```
$ pip install Flask-Babel
```

This extension uses **Babel**, **pytz**, and **speaklater** to add i18n and l10n support to the application.

We will use our catalog application from *Chapter 5, Webforms with WTForms*.

How to do it...

First, we will start with the configuration part by creating an instance of the `Babel` class using the `app` object. We will also specify what languages will be available here. French is added as the second language:

```python
from flask.ext.babel import Babel

ALLOWED_LANGUAGES = {
    'en': 'English',
    'fr': 'French',
}
babel = Babel(app)
```

Here, we used en and fr as the language codes. These refer to English (standard) and French (standard), respectively. If we intend to support multiple languages that are from the same standard language origin but differ on the basis of regions such as English (US) and English (GB), then we should use codes such as en-us and en-gb.

Next, we will create a file in the application folder called babel.cfg. The path of this file will be flask_catalog/my_app/babel.cfg, and it will have the following content:

```
[python: catalog/**.py]
[jinja2: templates/**.html]
extensions=jinja2.ext.autoescape,jinja2.ext.with_
```

Here, the first two lines tell Babel about the file name patterns that are to be searched for marked translatable text. The third one loads some extensions that make this searching of text in the files possible.

The locale of the application depends on the output of the method that is decorated with the @babel.localeselector decorator. Add the following method to the views file, that is, views.py:

```
from my_app import babel, ALLOWED_LANGUAGES

@babel.localeselector
def get_locale():
    return request.accept_languages.best_match(ALLOWED_LANGUAGES.keys())
```

The preceding method gets the Accept-Languages header from the request and finds the language that best matches the languages we allow.

It is pretty easy to change the language preferences in the browser. However, in any case, if you do not want to mess with the language preferences of the browser, simply return the expected language code from the get_locale() method.

Next, we will mark some text that is intended to be translated as per language mentioned. Let's start with the first text we see when we start our application, that is, in home.html:

```
{% block container %}
<h1>{{ _('Welcome to the Catalog Home') }}</h1>
  <a href="{{ url_for('products') }}" id="catalog_link">
  {{ _('Click here to see the catalog ') }}
  </a>
{% endblock %}
```

Here, _ is a shortcut for the `gettext` function provided by Babel to translate strings.

After this, we need to run the following commands so that the marked text is actually available as translated text in our template when it is rendered in the browser:

```
$ pybabel extract -F my_app/babel.cfg -o my_app/messages.pot
my_app
```

The preceding command traverses through the contents of the files; this command matches the patterns in `babel.cfg` and picks out the texts that have been marked as translatable. All these texts are placed in the `my_app/messages.pot` file. Consider the following command:

```
$ pybabel init -i my_app/messages.pot -d my_app/translations -l fr
```

The preceding `init` command creates a `.po` file, which will hold the translations for the texts to be translated. This file is created in the specified folder, `my_app/translations` as `fr/LC_MESSAGES/messages.po`. As we add more languages, more folders will be added.

Now, we need to add translations to the `messages.po` file. This can be manually done, or we can use GUI tools such as Poedit (`http://poedit.net/`). Using this tool, the translations will look like the following screenshot:

Manual editing of `messages.po` will look like the following code. Only one message translation is shown for demonstration:

```
#: my_app/templates/home.html:6
msgid "Click here to see the catalog "
msgstr "Cliquez ici pour voir le catalogue "
```

Save the `messages.po` file after the translations have been put in and run the following command:

```
$ pybabel compile -d my_app/translations
```

This will create a `messages.mo` file next to the `message.po` file, which will be used by the application to render the translated text.

Sometimes, the messages do not get compiled after running the preceding command. This is because the messages might be marked as fuzzy (starting with a #). These need to be looked at by a human and the # sign has to be removed if the message is OK to be updated by the compiler. To bypass this check, add a `-f` flag to the preceding `compile` command as it will force everything to get compiled.

How it works...

If we run the application with French set as the primary language in the browser, the home page will look like the following screenshot:

If the primary language is set to something other than French, then the content will be shown in English, which is the default language.

My browser language settings currently look like the ones shown in the following screenshot:

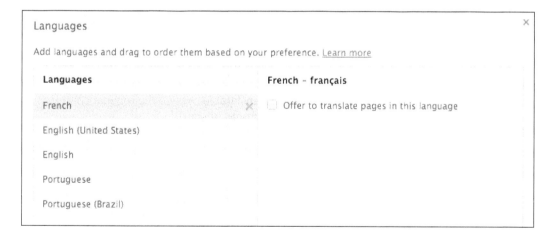

There's more...

Next time, if we need to update the translations in our `messages.po` file, we do not need to call the `init` command again. Instead, we can run an `update` command, which is as follows:

```
$ pybabel update -i my_app/messages.pot -d my_app/translations
```

After this, run the `compile` command as usual.

 It is often desired to change the language of a website based on the user IP and location (determined from the IP). This is regarded as an inferior way of handling localization as compared to the use of the Accept-Language header, as we did in our application.

See also

- The *Global language-switching action* recipe to allow the user to change the language directly from the application rather than doing it at the browser level.

- An important aspect of multiple languages is to be able to format the date, time, and currency accordingly. Babel handles this also pretty neatly. I urge you to try your hands at this by yourself. Refer to the Babel documentation available at `http://babel.pocoo.org/docs/` for this.

Lazy evaluation and the gettext/ngettext functions

Lazy evaluation is an evaluation strategy that delays the evaluation of an expression until its value is needed, that is, it is a call-by-need mechanism. In our application, there can be several instances of texts that are evaluated later while rendering the template. It usually happens when we have texts that are marked as translatable outside the request context, so we defer the evaluation of these until they are actually needed.

Getting ready

Let's start with the application from the previous recipe. Now, we want the labels in the product- and category-creation forms to show the translated values.

How to do it...

To mark all the field labels in the product and category forms as translatable, we will make the following changes to `models.py`:

```
from flask.ext.babel import _

class NameForm(Form):
    name = TextField(_('Name'), validators=[InputRequired()])

class ProductForm(NameForm):
    price = DecimalField(_('Price'), validators=[
        InputRequired(), NumberRange(min=Decimal('0.0'))
    ])
    category = CategoryField(
        _('Category'), validators=[InputRequired()], coerce=int
    )
    image = FileField(_('Product Image'))

class CategoryForm(NameForm):
    name = TextField(_('Name'), validators=[
        InputRequired(), check_duplicate_category()
    ])
```

Notice that all the field labels are enclosed within _() to be marked for translation.

Now, run the pybabel `extract` and `update` commands to update the `messages.po` file, and then fill in the relevant translations and run the `compile` command. Refer to the previous recipe, *Adding a new language*, for details.

Now, open the product-creation page using the link `http://127.0.0.1:5000/product-create`. However, does it work as expected? No! As most of us would have guessed by now, the reason for this behavior is that this text is marked for translation outside the request context.

To make this work, we just need to modify the `import` statement to the following:

```
from flask.ext.babel import lazy_gettext as _
```

Now, we have more text to translate. Let's say we want to translate the product-creation flash message content, which looks as follows:

```
flash('The product %s has been created' % name)
```

To mark it as translatable, we cannot just simply wrap the whole thing inside _() or gettext(). The gettext() function supports placeholders, which can be used as %(name)s. Using this, the preceding code will become something like:

```
flash(_('The product %(name)s has been created', name=name))
```

The resulting translated text for this will be like Le produit %(name)s a été créé.

There might be cases where we need to manage the translations based on the number of items, that is, singular or plural names. This is handled by the ngettext() method. Let's take an example where we want to show the number of pages in our products.html template. For this, we need to add the following:

```
{{ ngettext('%(num)d page', '%(num)d pages', products.pages) }}
```

Here, the template will render page if there is only page and pages if there is more than one page.

It is interesting to note how this translation looks in the messages.po file:

```
#: my_app/templates/products.html:20
#, python-format
msgid "%(num)d page"
msgid_plural "%(num)d pages"
msgstr[0] "%(num)d page"
msgstr[1] "%(num)d pages"
```

The preceding code makes the concept clear.

Global language-switching action

In the previous recipes, we saw that the languages change on the basis of the current language preferences in the browser. However, now, we want a mechanism where we can switch the language to be used irrespective of the language in the browser. For this, we need to handle the language at the application level.

Getting ready

We start by modifying the application from the last recipe, *Lazy evaluation and the gettext/ngettext functions*, to accommodate the changes to enable language switching. We will add an extra URL part to all our routes to add the current language. We can just change this language in the URL to switch between languages.

How to do it...

The first change that we need to do is modify all our URL rules to accommodate an extra URL part. So `@app.route('/')` will become `@app.route('/<lang>/')`, and `@app.route('/home')` will become `@app.route('/<lang>/home')`. Similarly, `@app.route('/product-search/<int:page>')` will become `@app.route('/<lang>/product-search/<int:page>')`. The same needs to be done for all the URL rules.

Now, we need to add a function that will add the language passed in the URL to the global proxy object g:

```
@app.before_request
def before():
    if request.view_args and 'lang' in request.view_args:
        g.current_lang = request.view_args['lang']
        request.view_args.pop('lang')
```

This method will run before each request and add the current language to g.

However, this will mean that all the `url_for()` calls in the application need to be modified to have an extra parameter called `lang` to be passed. Fortunately, there is an easy way out of this, which is as follows:

```
from flask import url_for as flask_url_for

@app.context_processor
def inject_url_for():
    return {
        'url_for': lambda endpoint, **kwargs: flask_url_for(
            endpoint, lang=g.current_lang, **kwargs
        )
    }

url_for = inject_url_for()['url_for']
```

In the preceding code, we first imported `url_for` from `flask` as `flask_url_for`. Then, we updated the application context processor to have the `url_for()` function, which is a modified version of `url_for()` provided by Flask to have `lang` as an extra parameter.

How it works...

Now, run the application as it is and you will notice that all the URLs will have a language part. The following two screenshots explain how the rendered templates will look.

On opening `http://127.0.0.1:5000/en/home`, we see the following:

The home page with English as the language

Now, just change the URL to `http://127.0.0.1:5000/fr/home`, and the home page will look like the following screenshot:

The home page with French as the language

See also

▶ The recipe, *Adding a new language*, to handle localization based on the language set in the browser (which is, by default, picked up from the language set at the OS level)

10
Debugging, Error Handling, and Testing

Until now, in this book, we have concentrated on developing applications and adding features to them one at a time. It is very important to know how robust our application is and keep track of how the application has been working and performing. This, in turn, gives rise to the need of being informed when something goes wrong in the application. It is normal to miss out on certain edge cases while developing an application, and usually, even the test cases miss them out. It will be great to know these edge cases whenever they occur so that they can be handled accordingly.

Testing in itself is a very huge topic, and has several books attributed to it. Here, we will try to understand the basics of testing with Flask.

In this chapter, we will cover the following recipes:

- Setting up basic file logging
- Sending e-mails on the occurrence of errors
- Using Sentry to monitor exceptions
- Debugging with pdb
- Creating our first simple test
- Writing more tests for views and logic
- Nose library integration
- Using mocking to avoid real API access
- Determining test coverage
- Using profiling to find bottlenecks

Introduction

Effective logging and the ability to debug quickly are some of the deciding factors to choose a framework for application development. The better the logging and debugging support from the framework, the quicker the process of application development and the easier the maintenance in future. It helps developers quickly find out the issues in the application, and many times, logging points out the issues even before they are identified by the end users. Effective error handling plays an important role in end user satisfaction and eases the pain of debugging at the developers' end. Even if the code is perfect, the application is bound to throw errors at times. Why? The answer is simple: the code might be perfect, but the world in which it works is not. There can be innumerable issues that can occur, and as developers, we always want to know the reason behind any anomaly. Writing test cases along with the application is one of the most important pillars of software writing.

Python's inbuilt logging system works pretty well with Flask. We will work with this logging system in this chapter before moving on to an awesome service called **Sentry**, which eases the pain of debugging and error logging to a huge extent.

As we have already talked about the importance of testing for application development, we will now see how to write test cases for a Flask application. We will also see how we can measure code coverage and profile our application to tackle any bottlenecks.

Setting up basic file logging

By default, Flask will not log anything for us anywhere, except for the errors with their stack traces, which are sent to the logger (we will see more of this in the remaining part of the chapter). This creates a lot of stack traces when we run the application in the development mode using `run.py`, but in production systems, we don't have this luxury. Thankfully, the logging library provides a whole lot of log handlers, which can be used as per our requirements.

Getting ready

We will start with our catalog application and add some basic logging to it using `FileHandler`, which logs messages to a specified file on the filesystem. We will start with a basic log format and then see how to format the log messages to be more informative.

How to do it...

As always, the first change is made to the `__init__.py` file, which serves as the application's configuration file:

```
app.config['LOG_FILE'] = 'application.log'

if not app.debug:
```

```
import logging
from logging import FileHandler
file_handler = FileHandler(app.config['LOG_FILE'])
file_handler.setLevel(logging.INFO)
app.logger.addHandler(file_handler)
```

Here, we added a configuration parameter to specify the logfile's location. This takes the relative path from the application folder, unless an absolute path is explicitly specified. Next, we will check whether the application is not already in the mode, and then, we will add a handler logging to a file with the logging level as INFO. DEBUG is the lowest logging level and will log everything at any level. For more details, refer to the logging library documentation (link available in the *See also* section).

After this, we just need to add loggers to our application wherever they are needed, and our application will start logging to the deputed file. Let's add a couple of loggers for demonstration to views.py:

```
@catalog.route('/')
@catalog.route('/<lang>/')
@catalog.route('/<lang>/home')
@template_or_json('home.html')
def home():
    products = Product.query.all()
    app.logger.info(
        'Home page with total of %d products' % len(products)
    )
    return {'count': len(products)}


@catalog.route('/<lang>/product/<id>')
def product(id):
    product = Product.query.filter_by(id=id).first()
    if not product:
        app.logger.warning('Requested product not found.')
        abort(404)
    return render_template('product.html', product=product)
```

In the preceding code, we have loggers to a couple of our view handlers. Notice that the first of the loggers in home() is of the info level and the other in product() is warning. If we set our log level in __init__.py as INFO, then both will be logged, and if we set the level as WARNING, then only the warning logger will be logged.

How it works...

The preceding piece of code will create a file called `application.log` at the root application folder. The logger statements as specified will be logged to this file and will look something like the following snippet, depending on the handler called; the first one being from `home` and the second from requesting a product that does not exist:

```
Home page with total of 1 products
Requested product not found.
```

There's more...

The information logged does not help much. It will be great to know when the issue was logged, with what level, which file caused the issue at what line number, and so on. This can be achieved using advanced logging formats. For this, we need to add a couple of statements to the configuration file, that is, `__init__.py`:

```python
if not app.debug:
    import logging
    from logging import FileHandler, Formatter
    file_handler = FileHandler(app.config['LOG_FILE'])
    file_handler.setLevel(logging.WARNING)
    app.logger.addHandler(file_handler)
    file_handler.setFormatter(Formatter(
        '%(asctime)s %(levelname)s: %(message)s '
        '[in %(pathname)s:%(lineno)d]'
    ))
```

In the preceding code, we added a formatter to `file_handler`, which will log the time, log level, message, file path, and line number. After this, the logged message will look as follows:

```
2014-08-02 15:18:21,154 WARNING: Requested product not found. [in /Users/
shalabhaggarwal/workspace/mydev/flask_catalog_testing_lgging/my_app/
catalog/views.py:50]
```

See also

► Read through Python's logging library documentation about handlers at `https://docs.python.org/dev/library/logging.handlers.html` to know more about logging handlers

Sending e-mails on the occurrence of errors

It is a good idea to receive errors when something unexpected happens with the application. Setting this up is pretty easy and adds a lot of convenience to the process of error handling.

Getting ready

We will take the application from the last recipe and add `mail_handler` to it to make our application send e-mails when an error occurs. Also, we will demonstrate how to set up these e-mails using Gmail as the SMTP server.

How to do it...

We will first add the handler to our configuration in `__init__.py`. This is similar to how we added `file_handler` in the last recipe:

```
RECEPIENTS = ['some_receiver@gmail.com']

if not app.debug:
    import logging
    from logging import FileHandler, Formatter
    from logging.handlers import SMTPHandler
    file_handler = FileHandler(app.config['LOG_FILE'])
    file_handler.setLevel(logging.INFO)
    app.logger.addHandler(file_handler)
    mail_handler = SMTPHandler(
        ("smtp.gmail.com", 587), 'sender@gmail.com', RECEPIENTS,
        'Error occurred in your application',
        ('sender@gmail.com', 'some_gmail_password'), secure=())
    mail_handler.setLevel(logging.ERROR)
    app.logger.addHandler(mail_handler)
    for handler in [file_handler, mail_handler]:
        handler.setFormatter(Formatter(
            '%(asctime)s %(levelname)s: %(message)s '
            '[in %(pathname)s:%(lineno)d]'
        ))
```

Here, we have a list of e-mail addresses to which the error notification e-mail will be sent. Also note that we have set the log level to ERROR in the case of `mail_handler`. This is because e-mails will be necessary only in the case of crucial and important matters.

For more details on the configuration of `SMTPHandler`, refer to the documentation.

Always make sure that you turn the `debug` flag off in `run.py` to enable the application to log and send e-mails for internal application errors (error 500).

How it works...

To cause an internal application error, just misspell a keyword in any of your handlers. You will receive an e-mail in your mailbox, with the formatting as set in the configuration and a complete stack trace for your reference.

There's more...

We might also want to log all the errors when a page is not found (error 404). For this, we can just tweak the `errorhandler` method a bit:

```
@app.errorhandler(404)
def page_not_found(e):
    app.logger.error(e)
    return render_template('404.html'), 404
```

Using Sentry to monitor exceptions

Sentry is a tool that eases the process of monitoring exceptions and also provides insights into the errors that the users of the application face while using it. It is highly possible that there are errors in logfiles that get missed out by the human eye. Sentry categorizes the errors under different categories and keeps a count of the recurrence of errors. This helps in understanding the severity of the errors on multiple criteria and helps us to handle them accordingly. It has a nice GUI that facilitates all of these features.

Getting ready

We will start with the Sentry installation and configuration procedure. There are multiple ways of installing and configuring Sentry as per our needs. Sentry also provides a SaaS-based hosted solution where you can just skip the installation part discussed ahead and move on directly to integration. You can get Sentry from `https://www.getsentry.com`.

Here, we will discuss a very basic version of the Sentry installation and configuration procedure, and the rest can be taken up by you when your level of familiarity with Sentry increases. We will use PostgreSQL as the database for Sentry, as it is highly recommended by the Sentry team itself, so we will run the following command:

```
$ pip install sentry[postgres]
```

Sentry is a server application that will need a client library to access it. The recommended client is **Raven**, which can be simply installed for a Flask-based setup by running the following command:

```
$ pip install raven[flask]
```

There is another library named **blinker** that is also needed. It is used to handle signals from the Flask application (this is out of the scope of this book, but you can read more about it at https://pypi.python.org/pypi/blinker). It can be installed using the following command:

```
$ pip install blinker
```

How to do it...

Following the installations, we need to do some configurations for the Sentry server. First, initialize the config file in a path of your choice. I prefer to initialize it inside a folder named etc in the current virtualenv. This can be done using the following command:

```
$ sentry init etc/sentry.conf.py
```

Then, the basic configuration will look something like the following code:

```
from sentry.conf.server import *

DATABASES = {
    'default': {
        'ENGINE': 'django.db.backends.postgresql_psycopg2',
        'NAME': 'sentry', # Name of the postgres database
        'USER': 'postgres', # Name of postgres user
        'PASSWORD': '',
        'HOST': '',
        'PORT': '',
        'OPTIONS': {
            'autocommit': True,
        }
    }
}
SENTRY_URL_PREFIX = 'http://localhost:9000'

SENTRY_WEB_HOST = '0.0.0.0'
SENTRY_WEB_PORT = 9000
SENTRY_WEB_OPTIONS = {
    'workers': 3,   # the number of gunicorn workers
    'limit_request_line': 0,   # required for raven-js
    'secure_scheme_headers': {'X-FORWARDED-PROTO': 'https'},
}
```

We can also configure the mail server details so that Sentry can send e-mails when errors are encountered and effectively take the overhead from the logging library, as we did in the last recipe. More about this can be read at `http://sentry.readthedocs.org/en/latest/quickstart/index.html#configure-outbound-mail`.

Now, in `postgres`, we need to create the database that we used in our Sentry configuration and upgrade the initial schema:

```
$ createdb -E utf-8 sentry
$ sentry --config=etc/sentry.conf.py upgrade
```

The upgrade process will create a default superuser. If it does not, do so yourself by running the following commands:

```
$ sentry --config=etc/sentry.conf.py createsuperuser
Username: sentry
Email address: someuser@example.com
Password:
Password (again):
Superuser created successfully.
$ sentry --config=etc/sentry.conf.py repair –owner=sentry
```

In the last command, `sentry` is the username that was chosen while creating the superuser.

Now, just start the Sentry server by running the following command:

```
$ sentry --config=etc/sentry.conf.py start
```

By default, Sentry runs on port 9000 and can be accessed at `http://localhost:9000/`.

Next, we need to create a team in Sentry using the GUI and then create a project to record our application's error logs. After you log in to Sentry using the superuser credentials, you will see a button, as shown in the following screenshot:

Create a team and project as the forms ask for. The project form will look like the following screenshot:

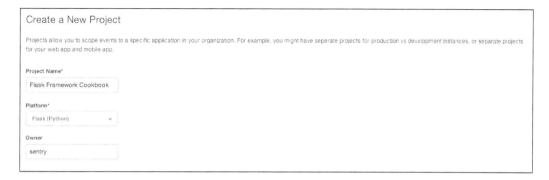

After this, a screen like the one in the following screenshot will be shown. The details here will be used in our Flask application's configuration.

Now, simply copy the details highlighted in the preceding screenshot and place them in the Flask configuration file. This will enable the logging of any uncaught errors to Sentry.

How it works...

An error logged in Sentry will look like the following screenshot:

It is also possible to log messages and user-defined exceptions in Sentry. I leave this to you to figure out by yourself.

Debugging with pdb

Most of the Python developers reading this book might already be aware of the usage of **pdb**, that is, the Python debugger. For those who are not aware of it, pdb is an interactive source code debugger for Python programs. We can set breakpoints wherever needed, debug using single-stepping at the source line level, and inspect the stack frames.

Many new developers might be of the opinion that the job of a debugger can be handled using a logger, but debuggers provide a much deeper insight into the flow of control and preserve the state at each step, and hence, save a lot of development time.

Getting ready

We will use Python's built-in pdb module for this recipe and use it in our application from the last recipe.

How to do it...

Using pdb is pretty simple in most cases. We just need to insert the following statement wherever we want to insert a breakpoint to inspect a certain block of code:

```
import pdb; pdb.set_trace()
```

This will trigger the application to break execution at this point, and then, we can step through the stack frames one by one using the debugger commands.

So, let's insert this statement in one of our methods, say, the handler for products:

```
def products(page=1):
    products = Product.query.paginate(page, 10)
    import pdb; pdb.set_trace()
    return render_template('products.html', products=products)
```

Whenever the control comes to this line, the debugger prompt will fire up; this will look as follows:

```
-> return render_template('products.html', products=product)
(Pdb) u
> /Users/shalabhaggarwal/workspace/flask_heroku/lib/python2.7/site-
packages/Flask-0.10.1-py2.7.egg/flask/app.py(1461)dispatch_request()
-> return self.view_functions[rule.endpoint](**req.view_args)
(Pdb) u
> /Users/shalabhaggarwal/workspace/flask_heroku/lib/python2.7/site-
packages/Flask-0.10.1-py2.7.egg/flask/app.py(1475)full_dispatch_request()
-> rv = self.dispatch_request()
(Pdb) u
> /Users/shalabhaggarwal/workspace/flask_heroku/lib/python2.7/site-
packages/Flask-0.10.1-py2.7.egg/flask/app.py(1817)wsgi_app()
-> response = self.full_dispatch_request()
```

Notice the u written against (Pdb). This signifies that I am moving the current frame one level up in the stack trace. All the variables, parameters, and properties used in that statement will be available in the same context to help figure out the issue or just understand the flow of code.

See also

- ▸ Check out the pdb module documentation at https://docs.python.org/2/library/pdb.html#debugger-commands to get hold of the various debugger commands

Creating our first simple test

Testing is one of the pillars of any software during development, and later during maintenance and expansion too. Especially in the case of web applications where the application will handle high traffic and be scrutinized by a large number of end users at all times, testing becomes pretty important, as the user feedback determines the fate of the application. In this recipe, we will see how to start with test writing and also see more complex tests in the recipes to follow.

Getting ready

We will start with the creation of a new test file named `app_tests.py` at the root application level, that is, alongside the `my_app` folder.

The `unittest2` Python library also needs to be installed using the following command:

```
$ pip install unittest2
```

How to do it...

To start with, the contents of the `app_tests.py` test file will be as follows:

```python
import os
from my_app import app, db
import unittest2 as unittest
import tempfile
```

The preceding code describes the imports needed for this test suite. We will use `unittest2` for our testing (install it using `pip` if not installed already). A `tempfile` is needed to create SQLite databases on the fly.

All the test cases need to subclass from `unitest.TestCase`:

```python
class CatalogTestCase(unittest.TestCase):

    def setUp(self):
        self.test_db_file = tempfile.mkstemp()[1]
        app.config['SQLALCHEMY_DATABASE_URI'] = 'sqlite:///' +
            self.test_db_file
        app.config['TESTING'] = True
        self.app = app.test_client()
        db.create_all()
```

The preceding method is run before each test is run and creates a new test client. A test is represented by the methods in this class that start with the `test_` prefix. Here, we set a database name in the app configuration, which is a timestamp that will always be unique. We also set the `TESTING` flag to `True`, which disables error catching to enable better testing. Finally, we ran the `create_all()` method on `db` to create all the tables from our application in the test database created. Consider the following code:

```python
    def tearDown(self):
        os.remove(self.test_db_file)
```

The preceding method is called after each test is run. Here, we will remove the current database file and use a fresh database file for each test. Consider the following code:

```
def test_home(self):
    rv = self.app.get('/')
    self.assertEqual(rv.status_code, 200)
```

The preceding code is our first test where we sent an HTTP GET request to our application at the / URL and tested the response for the status code, which should be 200; this represents a successful GET response.

```
if __name__ == '__main__':
    unittest.main()
```

How it works...

To run the test file, just execute the following command in the terminal:

$ python app_tests.py

The following screenshot shows the output that signifies the outcome of the tests:

See also

▶ Check out the next recipe, *Writing more tests for views and logic*, to see more on how to write complex tests

Writing more tests for views and logic

In the last recipe, we got started with writing tests for our Flask application. In this recipe, we will build upon the same test file and add more tests for our application; these tests will cover testing the views for behavior and logic.

Getting ready

We will build upon the test file named app_tests.py created in the last recipe.

How to do it...

Before we write any tests, we need to add a small bit of configuration to setUp() to disable the CSRF tokens, as they are not generated by default for test environments:

```
app.config['WTF_CSRF_ENABLED'] = False
```

The following are some tests that are created as a part of this recipe. Each test will be described as we go further:

```
def test_products(self):
    "Test Products list page"
    rv = self.app.get('/en/products')
    self.assertEqual(rv.status_code, 200)
    self.assertTrue('No Previous Page' in rv.data)
    self.assertTrue('No Next Page' in rv.data)
```

The preceding test sends a GET request to /products and asserts that the status code of the response is 200. It also asserts that there is no previous page and no next page (rendered as a part of template logic). Consider the following code:

```
def test_create_category(self):
    "Test creation of new category"
    rv = self.app.get('/en/category-create')
    self.assertEqual(rv.status_code, 200)

    rv = self.app.post('/en/category-create')
    self.assertEqual(rv.status_code, 200)
    self.assertTrue('This field is required.' in rv.data)

    rv = self.app.get('/en/categories')
    self.assertEqual(rv.status_code, 404)
    self.assertFalse('Phones' in rv.data)

    rv = self.app.post('/en/category-create', data={
        'name': 'Phones',
    })
    self.assertEqual(rv.status_code, 302)

    rv = self.app.get('/en/categories')
    self.assertEqual(rv.status_code, 200)
    self.assertTrue('Phones' in rv.data)

    rv = self.app.get('/en/category/1')
    self.assertEqual(rv.status_code, 200)
    self.assertTrue('Phones' in rv.data)
```

The preceding test creates a category and asserts for corresponding status messages. When a category is successfully created, we will redirect to the newly created category page, and hence, the status code will be 302. Consider the following code:

```
def test_create_product(self):
    "Test creation of new product"
    rv = self.app.get('/en/product-create')
    self.assertEqual(rv.status_code, 200)

    rv = self.app.post('/en/product-create')
    self.assertEqual(rv.status_code, 200)
    self.assertTrue('This field is required.' in rv.data)

    # Create a category to be used in product creation
    rv = self.app.post('/en/category-create', data={
        'name': 'Phones',
    })
    self.assertEqual(rv.status_code, 302)

    rv = self.app.post('/en/product-create', data={
        'name': 'iPhone 5',
        'price': 549.49,
        'company': 'Apple',
        'category': 1
    })
    self.assertEqual(rv.status_code, 302)

    rv = self.app.get('/en/products')
    self.assertEqual(rv.status_code, 200)
    self.assertTrue('iPhone 5' in rv.data)
```

The preceding test creates a product and asserts for corresponding status messages on each call.

As part of this test, we identified a small improvement in our `create_product()` method. What looked like `image = request.files['image']` earlier has now been replaced by `image = request.files` and `request.files['image']`. This is because in the case of an HTML form, we had an empty `request.files['image']` parameter, but in this case, we don't.

Consider the following code:

```
def test_search_product(self):
    "Test searching product"
    # Create a category to be used in product creation
    rv = self.app.post('/en/category-create', data={
        'name': 'Phones',
    })
    self.assertEqual(rv.status_code, 302)

    # Create a product
    rv = self.app.post('/en/product-create', data={
        'name': 'iPhone 5',
        'price': 549.49,
        'company': 'Apple',
        'category': 1
    })
    self.assertEqual(rv.status_code, 302)

    # Create another product
    rv = self.app.post('/en/product-create', data={
        'name': 'Galaxy S5',
        'price': 549.49,
        'company': 'Samsung',
        'category': 1
    })
    self.assertEqual(rv.status_code, 302)

    self.app.get('/')

    rv = self.app.get('/en/product-search?name=iPhone')
    self.assertEqual(rv.status_code, 200)
    self.assertTrue('iPhone 5' in rv.data)
    self.assertFalse('Galaxy S5' in rv.data)

    rv = self.app.get('/en/product-search?name=iPhone 6')
    self.assertEqual(rv.status_code, 200)
    self.assertFalse('iPhone 6' in rv.data)
```

The preceding test first creates a category and two products. Then, it searches for one product and makes sure that only the searched product is returned in the result.

How it works...

To run the test file, just execute the following command in the terminal:

```
$ python app_tests.py -v
test_create_category (__main__.CatalogTestCase)
Test creation of new category ... ok
test_create_product (__main__.CatalogTestCase)
Test creation of new product ... ok
test_home (__main__.CatalogTestCase)
Test home page ... ok
test_products (__main__.CatalogTestCase)
Test Products list page ... ok
test_search_product (__main__.CatalogTestCase)
Test searching product ... ok
----------------------------------------------------------------
Ran 5 tests in 0.189s

OK
```

What follows the command is the output that signifies the outcome of tests.

Nose library integration

Nose is a library that makes testing easier and much more fun. It provides a whole lot of tools to enhance our tests. Although Nose can be used for multiple purposes, the most important usage remains that of a test collector and runner. Nose automatically collects tests from Python source files, directories, and packages found in the current working directory. We will focus on how to run individual tests using Nose rather than the whole bunch of tests every time.

Getting ready

First, we need to install the Nose library:

```
$ pip install nose
```

How to do it...

We can execute all the tests in our application using Nose by running the following command:

```
$ nosetests -v
Test creation of new category ... ok
Test creation of new product ... ok
Test home page ... ok
Test Products list page ... ok
Test searching product ... ok
----------------------------------------------------------------
Ran 5 tests in 0.399s

OK
```

This will pick out all the tests in our application and run them even if we have multiple test files.

To run a single test file, we can simply run the following command:

```
$ nosetests app_tests.py
```

Now, if we want to run a single test, we simply need to run the following command:

```
$ nosetests app_tests:CatalogTestCase.test_home
```

This becomes important when we have a memory-intensive application and a large number of test cases. Then, the tests themselves can take a lot of time to run, and doing so every time can be very frustrating for a developer. Instead, we will prefer to run only those tests that concern the change made or the test that broke on a certain change.

See also

▶ There are many other ways of configuring Nose for optimal and effective usage as per our requirements. Refer to the Nose documentation at http://nose.readthedocs.org/en/latest/usage.html for more details.

Using mocking to avoid real API access

We are aware of how testing works, but now, let's say we have a third-party application/service integrated via API calls with our application. It will not be a great idea to make calls to this application/service every time tests are run. Sometimes, these can be paid too, and making calls during tests can not only be expensive, but also affect the statistics of that service. **Mocking** plays a very important role in such scenarios. The simplest example of this can be mocking SMTP for e-mails. In this recipe, we will integrate our application with the `geoip` library and then test it via mocking.

Getting ready

First, we need to install the `mock` and `geoip` libraries and the corresponding database:

```
$ pip install mock
$ pip install python-geoip
$ pip install python-geoip-geolite2
```

Now, let's say we want to store the location of the user who creates a product (think of a scenario where the application is administered via multiple locations around the globe).

We need to make some small changes to `models.py`, `views.py` and `templates/product.html`.

For `models.py`, we will add a new field named `user_timezone`:

```
class Product(db.Model):
    # .. Other fields ..
    user_timezone = db.Column(db.String(255))

    def __init__(self, name, price, category=None, image_path='',
            user_timezone=''):
        .. Other fields initialization ..
        self.user_timezone = user_timezone
```

For `views.py`, we will modify the `create_product()` method to include the timezone:

```
import geoip

def create_product():
    form = ProductForm(request.form)

    if request.method == 'POST' and form.validate():
        # .. Non changed code ..
        match = geoip.geolite2.lookup(request.remote_addr)
```

```
        product = Product(
            name, price, company, existing_category, filename,
            match and match.timezone or 'Localhost'
        )
        # .. Non changed code ..
```

Here, we fetched the geolocation data using an IP lookup and passed this during product creation. If no match is found, then the call is made from the localhost, or from 127.0.0.1 or 0.0.0.0.

Also, we will add this new field in our product template so that it becomes easy to verify in the test. For this, just add `{{ product.user_timezone }}` somewhere in the `product.html` template.

How to do it...

Modify `app_tests.py` to accommodate mocking of the `geoip` lookup:

```
from geoip import IPInfo
from mock import patch

class CatalogTestCase(unittest.TestCase):

    def setUp(self):
        # .. Non changed code ..
        self.lookup_patcher = patch('geoip.geolite2.lookup',
          autospec=True)
        PatchedLookup = self.lookup_patcher.start()
        PatchedLookup.return_value = IPInfo('17.0.0.1', {
            'location': {
                'time_zone': 'America/Los_Angeles'
            }
        })
        db.create_all()
```

First, we imported `IPInfo` from `geoip`, which is the class that defines the format in which the lookup data is to be created. Then, we patched `geoip.geolite2.lookup` and started the patcher. This means that whenever this call is made, it will be patched with `return_value`, which is set next. Consider the following code:

```
    def tearDown(self):
        self.lookup_patcher.stop()
        os.remove(self.test_db_file)
```

We stopped the mock patcher in `tearDown` so that the actual calls are not affected. Consider the following code:

```
def test_create_product(self):
    "Test creation of new product"
    # .. Non changed code ..

    rv = self.app.post('/en/product-create', data={
        'name': 'iPhone 5',
        'price': 549.49,
        'company': 'Apple',
        'category': 1
    })
    self.assertEqual(rv.status_code, 302)

    rv = self.app.get('/en/product/1')
    self.assertEqual(rv.status_code, 200)
    self.assertTrue('iPhone 5' in rv.data)
    self.assertTrue('America/Los_Angeles' in rv.data)
```

Here, after the creation of the product, we asserted that the `America/Los_Angeles` value is present somewhere in the product template that is rendered.

How it works...

Run the test and see whether it passes:

```
$ nosetests app_tests:CatalogTestCase.test_create_product -v
Test creation of new product ... ok


----------------------------------------------------

Ran 1 test in 0.095s


OK
```

See also

> ▶ There are multiple ways in which mocking can be done. I demonstrated just one of them. You can choose any method from the ones available.

Determining test coverage

In the previous recipes, test writing was covered, but there is an important aspect to testing called coverage. Coverage determines how much of our code has been covered by the tests. The higher the percentage of coverage, the better our tests (although it's not the only criterion for good tests). In this recipe, we will check the code coverage of our application.

Remember that 100 percent test coverage does not mean that the code is flawless. However, in any case, it is better than having no tests or lower coverage. Anything that is not tested is broken.

Getting ready

We will use a library called `coverage` for this recipe. The following is the installation command:

```
$ pip install coverage
```

How to do it...

The simplest way of getting the coverage details is to use the command line. Simply run the following command:

```
$ coverage run -source=../<Folder name of application> --omit=app_tests.
py,run.py app_tests.py
```

Here, `--source` indicates the directories that are to be considered in coverage, and `--omit` indicates the files that need to be omitted in the process.

Now, to print the report on the terminal itself, run the following command:

```
$ coverage report
```

The following screenshot shows the output:

Name	Stmts	Miss	Cover
my_app/__init__	31	0	100%
my_app/catalog/__init__	0	0	100%
my_app/catalog/models	69	6	91%
my_app/catalog/views	104	12	88%
TOTAL	204	18	91%

To get a nice HTML output of the coverage report, run the following command:

```
$ coverage html
```

This will create a new folder named `htmlcov` in your current working directory. Inside this, just open up `index.html` in a browser, and the full detailed view will be available.

Alternatively, we can include a piece of code in our test file and get the coverage report every time the tests are run. Add the following code snippets in `app_tests.py`:

Before anything else, add this:

```
import coverage

cov = coverage.coverage(
    omit = [
        '/Users/shalabhaggarwal/workspace/mydev/lib/python2.7/site-
packages/*',
        'app_tests.py'
    ]
)
cov.start()
```

Here, we imported the `coverage` library and created an object of it; this tells the library to omit all `site-packages` (by default, the coverage report is calculated for all dependencies as well) and the test file itself. Then, we started the process to determine the coverage.

Finally, modify the last block of code to the following:

```
if __name__ == '__main__':
    try:
        unittest.main()
    finally:
        cov.stop()
        cov.save()
        cov.report()
        cov.html_report(directory = 'coverage')
        cov.erase()
```

In the preceding code, we first put `unittest.main()` inside a `try..finally` block. This is because `unittest.main()` exits after all the tests are executed. Now, the coverage-specific code is forced to run after this method completes. We first stopped the coverage report, saved it, printed the report on the console, and then generated the HTML version of it before deleting the temporary `.coverage` file (this is created automatically as part of the process).

How it works...

If we run our tests after including the coverage-specific code, then we can run the following command:

```
$ python app_tests.py
```

The output will be as shown in the following screenshot:

Name	Stmts	Miss	Cover	Missing
my_app/__init__	31	0	100%	
my_app/catalog/__init__	0	0	100%	
my_app/catalog/models	69	6	91%	33, 44, 58, 62, 74, 90
my_app/catalog/views	104	12	88%	31, 53-54, 76, 78, 80, 89, 107-108, 147, 161-162
TOTAL	204	18	91%	

See also

▶ It is also possible to determine coverage using the Nose library that we discussed in the *Nose library integration* recipe. I leave it to you to explore this option yourself. Refer to `https://nose.readthedocs.org/en/latest/plugins/cover.html?highlight=coverage` for a head start.

Using profiling to find bottlenecks

Profiling is an important tool when we decide to scale the application. Before scaling, we want to know whether any process is a bottleneck and affects the overall performance. Python has an inbuilt profiler, `cProfile`, that can do the job for us, but to make life easier, Werkzeug has a `ProfilerMiddleware` of its own, which is written over cProfile. We will use this to determine whether there is anything that affects the performance.

Getting ready

We will use the application from the previous recipe and add `ProfilerMiddleware` in a new file named `generate_profile.py`.

How to do it...

Create a new file, `generate_profile.py`, alongside `run.py`, which works like `run.py` itself but with `ProfilerMiddleware`:

```
from werkzeug.contrib.profiler import ProfilerMiddleware
from my_app import app

app.wsgi_app = ProfilerMiddleware(app.wsgi_app, restrictions = [10])
app.run(debug=True)
```

Here, we imported `ProfilerMiddleware` from `werkzeug` and then modified `wsgi_app` on our Flask app to use it, with a restriction of the top 10 calls to be printed in the output.

How it works...

Now, we can run our application using `generate_profile.py`:

```
$ python generate_profile.py
```

We can then create a new product. Then, the output for that specific call will be like the following screenshot:

It is evident from the preceding screenshot that the most intensive call in this process is the call made to the geoip database. So, if we decide to improve the performance sometime down the line, then this is something that needs to be looked at first.

11
Deployment and Post Deployment

Up until now in the book, we have seen how to write Flask applications in different ways. Deployment of an application and managing the application post-deployment is as important as developing it. There can be various ways of deploying an application, where choosing the best way depends on the requirements. Deploying an application correctly is very important from the points of view of security and performance. There are multiple ways of monitoring an application after deployment of which some are paid and others are free to use. Using them again depends on requirements and features offered by them.

In this chapter, we will cover the following recipes:

- Deploying with Apache
- Deploying with uWSGI and Nginx
- Deploying with Gunicorn and Supervisor
- Deploying with Tornado
- Using Fabric for deployment
- S3 storage for file uploads
- Deploying with Heroku
- Deploying with AWS Elastic Beanstalk
- Application monitoring with Pingdom
- Application performance management and monitoring with New Relic

Introduction

In this chapter, we will talk about various application-deployment techniques, followed by some monitoring tools that are used post-deployment.

Each of the tools and techniques has its own set of features. For example, adding too much monitoring to an application can prove to be an extra overhead to the application and the developers as well. Similarly, missing out on monitoring can lead to undetected user errors and overall user dissatisfaction.

Hence, we should choose the tools wisely and they will ease our lives to the maximum.

In the post-deployment monitoring tools, we will discuss Pingdom and New Relic. Sentry is another tool that will prove to be the most beneficial of all from a developer's perspective. It has already been covered in the *Using Sentry to monitor exceptions* recipe in *Chapter 10, Debugging, Error Handling, and Testing*.

Deploying with Apache

First, we will learn how to deploy a Flask application with Apache, which is, unarguably, the most popular HTTP server. For Python web applications, we will use mod_wsgi, which implements a simple Apache module that can host any Python applications that support the WSGI interface.

 Remember that mod_wsgi is not the same as Apache and needs to be installed separately.

Getting ready

We will start with our catalog application and make appropriate changes to it to make it deployable using the Apache HTTP server.

First, we should make our application installable so that our application and all its libraries are on the Python load path. This can be done using a `setup.py` script, as seen in the *Making a Flask app installable using setuptools* recipe in *Chapter 1, Flask Configurations*. There will be a few changes to the script as per this application. The major changes are mentioned here:

```
packages=[
    'my_app',
    'my_app.catalog',
],
include_package_data=True,
zip_safe = False,
```

First, we mentioned all the packages that need to be installed as part of our application. Each of these needs to have an __init__.py file. The zip_safe flag tells the installer to not install this application as a ZIP file. The include_package_data statement reads from a MANIFEST.in file in the same folder and includes any package data mentioned here. Our MANIFEST.in file looks like:

```
recursive-include my_app/templates *
recursive-include my_app/static *
recursive-include my_app/translations *
```

Now, just install the application using the following command:

```
$ python setup.py install
```

> Installing mod_wsgi is usually OS-specific. Installing it on a Debian-based distribution should be as easy as just using the packaging tool, that is, apt or aptitude. For details, refer to https://code.google.com/p/modwsgi/wiki/InstallationInstructions and https://github.com/GrahamDumpleton/mod_wsgi.

How to do it...

We need to create some more files, the first one being app.wsgi. This loads our application as a WSGI application:

```
activate_this = '<Path to virtualenv>/bin/activate_this.py'
execfile(activate_this, dict(__file__=activate_this))

from my_app import app as application
import sys, logging
logging.basicConfig(stream = sys.stderr)
```

As we perform all our installations inside virtualenv, we need to activate the environment before our application is loaded. In the case of system-wide installations, the first two statements are not needed. Then, we need to import our app object as application, which is used as the application being served. The last two lines are optional, as they just stream the output to the standard logger, which is disabled by mod_wsgi by default.

> The app object needs to be imported as application, because mod_wsgi expects the application keyword.

Next comes a config file that will be used by the Apache HTTP server to serve our application correctly from specific locations. The file is named `apache_wsgi.conf`:

```
<VirtualHost *>

    WSGIScriptAlias / <Path to application>/flask_catalog_deployment/
app.wsgi

    <Directory <Path to application>/flask_catalog_deployment>
        Order allow,deny
        Allow from all
    </Directory>

</VirtualHost>
```

The preceding code is the Apache configuration, which tells the HTTP server about the various directories where the application has to be loaded from.

The final step is to add the `apache_wsgi.conf` file to `apache2/httpd.conf` so that our application is loaded when the server runs:

```
Include <Path to application>/flask_catalog_deployment/
apache_wsgi.conf
```

How it works...

Let's restart the Apache server service using the following command:

```
$ sudo apachectl restart
```

Open up `http://127.0.0.1/` in the browser to see the application's home page. Any errors coming up can be seen at `/var/log/apache2/error_log` (this path can differ depending on OS).

There's more...

After all this, it is possible that the product images uploaded as part of the product creation do not work. For this, we should make a small modification to our application's configuration:

```
app.config['UPLOAD_FOLDER'] = '<Some static absolute
    path>/flask_test_uploads'
```

We opted for a static path because we do not want it to change every time the application is modified or installed.

Now, we will include the path chosen in the preceding code to `apache_wsgi.conf`:

```
Alias /static/uploads/ "<Some static absolute
  path>/flask_test_uploads/"
<Directory "<Some static absolute path>/flask_test_uploads">
    Order allow,deny
    Options Indexes
    Allow from all
    IndexOptions FancyIndexing
</Directory>
```

After this, install the application and restart `apachectl`.

See also

- `http://httpd.apache.org/`

- `https://code.google.com/p/modwsgi/`

- `http://wsgi.readthedocs.org/en/latest/`

- `https://pythonhosted.org/setuptools/setuptools.html#setting-the-zip-safe-flag`

Deploying with uWSGI and Nginx

For those who are already aware of the usefulness of uWSGI and Nginx, there is not much that can be explained. uWSGI is a protocol as well as an application server and provides a complete stack to build hosting services. Nginx is a reverse proxy and HTTP server that is very lightweight and capable of handling virtually unlimited requests. Nginx works seamlessly with uWSGI and provides many under-the-hood optimizations for better performance.

Getting ready

We will use our application from the last recipe, *Deploying with Apache*, and use the same `app.wsgi`, `setup.py`, and `MANIFEST.in` files. Also, other changes made to the application's configuration in the last recipe will apply to this recipe as well.

 Disable any other HTTP servers that might be running, such as Apache and so on.

How to do it...

First, we need to install uWSGI and Nginx. On Debian-based distributions such as Ubuntu, they can be easily installed using the following commands:

```
# sudo apt-get install nginx
# sudo apt-get install uWSGI
```

 You can also install uWSGI inside a `virtualenv` using the `pip install uWSGI` command.

Again, these are OS-specific, so refer to the respective documentations as per the OS used.

Make sure that you have an `apps-enabled` folder for uWSGI, where we will keep our application-specific uWSGI configuration files, and a `sites-enabled` folder for Nginx, where we will keep our site-specific configuration files. Usually, these are already present in most installations in the `/etc/` folder. If not, refer to the OS-specific documentations to figure out the same.

Next, we will create a file named `uwsgi.ini` in our application:

```
[uwsgi]
http-socket    = :9090
plugin    = python
wsgi-file = <Path to application>/flask_catalog_deployment/app.wsgi
processes    = 3
```

To test whether uWSGI is working as expected, run the following command:

```
$ uwsgi --ini uwsgi.ini
```

The preceding file and command are equivalent to running the following command:

```
$ uwsgi --http-socket :9090 --plugin python --wsgi-file app.wsgi
```

Now, point your browser to `http://127.0.0.1:9090/`; this should open up the home page of the application.

Create a soft link of this file to the `apps-enabled` folder mentioned earlier using the following command:

```
$ ln -s <path/to/uwsgi.ini> <path/to/apps-enabled>
```

Before moving ahead, edit the preceding file to replace `http-socket` with `socket`. This changes the protocol from HTTP to uWSGI (read more about it at `http://uwsgi-docs.readthedocs.org/en/latest/Protocol.html`). Now, create a new file called `nginx-wsgi.conf`. This contains the Nginx configuration needed to serve our application and the static content:

```
location / {
    include uwsgi_params;
    uwsgi_pass 127.0.0.1:9090;
}
location /static/uploads/{
    alias <Some static absolute path>/flask_test_uploads/;
}
```

In the preceding code block, `uwsgi_pass` specifies the uWSGI server that needs to be mapped to the specified location.

Create a soft link of this file to the `sites-enabled` folder mentioned earlier using the following command:

$ ln -s <path/to/nginx-wsgi.conf> <path/to/sites-enabled>

Edit the `nginx.conf` file (usually found at `/etc/nginx/nginx.conf`) to add the following line inside the first server block before the last `}`:

```
include <path/to/sites-enabled>/*;
```

After all of this, reload the Nginx server using the following command:

$ sudo nginx -s reload

Point your browser to `http://127.0.0.1/` to see the application that is served via Nginx and uWSGI.

 The preceding instructions of this recipe can vary depending on the OS being used and different versions of the same OS can also impact the paths and commands used. Different versions of these packages can also have some variations in usage. Refer to the documentation links provided in the next section.

See also

- ▶ Refer to `http://uwsgi-docs.readthedocs.org/en/latest/` for more information on uWSGI.

- ▶ Refer to `http://nginx.com/` for more information on Nginx.

- ▶ There is a good article by DigitalOcean on this. I advise you to go through this to have a better understanding of the topic. It is available at `https://www.digitalocean.com/community/tutorials/how-to-deploy-python-wsgi-applications-using-uwsgi-web-server-with-nginx`.

- ▶ To get an insight into the difference between Apache and Nginx, I think the article by Anturis at `https://anturis.com/blog/nginx-vs-apache/` is pretty good.

Deploying with Gunicorn and Supervisor

Gunicorn is a WSGI HTTP server for Unix. It is very simple to implement, ultra light, and fairly speedy. Its simplicity lies in its broad compatibility with various web frameworks.

Supervisor is a monitoring tool that controls various child processes and handles the starting/restarting of these child processes when they exit abruptly due to some reason. It can be extended to control the processes via the XML-RPC API over remote locations without logging in to the server (we won't discuss this here as it is out of the scope of this book).

One thing to remember is that these tools can be used along with the other tools mentioned in the applications in the previous recipe, such as using Nginx as a proxy server. This is left to you to try on your own.

Getting ready

We will start with the installation of both the packages, that is, `gunicorn` and `supervisor`. Both can be directly installed using `pip`:

```
$ pip install gunicorn
$ pip install supervisor
```

How to do it...

To check whether the `gunicorn` package works as expected, just run the following command from inside our application folder:

```
$ gunicorn -w 4 -b 127.0.0.1:8000 my_app:app
```

After this, point your browser to `http://127.0.0.1:8000/` to see the application's home page.

Now, we need to do the same using Supervisor so that this runs as a daemon and will be controlled by Supervisor itself rather than human intervention. First of all, we need a Supervisor configuration file. This can be achieved by running the following command from `virtualenv`. Supervisor, by default, looks for an `etc` folder that has a file named `supervisord.conf`. In system-wide installations, this folder is `/etc/`, and in `virtualenv`, it will look for an `etc` folder in `virtualenv` and then fall back to `/etc/`:

```
$ echo_supervisord_conf > etc/supervisord.conf
```

 The `echo_supervisord_conf` program is provided by Supervisor; it prints a sample config file to the location specified.

This command will create a file named `supervisord.conf` in the `etc` folder. Add the following block in this file:

```
[program:flask_catalog]
command=<path/to/virtualenv>/bin/gunicorn -w 4 -b 127.0.0.1:8000 my_
app:app
directory=<path/to/virtualenv>/flask_catalog_deployment
user=someuser # Relevant user
autostart=true
autorestart=true
stdout_logfile=/tmp/app.log
stderr_logfile=/tmp/error.log
```

 Make a note that one should never run the applications as a root user. This is a huge security flaw in itself as the application crashes, which can harm the OS itself.

How it works...

Now, run the following commands:

```
$ supervisord
$ supervisorctl status
flask_catalog    RUNNING    pid 40466, uptime 0:00:03
```

The first command invokes the `supervisord` server, and the next one gives a status of all the child processes.

> The tools discussed in this recipe can be coupled with Nginx to serve as a reverse proxy server. I suggest that you try it by yourself.

Every time you make a change to your application and then wish to restart Gunicorn in order for it to reflect the changes, run the following command:

```
$ supervisorctl restart all
```

You can also give specific processes instead of restarting everything:

```
$ supervisorctl restart flask_catalog
```

See also

- http://gunicorn-docs.readthedocs.org/en/latest/index.html
- http://supervisord.org/index.html

Deploying with Tornado

Tornado is a complete web framework and a standalone web server in itself. Here, we will use Flask to create our application, which is basically a combination of URL routing and templating, and leave the server part to Tornado. Tornado is built to hold thousands of simultaneous standing connections and makes applications very scalable.

>
> Tornado has limitations while working with WSGI applications. So, choose wisely! Read more at http://www.tornadoweb.org/en/stable/wsgi.html#running-wsgi-apps-on-tornado-servers.

Getting ready

Installing Tornado can be simply done using `pip`:

```
$ pip install tornado
```

How to do it...

Next, create a file named `tornado_server.py` and put the following code in it:

```
from tornado.wsgi import WSGIContainer
from tornado.httpserver import HTTPServer
from tornado.ioloop import IOLoop
from my_app import app

http_server = HTTPServer(WSGIContainer(app))
http_server.listen(5000)
IOLoop.instance().start()
```

Here, we created a WSGI container for our application; this container is then used to create an HTTP server, and the application is hosted on port 5000.

How it works...

Run the Python file created in the previous section using the following command:

```
$ python tornado_server.py
```

Point your browser to `http://127.0.0.1:5000/` to see the home page being served.

 We can couple Tornado with Nginx (as a reverse proxy to serve static content) and Supervisor (as a process manager) for the best results. It is left for you to try this on your own.

Using Fabric for deployment

Fabric is a command-line tool in Python; it streamlines the use of SSH for application deployment or system-administration tasks. As it allows the execution of shell commands on remote servers, the overall process of deployment is simplified, as the whole process can now be condensed into a Python file, which can be run whenever needed. Therefore, it saves the pain of logging in to the server and manually running commands every time an update has to be made.

Getting ready

Installing Fabric can be simply done using `pip`:

```
$ pip install fabric
```

We will use the application from the *Deploying with Gunicorn and Supervisor* recipe. We will create a Fabric file to perform the same process to the remote server.

For simplicity, let's assume that the remote server setup has been already done and all the required packages have also been installed with a `virtualenv` environment, which has also been created.

How to do it...

First, we need to create a file called `fabfile.py` in our application, preferably at the application's root directory, that is, along with the `setup.py` and `run.py` files. Fabric, by default, expects this filename. If we use a different filename, then it will have to be explicitly specified while executing.

A basic Fabric file will look like:

```
from fabric.api import sudo, cd, prefix, run


def deploy_app():
    "Deploy to the server specified"
    root_path = '/usr/local/my_env'

    with cd(root_path):
        with prefix("source %s/bin/activate" % root_path):
            with cd('flask_catalog_deployment'):
                run('git pull')
                run('python setup.py install')

            sudo('bin/supervisorctl restart all')
```

Here, we first moved into our `virtualenv`, activated it, and then moved into our application. Then, the code is pulled from the Git repository, and the updated application code is installed using `setup.py install`. After this, we restarted the supervisor processes so that the updated application is now rendered by the server.

Most of the commands used here are self-explanatory, except `prefix`, which wraps all the succeeding commands in its block with the command provided. This means that the command to activate `virtualenv` will run first and then all the commands in the `with` block will execute with `virtualenv` activated. The `virtualenv` will be deactivated as soon as control goes out of the `with` block.

How it works...

To run this file, we need to provide the remote server where the script will be executed. So, the command will look something like:

```
$ fab -H my.remote.server deploy_app
```

Here, we specified the address of the remote host where we wish to deploy and the name of the method to be called from the `fab` script.

There's more...

We can also specify the remote host inside our `fab` script, and this can be good idea if the deployment server remains the same most of the times. To do this, add the following code to the `fab` script:

```
from fabric.api import settings

def deploy_app_to_server():
    "Deploy to the server hardcoded"
    with settings(host_string='my.remote.server'):
        deploy_app()
```

Here, we have hardcoded the host and then called the method we created earlier to start the deployment process.

S3 storage for file uploads

Amazon explains S3 as the storage for the Internet that is designed to make web-scale computing easier for developers. S3 provides a very simple interface via web services; this makes storage and retrieval of any amount of data very simple at any time from anywhere on the Internet. Until now, in our catalog application, we saw that there were issues in managing the product images uploaded as a part of the creating process. The whole headache will go away if the images are stored somewhere globally and are easily accessible from anywhere. We will use S3 for the same purpose.

Getting ready

Amazon offers **boto**, a complete Python library that interfaces with Amazon Web Services via web services. Almost all of the AWS features can be controlled using boto. It can be installed using `pip`:

```
$ pip install boto
```

How to do it...

Now, we should make some changes to our existing catalog application to accommodate support for file uploads and retrieval from S3.

First, we need to store the AWS-specific configuration to allow boto to make calls to S3. Add the following statements to the application's configuration file, that is, `my_app/__init__.py`:

```
app.config['AWS_ACCESS_KEY'] = 'Amazon Access Key'
app.config['AWS_SECRET_KEY'] = 'Amazon Secret Key'
app.config['AWS_BUCKET'] = 'flask-cookbook'
```

Next, we need to change our `views.py` file:

```
from boto.s3.connection import S3Connection
```

This is the import that we need from boto. Next, replace the following two lines in `create_product()`:

```
filename = secure_filename(image.filename)
image.save(os.path.join(app.config['UPLOAD_FOLDER'], filename))
```

Replace these two lines with:

```
filename = image.filename
conn = S3Connection(
    app.config['AWS_ACCESS_KEY'], app.config['AWS_SECRET_KEY']
)
bucket = conn.create_bucket(app.config['AWS_BUCKET'])
key = bucket.new_key(filename)
key.set_contents_from_file(image)
key.make_public()
key.set_metadata(
    'Content-Type', 'image/' + filename.split('.')[-1].lower()
)
```

The last change will go to our `product.html` template, where we need to change the image `src` path. Replace the original `img src` statement with the following statement:

```
<img src="{{ 'https://s3.amazonaws.com/' + config['AWS_BUCKET'] +
    '/' + product.image_path }}"/>
```

How it works...

Now, run the application as usual and create a product. When the created product is rendered, the product image will take a bit of time to come up as it is now being served from S3 (and not from a local machine). If this happens, then the integration with S3 has been successfully done.

See also

▸ The next recipe, *Deploying with Heroku*, to see how S3 is instrumental in easy deployment without the hassles of managing uploads on the server

Deploying with Heroku

Heroku is a cloud application platform that provides an easy and quick way to build and deploy web applications. Heroku manages the servers, deployment, and related operations while developers spend their time on developing applications. Deploying with Heroku is pretty simple with the help of the Heroku toolbelt, which is a bundle of some tools that make deployment with Heroku a cakewalk.

Getting ready

We will proceed with the application from the previous recipe that has S3 support for uploads.

As mentioned earlier, the first step will be to download the Heroku toolbelt, which can be downloaded as per the OS from `https://toolbelt.heroku.com/`.

Once the toolbelt is installed, a certain set of commands will be available at the terminal; we will see them later in this recipe.

 It is advised that you perform Heroku deployment from a fresh `virtualenv` where we have only the required packages for our application installed and nothing else. This will make the deployment process faster and easier.

Now, run the following command to log in to your Heroku account and sync your machined SSH key with the server:

```
$ heroku login
Enter your Heroku credentials.
Email: shalabh7777@gmail.com
Password (typing will be hidden):
Authentication successful.
```

You will be prompted to create a new SSH key if one does not exist. Proceed accordingly.

 Remember! Before all this, you need to have a Heroku account available on `https://www.heroku.com/`.

How to do it...

Now, we already have an application that needs to be deployed to Heroku. First, Heroku needs to know the command that it needs to run while deploying the application. This is done in a file named `Procfile`:

```
web: gunicorn -w 4 my_app:app
```

Here, we will tell Heroku to run this command to run our web application.

 There are a lot of different configurations and commands that can go into `Procfile`. For more details, read the Heroku documentation.

Heroku needs to know the dependencies that need to be installed in order to successfully install and run our application. This is done via the `requirements.txt` file:

```
Flask==0.10.1
Flask-Restless==0.14.0
Flask-SQLAlchemy==1.0
Flask-WTF==0.10.0
Jinja2==2.7.3
MarkupSafe==0.23
SQLAlchemy==0.9.7
WTForms==2.0.1
Werkzeug==0.9.6
boto==2.32.1
```

```
gunicorn==19.1.1
itsdangerous==0.24
mimerender==0.5.4
python-dateutil==2.2
python-geoip==1.2
python-geoip-geolite2==2014.0207
python-mimeparse==0.1.4
six==1.7.3
wsgiref==0.1.2
```

This file contains all the dependencies of our application, the dependencies of these dependencies, and so on. An easy way to generate this file is using the `pip freeze` command:

```
$ pip freeze > requirements.txt
```

This will create/update the `requirements.txt` file with all the packages installed in `virtualenv`.

Now, we need to create a Git repo of our application. For this, we will run the following commands:

```
$ git init
$ git add .
$ git commit -m "First Commit"
```

Now, we have a Git repo with all our files added.

> Make sure that you have a `.gitignore` file in your repo or at a global level to prevent temporary files such as `.pyc` from being added to the repo.

Now, we need to create a Heroku application and push our application to Heroku:

```
$ heroku create
Creating damp-tor-6795... done, stack is cedar
http://damp-tor-6795.herokuapp.com/ | git@heroku.com:damp-tor-6795.git
Git remote heroku added
$ git push heroku master
```

After the last command, a whole lot of stuff will get printed on the terminal; this will indicate all the packages being installed and finally, the application being launched.

How it works...

After the previous commands have successfully finished, just open up the URL provided by Heroku at the end of deployment in a browser or run the following command:

```
$ heroku open
```

This will open up the application's home page. Try creating a new product with an image and see the image being served from Amazon S3.

To see the logs of the application, run the following command:

```
$ heroku logs
```

There's more...

There is a glitch with the deployment we just did. Every time we update the deployment via the `git push` command, the SQLite database gets overwritten. The solution to this is to use the Postgres setup provided by Heroku itself. I urge you to try this by yourself.

Deploying with AWS Elastic Beanstalk

In the last recipe, we saw how deployment to servers becomes easy with Heroku. Similarly, Amazon has a service named Elastic Beanstalk, which allows developers to deploy their application to Amazon EC2 instances as easily as possible. With just a few configuration options, a Flask application can be deployed to AWS using Elastic Beanstalk in a couple of minutes.

Getting ready

We will start with our catalog application from the previous recipe, *Deploying with Heroku*. The only file that remains the same from this recipe is `requirement.txt`. The rest of the files that were added as a part of that recipe can be ignored or discarded for this recipe.

Now, the first thing that we need to do is download the AWS Elastic Beanstalk command-line tool library from the Amazon website (`http://aws.amazon.com/code/6752709412171743`). This will download a ZIP file that needs to be unzipped and placed in a suitable place, preferably your workspace home.

The path of this tool should be added to the `PATH` environment so that the commands are available throughout. This can be done via the `export` command as shown:

```
$ export PATH=$PATH:<path to unzipped EB CLI package>/eb/linux/python2.7/
```

This can also be added to the `~/.profile` or `~/.bash_profile` file using:

```
export PATH=$PATH:<path to unzipped EB CLI package>/eb/linux/
python2.7/
```

How to do it...

There are a few conventions that need to be followed in order to deploy using Beanstalk. Beanstalk assumes that there will be a file called `application.py`, which contains the application object (in our case, the `app` object). Beanstalk treats this file as the WSGI file, and this is used for deployment.

 In the *Deploying with Apache* recipe, we had a file named `app.wgsi` where we referred our `app` object as `application` because `apache/mod_wsgi` needed it to be so. The same thing happens here too because Amazon, by default, deploys using Apache behind the scenes.

The contents of this `application.py` file can be just a few lines as shown here:

```
from my_app import app as application
import sys, logging
logging.basicConfig(stream = sys.stderr)
```

Now, create a Git repo in the application and commit with all the files added:

```
$ git init
$ git add .
$ git commit -m "First Commit"
```

 Make sure that you have a `.gitignore` file in your repo or at a global level to prevent temporary files such as `.pyc` from being added to the repo.

Now, we need to deploy to Elastic Beanstalk. Run the following command to do this:

```
$ eb init
```

The preceding command initializes the process for the configuration of your Elastic Beanstalk instance. It will ask for the AWS credentials followed by a lot of other configuration options needed for the creation of the EC2 instance, which can be selected as needed. For more help on these options, refer to `http://docs.aws.amazon.com/elasticbeanstalk/latest/dg/create_deploy_Python_flask.html`.

After this is done, run the following command to trigger the creation of servers, followed by the deployment of the application:

```
$ eb start
```

 Behind the scenes, the preceding command creates the EC2 instance (a volume), assigns an elastic IP, and then runs the following command to push our application to the newly created server for deployment:
```
$ git aws.push
```

This will take a few minutes to complete. When done, you can check the status of your application using the following command:

```
$ eb status -verbose
```

Whenever you need to update your application, just commit your changes using the `git` and `push` commands as follows:

```
$ git aws.push
```

How it works...

When the deployment process finishes, it gives out the application URL. Point your browser to it to see the application being served.

Yet, you will find a small glitch with the application. The static content, that is, the CSS and JS code, is not being served. This is because the static path is not correctly comprehended by Beanstalk. This can be simply fixed by modifying the application's configuration on your application's monitoring/configuration page in the AWS management console. See the following screenshots to understand this better:

Click on the **Configuration** menu item in the left-hand side menu.

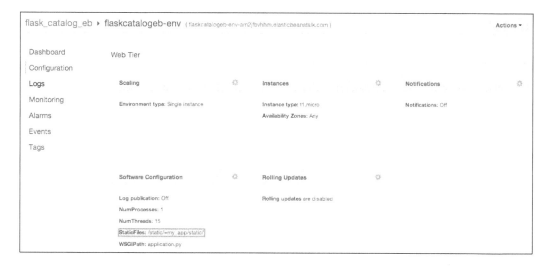

Notice the highlighted box in the preceding screenshot. This is what we need to change as per our application. Open **Software Settings**.

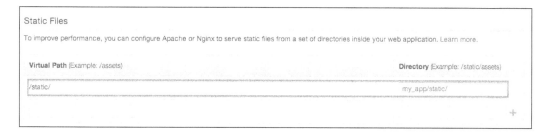

Change the virtual path for /static/, as shown in the preceding screenshot.

After this change is made, the environment created by Elastic Beanstalk will be updated automatically, although it will take a bit of time. When done, check the application again to see the static content also being served correctly.

Application monitoring with Pingdom

Pingdom is a website-monitoring tool that has the USP of notifying you as soon as your website goes down. The basic idea behind this tool is to constantly ping the website at a specific interval, say, 30 seconds. If a ping fails, it will notify you via an e-mail, SMS, tweet, or push notifications to mobile apps, which inform that your site is down. It will keep on pinging at a faster rate until the site is back up again. There are other monitoring features too, but we will limit ourselves to uptime checks in this book.

Getting ready

As Pingdom is a SaaS service, the first step will be to sign up for an account. Pingdom offers a free trial of 1 month in case you just want to try it out. The website for the service is `https://www.pingdom.com`.

We will use the application deployed to AWS in the *Deploying with AWS Elastic Beanstalk* recipe to check for uptime. Here, Pingdom will send an e-mail in case the application goes down and will send an e-mail again when it is back up.

How to do it...

After successful registration, create a check for time. Have a look at the following screenshot:

As you can see, I already added a check for the AWS instance. To create a new check, click on the **ADD NEW** button. Fill in the details asked by the form that comes up.

How it works...

After the check is successfully created, try to break the application by consciously making a mistake somewhere in the code and then deploying to AWS. As soon as the faulty application is deployed, you will get an e-mail notifying you of this. This e-mail will look like:

Once the application is fixed and put back up again, the next e-mail should look like:

You can also check how long the application has been up and the downtime instances from the Pingdom administration panel.

Application performance management and monitoring with New Relic

New Relic is an analytics software that provides near real-time operational and business analytics related to your application. It provides deep analytics on the behavior of the application from various aspects. It does the job of a profiler as well as eliminating the need to maintain extra moving parts in the application. It actually works in a scenario where our application sends data to New Relic rather than New Relic asking for statistics from our application.

Getting ready

We will use the application from the last recipe, which is deployed to AWS.

The first step will be to sign up with New Relic for an account. Follow the simple signup process, and upon completion and e-mail verification, it will lead to your dashboard. Here, you will have your license key available, which we will use later to connect our application to this account. The dashboard should look like the following screenshot:

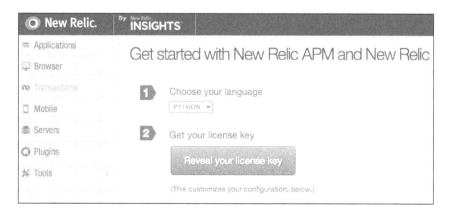

Here, click on the large button named **Reveal your license key**.

How to do it...

Once we have the license key, we need to install the `newrelic` Python library:

```
$ pip install newrelic
```

Now, we need to generate a file called `newrelic.ini`, which will contain details regarding the license key, the name of our application, and so on. This can be done using the following commands:

```
$ newrelic-admin generate-config LICENSE-KEY newrelic.ini
```

In the preceding command, replace `LICENSE-KEY` with the actual license key of your account. Now, we have a new file called `newrelic.ini`. Open and edit the file for the application name and anything else as needed.

To check whether the `newrelic.ini` file is working successfully, run the following command:

```
$ newrelic-admin validate-config newrelic.ini
```

This will tell us whether the validation was successful or not. If not, then check the license key and its validity.

Now, add the following lines at the top of the application's configuration file, that is, `my_app/__init__.py` in our case. Make sure that you add these lines before anything else is imported:

```
import newrelic.agent
newrelic.agent.initialize('newrelic.ini')
```

Now, we need to update the `requirements.txt` file. So, run the following command:

```
$ pip freeze > requirements.txt
```

After this, commit the changes and deploy the application to AWS using the following command:

```
$ git aws.push
```

How it works...

Once the application is successfully updated on AWS, it will start sending statistics to New Relic, and the dashboard will have a new application added to it.

Open the application-specific page, and a whole lot of statistics will come across. It will also show which calls have taken the most amount of time and how the application is performing. You will also see multiple tabs that correspond to a different type of monitoring to cover all the aspects.

See also

> ▸ The *Deploying with AWS Elastic Beanstalk* recipe to understand the deployment part used in this recipe

12

Other Tips and Tricks

This book has covered almost all the areas needed to be known for the creation of a web application using Flask. Much has been covered, and you need to explore more on your own. In this final chapter, we will go through some additional recipes that can be used to add value to the application, if necessary.

In this chapter, we will cover the following recipes:

-   ▸ Full-text search with Whoosh
-   ▸ Full-text search with Elasticsearch
-   ▸ Working with signals
-   ▸ Using caching with your application
-   ▸ E-mail support for Flask applications
-   ▸ Understanding asynchronous operations
-   ▸ Working with Celery

Introduction

In this chapter, we will first learn how to implement full-text search using Whoosh and Elasticsearch. Full-text search becomes important for a web application that offers a lot of content and options, such as an e-commerce site. Next, we will catch up on signals that help decouple applications by sending notifications (signals) when an action is performed somewhere in the application. This action is caught by a subscriber/receiver, which can perform an action accordingly. This is followed by implementing caching for our Flask application.

We will also see how e-mail support is added to our application and how e-mails can be sent directly from the application on different actions. We will then see how we can make our application asynchronous. By default, WSGI applications are synchronous and blocking, that is, by default, they do not serve multiple simultaneous requests together. We will see how to deal with this via a small example. We will also integrate Celery with our application and see how a task queue can be used to our application's benefit.

Full-text search with Whoosh

Whoosh is a fast, *featureful*, full-text indexing and searching library implemented in Python. It has a pure Pythonic API and allows developers to add search functionality to their applications easily and efficiently. In this recipe, we will use a package called Flask-WhooshAlchemy, which integrates the text-search functionality of Whoosh with SQLAlchemy for use in Flask applications.

Getting ready

The Flask-WhooshAlchemy package can be installed via `pip` using the following command:

```
$ pip install flask_whooshalchemy
```

This will install the required packages and dependencies.

How to do it...

Integrating Whoosh with Flask using SQLAlchemy is pretty straightforward. First, we need to provide the path to the Whoosh base directory where the index for our models will be created. This should be done in the application's configuration, that is, `my_app/__init__.py`:

```
app.config['WHOOSH_BASE'] = '/tmp/whoosh'
```

You can choose any path you prefer, and it can be absolute or relative.

Next, we need to make some changes to our `models.py` file to make the string/text fields searchable:

```
import flask.ext.whooshalchemy as whooshalchemy
from my_app import app

class Product(db.Model):
    __searchable__ = ['name', 'company']
    # … Rest of code as before … #

whooshalchemy.whoosh_index(app, Product)

class Category(db.Model):
```

```
__searchable__ = ['name']
# … Rest of code as before … #

whooshalchemy.whoosh_index(app, Category)
```

Notice the `__searchable__` statement that has been added to both the models. It tells Whoosh to create index on these fields. Remember that these fields should only be of the text or string type. The `whoosh_index` statements tell the application to create the index for these models if they are not already available.

After this is done, we can add a new handler to search using Whoosh. This is to be done in `views.py`:

```
@catalog.route('/product-search-whoosh')
@catalog.route('/product-search-whoosh/<int:page>')
def product_search_whoosh(page=1):
    q = request.args.get('q')
    products = Product.query.whoosh_search(q)
    return render_template(
        'products.html', products=products.paginate(page, 10)
    )
```

Here, we got the URL argument with the key as `q` and passed its value to the `whoosh_search()` method that does the full-text search in the `Product` model on the `name` and `company` fields, which we had made searchable in the models earlier.

How it works...

Those who have gone through the *SQL-based searching* recipe in *Chapter 4, Working with Views*, will recall that we implemented a method that performed a search on the basis of fields. However, here, in the case of Whoosh, we do not need to specify any field while searching. We can type any text and if this matches the searchable fields, the results will be shown, ordered in the rank of their relevance.

First, create some products in the application. Now, if we open `http://127.0.0.1:5000/product-search-whoosh?q=iPhone`, the resulting page will list all the products that have `iPhone` in their names.

 There are advanced options provided by Whoosh where we can control which fields to be searched for or how the result has to be ordered. You can explore them as per the needs of your application.

See also

▶ Refer to `https://pythonhosted.org/Whoosh/`

▶ Refer to `https://pypi.python.org/pypi/Flask-WhooshAlchemy`

Full-text search with Elasticsearch

Elasticsearch is a search server based on Lucene, which is an open source information-retrieval library. Elasticsearch provides a distributed full-text search engine with a RESTful web interface and schema-free JSON documents. In this recipe, we will implement full-text search using Elasticsearch for our Flask application.

Getting ready

We will use a Python library called `pyelasticsearch`, which makes dealing with Elasticsearch a lot easier:

```
$ pip install pyelasticsearch
```

We also need to install the Elasticsearch server itself. This can be downloaded from `http://www.elasticsearch.org/download/`. Unpack the package downloaded and run the following command:

```
$ bin/elasticsearch
```

This will start the Elasticsearch server on `http://localhost:9200/` by default.

How to do it...

To perform the integration, we will start by adding the Elasticsearch object to the application's configuration, that is, `my_app/__init__.py`:

```python
from pyelasticsearch import ElasticSearch
from pyelasticsearch.exceptions import IndexAlreadyExistsError

es = ElasticSearch('http://localhost:9200/')
try:
    es.create_index('catalog')
except IndexAlreadyExistsError, e:
    pass
```

Here, we created an `es` object from the `ElasticSearch` class, which accepts the server URL. Then, we created an index called `catalog`. This is done in a `try-except` block because if the index already exists, then `IndexAlreadyExistsError` is thrown, which we can just ignore.

Next, we need the ability to add a document to our Elasticsearch index. This can be done in views or models, but in my opinion, the best way will be to add it in the model layer. So, we will do this in the `models.py` file:

```python
from my_app import es

class Product(db.Model):

    def add_index_to_es(self):
        es.index('catalog', 'product', {
            'name': self.name,
            'category': self.category.name
        })
        es.refresh('catalog')

class Category(db.Model):

    def add_index_to_es(self):
        es.index('catalog', 'category', {
            'name': self.name,
        })
        es.refresh('catalog')
```

Here, in each of the models, we added a new method called `add_index_to_es()`, which will add the document that corresponds to the current `Product` or `Category` object to the `catalog` index with the relevant document type, that is, `product` or `category`. Finally, we refreshed our index so that the newly created index is available to be searched for.

The `add_index_to_es()` method can be called when we create, update, or delete a product or category. For demonstration purposes, I will just add this method while creating the product in `views.py`:

```python
from my_app import es

def create_product():
    #... normal product creation as always ...#
    db.session.commit()
    product.add_index_to_es()
    #... normal process as always ...#

@catalog.route('/product-search-es')
@catalog.route('/product-search-es/<int:page>')
def product_search_es(page=1):
    q = request.args.get('q')
    products = es.search(q)
    return products
```

Also, we added a `product_search_es()` method to allow searching on the Elasticsearch index we just created. Do the same in the `create_category()` method as well.

How to do it...

Now, let's say we created a few categories and products in each of the categories. Now, if we open `http://127.0.0.1:5000/product-search-es?q=galaxy`, then we will get a response like what is shown in the following screenshot:

```
{"hits": {"hits": [{"_score": 0.7554128, "_type": "product", "_id":
"ceuE9YqYSVO6LIz43acxVg", "_source": {"category": "Phones",
"company": "Samsung", "name": "Galaxy S5"}, "_index": "catalog"},
{"_score": 0.7554128, "_type": "product", "_id":
"xtLtchRzTCmyKZY91FTEew", "_source": {"category": "Phones", "name":
"Galaxy S5"}, "_index": "catalog"}], "total": 2, "max_score": 0.7554128},
"_shards": {"successful": 10, "failed": 0, "total": 10}, "took": 2, "timed_out":
false}
```

I encourage you to try and enhance the formatting and display of the page.

Working with signals

Signals can be thought of as events that happen in our application. These events can be subscribed by certain receivers who then invoke a function whenever the event occurs. The occurrence of events is broadcasted by senders who can specify the arguments that can be used by the function to be triggered by the receiver.

 You should refrain from modifying any application data in the signals because signals are not executed in a specified order and can easily lead to data corruption.

Getting ready

We will use a Python library called `blinker`, which provides the signals feature. Flask has inbuilt support for `blinker` and uses signaling to a good extent. There are certain core signals provided by Flask.

In this recipe, we will use the application from the *Full-text search with Elasticsearch* recipe and make the addition of the `product` and `category` documents to indexes work via signals.

How to do it...

First, we need to create signals for the product and category creation. This can be done in `models.py`. This can be done in any file we want, as signals are created on the global scope:

```
from blinker import Namespace

catalog_signals = Namespace()
product_created = catalog_signals.signal('product-created')
category_created = catalog_signals.signal('category-created')
```

We use `Namespace` to create signals, as it will create them in a custom namespace rather than in the global namespace and, thus, help in cleaner management of the signals. We created two signals where the intent of the use of both is clear by their names.

Then, we need to create subscribers to these signals and attach functions to them. For this, the `add_index_to_es()` methods have to be removed, and new functions on the global scope have to be created:

```
def add_product_index_to_es(sender, product):
    es.index('catalog', 'product', {
        'name': product.name,
        'category': product.category.name
    })
    es.refresh('catalog')

product_created.connect(add_product_index_to_es, app)

def add_category_index_to_es(sender, category):
    es.index('catalog', 'category', {
        'name': category.name,
    })
    es.refresh('catalog')

category_created.connect(add_category_index_to_es, app)
```

In the preceding code snippet, we created subscribers to the signals created earlier using `.connect()`. This method accepts the function that should be called when the event occurs; it also accepts the sender as an optional argument. The `app` object is provided as the sender because we do not want our function to be called every time the event is triggered anywhere in any application. This specifically holds true in the case of extensions, which can be used by multiple applications. The function that gets called by the receiver gets the sender as the first argument, which defaults to none if the sender is not provided. We provided the product/category as the second argument for which the record needs to be added to the Elasticsearch index.

Now, we just need to emit the signal that can be caught by the receiver. This needs to be done in `views.py`. For this, we just need to remove the calls to the `add_index_to_es()` methods and replace them with the `.send()` methods:

```
from my_app.catalog.models import product_created, category_created

def create_product():
    #... normal product creation as always ...#
    db.session.commit()
    product_created.send(app, product=product)
    # product.add_index_to_es()
    #... normal process as always ...#
```

Do the same in the `create_category()` method as well.

How it works...

Whenever a product is created, the `product_created` signal is emitted, with the `app` object as the sender and the product as the keyword argument. This is then caught in `models.py`, and the `add_product_index_to_es()` function is called, which adds the document to the catalog index.

See also

► The *Full-text search with Elasticsearch* recipe for background information on this recipe

► Refer to `https://pypi.python.org/pypi/blinker`

► Refer to `http://flask.pocoo.org/docs/0.10/signals/#core-signals`

► Signals provided by Flask-SQLAlchemy can be found at `https://pythonhosted.org/Flask-SQLAlchemy/signals.html`

Using caching with your application

Caching becomes an important and integral part of any web application when scaling or increasing the response time of your application becomes a question. Caching is the first thing that is implemented in these cases. Flask, by itself, does not provide any caching support by default, but Werkzeug does. Werkzeug has some basic support to cache with multiple backends, such as Memcached and Redis.

Getting ready

We will install a Flask extension called Flask-Cache, which simplifies the process of caching a lot:

```
$ pip install Flask-Cache
```

We will use our catalog application for this purpose and implement caching for some methods.

How to do it...

First, we need to initialize `Cache` to work with our application. This is done in the application's configuration, that is, `my_app/__init__.py`:

```
from flask.ext.cache import Cache

cache = Cache(app, config={'CACHE_TYPE': 'simple'})
```

Here, we used `simple` as the `Cache` type where the cache is stored in the memory. This is not advised for production environments. For production, we should use something such as Redis, Memcached, filesystem cache, and so on. Flask-Cache supports all of them with a couple more backends.

Next, we need to add caching to our methods; this is pretty simple to implement. We just need to add a `@cache.cached(timeout=<time in seconds>)` decorator to our view methods. A simple target can be the list of categories (we will do this in `views.py`):

```
from my_app import cache

@catalog.route('/categories')
@cache.cached(timeout=120)
def categories():
    # Fetch and display the list of categories
```

This way of caching stores the value of the output of this method in the cache in the form of a key-value pair, with the key as the request path.

How it works...

After adding the preceding code, to check whether the cache works as expected, first fetch the list of categories by pointing the browser to `http://127.0.0.1:5000/categories`. This will save a key-value pair for this URL in the cache. Now, create a new category quickly and navigate back to the same category list page. You will notice that the newly added category is not listed. Wait for a couple of minutes and then reload the page. The newly added category will be shown now. This is because the first time the category list was cached, it expired after 2 minutes, that is, 120 seconds.

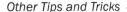

This might seem to be a fault with the application, but in the case of large applications, this becomes a boon where the hits to the database are reduced, and the overall application experience improves. Caching is usually implemented for those handlers whose results do not get updated frequently.

There's more...

Many of us might think that such caching will fail in the case of a single category or product page, where each record has a separate page. The solution to this is **memoization**. It is similar to cache with the difference that it stores the result of a method in the cache along with the information on the parameters passed. So, when a method is created with the same parameters multiple times, the result is loaded from the cache rather than making a database hit. Implementing memoization is again quite simple:

```
@catalog.route('/product/<id>')
@cache.memoize(120)
def product(id):
    # Fetch and display the product
```

Now, if we call a URL, say `http://127.0.0.1:5000/product/1` in our browser, the first time it will be loaded after making calls to the database. However, the next time, if we make the same call, the page will be loaded from the cache. On the other hand, if we open another product, say, `http://127.0.0.1:5000/product/2`, then it will be loaded after fetching the product details from the database.

See also

▶ Read more about Flask-Cache at `https://pythonhosted.org/Flask-Cache/`
▶ Read more about memoization at `http://en.wikipedia.org/wiki/Memoization`

E-mail support for Flask applications

The ability to send e-mails is usually one of the most basic functions of any web application. It is usually easy to implement with any application. With Python-based applications, it is also quite simple to implement with the help of smtplib. In the case of Flask, this is further simplified by an extension called **Flask-Mail**.

Getting ready

Flask-Mail can be easily installed via `pip`:

```
$ pip install Flask-Mail
```

Let's take a simple case where en e-mail will be sent to a catalog manager in the application whenever a new category is added.

How to do it...

First, we need to instantiate the `Mail` object in our application's configuration, that is, `my_app/__init__.py`:

```
from flask_mail import Mail

app.config['MAIL_SERVER'] = 'smtp.gmail.com'
app.config['MAIL_PORT'] = 587
app.config['MAIL_USE_TLS'] = True
app.config['MAIL_USERNAME'] = 'gmail_username'
app.config['MAIL_PASSWORD'] = 'gmail_password'
app.config['MAIL_DEFAULT_SENDER'] = ('Sender name', 'sender email')
mail = Mail(app)
```

Also, we need to do some configuration to set up the e-mail server and sender account. The preceding code is a sample configuration for Gmail accounts. Any SMTP server can be set up like this. There are several other options provided; they can be looked up in the Flask-Mail documentation at `https://pythonhosted.org/Flask-Mail`.

How it works...

To send an e-mail on category creation, we need to make the following changes in `views.py`:

```
from my_app import mail
from flask_mail import Message

@catalog.route('/category-create', methods=['GET', 'POST'])
def create_category():
    # … Create category … #
    db.session.commit()
    message = Message(
        "New category added",
        recipients=['some-receiver@domain.com']
    )
    message.body = 'New category "%s" has been created' %
      category.name
    mail.send(message)
    # … Rest of the process … #
```

Here, a new e-mail will be sent to the list of recipients from the default sender configuration that we created.

There's more...

Now, let's assume that we need to send a large e-mail with a lot of HTML content. Writing all this in our Python file will make the overall code ugly and unmanageable. A simple solution to this is to create templates and render their content while sending e-mails. I created two templates: one for the HTML content and one simply for text content.

The `category-create-email-text.html` template will look like this:

```
A new category has been added to the catalog.

The name of the category is {{ category.name }}.
Click on the URL below to access the same:
{{ url_for('catalog.category', id=category.id, _external = True) }}

This is an automated email. Do not reply to it.
```

The `category-create-email-html.html` template will look like this:

```
<p>A new category has been added to the catalog.</p>

<p>The name of the category is <a href="{{ url_for('catalog.category',
id=category.id, _external = True) }}">
    <h2>{{ category.name }}</h2>
  </a>.
</p>

<p>This is an automated email. Do not reply to it.</p>
```

After this, we need to modify our procedure of creating e-mail messages that we did earlier in the `views.py` file:

```
message.body = render_template(
    "category-create-email-text.html",
    category=category
)
message.html = render_template(
    "category-create-email-html.html",
    category=category
)
```

See also

▶ Read the next recipe, *Understanding asynchronous operations*, to see how we can delegate the time-consuming e-mail sending process to an asynchronous thread and speed up our application

Understanding asynchronous operations

Some of the operations in a web application can be time-consuming and make the overall application feel slow for the user, even though it's not actually slow. This decreases the user experience significantly. To deal with this, the simplest way to implement the asynchronous execution of operations is with the help of threads. In this recipe, we will implement it using the `thread` and `threading` libraries of Python. The `threading` library is simply an interface over `thread`; it provides more functionality and hides things that are normally not used by users.

Getting ready

We will use the application from the *E-mail support for Flask applications* recipe. Many of us will have noticed that while the e-mail is being sent, the application waits for the whole process to finish, which is actually unnecessary. E-mail sending can be easily done in the background, and our application can become available to the user instantaneously.

How to do it...

Doing an asynchronous execution with the `thread` library is very simple. Just add the following code to `views.py`:

```
import thread

def send_mail(message):
    with app.app_context():
        mail.send(message)

# Replace the line below in create_category()
#mail.send(message)
# by
thread.start_new_thread(send_mail, (message,))
```

As you can see, the sending of an e-mail happens in a new thread, which sends the message as a parameter to the newly created method. We need to create a new `send_mail()` method because our e-mail templates contain `url_for`, which can be executed only inside an application context; this won't be available in the newly created thread by default.

Alternatively, sending an e-mail can also be done using the `threading` library:

```
from threading import Thread

# Replace the previously added line in create_category() by
new_thread = Thread(target=send_mail, args=[message])
new_thread.start()
```

Effectively, the same thing happens as earlier but the `threading` library provides the flexibility of starting the thread whenever needed instead of creating and starting the thread at the same time.

How it works...

It is pretty simple to observe how this works. Compare the performance of this type of execution with the application in the previous recipe, *E-mail support for Flask applications*. You will notice that the application is more responsive. Another way can be to monitor the debug logs, where the newly created category's page will load before the e-mail is sent.

Working with Celery

Celery is a task queue for Python. Earlier, there used to be an extension to integrate Flask and Celery, but with Celery 3.0, it became obsolete. Now, Celery can be directly used with Flask by just using a bit of configuration. In the *Understanding asynchronous operations* recipe, we implemented asynchronous processing to send an e-mail. In this recipe, we will implement it using Celery.

Getting ready

Celery can be installed simply from PyPI:

```
$ pip install celery
```

To make Celery work with Flask, we will need to modify our Flask app config file a bit. Here, we will use Redis as the broker (thanks to its simplicity).

We will use the application from the previous recipe and implement Celery in it.

How to do it...

The first thing that we need to do is a bit of configuration in the application's configuration file, that is, `my_app/__init__.py`:

```
from celery import Celery

app.config.update(
    CELERY_BROKER_URL='redis://localhost:6379',
    CELERY_RESULT_BACKEND='redis://localhost:6379'
)

def make_celery(app):
    celery = Celery(
```

```
        app.import_name, broker=app.config['CELERY_BROKER_URL']
    )
    celery.conf.update(app.config)
    TaskBase = celery.Task
    class ContextTask(TaskBase):
        abstract = True
        def __call__(self, *args, **kwargs):
            with app.app_context():
                return TaskBase.__call__(self, *args, **kwargs)
    celery.Task = ContextTask
    return celery
```

The preceding snippet comes directly from the Flask website and can be used as is in your application in most cases:

```
celery = make_celery(app)
```

To run the Celery process, execute the following command:

$ celery worker -b redis://localhost:6379 --app=my_app.celery -l INFO

 Make sure that Redis is also running on the broker URL, as specified in the configuration.

Here, -b points to the broker, and –app points to the `celery` object that is created in the configuration file.

Now, we just need to use this `celery` object in our `views.py` file to send e-mails asynchronously:

```
from my_app import celery

@celery.task()
def send_mail(message):
    with app.app_context():
        mail.send(message)

# Add this line wherever the email needs to be sent
send_mail.apply_async((message,))
```

We add the `@celery.task` decorator to any method that we wish to be used as a Celery task. The Celery process will detect these methods automatically.

How it works...

Now, when we create a category and an e-mail is sent, we can see a task being run on the Celery process logs, which will look like this:

```
[2014-08-28 01:16:47,365: INFO/MainProcess] Received task: my_app.
catalog.views.send_mail[d2ca07ae-6b47-4b76-9935-17b826cdc340]
```

```
[2014-08-28 01:16:55,695: INFO/MainProcess] Task my_app.catalog.
views.send_mail[d2ca07ae-6b47-4b76-9935-17b826cdc340] succeeded in
8.329121886s: None
```

See also

▶ Refer to the *Understanding asynchronous operations* recipe to see how threads can be used for various purposes, in our case, to send e-mails

▶ Read more about Celery at `http://docs.celeryproject.org/en/latest/index.html`

Module 3

Mastering Flask

Gain expertise in Flask to create dynamic and powerful web applications

1
Getting Started

Python is a flexible language that gives programmers the freedom to structure their programming environment. However, a dangerous consequence of this freedom is the ability to not set up a new Python project right from the beginning in order to avoid problems down the road.

For example, you could be halfway through your project and realize that you deleted a file or piece of code five days ago that you need to use now. Consider another example where two of the packages that you wish to use require different versions of the same underlying package. Other than the tools introduced in this chapter, there will be a lot of extra work fixing problems that already have solutions. A little extra work in the beginning can save days of work in the future.

To this end, we will need to install three programs: **Git**, **pip**, and **virtualenv**.

Version control with Git

To protect our project against human error, we will use a version control system called Git. **Version control** is a tool that records changes in files over time. This allows a programmer to see how the code has changed from previous revisions and even revert the code to the previous state. Version control systems also make collaboration easier than ever, as changes can be shared between many different programmers and merged into the current version of the project automatically, without copying and pasting hundreds of lines of code.

Simply put, version control is like backups for your code, only more powerful.

Installing Git

Installing Git is very simple. Simply go to `http://www.git-scm.com/downloads` and click on the **Operating System** (**OS**) that is being run. A program will begin to download that will walk you through the basic installation process.

Git on Windows

Git was originally developed solely for Unix OSes (for example, Linux, Mac OS X). Consequently, using Git on Windows is not seamless. During the installation, the installer will ask whether you want to install Git alongside the normal Windows Command Prompt. Do not pick this option. Choose the default option that will install a new type of command line on your system named **Bash**, which is the same command line the Unix systems use. Bash is much more powerful than the default Windows command line, and this will be used in all the examples in this book.

 A good introduction to Bash for beginners is located at `http://linuxcommand.org/learning_the_shell.php#contents`.

Git basics

Git is a very complex tool; only the basics that are needed for this book will be covered here.

 To learn more, refer to the Git documentation at `http://www.git-scm.com/doc`.

Git does not track your changes automatically. In order for Git to run properly, we have to give it the following information:

- Which folders to track
- When to save the state of the code
- What to track and what not to

Before we can do anything, we tell Git to create a `git` instance in our directory. In your project directory, run the following in your terminal:

```
$ git init
```

Git will now start to track changes in our project. As `git` tracks our files, we can see the status of our tracked files, and any files that are not tracked, by typing the following command:

```
$ git status
```

Now we can save our first **commit**, which is a snapshot of your code at the time that you run the `commit` command.

```
# In Bash, comments are marked with a #, just like Python
# Add any files that have changes and you wish to save in this commit
$ git add main.py
# Commit the changes, add in your commit message with -m
$ git commit -m"Our first commit"
```

At any point in the future, we can return to this point in our project. Adding files to be committed is called **staging** files in Git. Remember to add stage files only if you are ready to commit them. Once the files are staged, any further changes will not be staged as well. For an example of more advanced Git usage, add any text to your `main.py` file with your text editor and then run the following:

```
# To see the changes from the last commit
$ git diff
# To see the history of your changes
$ git log
# As an example, we will stage main.py
# and then remove any added files from the stage
$ git add main.py
$ git status
$ git reset HEAD main.py
# After any complicated changes, be sure to run status
# to make sure everything went well
$ git status
# lets delete the changes to main.py, reverting to its state at the last commit
# This can only be run on files that aren't staged
$ git checkout -- main.py
```

Your terminal should look something like this:

```
● ○ ●                                 ⌂ lego — bash — 99×29
bash-3.2$ git diff
diff --git i/main.py w/main.py
index fc7d1c7..556ab4c 100644
--- i/main.py
+++ w/main.py
@@ -6,7 +6,7 @@ app.config.from_object(DevConfig)

 @app.route('/')
 def home():
-    return 'Hello World!'
+    return '<h1>Hello World!</h1>'

 if __name__ == '__main__':
     app.run()
bash-3.2$ git log
Thu Feb 19 21:11:42 2015 -0500 3d3508b (HEAD, master) Our first commit  [Jack Stouffer]
bash-3.2$ git add main.py
bash-3.2$ git status
On branch master
Changes to be committed:
        modified:   main.py
        new file:   manage.py

Untracked files:
        config.py
        config.pyc
        env/

bash-3.2$ ▊
```

The Git system's `checkout` command is rather advanced for this simple introduction, but it is used to change the current status of the Git system's HEAD pointer — that is, the current location of our code in the history of our project. This will be shown in the next example.

Now, to see the code in a previous commit, first run this:

```
$ git log
Fri Jan 23 19:16:43 2015 -0500 f01d1e2 Our first commit   [Jack Stouffer]
```

The string of characters next to our commit message, f01d1e2, is called the **hash** of our commit. It is the unique identifier of that commit that we can use to return to the saved state. Now, to take the project back to that state, run this:

```
$ git checkout f01d1e2
```

Your Git project is now in a special state where any changes or commits will neither be saved nor affect any commits that were made after the one you checked out. This state is just for viewing old code. To return to the normal mode of Git, run this:

```
$ git checkout master
```

Python package management with pip

In Python, programmers can download libraries from other programmers that extend the functionality of the standard Python library. As you already know from using Flask, a lot of Python's power comes from its large amount of community-created libraries.

However, installing third-party libraries can be a huge pain to do correctly. Say there is a package X that you wish to install. Simple enough, download the Zip file and run `setup.py`, right? Not quite. Package X relies on package Y, which in turn relies on Z and Q. None of this information was listed on package X's website, but they are required to be installed for X to work at all. You then have to find all of the packages one by one and install them, in the hope that the packages you are installing don't require any extra packages themselves.

In order to automate this process, we use **pip**, the Python package manager.

Installing the pip Python package manager on Windows

If you are on Windows, and your installed Python the current version, you already have pip! If your Python installation is not the most recent, the easiest thing to do is to simply reinstall it. Download the Python Windows installer at `https://www.python.org/downloads/`.

In Windows, the variable that controls which programs are accessible from the command line is **path**. To modify your path to include Python and pip, we have to add `C:\Python27` and `C:\Python27\Tools`. Edit the Windows path by opening the Windows menu, right-clicking on **Computer** and clicking on **Properties**. Under **Advanced system settings**, click **Environment Variables....** Scroll down until you find **Path**, double-click it, and add `;C:\Python27;C:\Python27\Tools` to the end.

To make sure you have modified your path correctly, close and reopen your terminal and type the following into the command line:

```
pip --help
```

Downloading the example code

You can download the example code files from your account at `http://www.packtpub.com` for all the Packt Publishing books you have purchased. If you purchased this book elsewhere, you can visit `http://www.packtpub.com/support` and register to have the files e-mailed directly to you.

`pip` should have printed its usage message as shown in the following screenshot:

```
MINGW32:/c/dashboard                                             _ □ ✕

jstouffer@PULSAR /c/dashboard (master)
$ pip --help

Usage:
  pip <command> [options]

Commands:
  install           Install packages.
  uninstall         Uninstall packages.
  freeze            Output installed packages in requirements format.
  list              List installed packages.
  show              Show information about installed packages.
  search            Search PyPI for packages.
  wheel             Build wheels from your requirements.
  zip               DEPRECATED. Zip individual packages.
  unzip             DEPRECATED. Unzip individual packages.
  help              Show help for commands.

General Options:
  -h, --help        Show help.
  --isolated        Run pip in an isolated mode, ignoring
                    environment variables and user configuration.
  -v, --verbose     Give more output. Option is additive, and can be
                    used up to 3 times.
```

Installing the pip Python package manager on Mac OS X and Linux

Some Python installations of Linux do not come with pip, and Mac OS X installations don't come with pip by default. To install it, download the `get-pip.py` file from `https://raw.githubusercontent.com/pypa/pip/master/contrib/get-pip.py`.

Once you have downloaded it, run it with elevated privileges using the following:

```
$ sudo python get-pip.py
```

Then pip will be installed automatically.

pip basics

To install a package with `pip`, follow this simple step:

```
$ pip install [package-name]
```

On Mac and Linux, because you are installing programs outside the user-owned folders, you might have to prepend `sudo` to the install commands. To install Flask, simply run this:

```
$ pip install flask
```

Then, all requirements of Flask will be installed for you.

If you want to remove a package that you are no longer using, run this:

```
$ pip uninstall [package-name]
```

If you wish to explore or find a package but don't know its exact name, you may use the search command:

```
$ pip search [search-term]
```

Now that we have a couple of packages installed, it is common courtesy in the Python community to create a list of packages that are required to run the project, so others can quickly install every thing required. This also has the added benefit that any new member of your project will be able to run your code quickly.

This list can be created with pip by running this:

```
$ pip freeze > requirements.txt
```

What exactly did this command do? `pip freeze` run by itself prints out a list of the installed packages and their versions as follows:

```
Flask==0.10.1
itsdangerous==0.24
Jinja2==2.7.3
MarkupSafe==0.23
Werkzeug==0.10.4
wheel==0.24.0
```

The > operator tells Bash to take everything printed by the last command and write it to this file. If you look into your project directory, you will see the new file named `requirements.txt` that contains the output of `pip freeze`.

To install all the packages from this file, a new project maintainer will have to run this:

```
$ pip install -r requirements.txt
```

This tells `pip` to read all the packages listed in `requirements.txt` and install them.

Dependency sandboxing with virtualenv

So you have installed all the packages you want for your new project. Great! But, what happens when we develop the second project some time later that will use newer versions of the same packages? What happens when a library that you wish to use depends on a library you installed for the first project, but it uses an older version? When newer versions of packages contain breaking changes, upgrading them will require extra development work on an older project that you may not be able to afford.

Thankfully, there is virtualenv, a tool that sandboxes your Python projects. The secret to virtualenv is tricking your computer into looking for and installing packages in the project directory rather than in the main Python directory, which allows you to keep them completely separate.

Now that we have pip, to install virtualenv just run this:

```
$ pip install virtualenv
```

virtualenv basics

Let's initialize virtualenv for our project as follows:

```
$ virtualenv env
```

The extra env tells virtualenv to store all the packages into a folder named env. virtualenv requires you to start it before it will sandbox your project:

```
$ source env/bin/activate
# Your prompt should now look like
(env) $
```

The source command tells Bash to run the script env/bin/activate in the context of the current directory. Let's reinstall Flask in our new sandbox as follows:

```
# you won't need sudo anymore
(env) $ pip install flask
# To return to the global Python
(env) $ deactivate
```

However, it goes against the best practices in Git to track what you don't own, so we should avoid tracking the changes in third-party packages. To ignore specific files in our project, the gitignore file is needed.

```
$ touch .gitignore
```

`touch` is the Bash command to create files, and the dot at the start of a file tells Bash to not list its existence unless specifically told to show hidden files. We will create the simple `gitignore` file for now:

```
env/
*.pyc
```

This tells Git to ignore the entire `env` directory and ignore all the files that end with `.pyc` (a *compiled* Python file). When used in this way, the `*` character is called a **wildcard**.

The beginning of our project

Finally, we can get to our first Flask project. In order to have a complex project at the end of the book, we will need a simple Flask project to start us off.

In the file named `config.py`, add the following:

```
class Config(object):
    pass

class ProdConfig(Config):
    pass

class DevConfig(Config):
    DEBUG = True
```

Now, in another file named `main.py`, add the following:

```
from flask import Flask
from config import DevConfig

app = Flask(__name__)
app.config.from_object(DevConfig)

@app.route('/')
def home():
    return '<h1>Hello World!</h1>'

if __name__ == '__main__':
    app.run()
```

For anyone who is familiar with the base Flask API, this program is very basic. It will just show `Hello World!` on the browser if we navigate to `http://127.0.0.1:5000/`. One point that may be unfamiliar to Flask users is `config.from_object`, rather than `app.config['DEBUG']`. We use `from_object` because in future, multiple configurations will be used, and manually changing every variable when we need to switch between configurations is tedious.

Remember to commit these changes in Git:

```
# The --all flag will tell git to stage all changes you have made
# including deletions and new files
$ git add --all
$ git commit -m "created the base application"
```

> Reminders will no longer be given on when to commit your changes to Git. It is up to readers to develop the habit of committing whenever you reach a stopping point. It is also assumed that you will be operating inside the virtual environment, so all command line prompts will not be prefixed with `(env)`.

Using Flask Script

In order to make next chapters easier for the reader, we will use the first of many **Flask extensions** (packages that extend the functionality of Flask) named **Flask Script**. Flask Script allows programmers to create commands that act within the **Application Context** of Flask—that is, the state in Flask that allows modification of the `Flask` object. Flask Script comes with some default commands to run the server and a python shell in the Application Context. To install Flask Script with `pip`, run this:

```
$ pip install flask-script
```

We will cover more advanced usage of Flask Script in *Chapter 10, Useful Flask Extensions*; for now, let's start with a simple script named `manage.py`. First import Flask Script's objects and your app as follows:

```
from flask.ext.script import Manager, Server
from main import app
```

Then, pass your app to the `Manager` object, which will initialize Flask Script:

```
manager = Manager(app)
```

Now we add our commands. The server is the same as the normal development server run through `main.py`. The `make_shell_context` function will create a Python shell that can be run within the app context. The returned dictionary will tell Flask Script what to import by default:

```
manager.add_command("server", Server())

@manager.shell
def make_shell_context():
    return dict(app=app)
```

 Running the shell through `manage.py` will become necessary later on when the Flask extensions will only initialize when a Flask app is created. Running the default Python shell will cause these extensions to return errors.

Then, end the file with the Python standard way of running only if the user ran this file:

```
if __name__ == "__main__":
    manager.run()
```

You will now be able to run the development server with:

```
$ python manage.py server
```

Use the shell with:

```
$ python manage.py shell
# Lets check if our app imported correctly
>>> app
<Flask 'main'>
```

Summary

Now that we have set up our development environment, we can move on to implementing advanced application features in Flask. Before we can do anything visual, we need something to display. In the next chapter, you will be introduced to, and then master working with, databases in Flask.

2
Creating Models with SQLAlchemy

As previously stated, **models** are a means of abstracting and giving a common interface to data. In most web applications, data is stored and retrieved from a **Relational Database Management System (RDBMS)**, which is a database that holds data in a tabular format with rows and columns and is able to compare data across tables. Some examples include MySQL, Postgres, Oracle, and MSSQL.

In order to create models on top of our database, we will use a Python package named **SQLAlchemy**. SQLAlchemy is a database API at its lowest level and performs **Object Relational Mapping (ORM)** at its highest level. An ORM is a technique to pass and convert data between two sources with different types of systems and data structures. In this case, it converts data between the large amount of types in databases versus the mix of types and objects in Python. Also, a programming language such as Python allows you to have different objects that hold references to each other, and get and set their attributes. An ORM, such as SQLAlchemy, helps translate that into a traditional database.

In order to tie SQLAlchemy into our application context, we will use Flask SQLAlchemy. Flask SQLAlchemy is a convenience layer on top of SQLAlchemy that provides useful defaults and Flask-specific functions. If you are already familiar with SQLAlchemy, then you are free to use it without Flask SQLAlchemy.

By the end of this chapter, we will have a full database schema of our blogging application as well as models interacting with that schema.

Setting up SQLAlchemy

In order to follow along in this chapter, you will need a running database if you do not already have one. If you have never installed a database or you do not have a preference, SQLite is the best option for beginners.

SQLite is a SQL that is fast, works without a server, and is entirely contained in one file. Also, SQLite is natively supported in python. If you choose to go with SQLite, a SQLite database will be created for you in the *Our first model* section.

Python packages

To install Flask SQLAlchemy with `pip`, run the following:

```
$ pip install flask-sqlalchemy
```

We will also need to install specific packages for the database you chose to use that will act as the connector for SQLAlchemy. SQLite users can skip this step:

```
# MySQL
$ pip install PyMySQL
# Postgres
$ pip install psycopg2
# MSSQL
$ pip install pyodbc
# Oracle
$ pip install cx_Oracle
```

Flask SQLAlchemy

Before we can abstract our data, we need to set up Flask SQLAlchemy. SQLAlchemy creates its database connection through a special database URI. This is a string that looks like a URL that contains all the information that SQLAlchemy needs to connect. It takes the general form of the following:

```
databasetype+driver://user:password@ip:port/db_name
```

For each driver you installed previously, the URI would be:

```
# SQLite
sqlite:///database.db
# MySQL
mysql+pymysql://user:password@ip:port/db_name
# Postgres
postgresql+psycopg2://user:password@ip:port/db_name
# MSSQL
mssql+pyodbc://user:password@dsn_name
# Oracle
oracle+cx_oracle://user:password@ip:port/db_name
```

In our `config.py` file, add the URI to the `DevConfig` class with:

```
class DevConfig(Config):
    debug = True
    SQLALCHEMY_DATABASE_URI = "YOUR URI"
```

Our first model

You may have noted that we did not actually create any tables in our database to abstract off of. This is because SQLAlchemy allows us to create either models from tables or tables from our models. This will be covered after we create the first model.

In our `main.py` file, SQLAlchemy must first be initialized with our app as follows:

```
from flask.ext.sqlalchemy import SQLAlchemy

app = Flask(__name__)
app.config.from_object(DevConfig)
db = SQLAlchemy(app)
```

SQLAlchemy will read our app's configuration and automatically connect to our database. Let's create a `User` model to interact with a user table in the `main.py` file:

```
class User(db.Model):
    id = db.Column(db.Integer(), primary_key=True)
    username = db.Column(db.String(255))
    password = db.Column(db.String(255))
```

```
    def __init__(self, username):
        self.username = username

    def __repr__(self):
        return "<User '{}'>".format(self.username)
```

What have we accomplished? We now have a model that is based on a user table with three columns. When we inherit from `db.Model`, the entire connection and communication with the database will be already handled for us.

Each class variable that is the `db.Column` instance represents a column in the database. There is an optional first argument in a `db.Column` instance that allows us to specify the name of the column in the database. Without it, SQLAlchemy assumes that the name of the variable is the same as the name of the column. Using this, optional variable would look like:

```
    username = db.Column('user_name', db.String(255))
```

The second argument to `db.Column` tells SQLAlchemy what type the column should be treated as. The main types that we will work with in this book are:

- `db.String`
- `db.Text`
- `db.Integer`
- `db.Float`
- `db.Boolean`
- `db.Date`
- `db.DateTime`
- `db.Time`

What each type represents is rather simple. The `String` and `Text` types take Python strings and translate them to the `varchar` and `text` type columns, respectively. The `Integer` and `Float` types take any Python number and translate them into the correct type before inserting them into the database. Boolean takes Python `True` or `False` statements and if the database has a `boolean` type, inserts a Boolean into the database. If there is no `boolean` type in the database, SQLAlchemy automatically translates between Python Booleans and a 0 or a 1 in the database. The `Date`, `DateTime`, and `Time` types use the Python types of the same name from the `datetime` native library and translate them into the database. The `String`, `Integer`, and `Float` types take an extra argument that tells SQLAlchemy the length limit on our column.

If you wish to truly understand how SQLAlchemy translates your code into SQL queries, add the following to the DevConfig file:

```
SQLALCHEMY_ECHO = True
```

This will print out the created queries to the terminal. You may wish to turn this feature off as you get further along in the book, as dozens of queries could be printed to the terminal every page load.

The argument `primary_key` tells SQLAlchemy that this column has the **primary key index** on it. Each SQLAlchemy model *requires* a primary key to function.

SQLAlchemy will assume that the name of your table is the lowercase version of your model class name. However, what if we want our table to be called something other than *users*? To tell SQLAlchemy what name to use, add the __tablename__ class variable. This is also how you connect to tables that already exist in your database. Just place the name of the table in the string.

```
class User(db.Model):
    __tablename__ = 'user_table_name'

    id = db.Column(db.Integer(), primary_key=True)
    username = db.Column(db.String(255))
    password = db.Column(db.String(255))
```

We don't have to include the __init__ or __repr__ functions. If we don't, then SQLAlchemy will automatically create an __init__ function that accepts the names and values of your columns as keyword arguments.

Creating the user table

Using SQLAlchemy to do the heavy lifting, we will now create the user table in our database. Update `manage.py` to:

```
from main import app, db, User
...
@manager.shell
def make_shell_context():
return dict(app=app, db=db, User=User)

Style - "db","User" in first line as Code Highlight
```

From now on, whenever we create a new model, import it and add it to the returned dict.

This will allow us to work with our models in the shell. Run the shell now and use `db.create_all()` to create all of the tables:

```
$ python manage.py shell
>>> db.create_all()
```

You should now see in your database a table called `users` with the columns specified. Also, if you are using SQLite, you should now see a file named `database.db` in your file structure.

CRUD

In every storage mechanism for data, there are four basic types of functions: **Create, Read, Update, and Delete (CRUD)**. These allow all the basic ways of manipulating and viewing data needed for our web apps. To use these functions, we will use an object on the database named the **session**. Sessions will be explained later in the chapter, but for now, think of them as a storage location for all of our changes to the database.

Creating models

To create a new row in your database using our models, add the model to the `session` and `commit` objects. Adding an object to the session marks its changes for saving, and committing is when the session is saved to the database as follows:

```
>>> user = User(username='fake_name')
>>> db.session.add(user)
>>> db.session.commit()
```

It is simple to add a new row to our table.

Reading models

After we have added data to our database, data can be queried using `Model.query`. For those who use SQLAlchemy, this is shorthand for `db.session.query(Model)`.

For our first example, use `all()` to get all rows in the database as a list.

```
>>> users = User.query.all()
>>> users
[<User 'fake_name'>]
```

When the number of items in the database increases, this query process becomes slower. In SQLAlchmey, as in SQL, we have the limit function to specify the total number of rows we wish to work with.

```
>>> users = User.query.limit(10).all()
```

By default, SQLAlchemy returns the records ordered by their primary keys. To control this, we have the `order_by` function, which is given as:

```
# asending
>>> users = User.query.order_by(User.username).all()
# desending
>>> users = User.query.order_by(User.username.desc()).all()
```

To return just one model, we use `first()` instead of `all()`:

```
>>> user = User.query.first()
>>> user.username
fake_name
```

To return one model by its primary key, use `query.get()`:

```
>>> user = User.query.get(1)
>>> user.username
fake_name
```

All these functions are chainable, which means that they can be appending on to each other to modify the return result. Those of you who are fluent in JavaScript will find this syntax familiar.

```
>>> users = User.query.order_by(
        User.username.desc()
    ).limit(10).first()
```

The `first()` and `all()` methods return a value and therefore end the chain.

There is also a Flask SQLAlchemy-specific method that is called **pagination**, which can be used rather than `first()` or `all()`. This is a convenience method designed to enable the pagination feature that most websites use while displaying a long list of items. The first parameter defines which page the query should return to and the second parameter is the number of items per page. So, if we passed 1 and 10 as the parameters, the first 10 objects would be returned. If we instead passed 2 and 10, objects 11-20 would be returned, and so on.

The pagination method is different from the `first()` and `all()` methods because it returns a pagination object rather than a list of models. For example, if we wanted to get the first 10 items of a fictional `Post` object for the first page in our blog:

```
>>> Post.query.paginate(1, 10)
<flask_sqlalchemy.Pagination at 0x105118f50>
```

This object has several useful properties:

```
>>> page = User.query.paginate(1, 10)
# return the models in the page
>>> page.items
[<User 'fake_name'>]
# what page does this object represent
>>> page.page
1
# How many pages are there
>>> page.pages
1
# are there enough models to make the next or previous page
>>> page.has_prev, page.has_next
(False, False)
# return the next or previous page pagination object
# if one does not exist returns the current page
>>> page.prev(), page.next()
(<flask_sqlalchemy.Pagination at 0x10812da50>,
 <flask_sqlalchemy.Pagination at 0x1081985d0>)
```

Filtering queries

Now we get to the actual power of SQL, that is, filtering results by a set of rules. To get a list of models that satisfy a set of equalities, we use the `query.filter_by` filter. The `query.filter_by` filter takes named arguments that represent the values we are looking for in each column in the database. To get a list of all users with a username of `fake_name`:

```
>>> users = User.query.filter_by(username='fake_name').all()
```

This example is filtering on one value, but multiple values can be passed to the `filter_by` filter. Just like our previous functions, `filter_by` is chainable:

```
>>> users = User.query.order_by(User.username.desc())
        .filter_by(username='fake_name')
        .limit(2)
        .all()
```

`query.filter_by` only works if you know the exact values that you are looking for. This is avoided by passing Python comparison statements to the query with `query.filter`:

```
>>> user = User.query.filter(
        User.id > 1
    ).all()
```

This is a simple example, but `query.filter` accepts any Python comparison. With common Python types, such as `integers`, `strings`, and `dates`, the `==` operator can be used for equality comparisons. If you had an `integer`, `float`, or `date` column, an inequality statement could also be passed with the `>`, `<`, `<=`, and `>=` operators.

We can also translate complex SQL queries with SQLAlchemy functions. For example, to use IN, OR, or NOT SQL comparisons:

```
>>> from sqlalchemy.sql.expression import not_, or_
>>> user = User.query.filter(
        User.username.in_(['fake_name']),
        User.password == None
    ).first()
# find all of the users with a password
>>> user = User.query.filter(
        not_(User.password == None)
    ).first()
# all of these methods are able to be combined
>>> user = User.query.filter(
        or_(not_(User.password == None), User.id >= 1)
    ).first()
```

In SQLAlchemy, comparisons to `None` are translated to comparisons to NULL.

Updating models

To update the values of models that already exist, apply the `update` method to a query object, that is, before you return the models with a method such as `first()` or `all()`:

```
>>> User.query.filter_by(username='fake_name').update({
        'password': 'test'
    })
# The updated models have already been added to the session
>>> db.session.commit()
```

Deleting models

If we wish to remove a model from the database:

```
>>> user = User.query.filter_by(username='fake_name').first()
>>> db.session.delete(user)
>>> db.session.commit()
```

Relationships between models

Relationships between models in SQLAlchemy are links between two or more models that allow models to reference each other automatically. This allows naturally related data, such as *comments to posts*, to be easily retrieved from the database with its related data. This is where the *R* in RDBMS comes from, and it gives this type of database a large amount of power.

Let's create our first relation. Our blogging website is going to need some blog posts. Each blog post is going to be written by one user, so it makes sense to link posts back to the user that wrote them to easily get all posts by a user. This is an example of a **one-to-many** relationship.

One-to-many

Let's add a model to represent blog posts on our website:

```
class Post(db.Model):
    id = db.Column(db.Integer(), primary_key=True)
    title = db.Column(db.String(255))
    text = db.Column(db.Text())
```

```
    publish_date = db.Column(db.DateTime())
    user_id = db.Column(db.Integer(), db.ForeignKey('user.id'))

    def __init__(self, title):
        self.title = title

    def __repr__(self):
        return "<Post '{}'>".format(self.title)
```

Note the column `user_id`. Those who are familiar with RDBMSes will know that this represents a **Foreign Key Constraint**. Foreign Key Constraint is a rule in the database that forces the value of `user_id` to exist in the `id` column in the user table. This is a check in the database to make sure that `Post` will always refer to an existing user. The parameter to `db.ForeignKey` is a string representation of the `user_id` field. If you have decided to call your user table with `__table_name__`, you must change this string. This string is used rather than a direct reference with `User.id` because during initialization of SQLAlchemy, the `User` object might not exist yet.

The `user_id` column itself is not enough to tell SQLAlchemy that we have a relationship. We must modify our `User` model as follows:

```
class User(db.Model):
    id = db.Column(db.Integer(), primary_key=True)
    username = db.Column(db.String(255))
    password = db.Column(db.String(255))
    posts = db.relationship(
        'Post',
        backref='user',
        lazy='dynamic'
    )
```

The `db.relationship` function creates a virtual column in SQLAlchemy that connects with `db.ForeignKey` in our `Post` model. The first parameter is the name of the class that we are referencing. We will cover what `backref` does soon, but what is the `lazy` parameter? The `lazy` parameter controls how SQLAlchemy will load our related objects. `subquery` would load our relations as soon as our `Post` object is loaded. This cuts down the number of queries, but will slow down when the number of returned items grows larger. In contrast, with the `dynamic` option, the related objects will be loaded on access and can be filtered down before returning. This is best if the number of returned objects is or will become large.

We may now access the `User.posts` variable that will return a list of all the posts whose `user_id` field equals our `User.id`. Let's try this now in our shell as follows:

```
>>> user = User.query.get(1)
>>> new_post = Post('Post Title')
>>> new_post.user_id = user.id
>>> user.posts
[]
>>> db.session.add(new_post)
>>> db.session.commit()
>>> user.posts
[<Post 'Post Title'>]
```

Note that we were not able to access our post from our relationship without committing our changes to the database.

The parameter `backref` gives us the ability to access and set our `User` class via `Post.user`. This is given by:

```
>>> second_post = Post('Second Title')
>>> second_post.user = user
>>> db.session.add(second_post)
>>> db.session.commit()
>>> user.posts
[<Post 'Post Title'>, <Post 'Second Title'>]
```

Because `user.posts` is a list, we could have also added our `Post` model to the list to save it automatically:

```
>>> second_post = Post('Second Title')
>>> user.posts.append(second_post)
>>> db.session.add(user)
>>> db.session.commit()
>>> user.posts
[<Post 'Post Title'>, <Post 'Second Title'>]
```

With the `backref` option as dynamic, we can treat our relation column as a query as well as a list:

```
>>> user.posts
[<Post 'Post Title'>, <Post 'Second Title'>]
>>> user.posts.order_by(Post.publish_date.desc()).all()
[<Post 'Second Title'>, <Post 'Post Title'>]
```

Before we move on to our next relationship type, let's add another model for user comments with a one-to-many relationship, which will be used in the book later on:

```python
class Post(db.Model):
    id = db.Column(db.Integer(), primary_key=True)
    title = db.Column(db.String(255))
    text = db.Column(db.Text())
    publish_date = db.Column(db.DateTime())
    comments = db.relationship(
        'Comment',
        backref='post',
        lazy='dynamic'
    )
    user_id = db.Column(db.Integer(), db.ForeignKey('user.id'))

    def __init__(self, title):
        self.title = title

    def __repr__(self):
        return "<Post '{}'>".format(self.title)

class Comment(db.Model):
    id = db.Column(db.Integer(), primary_key=True)
    name = db.Column(db.String(255))
    text = db.Column(db.Text())
    date = db.Column(db.DateTime())
    post_id = db.Column(db.Integer(), db.ForeignKey('post.id'))

    def __repr__(self):
        return "<Comment '{}'>".format(self.text[:15])
```

Many-to-many

What if we have two models that can reference each other, but each model needs to reference more than one of each type? For example, our blog posts will need tags in order for our users to easily group similar posts. Each tag can refer to many posts, but each post can have multiple tags. This type of relation is called a **many-to-many** relationship. Consider the following example:

```python
tags = db.Table('post_tags',
    db.Column('post_id', db.Integer, db.ForeignKey('post.id')),
    db.Column('tag_id', db.Integer, db.ForeignKey('tag.id'))
)

class Post(db.Model):
    id = db.Column(db.Integer(), primary_key=True)
    title = db.Column(db.String(255))
    text = db.Column(db.Text())
    publish_date = db.Column(db.DateTime())
    comments = db.relationship(
        'Comment',
        backref='post',
        lazy='dynamic'
    )
    user_id = db.Column(db.Integer(), db.ForeignKey('user.id'))
    tags = db.relationship(
        'Tag',
        secondary=tags,
        backref=db.backref('posts', lazy='dynamic')
    )

    def __init__(self, title):
        self.title = title

    def __repr__(self):
        return "<Post '{}'>".format(self.title)

class Tag(db.Model):
    id = db.Column(db.Integer(), primary_key=True)
    title = db.Column(db.String(255))

    def __init__(self, title):
        self.title = title

    def __repr__(self):
        return "<Tag '{}'>".format(self.title)
```

The db.Table object is a lower level access to the database than the abstraction of db.Model. The db.Model object rests on top of db.Table and provides a representation of specific rows in the table. The db.Table object is used because there is no need to access individual rows of the table.

The tags variable is used to represent the post_tags table, which contains two rows: one that represents the id of a post, and another that represents the id of a tag. To illustrate how this works, if the table had the following data:

```
post_id    tag_id
1          1
1          3
2          3
2          4
2          5
3          1
3          2
```

SQLAlchemy would translate this to:

- A post with an id of 1 has the tags with ids of 1 and 3
- A post with an id of 2 has the tags with ids of 3, 4, and 5
- A post with an id of 3 has the tags with ids of 1 and 2

You may describe this data as easily as tags being related to posts.

Before the db.relationship function sets up our relationship, but this time it has the secondary parameter. The secondary parameter tells SQLAlchemy that this relationship is stored in the tags table. Let's see this in the following code:

```
>>> post_one = Post.query.filter_by(title='Post Title').first()
>>> post_two = Post.query.filter_by(title='Second Title').first()
>>> tag_one = Tag('Python')
>>> tag_two = Tag('SQLAlchemy')
>>> tag_three = Tag('Flask')
>>> post_one.tags = [tag_two]
>>> post_two.tags = [tag_one, tag_two, tag_three]
>>> tag_two.posts
[<Post 'Post Title'>, <Post 'Second Title'>]
>>> db.session.add(post_one)
>>> db.session.add(post_two)
>>> db.session.commit()
```

As given in the one-to-many relationship, the main relationship column is just a list. The main difference being that the `backref` option is now also a list. Because it's a list, we may add posts to tags from the `tag` object as follows:

```
>>> tag_one.posts.append(post_one)
[<Post 'Post Title'>, <Post 'Second Title'>]
>>> post_one.tags
[<Tag 'SQLAlchemy'>, <Tag 'Python'>]
>>> db.session.add(tag_one)
>>> db.session.commit()
```

The convenience of SQLAlchemy sessions

Now that you understand the power of SQLAlchemy, you can also understand what the SQLAlchemy session object is and why web apps should never be made without them. As stated before, the session can be simply described as an object that tracks the changes in our models and commits them to the database when we tell it to. However, there is a bit more to it than this.

First, the session is the handler for **transactions**. Transactions are sets of changes that are flushed to the database on commit. Transactions provide a lot of hidden functionality. For example, transactions automatically determine which objects will be saved first when objects have relations. You might have noted this when we were saving tags in the previous section. When we added tags to the posts, the session automatically knew to save the tags first despite the fact that we did not add it to be committed. If we are working with raw SQL queries and a database connection, we would have to keep track of which rows are related to which other rows to avoid saving a foreign key reference to an object that does not exist.

Transactions also automatically mark data as stale when changes to an object are saved to the database. When we access the object next, a query is made to the database to update the data, but all happens behind the scenes. If we were not using SQLAlchemy, we would also need to manually track which rows need to updated. If we want to be resource efficient, we only need to query and update those rows.

Second, the session makes it impossible for there to be two different references to the same row in the database. This is accomplished by all queries going through the session (`Model.query` is actually `db.session.query(Model)`), and if the row has already been queried in this transaction, then the pointer to that object will be returned and not a new object. If this check did not exist, two objects that represent the same row could be saved to the database with different changes. This creates subtle bugs that might not be caught instantly.

Keep in mind that Flask SQLAlchemy creates a new session for every request and discards any changes that were not committed at the end of the request, so always remember to save your work.

 For an in-depth look at sessions, the creator of SQLAlchemy, Mike Bayer, gave a talk at PyCon Canada 2012. Refer to *The SQLAlchemy Session - In Depth*, here — `https://www.youtube.com/watch?v=PKAdehPHOMo`.

Database migrations with Alembic

The functionality of web apps change all the time, and with new functionality, we need to change the structure of our database. Whether it's adding or dropping new columns, or creation of new tables, our models will change throughout the life cycle of our app. However, problems quickly arise when the database changes often. When moving our changes from development to production, how can you be sure that you carried over every change without manually comparing each model and its corresponding table? Let's say that you wish to go back in your Git history to see if some earlier version of your app had the same bug that you are now encountering in production. How will you change your database back to the correct schema without a lot of extra work?

As programmers, we hate extra work. Thankfully, there is a tool called **Alembic**, which automatically creates and tracks database migrations from the changes in our SQLAlchemy models. **Database migrations** are records of all the changes of our schema. Alembic allows us to upgrade or downgrade our database to a specific saved version. Upgrading or downgrading by several versions will execute all the files between the two selected versions. The best part of Alembic is that its history files are only Python files. When we create our first migration, we can see how simple the Alembic syntax is.

Alembic does not capture every possible change. For example, it does not record changes on the SQL indexes. After every migration, the reader is encouraged to review the migration file and make any necessary corrections.

We won't work directly with Alembic; instead, we will use **Flask-Migrate**, which is an extension created specifically for SQLAlchemy and works with Flask Script. To install it with `pip`:

```
$ pip install Flask-Migrate
```

To get started, we need to add the command to our `manage.py` file as follows:

```
from flask.ext.script import Manager, Server
from flask.ext.migrate import Migrate, MigrateCommand

from main import app, db, User, Post, Tag

migrate = Migrate(app, db)

manager = Manager(app)
manager.add_command("server", Server())
manager.add_command('db', MigrateCommand)


@manager.shell
def make_shell_context():
    return dict(app=app, db=db, User=User, Post=Post, Tag=Tag)

if __name__ == "__main__":
    manager.run()
```

We initialized the `Migrate` object with our app and our SQLAlchemy instance, and we made the migrate command callable through `manage.py db`. To see a list of possible commands, run this:

```
$ python manage.py db
```

To start tracking our changes, we use the `init` command as follows:

```
$ python manage.py db init
```

This will create a new folder in our directory named `migrations` that will hold all of our history. Now we start with our first migration:

```
$ python manage.py  db migrate -m"initial migration"
```

This command will cause Alembic to scan our SQLAlchemy object and find all the tables and columns that did not exist before this commit. As this is our first commit, the migration file will be rather long. Be sure to specify the migration message with -m, as it's the easiest way to identify what each migration is doing. Each migration file is stored in the `migrations/versions/` folder.

To apply the migration to your database and change your schema, run the following:

```
$ python manage.py db upgrade
```

To return to the previous version, find the version number with the `history` command and pass it to the `downgrade` command:

```
$ python manage.py db history
<base> -> 7ded34bc4fb (head), initial migration
$ python manage.py db downgrade 7ded34bc4fb
```

Like Git, a hash marks each migration. This is the main functionality of Alembic, but it is only surface level. Try to align your migrations with your Git commits in order to make it easier to downgrade or upgrade when reverting commits.

Summary

Now that we have data control mastered, we can now move on to displaying our data in our application. The next chapter, *Chapter 3, Creating Views with Templates*, will dynamically cover creating HTML based on our models and adding models from our web interface.

3
Creating Views with Templates

Now that we have our data in an easily accessible format, displaying the information in a web page becomes much easier. In this chapter, we will use the included templating language for Flask Jinja, to dynamically create HTML from our SQLAlchemy models. We will also examine Jinja's methods to automate the creation of HTML and modify data for presentation inside a template. Then, the chapter will end with automatically creating and validating HTML forms with Jinja.

Jinja's syntax

Jinja is a templating language written in Python. A **templating language** is a simple format that is designed to help automate the creation of documents. In any templating language, variables passed to the template replace predefined locations in the template. In Jinja, variable substitutions are defined by {{ }}. The {{ }} syntax is called a **variable block**. There are also **control blocks** defined by {% %}, which declare language functions, such as **loops** or if statements. For example, when the Post model from the previous chapter is passed to it, we have the following Jinja code:

```
<h1>{{ post.title }}</h1>
```

This produces the following:

```
<h1>First Post</h1>
```

The variables displayed in a Jinja template can be any Python type or object, as long as they can be converted into a string via the Python function `str()`. For example, a dictionary or a list passed to a template can have its attributes displayed via:

```
{{ your_dict['key'] }}
{{ your_list[0] }}
```

Many programmers prefer to use JavaScript to template and dynamically create their HTML documents to take the HTML rendering load off of the server. This will not be covered in this chapter as it is an advanced JavaScript topic. However, many JavaScript templating engines use the `{{ }}` syntax as well. If you choose to combine Jinja and your JavaScript templates defined in your HTML files, then wrap the JavaScript templates in the `raw` control block to tell Jinja to ignore them:

```
{% raw %}
<script id="template" type="text/x-handlebars-template">
    <h1>{{title}}</h1>
    <div class="body">
        {{body}}
    </div>
</script>
{% endraw %}
```

Filters

It's a common mistake to believe that Jinja and Python's syntax is the same because of their similarity. However, there is a lot of differences. As you will see in this section, normal Python functions do not really exist. Instead, in Jinja, variables can be passed to built-in functions that modify the variables for display purposes. These functions, named filters, are called in the variable block with the pipe character `|`:

```
{{ variable | filter_name(*args) }}
```

Otherwise, if no arguments are passed to the filter, the parentheses can be omitted as follows:

```
{{ variable | filter_name }}
```

Filters can also be called control blocks to apply them to blocks of text:

```
{% filter filter_name %}
    A bunch of text
{% endfilter %}
```

There are many filters in Jinja; this book will cover only the most useful filters. For the sake of brevity, in each example, the output of each filter will be listed directly beneath the filter itself.

 For a full list of all the default filters in Jinja, visit `http://jinja.pocoo.org/docs/dev/templates/#list-of-builtin-filters`.

default

If the passed variable is `None`, then replace it with a default value as follows:

```
{{ post.date | default('2015-01-01') }}
2015-01-01
```

If you wish to replace the variable with the default value and if the variable evaluates to `False`, then pass `True` to the optional second parameter:

```
{{ '' | default('An empty string', True) }}
An empty string
```

escape

If the passed variable is a string of HTML, the &, <, >, ', and " characters will be printed as HTML escape sequences:

```
{{ "<h1>Title</h1>" | escape }}
&#60;h1&#62;Title&#60;/h1&#62;
```

float

This converts the passed value to a floating point number with the Python `float()` function as follows:

```
{{ 75 | float }}
75.0
```

int

This converts the passed value to an integer with the Python `int()` function as follows:

```
{{ 75.7 | int }}
75
```

join

This is a filter that joins elements of a list with a string and works exactly same as the `list` method of the same name. It is given as:

```
{{ ['Python', 'SQLAlchemy'] | join(',') }}
Python, SQLAlchemy
```

length

This is a filter that fills the same role as the Python `len()` function. It is given as:

```
Tag Count: {{ post.tags | length }}
Tag Count: 2
```

round

This rounds off a float to the specified precision:

```
{{ 3.14159265358979323862 | round(1) }}
3.1
```

You may also specify how you want the number to be rounded off:

```
{{ 4.7 | round(1, "common") }}
5
{{ 4.2 | round(1, "common") }}
4
{{ 4.7 | round(1, "floor") }}
4
{{ 4.2 | round(1, "ceil") }}
5
```

The `common` option rounds like a person would: anything at or above 0.5 is rounded up, and anything less than 0.5 is rounded down. The `floor` option always rounds the number down, and the `ceil` option always rounds up, regardless of the decimal.

safe

If you try to insert HTML into your page from a variable, for example, when you wish to display a blog post, Jinja will automatically try to add HTML escape sequences to the output. Look at the following example:

```
{{ "<h1>Post Title</h1>" }}
&lt;h1&gt;Post Title&lt;/h1&gt;
```

This is a necessary security feature. When an application has inputs that allow users to submit arbitrary text, it allows a malicious user to input HTML code. For example, if a user were to submit a script tag as a comment and Jinja didn't have this feature, the script would be executed on all the browsers that visited the page.

However, we still need a way to display HTML that we know is safe to show, such as the HTML of our blog posts. We can achieve this using the `safe` filter as follows:

```
{{ "<h1>Post Title</h1>" | safe }}
<h1>Post Title</h1>
```

title

We capitalize a string using title case format as follows:

```
{{ "post title" | title }}
Post Title
```

tojson

We can pass the variable to the Python `json.dumps` function. Remember that your passed object must be serializable by the `json` module.

```
{{ {'key': False, 'key2': None, 'key3': 45} | tojson }}
{key: false, key2: null, key3: 45}
```

This feature is most commonly used to pass SQLAlchemy models to JavaScript MVC frameworks on page load rather than waiting for an AJAX request. If you use `tojson` in this way, remember to pass the result to the `safe` filter as well to make sure that you don't get HTML escape sequences in your JavaScript. Here is an example with a `Backbone.js`, a popular JavaScript MVC framework, collection of models:

```
var collection = new PostCollection({{ posts | tojson | safe }});
```

truncate

This takes a long string and returns a string cutoff at the specified length in characters and appends an ellipses:

```
{{ "A Longer Post Body Than We Want" | truncate(10) }}
A Longer...
```

By default, any words that are cut in the middle are discarded. To disable this, pass `True` as an extra parameter:

```
{{ "A Longer Post Body Than We Want" | truncate(10, True) }}
A Longer P...
```

Custom filters

Adding your own filter into Jinja is as simple as writing a Python function. To understand custom filters, we will look at an example. Our simple filter will count the number of occurrences of a substring in a string and return it. Look at the following call:

```
{{ variable | filter_name("string") }}
```

This will be changed to:

```
filter_name(variable, "string")
```

We can define our filter as:

```
def count_substring(string, sub):
    return string.count(sub)
```

To add this function to the list of available filters, we have to manually add it to the `filters` dictionary of the `jinja_env` object in our `main.py` file:

```
app.jinja_env.filters['count_substring'] = count_substring
```

Comments

Comments in the template are defined by {# #}, will be ignored by Jinja, and will not be in the returned HTML code:

```
{# Note to the maintainers of this code #}
```

if statements

`if` statements in Jinja are similar to Python's `if` statements. Anything that returns, or is, a Boolean determines the flow of the code:

```
{%if user.is_logged_in() %}
    <a href='/logout'>Logout</a>
{% else %}
    <a href='/login'>Login</a>
{% endif %}
```

Filters can also be used in `if` statements:

```
{% if comments | length > 0 %}
    There are {{ comments | length }} comments
{% else %}
    There are no comments
{% endif %}
```

Loops

We can use loops in Jinja to iterate over any list or generator function:

```
{% for post in posts %}
    <div>
        <h1>{{ post.title }}</h1>
        <p>{{ post.text | safe }}</p>
    </div>
{% endfor %}
```

Loops and `if` statements can be combined to mimic the `break` functionality in Python loops. In this example, the loop will only use the post `if post.text` is not `None`:

```
{% for post in posts if post.text %}
    <div>
        <h1>{{ post.title }}</h1>
        <p>{{ post.text | safe }}</p>
    </div>
{% endfor %}
```

Inside the loop, you have access to a special variable named `loop`, which gives you access to information about the `for` loop. For example, if we want to know the current index of the current loop to emulate the `enumerate` function in Python, we may use the index variable of the loop variable as follows:

```
{% for post in posts %}
    {{ loop.index }}. {{ post.title }}
{% endfor %}
```

This will produce the following output:

```
1. Post Title
2. Second Post
```

All the variables and functions that the `loop` object exposes are listed in the following table:

Variable	Description
loop.index	The current iteration of the loop (1 indexed)
loop.index0	The current iteration of the loop (0 indexed)
loop.revindex	The number of iterations from the end of the loop (1 indexed)
loop.revindex0	The number of iterations from the end of the loop (0 indexed)
loop.first	True if the current item is first in the iterator
loop.last	True if the current item is last in the iterator
loop.length	The number of items in the iterator
loop.cycle	The helper function to cycle between the items in the iterator, which is explained later
loop.depth	Indicates how deep in a recursive loop the loop currently is (starts at level 1)
loop.depth0	Indicates how deep in a recursive loop the loop currently is (starts at level 0)

The `cycle` function is a function that goes through an iterator one item at a time at every loop. We may use the previous example to demonstrate:

```
{% for post in posts %}
    {{ loop.cycle('odd', 'even') }} {{ post.title }}
{% endfor %}
```

This will output:

```
odd Post Title
even Second Post
```

Macros

A **macro** is best understood as a function in Jinja that returns a template or HTML string. This is used to avoid code that is repeated over and over again and reduce it to one function call. For example, the following is a macro to add a Bootstrap CSS input and a label to your template:

```
{% macro input(name, label, value='', type='text') %}
    <div class="form-group">
        <label for"{{ name }}">{{ label }}</label>
```

```
        <input type="{{ type }}" name="{{ name }}"
            value="{{ value | escape }}" class="form-control">
    </div>
{% endmacro %}
```

Now to quickly add an input to a form in any template, call your macro using the following:

```
{{ input('name', 'Name') }}
```

This will output:

```
<div class="form-group">
    <label for"name">Name</label>
    <input type="text" name="name" value="" class="form-control">
</div>
```

Flask-specific variables and functions

Flask makes several functions and objects available to you by default in your template.

config

Flask makes the current `config` object available in templates:

```
{{ config.SQLALCHEMY_DATABASE_URI }}
sqlite:///database.db
```

request

This is the Flask `request` object for the current request.

```
{{ request.url }}
http://127.0.0.1/
```

session

The Flask `session` object is:

```
{{ session.new }}
True
```

url_for()

The `url_for` function returns the URL of a route by giving the route function name as a parameter. This allows URLs to be changed without worrying about where links will break.

```
{{ url_for('home') }}
/
```

If we had a route that had positional arguments in the URL, we pass them as `kwargs`. They will be filled in for us in the resulting URL as:

```
{{ url_for('post', post_id=1) }}
/post/1
```

get_flashed_messages()

This returns a list of all the messages passed through the `flash()` function in Flask. The `flash` function is a simple function that queues messages, which are just Python strings, for the `get_flashed_messages` function to consume.

```
{% for message in get_flashed_messages() %}
    {{ message }}
{% endfor %}
```

Creating our views

To get started, we need to create a new folder named `templates`, in our project directory. This folder will store all of our Jinja files, which are just HTML files with Jinja syntax mixed in. Our first template will be our home page, which will be a list of the first 10 posts with summaries. There will also be a view for a post that will just show the post content, comments on the page, links to the author user page, and links to tag pages. There will also be user and tag pages that show all the posts by a user and all the posts with a specific tag. Each page will also have a sidebar showing the five most recent posts and the top five most used tags.

The view function

Because each page will have the same sidebar information, we can break that into a separate function to simplify our code. In the `main.py` file, add the following code:

```
from sqlalchemy import func
```

```
...
def sidebar_data():
    recent = Post.query.order_by(
        Post.publish_date.desc()
    ).limit(5).all()
    top_tags = db.session.query(
        Tag, func.count(tags.c.post_id).label('total')
    ).join(
        tags
    ).group_by(Tag).order_by('total DESC').limit(5).all()

    return recent, top_tags
```

The most recent posts query is straight forward, but the most popular tags query looks somewhat familiar, yet a little odd. This is a bit beyond the scope of this book, but using the SQLAlchemy `func` library to return a count, we are able to order our tags by the most used tags. The `func` function is explained in detail at `http://docs.sqlalchemy.org/en/rel_1_0/core/sqlelement.html#sqlalchemy.sql.expression.func`.

The home page function in `main.py` will need all the posts in a pagination object and the sidebar information:

```
from flask import Flask, render_template
...
@app.route('/')
@app.route('/<int:page>')
def home(page=1):
    posts = Post.query.order_by(
        Post.publish_date.desc()
    ).paginate(page, 10)
    recent, top_tags = sidebar_data()

    return render_template(
```

```
    'home.html',
    posts=posts,
    recent=recent,
    top_tags=top_tags
)
```

Here, we finally see how Flask and Jinja tie together. The Flask function `render_template` takes the name of a file in the folder templates and passes all the `kwargs` to the template as variables. Also, our `home` function now has multiple routes to handle pagination and will default to the first page if there is nothing after the slash.

Now that you have all the pieces of knowledge that you need to write view functions, I challenge you to try to write the rest of the view functions based on the preceding descriptions. After you have tried, compare your results to the following:

```
@app.route('/post/<int:post_id>')
def post(post_id):
    post = Post.query.get_or_404(post_id)
    tags = post.tags
    comments = post.comments.order_by(Comment.date.desc()).all()
    recent, top_tags = sidebar_data()

    return render_template(
        'post.html',
        post=post,
        tags=tags,
        comments=comments,
        recent=recent,
        top_tags=top_tags
    )


@app.route('/tag/<string:tag_name>')
```

```
def tag(tag_name):
    tag = Tag.query.filter_by(title=tag_name).first_or_404()
    posts = tag.posts.order_by(Post.publish_date.desc()).all()
    recent, top_tags = sidebar_data()

    return render_template(
        'tag.html',
        tag=tag,
        posts=posts,
        recent=recent,
        top_tags=top_tags
    )


@app.route('/user/<string:username>')
def user(username):
    user = User.query.filter_by(username=username).first_or_404()
    posts = user.posts.order_by(Post.publish_date.desc()).all()
    recent, top_tags = sidebar_data()
    return render_template(
        'user.html',
        user=user,
        posts=posts,
        recent=recent,
        top_tags=top_tags
    )
```

After all of your views are written, the only thing left to do is to write the templates.

Writing the templates and inheritance

Because this book does not focus on interface design, we will use the CSS library Bootstrap and avoid writing custom CSS. If you have never used it before, **Bootstrap** is a set of default CSS rules that make your website work well across all browsers and has tools that allow you to easily control the layout of your website. To download Bootstrap, go to `http://getbootstrap.com/` and hit the button that says **Download Bootstrap**. Hit another button that says **Download Bootstrap** and you will start to download a Zip file. Unzip this file into your project directory and rename the folder to `static`. The `static` folder must be at the same directory level as the `main.py` file for Flask to automatically find the files. From now on, this is where we will keep our CSS, font, images, and JavaScript files.

Because every route will have a template assigned to it, each template will need the requisite HTML **boilerplate** code with our meta information, style sheets, common JavaScript libraries, and so on. To keep our templates **DRY** (**Don't Repeat Yourself**), we will use one of the most powerful features of Jinja, template inheritance. **Template inheritance** is when a child template can import a base template as a starting point and only replace marked sections in the base. To start our base template, we need a basic HTML skeleton as follows:

```
<!DOCTYPE html>
<html>
<head>
  <meta charset="utf-8">
  <meta http-equiv="X-UA-Compatible" content="IE=edge">
  <meta name="viewport" content="width=device-width, initial-
    scale=1">
  <title>{% block title %}Blog{% endblock %}</title>
  <link rel="stylesheet" href="{{ url_for('static',
    filename='css/bootstrap.min.css') }}">
</head>
<body>
  <div class="container">
    <div class="jumbotron">
      <h1><a href="{{ url_for('home') }}">My Blog</a></h1>
        <p>Welcome to the blog!</p>
    </div>
    {% block body %}
    {% endblock %}
  </div>
```

```
    <script src="{{ url_for('static', filename='js/jquery.min.js')
      }}">></script>
    <script src="{{ url_for('static',
      filename='js/bootstrap.min.js') }}">></script>
  </body>
  </html>
```

Save this as `base.html` in your `templates` directory. The `block` control block is used in inheritance to mark sections to be replaceable by the child template. Because we will use pagination in several different pages, let's create a macro to render a pagination widget:

```
{% macro render_pagination(pagination, endpoint) %}
  <nav>
    <ul class="pagination">
      <li>
        <a href="{{ url_for('home', page=pagination.prev().page)
          }}" aria-label="Previous">
          <span aria-hidden="true">&laquo;</span>
        </a>
      </li>
      {% for page in pagination.iter_pages() %}
        {% if page %}
          {% if page != pagination.page %}
            <li>
              <a href="{{ url_for(endpoint, page=page) }}">
                {{ page }}
              </a>
            </li>
          {% else %}
            <li><a href="">{{ page }}</a></li>
          {% endif %}
        {% else %}
          <li><a>…</a><li>
        {% endif %}
      {% endfor %}
      <li>
        <a href="{{ url_for('home', page=pagination.next().page)
          }}" aria-label="Next">
          <span aria-hidden="true">&raquo;</span>
        </a>
      </li>
    </ul>
  </nav>
{% endmacro %}
```

This macro takes a Flask SQLAlchemy pagination object and a view function name and constructs a Bootstrap list of page links. Add this to the top of `base.html` so that all the pages that inherit from it will have access to it.

The home page template

To inherit a template, the `extends` control block is used:

```
{% extends "base.html" %}
{% block title %}Home{% endblock %}
```

This template will use all the HTML `base.html` but replace the data in the `title` block. If we do not declare a `title` block, the content in `base.html` would remain unchanged. Save this template as `home.html`. Now we can see this in action. Open `http://127.0.0.1:5000/` on your browser and you should see the following:

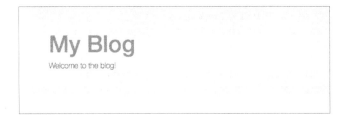

At this point, it is easier to develop and mock UIs if you have representative fake data. Because we only have two posts and manually adding a large amount of models from the command line is tedious (which we shall fix in *Chapter 10, Useful Flash Extensions*), let's use the following script to add 100 example posts:

```
import random
import datetime

user = User.query.get(1)

tag_one = Tag('Python')
tag_two = Tag('Flask')
tag_three = Tag('SQLAlechemy')
tag_four = Tag('Jinja')
tag_list = [tag_one, tag_two, tag_three, tag_four]

s = "Example text"

for i in xrange(100):
```

```
    new_post = Post("Post " + str(i))
    new_post.user = user
    new_post.publish_date = datetime.datetime.now()
    new_post.text = s
    new_post.tags = random.sample(tag_list, random.randint(1, 3))
    db.session.add(new_post)

db.session.commit()
```

This script is simple for loop that sets all the attributes of a new post and randomizes what tags the post has. Now, to begin developing our templates in earnest, we will start by adding the following to the home page: summaries of our blog posts with links, the most recent blog posts, and the most commonly used tags.

Now, let's add our content to home.html:

```
{% block body %}
<div class="row">
  <div class="col-lg-9">
    {% for post in posts.items %}
    <div class="row">
      <div class="col-lg-12">
        <h1>{{ post.title }}</h1>
      </div>
    </div>
    <div class="row">
      <div class="col-lg-12">
        {{ post.text | truncate(255) | safe }}
        <a href="{{
          url_for('posts', post_id=post.id)
          }}">Read More</a>
      </div>
    </div>
    {% endfor %}
  </div>
  <div class="col-lg-3">
    <div class="row">
      <h5>Recent Posts</h5>
      <ul>
        {% for post in recent %}
        <li><a href="{{
          url_for('post', post_id=post.id)
```

```
            }}">{{ post.title }}</a></li>
        {% endfor %}
      </ul>
    </div>
    <div class="row">
      <h5>Popular Tags</h5>
      <ul>
        {% for tag in top_tags %}
        <li><a href="{{ url_for('tag', tag_name=tag[0].title
          }}">{{ tag[0].title }}</a></li>
        {% endfor %}
      </ul>
    </div>
  </div>
</div>
{% endblock %}
```

All the other pages will take this general form of content in the middle with a sidebar of links to popular content.

Writing the other templates

Now that you know the ins and outs of inheritance and you know which data is going to go to each template, I will pose the same challenge as the previous section. Try to write the content sections of the remaining templates. After finishing it, you should be able to freely navigate around your blog, click on posts, and view user pages. There is one final bit of functionality to add in this chapter — the ability for readers to add comments.

Flask WTForms

Adding forms in your application seems to be an easy task, but when you start coding the server-side code, the task of validating user input grows bigger and bigger as the form becomes more complex. Security is paramount as the data is from an untrustworthy source and is going to be entered in the database. **WTForms** is a library that handles server form validation for you by checking input against common form types. Flask WTForms is a Flask extension on top of WTForms that add features, such as Jinja HTML rendering, and protects you against attacks, such as **SQL injection** and **cross-site request forgery**. To install Flask WTForms and WTForms, we have:

```
$ pip install Flask-WTF
```

Protecting yourself against SQL injection and cross-site request forgery is extremely important, as these are the most common forms of attacks your website will receive. To learn more about these attacks, visit https://en.wikipedia.org/wiki/SQL_injection and https://en.wikipedia.org/wiki/Cross-site_request_forgery for SQL injection and cross-site request forgery, respectively.

To have Flask WTForms' security measures working properly, we will need a secret key. A **secret key** is a random string of characters that will be used to cryptographically sign anything that needs to be tested for its authenticity. This cannot be any string; it must be randomized to avoid weakening the strength of the security protections. To generate a random string, type the following into Bash:

```
$ cat /dev/urandom | tr -cd 'a-f0-9' | head -c 32
```

If you are using Mac, type the following:

```
cat /dev/urandom | env LC_CTYPE=C tr -cd 'a-f0-9' | head -c 32
```

Add the output in `config.py` on the `Config` object:

```
class Config(object):
    SECRET_KEY = 'Your key here'
```

WTForms basics

There are three main parts of WTForms—**forms**, **fields**, and **validators**. Fields are representations of input fields and do rudimentary type checking, and validators are functions attached to fields that make sure that the data submitted in the form is within our constraints. The form is a class that contains fields and validators and validates itself on a POST request. Let's see this in action to get a better idea. In the `main.py` file, add the following:

```
from flask_wtf import Form
from wtforms import StringField, TextAreaField
from wtforms.validators import DataRequired, Length
...
class CommentForm(Form):
    name = StringField(
        'Name',
        validators=[DataRequired(), Length(max=255)]
    )
    text = TextAreaField(u'Comment', validators=[DataRequired()])
```

Here we have a class that inherits from Flask WTForm's `Form` object and defines inputs with class variables that equal WTForm fields. The fields take an optional parameter `validators`, a list of WTForm validators that will be applied to our data. The most commonly used fields are:

- `fields.DateField`

  This represents a Python `Date` object and takes an optional parameter format that takes a `stftime` format string to translate the data.

- `fields.IntegerField`

  This attempts to coerce passed data to an integer and is rendered in the template as a number input.

- `fields.FloatField`

  This attempts to coerce passed data to a float and is rendered in the template as a number input.

- `fields.RadioField`

  This represents a set of radio inputs and takes a parameter `choices`, that is, a list of tuples that act as the displayed value and the returned value.

- `fields.SelectField`

  Along with `SelectMultipleField`, it represents a set of radio inputs. Takes a parameter `choices`, that is, a list of tuples that act as the displayed and returned values.

- `fields.StringField`

  This represents a normal text input and will attempt to coerce the returned data to a string.

 For a full list of validators and fields, visit the WTForms documentation at `http://wtforms.readthedocs.org`.

The most common validators are as follows:

- `validators.DataRequired()`
- `validators.Email()`
- `validators.Length(min=-1, max=-1)`

- `validators.NumberRange(min=None, max=None)`
- `validators.Optional()`
- `validators.Regexp(regex)`
- `validators.URL()`

Each of these validations follows the Pythonic naming scheme. Therefore, they are rather straight forward on what they do. All validators take an optional parameter named `message`, which is the error message that will be returned if the validator fails. If message is not set, it uses same defaults.

Custom validators

Writing a custom validation function is very simple. All that is required is to write a function that takes the `form` object and the `field` object as parameters and raises a WTForm.`ValidationError` if the data does not pass the test. Here is an example of a custom e-mail validator:

```
import re
import wtforms
def custom_email(form, field):
    if not re.match(r"[^@]+@[^@]+\.[^@]+", field.data):
        raise wtforms.ValidationError('Field must be a valid email
            address.')
```

To use this function, just add it to the list of validators for your field.

Posting comments

Now that we have our comment form and we understand how to build it, we need to add it to the start of our post view:

```
@app.route('/post/<int:post_id>', methods=('GET', 'POST'))
def post(post_id):
form = CommentForm()
if form.validate_on_submit():
        new_comment = Comment()
    new_comment.name = form.name.data
    new_comment.text = form.text.data
    new_comment.post_id = post_id
    new_comment.date = datetime.datetime.now()
```

```
db.session.add(new_comment)
db.session.commit()
post = Post.query.get_or_404(post_id)
tags = post.tags
comments = post.comments.order_by(Comment.date.desc()).all()
recent, top_tags = sidebar_data()

return render_template(
    'post.html',
    post=post,
    tags=tags,
    comments=comments,
    recent=recent,
    top_tags=top_tags,
    form=form
)
```

First, we add the POST method to the list of allowed method to our view. Then, a new instance of our form object is created. The validate_on_submit() method then checks whether the Flask request is a POST request. If it is a POST request, it sends the request form data to the form object. If the data is validated, then validate_on_submit() returns True and adds the data to the form object. We then take the data from each field, populate a new comment, and add it to the database. Finally, we add the form to the variable to be sent to the template, so we can add the form to our post.html file:

```
<div class="col-lg-12">
  <h3>New Comment:</h3>
  <form method="POST" action="{{ url_for('post', post_id=post.id)
    }}">
    {{ form.hidden_tag() }}
    <div class="form-group">
      {{ form.name.label }}
      {% if form.name.errors %}
        {% for e in form.name.errors %}
          <p class="help-block">{{ e }}</p>
        {% endfor %}
      {% endif %}
      {{ form.name(class_='form-control') }}
    </div>
    <div class="form-group">
      {{ form.text.label }}
      {% if form.text.errors %}
```

```
        {% for e in form.text.errors %}
          <p class="help-block">{{ e }}</p>
        {% endfor %}
      {% endif %}
      {{ form.text(class_='form-control') }}
    </div>
    <input class="btn btn-primary" type="submit" value="Add
      Comment">
  </form>
</div>
```

There are several new things happing here. First, the `form.hidden_tag()` method
adds an anti-cross-site request forgery measure automatically. Second, the `field.`
`errors` list is used to render any messages that our validators send if validation fails.
Third, calling the field itself as a method will render the HTML code of that field.
Finally, calling `field.label` will automatically create an HTML label for our input.
Now, adding information to the fields and pressing the submit button should add
your comment!

This would look like the following screenshot:

One final challenge for the reader is to make a macro that takes a `form` object and an
endpoint to send the `POST` request to and autogenerate HTML for the entire form tag.
Refer to the WTForms documents if you get stuck. It's tricky, but not too difficult.

Summary

Now, after only three chapters, you already have a fully functional blog. This is where a lot of books on web development technologies would end. However, there are still 10 more chapters to go to turn your utilitarian blog into something that a user would actually use for their website. In the next chapter, we will focus on structuring Flask apps to accommodate long-term development and larger scale projects.

4
Creating Controllers with Blueprints

The final piece of the **Model View Controller (MVC)** equation is controllers. We have already seen the basic usage of the view functions in our main.py file. Now, the more complex and powerful versions will be introduced, and we will turn our disparate view functions in cohesive wholes. We will also discuss the internals of how Flask handles the lifetime of an HTTP request and advanced ways to define Flask views.

Request setup, teardown, and application globals

In some cases, a request-specific variable is needed across all view functions and needs to be accessed from the template as well. To achieve this, we can use Flask's decorator function @app.before_request and the object g. The function @app.before_request is executed every time before a new request is made. The Flask object g is a thread-safe store of any data that needs to be kept for each specific request. At the end of the request, the object is destroyed, and a new object is spawned at the start of a new request. For example, the following code checks whether the Flask session variable contains an entry for a logged in user; if it exists, it adds the User object to g:

```
from flask import g, session, abort, render_template

@app.before_request
def before_request():
    if 'user_id' in session:
```

```
        g.user = User.query.get(session['user_id'])

@app.route('/restricted')
def admin():
    if g.user is None:
        abort(403)
    return render_template('admin.html')
```

Multiple functions can be decorated with `@app.before_request`, and they all will be executed before the requested view function is executed. There also exists a decorator `@app.teardown_request`, called after the end of every request. Keep in mind that this method of handling user logins is meant as an example and is not secure. The recommend method is covered in *Chapter 6, Securing Your App*.

Error pages

Displaying a browser's default error pages to the end user is jarring as the user loses all context of your app, and they must hit the *back* button to return to your site. To display your own templates when an error is returned with the Flask `abort()` function, use the `errorhandler` decorator function:

```
@app.errorhandler(404)
def page_not_found(error):
    return render_template('page_not_found.html'), 404
```

The `errorhandler` is also useful to translate internal server errors and HTTP 500 code into user-friendly error pages. The `app.errorhandler()` function may take either one or many HTTP status codes to define which code it will act on. The returning of a tuple instead of just an HTML string allows you to define the HTTP status code of the `Response` object. By default, this is set to `200`.

Class-based views

In most Flask apps, views are handled by functions. However, when many views share common functionality or there are pieces of code that could be broken out into separate functions, it would be useful to implement our views as classes to take advantage of inheritance.

For example, if we have views that render a template, we could create a generic view class that keeps our code *DRY*:

```python
from flask.views import View

class GenericView(View):
    def __init__(self, template):
        self.template = template
        super(GenericView, self).__init__()

    def dispatch_request(self):
        return render_template(self.template)

app.add_url_rule(
    '/', view_func=GenericView.as_view(
        'home', template='home.html'
    )
)
```

The first thing to note about this code is the `dispatch_request()` function in our view class. This is the function in our view that acts as the normal view function and returns an HTML string. The `app.add_url_rule()` function mimics the `app.route()` function as it ties a route to a function call. The first argument defines the route of the function, and the `view_func` parameter defines the function that handles the route. The `View.as_view()` method is passed to the `view_func` parameter because it transforms the `View` class into a view function. The first argument defines the name of the view function, so functions such as `url_for()` can route to it. The remaining parameters are passed to the `__init__` function of the `View` class.

Like the normal view functions, HTTP methods other than GET must be explicitly allowed for the `View` class. To allow other methods, a class variable containing the list of named methods must be added:

```python
class GenericView(View):
    methods = ['GET', 'POST']
    ...
    def dispatch_request(self):
        if request.method == 'GET':
            return render_template(self.template)
        elif request.method == 'POST':
            ...
```

Method class views

Often, when functions handle multiple HTTP methods, the code can become difficult to read due to large sections of code nested within `if` statements:

```
@app.route('/user', methods=['GET', 'POST', 'PUT', 'DELETE'])
def users():
    if request.method == 'GET':
        ...
    elif request.method == 'POST':
        ...
    elif request.method == 'PUT':
        ...
    elif request.method == 'DELETE':
        ...
```

This can be solved with the `MethodView` class. `MethodView` allows each method to be handled by a different class method to separate concerns:

```
from flask.views import MethodView

class UserView(MethodView):
    def get(self):
        ...
    def post(self):
        ...
    def put(self):
        ...
    def delete(self):
        ...

app.add_url_rule(
    '/user',
    view_func=UserView.as_view('user')
)
```

Blueprints

In Flask, a **blueprint** is a method of extending an existing Flask app. Blueprints provide a way of combining groups of views with common functionality and allow developers to break their app down into different components. In our architecture, blueprints will act as our *controllers*.

Views are registered to a blueprint; a separate template and static folder can be defined for it, and when it has all the desired content on it, it can be registered on the main Flask app to add blueprint content. A blueprint acts much like a Flask app object, but is not actually a self-contained app. This is how Flask extensions provide view functions. To get an idea of what blueprints are, here is a very simple example:

```
from flask import Blueprint
example = Blueprint(
    'example',
    __name__,
    template_folder='templates/example',
    static_folder='static/example',
    url_prefix="/example"
)

@example.route('/')
def home():
    return render_template('home.html')
```

The blueprint takes two required parameters—the name of the blueprint and the name of the package—that are used internally in Flask; passing __name__ to it will suffice.

The other parameters are optional and define where the blueprint will look for files. Because `templates_folder` was specified, the blueprint will not look in the default template folder, and the route will render `templates/example/home.html` and not `templates/home.html`. The `url_prefix` option automatically adds the provided URI to the start of every route in the blueprint. So, the URL for the home view is actually `/example/`.

The `url_for()` function will now have to be told which blueprint the requested route is in:

```
{{ url_for('example.home') }}
```

Also, the `url_for()` function will now have to be told whether the view is being rendered from within the same blueprint:

```
{{ url_for('.home') }}
```

The `url_for()` function will also look for static files in the specified static folder.

To add the blueprint to our app:

```
app.register_blueprint(example)
```

Let's transform our current app to one that uses blueprints. We will first need to define our blueprint before all of our routes:

```
blog_blueprint = Blueprint(
    'blog',
    __name__,
    template_folder='templates/blog',
    url_prefix="/blog"
)
```

Now, because the templates folder was defined, we need to move all of our templates into a subfolder of the templates folder named blog. Next, all of our routes need to have the `@app.route` changed to `@blog_blueprint.route`, and any class view assignments now need to be registered to `blog_blueprint`. Remember that `url_for()` function calls in the templates will also have to be changed to have a period prepended to then to indicate that the route is in the same blueprint.

At the end of the file, right before the `if __name__ == '__main__':` statement, add the following:

```
app.register_blueprint(blog_blueprint)
```

Now all of our content is back on the app, which is registered under the blueprint. Because our base app no longer has any views, let's add a redirect on the base URL:

```
@app.route('/')
def index():
    return redirect(url_for('blog.home'))
```

Why blog and not `blog_blueprint`? Because blog is the name of the blueprint and the name is what Flask uses internally for routing. `blog_blueprint` is the name of the variable in the Python file.

Summary

We now have our app working inside a blueprint, but what does this give us? Let's say that we wanted to add a photo sharing function to our site; we would be able to group all the view functions into one blueprint with its own templates, static folder, and URL prefix without any fear of disrupting the functionality of the rest of the site. In the next chapter, blueprints will be made even more powerful by separating them into different files after upgrading our file and code structure.

5
Advanced Application Structure

Our application has gone from a very simple example to an extendable foundation on which powerful features can easily be built. However, having our application entirely resided in one file needlessly clutters our code. To make the application code clearer and more comprehensible, we will transform the entire code into a Python module and split the code into multiple files.

The project as a module

Currently, your folder structure should look like this:

```
webapp/
  config.py
  database.db
  main.py
  manage.py
  env/
  migrations/
    versions/
  static/
    css/
    js/
  templates/
    blog/
```

To convert our code to a module, our files will be converted to this folder structure:

```
webapp/
   manage.py
   database.db
   webapp/
      __init__.py
      config.py
      forms.py
      models.py
      controllers/
         __init__.py
         blog.py
      static/
         css/
         js/
      templates/
         blog/
   migrations/
      versions/
```

We will create this folder structure step by step. The first change to make is to create a folder in your application that will hold the module. In this example, it will be called webapp, but can be called anything except a blog, because the controllers are called blogs. If there are two blog objects to import from, Python will not import objects correctly from the parent directory while importing inside the blog.py file.

Next move main.py and config.py — the static and template folders, respectively — into your project folder and create a controllers folder as well. We will also need to create the files forms.py and models.py in the project folder, and a blog.py file in the controllers folder. Also, the main.py file will need to be renamed __init__.py.

The filename __init__.py looks odd, but it has a specific function. In Python, a folder can be marked as a module by placing a file named __init__.py inside it. This allows programs to import objects and variables from the Python files in the folder.

To learn more about organizing Python code in a module, refer to the official documentation at https://docs.python.org/2/tutorial/modules.html#packages.

Refactoring the code

Let's begin moving our SQLAlchemy code to the `models.py` file. Cut all the model declarations, the table of tags, and the database object from `__init__.py` and copy them to the `models.py` file along with the SQLAlchemy import. Also, our db object will no longer be initialized with the app object as a parameter because the `app` object is not present in the `models.py` file, and importing it would result in a cyclical import. Instead, we will have the app object added on to the db object after our models are initialized. This will be achieved later in our `__init__.py` file.

Your `models.py` file should now look like this:

```
from flask.ext.sqlalchemy import SQLAlchemy

db = SQLAlchemy()

tags = db.Table(
    'post_tags',
    db.Column('post_id', db.Integer, db.ForeignKey('post.id')),
    db.Column('tag_id', db.Integer, db.ForeignKey('tag.id'))
)

class User(db.Model):
    ...

class Post(db.Model):
    ...

class Comment(db.Model):
    ...

class Tag(db.Model):
    ...
```

Next, the `CommentForm` object, along with all the WTForms imports, should be moved to the `forms.py` file. The `forms.py` file will hold all the WTForms objects in their own file.

The `forms.py` file should look like this:

```
from flask_wtf import Form
from wtforms import StringField, TextAreaField
from wtforms.validators import DataRequired, Length


class CommentForm(Form):
    ...
```

The `blog_blueprint` data function, all its routes, and the `sidebar_data` data function need to be moved to the `blog.py` file in the controllers folder.

The `blog.py` file should now look like this:

```
import datetime
from os import path
from sqlalchemy import func
from flask import render_template, Blueprint

from webapp.models import db, Post, Tag, Comment, User, tags
from webapp.forms import CommentForm

blog_blueprint = Blueprint(
    'blog',
    __name__,
    template_folder=path.join(path.pardir, 'templates', 'blog')
    url_prefix="/blog"
)

def sidebar_data():
    ...
```

Now, whenever a new blueprint is made, a new file in the controllers folder can be made for it, breaking down the application code into logical groups. Also, we need an empty __init__.py file in the controllers folder in order to mark it as a module.

Finally, we focus on our __init__.py file. All that should remain in the __init__.py file is the app object creation, the index route, and the `blog_blueprint` registration on the app object. However, there is one thing to add—the database initialization. With the `db.init_app()` function, we will add the app object to the db object after it's imported:

```
from flask import Flask, redirect, url_for
from config import DevConfig

from models import db
from controllers.blog import blog_blueprint

app = Flask(__name__)
app.config.from_object(DevConfig)

db.init_app(app)

@app.route('/')
def index():
    return redirect(url_for('blog.home'))

app.register_blueprint(blog_blueprint)

if __name__ == '__main__':
    app.run()
```

There are two final things to fix before our new structure works if you are using SQLite—the SQLAlchemy database URL in `config.py` needs to be updated and the imports in `manage.py` need to be updated. Because the SQLAlchemy URL for a SQLite database is a relative file path, it has to be changed to:

```
from os import path

class DevConfig(object):
    SQLALCHEMY_DATABASE_URI = 'sqlite://' + path.join(
        path.pardir,
        'database.db'
    )
```

To fix the `manage.py` imports, replace the imports from `main.py` with:

```
from webapp import app
from webapp.models import db, User, Post, Tag, Comment
```

Now if you run `manage.py` file, your app will run with the new structure.

Application factories

Now that we are using blueprints in a modular manner, however, there is another improvement we can make to our abstraction, which creates a **factory** for our application. The concept of a factory comes from the **object-oriented programming (OOP)** world, and it simply means a function or an object that creates another object. Our application factory will take one of our `config` objects, which we created at the beginning of the book and returned a Flask application object.

 The object factory design was popularized by the now famous book, *Design Patterns: Elements of Reusable Object-Oriented Software*, by the Gang of Four. To learn more about these design patterns and how they can help simplify a project's code, look at `https://en.wikipedia.org/wiki/Structural_pattern`.

Creating a factory function for our application object has several benefits. First, it allows the context of the environment to change the configuration of the application. When your server creates the application object to serve, it can take into account any changes in the server necessary and change the configuration object given to the app accordingly. Second, it makes testing much easier because it allows differently configured applications to be tested quickly. Third, multiple instances of the same application using the same configuration can be created very easily. This is useful for situations where web traffic is balanced across several different servers.

Now that the benefits of application factories are clear, let's modify our __init__.py file to implement it:

```
from flask import Flask, redirect, url_for
from models import db
from controllers.blog import blog_blueprint

def create_app(object_name):
    app = Flask(__name__)
    app.config.from_object(object_name)

    db.init_app(app)

    @app.route('/')
    def index():
        return redirect(url_for('blog.home'))

    app.register_blueprint(blog_blueprint)

    return app
```

The change to the file is very simple; we contained our code in a function that takes a `config` object and returns an application object. We will need to modify our `manage.py` file in order to work with the `create_app` function as follows:

```
import os
from flask.ext.script import Manager, Server
from flask.ext.migrate import Migrate, MigrateCommand
from webapp import create_app
from webapp.models import db, User, Post, Tag, Comment

# default to dev config
env = os.environ.get('WEBAPP_ENV', 'dev')
app = create_app('webapp.config.%sConfig' % env.capitalize())
...
manager = Manager(app)
manager.add_command("server", Server())
```

When we created our configuration objects it was mentioned that the environment that the application is running in could change the configuration of the application. This code has a very simple example of that functionality where an environment variable is loaded and determines which `config` object to give to the `create_app` function. Environment variables are **global variables** in Bash that can be accessed by many different programs. They can be set in Bash with the following syntax:

```
$ export WEBAPP_ENV="dev"
```

To read a variable:

```
$ echo $WEBAPP_ENV
dev
```

You can also delete the variable easily as follows:

```
$ unset $WEBAPP_ENV
$ echo $WEBAPP_ENV
```

On your production server, you would set WEBAPP_ENV to prod. The true power of this setup will become clearer once you deploy to production in *Chapter 13, Deploying Flask Apps*, and when we get to *Chapter 12, Testing Flask Apps*, which covers testing our project.

Summary

We have transformed our application into a much more manageable and scalable structure, which will save us a lot of headaches as we move further through the book and add more advanced features. In the next chapter, we will add a login and registration system to our application, and other features to make our site more secure.

6
Securing Your App

We have a mostly functioning blog app, but it is missing some crucial features, such as user login, registration, and adding and editing posts from the browser. The user login functionality can be created in many different ways, so each of the sections demonstrates mutually exclusive methods to create logins. The first way is directly using the browser's cookies, and the second way is using a Flask extension named **Flask Login**.

Setting up

Before we jump right into making a user authentication system, there is a lot of setup code. To run any type of authentication, our app will need the following elements common to all:

- First, the user models will need proper password hashing

- Second, a login form and a registration form will be needed to validate user input

- Third, a login view and a registration view with templates for each will be needed

- Fourth, various social logins need to be set up in order to tie them into the login system when it is implemented

Updating the models

Until now, our users had their passwords stored as a plain text in the database. This is a major security flaw. If any malicious user were to gain access to the data in the database, they could log in to any account. The fallout of such a breach would be greater than our site. Large amounts of people on the Internet use a common password for many sites.

If an attacker had access to an e-mail and password combination, it is very likely that this information could be used to log in to a Facebook account or even a bank account.

To protect our user passwords, they will be encrypted with a one-way encryption method named a **hashing algorithm**. A one-way encryption means that after information is encrypted, the original information cannot be regained from the result. However, given the same data, the hashing algorithm will always produce the same result. The data given to the hashing algorithm can be anything from a text file to a movie file. In this case, the data is just a string of characters. With this functionality, our passwords can be stored as **hashes** (data that has been hashed). Then, when a user enters their password in the login or registration page, the text entered for the password will be sent through the same hashing algorithm, and the stored hash and the entered hash will be verified.

There are many hashing algorithms, most of which are not secure because they are easy to **brute force**. Hackers continuously try sending data through a hashing algorithm until something matches. To best protect the user passwords, bcrypt will be our hashing algorithm of choice. **Bcrypt** is purposely designed to be inefficient and slow (milliseconds vs. microseconds) for the computer to process, thereby making it harder to brute force. To add bcrypt to our project, the package **Flask Bcrypt** will need to be installed as follows:

```
$ pip install Flask-Bcrypt
```

This is the second Flask extension that will be initialized on the app object, the other being the SQLAlchemy object. The db object was stored in the models.py file, but there is no obvious place to initialize Flask Bcrypt. To hold all future extensions, add the file named extensions.py in the same directory as the __init__.py file. Inside, Flask Bcrypt will have to be initialized:

```
from flask.ext.bcrypt import Bcrypt
bcrypt = Bcrypt()
```

It is then added to the app object:

```
from webapp.extensions import bcrypt

def create_app(object_name):
    app = Flask(__name__)
    app.config.from_object(object_name)

    db.init_app(app)
    bcrypt.init_app(app)
```

Bcrypt is now ready to use. To have our `User` object use bcrypt, we will add two methods that set the password and check if a string matches the stored hash:

```
from webapp.extensions import bcrypt

class User(db.Model):
    id = db.Column(db.Integer(), primary_key=True)
    username = db.Column(db.String(255))
    password = db.Column(db.String(255))
    posts = db.relationship(
        'Post',
        backref='user',
        lazy='dynamic'
    )

    def __init__(self, username):
        self.username = username

    def __repr__(self):
        return '<User {}>'.format(self.username)

    def set_password(self, password):
        self.password = bcrypt.generate_password_hash(password)

    def check_password(self, password):
        return bcrypt.check_password_hash(self.password, password)
```

Now, our `User` models can store passwords securely. Next, our login process needs to use these methods to create new users and check passwords.

Creating the forms

Three forms are required: a login form, a registration form, and a form for our **post creation** page. The login form will have username and password fields:

```
from wtforms import (
    StringField,
    TextAreaField,
    PasswordField,
    BooleanField
)
from wtforms.validators import DataRequired, Length, EqualTo, URL

class LoginForm(Form):
    username = StringField('Username', [
        DataRequired(), Length(max=255)
    ])
```

```
            password = PasswordField('Password', [DataRequired()])

        def validate(self):
            check_validate = super(LoginForm, self).validate()

            # if our validators do not pass
            if not check_validate:
                return False

            # Does our the exist
            user = User.query.filter_by(
                username=self.username.data
            ).first()
            if not user:
                self.username.errors.append(
                    'Invalid username or password'
                )
                return False

            # Do the passwords match
            if not self.user.check_password(self.password.data):
                self.username.errors.append(
                    'Invalid username or password'
                )
                return False

        return True
```

Along with the normal validations, our `LoginForm` method will also check whether the username passed exists and will use the `check_password()` method to check the hashes.

Protecting your form from spam with reCAPTCHA

The registration form will have a username field, a password field with a confirmation field, and a special field named a reCAPTCHA field. A CAPTCHA is a special field on a web form that checks whether whoever is entering data into the form is actually a person, or an automated program that is spamming your site. reCAPTCHA is simply one implementation of a CAPTCHA. reCAPTCHA has been integrated into WTForms as it is the most popular implementation on the Web.

To use reCAPTCHA, you will need a reCAPTCHA login from `https://www.google.com/recaptcha/intro/index.html`. As reCAPTCHA is a Google product, you can log in with your Google account.

Once you log in, it will ask you to add a site. In this case, any name will do, but the domain field must have `localhost` as an entry. Once you deploy your site, your domain must also be added to this list.

Now that you have added a site, dropdowns with instructions on server and client integration will appear. The given `script` tag will need to be added to the templates of our login and registration views when we create them. What WTForms needs from this page are the keys, as shown in the following screenshot:

Remember to never show these keys to public. As these keys are only registered to `localhost`, they can be shown here without recourse.

Add these keys to the `config` object in the `config.py` file so that WTForms can access them as follows:

```
class Config(object):
    SECRET_KEY = 'Key Here'
    RECAPTCHA_PUBLIC_KEY =
"6LdKkQQTAAAAAEH0GFj7NLg5tGicaoOus7G9Q5Uw"
    RECAPTCHA_PRIVATE_KEY =
'6LdKkQQTAAAAAMYroksPTJ7pWhobYb88fTAcxcYn'
```

The following is our registration form:

```
class RegisterForm(Form):
    username = StringField('Username', [
        DataRequired(),
        Length(max=255)
    ])
    password = PasswordField('Password', [
        DataRequired(),
        Length(min=8)
    ])
    confirm = PasswordField('Confirm Password', [
        DataRequired(),
        EqualTo('password')
    ])
```

```
    recaptcha = RecaptchaField()

    def validate(self):
        check_validate = super(RegisterForm, self).validate()

        # if our validators do not pass
        if not check_validate:
            return False

        user = User.query.filter_by(
            username=self.username.data
        ).first()

        # Is the username already being used
        if user:
            self.username.errors.append(
                "User with that name already exists"
            )
            return False

        return True
```

The post creation form will just contain a text input for the title and a text area input for the post content:

```
class PostForm(Form):
    title = StringField('Title', [
        DataRequired(),
        Length(max=255)
    ])
    text = TextAreaField('Content', [DataRequired()])
```

Creating views

In the previous chapter, the index view containing the redirect to the blog home was stored in the `create_app` function. That was alright for one view. Now, this section is going to add many views on the base URL of the site. As such, we need a new controller in `controllers/main.py`:

```
main_blueprint = Blueprint(
    'main',
    __name__,
```

```
        template_folder='../templates/main'
)

@main_blueprint.route('/')
def index():
    return redirect(url_for('blog.home'))
```

The login and registration views will create our form objects and pass them to the templates. For now, the login form will not do anything if the data passed validates. The actual login functionality will be added in the next section. However, the registration view will create a new user if the data passes validation. Along with the login and registration views, there needs to be a logout view, which will do nothing for now as well.

In the main.py controller, add the following:

```
from webapp.forms import LoginForm, RegisterForm

@main_blueprint.route('/login', methods=['GET', 'POST'])
def login():
    form = LoginForm()

    if form.validate_on_submit():
        flash("You have been logged in.", category="success")
        return redirect(url_for('blog.home'))

    return render_template('login.html', form=form)

@main_blueprint.route('/logout', methods=['GET', 'POST'])
def logout():
    flash("You have been logged out.", category="success")
    return redirect(url_for('.home'))

@main_blueprint.route('/register', methods=['GET', 'POST'])
def register():
    form = RegisterForm()

    if form.validate_on_submit():
        new_user = User()
        new_user.username = form.username.data
        new_user.set_password(form.username.data)
```

```
        db.session.add(new_user)
        db.session.commit()

        flash(
            "Your user has been created, please login.",
            category="success"
        )

        return redirect(url_for('.login'))

    return render_template('register.html', form=form)
```

The `login.html` and `register.html` templates used in the preceding code (placed in the `templates/main` folder) can be made with the `form` macro created in *Chapter 3, Creating Views with Templates*, but the `script` tag from reCAPTCHA cannot be added to `register.html` yet.

First, there needs to be a way for our child templates to add new JavaScript files to the `base.html` template. There also needs to be a way for our views to flash messages to the user with the Flask `flash` function. A new content block has to be added to the `base.html` file along with a loop over the messages:

```html
<body>
  <div class="container">
    <div class="jumbotron">
      <h1><a href="{{ url_for('blog.home') }}">My Blog</a></h1>
      <p>Welcome to the blog!</p>
    </div>
    {% with messages = get_flashed_messages(with_categories=true) %}
      {% if messages %}
        {% for category, message in messages %}
          <div class="alert alert-{{ category }} alert-dismissible"
            role="alert">
          <button type="button" class="close" data-dismiss="alert"
aria-label="Close"><span aria-hidden="true">&times;</span></button>

          {{ message }}
          </div>
        {% endfor %}
      {% endif %}
    {% endwith %}
    {% block body %}
    {% endblock %}
  </div>
```

```
<script
  src="https://ajax.googleapis.com/ajax/libs/jquery/1.11.2/jquery.
min.js">
  </script>
<script
  src="https://maxcdn.bootstrapcdn.com/bootstrap/3.3.2/js/bootstrap.
min.js">
  </script>
{% block js %}
{% endblock %}
</body>
```

Your login page should now resemble the following:

Your registration page should look like this:

Now we need to create the post creation and editing page so something can be secured. The two pages will need to transform the text area field into a **WYSIWYG** (short for **What You See Is What You Get**) editor to handle wrapping the post text in HTML. In the `blog.py` controller, add the following views:

```
from webapp.forms import CommentForm, PostForm

@blog_blueprint.route('/new', methods=['GET', 'POST'])
def new_post():
    form = PostForm()

    if form.validate_on_submit():
        new_post = Post(form.title.data)
        new_post.text = form.text.data
        new_post.publish_date = datetime.datetime.now()

        db.session.add(new_post)
        db.session.commit()

    return render_template('new.html', form=form)

@blog_blueprint.route('/edit/<int:id>', methods=['GET', 'POST'])
def edit_post(id):

    post = Post.query.get_or_404(id)
    form = PostForm()

    if form.validate_on_submit():
        post.title = form.title.data
        post.text = form.text.data
        post.publish_date = datetime.datetime.now()

        db.session.add(post)
        db.session.commit()

        return redirect(url_for('.post', post_id=post.id))

    form.text.data = post.text

    return render_template('edit.html', form=form, post=post)
```

This functionality is much like the code used to add new comments. The data of the text field is set in the view because there is no easy way to set the contents of `TextAreaField` inside a template.

The `new.html` template will need a JavaScript file for the WYSIWYG editor. **CKEditor** is very simple to install and use. Now, our `new.html` file can be created as follows:

```
{% extends "base.html" %}
{% block title %}Post Creation{% endblock %}
{% block body %}
<div class="row">
  <h1 class="text-center">Create A New Post</h1>
  <form method="POST" action="{{ url_for('.new_post') }}">
    {{ form.hidden_tag() }}
    <div class="form-group">
      {{ form.title.label }}
      {% if form.title.errors %}
        {% for e in form.title.errors %}
          <p class="help-block">{{ e }}</p>
        {% endfor %}
      {% endif %}
      {{ form.title(class_='form-control') }}
    </div>
    <div class="form-group">
      {{ form.text.label }}
      {% if form.text.errors %}
        {% for e in form.text.errors %}
          <p class="help-block">{{ e }}</p>
        {% endfor %}
      {% endif %}
      {{ form.text(id="editor", class_='form-control') }}
    </div>
    <input class="btn btn-primary" type="submit" value="Submit">
  </form>
</div>
{% endblock %}

{% block js %}
<script src="//cdn.ckeditor.com/4.4.7/standard/ckeditor.js"></script>
<script>
```

```
        CKEDITOR.replace('editor');
    </script>
    {% endblock %}
```

This is all that is needed to have the user's input stored as HTML in the database. Because we passed the safe filter in our post template, the HTML code appears correctly on our post pages. The edit.html template is similar to the new.html template. The only difference is the form opening tag and the creation of the title field:

```
    <form method="POST" action="{{ url_for('.edit_post', id=post.id)
      }}">
    ...
    {{ form.title(class_='form-control', value=post.title) }}
    ...
    </form>
```

The post.html template will need a button for authors to link them to the edit page:

```
    <div class="row">
      <div class="col-lg-6">
        <p>Written By <a href="{{ url_for('.user', username=post.user.
    username)
          }}">{{ post.user.username }}</a> on {{ post.publish_date }}</p>
      </div>
      ...
      <div class="row">
        <div class="col-lg-2">
        <a href="{{ url_for('.edit_post', id=post.id) }}" class="btn btn-
          primary">Edit</a>
      </div>
    </div>
```

When we are able to detect the current user, the edit button will only be shown to the user who created the post.

Social logins

Integrating alternative login and registration options into your site becomes more important as time goes on. Every month, there is another announcement that passwords have been stolen from a popular website. Implementing the following login options means that our site's database never stores a password for that user.

Verification is handled by a large brand name company, which the user already places their trust in. By using social logins, the amount of trust a user has to place in the website they are using is much lower. Your login process also becomes much shorter for the user, decreasing the barrier to entry to your app.

Socially authenticated users act as normal users, and unlike the password-based login methods, they all can be used in tandem.

OpenID

OpenID is an open protocol that allows users on one site to be authenticated by any third-party site that implements the protocol, which are called **Relaying Parties (RPs)**. An OpenID login is represented as a URL from one of the RPs, typically the profile page of the website.

 To know a full list of sites that use OpenID and how to use each, go to http://openid.net/get-an-openid/.

To add OpenID to Flask, a Flask extension named **Flask-OpenID** will be needed:

```
$ pip install Flask-OpenID
```

Our app will need a couple of things to implement OpenID:

- A new form object
- The form validation on the login and registration pages
- A callback after the form submission to log the user in or create a new user

In the extensions.py file, the OpenID object can be initialized as follows:

```
from flask.ext.bcrypt import Bcrypt
from flask.ext.openid import OpenID
bcrypt = Bcrypt()
oid = OpenID()
```

In the __init__.py file, the oid object is registered to the app object:

```
from .models import db

def create_app(object_name):
    app = Flask(__name__)
    app.config.from_object(object_name)
```

```
db.init_app(app)
bcrypt.init_app(app)
oid.init_app(app)
```

The new `form` object will only need the URL of the RP:

```
from wtforms.validators import DataRequired, Length, EqualTo, URL

class OpenIDForm(Form):
    openid = StringField('OpenID URL', [DataRequired(), URL()])
```

On the login and registration views, `OpenIDForm()` will be initialized, and if the data is valid, a login request will be sent:

```
from webapp.extensions import oid
...


@main_blueprint.route('/login', methods=['GET', 'POST'])
@oid.loginhandler
def login():
    form = LoginForm()
    openid_form = OpenIDForm()

    if openid_form.validate_on_submit():
        return oid.try_login(
            openid_form.openid.data,
            ask_for=['nickname', 'email'],
            ask_for_optional=['fullname']
        )

    if form.validate_on_submit():
        flash("You have been logged in.", category="success")
        return redirect(url_for('blog.home'))

    openid_errors = oid.fetch_error()
    if openid_errors:
        flash(openid_errors, category="danger")

    return render_template(
        'login.html',
        form=form,
        openid_form=openid_form
    )
```

```
@main_blueprint.route('/register', methods=['GET', 'POST'])
@oid.loginhandler
def register():
    form = RegisterForm()
    openid_form = OpenIDForm()

    if openid_form.validate_on_submit():
        return oid.try_login(
            openid_form.openid.data,
            ask_for=['nickname', 'email'],
            ask_for_optional=['fullname']
        )

    if form.validate_on_submit():
        new_user = User(form.username.data)
        new_user.set_password(form.password.data)

        db.session.add(new_user)
        db.session.commit()

        flash(
            "Your user has been created, please login.",
            category="success"
        )

        return redirect(url_for('.login'))

    openid_errors = oid.fetch_error()
    if openid_errors:
        flash(openid_errors, category="danger")

    return render_template(
        'register.html',
        form=form,
        openid_form=openid_form
    )
```

Both the views have the new decorator `@oid.loginhandler`, which tells Flask-OpenID to listen for authentication information coming back from the RP. With OpenID, logging in and registering are the same. It is possible to create a user from the login form and to log in from the registration form. The same field appears on both pages to avoid user confusion.

To handle the user creation and login, a new function in the `extensions.py` file is needed:

```
@oid.after_login
def create_or_login(resp):
    from models import db, User
    username = resp.fullname or resp.nickname or resp.email
    if not username:
        flash('Invalid login. Please try again.', 'danger')
        return redirect(url_for('main.login'))

    user = User.query.filter_by(username=username).first()
    if user is None:
        user = User(username)
        db.session.add(user)
        db.session.commit()

    # Log the user in here
    return redirect(url_for('blog.home'))
```

This function is called after every successful response from the RP. If the login is successful and a user object does not exist for the identity, this function creates a new `User` object. If one already exists, the upcoming authentication methods will log the user in. OpenID does not require all possible information to be returned, so it is possible that rather than a full name, only an e-mail will be returned. This is why the username can be the nickname, full name, or e-mail. The `db` and `User` object are imported inside the function to avoid cyclical imports from the `models.py` file importing the `bcrypt` object.

Facebook

To log in with Facebook, and later Twitter, a protocol named **OAuth** is used. Our app will not use OAuth directly, instead another Flask extension will be used named **Flask OAuth**:

$ pip install Flask-OAuth

To use Facebook login, our app needs to define a Facebook OAuth object with our app's keys. Define a view that redirects the user to the login authorization process on Facebook's server, and a function on the Facebook method to load the `auth` token from the login process.

First, a Facebook app needs to be created at `http://developers.facebook.com`. Once you create a new app, look for the panel that lists your app's id and secret key.

Use these values while adding the following code to `extensions.py`:

```
from flask_oauth import OAuth

bcrypt = Bcrypt()
oid = OpenID()
oauth = OAuth()

...

facebook = oauth.remote_app(
    'facebook',
    base_url='https://graph.facebook.com/',
    request_token_url=None,
    access_token_url='/oauth/access_token',
    authorize_url='https://www.facebook.com/dialog/oauth',
    consumer_key=' FACEBOOK_APP_ID',
    consumer_secret=' FACEBOOK_APP_SECRET',
    request_token_params={'scope': 'email'}
)
@facebook.tokengetter
def get_facebook_oauth_token():
    return session.get('facebook_oauth_token')
```

In the Facebook developer interface, be sure to add a new authorized website as `http://localhost:5000/` or the login will not work. In the `main.py` controller, add the following code:

```python
from webapp.extensions import oid, facebook

...


@main_blueprint.route('/facebook')
def facebook_login():
    return facebook.authorize(
        callback=url_for(
            '.facebook_authorized',
            next=request.referrer or None,
            _external=True
        )
    )


@main_blueprint.route('/facebook/authorized')
@facebook.authorized_handler
def facebook_authorized(resp):
    if resp is None:
        return 'Access denied: reason=%s error=%s' % (
            request.args['error_reason'],
            request.args['error_description']
        )

    session['facebook_oauth_token'] = (resp['access_token'], '')

    me = facebook.get('/me')
    user = User.query.filter_by(
        username=me.data['first_name'] + " " + me.data['last_name']
    ).first()

    if not user:
        user = User(me.data['first_name'] + " " + me.data['last_
name'])
        db.session.add(user)
        db.session.commit()

    # Login User here
```

```
        flash("You have been logged in.", category="success")

        return redirect(
            request.args.get('next') or url_for('blog.home')
        )
```

The first route, `facebook_login`, is just a redirect to the login process on Facebook's website. The `facebook_authorized` view receives the response from Facebook's servers and, just like the OpenID process, either creates a new user or logs the user in. Now to start the process, add the following link to the registration and login templates:

```
<h2 class="text-center">Register With Facebook</h2>
<a href="{{ url_for('.facebook_login') }}">Login via Facebook</a>
```

Twitter

The Twitter login process is very similar. To create a Twitter app and receive your keys, go to `https://apps.twitter.com/`. In `extensions.py`:

```
twitter = oauth.remote_app(
    'twitter',
    base_url='https://api.twitter.com/1.1/',
    request_token_url='https://api.twitter.com/oauth/request_token',
    access_token_url='https://api.twitter.com/oauth/access_token',
    authorize_url='https://api.twitter.com/oauth/authenticate',
    consumer_key='',
    consumer_secret=''
)

@twitter.tokengetter
def get_twitter_oauth_token():
    return session.get('twitter_oauth_token')
```

In the `main.py` controller, add the following views:

```
@main_blueprint.route('/twitter-login')
def twitter_login():
    return twitter.authorize(
        callback=url_for(
            '.twitter_authorized',
            next=request.referrer or None,
            _external=True
        )
    )
```

```
@main_blueprint.route('/twitter-login/authorized')
@twitter.authorized_handler
def twitter_authorized(resp):
    if resp is None:
        return 'Access denied: reason: {} error: {}'.format(
            request.args['error_reason'],
            request.args['error_description']
        )

    session['twitter_oauth_token'] = resp['oauth_token'] + \
        resp['oauth_token_secret']

    user = User.query.filter_by(
        username=resp['screen_name']
    ).first()

    if not user:
        user = User(resp['screen_name'], '')
        db.session.add(user)
        db.session.commit()

    # Login User here
    flash("You have been logged in.", category="success")

    return redirect(
        request.args.get('next') or url_for('blog.home')
    )
```

These views perform the same function as their Facebook counterparts. Finally, in the register and login templates, add the following link to start the login process:

```
<h2 class="text-center">Register With Twitter</h2>
<a href="{{ url_for('.twitter_login') }}">Login</a>
```

Using the session

One way to create authentication in Flask is to use the session object. The session object is an object in Flask that creates an easy way for the server to store information in the user's browser with cookies. The stored data is cryptographically signed with the app's secret key. If the user attempts to modify the cookie, then the sign will no longer be valid and the cookie will not be read.

The session object has the same API as a `dict` object. To add data to it, simply use this:

```
session['key'] = data
```

To retrieve data, use this:

```
session['key']
```

To log a user in, a username key will be added to the session and set to the username of the current user.

```
@main_blueprint.route('/login', methods=['GET', 'POST'])
def login():
    form = LoginForm()

    if form.validate_on_submit():
        # Add the user's name to the cookie
        session['username'] = form.username.data

    return render_template('login.html', form=form)
```

To log the user out, the key can be popped from the session:

```
@main_blueprint.route('/logout', methods=['GET', 'POST'])
def logout():
    # Remove the username from the cookie
    session.pop('username', None)
    return redirect(url_for('.login'))
```

To check whether a user is currently logged in, the view can test if the username key exists in the session. Consider the following new post view:

```
@blog_blueprint.route('/new', methods=['GET', 'POST'])
def new_post ():
    if 'username' not in session:
        return redirect(url_for('main.login'))
    ...
```

Some of our templates will need access to the current user object. At the start of every request, our `blog` blueprint can check whether the username is in the session. If so, add the `User` object to the `g` object, which is accessible through the templates.

```
@blog_blueprint.before_request
def check_user():
    if 'username' in session:
```

```
        g.current_user = User.query.filter_by(
            username=session['username']
        ).one()
    else:
        g.current_user = None
```

Our login check can be changed to:

```
@blog_blueprint.route('/new', methods=['GET', 'POST'])
def new_post():
    if not g.current_user:
        return redirect(url_for('main.login'))
    ...
```

Also, the edit button on the post page should only appear when the current user is the author:

```
{% if g.current_user == post.user %}
<div class="row">
  <div class="col-lg-2">
    <a href="{{ url_for('.edit_post', id=post.id) }}" class="btn btn-
      primary">Edit</a>
  </div>
</div>
{% endif %}
```

The edit page itself should also perform the following check:

```
@blog_blueprint.route('/edit/<int:id>', methods=['GET', 'POST'])
def edit_post(id):
    if not g.current_user:
        return redirect(url_for('main.login'))

    post = Post.query.get_or_404(id)

    if g.current_user != post.user:
        abort(403)
    ...
```

Now our app has a fully featured login system with a traditional username and password combination and many social logins as well. However, there are some features that are not covered in this system. For example, what if we wanted some users to be able to only comment while giving others permission to create posts? Also, our login system does not implement a Remember Me function. To cover this functionality, we will refactor our app to use a Flask extension named **Flask Login** instead of directly using the session.

Flask Login

To start using Flask Login, it needs to be downloaded first:

```
$ pip install flask-login
```

The main Flask Login object is the `LoginManager` object. Like the other Flask extensions, initialize the `LoginManager` object in `extensions.py`:

```
from flask.ext.login import LoginManager
...
login_manager = LoginManager()
```

There are some configuration options that need to be changed on the object:

```
login_manager.login_view = "main.login"
login_manager.session_protection = "strong"
login_manager.login_message = "Please login to access this page"
login_manager.login_message_category = "info"


@login_manager.user_loader
def load_user(userid):
    from models import User
    return User.query.get(userid)
```

The preceding configuration values define which view should be treated as the login page and what the message to the user while logging in should look like. Setting the option `session_protection` to `strong` better protects against malicious users tampering with their cookies. When a tampered cookie is identified, the session object for that user is deleted and the user is forced to log back in. The `load_user` function takes an id and returns the `User` object. It's for Flask Login to check whether an id identifies the correct user object.

The `User` model needs to be updated to include some methods for Flask Login. First is `is_authenticated` to check whether the `User` object has been logged in. Next is `is_active`, which checks whether the user has gone through some sort of activation process, such as an e-mail confirmation. Otherwise, it allows site administrators to ban a user without deleting their data. Then, `is_anonymous` checks whether this user is anonymous and not logged in. Finally, a `get_id` function returns a unique `unicode` identifier for that `User` object.

This app will use a simple implementation for this functionality:

```
from flask.ext.login import AnonymousUserMixin
...


class User(db.Model):
    id = db.Column(db.Integer(), primary_key=True)
    username = db.Column(db.String(255))
    password = db.Column(db.String(255))
    posts = db.relationship(
        'Post',
        backref='user',
        lazy='dynamic'
    )

    def __init__(self, username):
        self.username = username

    def __repr__(self):
        return '<User {}>'.format(self.username)

    def set_password(self, password):
        self.password = bcrypt.generate_password_hash(password)

    def check_password(self, password):
        return bcrypt.check_password_hash(self.password, password)

    def is_authenticated(self):
        if isinstance(self, AnonymousUserMixin):
            return False
        else:
            return True

    def is_active(self):
        return True

    def is_anonymous(self):
        if isinstance(self, AnonymousUserMixin):
            return True
        else:
            return False

    def get_id(self):
        return unicode(self.id)
```

In Flask Login, every user on the site inherits from some user object. By default, they inherit an AnonymousUserMixin object. If your site needs some functionality with anonymous users, you can create a class that inherits from AnonymousUserMixin and set it as the default user class with the following:

```
login_manager.anonymous_user = CustomAnonymousUser
```

 To better understand the concept of **mixins**, visit https://en.wikipedia.org/wiki/Mixin.

To log in a user with Flask Login, use:

```
from flask.ext.login import login_user
login_user(user_object)
```

Flask Login then takes care of all of the session handling. To have the user be remembered, add remember=True, to the login_user call. A checkbox can be added to the login form to give users the choice:

```
from wtforms import (
    StringField,
    TextAreaField,
    PasswordField,
    BooleanField
)

class LoginForm(Form):
    username = StringField('Username', [
        DataRequired(),
        Length(max=255)
    ])
    password = PasswordField('Password', [DataRequired()])
    remember = BooleanField("Remember Me")
    ...
```

In the login view, add this:

```
if form.validate_on_submit():
    user = User.query.filter_by(
        username=form.username.data
    ).one()
    login_user(user, remember=form.remember.data)
```

To log the current user out, use the following:

```
from flask.ext.login import login_user, logout_user
logout_user()
```

To protect a view from unauthorized users and send them to the login page, add the `login_required` decorator as follows:

```
from flask.ext.login import login_required

@blog_blueprint.route('/new', methods=['GET', 'POST'])
@login_required
def new_post():
    form = PostForm()
    ...
```

Flask Login also provides a proxy to the logged in user with `current_user`. This proxy is available in views and templates alike. So, in our blog controller, the custom `before_request` handler can be deleted, and our calls to `g.current_user` should be replaced with `current_user`.

Now, with Flask Login, our app's login system is more Pythonic and secure. There is one last feature to implement: user roles and permissions.

User roles

To add user permissions to our application, our `User` model will need a many-to-many relationship to a `Role` object, and it will need another Flask extension named **Flask Principal**.

With our code from *Chapter 2, Creating Models with SQLAlchemy*, adding a many-to-many relationship to the `User` object is easy:

```
roles = db.Table(
    'role_users',
    db.Column('user_id', db.Integer, db.ForeignKey('user.id')),
    db.Column('role_id', db.Integer, db.ForeignKey('role.id'))
)

class User(db.Model):
    id = db.Column(db.Integer(), primary_key=True)
```

```
    username = db.Column(db.String(255), unique=True)
    password = db.Column(db.String(255))
    posts = db.relationship(
        'Post',
        backref='user',
        lazy='dynamic'
    )
    roles = db.relationship(
        'Role',
        secondary=roles,
        backref=db.backref('users', lazy='dynamic')
    )

    def __init__(self, username):
        self.username = username

        default = Role.query.filter_by(name="default").one()
        self.roles.append(default)
    ...

class Role(db.Model):
    id = db.Column(db.Integer(), primary_key=True)
    name = db.Column(db.String(80), unique=True)
    description = db.Column(db.String(255))

    def __init__(self, name):
        self.name = name

    def __repr__(self):
        return '<Role {}>'.format(self.name)
```

From the command line, populate the roles table with three roles: admin, poster, and default. These will act as the main permissions for Flask Principal.

Flask Principal works around the idea of an identity. Something in the application, a User object in our case, has an identity associated with it. The identity provides Need objects, which at their core are just named tuples. Needs define what the identity can do. Permissions are initialized with Need, and they define what Need objects a resource needs to be accessed.

Flask Principal provides two convenient `Need` objects: `UserNeed` and `RoleNeed`, which are exactly what is needed for our app. In `extensions.py`, Flask Principal will be initialized and our `RoleNeed` objects will be created:

```
from flask.ext.principal import Principal, Permission, RoleNeed
principals = Principal()
admin_permission = Permission(RoleNeed('admin'))
poster_permission = Permission(RoleNeed('poster'))
default_permission = Permission(RoleNeed('default'))
```

Flask Principal requires a function that adds `Need` objects to it after the identity has changed. Because this function requires access to the `app` object, this function will reside in the `__init__.py` file:

```
from flask.ext.principal import identity_loaded, UserNeed, RoleNeed
from extensions import bcrypt, oid, login_manager, principals
def create_app(object_name):
    app = Flask(__name__)
    app.config.from_object(object_name)

    db.init_app(app)
    bcrypt.init_app(app)
    oid.init_app(app)
    login_manager.init_app(app)
    principals.init_app(app)

    @identity_loaded.connect_via(app)
    def on_identity_loaded(sender, identity):
        # Set the identity user object
        identity.user = current_user

        # Add the UserNeed to the identity
        if hasattr(current_user, 'id'):
            identity.provides.add(UserNeed(current_user.id))

        # Add each role to the identity
        if hasattr(current_user, 'roles'):
            for role in current_user.roles:
                identity.provides.add(RoleNeed(role.name))
    ...
```

Now when the identity is changed, it will add a `UserNeed` and all of the `RoleNeed` objects as well. The identity changes when the user logs in or logs out:

```python
from flask.ext.principal import (
    Identity,
    AnonymousIdentity,
    identity_changed
)
@main_blueprint.route('/login', methods=['GET', 'POST'])
@oid.loginhandler
def login():
    ...

    if form.validate_on_submit():
        user = User.query.filter_by(
            username=form.username.data
        ).one()
        login_user(user, remember=form.remember.data)

        identity_changed.send(
            current_app._get_current_object(),
            identity=Identity(user.id)
        )

        flash("You have been logged in.", category="success")
        return redirect(url_for('blog.home'))
@main_blueprint.route('/logout', methods=['GET', 'POST'])
def logout():
    logout_user()

    identity_changed.send(
        current_app._get_current_object(),
        identity=AnonymousIdentity()
    )

    flash("You have been logged out.", category="success")
    return redirect(url_for('.login'))
```

When the user logs in, their identity will trigger the `on_identity_loaded` method, and set their `Need` objects up. Now if we had a page that we wanted only posters to have access to:

```
from webapp.extensions import poster_permission
@blog_blueprint.route('/edit/<int:id>', methods=['GET', 'POST'])
@login_required
@poster_permission.require(http_exception=403)
def edit_post(id):
    ...
```

We could also replace our user check in the same view with a `UserNeed` check as follows:

```
from webapp.extensions import poster_permission, admin_permission

@blog_blueprint.route('/edit/<int:id>', methods=['GET', 'POST'])
@login_required
@poster_permission.require(http_exception=403)
def edit_post(id):
    post = Post.query.get_or_404(id)
    permission = Permission(UserNeed(post.user.id))

    # We want admins to be able to edit any post
    if permission.can() or admin_permission.can():
        form = PostForm()

        if form.validate_on_submit():
            post.title = form.title.data
            post.text = form.text.data
            post.publish_date = datetime.datetime.now()

            db.session.add(post)
            db.session.commit()

            return redirect(url_for('.post', post_id=post.id))

        form.text.data = post.text
        return render_template('edit.html', form=form, post=post)

    abort(403)
```

 Visit the documentation of Flask Principal at `https://pythonhosted.org/Flask-Principal/` to understand how to create much more complex `Need` objects.

Summary

Our users now have secure logins, multiple login and registration options, and explicit access permissions. Our app has everything that is needed to be a full-fledged blog app. In the next chapter, the book will stop following this example application in order to introduce a technology called **NoSQL**.

7
Using NoSQL with Flask

A **NoSQL** (short for **Not Only SQL**) database is any nonrelational data store. It usually focuses on speed and scalability. NoSQL has been taking the web development world by storm for the past 7 years. Huge companies, such as Netflix and Google, announced that they were moving many of their services to NoSQL databases, and many smaller companies followed this.

This chapter will deviate from the rest of the book in which Flask will not be the main focus. The focus on database design might seem odd in a book about Flask, but choosing the correct database for your application is arguably the most important decision while designing your technology stack. In the vast majority of web applications, the database is the bottleneck, so the database you pick will determine the overall speed of your app. A study conducted by Amazon showed that even a 100-ms delay caused a 1 percent reduction in sales, so speed should always be one of the main concerns of a web developer. Also, there is an abundance of horror stories in the programmer community of web developers about choosing a popular NoSQL database and then not really understanding what the database required in terms of administration. This leads to large amounts of data loss and crashes, which in turn means losing customers. All in all, it's no exaggeration to say that your choice of database for your application can be the difference between your app succeeding or failing.

To illustrate the strengths and weaknesses of NoSQL databases, each type of NoSQL database will be examined, and the differences between NoSQL and traditional databases will be laid out.

Types of NoSQL databases

NoSQL is a blanket term used to describe nontraditional methods of storing data in a database. To make matters more confusing, NoSQL may also mean the databases that are relational but did not use SQL as a query language, for example, **RethinkDB**. The vast majority of NoSQL databases are not relational, unlike RDBMS, which means that they cannot perform operations such as JOIN. The lack of a JOIN operation is a trade-off because it allows faster reads and easier decentralization by spreading data across several servers or even separate data centers.

Modern NoSQL databases include key-value stores, document stores, column family stores, and graph databases.

Key-value stores

A **key-value** NoSQL database acts much like a dictionary in Python. A single value is associated with one key and is accessed via that key. Also, like a Python dictionary, most key-value databases have the same read speed regardless of how many entries there are. Advanced programmers would know this as **O(1) reads**. In some key-value stores, only one key can be retrieved at a time, rather than multiple rows in traditional SQL databases. In most key-value stores, the content of the value is not *queryable*, but the keys are. Values are just binary blobs; they can be literally anything from a string to a movie file. However, some key-value stores give default types, such as strings, lists, sets, and dictionaries, while still giving the option of adding binary data.

Because of their simplicity, key-value stores are typically very fast. However, their simplicity makes them unsuitable as the main database for most applications. As such, most key-value store use cases are storing simple objects that need to expire after a given amount of time. Two common examples of this pattern are storing user's session data and shopping cart data. Also, key-value stores are commonly used as caches for the application or for other databases. For example, results from a commonly run, or CPU-intensive, query or function are stored with the query or function name as a key. The application will check the cache in the key-value store before running the query on the database, thereby decreasing page load times and stress on the database. An example of this functionality will be shown in *Chapter 10, Useful Flask Extensions*.

The most popular key-value stores are **Redis**, **Riak**, and **Amazon DynamoDB**.

Document stores

Document store is one of the most popular NoSQL database types and what typically replaces an RDBMS. Databases store data in collections of key-value pairs called documents. These documents are schema-less, meaning no document must follow the structure of another document. Also, extra keys may be appended to the document after its creation. Most document stores store data in **JSON (JavaScript Object Notation)**, a superset of JSON, or XML. For example, the following are two different post objects stored in JSON:

```
{
    "title": "First Post",
    "text": "Lorem ipsum...",
    "date": "2015-01-20",
    "user_id": 45
}
{
    "title": "Second Post",
    "text": "Lorem ipsum...",
    "date": "2015-01-20",
    "user_id": 45,
    "comments": [
        {
            "name": "Anonymous",
            "text": "I love this post."
        }
    ]
}
```

Note that the first document has no comments array. As stated before, documents are schema-less, so this format is perfectly valid. The lack of a schema also means that there are no type checks at the database level. There is nothing on the database to stop an integer from being entered into the title field of a post. Schema-less data is the most powerful feature of document stores and draws many to adopt one for their apps. However, it can also be considered very dangerous, as there is one less check stopping faulty or malformed data from getting into your database.

Some document stores collect similar objects in collections of documents to make querying objects easier. However, in some document stores, all objects are queried at once. Document stores store the metadata of each object, which allows all of the values in each document to be queried and return matching documents.

The most popular document stores are **MongoDB**, **CouchDB**, and **Couchbase**.

Column family stores

Column family stores, also known as wide column stores, have many things in common with both key-value stores and document stores. Column family stores are the fastest type of NoSQL database because they are designed for large applications. Their main advantage is their ability to handle terabytes of data and still have very fast read and write speeds by distributing the data across several servers in an intelligent way.

Column family stores are also the hardest to understand, due in part to the vernacular of column family stores, as they use many of the same terms as an RDBMS, with wildly different meanings. In order to understand what a column family store is clearly, let's jump straight to an example. Let's create a simple *user to posts* association in a typical column family store.

First, we need a user table. In column family stores, data is stored and accessed via a unique key, such as a key-value store, but the contents are unstructured columns, such as a document store. Consider the following user table:

Key	Jack			John	
Column	**Full Name**	**Bio**	**Location**	**Full Name**	**Bio**
Value	Jack Stouffer	This is my about me	Michigan, USA	John Doe	This is my about me

Note that each key holds columns, which are key-value pairs as well. Also, it is not required that each key has the same number or types of columns. Each key can store hundreds of unique columns, or they can all have the same number of columns to make application development easier. This is in contrast to key-value stores, which can hold any type of data with each key. This is also slightly different to document stores, which can store types, such as arrays and dictionaries in each document. Now let's create our posts' table:

Key	Post/1			Post/2		
Column	**Title**	**Date**	**Text**	**Title**	**Date**	**Text**
Value	Hello World	2015-01-01	Post text...	Still Here	2015-02-01	Post text...

There are several things to understand about column family stores before we continue. First, in column family stores, data can only be selected via a single key or key range; there is no way to query the contents of the columns. To get around this, many programmers use an external search tool with their database, such as **Elasticsearch**, that stores the contents of columns in a searchable format and returns matching keys to be queried on the database. This limitation is why proper *schema* design is so crucial in column family stores, and must be carefully thought through before storing any data.

Second, data cannot be ordered by the content of the columns. Data can only be ordered by key, which is why the keys to the posts are integers. This allows the posts to be returned in the order in which they were entered. This was not a requirement for the user table because there is no need to sequentially order users.

Third, there are no JOIN operators and we cannot query for a column that would hold a user key. With our current schema, there is no way to associate a post with a user. To create this functionality, we need a third table that holds the user to post associations:

Key	Jack		
Column	Posts	Posts/1	Post/1
Value		Posts/2	Post/2

This is slightly different from the other tables we have seen so far. The Posts column is named a super column, which is a column that holds other columns. In this table, a super column is associated with our user key, which is holding an association of the position of a post to one post. Clever readers might ask why we wouldn't just store this association in our user table, much like how the problem would be solved in document stores. This is because regular columns and super columns cannot be held in the same table. You must choose one at the creation of each table.

To get a list of all the posts by a user, we would first have to query the post association table with our user key, use the returned list of associations to get all of the keys in the posts table, and query the post table with the keys.

If that query seems like a roundabout process to you that's because it is, and it is that way by design. The limiting nature of a column family store is what allows it to be so fast and handle so much data. Removing features such as searching by value and column name give column family stores the ability to handle hundreds of terabytes of data. It's not an exaggeration to say that SQLite is a more complex database for the programmer than a typical column family store.

For this reason, most Flask developers should steer clear of column family stores as it adds complexity to applications that isn't necessary. Unless your application is going to handle millions of reads and writes a second, using a column family store is like pounding in a nail with an atomic bomb.

The most popular column family stores are **BigTable**, **Cassandra**, and **HBase**.

Graph databases

Designed to describe and then query relationships, graph databases are like document stores but have mechanisms to create and describe links between two **nodes**.

A node in a graph store is a single piece of data, usually a collection of key-value pairs or a JSON document. Nodes can be given labels to mark them as part of a category, for example, a user or a group. After your nodes have been defined, an arbitrary number of one-way relationships between the nodes, named **links**, can be created with their own attributes. For example, if our data had two user nodes and each of the two users knew each other, we would define two "knows" links between them to describe that relationship. This would allow you to query all the people that know one user or all the people that a user knows.

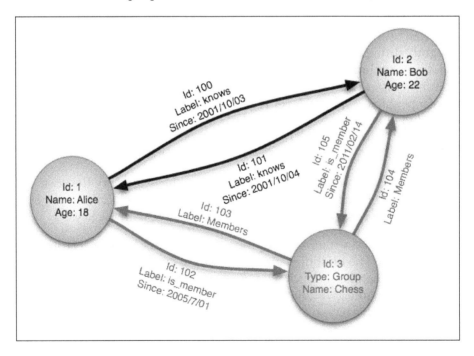

Graph stores also allow you to query by the link's attributes. This allows you to easily create otherwise complex queries, such as all of the users that one user marked as known in October 2001. Graph stores can follow links from node to node to create even more complex queries. If this example dataset had more groups, we could query for groups that people we know have joined but we haven't joined. Otherwise, we could query for people who are in the same groups as a user, but the user doesn't know them. Queries in a graph store can also follow a large number of links to answer complex questions, such as "which restaurants, that have a three-star rating or more, in New York, that serve burgers, have my friends liked?"

The most common use case for a graph database is to build a recommendation engine. For example, say we had a graph store filled with our friend data from a social networking site. Using this data, we could build a mutual friend finder by querying for users where more than two of our friends have marked them as a friend.

It is very rare for a graph database to be used as the primary data store of an application. Most uses of graph stores have each node acting as a representation of a piece of data in their main database by storing its unique identifier and a small amount of other identifying information.

The most popular graph stores are **Neo4j** and **InfoGrid**.

RDBMS versus NoSQL

NoSQL is a tool, and like any tool is has specific use cases where it excels, and use cases where some other tool would be a better fit. No one would use a screwdriver to pound in a nail. It's possible, but using a hammer would make the job easier. One large problem with NoSQL databases is that people adopt them when an RDBMS would solve the problem just as well or better.

To understand which tool to be used when, we must understand the strengths and weaknesses of both systems.

The strengths of RDBMS databases

One of the biggest strengths of an RDBMS is its maturity. The technology behind an RDBMS has existed for over 40 years and is based on the solid theory of relational algebra and relational calculus. Because of their maturity, they have a long, proven track record across many different industries of handling data in a safe and secure way.

Data safety

Safety is also one of the biggest selling points of an RDBMS. A RDBMS has several methods in place to ensure that the data entered into the database will not only be correct, but that data loss is practically nonexistent. These methods combine to form what is known as **ACID**, which stands for Atomicity, Consistency, Isolation, and Durability. ACID is a set of rules for transactions that guarantee that the transaction is handled safely.

First, atomicity requires that each transaction is all or nothing. If one part of the transaction fails, the entire transaction fails. This is much like the mentality in the Zen of Python: "Errors should never pass silently. Unless explicitly silenced." If there is a problem with the data changed or entered, the transaction should not keep operating because the proceeding operations most likely require that the previous operations were successful.

Second, consistency requires that any data the transaction modifies or adds follow the rules of each table. Such rules include type checks, user-defined constraints, such as FOREIGN KEY, cascade rules, and triggers. If any of the rules are broken, then by the atomicity rule, the transaction is thrown out.

Third, isolation requires that if the database runs transactions concurrently to speed up writes, that the outcome of the transactions would be the same if they were run serially. This is mostly a rule for database programmers and not something that web developers need to worry about.

Finally, durability requires that once a transaction is accepted, the data must never be lost, barring a hard drive failure after the transaction is accepted. If the database crashes or loses power, the durability principle requires that any data written before the problem occurred still be present when the server is backed up. This essentially means that all transactions must be written to the disk once they are accepted.

Speed and scale

A common misconception is that the ACID principle makes an RDBMS unable to scale and slow. This is only half true; it is completely possible for an RDBMS to scale. For example, an Oracle database configured by a professional database administrator can handle tens of thousands of complex queries a second. Huge companies, such as Facebook, Twitter, Tumblr, and Yahoo!, are using MySQL to great effect, and PostgreSQL is emerging as a favorite of many programmers due to its speed advantage over MySQL.

However, the largest weakness of an RDBMS is the inability to easily scale by splitting the data across several databases working in tandem. It's not impossible, as some detractors seem to imply, it's just harder than a NoSQL database. This is due to the nature of `JOIN`, which requires a scan of the entire data in a table, even if it is split across multiple servers. Several tools exist to help creation of a partitioned setup, but it is still mostly a job for professional database administrators.

Tools

When evaluating a programming language, the strongest points for or against adopting it are the size and activity of its community. A larger and more active community means more help if you get stuck, and more open source tools are available to use in your projects.

It's no different with databases. An RDBMS, such as MySQL or PostgreSQL, has official libraries for almost every language that is used in commercial environments and unofficial libraries for everything else. Tools, such as Excel, can easily download the latest data from one of these databases and allow the user to treat it like it was any other dataset. Several free desktop GUIs exist for each database, and some are officially supported by the databases' corporate sponsor.

The strengths of NoSQL databases

The main reason that many use NoSQL databases is its speed advantage over traditional databases. Out of the box, many NoSQL databases can outperform an RDBMS by a large amount. However, the speed comes at a cost. Many NoSQL databases, especially document stores, sacrifice consistency for availability. This means that they can handle many concurrent reads and writes, but those writes may be in conflict with one another. These databases promise "eventual consistency" rather than consistency checks on each write. In short, many NoSQL databases do not provide ACID transactions, or they are turned off by default. Once ACID checks are enabled, the speed of the database drops to near the performance of traditional databases. Every NoSQL database handles data safety differently, so it's important to read the documentation carefully before choosing one over another.

The second feature that pulls people to NoSQL is its ability to handle unformatted data. Storing data in XML or JSON allows an arbitrary structure for each document. Applications that store user-designed data have benefited greatly from the adoption of NoSQL. For example, a video game that allows players to submit their custom levels to some central repository can now store the data in a queryable format rather than in a binary blob.

The third feature that draws people to NoSQL is the ease of creating a cluster of databases working in tandem. Not having JOINs or only accessing values via keys makes splitting the data across servers a rather trivial task when compared with an RDBMS. This is due to the fact that JOINs requires a scan of the entire table, even if it is split across many different servers. JOINs become even slower when documents or keys can be assigned to a server by an algorithm as simple as the starting character of its unique identifier. For example, everything that starts with the letters A-H is sent to server one, I-P to server two, and Q-Z to server three. This makes looking up the location of data for a connected client very fast.

What database to use when

So, each database has different uses. It was stated at the beginning of the section that the main problem when programmers choose a NoSQL database for their technology stack is that they choose it when an RDBMS would work just as well. This is born out of some common misconceptions. First, people try to use a relational mindset and data model and think that they will work just as well in a NoSQL database. People usually come to this misunderstanding because the marketing on websites for NoSQL databases is misleading and encourages users to drop their current database without considering if a nonrelational model would work for their project.

Second, people believe that you must use only one data store for their application. Many applications can benefit from using more than one data store. Using a Facebook clone as an example, it could use MySQL for holding user data, redis to store session data, a document store to hold the data for the quizzes and surveys that people share with each other, and a graph database to implement a find friends feature.

If an application feature needs very fast writes, and write safety is not a primary concern, then use a document store database. If you need to store and query schema-less data, then you should use a document store database.

If an application feature needs to store something that deletes itself after a specified time, or the data does not need to be searched, then use a key-value store.

If an application feature relies on finding or describing complex relationships between two or more sets of data, then use a graph store.

If an application feature needs guaranteed write safety, each entry can fix into a specified schema, different sets of data in the database need to be compared using JOINs, or it needs constraints on the entered data, then use an RDBMS.

MongoDB in Flask

MongoDB is far and away the most popular NoSQL database. MongoDB is also the best-supported NoSQL database for Flask and Python in general. Therefore, our examples will focus on MongoDB.

MongoDB is a document store NoSQL database. Documents are stored in collections, which allow grouping of similar documents, but no similarities between documents are necessary to store a document in a collection. Documents are defined in a JSON superset named BSON, which stands for Binary JSON. BSON allows JSON to be stored in binary format rather than in string format, saving a lot of space. BSON also distinguishes between several different ways of storing numbers, such as 32-bit integers and doubles.

To understand the basics of MongoDB, we will use Flask-MongoEngine to cover the same functionality of Flask-SQLAlchemy in the previous chapters. Remember that these are just examples. There is no benefit in refactoring our current code to use MongoDB because MongoDB cannot offer any new functionality for our use case. New functionality with MongoDB will be shown in the next section.

Installing MongoDB

To install MongoDB, go to `https://www.mongodb.org/downloads` and select your OS from the tabs under the heading "Download and Run MongoDB Yourself". Every OS that has a supported version has installation instructions listed next to the download button of the installer.

To run MongoDB, go to bash and run:

```
$ mongod
```

This will run a server for as long as the window is open.

Setting Up MongoEngine

MongoEngine needs to be installed with pip before we can get started:

```
$ pip install Flask-MongoEngine
```

In the `models.py` file, a mongo object will be created that represents our database:

```
from flask.ext.mongoengine import MongoEngine
...
db = SQLAlchemy()
mongo = MongoEngine()
```

Just like the SQLAlchemy object, our mongo object needs to be initialized on the app object in __init__.py:

```
from models import db, mongo
...
db.init_app(app)
mongo.init_app(app)
```

Before our app will run, our DevConfig object in config.py needs to set up the parameters of the mongo connection:

```
MONGODB_SETTINGS = {
    'db': 'local',
    'host': 'localhost',
    'port': 27017
}
```

These are the defaults for a brand new MongoDB installation.

Defining documents

MongoEngine is an ORM based around Python's object system, specifically for MongoDB. Unfortunately, there exists no SQLAlchemy style wrapper that supports all NoSQL drivers. In an RDBMS, the implementations of SQL are so similar that creating a universal interface is possible. However, the underlying implementations of each document store are different enough that the task of creating a similar interface would be more trouble than it is worth.

Each collection in your mongo database is represented by a class that inherits from mongo.Document:

```
class Post(mongo.Document):
    title = mongo.StringField(required=True)
    text = mongo.StringField()
    publish_date = mongo.DateTimeField(
        default=datetime.datetime.now()
    )

    def __repr__(self):
        return "<Post '{}'>".format(self.title)
```

Each class variable is a representation of a key belonging to a document, which is represented in this example of a Post class. The class variable name is used as the key in the document.

Unlike SQLAlchemy, there is no need to define a primary key. A unique ID will be generated for you under the ID attribute. The preceding code would generate a BSON document that would resemble the following:

```
{
    "_id": "55366ede8b84eb00232da905",
    "title": "Post 0",
    "text": "<p>Lorem ipsum dolor...",
    "publish_date": {"$date": 1425255876037}
}
```

Field types

There are a large number of fields such that each represents a distinct category of data in Mongo. Unlike the underlying database, each field provides a type check before the document is allowed to be saved or altered. The most used fields are as follows:

- BooleanField
- DateTimeField
- DictField
- DynamicField
- EmbeddedDocumentField
- FloatField
- IntField
- ListField
- ObjectIdField
- ReferenceField
- StringField

 For a full list of fields and a detailed documentation, go to the MongoEngine website at http://docs.mongoengine.org.

The majority of these are named for the Python type they accept, and work the same as the SQLAlchemy types. However, there are some new types that have a counterpart in SQLAlchemy. DynamicField is a field that can hold any type of value and performs no type checks on values. DictField can store any Python dictionary that can be serialized by json.dumps(). The ReferenceField simply stores the unique ID of a document, and when queried, MongoEngine will return the referenced document. Counter to ReferenceField, EmbeddedDocumentField stores the passed document in the parent document, so there is no need for a second query. The ListField type represents a list of fields of a specific type.

This is typically used to store a list of references to other documents or a list of embedded documents to create a one-to-many relationship. If a list of unknown types is needed, DynamicField can be used. Each field type takes some common arguments, as shown in the following.

```
Field(
    primary_key=None
    db_field=None,
    required=False,
    default=None,
    unique=False,
    unique_with=None,
    choices=None
)
```

The primary_key argument specifies that you do not want MongoEngine to autogenerate a unique key, but the value of the field should be used as the ID. The value of this field will now be accessible from both the id attribute and the name of the field.

db_field defines what the key will be named in each document. If not set, it will default to the name of the class variable.

If required is defined as True, then that key must be present in the document. Otherwise, the key does not have to exist for documents of that type. When a class defined, nonexistent key is queried, it will return None.

default specifies the value that this field will be given if no value is defined.

If unique is set to True, MongoEngine checks to make sure that no other documents in the collection will have the same value for this field.

When passed a list of field names, `unique_with` will make sure that when taken in combination the values of all the fields will be unique for each document. This is much like multicolumn `UNIQUE` indexes in an RDBMS.

Finally, when given a list, the `choices` option limits the allowable values for that field to the elements in the list.

Types of documents

MongoEngine's method to define documents allows either flexibility or rigidity on a collection-by-collection basis. Inheriting from `mongo.Document` means that only the keys defined in the class can be saved to the database. Those keys defined in the class can be empty, but everything else will be ignored. On the other hand, if your class inherits `mongo.DynamicDocument`, any extra fields set will be treated as `DynamicFields` and will be saved with the document.

```
class Post(mongo.DynamicDocument):
    title = mongo.StringField(required=True, unique=True)
    text = mongo.StringField()
    ...
```

To show the not recommended extreme, the following class is perfectly valid; it has no required fields and allows any fields to be set:

```
class Post(mongo.DynamicDocument):
    pass
```

The last type of document is the `EmbeddedDocument`. The `EmbeddedDocument` is simply a document that is passed to an `EmbeddedDocumentField` and stored as is in the document as follows:

```
class Comment(mongo.EmbeddedDocument):
    name = mongo.StringField(required=True)
    text = mongo.StringField(required=True)
    date = mongo.DateTimeField(
        default=datetime.datetime.now()
    )
```

Why use the `EmbeddedDocumentField` over the `DictField` when they seem to perform the same function? The end result of using each is the same. However, an embedded document defines a structure for the data, while a `DictField` can be anything. for better understanding, think of it this way: `Document` is to `DynamicDocument` as `EmbeddedDocument` is to `DictField`.

The meta attribute

Using the `meta` class variable, many attributes of a document can be manually set. If you are working with an existing set of data and want to connect your classes to the collections, set the collection key of the `meta` dictionary:

```
class Post(mongo.Document):
    ...
    meta = {'collection': 'user_posts'}
```

You can also manually set the max number of documents in the collection and how large each document can be. In this example, there can be only 10,000 documents, and each document can't be larger than 2 MB:

```
class Post(mongo.Document):
    ...
    meta = {
        'collection': 'user_posts',
        'max_documents': 10000,
        'max_size': 2000000
    }
```

Indexes can also be set through MongoEngine. Indexes can be single field by using a string or multifield using a tuple:

```
class Post(mongo.Document):
    ...
    meta = {
        'collection': 'user_posts',
        'max_documents': 10000,
        'max_size': 2000000,
        'indexes': [
            'title',
            ('title', 'user')
        ]
    }
```

The default ordering of a collection can be set through the `meta` variable with the **ordering key**. When – is prepended, it tells MongoEngine to order results by descending order of that field. If + is prepended, it tells MongoEngine to order results by ascending order of that field. This default behavior is overridden if the `order_by` function is specified in a query, which will be shown in the *CRUD* section.

```
class Post(mongo.Document):
    ...
```

```
meta = {
    'collection': 'user_posts',
    'max_documents': 10000,
    'max_size': 2000000,
    'indexes': [
        'title',
        ('title', 'user')
    ],
    'ordering': ['-publish_date']
}
```

The `meta` variable can also enable user-defined documents to be inherited from, which is disabled by default. The subclass of the original document will be treated as a member of the parent class and will be stored in the same collection as follows:

```
class Post(mongo.Document):
    ...
    meta = {'allow_inheritance': True}

class Announcement(Post):
    ...
```

CRUD

As stated in *Chapter 2*, Creating Models with SQLAlchemy, there are four main forms of data manipulation that any data store must implement. They are creation of new data, reading existing data, updating existing data, and deleting data.

Create

To create a new document, just create a new instance of the class and call the `save` method.

```
>>> post = Post()
>>> post.title = "Post From The Console"
>>> post.text = "Lorem Ipsum..."
>>> post.save()
```

Otherwise, the values can be passed as keywords in the object creation:

```
>>> post = Post(title="Post From Console", text="Lorem Ipsum...")
```

Unlike SQLAlchemy, MongoEngine does not automatically save related objects stored in `ReferenceFields`. To save any changes to referenced documents along with the changes to the current document, pass `cascade` as `True`:

```
>>> post.save(cascade=True)
```

If you wish to insert a document and skip its checks against the defined parameters in the class definition, then pass validate as `False`.

```
>>> post.save(validate=False)
```

 Remember that these checks exist for a reason. Turn this off only for a very good reason

Write safety

By default, MongoDB does not wait for the data to be written to disk before acknowledging that the write occurred. This means that it is possible for writes that were acknowledged to have failed, either by hardware failure or some error when the write occurred. To ensure that the data is written to disk before Mongo confirms the write, use the `write_concern` keyword. The **write concern** tells Mongo when it should return with an acknowledgement of the write:

```
# will not wait for write and not notify client if there was an error
>>> post.save(write_concern={"w": 0})
# default behavior, will not wait for write
>>> post.save(write_concern={"w": 1})
# will wait for write
>>> post.save(write_concern={"w": 1, "j": True})
```

 As stated in the RDBMS versus NoSQL section, it's very important that you understand how the NoSQL database that you are using treats writes. To learn more about MongoDB's write concern, go to http://docs.mongodb.org/manual/reference/write-concern/.

Read

To access the documents from the database, the `objects` attribute is used. To read all of the documents in a collection, use the `all` method:

```
>>> Post.objects.all()
[<Post: "Post From The Console">]
```

To limit the number of items returned, use the `limit` method:

```
# only return five items
>>> Post.objects.limit(5).all()
```

This `limit` command is slightly different than the SQL version. In SQL, the `limit` command can also be used to skip the first results. To replicate this functionality, use the `skip` method as follows:

```
# skip the first 5 items and return items 6-10
>>> Post.objects.skip(5).limit(5).all()
```

By default, MongoDB returns the results ordered by the time of their creation. To control this, there is the `order_by` function:

```
# ascending
>>> Post.objects.order_by("+publish_date").all()
# descending
>>> Post.objects.order_by("-publish_date").all()
```

If you want only the first result from a query, use the `first` method. If your query returns nothing, and you expected it to, then use `first_or_404` to automatically abort with a 404 error. This acts exactly the same as its Flask-SQLAlchemy counterpart and is provided by Flask-MongoEngine.

```
>>> Post.objects.first()
<Post: "Post From The Console">
>>> Post.objects.first_or_404()
<Post: "Post From The Console">
```

The same behavior is available for the `get` method, which expects the query will only return one result and will raise an exception otherwise:

```
# The id value will be different your document
>>> Post.objects(id="5534451d8b84ebf422c2e4c8").get()
<Post: "Post From The Console">
>>> Post.objects(id="5534451d8b84ebf422c2e4c8").get_or_404()
<Post: "Post From The Console">
```

The `paginate` method is also present and has the exact same API as its Flask-SQLAlchemy counterpart:

```
>>> page = Post.objects.paginate(1, 10)
>>> page.items()
[<Post: "Post From The Console">]
```

Also, if your document has a `ListField` method, the `paginate_field` method on the document object can be used to paginate through the items of the list.

Filtering

If you know the exact value of the field you wish to filter by, pass its value as a keyword to the `objects` method:

```
>>> Post.objects(title="Post From The Console").first()
<Post: "Post From The Console">
```

Unlike SQLAlchemy, we cannot pass truth tests to filter our results. Instead, special keyword arguments are used to test values. For example, to find all posts published after January 1, 2015:

```
>>> Post.objects(
        publish_date__gt=datetime.datetime(2015, 1, 1)
    ).all()
[<Post: "Post From The Console">]
```

The `__gt` appended to the end of the keyword is called an operator. MongoEngine supports the following operators:

- `ne`: not equal to
- `lt`: less than
- `lte`: less than or equal to
- `gt`: greater than
- `gte`: greater than or equal to
- `not`: negate a operator, for example, `publish_date__not__gt`
- `in`: value is in list
- `nin`: value is not in list
- `mod`: *value % a == b, a* and *b* are passed as (*a, b*)
- `all`: every item in list of values provided is in the field
- `size`: the size of the list
- `exists`: value for field exists

MongoEngine also provides the following operators to test string values:

- `exact`: string equals the value

- `iexact`: string equals the value (case insensitive)

- `contains`: string contains the value

- `icontains`: string contains the value (case insensitive)

- `startswith`: string starts with the value

- `istartswith`: string starts with the value (case insensitive)

- `endswith`: string ends with the value

- `iendswith`: string ends with the value (case insensitive) Update

These operators can be combined to create the same powerful queries that were created in the previous sections. For example, to find all of the posts that were created after January 1, 2015 that don't have the word `post` in the title, the body text starts with the word `Lorem`, and ordered by the publish date with the latest one:

```
>>> Post.objects(
    title__not__icontains="post",
    text__istartswith="Lorem",
    publish_date__gt=datetime.datetime(2015, 1, 1),
).order_by("-publish_date").all()
```

However, if there is some complex query that cannot be represented by these tools, then a raw Mongo query can be passed as well:

```
>>> Post.objects(__raw__={"title": "Post From The Console"})
```

Update

To update objects, the `update` method is called on the results of a query.

```
>>> Post.objects(
        id="5534451d8b84ebf422c2e4c8"
    ).update(text="Ipsum lorem")
```

If your query should only return one value, then use `update_one` to only modify the first result:

```
>>> Post.objects(
        id="5534451d8b84ebf422c2e4c8"
    ).update_one(text="Ipsum lorem")
```

Unlike traditional SQL, there are many different ways to change a value in MongoDB. Operators are used to change the values of a field in different ways:

- `set`: This sets a value (same as given earlier)
- `unset`: This deletes a value and removes the key
- `inc`: This increments a value
- `dec`: This decrements a value
- `push`: This appends a value to a list
- `push_all`: This appends several values to a list
- `pop`: This removes the first or last element of a list
- `pull`: This removes a value from a list
- `pull_all`: This removes several values from a list
- `add_to_set`: This adds value to a list only if its not in the list already

For example, if a `Python` value needs to be added to a `ListField` named tags for all `Post` documents that have the `MongoEngine` tag:

```
>>> Post.objects(
        tags__in="MongoEngine",
        tags__not__in="Python"
    ).update(push__tags="Python")
```

The same write concern parameters to save exist for updates.

```
>>> Post.objects(
        tags__in="MongoEngine"
    ).update(push__tags="Python", write_concern={"w": 1, "j": True})
```

Delete

To delete a document instance, call its `delete` method:

```
>>> post = Post.objects(
        id="5534451d8b84ebf422c2e4c8"
    ).first()
>>> post.delete()
```

Relationships in NoSQL

As we created relationships in SQLAlchemy, we can create relationships between objects in MongoEngine. Only with MongoEngine, we will be doing so without `JOIN` operators.

One-to-many relationships

There are two ways to create a one-to-many relationship in MongoEngine. The first method is to create a relationship between two documents by using a `ReferenceField` to point to the ID of another object.

```
class Post(mongo.Document):
    ...
    user = mongo.ReferenceField(User)
```

Accessing the property of the `ReferenceField` gives direct access to the referenced object as follows:

```
>>> user = User.objects.first()
>>> post = Post.objects.first()
>>> post.user = user
>>> post.save()
>>> post.user
<User Jack>
```

Unlike SQLAlchemy, MongoEngine has no way to access objects that have relationships to another object. With SQLAlchemy, a `db.relationship` variable could be declared, which allows a user object to access all of the posts with a matching `user_id` column. No such parallel exists in MongoEngine.

A solution is to get the user ID for the posts you wish to search for and filter with the user field. This is the same thing as SQLAlchemy did behind the scenes, but we are just doing it manually:

```
>>> user = User.objects.first()
>>> Post.objects(user__id=user.id)
```

The second way to create a one-to-many relationship is to use an `EmbeddedDocumentField` with an `EmbeddedDocument`:

```
class Post(mongo.Document):
    title = mongo.StringField(required=True)
    text = mongo.StringField()
```

```
    publish_date = mongo.DateTimeField(
        default=datetime.datetime.now()
    )
    user = mongo.ReferenceField(User)
    comments = mongo.ListField(
        mongo.EmbeddedDocumentField(Comment)
    )
```

Accessing the comments property gives a list of all the embedded documents. To add a new comment to the post, treat it like a list and append comment documents to it:

```
>>> comment = Comment()
>>> comment.name = "Jack"
>>> comment.text = "I really like this post!"
>>> post.comments.append(comment)
>>> post.save()
>>> post.comments
[<Comment 'I really like this post!'>]
```

Note that there was no call to a save method on the comment variable. This is because the comment document is not a real document, it is only an abstraction of the DictField. Also, keep in mind that documents can only be 16 MB large, so be careful how many EmbeddedDocumentFields are on each document and how many EmbeddedDocuments each one is holding.

Many-to-many relationships

The concept of a many-to-many relationship does not exist in document store databases. This is because with ListFields they become completely irrelevant. To idiomatically create the tag feature for the Post object, add a list of strings:

```
class Post(mongo.Document):
    title = mongo.StringField(required=True)
    text = mongo.StringField()
    publish_date = mongo.DateTimeField(
        default=datetime.datetime.now()
    )
    user = mongo.ReferenceField(User)
    comments = mongo.ListField(
        mongo.EmbeddedDocumentField(Comment)
    )
    tags = mongo.ListField(mongo.StringField())
```

Now when we wish to query for all of the `Post` objects that have a specific tag, or many tags, it is a simple query:

```
>>> Post.objects(tags__in="Python").all()
>>> Post.objects(tags__all=["Python", "MongoEngine"]).all()
```

For the list of roles on each user object, the optional choices argument can be given to restrict the possible roles:

```
available_roles = ('admin', 'poster', 'default')

class User(mongo.Document):
    username = mongo.StringField(required=True)
    password = mongo.StringField(required=True)
    roles = mongo.ListField(
        mongo.StringField(choices=available_roles)
    )

    def __repr__(self):
        return '<User {}>'.format(self.username)
```

Leveraging the power of NoSQL

So far, our MongoEngine code should look like the following:

```
available_roles = ('admin', 'poster', 'default')

class User(mongo.Document):
    username = mongo.StringField(required=True)
    password = mongo.StringField(required=True)
    roles = mongo.ListField(
        mongo.StringField(choices=available_roles)
    )

    def __repr__(self):
        return '<User {}>'.format(self.username)


class Comment(mongo.EmbeddedDocument):
    name = mongo.StringField(required=True)
    text = mongo.StringField(required=True)
    date = mongo.DateTimeField(
```

```
                default=datetime.datetime.now()
        )

        def __repr__(self):
            return "<Comment '{}'>".format(self.text[:15])


    class Post(mongo.Document):
        title = mongo.StringField(required=True)
        text = mongo.StringField()
        publish_date = mongo.DateTimeField(
            default=datetime.datetime.now()
        )
        user = mongo.ReferenceField(User)
        comments = mongo.ListField(
            mongo.EmbeddedDocumentField(Comment)
        )
        tags = mongo.ListField(mongo.StringField())

        def __repr__(self):
            return "<Post '{}'>".format(self.title)
```

This code implements the same functionality as the SQLAlchemy models. To show the unique power of NoSQL, let's add a feature that would be possible with SQLAlchemy, but that is much more difficult: different post types, each with their own custom bodies. This will be much like the functionality of the popular blog platform, Tumblr.

To begin, allow your post type to act as a parent class and remove the text field from the Post class as not all posts will have text on them:

```
    class Post(mongo.Document):
        title = mongo.StringField(required=True)
        publish_date = mongo.DateTimeField(
            default=datetime.datetime.now()
        )
        user = mongo.ReferenceField(Userm)
        comments = mongo.ListField(
            mongo.EmbeddedDocumentField(Commentm)
        )
        tags = mongo.ListField(mongo.StringField())

        meta = {
            'allow_inheritance': True
        }
```

Each post type will inherit from the Post class. Doing so will allow the code to treat any Post subclass as if it were a Post. Our blogging app will have four types of posts: a normal blog post, an image post, a video post, and a quote post.

```
class BlogPost(Post):
    text = db.StringField(required=True)

    @property
    def type(self):
        return "blog"

class VideoPost(Post):
    url = db.StringField(required=True)

    @property
    def type(self):
        return "video"

class ImagePost(Post):
    image_url = db.StringField(required=True)

    @property
    def type(self):
        return "image"

class QuotePost(Post):
    quote = db.StringField(required=True)
    author = db.StringField(required=True)

    @property
    def type(self):
        return "quote"
```

Our post creation page needs to be able to create each of these post types. The PostForm object in forms.py, which handles post creation, will need to be modified to handle the new fields first. We will add a selection field that determines the type of post, an author field for the quote type, an image field to hold a URL, and a video field that will hold the embedded HTML iframe. The quote and blog post content will both share the text field as follows:

```
class PostForm(Form):
    title = StringField('Title', [
        DataRequired(),
        Length(max=255)
    ])
```

```
type = SelectField('Post Type', choices=[
    ('blog', 'Blog Post'),
    ('image', 'Image'),
    ('video', 'Video'),
    ('quote', 'Quote')
])
text = TextAreaField('Content')
image = StringField('Image URL', [URL(), Length(max=255)])
video = StringField('Video Code', [Length(max=255)])
author = StringField('Author', [Length(max=255)])
```

The `new_post` view function in the `blog.py` controller will also need to be updated to handle the new post types:

```
@blog_blueprint.route('/new', methods=['GET', 'POST'])
@login_required
@poster_permission.require(http_exception=403)
def new_post():
    form = PostForm()

    if form.validate_on_submit():
        if form.type.data == "blog":
            new_post = BlogPost()
            new_post.text = form.text.data
        elif form.type.data == "image":
            new_post = ImagePost()
            new_post.image_url = form.image.data
        elif form.type.data == "video":
            new_post = VideoPost()
            new_post.video_object = form.video.data
        elif form.type.data == "quote":
            new_post = QuotePost()
            new_post.text = form.text.data
            new_post.author = form.author.data

        new_post.title = form.title.data
        new_post.user = User.objects(
            username=current_user.username
        ).one()

        new_post.save()

    return render_template('new.html', form=form)
```

The `new.html` file that renders our form object will need to display the new fields added to the form:

```
<form method="POST" action="{{ url_for('.new_post') }}">
...
<div class="form-group">
    {{ form.type.label }}
    {% if form.type.errors %}
        {% for e in form.type.errors %}
            <p class="help-block">{{ e }}</p>
        {% endfor %}
    {% endif %}
    {{ form.type(class_='form-control') }}
</div>
...
<div id="image_group" class="form-group">
    {{ form.image.label }}
    {% if form.image.errors %}
        {% for e in form.image.errors %}
            <p class="help-block">{{ e }}</p>
        {% endfor %}
    {% endif %}
    {{ form.image(class_='form-control') }}
</div>
<div id="video_group" class="form-group">
    {{ form.video.label }}
    {% if form.video.errors %}
        {% for e in form.video.errors %}
            <p class="help-block">{{ e }}</p>
        {% endfor %}
    {% endif %}
    {{ form.video(class_='form-control') }}
</div>
<div id="author_group" class="form-group">
    {{ form.author.label }}
        {% if form.author.errors %}
            {% for e in form.author.errors %}
                <p class="help-block">{{ e }}</p>
            {% endfor %}
        {% endif %}
        {{ form.author(class_='form-control') }}
</div>
<input class="btn btn-primary" type="submit" value="Submit">
</form>
```

Now that we have our new inputs, we can add in some JavaScript to show and hide the fields based on the type of post:

```
{% block js %}
<script src="//cdn.ckeditor.com/4.4.7/standard/ckeditor.js"></script>
<script>
    CKEDITOR.replace('editor');

    $(function () {
        $("#image_group").hide();
        $("#video_group").hide();
        $("#author_group").hide();

        $("#type").on("change", function () {
            switch ($(this).val()) {
                case "blog":
                    $("#text_group").show();
                    $("#image_group").hide();
                    $("#video_group").hide();
                    $("#author_group").hide();
                    break;
                case "image":
                    $("#text_group").hide();
                    $("#image_group").show();
                    $("#video_group").hide();
                    $("#author_group").hide();
                    break;
                case "video":
                    $("#text_group").hide();
                    $("#image_group").hide();
                    $("#video_group").show();
                    $("#author_group").hide();
                    break;
                case "quote":
                    $("#text_group").show();
                    $("#image_group").hide();
                    $("#video_group").hide();
                    $("#author_group").show();
                    break;
            }
```

```
        });
    })
</script>
{% endblock %}
```

Finally, the `post.html` needs to be able to display our post types correctly. We have the following:

```
<div class="col-lg-12">
    {{ post.text | safe }}
</div>
All that is needed is to replace this with:
<div class="col-lg-12">
    {% if post.type == "blog" %}
        {{ post.text | safe }}
    {% elif post.type == "image" %}
        <img src="{{ post.image_url }}" alt="{{ post.title }}">
    {% elif post.type == "video" %}
        {{ post.video_object | safe }}
    {% elif post.type == "quote" %}
        <blockquote>
            {{ post.text | safe }}
        </blockquote>
        <p>{{ post.author }}</p>
    {% endif %}
</div>
```

Summary

In this chapter, the fundamental differences between NoSQL and traditional SQL systems were laid out. We explored the main types of NoSQL systems and why an application might need, or not need, to be designed with a NoSQL database. Using our app's models as a base, the power of MongoDB and MongoEngine was shown by how simple it was to set up complex relationships and inheritance. In the next chapter, our blogging application will be extended with a feature designed for other programmers who wish to use our site to build their own service, that is, RESTful endpoints.

8
Building RESTful APIs

Representational State Transfer, or **REST**, is a method of transferring information between a client and a server. On the Web, REST is used on top of HTTP and allows browsers and servers to easily communicate by leveraging basic HTTP commands. By using HTTP commands, REST is platform and programming language agnostic, and decouples the client and the server for easier development. This is typically used in JavaScript applications that need to pull or update user information on the server. REST is also used to provide outside developers with a common interface to user data. For example, Facebook and Twitter use REST in their application program interface (**API**), to allow developers to get information without having to parse the website's HTML.

What is REST

Before getting into the details of REST, let's look at an example. With a client, in this case, a web browser, and a server, the client sends a request to the server over HTTP for some models as follows:

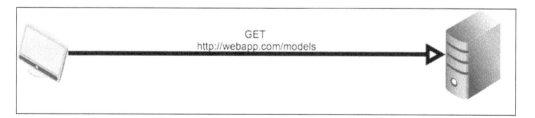

The server will then respond with a document containing all the models.

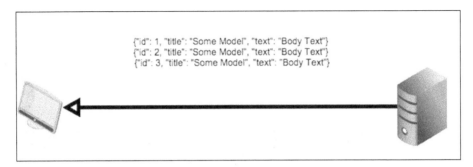

The client can then modify the data on the server through a PUT HTTP request:

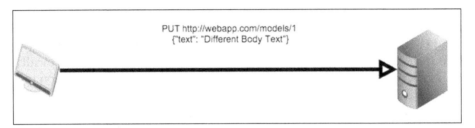

Then the server will respond that it has modified the data. This is a very simplified example, but it will serve as a backdrop to how REST is defined.

Rather than a strict standard, REST lays out a set of constraints on communications to define a methodology that can be implemented in many ways. These constraints are born out of years of trial and error with other communication protocols, such as **Remote Procedure Call (RPC)** or **Simple Object Access Protocol (SOAP)**. These protocols fell by the wayside due to their strictness, verboseness, and the difficulty in creating APIs with them. The issues with these systems were identified, and REST's constraints were created to keep these issues from happening again.

The first constraint requires that the client and the server must have a separation of concerns. The client cannot handle permanent data storage, and the server cannot handle anything with the user interface.

The second constraint is that the server must be stateless. What this means is that any information that is necessary to handle requests is stored in the request itself or by the client. An example of the server being stateless is the session object in Flask. The session object does not store its information on the server, but stores it on the client in a cookie. The cookie is sent along with every request for the server to parse and determine if the necessary data for the requested resource is stored inside it rather than the server storing session information for every user.

The third constraint is that all resources provided must have a uniform interface. There are many different parts to this constraint, which are as follows:

- The interface is based around resources, which are models in our case.

- Data sent by the server is not the actual data in the server, but a representation. For example, the actual database is not sent with each request, but a JSON abstraction of the data.

- The data sent by the server is enough to allow the client to modify the data on the server. In the preceding example, the IDs passed to the client filled this role.

- Every resource provided by the API must be represented and accessed in the same manner. For example, one resource cannot be represented in XML and one in JSON, one over raw TCP and one over HTTP.

The final constraint is that the system must allow for layers. Load balancers, proxies, caches, and other servers and services can act between the client and the server as long as the final result is the same as if they were not there.

When a system adheres to all these constraints, it is considered to be a RESTful system. The most common forms of RESTful systems are built of HTTP and JSON. Each resource is located on its own URL path and modified with different HTTP request types. Generally, it takes the following form:

HTTP method	URL	Action
GET	http://host/resource	Get all the resource representations
GET	http://host/resource/1	Get the resource with an ID of one
POST	http://host/resource	Create a new resource from the form data in the POST
PUT	http://host/resource/1	Modify the existing data of the resource with the ID of one
DELETE	http://host/resource/1	Delete the resource with the ID of one

As an example, a response to the second GET request would look like the following:

```
{
    "id": 100,
    "date": "2015-03-02T00:24:36+00:00",
    "title": "Resource #98"
}
```

In REST APIs, it is also very important to return the correct HTTP status code with the response data, to notify the clients of what actually happened on the server without the client resorting to parsing the returned message. Here is the list of the main HTTP codes used in REST APIs and their meaning.

HTTP code	Name	Meaning
200	OK	The default code of HTTP. The request was successful, and the data was returned.
201	Created	The request was successful, and a new resource was created on the server.
204	No content	The request was successful, but the response returned no content.
400	Bad request	The request was denied because of some perceived client error — either a malformed request or missing required data.
401	Unauthorized	The request was denied because the client is not authenticated and should authenticate before requesting this resource again.
403	Forbidden	The request was denied because the client does not have permission to access this resource. This is in contrast to the 401 code, which assumes that the user is not authenticated. The 403 code says the resource is not accessible regardless of authentication.
404	Not found	The requested resource does not exist.
405	Method not allowed	The request was denied because the HTTP method is not available for the URL.

Setting up a RESTful Flask API

In our app, we will create a RESTful interface to the blog post data in our database. The representations of the data will be sent as JSON. The data will be retrieved and modified using the general form in the preceding table, but the URI will be /api/posts.

We could just use the standard Flask views to create the API, but the Flask extension **Flask Restful** makes the task much easier.

To install Flask Restful:

```
$ pip install Flask-Restful
```

In the `extensions.py` file, initialize the `Api` object that will handle all the routes:

```
from flask.ext.restful import Api
…
rest_api = Api()
```

The control logic and views for our Post API should be stored in a new folder named `rest` in the `controllers` folder. In this folder, we will need an empty `__init__.py` and a file named `post.py`. Inside `post.py`, let's create a simple *Hello World* example:

```
from flask.ext.restful import Resource


class PostApi(Resource):
    def get(self):
        return {'hello': 'world'}
```

In Flask Restful, every REST resource is defined as a class that inherits from the `Resource` object. Much like the `MethodView` object shown in *Chapter 4, Creating Controllers with Blueprints*, any class that inherits from the `Resource` object defines its logic with methods named after the HTTP methods. For example, when the GET HTTP method hits the `PostApi` class, the `get` method will be executed.

Just like the other Flask extensions we used, the `Api` object will need to be initialized on the app object in the `__init__.py` file, which holds the `create_app` function. The `PostApi` class will also have its route defined with the `add_resource()` method of the `Api` object:

```
from .extensions import (
    bcrypt,
    oid,
    login_manager,
    principals,
    rest_api
)
from .controllers.rest.post import PostApi


def create_app(object_name):
    …
    rest_api.add_resource(PostApi, '/api/post')
    rest_api.init_app(app)
```

Now, if you open the `/api/post` URI in the browser, the *Hello World* JSON will be displayed.

GET requests

For some of our GET, PUT, and DELETE requests, our API will need the ID of the Post to modify. The add_resource method can take multiple routes, so let's add the second route that captures the passed ID:

```
rest_api.add_resource(
    PostApi,
    '/api/post',
    '/api/post/<int:post_id>',
    endpoint='api'
)
```

Now the get method will need to accept post_id as a keyword argument:

```
class PostApi(Resource):
    def get(self, post_id=None):
        if post_id:
            return {"id": post_id}

        return {"hello": "world"}
```

The data to be sent to the client must be a representation of the Post objects in JSON, so how will our Post objects be translated? Flask Restful provides a way of translating any object to JSON through the fields object and the marshal_with function decorator.

Output formatting

The output format is defined by creating a dictionary of field objects that represent basic types. The key of the field defines what attribute the field will try to translate. By passing the dictionary to the marshal_with decorator, any object the get method attempts to return will be first translated with the dictionary. This also works for lists of objects:

```
from flask import abort
from flask.ext.restful import Resource, fields, marshal_with
from webapp.models import Post

post_fields = {
    'title': fields.String(),
    'text': fields.String(),
    'publish_date': fields.DateTime(dt_format='iso8601')
```

```
}

class PostApi(Resource):
    @marshal_with(post_fields)
    def get(self, post_id=None):
        if post_id:
            post = Post.query.get(post_id)
            if not post:
                abort(404)

            return post
        else:
            posts = Post.query.all()
            return posts
```

While reloading the API in the browser, every Post object will be shown in JSON format. However, the problem is that the API should not return the HTML from the WYSIWYG editor in the post creation form. As stated earlier, the server should not be concerned with UI, and HTML is purely for output specification. To solve this, we will need a custom field object that strips HTML from strings. In a new file in the rest folder named fields.py, add the following:

```
from HTMLParser import HTMLParser
from flask.ext.restful import fields

class HTMLStripper(HTMLParser):
    def __init__(self):
        self.reset()
        self.fed = []

    def handle_data(self, d):
        self.fed.append(d)

    def get_data(self):
        return ''.join(self.fed)

    def strip_tags(html):
        s = HTMLStripper()
        s.feed(html)

    return s.get_data()

class HTMLField(fields.Raw):
    def format(self, value):
        return strip_tags(str(value))
```

Now, our `post_fields` dictionary should be updated to work with the new field:

```
from .fields import HTMLField

post_fields = {
    'title': fields.String(),
    'text': HTMLField(),
    'publish_date': fields.DateTime(dt_format='iso8601')
}
```

Using the standard library `HTMLParser` module, we now have a `strip_tags` function that will return any string cleaned of HTML tags. A new field type `HTMLfield` is defined by inheriting from the `fields.Raw` class and sending values through the `strip_tags` function. If the page is reloaded once again, all the HTML is gone and just the text remains.

Flask Restful provides many default fields:

- `fields.String`: This converts the value using `str()`.
- `fields.FormattedString`: This passes formatted string in Python with the variable name in brackets.
- `fields.Url`: This provides the same functionality as the Flask `url_for` function.
- `fields.DateTime`: This converts a Python `date` or `datetime` object to a string. The format keyword argument specifies if the string should be an `ISO8601` date or an `RFC822` date.
- `fields.Float`: This converts the value to a string representation of a float.
- `fields.Integer`: This converts the value to a string representation of an integer.
- `fields.Nested`: This allows nested objects to be represented by another dictionary of field objects.
- `fields.List`: Much like the MongoEngine API, this field takes another field type as an argument and tries to convert a list of values into a JSON list of the field types.
- `fields.Boolean`: This converts the value to a string representation of a boolean argument.

There are two more fields that should be added to the returned data: the author and the tags. The comments will be left out because they should be contained under their own resource.

```
nested_tag_fields = {
```

```
    'id': fields.Integer(),
    'title': fields.String()
}

post_fields = {
    'author': fields.String(attribute=lambda x: x.user.username),
    'title': fields.String(),
    'text': HTMLField(),
    'tags': fields.List(fields.Nested(nested_tag_fields)),
    'publish_date': fields.DateTime(dt_format='iso8601')
}
```

The `author` field uses the attribute keyword argument of the `field` class. This allows any attribute of the object to be represented rather than just base-level properties. Because the many-to-many relationship of the tags returns a list of objects, the same solution cannot be used with the tags. Using the `NestedField` type inside a `ListField` and another dictionary of fields, a list of tag dictionaries can now be returned. This has the added benefit for the end users of the API of giving them a tag ID to easily query as if there was a tag API.

Request arguments

While sending a GET request to the base of the resource, our API currently sends all the Post objects in the database. This is acceptable if the number of objects is low or the number of people using the API is low. However, if either increases, the API will put a large amount of stress on the database. Much like the Web interface, the API should be paginated as well.

In order to achieve this, our API will need to accept a GET query string parameter `page` that specifies which page to load. Flask Restful provides a method to grab request data and parse it. If the required arguments aren't there, or the types don't match, Flask Restful will autocreate a JSON error message. In a new file in the `rest` folder named `parsers.py`, add the following code:

```
from flask.ext.restful import reqparse

post_get_parser = reqparse.RequestParser()
post_get_parser.add_argument(
    'page',
    type=int,
    location=['args', 'headers'],
    required=False
)
```

Now the `PostApi` class will need to be updated to work with our parser:

```
from .parsers import post_get_parser


class PostApi(Resource):
    @marshal_with(post_fields)
    def get(self, post_id=None):
        if post_id:
            post = Post.query.get(post_id)
            if not post:
                abort(404)

            return post
        else:
            args = post_get_parser.parse_args()
            page = args['page'] or 1
            posts = Post.query.order_by(
                Post.publish_date.desc()
            ).paginate(page, 30)

            return posts.items
```

In the preceding example, the `RequestParser` looks for the `page` variable in either the query string or the request header and returns the page of Post objects from that page.

After a parser object is created with `RequestParser`, arguments can be added using the `add_argument` method. The first argument of `add_argument` is the key of the argument to parse, but `add_argument` also takes a lot of keyword arguments:

- `action`: This is what the parser does with the value after it has been successfully parsed. The two available options are `store` and `append`. `store` adds the parsed value to the returned dictionary. `append` adds the parsed value to the end of a list in the dictionary.

- `case_sensitive`: This is a `boolean` argument to allow or disallow the keys to be case insensitive.

- `choices`: This is like MongoEngine, a list of the allowed values for the argument.

- `default`: This is the value produced if the argument is absent from the request.

- `dest`: This is the key to add the parsed value in the return data.

- `help`: This is a message to return to the user if validation fails.
- `ignore`: This is a `boolean` argument to allow or disallow failures of the type conversion.
- `location`: this indicates where to look for the data. The locations available are:
  - ° `args` to look in the GET query string
  - ° `headers` to look in the HTTP request headers
  - ° `form` to look in the HTTP POST data
  - ° `cookies` to look in the HTTP cookies
  - ° `json` to look in any sent JSON
  - ° `files` to look in the POST file data
- required: this is a `boolean` argument to determine if the argument is optional.
- store_missing: this is a `boolean` argument to determine if the default value should be stored if the argument is not in the request.
- type: this is the Python type to convert the passed value.

Using the Flask Restful parser, it is very easy to add new parameters to the API. For example, let's add a user argument that allows us to search for all posts by a user. First, in the `parsers.py` file, add the following:

```
post_get_parser = reqparse.RequestParser()
post_get_parser.add_argument(
    'page',
    type=int,
    location=['json', 'args', 'headers']
)
post_get_parser.add_argument(
    'user',
    type=str,
    location=['json', 'args', 'headers']
)
```

Then, in `post.py`, add the following:

```
class PostApi(Resource):
    @marshal_with(post_fields)
    def get(self, post_id=None):
        if post_id:
            post = Post.query.get(post_id)
            if not post:
```

```
                        abort(404)

            return post
        else:
            args = post_get_parser.parse_args()
            page = args['page'] or 1

            if args['user']:
                user = User.query.filter_by(
                    username=args['user']
                ).first()
                if not user:
                    abort(404)

                posts = user.posts.order_by(
                    Post.publish_date.desc()
                ).paginate(page, 30)
            else:
                posts = Post.query.order_by(
                    Post.publish_date.desc()
                ).paginate(page, 30)

            return posts.items
```

When the Flask `abort` function is called from a `Resource`, Flask Restful will automatically create an error message to be returned with the status code.

POST requests

Using our new knowledge of the Flask Restful parser, the `POST` endpoint can be added. First, we will need a parser that will take a title, the body text, and a list of tags. In the `parser.py` file, add the following:

```
post_post_parser = reqparse.RequestParser()
post_post_parser.add_argument(
    'title',
    type=str,
    required=True,
    help="Title is required"
)
post_post_parser.add_argument(
    'text',
```

```
        type=str,
        required=True,
        help="Body text is required"
    )
post_post_parser.add_argument(
        'tags',
        type=str,
        action='append'
    )
```

Next, the `PostApi` class will need a `post` method to handle incoming requests. The `post` method will use the given values for the title and body text. Also, if the tags key exists, then add the tags to the post, which creates new tags if the passed ones do not exist:

```
import datetime
from .parsers import (
    post_get_parser,
    post_post_parser
)
from webapp.models import db, User, Post, Tag


class PostApi(Resource):
    ...
    def post(self, post_id=None):
        if post_id:
            abort(400)
        else:
            args = post_post_parser.parse_args(strict=True)
            new_post = Post(args['title'])
            new_post.date = datetime.datetime.now()
            new_post.text = args['text']

            if args['tags']:
                for item in args['tags']:
                    tag = Tag.query.filter_by(title=item).first()

                    # Add the tag if it exists.
                    # If not, make a new tag
                    if tag:
                        new_post.tags.append(tag)
                    else:
```

```
                            new_tag = Tag(item)
                            new_post.tags.append(new_tag)

                    db.session.add(new_post)
                    db.session.commit()
                    return new_post.id, 201
```

At the `return` statement, if a tuple is returned, the second argument is treated as the status code. There is also a third value that acts as extra header values by passing a dictionary.

In order to test this code, a different tool than the web browser has to be used, as creating custom POST requests without a browser plugin is very difficult in a browser. A tool named curl will be used instead. **Curl** is a command-line tool included in Bash that allows for creation and manipulation of HTTP requests. To perform a GET request with curl, just pass the URL:

```
$ curl http://localhost:5000/api/post/1
```

To pass POST variables, the d flag is used:

```
$ curl -d "title=From REST" \
-d "text=The body text from REST" \
-d "tag=Python" \
http://localhost:5000/api/post
```

The id of the newly created post should be returned. However, if you now load the post you created in the browser, an error should appear. This is because our `Post` object had no user associated with it. In order to have Post objects assigned to users and for only authenticated users of the website to have permission to POST posts, we need to create an authentication system.

Authentication

To solve our authentication problems, Flask-Login could be used and the cookie data from the login could be checked. However, this would require developers who wish to use our API to have their program login through the web interface. We could also have developers send their login data with every request, but it's a good design practice to only send sensitive information when absolutely necessary. Instead, our API will provide an `auth` endpoint that allows them to send login credentials and get an access token back.

This access token will be created by the Python library *it's dangerous*, which Flask uses to encode the session data on a cookie, so it should already be installed. The token will be a Python dictionary cryptographically signed by the app's secret key containing the id of the user. This token has an expiration date encoded inside it that will not allow it to be used after it expires. This means that even if the token is stolen by a malicious user, it will only be useful for a limited amount of time before the client has to reauthenticate. First, a new parser is needed to handle parsing the username and password data:

```
user_post_parser = reqparse.RequestParser()
user_post_parser.add_argument('username', type=str, required=True)
user_post_parser.add_argument('password', type=str, required=True)
```

In a new file named auth.py inside the rest folder, add the following code:

```
from flask import abort, current_app

from .parsers import user_post_parser
from itsdangerous import TimedJSONWebSignatureSerializer as Serializer

class AuthApi(Resource):
    def post(self):
        args = user_post_parser.parse_args()
        user = User.query.filter_by(
            username=args['username']
        ).one()

        if user.check_password(args['password']):
            s = Serializer(
                current_app.config['SECRET_KEY'],
                expires_in=600
            )
            return {"token": s.dumps({'id': user.id})}
        else:
            abort(401)
```

 Do not allow users to send their login credentials across an unsecured connection! HTTPS is required if you wish to protect your user's data. The best solution would be to require HTTPS for your entire app to avoid the possibility.

Users of our API will have to pass the token received from this resource to any method that requires user credentials. However, first we need a function that verifies the token. In the `models.py` file, the `verify_auth_token` will be a `staticmethod` on the `User` object:

```python
from itsdangerous import (
    TimedJSONWebSignatureSerializer as Serializer,
    BadSignature,
    SignatureExpired
)
from flask import current_app

class User(db.Model):
    ...

    @staticmethod
    def verify_auth_token(token):
        s = Serializer(current_app.config['SECRET_KEY'])

        try:
            data = s.loads(token)
        except SignatureExpired:
            return None
        except BadSignature:
            return None

        user = User.query.get(data['id'])
        return user
```

Our POST parser needs a token argument to accept the `auth` token:

```python
post_post_parser = reqparse.RequestParser()
post_post_parser.add_argument(
    'token',
    type=str,
    required=True,
    help="Auth Token is required to create posts"
)
```

Now, our `post` method can properly add new posts as follows:

```python
class PostApi(Resource):
    def get(self, post_id=None):
        ...

    def post(self, post_id=None):
        if post_id:
```

```
        abort(405)
    else:
        args = post_post_parser.parse_args(strict=True)

        user = User.verify_auth_token(args['token'])
        if not user:
            abort(401)

        new_post = Post(args['title'])
        new_post.user = user
        ...
```

Using curl, our `auth` and `post` APIs can now be tested. For the sake of brevity, the token is omitted here as it is very long:

```
$ curl -d "username=user" \
-d "password=password" \
http://localhost:5000/api/auth


{token: <the token>}


$ curl -d "title=From REST" \
-d "text=this is from REST" \
-d "token=<the token>" \
-d "tags=Python" \
-d "tags=Flask" \
http://localhost:5000/api/post
```

PUT requests

As listed in the table at the beginning of this chapter, PUT requests are for changing the values of existing resources. Like the `post` method, the first thing to be done is to create a new parser in `parsers.py`:

```
post_put_parser = reqparse.RequestParser()
post_put_parser.add_argument(
    'token',
    type=str,
    required=True,
    help="Auth Token is required to edit posts"
)
post_put_parser.add_argument(
```

```
        'title',
        type=str
    )
    post_put_parser.add_argument(
        'text',
        type=str
    )
    post_put_parser.add_argument(
        'tags',
        type=str,
        action='append'
    )
```

The logic for the `put` method is very similar to the `post` method. The main difference is that each change is optional and any request that does not provide a `post_id` is denied:

```python
from .parsers import (
    post_get_parser,
    post_post_parser,
    post_put_parser
)


class PostApi(Resource):
    @marshal_with(post_fields)
    def get(self, post_id=None):
        ...

    def post(self, post_id=None):
        ...

    def put(self, post_id=None):
        if not post_id:
            abort(400)

        post = Post.query.get(post_id)
        if not post:
            abort(404)

        args = post_put_parser.parse_args(strict=True)
        user = User.verify_auth_token(args['token'])
        if not user:
```

```
        abort(401)
    if user != post.user:
        abort(403)

    if args['title']:
        post.title = args['title']

    if args['text']:
        post.text = args['text']

    if args['tags']:
        for item in args['tags']:
            tag = Tag.query.filter_by(title=item).first()

            # Add the tag if it exists. If not, make a new tag
            if tag:
                post.tags.append(tag)
            else:
                new_tag = Tag(item)
                post.tags.append(new_tag)

    db.session.add(post)
    db.session.commit()
    return post.id, 201
```

To test this method, curl can also create PUT requests with the -x flag:

```
$ curl -X PUT \
-d "title=Modified From REST" \
-d "text=this is from REST" \
-d "token=<the token>" \
-d "tags=Python" -d "tags=Flask" -d "tags=REST" \
http://localhost:5000/api/post/101
```

DELETE requests

Finally, we have the DELETE request, which is the simplest of the four supported methods. The main difference with the delete method is that it returns no content, which is the accepted standard with DELETE requests:

```
class PostApi(Resource):
    @marshal_with(post_fields)
```

```
def get(self, post_id=None):
    ...

def post(self, post_id=None):
    ...

def put(self, post_id=None):
    ...

def delete(self, post_id=None):
    if not post_id:
        abort(400)

    post = Post.query.get(post_id)
    if not post:
        abort(404)

    args = post_delete_parser.parse_args(strict=True)
    user = verify_auth_token(args['token'])
    if user != post.user:
        abort(403)

    db.session.delete(post)
    db.session.commit()
    return "", 204
```

Again, we can test with:

```
$ curl -X DELETE\
-d "token=<the token>"\
http://localhost:5000/api/post/102
```

If everything is successfully deleted, you should receive a 204 status code and nothing should show up.

Before we move on from REST completely, there is one final challenge to the reader to test your understanding of Flask Restful. Try to create a comments API that is not only modifiable from `http://localhost:5000/api/comments`, but also allow developers to modify only those comments on a specific post by using the URL `http://localhost:5000/api/post/<int:post_id>/comments`.

Summary

Our Post API is now a complete feature. If a developer wants, they can create a desktop or mobile application using this API, all without using HTML scraping, which is a very tedious and long process. Giving the developers who wish to use your website as a platform the ability to do so will increase your site's popularity, as they will essentially give you free advertising with their app or website.

In the next chapter, we will use the popular program Celery to run programs and tasks asynchronously with our application.

Creating Asynchronous Tasks with Celery

While creating web apps, it is vital to keep the time that a request takes to process below or around 50 ms. As the majority of response times are occupied by waiting for users' connection, and extra processing time may hang the server. Any extra processing on the server that can be avoided should be avoided. However, it is quite common for several operations in a web app to take longer than a couple of seconds, especially when complex database operations or image processing are involved. To save our user experience, a task queue named Celery will be used to move these operations out of the Flask process.

What is Celery?

Celery is an asynchronous task queue written in Python. Celery runs tasks, which are user-defined functions, *concurrently*—multiple tasks at once—through the Python multiprocessing library. Celery receives messages that tell it to start a task from a **broker**, which is usually called a message queue as shown in the following diagram:

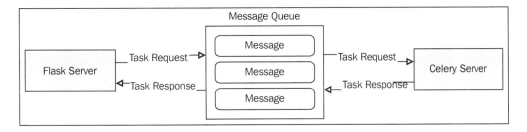

A **message queue** is a system specifically designed to send data between producer processes and consumer processes. **Producer processes** are any programs that create messages to be sent in the queue, and **consumer processes** are any programs that take the messages out of the queue. Messages sent from a producer are stored in a **First In First Out** (FIFO) queue, where the oldest items are retrieved first. Messages are stored until a consumer receives the message, after which it is deleted. Message queues provide real-time messaging without relying on polling, the process of continuously checking the status of a process. When messages are sent from producers, consumers are *listening* on their connection to the message queue for new messages; the consumer is not constantly contacting the queue. This difference is like the difference between **AJAX** and **WebSockets**; AJAX requires constant contact with the server while WebSockets are just a continuous stream.

It is possible to replace the message queue with a traditional database. Celery even comes with built-in support for SQLAlchemy to allow this. However, using a database as a broker for Celery is highly discouraged. Using a database in place of a message queue requires the consumer to constantly poll the database for updates. Also, because Celery uses multiprocessing for concurrency, the number of connections making lots of reads goes up quickly. Under medium loads, using a database requires the producer to make lots of writes to the database at the same time as the consumer is reading. Databases cannot have too many connections making reads, writes, and updates at the same time on the same data. When this happens, tables are often locked and all other connections are left waiting for each write to finish before anything can read the data, and vice versa. Even worse, it can lead to race conditions, which are situations where concurrent events change and read the same resource, and each concurrent operation started using a stale version of the data. Specific to Celery, this can lead to the same operation being run multiple times for the same message.

It is also possible to use a message queue as a broker and a database to store the results of the tasks. In the preceding diagram, the message queue was used for sending task requests and task results.

However, using a database to store the end result of the task allows the final product to be stored indefinitely, whereas the message queue will throw out the data as soon as the producer receives the data as shown in the following diagram:

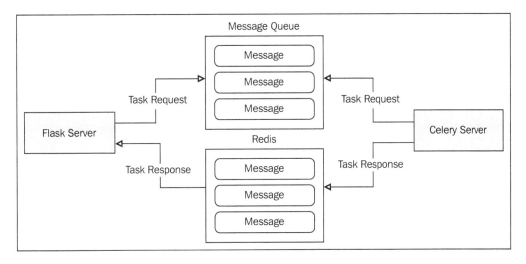

This database is often a key-value NoSQL store to help handle the load. This is useful if you plan on doing analytics on previously run tasks; otherwise, it's safer to just stick with the message queue.

There is even an option to drop the results of tasks entirely and not have the results of tasks returned. This has the downside that the producer has no way of knowing if a task was successful or not, but often this is enough in smaller projects.

For our stack, we will use **RabbitMQ** as the message broker. RabbitMQ runs on all major OSes and is very simple to set up and run. Celery also supports RabbitMQ without any extra libraries and is the recommended message queue in the Celery documentation.

> At the time of writing, there is no way to use RabbitMQ with Celery in Python 3. You can use Redis instead of RabbitMQ. The only difference will be the connection strings. For more information, see `http://docs.celeryproject.org/en/latest/getting-started/brokers/redis.html`.

Setting up Celery and RabbitMQ

To install Celery with `pip`, run the following:

```
$ pip install Celery
```

We will also need a Flask extension to help handle initializing Celery:

```
$ pip install Flask-Celery-Helper
```

The Flask documentation states that Flask extensions for Celery are unnecessary. However, getting the Celery server to work with Flask's application context when your app is organized with an application factory is significant. So, we will use **Flask-Celery-Helper** to do the heavy lifting.

Next, RabbitMQ needs to be installed. RabbitMQ is not written in Python; therefore, installation instructions will be different for every OS. Thankfully, RabbitMQ maintains a detailed list of instructions for each OS at `https://www.rabbitmq.com/download.html`.

After RabbitMQ is installed, go to a terminal window and run the following:

```
$ rabbitmq-server
```

This will start a RabbitMQ server with a user of guest and a password of guest. By default, RabbitMQ only accepts connections on localhost, so this setup is okay for the development.

Creating tasks in Celery

As stated before, Celery tasks are just user-defined functions that perform some operations. But before any tasks can be written, our Celery object needs to be created. This is the object that the Celery server will import to handle running and scheduling all of the tasks.

At a bare minimum, Celery needs one configuration variable to run: the connection to the message broker. The connection is defined like the SQLAlchemy connection, as a URL. The backend, what stores our tasks' results, is also defined as a URL as shown in the following code:

```
class DevConfig(Config):
    DEBUG = True
    SQLALCHEMY_DATABASE_URI = 'sqlite:///../database.db'
    CELERY_BROKER_URL = "amqp://guest:guest@localhost:5672//"
```

```
    CELERY_BACKEND = "amqp://guest:guest@localhost:5672//"
```

In the extensions.py file, the Celery class from Flask-Celery-Helper will be initialized:

```
from flask.ext.celery import Celery
celery = Celery()
```

So, in order for our Celery process to work with the database and any other Flask extensions, it needs to work within our application context. In order to do so, Celery will need to create a new instance of our application for each process. Unlike most Celery apps, we need a Celery factory to create an application instance and register our Celery instance on it. In a new file in the top-level directory, the same location where manage.py resides, named celery_runner.py, add the following:

```
import os
from webapp import create_app
from celery import Celery
from webapp.tasks import log

def make_celery(app):
    celery = Celery(
        app.import_name,
        broker=app.config['CELERY_BROKER_URL'],
        backend=app.config['CELERY_BACKEND_URL']
    )
    celery.conf.update(app.config)
    TaskBase = celery.Task

    class ContextTask(TaskBase):
        abstract = True

        def __call__(self, *args, **kwargs):
            with app.app_context():
                return TaskBase.__call__(self, *args, **kwargs)

    celery.Task = ContextTask

    return celery

env = os.environ.get('WEBAPP_ENV', 'dev')
flask_app = create_app(
    'webapp.config.%sConfig' % env.capitalize()
)
celery = make_celery(flask_app)
```

What the `make_celery` function does is wraps every call to each Celery task in a Python `with` block. This makes sure that every call to any Flask extension will work as it is working with our app. Also, make sure not to name the Flask app instance `app`, as Celery tries to import any object named `app` or `celery` as the Celery application instance. So, naming your Flask object `app` will cause Celery to try to use it as a Celery object.

Now, we can write our first task. It will be a simple task to start with, one that just returns any string passed to it. In a new file in the application directory named `tasks.py`, add the following:

```
from webapp.extensions import celeryfrom webapp.extensions import
celery
@celery.task()
def log(msg):
    return msg
```

Now, the final piece of the puzzle is to run the Celery process, which is called a **worker**, in a new terminal window. Again, this is the process that will be listening to our message broker for commands to start new tasks:

```
$ celery worker -A celery_runner --loglevel=info
```

The `loglevel` flag is there, so you can see the confirmation that a task was received and its output was available in the terminal window.

Now, we can send commands to our Celery worker. Open the `manage.py` shell and import the `log` task:

```
>>> from webapp.tasks import log
>>> log("Message")
Message
>>> result = log.delay("Message")
```

The function can be called as if it were any other function; doing so will execute the function in the current process. However, calling the `delay` method on the task will send a message to the worker process to execute the function with the given arguments.

In the terminal window that is running the Celery worker, you should see something like the following:

```
Task tasks.log succeeded in 0.0005873600021s: 'Message'
```

With any asynchronous task, the `ready` method can be used to tell if the task has successfully completed. If true, the `get` method can be used to retrieve the result of the tasks.

```
>>> result.ready()
True
>>> result.get()
"Message"
```

The `get` method causes the current process to wait until the `ready` function returns `True` to retrieve the result. So, calling `get` immediately after calling the task essentially makes the task synchronous. Because of this, it's rather rare for tasks to actually return a value to the producer. The vast majority of tasks perform some operation and then exit.

When a task is run on the Celery worker, the state of the task can be accessed via the `state` attribute. This allows for a more fine-grained understanding of what the task is currently doing in the worker process. The available states are as follows:

- `FAILURE`: The task failed and all of the retries failed as well
- `PENDING`: The task has not yet been received by the worker
- `RECEIVED`: The task has been received by the worker and is not yet processing
- `RETRY`: The task failed and is waiting to be retried
- `REVOKED`: The task was stopped
- `STARTED`: The worker has started processing the task
- `SUCCESS`: The task completed successfully

In Celery, if a task fails, then the task can recall itself with the `retry` method as follows:

```
@celery.task(bind=True)
def task(self, param):
    try:
        some_code
    except Exception, e:
        self.retry(exc=e)
```

The `bind` parameter in the decorator function tells Celery to pass a reference to the task object as the first parameter in the function. Using the `self` parameter, the `retry` method can be called, which will rerun the task with the same parameters. There are several other parameters that can be passed to the function decorator to change the behavior of the task:

- `max_retries`: This is the maximum number of times the task can be retried before it is declared as failed.

- `default_retry_delay`: This is the time in seconds to wait before running the task again. It's good idea to keep this at somewhere around a minute or so if you expect that the conditions that led to the task failing are transitory — for example, network errors.

- `rate_limit`: This specifies the total number of unique calls to this task that are allowed to run in a given interval. If the value is an integer, it is the total number of this task that is allowed to run per second. The value can also be a string in the form of *x/m* for *x* number of tasks per minute or *x/h* for *x* number of tasks per hour. For example, passing in *5/m* will only allow this task to be called five times a minute.

- `time_limit`: If specified, the task will be killed if it runs longer than this number of seconds.

- `ignore_result`: If the task's return value isn't used, then don't send it back.

It's a good idea to specify all of these for each task to avoid any chance that a task will not be run.

Running Celery tasks

The `delay` method is a shorthand version of the `apply_async` method, which is called in this format:

```
task.apply_async(
    args=[1, 2],
    kwargs={'kwarg1': '1', 'kwarg2': '2'}
)
```

However, the `args` keyword can be implicit:

```
apply_async([1, 2], kwargs={'kwarg1': '1', 'kwarg2': '2'})
```

Calling `apply_async` allows you to define some extra functionality in the task call that you cannot specify in the `delay` method. First, the `countdown` option specifies the amount of time in seconds the worker should wait to run the task after receiving it:

```
>>> from webapp.tasks import log
>>> log.apply_async(["Message"], countdown=600)
```

`countdown` is not a guarantee that the task will be run after `600` seconds. `countdown` only says that the task is up for processing after *x* number of seconds. If all of the worker processes are busy with the other tasks, then it will not be run immediately.

Another keyword argument that `apply_async` gives is the `eta` argument. `eta` is passed through a Python `datetime` object that specifies exactly when the task should be run. Again, `eta` is not reliable.

```
>>> import datetime
>>> from webapp.tasks import log
# Run the task one hour from now
>>> eta = datetime.datetime.now() + datetime.timedelta(hours=1)
>>> log.apply_async(["Message"], eta=eta)
```

Celery workflows

Celery provides many ways to group multiple, dependent tasks together or to execute many tasks in parallel. These methods take a large amount of influence from language features found in functional programming languages. However, to understand how this works, we first need to understand signatures. Consider the following task:

```
@celery.task()
def multiply(x, y):
    return x * y
```

Let's see a **signature** in action to understand it. Open up the `manage.py` shell:

```
>>> from celery import signature
>>> from webapp.tasks import multiply
# Takes the same keyword args as apply_async
>>> signature('webapp.tasks.multiply', args=(4, 4) , countdown=10)
webapp.tasks.multiply(4, 4)
# same as above
```

```
>>> from webapp.tasks import multiply
>>> multiply.subtask((4, 4), countdown=10)
webapp.tasks.multiply(4, 4)
# shorthand for above, like delay in that it doesn't take
# apply_async's keyword args
>>> multiply.s(4, 4)
webapp.tasks.multiply(4, 4)
>>> multiply.s(4, 4)()
16
>>> multiply.s(4, 4).delay()
```

Calling a signature, or sometimes called a **subtask**, of a task creates a function that can be passed to the other functions to be executed. Executing the signature, like the third-to-last line in the example, executes the function in the current process and not in the worker.

Partials

The first application of task signatures is functional programming style partials. **Partials** are functions that originally take many arguments; however an operation is applied to the original function to return a new function, so the first n arguments are always the same. An example would be a `multiply` function that is not a task:

```
>>> new_multiply = multiply(2)
>>> new_multiply(5)
10
# The first function is unaffected
>>> multiply(2, 2)
4
```

This is a fictional API, but this is very close to the Celery version:

```
>>> partial = multiply.s(4)
>>> partial.delay(4)
```

The output in the worker window should show **16**. Basically, we created a new function that was saved to partial and that will always multiply its input by four.

Callbacks

Once a task is completed, it is very common to have another task run based on the output of the previous tasks. To achieve this, the `apply_async` function has a `link` method:

```
>>> multiply.apply_async((4, 4), link=log.s())
```

The worker output should show that both the `multiply` task and the `log` task returned **16**.

If you have a function that does not take input, or your callback does not need the result of the original method, the task signature must be marked as immutable with the `si` method:

```
>>> multiply.apply_async((4, 4), link=log.si("Message"))
```

Callbacks can be used to solve real-world problems. If we wanted to send a welcome e-mail every time a task created a new user, then we could produce that effect with the following call:

```
>>> create_user.apply_async(("John Doe", password), link=welcome.s())
```

Partials and callbacks can be combined to produce some powerful effects:

```
>>> multiply.apply_async((4, 4), link=multiply.s(4))
```

It's important to note that if this call was saved and the `get` method was called on it, the result would be **16** rather than **64**. This is because the `get` method does not return the results for callback methods. This will be solved with later methods.

Group

The `group` function takes a list of signatures and creates a callable function to execute all of the signatures in parallel and then return a list of all of the results:

```
>>> from celery import group
>>> sig = group(multiply.s(i, i+5) for i in range(10))
>>> result = sig.delay()
>>> result.get()
[0, 6, 14, 24, 36, 50, 66, 84, 104, 126]
```

Chain

The `chain` function takes task signatures and passes the value of each result to the next value in the chain, returning one result as follows:

```
>>> from celery import chain
>>> sig = chain(multiply.s(10, 10), multiply.s(4), multiply.s(20))
# same as above
>>> sig = (multiply.s(10, 10) | multiply.s(4) | multiply.s(20))
>>> result = sig.delay()
>>> result.get()
8000
```

Chains and partials can be taken a bit further. Chains can be used to create new functions when using partials, and chains can be nested as follows:

```
# combining partials in chains
>>> func = (multiply.s(10) | multiply.s(2))
>>> result = func.delay(16)
>>> result.get()
200
# chains can be nested
>>> func = (
    multiply.s(10) | multiply.s(2) | (multiply.s(4) | multiply.s(5))
)
>>> result = func.delay(16)
>>> result.get()
800
```

Chord

The `chord` function creates a signature that will execute a `group` of signatures and pass the final result to a callback:

```
>>> from celery import chord
>>> sig = chord(
    group(multiply.s(i, i+5) for i in range(10)),
    log.s()
)
```

```
>>> result = sig.delay()
>>> result.get()
[0, 6, 14, 24, 36, 50, 66, 84, 104, 126]
```

Just like the link argument, the callback is not returned with the `get` method.

Using the `chain` syntax with a group and a callback automatically creates a chord signature:

```
# same as above
>>> sig = (group(multiply.s(i, i+5) for i in range(10)) | log.s())
>>> result = sig.delay()
>>> result.get()
[0, 6, 14, 24, 36, 50, 66, 84, 104, 126]
```

Running tasks periodically

Celery also has the ability to call tasks periodically. For those familiar with ***nix** OSes, this system is a lot like the command-line utility `cron`, but it has the added benefit of being defined in our source code rather than on some system file. As such, it will be much easier to update when our code is ready for publishing to production in *Chapter 13, Deploying Flask Apps,*. In addition, all of the tasks are run within the application context, whereas a Python script called by `cron` would not be.

To add periodic tasks, add the following to the `DevConfig` configuration object:

```
import datetime
...

CELERYBEAT_SCHEDULE = {
    'log-every-30-seconds': {
        'task': 'webapp.tasks.log',
        'schedule': datetime.timedelta(seconds=30),
        'args': ("Message",)
    },
}
```

This `configuration` variable defines that the `log` task should be run every 30 seconds with the `args` tuple passed as the parameters. Any `timedelta` object can be used to define the interval to run the task on.

To run periodic tasks, another specialized worker named a `beat` worker is needed. In another terminal window, run the following:

```
$ celery -A celery_runner beat
```

If you now watch the terminal output in the main `Celery` worker, you should now see a log event every 30 seconds.

What if your task needs to run at much more specific intervals, for example, every Tuesday in June at 3 am and 5 pm? For very specific intervals, there is the Celery `crontab` object.

To illustrate how the `crontab` object represents intervals, here are some examples:

```
>>> from celery.schedules import crontab
# Every midnight
>>> crontab(minute=0, hour=0)
# Once a 5AM, then 10AM, then 3PM, then 8PM
>>> crontab(minute=0, hour=[5, 10, 15, 20])
# Every half hour
>>> crontab(minute='*/30')
# Every Monday at even numbered hours and 1AM
>>> crontab(day_of_week=1, hour ='*/2, 1')
```

The object has the following arguments:

- minute
- hour
- day_of_week
- day_of_month
- month_of_year

Each of these arguments can take various inputs. With plain integers, they operate much like the `timedelta` object, but they can also take strings and lists. When passed a list, the task will execute on every moment that is in the list. When passed a string in the form of */x, the task will execute every moment that the modulo operation returns zero. Also, the two forms can be combined to form a comma-separated string of integers and divisions.

Monitoring Celery

When our code is pushed to the server, our `Celery` worker will not be run in the terminal window, it will be run as a background task. Because of this, Celery provides many command-line arguments to monitor the status of your `Celery` worker and tasks. These commands take the following form:

```
$ celery -A celery_runner <command>
```

The main tasks to view the status of your workers are as follows:

- `status`: This prints the running workers and if they are up
- `result`: When passed a task id, this shows the return value and final status of the task
- `purge`: Using this, all messages in the broker will be deleted
- `inspect active`: This lists all active tasks
- `inspect scheduled`: This lists all tasks that have been scheduled with the `eta` argument
- `inspect registered`: This lists all of the tasks waiting to be processed
- `inspect stats`: This returns a dictionary full of statistics on the currently running workers and the broker

Web-based monitoring with Flower

Flower is a web-based, real-time management tool for Celery. In Flower, all active, queued, and completed tasks can be monitored. Flower also provides graphs and stats on how long each graph has been sitting in the queue versus how long its execution took and the arguments to each of those tasks.

To install Flower, use `pip` as follows:

```
$ pip install flower
```

To run it, just treat `flower` as a Celery command as follows:

```
$ celery flower -A celery_runner --loglevel=info
```

Now, open your browser to `http://localhost:5555`. It's best to familiarize yourself with the interface while tasks are running, so go to the command line and type the following:

```
>>> sig = chord(
    group(multiply.s(i, i+5) for i in xrange(10000)),
    log.s()
)
>>> sig.delay()
```

Your worker process will now start processing 10,000 tasks. Browse around the different pages while the tasks are running to see how Flower interacts with your worker while it is really churning.

Creating a reminder app

Let's get into some real-world examples in Celery. Suppose another page on our site now requires a reminder feature. Users can create reminders that will send an e-mail to a specified location at the time specified. We will need a model, a task, and a way to call our task automatically every time a model is created.

Let's start with the following basic SQLAlchemy model:

```
class Reminder(db.Model):
    id = db.Column(db.Integer(), primary_key=True)
    date = db.Column(db.DateTime())
    email = db.Column(db.String())
    text = db.Column(db.Text())

    def __repr__(self):
        return "<Reminder '{}'>".format(self.text[:20])
```

Now we need a task that will send an e-mail to the location in the model. In our `tasks.py` file, add the following task:

```
import smtplib
from email.mime.text import MIMEText

@celery.task(
    bind=True,
    ignore_result=True,
```

```
        default_retry_delay=300,
        max_retries=5
)
def remind(self, pk):
    reminder = Reminder.query.get(pk)
    msg = MIMEText(reminder.text)

    msg['Subject'] = "Your reminder"
    msg['From'] = your_email
    msg['To'] = reminder.email

    try:
        smtp_server = smtplib.SMTP('localhost')
        smtp_server.starttls()
        smtp_server.login(user, password)
        smtp_server.sendmail(
            your_email,
            [reminder.email],
            msg.as_string()
        )
        smtp_server.close()

        return
    except Exception, e:
        self.retry(exc=e)
```

Note that our task takes a primary key rather than a model. This is a hedge against a race condition, as a passed model could be stale by the time the worker finally gets around to processing it. You will also have to replace the placeholder e-mails and login with your own login info.

How do we have our task called when the user creates a reminder model? We will use a SQLAlchemy feature named `events`. SQLAlchemy allows us to register callbacks on our models that will be called when specific changes are made to our models. Our task will use the `after_insert` event, which is called after new data is entered into the database, whether the model is brand new or being updated.

We need a callback in `tasks.py`:

```
def on_reminder_save(mapper, connect, self):
    remind.apply_async(args=(self.id,), eta=self.date)
```

Now, in __init__.py, we will register our callback on our model:

```
from sqlalchemy import event
from .tasks import on_reminder_save

def create_app(object_name):
    app = Flask(__name__)
    app.config.from_object(object_name)

    db.init_app(app)
    event.listen(Reminder, 'after_insert', on_reminder_save)
    ...
```

Now, every time a model is saved, a task is registered that will send an e-mail to our user.

Creating a weekly digest

Say our blog has a lot of people who don't use RSS and prefer mailing lists, which is a large number of users. We need some way to create a list of new posts at the end of every week to increase our site's traffic. To solve this problem, we will create a digest task that will be called by a beat worker at 10 am every Saturday.

First, in tasks.py, let's create our task as follows:

```
@celery.task(
    bind=True,
    ignore_result=True,
    default_retry_delay=300,
    max_retries=5
)
def digest(self):
    # find the start and end of this week
    year, week = datetime.datetime.now().isocalendar()[0:2]
    date = datetime.date(year, 1, 1)
    if (date.weekday() > 3):
        date = date + datetime.timedelta(days=7 - date.weekday())
    else:
        date = date - datetime.timedelta(days=date.weekday())
    delta = datetime.timedelta(days=(week - 1) * 7)
```

```
start, end = date + delta, date + delta +
    datetime.timedelta(days=6)

posts = Post.query.filter(
    Post.publish_date >= start,
    Post.publish_date <= end
).all()

if (len(posts) == 0):
    return

msg = MIMEText(
    render_template("digest.html", posts=posts),
    'html'
)

msg['Subject'] = "Weekly Digest"
msg['From'] = your_email

try:
    smtp_server = smtplib.SMTP('localhost')
    smtp_server.starttls()
    smtp_server.login(user, password)
    smtp_server.sendmail(
        your_email,
        [recipients],
        msg.as_string()
    )
    smtp_server.close()

    return
except Exception, e:
    self.retry(exc=e)
```

We will also need to add a periodic schedule to our configuration object in `config.py` to manage our task:

```
CELERYBEAT_SCHEDULE = {
    'weekly-digest': {
        'task': 'tasks.digest',
        'schedule': crontab(day_of_week=6, hour='10')
    },
}
```

Finally, we need our e-mail template. Unfortunately, HTML in e-mail clients is terribly outdated. Every single e-mail client has different rendering bugs and quirks, and the only way to find them is to open your e-mail in all the clients. Many e-mail clients don't even support CSS, and those that do support a very small amount of selectors and attributes. In order to compensate, we have to use the web development methods of 10 years ago, that is, designing with tables with inline styles. Here is our `digest.html`:

```
"http://www.w3.org/TR/xhtml1/DTD/xhtml1-transitional.dtd">
<html xmlns="http://www.w3.org/1999/xhtml">
    <head>
        <meta http-equiv="Content-Type"
            content="text/html; charset=UTF-8" />
        <meta name="viewport"
            content="width=device-width, initial-scale=1.0"/>
        <title>Weekly Digest</title>
    </head>
    <body>
        <table align="center"
            border="0"
            cellpadding="0"
            cellspacing="0"
            width="500px">
        <tr>
            <td style="font-size: 32px;
                    font-family: Helvetica, sans-serif;
                    color: #444;
                    text-align: center;
                    line-height: 1.65">
                Weekly Digest
            </td>
        </tr>
        {% for post in posts %}
            <tr>
                <td style="font-size: 24px;
                        font-family: sans-serif;
                        color: #444;
                        text-align: center;
                        line-height: 1.65">
                    {{ post.title }}
                </td>
```

```
        </tr>
        <tr>
            <td style="font-size: 14px;
                        font-family: serif;
                        color: #444;
                        line-height:1.65">
                {{ post.text | truncate(500) | safe }}
            </td>
        </tr>
        <tr>
            <td style="font-size: 12px;
                        font-family: serif;
                        color: blue;
                        margin-bottom: 20px">
                <a href="{{ url_for('.post',
                   post_id=post.id) }}">Read More</a>
            </td>
        </tr>
        {% endfor %}
    </table>
</body>
</html>
```

Now, at the end of every week, our digest task will be called and it will send an
e-mail to all the users present in our mailing list.

Summary

Celery is a very powerful task queue that allows programmers to defer the
processing of slower tasks to another process. Now that you understand how to
move complex tasks out of the Flask process, we will take a look at a collection of
Flask extensions that simplify some common tasks seen in Flask apps.

10
Useful Flask Extensions

As we have seen throughout this book, Flask is designed to be as small as possible while still giving you the flexibility and tools needed to create web applications. However, there are a lot of features that are common to many web applications, which means that many applications will require writing code that does the same task for each web application. To solve this problem, people have created extensions to Flask to avoid reinventing the wheel, and we have seen many Flask extensions already throughout the book. This chapter will focus on some of the more useful Flask extensions that don't have enough content to separate them out into their own chapter, but will save you a lot of time and frustration.

Flask Script

In *Chapter 1*, *Getting Started*, we created a basic manage script with the Flask extension Flask Script to allow easy running of the server and debugging with the shell. In this chapter, we will cover the features that were not covered in that basic introduction.

In Flask Script, you can create custom commands to be run within the application context. All that is needed is to create a command to decorate a normal Python function with a decorator function provided by Flask Script. For example, if we wanted a task that would return the string "Hello, World!" we would add the following to `manage.py`:

```
@manager.command
def test():
    print "Hello, World!"
```

From the command line, the `test` command can now be run using the following:

```
$ python manage.py test
Hello, World!
```

Delete the test command, and let's create a simple command to help set up new developers on our application by creating their SQLite database and filling it with test data. This command is partially lifted from the script created in *Chapter 4, Creating Controllers with Blueprints*:

```python
@manager.command
def setup_db():
    db.create_all()

    admin_role = Role()
    admin_role.name = "admin"
    admin_role.description = "admin"
    db.session.add(admin_role)

    default_role = Role()
    default_role.name = "default"
    default_role.description = "default"
    db.session.add(default_role)

    admin = User()
    admin.username = "admin"
    admin.set_password("password")
    admin.roles.append(admin_role)
    admin.roles.append(default_role)
    db.session.add(admin)

    tag_one = Tag('Python')
    tag_two = Tag('Flask')
    tag_three = Tag('SQLAlechemy')
    tag_four = Tag('Jinja')
    tag_list = [tag_one, tag_two, tag_three, tag_four]

    s = "Body text"

    for i in xrange(100):
        new_post = Post("Post {}".format(i))
        new_post.user = admin
```

```
        new_post.publish_date = datetime.datetime.now()
        new_post.text = s
        new_post.tags = random.sample(
            tag_list,
            random.randint(1, 3)
        )
        db.session.add(new_post)

    db.session.commit()
```

Now if a new developer is assigned the project, they could download the `git repo` from our server, install the `pip` libraries, run the `setup_db` command, and would be able to run the project with everything they need.

Flask Script also provides two utility functions that can be easily added to our project.

```
from flask.ext.script.commands import ShowUrls, Clean
...
manager = Manager(app)
manager.add_command("server", Server())
manager.add_command("show-urls", ShowUrls())
manager.add_command("clean", Clean())
```

The `show-urls` command lists all of the routes registered on the `app` object and the URL tied to that route. This is very useful while debugging Flask extensions, as it becomes trivial to see whether the registration of its blueprints is working or not. The Clean command just removes the `.pyc` and `.pyo` compiled Python files from our working directory.

Flask Debug Toolbar

Flask Debug Toolbar is a Flask extension that aids development by adding debugging tools into the web view of your application. It gives you information such as the bottlenecks in your view rendering code, and how many SQLAlchemy queries it took to render the view.

As always, we will use `pip` to install Flask Debug Toolbar:

```
$ pip install flask-debugtoolbar
```

Next, we need to add Flask Debug Toolbar to the extensions.py file. As we will be modifying this file a lot in this chapter, here is the start of the file so far along with the code to initialize Flask Debug Toolbar:

```
from flask import flash, redirect, url_for, session
from flask.ext.bcrypt import Bcrypt
from flask.ext.openid import OpenID
from flask_oauth import OAuth
from flask.ext.login import LoginManager
from flask.ext.principal import Principal, Permission, RoleNeed
from flask.ext.restful import Api
from flask.ext.celery import Celery
from flask.ext.debugtoolbar import DebugToolbarExtension

bcrypt = Bcrypt()
oid = OpenID()
oauth = OAuth()
principals = Principal()
celery = Celery()
debug_toolbar = DebugToolbarExtension()
```

Now, the initialization function needs to be called in our create_app function in __init__.py:

```
from .extensions import (
    bcrypt,
    oid,
    login_manager,
    principals,
    rest_api,
    celery,
    debug_toolbar,
)

def create_app(object_name):

    debug_toolbar.init_app(app)
```

This is all that is needed to get Flask Debug Toolbar up and running. If the `DEBUG` variable in your app's `config` is set to *true*, the toolbar will appear. If `DEBUG` is not set to *true*, the toolbar will not be injected into the page.

On the right-hand side of the screen, you will see the toolbar. Each section is a link that will display a table of values on the page. To get a list of all the functions that were called in order to render the view, click the checkmark next to **Profiler** to enable it, reload the page, and click on **Profiler**. This view easily allows you to quickly diagnose which parts of your apps are the slowest or are called the most.

By default, Flask Debug Toolbar intercepts `HTTP 302 redirect` requests. To disable this, add the following to your configuration:

```
class DevConfig(Config):
    DEBUG = True
    DEBUG_TB_INTERCEPT_REDIRECTS = False
```

Also, if you are using Flask-MongoEngine, you can view all of the queries that were made to render the page by overriding which panels are rendered and adding MongoEngine's custom panel.

```
class DevConfig(Config):
    DEBUG = True
    DEBUG_TB_PANELS = [
        'flask_debugtoolbar.panels.versions.VersionDebugPanel',
        'flask_debugtoolbar.panels.timer.TimerDebugPanel',
        'flask_debugtoolbar.panels.headers.HeaderDebugPanel',
        'flask_debugtoolbar.panels.
        request_vars.RequestVarsDebugPanel',
        'flask_debugtoolbar.panels.config_vars.
        ConfigVarsDebugPanel ',
        'flask_debugtoolbar.panels.template.
        TemplateDebugPanel',
        'flask_debugtoolbar.panels.
        logger.LoggingPanel',
        'flask_debugtoolbar.panels.
        route_list.RouteListDebugPanel'
        'flask_debugtoolbar.panels.profiler.
        ProfilerDebugPanel',
        'flask.ext.mongoengine.panels.
        MongoDebugPanel'
    ]
    DEBUG_TB_INTERCEPT_REDIRECTS = False
```

This will add a panel to the toolbar that is very similar to the default SQLAlchemy one.

Flask Cache

In *Chapter 7, Using NoSQL with Flask*, we learned that page load time is one of the most important factors to determine the success of your web app. Despite the fact that our pages do not change very often and due to the fact that new posts will not be made very often, we still render the template and query the database every single time the page is asked for by our user's browsers.

Flask Cache solves this problem by allowing us to store the results of our view functions and return the stored results rather than render the template again. First, we need to install Flask Cache from `pip`:

```
$ pip install Flask-Cache
```

Next, initialize it in `extensions.py`:

```
from flask.ext.cache import Cache

cache = Cache()
```

Then, register the `Cache` object on the application, in the `create_app` function in `__init__.py`:

```
from .extensions import (
    bcrypt,
    oid,
    login_manager,
    principals,
    rest_api,
    celery,
    debug_toolbar,
    cache
)

def create_app(object_name):
    ...
    cache.init_app(app)
```

Before we can start caching our views, there is a need to tell Flash Cache how we want to store the results of our new functions.

```
class DevConfig(Config):
    ...
    CACHE_TYPE = 'simple'
```

The `simple` option tells Flask Cache to store the results in memory in a Python dictionary, which for the vast majority of Flask apps is adequate. We'll cover more types of Cache backends later in this section.

Caching views and functions

In order to cache the results of a view function, simply add a decorator to any function:

```
@blog_blueprint.route('/')
@blog_blueprint.route('/<int:page>')
@cache.cached(timeout=60)
def home(page=1):
```

```
posts = Post.query.order_by(
    Post.publish_date.desc()
).paginate(page, 10)
recent, top_tags = sidebar_data()

return render_template(
    'home.html',
    posts=posts,
    recent=recent,
    top_tags=top_tags
)
```

The `timeout` parameter specifies how many seconds the cached result should last before the function should be run again and stored again. To confirm that the view is actually being cached, check the SQLAlchemy section on the Debug Toolbar. Also, we can see that the impact caching has on page load times by activating the profiler and comparing the times before and after. On the author's top of the line laptop, the main blog page takes 34 ms to render, mainly due to the eight different queries that are made to the database. But after the cache is activated, this decreases to .08 ms. That's a 462.5 percent increase in speed!

View functions are not the only thing that can be cached. To cache any Python function, simply add a similar decorator to the function definition as follows:

```
@cache.cached(timeout=7200, key_prefix='sidebar_data')
def sidebar_data():
    recent = Post.query.order_by(
        Post.publish_date.desc()
    ).limit(5).all()

    top_tags = db.session.query(
        Tag, func.count(tags.c.post_id).label('total')
    ).join(
        tags
    ).group_by(
        Tag
    ).order_by('total DESC').limit(5).all()

    return recent, top_tags
```

The keyword argument `key_prefix` is necessary for non view functions in order for Flask Cache to properly store the results of the function. This needs to be unique for every function cached, or the results of the functions will override each other. Also, note that the timeout for this function is set to 2 hours rather than the 60 seconds in the previous examples. This is because the results for this function are less likely to change than the view functions, and if the data is stale, it is not as big an issue.

Caching functions with parameters

However, the normal cache decorator does not take function parameters into account. If we cached a function that took parameters with the normal cache decorator, it would return the same result for every parameter set. In order to fix this, we use the memoize function:

```
class User(db.Model):
    ...

    @staticmethod
    @cache.memoize(60)
    def verify_auth_token(token):
        s = Serializer(current_app.config['SECRET_KEY'])

        try:
            data = s.loads(token)
        except SignatureExpired:
            return None
        except BadSignature:
            return None

        user = User.query.get(data['id'])
        return user
```

Memoize stores the parameters passed to the function as well as the result. In the preceding example, memoize is being used to store the result of the verify_auth_token method, which is called many times and queries the database every single time. This method can safely be memoized because it returns the same result every time if the same token is passed to it. The only exception to this rule is if the user object gets deleted during the 60 seconds that the function is stored, but this is very unlikely.

Be careful not to memoize or cache functions that rely on either globally scoped variables or on constantly changing data. This can lead to some very subtle bugs, and in the worst case, data race. The best candidates for memoization are what are referred to as pure functions. Pure functions are functions that will produce the same result when the same parameters are passed to them. It does not matter how many times the function is run. Pure functions also do not have any side effects, which means that they do not change globally scoped variables. This also means that pure functions cannot do any IO operations. While the verify_auth_token function is not pure because it does database IO, it is ok because as was stated before it is very unlikely that the underlying data will change.

While we are developing the application, we do not want the view functions to be cached because results will be changing all the time. To fix this, set the CACHE_ TYPE variable to null and set the CACHE_TYPE variable to simple in the production configuration, so when the app is deployed everything works as expected:

```
class ProdConfig(Config):
    ...
    CACHE_TYPE = 'simple'

class DevConfig(Config):
    ...
    CACHE_TYPE = 'null'
```

Caching routes with query strings

Some routes, such as our home and post routes, take the parameters through the URL and return content specific to those parameters. We run into a problem if routes like these are cached, as the first rendering of the route will be returned for all requests regardless of the URL parameters. The solution is rather simple. The key_ prefix keyword argument in the cache method can be either a string or a function, which will be executed to dynamically generate a key. This means that a function can be created to generate a key that is tied to the URL parameters, so each request only returns a cached page if that specific combination of parameters has been called before. In the blog.py file, add the following:

```
def make_cache_key(*args, **kwargs):
    path = request.path
    args = str(hash(frozenset(request.args.items())))
    lang = get_locale()
    return (path + args + lang).encode('utf-8')


@blog_blueprint.route(
    '/post/<int:post_id>',
    methods=('GET', 'POST')
)
@cache.cached(timeout=600, key_prefix=make_cache_key)
def post(post_id):
    ...
```

Now, each individual post page will be cached for 10 minutes.

Using Redis as a cache backend

If the amount of view functions or the number of unique parameters passed to your cached functions becomes too large for memory, you can use a different backend for the cache. As was mentioned in *Chapter 7*, *Using NoSQL with Flask*, Redis can be used as a backend for the cache. To implement that functionality, all that needs to be done is to add the following configuration variables to the `ProdConfig` class as follows:

```
class ProdConfig(Config):
    ...
    CACHE_TYPE = 'redis'
    CACHE_REDIS_HOST = 'localhost'
    CACHE_REDIS_PORT = '6379'
    CACHE_REDIS_PASSWORD = 'password'
    CACHE_REDIS_DB = '0'
```

If you replace the values of the variables with your own data, Flask Cache will automatically create a connection to your `redis` database and use it to store the results of the functions. All that is needed is to install the Python `redis` library:

```
$ pip install redis
```

Using memcached as a cache backend

Just like the `redis` backend, the `memcached` backend provides an alternative way of storing results if the memory option is too limiting. In contrast to `redis`, `memcached` is designed to `cache` objects for later use and reduce load on the database. Both `redis` and `memcached` can serve the same purpose, and choosing one over the other comes down to personal preference. To use `memcached`, we need to install its Python library:

```
$ pip install memcache
```

Connecting to your `memcached` server is handled in the configuration object, just like the `redis` setup:

```
class ProdConfig(Config):
    ...
    CACHE_TYPE = 'memcached'
    CACHE_KEY_PREFIX = 'flask_cache'
    CACHE_MEMCACHED_SERVERS = ['localhost:11211']
```

Flask Assets

Another bottleneck in web applications are the amount of HTTP requests required to download the CSS and JavaScript libraries for the page. The extra files can only be downloaded after HTML for the page has been loaded and parsed. To combat this, many modern browsers download many of these libraries at once, but there is a limit to how many simultaneous requests the browser makes.

Several things can be done on the server to reduce the amount of time spent downloading these files. The main technique that developers use is to concatenate all of the JavaScript libraries into one file and all of the CSS libraries into another while removing all of the whitespace and carriage returns from the resulting files. This reduces the overhead of multiple HTTP requests, and removing the unnecessary whitespace and carriage returns can reduce a file's size by up to 30 percent. Another technique is to tell the browser to cache the files locally with specialized HTTP headers, so the file is only loaded again once it changes. These can be tedious to do manually because they need to be done after every deployment to the server.

Thankfully, Flask Assets implements all the above techniques. Flask Assets works by giving it a list of files and a way to concatenate them, and then adding a special control block into your templates in place of the normal link and script tags. Flask Assets will then add in a link or a script tag that links to the newly generated file. To get started, Flask Assets needs to be installed. We also need to install `cssmin` and `jsmin`, which are Python libraries that handle the modification of the files:

```
$ pip install Flask-Assets cssmin jsmin
```

Now, the collections of files to be concatenated, named bundles, need to be created. In `extensions.py`, add the following:

```python
from flask_assets import Environment, Bundle

assets_env = Environment()

main_css = Bundle(
    'css/bootstrap.css',
    filters='cssmin',
    output='css/common.css'
)

main_js = Bundle(
    'js/jquery.js',
    'js/bootstrap.js',
    filters='jsmin',
    output='js/common.js'
)
```

Each `Bundle` object takes an infinite number of files as positional arguments to define the files to be bundled, a keyword argument `filters` to define the filters to send the files through, and an `output` that defines the filename in the `static` folder to save the result to.

 The `filters` keyword can be a single value or a list. To get the full list of available filters, including automatic Less and CSS compliers, see the docs at `http://webassets.readthedocs.org/en/latest/`.

While it's true that because our site is light on styles the CSS bundle has only one file in it. It's still a good idea to put the file in a bundle for two reasons.

While we are in development, we can use the un-minified versions of the libraries, which makes debugging easier. When the app is deployed to production, the libraries are automatically minified.

These libraries will be sent to the browser with the cache headers, when linking them in HTML normally would not.

Before Flask Assets can be tested, three more changes need to be made. First, in the `__init__.py` format, the extension and bundles need to be registered:

```
from .extensions import (
    bcrypt,
    oid,
    login_manager,
    principals,
    rest_api,
    celery,
    debug_toolbar,
    cache,
    assets_env,
    main_js,
    main_css
)

def create_app(object_name):
    ...
    assets_env.init_app(app)

    assets_env.register("main_js", main_js)
    assets_env.register("main_css", main_css)
```

Next, the `DevConfig` class needs an extra variable to tell Flask Assets to not compile the libraries while in development:

```
class DevConfig(Config):
    DEBUG = True
    DEBUG_TB_INTERCEPT_REDIRECTS = False

    ASSETS_DEBUG = True
```

Finally, the link and script tags in both of the `base.html` files need to be replaced with the control block from Flask Assets. We have the following:

```
<link rel="stylesheet"
href=https://maxcdn.bootstrapcdn.com/bootstrap/3.3.2/css/bootst
rap.min.css>
```

Replace this with the following:

```
{% assets "main_css" %}
<link rel="stylesheet" type="text/css" href="{{ ASSET_URL }}"
/>
{% endassets %}
```

We also have the following:

```
<script
src="https://ajax.googleapis.com/ajax/libs/jquery/1.11.2/jquery
.min.js"></script>
<script
src="https://maxcdn.bootstrapcdn.com/bootstrap/3.3.2/js/bootstr
ap.min.js"></script>
```

Replace this with the following:

```
{% assets "main_js" %}
<script src="{{ ASSET_URL }}"></script>
{% endassets %}
```

Now, if you reload the page, all of the CSS and JavaScript will now be handled by Flask Assets.

Flask Admin

In *Chapter 6, Securing Your App,* we created an interface to allow users to create and edit blog posts without having to use the command line. This was adequate to demonstrate the security measures presented in the chapter, but there is still no way for posts to be deleted or tags assigned to them using the interface. We also do not have a way to delete or edit comments that we would rather not have common users see. What our app needs is a fully featured administrator interface in the same vein as the WordPress interface. This is such a common requirement for apps that a Flask extension name Flask Admin was created to easily create administrator interfaces. To get started, install Flask Admin with `pip`:

$ pip install Flask-Admin

As usual, we need to create the `extension` object in `extensions.py`:

```
from flask.ext.admin import Admin

admin = Admin()
```

Then, the object needs to be registered on the `app` object in `__init__.py`:

```
from .extensions import (
    bcrypt,
    oid,
    login_manager,
    principals,
    rest_api,
    celery,
    debug_toolbar,
    cache,
    assets_env,
    main_js,
    main_css,
    admin
)

def create_app(object_name):
    ...
    admin.init_app(app)
```

If you navigate to `localhost:5000/admin`, you should now see the empty Flask Admin interface:

Flask Admin works by registering view classes on the `admin` object that define one or more routes. Flask Admin has three main types of views: the `ModelView`, `FileAdmin`, and `BaseView` views.

Creating basic admin pages

The `BaseView` class allows normal Flask pages to be added to your `admin` interface. This is normally the least used type of view in Flask Admin setups, but if you wish to include something like custom reporting with JavaScript charting libraries, you would do it with just a base view. In a new file in the controllers folder named `admin.py`, add the following:

```
from flask.ext.admin import BaseView, expose

class CustomView(BaseView):
    @expose('/')
    def index(self):
        return self.render('admin/custom.html')

    @expose('/second_page')
    def second_page(self):
        return self.render('admin/second_page.html')
```

In a subclass of `BaseView`, multiple views can be registered at once if they are defined together. Keep in mind, however, that each subclass of `BaseView` requires at least one exposed method on the path /. Also, methods other than the method within the path / will not be in the navigation of the administrator interface, and will have to be linked to the other pages in the class. The `expose` and `self.render` functions work exactly the same as their counterparts in the normal Flask API.

To have your templates inherit the default styles of Flask Admin, create a new folder in the templates directory named `admin` with a file named `custom.html` and add the following Jinja code:

```
{% extends 'admin/master.html' %}
{% block body %}
    This is the custom view!
    <a href="{{ url_for('.second_page') }}">Link</a>
{% endblock %}
```

To view this template, an instance of `CustomView` needs to be registered on the `admin` object. This will be done in the `create_app` function rather than in the `extensions.py` file because some of our admin pages will need the database object, which would lead to circular imports if the registrations were in `extensions.py`. In `__init__.py`, add the following code to register the class:

```
from webapp.controllers.admin import CustomView

...

def create_app(object_name):

    ...

    admin.add_view(CustomView(name='Custom'))
```

The `name` keyword argument specifies that the label used in the navigation bar on the top of the `admin` interface should read `Custom`. After you have registered `CustomView` to the `admin` object, your `admin` interface should now have a second link in the navigation bar as follows.

Creating database admin pages

The main power of Flask Admin comes from the fact that you can automatically create administrator pages for your data by giving Flask Admin your SQLAlchemy or MongoEngine models. Creating these pages is very easy; in `admin.py`, just add the following code:

```
from flask.ext.admin.contrib.sqla import ModelView
# or, if you use MongoEngine
from flask.ext.admin.contrib.mongoengine import ModelView

class CustomModelView(ModelView):
    pass
```

Then, in `__init__.py`, register the class with the model you wish to use and the database `session` object as follows:

```
from controllers.admin import CustomView, CustomModelView
from .models import db, Reminder, User, Role, Post, Comment, Tag

def create_app(object_name):

    admin.add_view(CustomView(name='Custom'))
    models = [User, Role, Post, Comment, Tag, Reminder]

    for model in models:
        admin.add_view(
            CustomModelView(model, db.session,
            category='models')
        )
```

The `category` keyword tells Flask Admin to put all of the views with the same category value into the same dropdown on the navigation bar.

If you go to the browser now, you will see a new drop-down menu labeled **Models** with links to the admin pages of all of the tables in the database as follows:

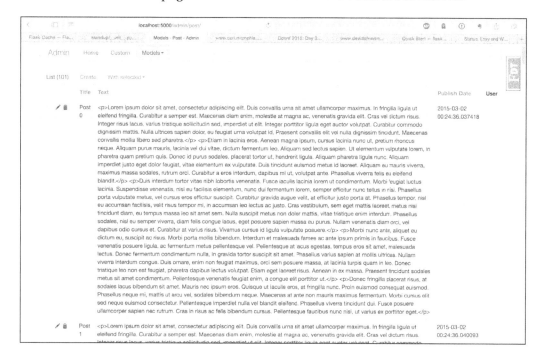

The generated interface for each model provides a lot of functionality. New posts can be created, and the existing posts can be deleted in bulk. All of the fields can be set from this interface, including the relationship fields, which are implemented as searchable drop-down menus. The date and datetime fields even have custom JavaScript inputs with calendar dropdowns. Overall, this is a huge improvement to the hand-created interface that was created in *Chapter 6, Securing Your App*.

Enhancing the post's administration

While this interface is a huge step-up in quality, there are some features missing. We no longer have the WYSIWYG editor that was available in the original interface, and this page can be improved by enabling some of the more powerful Flask Admin features.

To add the WYSIWYG editor back into the `post` creation page, we will need a new `WTForms` field, as Flask Admin constructs its forms with Flask WTF. We will also need to override the `textarea` field in the `post` edit and creation page with this new field type. The first thing that needs to be done is to create the new field type in `forms.py` by using the `textarea` field as a base:

```
from wtforms import (
    widgets,
    StringField,
    TextAreaField,
    PasswordField,
    BooleanField
)

class CKTextAreaWidget(widgets.TextArea):
    def __call__(self, field, **kwargs):
        kwargs.setdefault('class_', 'ckeditor')
        return super(CKTextAreaWidget, self).__call__(field,
        **kwargs)

class CKTextAreaField(TextAreaField):
    widget = CKTextAreaWidget()
```

In this code, we created a new field type `CKTextAreaField` that adds a widget to the `textarea`, and all that the widget does is adds a class to the HTML tag. Now, to add this field to the `Post` admin page, the `Post` will need its own `ModelView`:

```
from webapp.forms import CKTextAreaField

class PostView(CustomModelView):
    form_overrides = dict(text=CKTextAreaField)
    column_searchable_list = ('text', 'title')
    column_filters = ('publish_date',)

    create_template = 'admin/post_edit.html'
    edit_template = 'admin/post_edit.html'
```

There are several new things in this code. First, the `form_overrides` class variable tells Flask Admin to override the field type of the name text with this new field type. The `column_searchable_list` function defines which columns are searchable via text. Adding this will allow Flask Admin to include a search field on the overview page that searches the values of the defined fields. Next, the `column_filters` class variable tells Flask Admin to create a `filters` interface on the overview page of this model. The `filters` interface allows columns that are not text to be filtered down by adding conditions to the shown rows. An example with the preceding code is to create a filter that shows all rows with `publish_date` values greater than January 1, 2015. Finally, the `create_template` and `edit_template` class variables allow you to define custom templates for Flask Admin to use. For the custom template that we will be using, we need to create a new file `post_edit.html` in the admin folder. In this template, we will include the same JavaScript library that was used in *Chapter 6, Securing Your App*:

```
{% extends 'admin/model/edit.html' %}
{% block tail %}
    {{ super() }}
    <script
        src="//cdn.ckeditor.com/4.4.7/standard/ckeditor.js">
    </script>
{% endblock %}
```

The tail block of the inherited template is located at the end of the file. Once the template is created, your `post` edit and creation page should look like this:

Creating file system admin pages

Another common function that most `admin` interfaces cover is being able to access the server's file system from the web. Thankfully, Flask Admin includes this feature with the `FileAdmin` class

```
class CustomFileAdmin(FileAdmin):
    pass
```

Now, just import the new class into your `__init__.py` file and pass in the path that you wish to be accessible from the web:

```
import os
from controllers.admin import (
    CustomView,
    CustomModelView,
    PostView,
    CustomFileAdmin
)


def create_app(object_name):

    admin.add_view(
        CustomFileAdmin(
            os.path.join(os.path.dirname(__file__), 'static'),
            '/static/',
            name='Static Files'
        )
    )
```

Securing Flask Admin

Currently, the entire `admin` interface is accessible to the world; let's fix that. The routes in the `CustomView` can be secured just like any other route:

```
class CustomView(BaseView):
    @expose('/')
    @login_required
    @admin_permission.require(http_exception=403)
    def index(self):
        return self.render('admin/custom.html')

    @expose('/second_page')
    @login_required
```

```
    @admin_permission.require(http_exception=403)
    def second_page(self):
        return self.render('admin/second_page.html')
```

To secure the `ModeView` and `FileAdmin` subclasses, they need to have a method named `is_accessible` defined, which either returns *true* or *false*.

```
class CustomModelView(ModelView):
    def is_accessible(self):
        return current_user.is_authenticated() and\
                admin_permission.can()

class CustomFileAdmin(FileAdmin):
    def is_accessible(self):
        return current_user.is_authenticated() and\
                admin_permission.can()
```

Because we set up our authentication correctly in *Chapter 6, Securing Your App*, this task was trivial.

Flask Mail

The final Flask extension that this chapter will cover is Flask Mail, which allows you to connect and configure your SMTP client from Flask's configuration. Flask Mail will also help to simplify application testing in *Chapter 12, Testing Flask Apps*. The first step is to install Flask Mail with `pip`:

$ pip install Flask-Mail

Next, the `Mail` object needs to be initialized in the `extentions.py` file:

```
from flask_mail import Mail

mail = Mail()
```

`flask_mail` will connect to our SMTP server of choice by reading the configuration variables in our `app` object, so we need to add those values to our `config` object:

```
class DevConfig(Config):

    MAIL_SERVER = 'localhost'
    MAIL_PORT = 25
    MAIL_USERNAME = 'username'
    MAIL_PASSWORD = 'password'
```

Finally, the `mail` object is initialized on the `app` object in `__init__.py`:

```
from .extensions import (
    bcrypt,
    oid,
    login_manager,
    principals,
    rest_api,
    celery,
    debug_toolbar,
    cache,
    assets_env,
    main_js,
    main_css,
    admin,
    mail
)


def create_app(object_name):

    mail.init_app(app)
```

To see how Flask Mail can simplify our e-mailing code, this is the remind task created in *Chapter 9, Creating Asynchronous Tasks with Celery*, but using Flask Mail instead of the standard library SMTP module:

```
from flask_mail import Message
from webapp.extensions import celery, mail

@celery.task(
    bind=True,
    ignore_result=True,
    default_retry_delay=300,
    max_retries=5
)
def remind(self, pk):
    reminder = Reminder.query.get(pk)
    msg = MIMEText(reminder.text)
    msg = Message("Your reminder",
                  sender="from@example.com",
                  recipients=[reminder.email])

    msg.body = reminder.text
    mail.send(msg)
```

Summary

This chapter has created a large increase in the functionality of our app. We now have a fully featured administrator interface, a useful debugging tool in the browser, two tools that greatly speed up page load times, and a utility to make sending e-mails less of a headache.

As was stated at the start of this chapter, Flask is bare-bones and allows you to pick and choose the functionality that you want. Therefore, it is important to keep in mind that it is not necessary to include all of these extensions in you app. If you are the only content creator of your app, maybe the command-line interface is all you need because adding in these features takes development time and maintenance time when they inevitably break. This warning is given at the end of the chapter because one of the main reasons many Flask apps become unwieldy is because they include so many extensions that testing and maintaining all of them becomes a very large task.

In the next chapter, you will learn the internals of how an extension works and how to create your own extension.

11
Building Your Own Extension

From the first chapter of this book, we have been adding Flask extensions to our app in order to add new features and save us from spending lots of time to reinvent the wheel. Up to this point, it was unknown how these Flask extensions worked. In this chapter, we will create two simple Flask extensions in order to better understand Flask's internals and allow you to extend Flask with your own functionality.

Creating a YouTube Flask extension

To begin, the first extension we are going to create is a simple extension that allows embedding YouTube videos in Jinja templates with the following tag:

```
{{ youtube(video_id) }}
```

The video_id object is the code after the v in any YouTube URL. For example, in the URL https://www.youtube.com/watch?v=_OBlgSz8sSM, the video_id object would be _OBlgSz8sSM.

For now, the code for this extension will reside in extensions.py. However, this is only for development and debugging purposes. When the code is ready to be shared, it will be moved into its own project directory.

The first thing that any Flask extension needs is the object that will be initialized on the app. This object will handle adding its Blueprint object to the app and registering the youtube function on Jinja:

```
from flask import Blueprint

class Youtube(object):
    def __init__(self, app=None, **kwargs):
        if app:
            self.init_app(app)
```

```
def init_app(self, app):
    self.register_blueprint(app)

def register_blueprint(self, app):
    module = Blueprint(
        "youtube",
        __name__,
        template_folder="templates"
    )
    app.register_blueprint(module)
    return module
```

So far, the only thing this code does is initialize an empty blueprint on the `app` object. The next piece of code needed is a representation of a video. The following will be a class that will handle the parameters from the Jinja function and render HTML to display in the template:

```
from flask import (
    flash,
    redirect,
    url_for,
    session,
    render_template,
    Blueprint,
    Markup
)

class Video(object):
    def __init__(self, video_id, cls="youtube"):
        self.video_id = video_id
        self.cls = cls

    def render(self, *args, **kwargs):
        return render_template(*args, **kwargs)

    @property
    def html(self):
        return Markup(
            self.render('youtube/video.html', video=self)
        )
```

This object will be created from the `youtube` function in the template, and any arguments passed in the template will be given to this object to render HTML. There is also a new object in this code, `Markup`, which we never used before. The `Markup` class is Flask's way of automatically escaping HTML or marking it as safe to include in the template. If we just returned HTML, Jinja would autoescape it because it does not know whether it is safe or not. This is Flask's way of protecting your site from **cross-site scripting attacks**.

The next step is to create the function that will be registered in Jinja:

```
def youtube(*args, **kwargs):
    video = Video(*args, **kwargs)
    return video.html
```

In the YouTube class, we have to register the function to Jinja in the init_app method:

```
class Youtube(object):
    def __init__(self, app=None, **kwargs):
        if app:
            self.init_app(app)

    def init_app(self, app):
        self.register_blueprint(app)
        app.add_template_global(youtube)
```

Finally, we have to create HTML that will add the video to the page. In a new folder named youtube in the templates directory, create a new HTML file named video.html and add the following code to it:

```
<iframe
    class="{{ video.cls }}"
    width="560"
    height="315"
    src="https://www.youtube.com/embed/{{ video.video_id }}"
    frameborder="0"
    allowfullscreen>
</iframe>
```

This is all the code that's needed to embed YouTube videos in your templates. Let's test this out now. In extensions.py, initialize the Youtube class below the Youtube class definition:

```
youtube_ext = Youtube()
```

In __init__.py, import the youtube_ext variable and use the init_app method we created to register it on the app:

```
from .extensions import (
    bcrypt,
    oid,
    login_manager,
    principals,
    rest_api,
```

```
        celery,
        debug_toolbar,
        cache,
        assets_env,
        main_js,
        main_css,
        admin,
        mail,
        youtube_ext
    )

    def create_app(object_name):
        ...
        youtube_ext.init_app(app)
```

Now, as a simple example, add the `youtube` function to the top of the blog home page:

```
{{ youtube("_OB1gSz8sSM") }}
```

This will have the following result:

Creating a Python package

In order to make our new Flask extension available to others, we have to create an installable Python package from the code we have written so far. To begin, we need a new project directory outside our current application directory. We will need two things: a setup.py file, which we will fill in later, and a folder named flask_youtube. In the flask_youtube directory, we will have an __init__.py file, which will contain all the code that we wrote for our extension.

Here is the final version of that code contained in the __init__.py file:

```python
from flask import render_template, Blueprint, Markup

class Video(object):
    def __init__(self, video_id, cls="youtube"):
        self.video_id = video_id
        self.cls = cls

    def render(self, *args, **kwargs):
        return render_template(*args, **kwargs)

    @property
    def html(self):
        return Markup(
            self.render('youtube/video.html', video=self)
        )

def youtube(*args, **kwargs):
    video = Video(*args, **kwargs)
    return video.html

class Youtube(object):
    def __init__(self, app=None, **kwargs):
        if app:
            self.init_app(app)

    def init_app(self, app):
        self.register_blueprint(app)
        app.add_template_global(youtube)

    def register_blueprint(self, app):
        module = Blueprint(
            "youtube",
            __name__,
            template_folder="templates"
        )
        app.register_blueprint(module)
        return module
```

Also inside the `flask_youtube` directory, we will need a `templates` directory, which will hold the `youtube` directory that we put in our app's `templates` directory.

In order to turn this code into a Python package, we will use the library named `setuptools`. `setuptools` is a Python package that allows developers to easily create installable packages for their code. `setuptools` will bundle code so that `pip` and `easy_install` can automatically install them, and will even upload your package to the **Python Package Index (PyPI)**.

 All the packages that we have been installing from `pip` have come from PyPI. To see all the available packages, go to `https://pypi.python.org/pypi`.

All that is needed to get this functionality is to fill out the `setup.py` file:

```
from setuptools import setup, find_packages
setup(
    name='Flask-YouTube',
    version='0.1',
    license='MIT',
    description='Flask extension to allow easy embedding of YouTube
videos',
    author='Jack Stouffer',
    author_email='example@gmail.com',
    platforms='any',
    install_requires=['Flask'],
    packages=find_packages()
)
```

This code uses the `setup` function from `setuptools` to find your source code and make sure that the machine that is installing your code has the required packages. Most of the attributes are rather self-explanatory, except the package attribute, which uses the `find_packages` function from `setuptools`. What the `package` attribute does is it finds which parts of our source code are part of the package to be released. We use the `find_packages` method to automatically find which parts of the code to include. This is based on some sane defaults, such as looking for directories with `__init__.py` files and excluding common file extensions.

Although it is not mandatory, this setup also contains metadata about the author and the license, which would be included on the PyPI page if we were to upload this there. There is a lot more customization available in the `setup` function, so I encourage you to read the documentation at `http://pythonhosted.org/setuptools/`.

You can now install this package on your machine by running the following commands:

```
$ python setup.py build
$ python setup.py install
```

This will install your code into your Python `packages` directory, or if you're using `virtualenv`, it will install it to the local `packages` directory. Then, you can import your place on package via:

```
from flask_youtube import Youtube
```

Modifying the response with Flask extensions

So, we have created an extension that adds new functionality to our templates. But how would we create an extension which modifies the behavior of our app at the request level? To demonstrate this, let's create an extension that modifies all the responses from Flask by compressing the contents of the response. This is a common practice in web development in order to speed up page load times, as compressing objects with a method like **gzip** is very fast and relatively cheap CPU-wise. Normally, this would be handled at the server level. So, unless you wish to host your app with only Python code, which is possible and will be covered in *Chapter 13, Deploying Flask Apps*, this extension really doesn't have much use in the real world.

To achieve this, we will use the `gzip` module in the Python standard library to compress the contents after each request is processed. We will also have to add special HTTP headers into the response in order for the browser to know that the content is compressed. We will also need to check in the HTTP request headers whether the browser can accept gzipped contents.

Just as before, our content will initially reside in the `extensions.py` file:

```
from flask import request
from gzip import GzipFile
from io import BytesIO
...

class GZip(object):
    def __init__(self, app=None):
        self.app = app
        if app is not None:
            self.init_app(app)
```

```
        def init_app(self, app):
            app.after_request(self.after_request)

        def after_request(self, response):
            encoding = request.headers.get('Accept-Encoding', '')

            if 'gzip' not in encoding or \
               not response.status_code in (200, 201):
                return response

            response.direct_passthrough = False

            contents = BytesIO()
            with GzipFile(
                mode='wb',
                compresslevel=5,
                fileobj=contents) as gzip_file:
                gzip_file.write(response.get_data())

            response.set_data(bytes(contents.getvalue()))

            response.headers['Content-Encoding'] = 'gzip'
            response.headers['Content-Length'] = response.content_length

            return response

    flask_gzip = GZip()
```

Just as with the previous extension, our initializer for the compress object accommodates both the normal Flask setup and the application factory setup. In the `after_request` method, instead of registering a blueprint, we register a new function on the after-request event so that our extension can compress the results.

The `after_request` method is where the real logic of the extension comes into play. First, it checks whether the browser accepts gzip encoding by looking at the `Accept-Encoding` value in the request header. If the browser does not accept gzip, or did not return a successful response, the function just returns the contents and makes no modifications to it. However, if the browser does accept our content and the response was successful, then we will compress the content. We use another standard library class named `BytesIO`, which allows file streams to be written and stored in memory, and not in an intermediate file. This is necessary because the `GzipFile` object expects to write to a file object.

After the data is compressed, we set the response objects' data to the results of the compression and set the necessary HTTP header values in the response as well. Finally, the gzip contents are returned to the browser, and the browser then decompresses the contents, significantly speeding up the page load times.

In order to test the functionality in your browser, you have to disable **Flask Debug Toolbar**, because at the time of writing there is a bug in its code where it expects all responses to be encoded in UTF-8.

If you reload the page nothing should look different. However, if you use the developer tools in the browser of your choice and inspect the responses, you will see that they are compressed.

Summary

Now that we went through two different examples of different types of Flask extensions, you should have a very clear understanding of how most of the Flask extensions that we used work. Using the knowledge that you have now, you should be able to add any extra functionality to Flask that you need for your specific application.

In the next chapter, we are going to look at how to add testing to our application to take out the guesswork of whether changes we made to the code have broken any of the functionality of our application.

12
Testing Flask Apps

Throughout this book, every time that we have made a modification to our application's code, we have had to manually load the affected web pages into our browser to test if the code was working correctly. As the application grows, this process becomes more and more tedious, especially if you change something that is of low level and used everywhere, such as SQLAlchemy model code.

In order to automate the process of verifying that our code works the way we want it to, we will use a built-in feature of Python that allows us to write tests, normally named unit tests, which are checked against our application's code.

What are unit tests?

Testing a program is very simple. All it involves is running particular pieces of your program and saying what you expect the results to be and comparing it to what the results from the piece of the program actually are. If the results are the same, the test passes. If the results are different, the test fails. Typically, these tests are run before code is committed to the Git repository and before code is deployed to the live server in order to make sure that broken code doesn't make it into either of those systems.

In program testing, there are three main types of tests. Unit tests are tests that verify the correctness of individual pieces of code, such as functions. Second is integration testing, which tests the correctness of various units of programs working in tandem. The last type of testing is system testing, which tests the correctness of the whole system at once rather than in individual pieces.

In this chapter, we will be using unit testing and system testing in order to verify that our code is working as planned. We will not do integration testing in this chapter because the way in which various parts of the code work in tandem are not handled by the code we have written. For example, the way SQLAlchemy worked with Flask is not handled by our code. Flask SQLAlchemy handles it.

This brings us to one of the first rules of code testing. Write tests for code that you own. The first reason for this is it's very likely that a test for this could have already been written. The second reason is that any bugs in the libraries that you use will surface in your tests when you want to use that library's functionality.

How does testing work?

Let's start with a very simple Python function for us to test.

```
def square(x):
    return x * x
```

In order to verify the correctness of this code, we pass a value and we will test if the result of the function is what we expect. For example, we would give it an input of five and would expect the result to be 25.

To illustrate the concept, we can manually test this function in the command line using the `assert` statement. The `assert` statement in Python simply says that if the conditional statement after the `assert` keyword returns `False`, throw an exception as follows:

```
$ python
>>> def square(x):
...     return x * x
>>> assert square(5) == 25
>>> assert square(7) == 49
>>> assert square(10) == 100
>>> assert square(10) == 0
Traceback (most recent call last):
  File "<stdin>", line 1, in <module>
AssertionError
```

Using these `assert` statements, we verified that the square function was working as intended.

Unit testing the application

Unit testing in Python works by combining `assert` statements into their own functions inside a class. This collection of testing functions inside the class is called a test case. Each function inside the test case should test only one thing, which is the main idea behind unit testing. Testing only one thing in your unit tests forces you to verify each piece of code individually and not gloss over any of the functionality of your code. If you write your unit tests correctly, you will end up with lots and lots of them. While this may seem overly verbose, it will save you from headaches down the road.

Before we can build our test cases, we need another configuration object specifically to set up the app for testing. In this configuration, we will use the Python `tempfile` module in the standard library in order to create a test SQLite database in a file that will automatically delete itself when the tests are over. This allows us to guarantee that the tests will not interfere with our actual database. Also, the configuration disables WTForms CSRF checks to allow us to submit forms from the tests without the CSRF token.

```
import tempfile

class TestConfig(Config):
    db_file = tempfile.NamedTemporaryFile()

    DEBUG = True
    DEBUG_TB_ENABLED = False

    SQLALCHEMY_DATABASE_URI = 'sqlite:///' + db_file.name

    CACHE_TYPE = 'null'
    WTF_CSRF_ENABLED = False

    CELERY_BROKER_URL = "amqp://guest:guest@localhost:5672//"
    CELERY_BACKEND_URL = "amqp://guest:guest@localhost:5672//"

    MAIL_SERVER = 'localhost'
    MAIL_PORT = 25
    MAIL_USERNAME = 'username'
    MAIL_PASSWORD = 'password'
```

Testing the route functions

Let's build our first test case. In this test case, we will be testing if the route functions successfully return a response if we access their URL. In a new directory at the root of the project directory named `tests`, create a new file named `test_urls.py`, which will hold all of the unit tests for the routes. Each test case should have its own file, and each test case should focus on one area of the code you are testing.

In `test_urls.py`, let's start creating what the built-in Python `unittest` library needs. The code will use the `unittest` library from Python in order to run all the tests that we create in the test case.

```
import unittest

class TestURLs(unittest.TestCase):
    pass

if __name__ == '__main__':
    unittest.main()
```

Let's see what happens when this code is run. We will use the `unittest` library's ability to automatically find our test cases to run the tests. The pattern the `unittest` library looks for is `test*.py`:

```
$ python -m unittest discover


----------------------------------------------------------------

Ran 0 tests in 0.000s


OK
```

Because there are no tests in the test case, the test case passed successfully.

> The test script was run from the parent directory of the script and not in the test folder itself. This is to allow imports of the application code inside the test scripts.

In order to test the URLs, we need to have a way to query the application's routes without actually running a server, so our requests are returned. Flask provides a way of accessing routes in tests named the test client. The test client gives methods to create HTTP requests on our routes without having to actually run the application with `app.run()`.

We will need the test client object for each of the tests in this test case, but adding in code in each `unittest` to create the test client doesn't make much sense when we have the `setUp` method. The `setUp` method is run before each unit test and can attach variables to self in order for the test method to have access to them. In our `setUp` method, we need to create the application object with our `TestConfig` object and create the test client.

Also, there are three bugs that we need to work around. The first two are in the Flask Admin and Flask Restful extensions, which do not remove the Blueprint objects stored internally when the application object they are applied to is destroyed. Third, Flask SQLAlchemy's initializer doesn't correctly add the application object while outside the `webapp` directory:

```
class TestURLs(unittest.TestCase):
    def setUp(self):
        # Bug workarounds
        admin._views = []
        rest_api.resources = []

        app = create_app('webapp.config.TestConfig')
        self.client = app.test_client()

        # Bug workaround
        db.app = app

        db.create_all()
```

 All of the bugs previously listed exist at the time of writing and may no longer exist when you read this chapter.

Along with the `setUp` method, there is also the `tearDown` method, which is run every time a unit test ends. The `tearDown` method is to destroy any objects that were created in the `setUp` method that cannot be automatically garbage collected. In our case, we will use the `tearDown` method in order to delete the tables in the test database in order to have a clean slate for each test.

```
class TestURLs(unittest.TestCase):
    def setUp(self):
        ...

    def tearDown(self):
        db.session.remove()
        db.drop_all()
```

Now we can create our first unit test. The first test will test whether accessing the root of our application will return a `302 redirect` to the blog home page as follows:

```
class TestURLs(unittest.TestCase):
    def setUp(self):
        ...

    def tearDown(self):
        ...

    def test_root_redirect(self):
        """ Tests if the root URL gives a 302 """

        result = self.client.get('/')
        assert result.status_code == 302
        assert "/blog/" in result.headers['Location']
```

Each unit test must start with the word `test` to tell the `unittest` library that the function is a unit test and not just some utility function inside the test case class.

Now if we run the tests again, we see our test being run and passing the checks:

```
$ python -m unittest discover
.
-------------------------------------------------------------------
Ran 1 tests in 0.128s


OK
```

The best way to write tests is to ask yourself what you are looking for ahead of time, write the `assert` statements, and write the code needed to execute those asserts. This forces you to ask what you are really testing before you start writing the test. It's also the best practice to write a Python doc string for each unit test, as it will be printed with the name of the test whenever the test fails, and after you write 50+ tests, it can be helpful to know exactly what the test is for.

Rather than using the built-in `assert` keyword from Python, we can use some of the methods provided by the `unittest` library. These methods provide specialized error messages and debug information when the `assert` statements inside these functions fail.

The following is a list of all of the special `assert` statements given by the `unittest` library and what they do:

- `assertEqual(x, y)`: Assert x `==` y
- `assertNotEqual(x, y)`: Assert x `!=` y
- `assertTrue(x)`: Assert x is `True`
- `assertFalse(x)`: Assert x is `False`
- `assertIs(x, y)`: Assert x is y
- `assertIsNot(x, y)`: Assert x is not y
- `assertIsNone(x)`: Assert x is `None`
- `assertIsNotNone(x)`: Assert x is not `None`
- `assertIn(x, y)`: Assert x in y
- `assertNotIn(x, y)`: Assert x not in y
- `assertIsInstance(x, y)`: Assert `isinstance(x, y)`
- `assertNotIsInstance(x, y)`: Assert not `isinstance(x, y)`

If we wanted to test the return value of a normal page, the unit test would look like this:

```
class TestURLs(unittest.TestCase):
    def setUp(self):
        ...

    def tearDown(self):
        ...

    def test_root_redirect(self):
        ...
```

Remember that this code is only testing if the URLs give returns successfully. The content of the return to data is not part of these tests.

If we wanted to test submitting a form like the login form, we can use the post method of the test client. Let's create a `test_login` method to see if the login form works correctly:

```python
class TestURLs(unittest.TestCase):
    ...

    def test_login(self):
        """ Tests if the login form works correctly """

        test_role = Role("default")
        db.session.add(test_role)
        db.session.commit()

        test_user = User("test")
        test_user.set_password("test")
        db.session.add(test_user)
        db.session.commit()

        result = self.client.post('/login', data=dict(
            username='test',
            password="test"
        ), follow_redirects=True)

        self.assertEqual(result.status_code, 200)
        self.assertIn('You have been logged in', result.data)
```

The additional check for the string in the return data exists because the return code is not affected by the validity of the entered data. The post method will work for testing any of the form objects we have created throughout the book.

Now that you understand the mechanics of unit testing, you can use unit testing in order to test all the parts of your application. For example, testing all the routes in the application, testing any utility function that we have made like `sidebar_data`, testing if users with certain permissions can or cannot access a page, and so on.

If your application's code has a feature, no matter how small, you should have a test for it. Why? Because whatever can go wrong, will go wrong. If the validity of your application's code relies entirely on manual testing, then something is going to get overlooked as your app grows. When something gets overlooked, then broken code is deployed to live servers, which annoys your users.

User interface testing

In order to test the high level of our application's code, and to create system tests, we will write tests that work with browsers and verify that the UI code is functioning properly. Using a tool called Selenium, we will create Python code that hooks into a browser and controls it purely from code. You find elements on the screen and then perform actions on those elements by having Selenium. Click on it or input keystrokes. Also, Selenium allows you to perform checks on the page content by giving you access to the elements' content, such as its attributes and its inner text. For more advanced checks, Selenium even gives an interface to run arbitrary JavaScript on the page. If the JavaScript returns a value, it is automatically converted into a Python type.

Before we touch the code, Selenium needs to be installed:

```
$ pip install selenium
```

To begin with the code, our UI tests need a file of their own in the tests directory named test_ui.py. Because system tests do not test one specific thing, the best way to write user interface tests is to think of the test as going through a typical user's flow. Before you write the test, write down specific steps that our fake user is going to simulate:

```
import unittest

class TestURLs(unittest.TestCase):
    def setUp(self):
        pass

    def tearDown(self):
        pass

    def test_add_new_post(self):
        """ Tests if the new post page saves a Post object to the
            database

            1. Log the user in
            2. Go to the new_post page
            3. Fill out the fields and submit the form
            4. Go to the blog home page and verify that the post
               is on the page
        """
        pass
```

Now that we know exactly what our test is going to do, let's start adding in Selenium code. In the `setUp` and `tearDown` methods, we need code to start up a web browser that Selenium controls and then close it when the test is over.

```python
import unittest
from selenium import webdriver
class TestURLs(unittest.TestCase):
    def setUp(self):
        self.driver = webdriver.Firefox()
    def tearDown(self):
        self.driver.close()
```

This code spawns a new Firefox window with Selenium controlling it. For this to work of course, you need Firefox installed on your computer. There is support for other browsers, but they all require an extra program for them to work correctly. Firefox has the best support out of all of the browsers.

Before we write the code for the test, let's explore the Selenium API as follows:

```python
$ python
>>> from selenium import webdriver
>>> driver = webdriver.Firefox()
# load the Google homepage
>>> driver.get("http://www.google.com")
# find a element by its class
>>> search_field = driver.find_element_by_class_name("gsfi")
# find a element by its name
>>> search_field = driver.find_element_by_name("q")
# find an element by its id
>>> search_field = driver.find_element_by_id("lst-ib")
# find an element with JavaScript
>>> search_field = driver.execute_script(
    "return document.querySelector('#lst-ib')"
)
# search for flask
>>> search_field.send_keys("flask")
>>> search_button = driver.find_element_by_name("btnK")
>>> search_button.click()
```

These are the main functions from Selenium that we will be using, but there are many other ways to find and interact with elements on the web page. For the full list of available features, refer to the Selenium-Python documentation at `http://selenium-python.readthedocs.org`.

There are two gotchas in Selenium that need to be kept in mind while writing your tests, or you will run into very odd bugs that are almost impossible to debug from their error messages:

1. Selenium is designed to work like there is an actual person controlling the browser. This means that if an element cannot be seen on the page, Selenium cannot interact with it. For example, if an element covers another element you wish to click, say a modal window is in front of a button, then the button cannot be pushed. If the element's CSS has its display set to `none` or visibility set to `hidden`, the results will be the same.

2. All of the variables that point toward elements on the screen are stored as pointers to those elements in the browser, which means that they are not stored in Python's memory. If the page changes without using the `get` method, like when a link is clicked and a new element pointer is created, then the test will crash. This happens because the driver will be continuously looking for the elements on the previous page and not finding them on the new one. The `get` method of the driver clears out all those references.

In the previous tests, we used the test client in order to simulate a request to the application object. However, because we are now using something that needs to directly interface with the application through a web browser, we need an actual server to be running. This server needs to be run in a separate terminal window before the user interface tests are run so that they have something to request. To do this, we need a separate Python file in order to run the server with our test configuration, as well as setting up some models for our UI tests to use. In a new file at the root of the project directory named `run_test_server.py`, add the following:

```
from webapp import create_app
from webapp.models import db, User, Role

app = create_app('webapp.config.TestConfig')

db.app = app
db.create_all()
```

```
default = Role("default")
poster = Role("poster")
db.session.add(default)
db.session.add(poster)
db.session.commit()

test_user = User("test")
test_user.set_password("test")
test_user.roles.append(poster)
db.session.add(test_user)
db.session.commit()

app.run()
```

Now that we have both the test server script and the knowledge of Selenium's API, we can finally write the code for our test:

```
class TestURLs(unittest.TestCase):
    def setUp(self):
        ...

    def tearDown(self):
        ...

    def test_add_new_post(self):
        """ Tests if the new post page saves a Post object to the
            database

            1. Log the user in
            2. Go to the new_post page
            3. Fill out the fields and submit the form
            4. Go to the blog home page and verify that
               the post is on the page
        """
        # login
        self.driver.get("http://localhost:5000/login")

        username_field = self.driver.find_element_by_name(
            "username"
        )
        username_field.send_keys("test")
```

```
password_field = self.driver.find_element_by_name(
    "password"
)
password_field.send_keys("test")

login_button = self.driver.find_element_by_id(
    "login_button"
)
login_button.click()

# fill out the form
self.driver.get("http://localhost:5000/blog/new")

title_field = self.driver.find_element_by_name("title")
title_field.send_keys("Test Title")

# find the editor in the iframe
self.driver.switch_to.frame(
    self.driver.find_element_by_tag_name("iframe")
)
post_field = self.driver.find_element_by_class_name(
    "cke_editable"
)
post_field.send_keys("Test content")
self.driver.switch_to.parent_frame()

post_button = self.driver.find_element_by_class_name(
    "btn-primary"
)
post_button.click()

# verify the post was created
self.driver.get("http://localhost:5000/blog")
self.assertIn("Test Title", self.driver.page_source)
self.assertIn("Test content", self.driver.page_source)
```

Most of this test uses the methods that we introduced earlier. However, there is a new method in this test named `switch_to`. The `switch_to` method is the context of the driver to allow the selection of elements inside an `iframe` element. Normally, it's impossible for the parent window to select any elements inside an `iframe` using JavaScript, but because we are directly interfacing into the browser itself, we can access `iframe` element's contents. We need to switch contacts like these because the WYSIWYG editor inside the post creation page uses `iframe` in order to create itself. After we are done with selecting elements within the `iframe`, we need to switch back to the parent context with the `parent_frame` method.

You now have the tools that you need to test both your server code and your user interface code completely. For the rest of the chapter, we will focus on tools and methodologies in order to make your testing even more effective in ensuring your application's correctness.

Test coverage

Now that our tests have been written, we have to know whether our code is sufficiently tested. The concept of test coverage, also known as code coverage, was invented to solve this issue. In any project, the test coverage represents what percentage of the code in the project was executed when the tests were run, and which lines were never run. This gives an idea of what parts of the project aren't being tested in our unit tests. To add coverage reports to our project, install the coverage library with pip as follows:

```
$ pip install coverage
```

The coverage library can be run as a command-line program that will run your test suite and take its measurements while the tests are running.

```
$ coverage run --source webapp --branch -m unittest discover
```

The `--source` flag tells coverage to only report on the coverage for the files in the `webapp` directory. If that weren't included, the percentages for all the libraries used in the app would be included as well. By default, if any code in an `if` statement is executed, the entire `if` statement is said to have executed. The `--branch` flag tells `coverage` to disable this and measure everything.

After `coverage` runs our tests and takes its measurements, we can see a report of its findings in two ways. The first is to see a print out of each file's coverage percentage on the command line:

```
$ coverage report
Name                                    Stmts    Miss  Branch  BrMiss   Cover
-----------------------------------------------------------------
webapp/__init__                            51       0       6       0    100%
webapp/config                              37       0       0       0    100%
webapp/controllers/__init__                 0       0       0       0    100%
webapp/controllers/admin                   27       4       0       0     85%
webapp/controllers/blog                    77      45       8       8     38%
webapp/controllers/main                    78      42      20      16     41%
webapp/controllers/rest/__init__            0       0       0       0    100%
webapp/controllers/rest/auth               13       6       2       2     47%
webapp/controllers/rest/fields             17       8       0       0     53%
webapp/controllers/rest/parsers            19       0       0       0    100%
webapp/controllers/rest/post               85      71      44      43     12%
webapp/extensions                          56      14       4       4     70%
webapp/forms                               48      15      10       7     62%
webapp/models                              89      21       4       3     74%
webapp/tasks                               41      29       4       4     27%
-----------------------------------------------------------------
TOTAL                                     638     255     102      87     54%
```

The second is to use coverage's HTML generating ability to see a detailed breakdown of each file in the browser.

```
$ coverage html
```

The preceding command creates a directory named `htmlcov`. When the `index.html` file is opened in the browser, each file name can be clicked on to reveal the breakdown of what lines were and were not run during the tests.

```
43          recent=recent,
44          top_tags=top_tags
45      }
46

47
48  @blog_blueprint.route('/post/<int:post_id>', methods=['GET', 'POST'])
49  @cache.cached(timeout=60)
50  def post(post_id):
51      form = CommentForm()
52
53      if form.validate_on_submit():
54          new_comment = Comment()
55          new_comment.name = form.name.data
56          new_comment.text = form.text.data
57          new_comment.post_id = post_id
58          new_comment.date = datetime.datetime.now()
59
60          db.session.add(new_comment)
61          db.session.commit()
62
63      post = Post.query.get_or_404(post_id)
64      tags = post.tags
65      comments = post.comments.order_by(Comment.date.desc()).all()
66      recent, top_tags = sidebar_data()
67
68      return render_template(
69          'post.html',
70          post=post,
71          tags=tags,
72          comments=comments,
73          recent=recent,
74          top_tags=top_tags,
75          form=form
76      }
77

78
79  @blog_blueprint.route('/new', methods=['GET', 'POST'])
80  @login_required
81  @poster_permission.require(http_exception=403)
82  def new_post():
83      form = PostForm()
84
85      if form.validate_on_submit():
86          new_post = Post(form.title.data)
```

In the preceding screenshot, the `blog.py` file was opened, and the coverage report clearly shows that the post route was never executed. However, this also gives some false negatives. As the user interface tests are not testing code that is being run by the coverage program, it doesn't count toward our coverage report. In order to fix this, just to make sure that you have tests in your test cases, test each individual function that would have been tested in the user interface tests.

In most projects, the percentage to aim for is around 90% code coverage. It's very rare that a project will have 100% of its code testable, and this possibility decreases as the size of the project increases.

Test-driven development

Now that we have our tests written, how can they be integrated into the development process? Currently, we are using our tests in order to ensure code correctness after we create some feature. But, what if we flipped the order and used tests in order to create correct code from the beginning? This is what **test-driven development** (TDD) advocates.

TDD follows a simple loop to write the code of a new feature in your application:

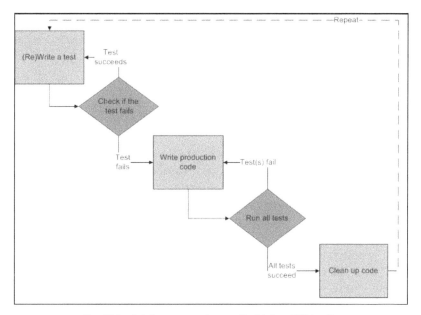

Credit for this image goes to user Excirial on Wikipedia

In a project that uses TDD, the first thing that you write, before any of the code that controls what you are actually building, is the tests. What this forces the programmers on the project to do is to plan out the project's scope, design, and requirements before writing any code. While designing APIs, it also forces the programmer to design the interface of the API from a consumer's perspective rather than design the interface after all the backend code has been written.

In TDD, tests are designed to fail the first time that you run them. There is a saying in TDD that if your tests don't fail the first time that you run them, you're not really testing anything. What this means is that you are most likely testing to what the tested unit gives rather than what it should give while writing tests after the fact.

After your tests fail the first time, you continuously write code until all the tests pass. This process is repeated for each new feature.

Once all of the original tests pass and the code is cleaned up, TDD tells you to stop writing code. By only writing code until the tests pass, TDD also enforces the **You Aren't Going To Need It (YAGNI)** philosophy, which states that programmers should only implement what they actually need rather than what they perceive they will need. A huge amount of wasted effort is made during development when programmers try to preemptively add functionality when no one needed it.

For example, on a PHP project that I worked on, I found the following code that looked for images in a directory:

```
$images = glob(
    $img_directory . "{*.jpg, *.jpeg, *.gif, *.png, *.PNG, *.Png,
*.PnG, *.pNG, *.pnG, *.pNg, *.PNg}",
    GLOB_BRACE
);
```

In PHP, glob is a function that looks through the contents of a directory to find files that match the pattern. I confronted the programmer who wrote it. His explanation for all the different versions of the .png extension was that some user uploaded a file with a .PNG extension, and the function didn't find it because it was only looking for the lowercase versions of the extensions. Instead of adding the uppercase versions to fix the problem at hand, he tried to fix a problem that didn't exist to make sure that he didn't have to touch this code again. We may feel like wasting a small amount of time, but this code was a microcosm of the entire code base. If this project followed TDD, a test case would have been added for the uppercase file extensions, the code added to pass the test, and that would have been the end of it.

TDD also promotes the idea of **Keep It Simple, Stupid** (**KISS**), which dictates that simplicity should be a design goal from the beginning. TDD promotes KISS because it requires small, testable units of code that can be separated from each other and don't rely on a shared global state.

Also, in projects that follow TDD, there is an always-current documentation through the tests. One of the axioms of programming is that with any sufficiently large program, the documentation will always be out of date. This is because the documentation is one of the last things on the mind of the programmer when he/she is changing the code. However, with tests there are clear examples of each piece of functionality in the project (if the project has a large code coverage percentage). The tests are updated all the time and therefore show good examples of how the functions and API of the program should work.

Now that you understand Flask's functionality and how to write tests for Flask, the next project that you create in Flask can be entirely made with TDD.

Summary

Now that you understand testing and what it can do for your application, you can create applications that are guaranteed to be less bug-ridden. You will spend less time fixing bugs and more time adding features that are requested by your users.

In the next chapter, we will finish the book by going over ways to deploy your application into a production environment on a server.

As a final challenge to the reader, before moving onto the next chapter try to get your code coverage over 95%.

13
Deploying Flask Apps

Now that we have reached the last chapter of the book and have a fully functioning web app made in Flask, the final step to take in our development is to make the app available for the world. There are many different approaches to host your Flask app, each of them with their own pros and cons. This chapter will cover the best solutions and guide you in what situations you should choose one over the other.

Note that, in this chapter, the term server is used to refer to the physical machine that is running the operating system. But, when the term web server is used, it refers to the program on the server that receives HTTP requests and sends responses.

Deploying on your own server

The most common way to deploy any web app is to run it on a server that you have control over. In this case, control means access to a terminal on the server with an administrator account. This type of deployment gives you the most amount of freedom out of the other choices as it allows you to install any program or tool you wish. This is in contrast to other hosting solutions where the web server and database are chosen for you. This type of deployment also happens to be the least expensive option.

The downside to this freedom is that you take the responsibility of keeping the server up, backing up user data, keeping the software on the server up to date to avoid security issues, and so on. All books have been written on good server management. So if this is not a responsibility that you believe you or your company can handle, it would be best if you choose one of the other deployment options.

This section will be based on a Debian Linux-based server, as Linux is far and away the most popular OS to run web servers and Debian is the most popular Linux distro (a particular combination of software and the Linux kernel released as a package). Any OS with bash and a program named SSH (which will be introduced in the next section) will work for this chapter. The only differences will be the command-line programs to install software on the server.

Each of these web servers will use a protocol named **Web Server Gateway Interface (WSGI)**, which is a standard designed to allow Python web applications to easily communicate with web servers. We will never directly work with WSGI, but most of the web server interfaces we will be using will have WSGI in their name and it can be confusing if you don't know what it is.

Pushing code to your server with fabric

To automate the process of setting up and pushing our application code to the server, we will use a Python tool named fabric. Fabric is a command-line program that reads and executes Python scripts on remote servers using a tool named SSH. SSH is a protocol that allows a user of one computer to remotely log in to another computer and execute commands on the command line, provided that the user has an account on the remote machine.

To install `fabric`, we will use `pip` as follows:

```
$ pip install fabric
```

`fabric` commands are collections of command-line programs to be run on the remote machine's shell, in this case, bash. We are going to make three different commands: one to run our unit tests, one to set up a brand new server to our specifications, and one to have the server update its copy of the application code with `git`. We will store these commands in a new file at the root of our project directory named `fabfile.py`.

As it's the easiest to create, let's make the test command first:

```
from fabric.api import local

def test():
    local('python -m unittest discover')
```

To run this function from the command line, we can use `fabric` command-line interface by passing the name of the command to run:

```
$ fab test
[localhost] local: python -m unittest discover

.....

------------------------------------------------------------------

Ran 5 tests in 6.028s
OK
```

Fabric has three main commands: `local`, `run`, and `sudo`. The `local` function, as seen in the preceding function, `run` commands on the local computer. The `run` and `sudo` functions run commands on a remote machine, but `sudo` runs commands as an administrator. All of these functions notify fabric whether the command ran successfully or not. If the command didn't run successfully, which means that, in this case, our tests failed, any other commands in the function will not be run. This is useful for our commands because it allows us to force ourselves not to push any code to the server that does not pass our tests.

Now we need to create the command to set up a new server from scratch. What this command will do is install the software that our production environment needs as well as downloads the code from our centralized `git` repository. It will also create a new user that will act as the runner of the web server as well as the owner of the code repository.

 Do not run your web server or have your code deployed by the root user. This opens your application to a whole host of security vulnerabilities.

This command will differ based on your operating system, and we will be adding this command in the rest of the chapter based on what server you choose:

```python
from fabric.api import env, local, run, sudo, cd

env.hosts = ['deploy@[your IP]']

def upgrade_libs():
    sudo("apt-get update")
    sudo("apt-get upgrade")
```

```
def setup():
    test()
    upgrade_libs()

    # necessary to install many Python libraries
    sudo("apt-get install -y build-essential")
    sudo("apt-get install -y git")
    sudo("apt-get install -y python")
    sudo("apt-get install -y python-pip")
    # necessary to install many Python libraries
    sudo("apt-get install -y python-all-dev")

    run("useradd -d /home/deploy/ deploy")
    run("gpasswd -a deploy sudo")

    # allows Python packages to be installed by the deploy user
    sudo("chown -R deploy /usr/local/")
    sudo("chown -R deploy /usr/lib/python2.7/")

    run("git config --global credential.helper store")

    with cd("/home/deploy/"):
        run("git clone [your repo URL]")

    with cd('/home/deploy/webapp'):
        run("pip install -r requirements.txt")
        run("python manage.py createdb")
```

There are two new fabric features in this script. The first is the `env.hosts` assignment, which tells fabric the user and IP address of the machine it should be logging in to. Second, there is the `cd` function used in conjunction with the with keyword, which executes any functions in the context of that directory instead of the home directory of the deploy user. The line that modifies the `git` configuration is there to tell `git` to remember your repository's username and password, so you do not have to enter it every time you wish to push code to the server. Also, before the server is set up, we make sure to update the server's software to keep the server up to date.

Finally, we have the function to push our new code to the server. In time, this command will also restart the web server and reload any configuration files that come from our code. But that depends on the server you choose, so this is filled out in the subsequent sections.

```
def deploy():
    test()
    upgrade_libs()
    with cd('/home/deploy/webapp'):
        run("git pull")
        run("pip install -r requirements.txt")
```

So, if we were to begin working on a new server, all we would need to do to set it up is to run the following commands:

```
$ fabric setup
$ fabric deploy
```

Running your web server with supervisor

Now that we have automated our updating process, we need some program on the server to make sure that our web server, and database if you aren't using SQLite, is running. To do this, we will use a simple program called supervisor. All that supervisor does is automatically runs command-line programs in background processes and allows you to see the status of the running programs. Supervisor also monitors all of the processes it's running, and if the process dies, it tries to restart it.

To install supervisor, we need to add it to the setup command in our fabfile.py:

```
def setup():
    ...
    sudo("apt-get install -y supervisor")
```

To tell supervisor what to do, we need to create a configuration file and then copy it to the /etc/supervisor/conf.d/ directory of our server during the deploy fabric command. Supervisor will load all of the files in this directory when it starts and attempts to run them.

In a new file in the root of our project directory named `supervisor.conf`, add the following:

```
[program:webapp]
command=
directory=/home/deploy/webapp
user=deploy

[program:rabbitmq]
command=rabbitmq-server
user=deploy

[program:celery]
command=celery worker -A celery_runner
directory=/home/deploy/webapp
user=deploy
```

> This is the bare minimum configuration needed to get a web server up and running. But, supervisor has a lot more configuration options. To view all of the customizations, go to the supervisor documentation at `http://supervisord.org/`.

This configuration tells `supervisor` to run a command in the context of `/home/deploy/webapp` under the `deploy` user. The right hand of the command value is empty because it depends on what server you are running and will be filled in for each section.

Now we need to add a `sudo` call in the deploy command to copy this configuration file to the `/etc/supervisor/conf.d/` directory as follows.

```
def deploy():
    ...
    with cd('/home/deploy/webapp'):
        ...
        sudo("cp supervisord.conf /etc/supervisor/conf.d/webapp.conf")

    sudo('service supervisor restart')
```

A lot of projects just create the files on the server and forget about them, but having the configuration file stored in our `git` repository and copied on every deployment gives several advantages. First, this means that it is easy to revert changes if something goes wrong using `git`. Second, it means that we don't have to log in to our server in order to make changes to the files.

 Don't use the Flask development server in production. It not only fails to handle concurrent connections but also allows arbitrary Python code to be run on your server.

Gevent

The simplest option to get a web server up and running is to use a Python library named gevent to host your application. Gevent is a Python library that adds an alternative way of doing concurrent programming outside the Python threading library called **co-routines**. Gevent has an interface to run WSGI applications that is both simple and has good performance. A simple gevent server can easily handle hundreds of concurrent users, which is 99% more than the users of websites on the Internet will ever have. The downside to this option is that its simplicity means a lack of configuration options. There is no way, for example, to add rate limiting to the server or to add HTTPS traffic. This deployment option is purely for sites that you don't expect to receive a huge amount of traffic. Remember YAGNI; only upgrade to a different web server if you really need to.

 Co-routines are a bit outside of the scope of this book, so a good explanation can be found at `https://en.wikipedia.org/wiki/Coroutine`.

To install gevent, we will use pip:

```
$ pip install gevent
```

In a new file in the root of the project directory named gserver.py, add the following:

```
from gevent.wsgi import WSGIServer
from webapp import create_app

app = create_app('webapp.config.ProdConfig')

server = WSGIServer(('', 80), app)
server.serve_forever()
```

To run the server with supervisor, just change the command value to the following:

```
[program:webapp]
command=python gserver.py
directory=/home/deploy/webapp
user=deploy
```

Now when you deploy, gevent will be automatically installed for you by running your requirements.txt on every deployment, that is, if you are properly pip freezing after every new dependency is added.

Tornado

Tornado is another very simple way to deploy WSGI apps purely with Python. Tornado is a web server that is designed to handle thousands of simultaneous connections. If your application needs real-time data, Tornado also supports WebSockets for continuous, long-lived connections to the server.

 Do not use Tornado in production on a Windows server. The Windows version of Tornado is not only much slower, but it is considered beta quality software.

To use Tornado with our application, we will use Tornado's WSGIContainer in order to wrap the application object to make it Tornado compatible. Then, Tornado will start to listen on port *80* for requests until the process is terminated. In a new file named tserver.py, add the following:

```
from tornado.wsgi import WSGIContainer
from tornado.httpserver import HTTPServer
from tornado.ioloop import IOLoop
from webapp import create_app
app = WSGIContainer(create_app("webapp.config.ProdConfig"))
http_server = HTTPServer(app)
http_server.listen(80)
IOLoop.instance().start()
```

To run the Tornado with supervisor, just change the command value to the following:

```
[program:webapp]
command=python tserver.py
directory=/home/deploy/webapp
user=deploy
```

Nginx and uWSGI

If you need more performance or customization, the most popular way to deploy a Python web application is to use the web server Nginx as a frontend for the WSGI server uWSGI by using a reverse proxy. A reverse proxy is a program in networks that retrieves contents for a client from a server as if they returned from the proxy itself:

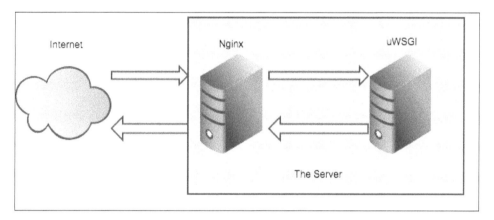

Nginx and uWSGI are used in this way because we get the power of the Nginx frontend while having the customization of uWSGI.

Nginx is a very powerful web server that became popular by providing the best combination of speed and customization. Nginx is consistently faster than other web severs such as Apache httpd and has native support for WSGI applications. The way it achieves this speed is several good architecture decisions as well as the decision early on that they were not going to try to cover a large amount of use cases like Apache does. Having a smaller feature set makes it much easier to maintain and optimize the code. From a programmer's perspective, it is also much easier to configure Nginx, as there is no giant default configuration file (`httpd.conf`) that needs to be overridden with `.htaccess` files in each of your project directories.

One downside is that Nginx has a much smaller community than Apache, so if you have an obscure problem, you are less likely to be able to find answers online. Also, it's possible that a feature that most programmers are used to in Apache isn't supported in Nginx.

uWSGI is a web server that supports several different types of server interfaces, including WSGI. uWSGI handles severing the application content as well as things such as load balancing traffic across several different processes and threads.

To install uWSGI, we will use `pip`:

```
$ pip install uwsgi
```

In order to run our application, uWSGI needs a file with an accessible WSGI application. In a new file named `wsgi.py` in the top level of the project directory, add the following:

```
from webapp import create_app

app = create_app("webapp.config.ProdConfig")
```

To test uWSGI, we can run it from the command line with the following:

```
$ uwsgi --socket 127.0.0.1:8080 \
--wsgi-file wsgi.py \
--callable app \
--processes 4 \
--threads 2
```

If you are running this on your server, you should be able to access port *8080* and see your app (if you don't have a firewall that is).

What this command does is load the app object from the `wsgi.py` file and makes it accessible from `localhost` on port *8080*. It also spawns four different processes with two threads each, which are automatically load balanced by a master process. This amount of processes is overkill for the vast, vast majority of websites. To start off, use a single process with two threads and scale up from there.

Instead of adding all of the configuration options on the command line, we can create a text file to hold our configuration, which brings the same benefits for configuration that were listed in the section on supervisor.

In a new file in the root of the project directory named `uwsgi.ini`, add the following code:

```
[uwsgi]
socket = 127.0.0.1:8080
wsgi-file = wsgi.py
callable = app
processes = 4
threads = 2
```

 uWSGI supports hundreds of configuration options as well as several official and unofficial plugins. To leverage the full power of uWSGI, you can explore the documentation at `http://uwsgi-docs.readthedocs.org/`.

Let's run the server now from supervisor:

```
[program:webapp]
command=uwsgi uwsgi.ini
directory=/home/deploy/webapp
user=deploy
```

We also need to install Nginx within the setup function:

```
def setup():
    ...
    sudo("apt-get install -y nginx")
```

Because we are installing Nginx from the OS's package manager, the OS will handle running of Nginx for us.

 At the time of writing, the Nginx version in the official Debian package manager is several years old. To install the most recent version, follow the instructions here: `http://wiki.nginx.org/Install`.

Next, we need to create an Nginx configuration file and then copy it to the
`/etc/nginx/sites-available/` directory when we push the code. In a new
file in the root of the project directory named `nginx.conf`, add the following:

```
server {
    listen 80;
    server_name your_domain_name;

    location / {
        include uwsgi_params;
        uwsgi_pass 127.0.0.1:8080;
    }

    location /static {
        alias /home/deploy/webapp/webapp/static;
    }
}
```

What this configuration file does is it tells Nginx to listen for incoming requests on
port *80*, and forwards all requests to the WSGI application that is listening on port
8080. Also, it makes an exception for any requests for static files and instead sends
those requests directly to the file system. Bypassing uWSGI for static files gives a
great performance boost, as Nginx is really good at serving static files quickly.

Finally, in the `fabfile.py` file:

```
def deploy():
    ...
    with cd('/home/deploy/webapp'):
        ...
        sudo("cp nginx.conf "
            "/etc/nginx/sites-available/[your_domain]")
        sudo("ln -sf /etc/nginx/sites-available/your_domain "
            "/etc/nginx/sites-enabled/[your_domain]")

    sudo("service nginx restart")
```

Apache and uWSGI

Using Apache httpd with uWSGI has mostly the same setup. First off, we need an apache configuration file in a new file in the root of our project directory named `apache.conf`:

```
<VirtualHost *:80>
    <Location />
        ProxyPass / uwsgi://127.0.0.1:8080/
    </Location>
</VirtualHost>
```

This file just tells Apache to pass all requests on port *80* to the uWSGI web server listening on port *8080*. However, this functionality requires an extra Apache plugin from uWSGI named `mod-proxy-uwsgi`. We can install this as well as Apache in the set command:

```
def setup():

    sudo("apt-get install -y apache2")
    sudo("apt-get install -y libapache2-mod-proxy-uwsgi")
```

Finally, in the `deploy` command, we need to copy our Apache configuration file into Apache's configuration directory:

```
def deploy():
    ...
    with cd('/home/deploy/webapp'):
        ...
        sudo("cp apache.conf "
            "/etc/apache2/sites-available/[your_domain]")
        sudo("ln -sf /etc/apache2/sites-available/[your_domain] "
            "/etc/apache2/sites-enabled/[your_domain]")

        sudo("service apache2 restart")
```

Deploying on Heroku

Heroku is the first of the **Platform as a Service (PaaS)** providers that this chapter will cover. PaaS is a service given to web developers that allows them to host their websites on a platform that is controlled and maintained by someone else. At the cost of freedom, you gain assurances that your website will automatically scale with the number of users your site has with no extra work on your part. Using PaaS also tends to be more expensive than running your own servers.

Heroku is PaaS that aims to be easy to use for web developers by hooking into already existing tools and not requiring any large changes in the app. Heroku works by reading the file named `Procfile`, which contains commands that your Heroku dyno basically a virtual machine sitting on a server, will run. Before we begin, you will need a Heroku account. If you wish to just experiment, there is a free account available.

In a new file named `Procfile` in the root of the directory, add the following:

```
web: uwsgi uwsgi.ini
```

This tells Heroku that we have a process named web, which will run the uWSGI command and pass the `uwsgi.ini` file. Heroku also needs a file named `runtime.txt`, which will tell it what Python runtime you wish to use, (at the time of writing, the latest Python release is 2.7.10):

```
python-2.7.10
```

Finally, we need to make some modifications to the `uwsgi.ini` file that we made earlier:

```
[uwsgi]
http-socket = :$(PORT)
die-on-term = true
wsgi-file = wsgi.py
callable = app
processes = 4
threads = 2
```

We set the port at uWSGI listens to the environment variable port because Heroku does not directly expose the dyno to the Internet. Instead, it has a very complicated load balancer and reverse proxy system, so we need to have uWSGI listen on the port that Heroku needs us to listen on. Also, we set **die-on-term** to true so that uWSGI listens for a signal termination event from the OS correctly.

To work with Heroku's command-line tools, we first need to install them, which can be done from `https://toolbelt.heroku.com`.

Next, you need to log in to your account:

```
$ heroku login
```

We can test our setup to make sure that it will work on Heroku before we deploy it by using the foreman command:

```
$ foreman start web
```

Foreman command simulates the same production environment that Heroku uses run our app. To create the dyno, which will run the application on Heroku's servers, we will use the `create` command. Then, we can push to the remote branch Heroku on our `git` repository to have Heroku servers automatically pull down our changes.

```
$ heroku create
```
```
$ git push heroku master
```

If everything went well, you should have a working application on your new Heroku dyno. You can open a new tab to your new web application with the following command:

```
$ heroku open
```

To see the app on a Heroku deployment in action, visit `https://mastering-flask.herokuapp.com/`.

Using Heroku Postgres

Maintaining a database properly is a full-time job. Thankfully, we can use one of Heroku's built-in features in order to automate this process for us. Heroku Postgres is a Postgres database that is maintained and hosted entirely by Heroku. Because we are using SQLAlchemy, using Heroku Postgres is trivial. In your dyno's dashboard, there is a link to your **Heroku Postgres** information. By clicking on it, you will be taken to a page as the one shown here:

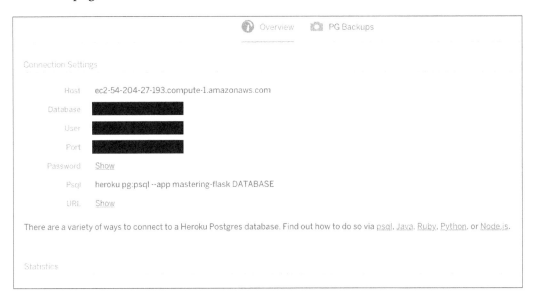

By clicking on the **URL** field, you will have an SQLAlchemy URL, which you can directly copy to your production configuration object.

Using Celery on Heroku

We have our production web server and database setup, but we still need to set up Celery. Using one of Heroku's many plugins, we can host a RabbitMQ instance in the cloud while running the Celery worker on the dyno.

The first step is to tell Heroku to run your celery worker in the `Procfile`:

```
web: uwsgi uwsgi.ini
celery: celery worker -A celery_runner
```

Next, to install the Heroku RabbitMQ plugin with the free plan (named the `lemur` plan), use the following command:

```
$   heroku addons:create cloudamqp:lemur
```

 To get the full list of Heroku add-ons, go to `https://elements.heroku.com/addons`.

At the same location on the dashboard where Heroku Postgres was listed, you will now find **CloudAMQP**:

Clicking on it will also give you a screen with a copiable URL, which you can paste into your production configuration:

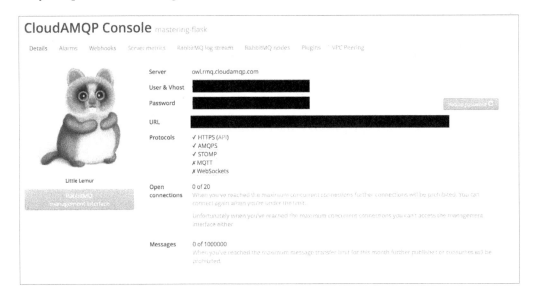

Deploying on Amazon web services

Amazon Web Services (**AWS**) is a collection of application platforms maintained by Amazon and built on top of the same infrastructure that runs amazon.com. To deploy our Flask code, we will be using Amazon Elastic Beanstalk, while the database will be hosted on Amazon Relational Database Service, and our messaging queue for Celery will be hosted on Amazon Simple Queue Service.

Using Flask on Amazon Elastic Beanstalk

Elastic Beanstalk is a platform for web applications that offers many powerful features for developers, so web developers do not have to worry about maintaining servers.

For example, your Elastic Beanstalk application will automatically scale by utilizing more and more servers as the number of people using your app at once grows. For Python apps, Elastic Beanstalk uses Apache in combination with mod_wsgi to connect to WSGI applications, so there is no extra configuration needed.

Before we begin, you will need an Amazon.com account and log in to http://aws.amazon.com/elasticbeanstalk. When you are logged in, you will see a screen like the following image:

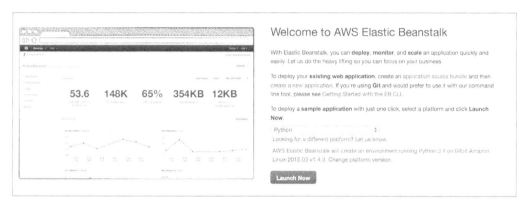

Click on the dropdown to select Python, and if your application needs a specific Python version, be sure to click on **Change platform version** and select the Python version you need. You will be taken through a setup process, and finally your app will go through an initialization process on Amazon's servers. While this is working, we can install the Elastic Beanstalk command-line tools. These tools will allow us to automatically deploy new versions of our application. To install them, use pip:

```
$ pip install awsebcli
```

Before we can deploy the application, you will need an AWS Id and access key. To do this, click on the dropdown that displays your username at the top of the page and click on **Security Credentials**.

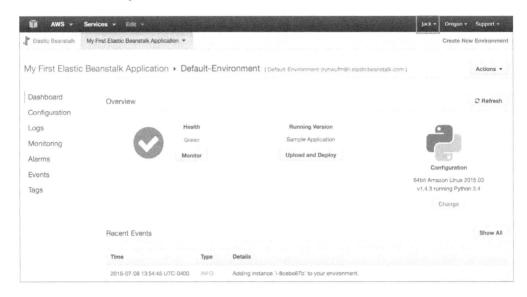

Then, click on the gray box that says **Access Keys** to get your ID and key pair:

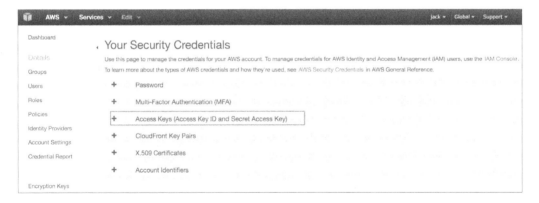

Once you have your key pair, do not share it with anyone because it will give anyone access to have a complete control over all of your platform instances on AWS. Now we can set up the command-line tools. In your project directory, run the following command:

```
$ eb init
```

Select the application that you created earlier to tie this directory to that application. We can see what is running on the application instance now by running the following:

```
$ eb open
```

Right now, you should just see a placeholder application. Let's change that by deploying our app. Elastic Beanstalk looks for a file named `application.py` in your project directory, and it expects a WSGI application named application in that file, so let's create that file now:

```
from webapp import create_app
application = create_app("webapp.config.ProdConfig")
```

Once that file is created, we can finally deploy the application:

```
$ eb deploy
```

This is needed to run Flask on AWS. To see the book's application running on Elastic Beanstalk, go to `http://masteringflask.elasticbeanstalk.com`.

Using Amazon Relational Database Service

Amazon Relational Database Service is a database hosting platform in the cloud that automatically manages several things, such as recovery on node failure and keeping several nodes in different locations in sync.

To use RDS, go to the services tab and click on Relational Database Service. To create your database, click on **Get Started**, which will take you though a simple setup process.

Once your database has been configured and created, you can use the **endpoint** variable listed on the RDS dashboard and the database name and password to create the SQLAlchemy URL in your production configuration object:

This's all that it takes to create a very resilient database on the cloud with Flask!

Using Celery with Amazon Simple Queue Service

In order to use Celery on AWS, we need to have our Elastic Beanstalk instance run our Celery worker in the background as well as set up **a Simple Queue Service (SQS)** messaging queue. For Celery to support SQS, it needs to install a helper library from `pip`:

```
$ pip install boto
```

Setting up a new messaging queue on SQS is very easy. Go to the services tab and click on **Simple Queue Service** in the applications tab and then click on **Create New Queue.** After a very short configuration screen, you should see a screen much like the following:

Now we have to change our CELERY_BROKER_URL and CELERY_BACKEND_URL to the new URL, which takes the following format:

```
sqs://aws_access_key_id:aws_secret_access_key@
```

This uses the key pair you created in the Elastic Beanstalk section.

Finally, we need to tell Elastic Beanstalk to run a Celery worker in the background. We can do this with the .conf file in a new directory at the root of the project named .ebextensions (note the period at the start of the folder name). In a file in this new directory, it can be called whatever you wish, add the following commands:

```
celery_start:
    command: celery multi start worker1 -A celery_runner
```

Now whenever the instance reboots, this command will be run before the server is run.

Summary

As this chapter explained, there are many different options to hosting your application, each having their own pros and cons. Deciding on one depends on the amount of time and money you are willing to spend as well as the total number of users you expect.

Now we have reached the conclusion of the book. I hope that this book was helpful to build your understanding of Flask and how it can be used to create applications of any complexity with ease and with simple maintainability.

Bibliography

This course is a blend of different projects and texts all packaged up keeping your journey in mind. It includes the content from the following Packt products:

- *Flask By Example – Gareth Dwyer*
- *Flask Framework Cookbook – Shalabh Aggarwal*
- *Mastering Flask – Jack Stouffer*

Index

G

get-pip.py file
  reference 5
Get Requests
  defining 614
  output formatting 614-617
  request arguments 617-620
Gevent 715
Git
  defining 475-478
  installing 11-13, 476
  installing, on Windows 476
  reference 476
  using 11-13
GitHub
  reference 12
git repository
  local project structure, setting up 145, 146
  project, setting up on VPS 146, 147
  setting up 145
Git repository
  setting up 20, 80
global language-switching action
  implementing 402-404
global variables 542
Google
  using, for authentication 355-357
Google Analytics
  reference 234
Google developer console
  reference 355
Google Map markers
  customizing 123
  reference 123
Google Maps 99
graph databases 582, 583
group function 641
Gunicorn
  about 438
  Flask app, deploying with 438, 439
gzip 685

H

hamburger icon 152
hash 478
hashing algorithm 546

hash reversal
  website link 164
Headlines application
  cookies, adding 67
  cookies, using with Flask 67
  CSS, adding 72
  issues 67
Hello application 12
Hello, World!
  code, running 7
  code, writing 5, 6
  writing 5
Heroku
  about 445, 722
  Celery, using on 724, 726
  deploying on 722, 723
  reference 446
  used, for deploying Flask app 445-447
Heroku add-ons
  reference 725
Heroku Postgres
  using 724
Heroku toolbelt
  download link 445
HTML 5
  reference 23
HTML boilerplate code 520
HTTP codes
  used, in REST APIs 612
HTTP cookies
  reference 66
HTTP GET
  used, for obtaining user input 41-43
HTTP POST
  used, for obtaining user input 44
HTTP requests
  DELETE 362
  GET 362
  PATCH 362
  POST 362
  PUT 362
HTTP request types
  references 611
Hyper Text Markup Language 23
Hyper Text Transport Protocol Secure
  (HTTPS) 232

I

PyMySQL 83

N

New Relic
about 453
used, for monitoring application 453, 454
new request
reference 188
Nginx
about 435, 717-719
references 437, 719
used, for deploying Flask app 435-437
nodes 582
Nose
about 421
reference, for documentation 422
used, for executing tests 421, 422
NoSQL
about 289
opting, with MongoDB 289-292
versus RDBMS 583
NoSQL databases
about 578
column family stores 580-582
document stores 579
graph databases 582, 583
key-value stores 578
strengths 585
types 578
Not Only SQL (NoSQL) 577

O

OAuth 351, 560
Object Oriented Programming 178
object-oriented programming (OOP) 541
Object Relational Mapping (ORM) 80, 487
one-to-many relationship
defining 496-499
Open Exchange Rates API
API key, obtaining 56
reference 56
using 57
OpenID
about 346, 557-560
reference 346
used, for authentication 346-350

OpenWeatherMap
reference 48
OpenWeatherMap API
about 48
duplicate city names, handling 55
key, retrieving 49
reference 48
used, for signing up 48
OpenWeatherMap API key
reference 49
retrieving 49
Open Web Application Security Project (OWASP)
about 199
reference 163

P

paginate() method
about 300
error_out argument 300
page argument 300
per_page argument 300
pagination 493
partials 640
passwords management, cryptographic hashes used
about 162
hashes, reversing 164, 165
passwords, salting 165, 166
Python hashlib 163
path 479
pdb
reference, for documentation 415
using, for debugging 414, 415
Pingdom
about 451
reference 452
used, for monitoring application 451-453
pip
defining 475, 480, 481
installing 4
pip Python package manager
installing, on Linux 480
installing, on Mac OS X 480
installing, on Windows 479
Platform as a Service (PaaS) 722

Thank you for buying

Flask: Building Python Web Services

About Packt Publishing

Packt, pronounced 'packed', published its first book, *Mastering phpMyAdmin for Effective MySQL Management*, in April 2004, and subsequently continued to specialize in publishing highly focused books on specific technologies and solutions.

Our books and publications share the experiences of your fellow IT professionals in adapting and customizing today's systems, applications, and frameworks. Our solution-based books give you the knowledge and power to customize the software and technologies you're using to get the job done. Packt books are more specific and less general than the IT books you have seen in the past. Our unique business model allows us to bring you more focused information, giving you more of what you need to know, and less of what you don't.

Packt is a modern yet unique publishing company that focuses on producing quality, cutting-edge books for communities of developers, administrators, and newbies alike. For more information, please visit our website at www.packtpub.com.

Writing for Packt

We welcome all inquiries from people who are interested in authoring. Book proposals should be sent to author@packtpub.com. If your book idea is still at an early stage and you would like to discuss it first before writing a formal book proposal, then please contact us; one of our commissioning editors will get in touch with you.

We're not just looking for published authors; if you have strong technical skills but no writing experience, our experienced editors can help you develop a writing career, or simply get some additional reward for your expertise.

Please check www.PacktPub.com for information on our titles

CPSIA information can be obtained
at www.ICGtesting.com
Printed in the USA
BVHW080412291118
534282BV00003B/19/P